Inventing Arguments

FOURTH EDITION
2016 MLA UPDATE EDITION

Inventing Arguments

FOURTH EDITION
2016 MLA UPDATE EDITION

John Mauk
Miami University

John Metz
Kent State University at Geauga

CENGAGE
Learning®

Australia • Brazil • Mexico • Singapore • United Kingdom • United States

**Inventing Arguments,
Fourth Edition**
2016 MLA Update Edition

John Mauk, John Metz

Product Director: Monica
Eckman

Product Team Manager:
Christopher Bennem

Product Manager: Kate Derrick

Senior Content Developer:
Leslie Taggart

Associate Content Developer:
Erin Bosco

Product Assistant: Kerry DeVito

Senior Managing Media
Developer: Cara Douglass-Graff

Marketing Manager: Erin
Parkins

Senior Content Project
Manager: Andrea Wagner

Senior Art Director: Marissa
Falco

Manufacturing Planner: Betsy
Donaghey

IP Analyst: Ann Hoffman

IP Project Manager: Farah Fard

Production Service/Compositor:
MPS Limited

Text Designer: Dare Porter, Real
Time Design

Cover Designer: Deborah
Dutton

Cover Image: Jonathan Poore/
Cengage Learning

For product information and technology assistance, contact us at
Cengage Learning Customer & Sales Support, 1-800-354-9706

For permission to use material from this text or product,
submit all requests online at **www.cengage.com/permissions**.
Further permissions questions can be emailed to
permissionrequest@cengage.com.

Library of Congress Control Number: 2014957551

Student edition: 978-1-337-28085-3
Loose-leaf edition: 978-1-337-28087-7

Cengage Learning
20 Channel Center Street
Boston, MA 02210
USA

Cengage Learning is a leading provider of customized learning solutions with office
locations around the globe, including Singapore, the United Kingdom, Australia,
Mexico, Brazil, and Japan. Locate your local office at **www.cengage.com/global**.

Cengage Learning products are represented in Canada by Nelson Education, Ltd.

To learn more about Cengage Learning Solutions, visit
www.cengage.com.

Purchase any of our products at your local college store or at our preferred online store
www.cengagebrain.com.

Printed in the United States of America
Print Number: 01   Print Year: 2016

"Knowledge emerges only
through invention and re-invention,
through the restless, impatient,
continuing, hopeful inquiry human beings
pursue in the world, with the world,
and with each other."

—Paulo Freire, *Pedagogy of the Oppressed*

Part One: Entering Argument 1

Part Two: Inventing Argument 109

Part Three: Research 307

Part Four: Argument Anthology 393

CONTENTS

Part Two: Inventing Argument   109

Part Three: Research   307

Part Four: Argument Anthology   393

NOTE TO INSTRUCTORS

Teaching argument to first- and second-year college students requires a good amount of distillation: various theories must be condensed into a reasonable number of terms and concepts. Instructors face the dilemma of how much time to spend on argument intricacies versus student ideas. (Ultimately, these courses are about student writing, after all.) We've tried to address this tension head on, creating what we think of as a *syllabus-able* argument text—one that has a kind of practical logic but that also does justice to the complexities of the rhetorical tradition.

Most college writing teachers accept the premise that argument is always tied to particular rhetorical situations. Continuing with the Sophistic tradition, most of us believe that the study of argumentative public discourse must emerge from public situations. Therefore, *Inventing Arguments* draws attention to the real material and intellectual affairs of student writers. It teaches students to build arguments from the rhetorical matter swirling around them, including but not limited to the essays, articles, reports, and images they encounter in the classroom.

As instructors ourselves, we've found that students need help getting beyond common argument topics and lifeless support strategies. To succeed in academic argument, and the critical thinking it requires, students must go beyond announcing common opinions and relying on basic factual support. They need help inventing unique positions, developing appeals, and coming to revelatory insights. To these ends, *Inventing Arguments* has three major pedagogical goals:

1. To help students recognize the rhetorical moves they encounter daily and understand how those moves animate their lives.

2. To foreground the *invention* of arguments (the discovery and development of increasingly complex claims and counterarguments).

3. To help students enter arguments in a sophisticated fashion—by attending to the voices and tensions already lurking within and around a topic. When students tune in to the claims, values, and beliefs of others, their own arguments gain intensity and complexity.

> The structure of *Inventing Arguments* reflects the best way we know to help students enter rhetorical situations and invent arguments.

Part One: Entering Argument

Chapter 1 introduces basic terms (*argument, rhetoric, invention*) and offers assignments to help students genuinely engage the concepts. The activities throughout, we hope, put students in a powerful intellectual place where they can examine some basic assumptions about rhetoric, their relationship to argument, and the opinions swirling around their lives. Thereafter, the chapters of Part One walk through the main elements of argument—from the most to the least explicit: Claims, Support, Opposition, Values and Assumptions. We hope that these initial chapters distill the most important concepts: three types of claims, three major forms of support, three ways to engage opposition, and the role of values and assumptions in the structure of argument.

The assignments at the end of each brief chapter grow in complexity. First students identify major elements of arguments (in Chapters 1 and 2), then summarize arguments (in Chapters 3 and 4), and then work toward analyzing arguments (in Chapters 5 and 6). In other words, the assignments walk students slowly up to formal rhetorical analysis—which is the focus of Chapter 6.

Part Two: Inventing Argument

We hope that students get one primary point from this book: *Arguments make ideas.* In other words, we hope students learn not only to assert and defend claims but also to develop increasingly complex ideas. Chapters 7–12 help students transform initial opinions into thoughtful academic arguments. The Invention sections, in particular, *model* and *dramatize* the intellectual acts behind academic writing. (Generally, we've always thought it unfair to value intellectual complexity, or even demand it from students, without teaching it—without modeling and dramatizing it.) We hope the particular prompts, questions, and activities help animate your classrooms and vitalize student projects.

Beyond the writing prompts, *Inventing Arguments* offers a range of sample essays and arguments. Students often yearn for models, while instructors want students to explore beyond models. It's a constant pedagogical tension. We tried to address this tension by including sample essays in each chapter, but also displaying the intensive thinking behind those models. We've also found that students can easily become lost in a sea of readings—that too many readings can steal time and energy away from writing projects. Therefore, we've limited the essays in Chapters 7–12 to four samples, including one annotated piece of student or commissioned writing. (Additional readings are now in Part Four.)

Part Three: Research

We designed the research section with the student in mind—not only with the common questions and problems that students experience but also with the resources and opportunities available to them. We hope that this section teaches students to think of research as a process of reading, entering, and inventing arguments. It includes the common strategies for primary research, print and electronic research, and offers crucial advice for evaluating sources that rely on the use of statistics.

Part Four: Argument Anthology

To help instructors create synthesis assignments and to give students resources for their own writing projects, we offer a wide selection of voices, political perspectives, and topics in the Argument Anthology. The anthology features a range of readings (essays, articles, reports, and images) within thematic categories: Politics, Men and Women, Race, Environment, Education, Consumption, Popular Culture and Media, Technology, and Philosophy and Humanity. Each reading offers follow-up analysis questions that focus on rhetorical moves working in the argument and quiet connections with other readings in the book.

New to the Fourth Edition

- A new discussion of Classical, Rogerian, and Toulmin Argument in Chapter 1 helps students understand different ways of thinking about argument.

- Increased coverage of Rogerian argument in Chapter 4 includes Carl Rogers' essay "Communication: Its Blocking and Its Facilitation" and an opportunity for students to approach a rhetorical situation from a Rogerian perspective, one based on cooperation and understanding.

- Increased coverage of Toulminian terms in Chapter 5 helps students to better analyze—to dig further into the evasive layers of practical arguments.

- A new name for Chapter 5, "Assumptions and Values," better reflects its coverage.

- Types of claims (fact, value, and policy) introduced in Chapter 2 are more clearly related to the writing projects in Part Two: Arguing Definitions, Arguing Causes, Arguing Value, Arguing Crisis, Arguing the Past, and Arguing the Future.

- Part Three, Research, is now divided into two chapters: Chapter 13, The Research Path, and Chapter 14, Documenting Styles.

- Updated and new citations have been added to both the MLA and APA sections of Chapter 14. A new design better distinguishes the two citation styles for easier reference. The chapter includes the updated documentation guidelines put forth in the eighth edition of the *MLA Handbook* (2016).

Unique Pedagogical Tools

WHAT DO OTHERS CLAIM? WHAT DO I CLAIM?

This activity in each Part Two chapter helps students understand the rhetorical situation and reinforces an essential and often overlooked skill: distinguishing one's own thinking from other voices. These questions also get at the rhetorical theory at the center of the book, namely that better ideas emerge from the juxtaposition of (and tension between) perspectives.

MORE SAMPLE CLAIMS

Each chapter features an "Inventing a Claim" section, which helps students with the heavy intellectual work of narrowing their ideas to a revelatory thesis—one that reveals a new dimension to a topic. And each chapter offers a list of revelatory thesis statements about a variety of topics—so students can see the possibilities for their own projects.

INVENTION QUESTIONS/INVENTION WORKSHOPS

Each chapter in Part Two relies on key questions. These questions are well marked within each section so that you can assign them in class or as homework. The questions are also featured in Invention Workshops—classroom activities designed to help students maximize the rhetorical situation of the classroom. (We've found, and heard, that these workshops animate classroom sessions while keeping the focus on student projects.)

A Final Note

As college composition instructors, we are always in danger of becoming custodians of grammar and arrangement—of format, style, and conformity. We are always (and already) in danger of losing the vitality of the Sophistic tradition, which emphasized invention and rhetorical situation. In writing this pedagogy, we tried to remind ourselves that the formal study of argument emerged from roughly the same place and the same time in history as the practice of democracy. We hope this book does justice to the critical work of the composition classroom—work that keeps both rhetoric and democracy alive.

ACKNOWLEDGMENTS

For years, we have thought that invention is the key to good writing. But in developing this book, we have come to believe that invention can change the world. In the process of indulging and promoting this belief, we have been fortunate for the support and contributions of savvy cohorts. We offer our humble gratitude to everyone involved in the creation and revision of this book:

Julie McBurney, content developer

Leslie Taggart, Senior Content Developer

Kate Derrick, Product Manager

Michael Lepera, Senior Content Production Manager

Edward Dionne, Production Manager at MPS North America

Ann Hoffman and Farah Fard in the Intellectual Property department

Marissa Falco, Senior Art Director

Rosemary Winfield, Senior Content Project Manager

Thanks also to our students and colleagues who have graciously joined us in our efforts to transcend what is and to invent what could be. Finally, thanks to our families and friends for enduring another edition.

Any textbook project requires hearty professionals who offer their time and energy to help steer the pedagogy in valuable directions. Once again, we relied heavily on the insights of our reviewers and were often humbled at their prowess. We are indebted to the following teachers, theorists, rhetoricians, and scholars:

John Boyd, Ball State University

Ludger Brinker, Macomb Community College

Glenda Buenger, William Penn University

Katawna Caldwell, Eastfield College

Anne Cassia, Merritt College

Naomi Clark, University of Missouri

Maureen Connolly, Elmhurst College

Robert Cooper, Eastfield College–Dallas County Community College

Joseph Couch, Montgomery College

Drucella Crutchfield, Southeastern University

Susan Davis, Arizona State University

Gwyn Enright, San Diego City College

Brooke Eubanks, Central Arizona College

Cassie Falke, East Texas Baptist University

Madelyn Flammia, University of Central Florida

Clarence Hundley, Thomas Nelson Community College

Elizabeth Huston, Eastfield College

Silas Gossman, Camden County College

Melanie Jenkins, Snow College

Elizabeth Joseph, Eastfield College

Cecilia Kennedy, Clark State Community College

Diane Martin, Brookhaven College

Theodore Matula, University of San Francisco

Ronald Miller, Francis Marion University

Shawn Miller, Francis Marion University

Dan Morgan, Scott Community College

Michael Morris, Eastfield College

Susan Nyikos, Utah State University

Ildiko Olasz, Northwest Missouri State University

Elizabeth Oldfield, Southeastern Community College

Thomas Owen, Eastfield College

Yolanda Page, University of Arkansas at Pine Bluff

Amy Ratto Parks, University of Montana

Amy Patrick, Western Illinois University

Martha Payne, Ball State University

Luke Rolfes, Northwest Missouri State University

Rod Romesburg, Rollins College

Nancy Rowe, Loyola University

Greg Siering, Ball State University

Shawn Smolen-Morton, Francis Marion University

Susan Swanson, Owensboro Community College

Bobby Vasquez, University of Nebraska – Omaha

Larissa Washington, Eastfield College

Sandra Young, Sacred Heart University

Will Zhang, Des Moines Area Community College

Online Resources

MINDTAP FOR INVENTING ARGUMENTS, FOURTH EDITION

The new *MindTap for Inventing Arguments,* Fourth Edition allows you to personalize your teaching through a Learning Path built with key student objectives and your syllabus in mind. The MindTap includes an ebook exactly like the print book, along with additional media and activities. The course is as flexible as you want it to be: you can add your own activities, PowerPoints, videos, and Google docs or simply select from the available content, and you can rearrange the parts to suit the needs of the course. Analytics and reports provide a snapshot of class progress, time in course, engagement, and completion rates.

The Insite App in MindTap provides students with an easy way to upload papers for peer review, instructor comments, and if desired, an originality check. You can comment on student papers using prepopulated comments or write your own; create your own library of comments that can then be reused; or respond to student papers in a video, which is especially useful in an online course to personalize your interaction with students. The Aplia App has a variety of grammar activities that you can assign if the class needs them, and these activities are autogradable.

ONLINE INSTRUCTOR'S MANUAL

Available for download on the password-protected instructor companion site, this manual contains invaluable syllabus planning and teaching tips, as well as outlines that make it easier to prepare for your course.

NOTE TO STUDENTS

Many thousands of students across the country are presently taking a course on argumentation and academic writing. Since it's a requirement for nearly all two-year and four-year college degrees in America, a fair question would be *What's so important about argument?* Among all the possible answers, instructors seem to give a few consistently:

- Because argumentation is a vital tool for thriving in academic life.
- Because supporting assertions in public and professional situations will define much of students' post-college life.
- Because sound argumentation is essential for maintaining a democracy.
- Because students need training in argument to defend against government and corporate propaganda.

- Because getting things done requires bringing others into your way of thinking.
- Because adept arguers are adept thinkers (and vice versa).

In short, most of us who teach these courses know that once you enter public life, you enter argumentative life. Chances are you will be called on almost daily to make assertions about your work, your rights, your faith, your freedom to be without faith, your family, your country, your own hopes. You will have to argue for yourself and others, and for the world that you want to inhabit. And even if you don't make such arguments, others will. Voices all around you will try to define how you should live and think and even hope.

With these ideas in mind, we have tried to create an argumentative experience—a series of chapters that will immerse you in the complexities and nuances of argument. We hoped to create an experience for and *about* students—about the real situations that surround you and define your lives.

Part One: Entering Argument

These chapters introduce the basic and not-so-basic layers of argument. As you will see, there are many terms and tools—and your instructor may highlight some more than others. As the chapters in this section proceed, they increase in complexity—beginning with the most essential and visible layers of argument and evolving into the most evasive or hidden aspects. We have tried to keep the main and most common terms as headings. In other words, if you understand (and know how to apply) the terms in bold throughout these chapters, you will be well on your way to understanding the function and power of academic argument.

Part Two: Inventing Argument

From our perspective, this is the heart of the book. It's where you, the writer, develop arguments from the ground up. We consider these chapters the big assignment projects in the book—where you will apply the tools learned in Part One. Of course, the projects you take on will depend upon your course, your instructor, and your college's particular objectives, but we designed these chapters to facilitate real arguments in your life. Following the ancient Greeks (who invented this whole study), you will learn the most from arguing in real situations. And don't forget, the classroom is a real situation. We hope you'll see these chapters as opportunities to dig up, reveal, and argue about something that matters in your community.

Part Three: Research

If your college course is like most throughout the country, you will be responsible for learning the nuances of formal research and documentation. It may sound intimidating—or wildly boring. But it doesn't have to be. We see research as another part of invention. The strategies offered in this section can be applied to any of the writing projects in Chapters 7–12. The research chapters will help you to work with interviews, surveys, print sources (such as books, journals, magazines, and newspapers), and electronic sources (such as websites, databases, and online books). These chapters also explain important skills such as paraphrase, summary, and quotation and cover documentation formats for the Modern Language Association (MLA) and the American Psychological Association (APA).

Part Four: Argument Anthology

Some instructors encourage their students to explore particular -topics—to get immersed in arguments about one particular issue; for example, environmental resources, election politics, racial tension, advertising in popular culture, and so on. We designed this Anthology for that purpose—so that students could follow up with a particular issue, synthesize a group of readings, and find the quiet connections among them. While you could easily develop nuanced and successful arguments with the readings in this book, we also suggest that you launch outward and find more essays, articles, reports, and images that help give meaning to your projects.

Peace,
John Mauk and John Metz

Argumentation: *(1) The act of asserting, supporting, and defending a claim;*
(2) The art of discovering and defending what should be thought, what should be done;
(3) The art of changing others' minds while not losing your own.

PART ONE

Entering Argument

Inventive writers learn to see
the lurking arguments.

Library of Congress Prints & Photographs Division

1

Inventing Arguments

WHAT IS ARGUMENT?

Argument is the act of asserting, supporting, and defending a claim. It is an intellectual and a social process. People are surrounded by argument. It can be said that public life is argumentative—that people are vying to be heard, trying to assert their vision of the world to anyone who will hear it. But argument can work in more subtle ways in the form of advertisements, songs, billboards, posters, slogans, and stories. While our daily language may not be full of explicit debate, it is full of underlying values and unstated assumptions. When people make a point about a favorite song or an interesting class, they are hinting at an entire argument, which entails a set of values and assumptions about social worth.

American history can be seen, and is often taught, as a series of arguments. The Founding Fathers were exemplary arguers, and Thomas Jefferson's Declaration of Independence may be one of the most politically significant arguments the world has seen. Arguments have driven American history: the evolution of its colonies and states, the development of a federal government, the drawing of borders, the accumulation of territory, the removal of Native Americans, the institution of slavery, the abolitionist movement, the South's secession from the Union, the Civil War, Reconstruction, the emergence of public education, the extension of voting rights, the Industrial Revolution, the development of unions, the rise of monopoly capitalism, the Works Progress Administration during the Great Depression, the nation's role in World War I and II, the Japanese-American internment camps, the Civil Rights movement, the Vietnam War, *Roe vs. Wade,* Watergate, the L.A. riots, the Iran-Contra scandal, the war on drugs, biotechnology, the nation's intervention in Iraq, state marriage amendments, ballot counting—the list goes on and on. All of these events and situations have been layered with fevered arguments and advocates competing to take the country in one direction instead of another. Today, we need only to turn on the television to hear argument stacked atop argument. From CNN to Comedy Central, news anchors and standup comedians alike are leading participants in collective arguments.

WHAT IS ACADEMIC ARGUMENT?

Although history seems fraught with bold arguments among classes, religions, rulers, and countries, the vast majority of arguments are subtler: small exchanges of ideas with participants urging others to accept their positions. Most often, argument does *not* include beating an opponent, taking up arms, or preaching to an audience, but involves making a debatable position appear reasonable or acceptable. And this is the primary motive behind academic argument: *to make others see the wisdom of a position or perspective.*

Academic disciplines are arenas of argument. Many college students are surprised to discover the degree to which their fields of study have grown from internal debates. In composition studies, for instance, some scholars, called expressionists, have argued that ideas come from inside a writer's consciousness; other scholars, known as social constructionists, have argued that ideas emerge from the influence of social conditions that surround a writer; still other scholars have tried to combine these views. Or consider psychology: Sigmund Freud did not simply announce his theories on psychoanalysis to receptive audiences. He presented his theories as arguments. In fact, every major figure in a field of study, from chemistry to engineering, has been an arguer as much as anything else.

Many scholars say that academic disciplines provide their own language of argument. In other words, engineers learn how to make arguments within the framework of engineering, chemists learn how to argue using the language of chemistry, and so forth. They learn the formulas, language, and equations required to enter the ongoing arguments of their discipline. It might even be said that academic disciplines teach students how to view the world. Biologists, for instance, may come to believe that the world is knowable and that the origins of life can be discovered. Philosophers may come to believe that nothing can be known outside of a particular time and place. Psychologists may come to believe that people have control over their decisions. These beliefs and assumptions may rest quietly beneath the daily thoughts and work of biologists, philosophers, and psychologists, but they have significant impact on what gets said and done. And eventually, all those who practice within a discipline are affected by the assumptions (and the arguments) that have accumulated during their studies.

Outside the academic tradition is a popular saying: "People are entitled to their own opinions." But we should investigate this statement because it poses a problem for those interested in the study of argument. It suggests that people's opinions are set in stone. But people do not simply keep their opinions. Instead, they trade them for others. Thus, to say that *people are entitled to their own opinions* greatly oversimplifies the human consciousness, which is actually a complex process of building, transforming, and trading opinions. It ignores how people really work in the world of ideas, and it ignores the power of language to shape our perspectives on the world around us.

Although the saying "People are entitled to their own opinions" seems open-minded, the statement most often means, "What other people think doesn't matter to me." This statement is often used to dismiss others' opinions; it is used to stop exploration and cut people off from others' arguments. But in a democratic society, in which everyday citizens help constitute policy, vote for political agendas, and conclude verdicts, other people's opinions do matter. What people think about labor, war, abortion, human rights, water pollution, corporate power, and so forth impacts the civilization that we all inhabit. More than anything else (more than money, weapons, or even good looks), other people's opinions influence how we live. Because most of us do not live on our own islands, cut off from the influence of culture, law, and policy, others' opinions directly filter into our everyday behaviors and thoughts. And that is why argument is so important.

Argument has been studied and taught since antiquity. In college classes today, different ideas from ancient and current traditions help students to understand and invent arguments.

CLASSICAL ARGUMENT Rhetoricians from ancient Greece and Rome taught a wide range of argument methods, terms, and concepts. As in the United States today, argument was a major part of public life—a way of developing policy, deciding on laws, and determining courses of action. While many ancient ideas have been carried forward over the millennia, the following will be especially important throughout this text:

Ancient rhetoricians such as Aristotle divided argumentative assertions into three categories: One could make a claim about the existence or nature of something (a claim of **fact**), the intensity or worth of something (a claim of **value**), and what can or might be done about something (a claim of **policy**). These categories, explained more thoroughly in Chapter 2, have held up through history. Modern rhetoricians and teachers still use the distinctions to make sense of different arguments.

The ancients also categorized support strategies or what are sometimes called proofs. While there were different names and grids, three categories were consistent: evidence, examples, and appeals. Like the distinctions among claims, these categories are still in place today. They are explained thoroughly in Chapter 3.

The final support category, appeals, was especially critical to ancient rhetoricians, who saw the act of engaging an audience as an art form—a delicate process of connecting a topic to people's beliefs and emotions. They created three general categories for this artistic process: **ethos**, an appeal based on the presenter's character and credibility; **pathos**, an appeal to emotion; and **logos**, an appeal to reason or logic. In other words, arguers could support their claims by foregrounding their own character, tapping into a shared emotion, or developing a logical case. These categories are also explained more thoroughly in Chapter 3.

As this chapter explains, many other terms and concepts come to us from ancient Greek and Roman scholars, but the following are essential:

Three Claims: Fact, Value, Policy

Three Kinds of Support: Evidence, Examples, Appeals

Three Appeals: Ethos, Pathos, Logos

ROGERIAN ARGUMENT In "Communication: Its Blocking and Its Facilitation" (1961), psychologist Carl Rogers proposed a type of communication based on finding common ground. As a psychologist, Rogers believed the major barrier to interpersonal communication was one's tendency to quickly form an evaluation in response to someone else's statement. Rogers proposed listening with understanding first and then accurately restating the other person's position before responding. He writes,

> Each person can speak up for himself only when he has first restated the ideas and feelings of the previous speaker accurately, and to that speaker's satisfaction. You see what this would mean. It would simply mean that before presenting your own point of view, it would be necessary for you to really achieve the other speaker's frame of reference to understand his thoughts and feelings so well that you could summarize them for him.

According to Rogers, this approach takes the emotion out of the discussion, which leads to a more rational exchange and a better chance of mutual understanding. Taking a Rogerian approach means trying to really understand someone else's position before responding. And by doing this, *your* position, not just theirs, is likely to change. Rogerian argument is discussed further in Chapter 4, Opposition.

TOULMIN ARGUMENT In *The Uses of Argument* (1958) and *An Introduction to Reasoning* (1979), philosopher and educator Stephen Toulmin provides an explanation of practical reasoning and argumentation. Toulmin explains that while trains, or lines, of reasoning vary from situation to situation, all situations share certain features. The Toulmin model describes those common features: claim, grounds, warrant, backing, rebuttal, and qualifier.

In addition to describing these six features, Toulmin explains that reasoning can be used for **inquiry** and for **advocacy**. Using reasoning for inquiry leads to *discovering* new ideas, and using reasoning for advocacy involves *supporting* an existing idea. Using reasoning for inquiry is what Ancient rhetoricians, like Aristotle, called *invention*. This is using language (reasoning) to explore, discover, and develop ideas; to explore into the complexities of ideas; and to complicate one's thinking about a topic.

We use reasoning to invent, through writing and speaking, and alone as we think. In *An Introduction to Reasoning*, Toulmin explains:

> [W]e often begin to test our ideas in a critical manner and think over the available reasons for or against them as soon as we first have the ideas. In a form of thinking that might be called *intrapersonal communication*, we imagine ourselves sharing an idea with other people and rehearse the questions they might ask and the challenges they might make to our supporting reasons.

When you have an imaginary discussion (a debate or argument) with someone (a friend, coworker, family member), you are using reasoning to think through what you *might* think about an issue. This is a common act of invention: we all do it, probably every day. And this is one way, perhaps the main way, that we arrive at the positions we take in life. Toulmin's model helps us invent ideas and then advocates for them. This model—and how the six parts of it function—is discussed in more depth in Chapter 5, Values and Assumptions.

Activities

1. With several others, debate the following: *Why do opinions change?* Share your initial thinking, and then explore other possibilities. Consider particular opinions you once held but that changed.

2. In a small group, make a list of careers that people prepare for in college, such as doctor, accountant, marketing specialist, nutritionist, and so on. Then discuss how a college education teaches students in each field to view the world in a particular way.

3. What arguments make up the national debate about the war in Afghanistan?

4. What arguments are put forth in the preamble of the Declaration of Independence?

WHAT IS RHETORIC?

Rhetoric is a process of recognizing and using the most effective strategies for influencing thought. The Greek philosopher Aristotle defined rhetoric as the ability to see the available means of persuasion for each particular case. In other words, rhetoric is more than a tool for changing people's minds; it is also the study of how people are persuaded into their beliefs. People who study rhetoric and writing are interested in how opinions form and change. They study the relationship between language and belief, and they examine the cultural conditions around people and their everyday use of language.

In its classical Greek origins (circa fifth-century BCE), rhetoric was a primary field of study. In many ways, it was the glue between various academic pursuits because it focused on how ideas (regardless of content) are used, shared, communicated, implemented, and manipulated. The study of rhetoric was the study of social and intellectual activity. Today, in popular use, rhetoric has a significantly smaller domain and is sometimes narrowly associated with empty or dishonest language.

Greek philosopher Aristotle.

The cartoon on the next page may point to a truth about politics, but *rhetoric is not about dishonesty*. Rhetoric is most often used honestly to communicate ideas and to bring others into one's own perspective. In this sense, everyone uses rhetoric. A child learns that adding "please" to his request for a cookie gets better results than screaming, "Cookie!" A teenager knows that asking for the family car should involve some mention of her intentions to be home early. Imagine the following exchange between an employee and his boss:

> "Hey, I need to leave early today."
>
> "Well, Vick, you can't."

Then notice the added layers of rhetoric in the following:

> "Excuse me, Kim. My daughter has an important doctor's appointment, and I was wondering if I could leave early today to be with her."
>
> "Sure, Vick. Can you come in early tomorrow to make up for the lost time?"

We might call the second exchange more polite or more respectful. But the layer of respect is also a layer of rhetoric, a strategy for inviting the audience (Kim) into the speaker's perspective. Vick is not being dishonest in the second example—at least, we cannot assume he is. He merely gives some information that helps make his request seem valid. In fact, anytime someone offers information, describes something a particular way, or arranges information in a particular way so that someone else will accept a claim, he or she is making rhetorical decisions.

PRESCRIPTION DRUG BENEFIT!

PATIENTS BILL OF RIGHTS!

BLAH, BLAH, BLAH, BLAH, BLAH,...

CONGRESS

EMPTY RHETORIC

Huck/Konopacki Labor Cartoons

But the preceding examples are rather basic. The child who says "please" and the worker who nuances his request are not *studying* rhetoric. They are simply using the available means of persuasion. The student of rhetoric explores the ways in which different uses of language impact people in various situations. That is, students of rhetoric ask questions about particular situations:

- What is happening? Why should someone speak out?
- Who is present? Who is the audience?
- What are the audience's values and beliefs?
- What kind of language would best appeal to those beliefs?

When we try to make a point seem reasonable, ethical, or emotional for a particular audience, we are involved in a rhetorical effort. That effort can be dramatic, such as when a lawyer is trying to persuade a jury to see facts in a particular way or when a politician gives an impassioned speech. Sometimes, the rhetorical effort can be subtle. For instance, when scientists arrange information on a laboratory report, they present their findings so that their work appears coherent and logical. The scientists may not make a dramatic point about their own thinking, but the report may still have a rhetorical dimension:

> Results: Overall, beavers showed a preference for certain species of trees, and their preference was based on distance from the central place. Measurements taken at the study site show that beavers avoided oaks and musclewood . . . and show a significant food preference ($x_- = 447.26$, d.f. $= 9$, $P < .05$). No avoidance or particular preference was observed for the other tree species. (http://www.ncsu.edu/labwrite/res /labreport/res-sample-labrep.html) – Copyright © 2004 by NC State University.

One of the most obvious uses of rhetoric is in advertising. Television, radio, magazine, Internet, and even restroom advertisements use language and graphics to persuade us to buy things. It works. Americans are profoundly influenced by advertising rhetoric—so much so that it has become an art form. Companies spend billions of dollars each year in a rhetorical race for our attention. They shape every sentence and carefully select every image so each ad will have the most dramatic effect on its audience. Rhetoric is a powerful aspect of language, perhaps the most powerful. When used for positive purposes, it can help people share ideas, values, and visions. When used for negative purposes, it can prompt people to waste money on useless trinkets or lead them into treachery.

Rhetoric is more than the selection and arrangement of words. It also is a deeper exploration of thought and language. Students and scholars of rhetoric can ask theoretical questions:

- What is the relationship between thought and language?
- How does a particular type of language influence consciousness?

- How do particular values or beliefs stay in place over time?
- How do some values or beliefs get dismissed or overrun?

The study of rhetoric is still at the heart of writing classes today. Students learn not just about correct grammar but also about the relationship between language and thought, the processes of analyzing and creating *discourse* (language in use). The goal of studying rhetoric is to examine the nuances of persuasive language as they appear in essays, reports, literature, slogans, advertisements, speeches, memos, policies, art, entertainment, and even actions. Rhetoric is key to the study of argument. In a sense, there can be no argument without rhetoric.

The ancient Greek lessons on rhetoric still apply today. In writing, debate, communication, and speech courses, students study the five categories, or canons, of rhetoric passed down from the ancient Greeks:

Jason Smith/Getty Images for NASCAR/Getty Images Sport

Driver Tony Stewart in victory lane after winning the NASCAR Sprint Cup Series Pepsi Max 400.

- **Invention:** the discovery and development of ideas
- **Arrangement:** the organization of ideas in a coherent and engaging fashion
- **Style or voice:** the personal or individualized use of language conventions, with attention to appropriateness, situation, and audience
- **Memory:** the recollection of prepared points
- **Delivery:** the presentation of ideas

These canons are used as intellectual tools for developing, extending, and shaping ideas. Because discovering and developing ideas is so important to academic writing, invention is an extensive part of the process, and it has a primary place in this book. As you will see in Chapters 7–12, arrangement and voice are also important components.

Rhetorical situation refers to an opportunity to address a particular audience about a disputed or disputable issue. Looking back at the definition of *rhetoric,* we might say that the rhetorical situation is an opportunity to gather and use the available means of persuasion. A rhetorical situation involves an **exigence**—an occasion when something happens or does not happen that results in some uncertainty. The rhetorical situation also involves a speaker/writer, an

---

Rhetorical Situation

The rhetorical situation includes the

- tension or "exigence"
- arguer (speaker/writer)
- audience
- method of communication
- rules of communication
- text or message

---

audience, a method of communication, and the rules of communication (whether directly stated or implied), as well as the text, or message. All elements of the rhetorical situation exist in time and place, which impact what can and should be said. Good rhetoricians (good writers) know how to seize upon all the particular elements of time and place. They build points out of the raw social materials around them.

Academic essays have their own rhetorical situation. The student is the speaker/writer; the audience is usually defined by a group of peers and an instructor; the rules of communication are explicitly defined (and even evaluated) on a syllabus and assignment prompt; and the assignment itself is the exigence—the opportunity to address the audience, to assert a way of thinking about a topic. (Imagine seeing an assignment as a rhetorical opportunity!) In academic settings, writers should assume that their audiences are attentive, informed, and tuned in to all the layers of an argument. Academic readers are constantly thinking about the messages being sent and the way the ideas can be received. As a result, they expect rhetorical moves that are not common in many popular culture arguments:

- **Revelatory rather than familiar points:** While popular culture attempts to make audiences comfortable by repeating familiar phrases and announcing widely held opinions, academic argument attempts to give the audience a new way of seeing the topic. Academic argument attempts to reveal previously unseen layers of ideas.

- **Appeals to logic rather than emotion:** While the goal of much popular culture, from news programs to MTV, is to engage our emotions (such as fear or desire), academic argument appeals more to the audience's ability to reason and think through difficult or complex issues. This is not to say that academic argument avoids emotional appeals, but it uses them sparingly.

- **Analysis rather than packaging:** While popular culture packages ideas into slogans, academic argument seeks to *unpack* ideas, breaking open familiar phrases and concepts.

- **Inclusion rather than exclusion:** Many arguments in popular culture exclude groups of people. Some political talk show hosts, for example, will deride liberals or conservatives, thereby confirming their audience's beliefs. But academic arguments attempt to place less focus on people's individual qualities and instead invite the audience into a way of thinking.

Activities

1. Think of a recent college class. Make a list of all the rhetorical strategies of the instructor and the students. Consider all the subtle and explicit ways that instructors work to bring students into a way of thinking— about the class, the rules, the rewards, the penalties. And consider how students work to persuade instructors of their abilities, their dedication, or even their apathy about the course. Consider particular language, phrasing, words, suggestions.

2. Make a list of situations from history or current events in which rhetoric has been used for good or bad purposes.

3. Describe a situation in the past twenty-four hours in which you made a rhetorical decision.

WHAT IS INVENTION?

Invention is the discovery and development of ideas. It is the engine of argument: It moves everyone involved (arguer and audience) away from worn-out statements and toward new territory and vital ideas. Without it, arguers end up reasserting tired statements, going around in circles, or simply projecting their initial opinions on a given topic. Invention allows arguers to discover, for themselves and their audiences, something worthy of their attention.

Beginning writers sometimes assume that invention means merely brainstorming for a topic—tricks such as clustering or free writing. Once they have a topic that seems like it might generate lots of ideas, they stop inventing and start drafting. But this strategy is flawed in two important ways. First, invention is not necessarily a chaotic storm in the brain, a mysterious and random array of lightning strikes. (If that's all it were, writing would be a complete disaster.) Invention can be a deliberate process, a challenging journey driven by probing questions and strategic intellectual moves. Second, invention is not something that ends once someone finds a topic and takes a stand. In fact, the real thinking and the most intensive intellectual probing begin once a topic is found: a writer must develop support (evidence, examples, and appeals) that adds dimension and substance to a position.

A common misconception about argument, and about academic writing in general, is that opinions must be proven with facts based on some form of research. According to this view, the best arguments must be those that have lots of statistics and data to support claims. Because of this, writers may feel inclined to depend on others' words and ideas, and they might have difficulty developing points on their own. But those who know key invention strategies can use research more strategically than those who rely on it to make every point for them. And those who know how to invent can get beyond their initial opinions about a topic and develop thoughts that shed new light on hidden layers. Notice how the following discussion goes from an initial opinion to a more complex insight:

Jack: Old people should stay off the roads.

Linda: Just because they drive slowly?

Jack: No, because they drive slowly and they hold up other people. And because everyone else is in a hurry, the older drivers make driving hazardous.

Diana: So the people in a hurry aren't the hazards?

Jack: Well, of course they are, but the slower drivers just frustrate everyone who wants to go the speed limit.

Diana: Or faster?

Jack: Yes . . . or faster.

Linda: If everyone on the roads had no obstacles and they could speed to where they needed to be, would the roads be safer? Would people drive any better?

Jack: Well, maybe not.

Linda: So is the problem really "old people"?

Jack: The problem is that everyone—those people in a hurry and those who aren't—have to share the roads.

Diana: And most people aren't very good at sharing space.

Jack: In general, people have their own cars, their own homes, their own lawnmowers, their own . . . everything. But suddenly, they pull out into the street, and they're in shared space.

Linda: So you're saying that the problem isn't with only one group of drivers—it's with an attitude that might include all groups?

The conversation develops into something more insightful than Jack's first personal opinion. As the three writers talk, they invent increasingly layered ideas. They ask questions about their own claims and thereby open up intellectual possibilities that they could not previously have imagined. They do not merely express opinions or give answers. Instead, they assert an idea and then interrogate it. In this way, inventive writers learn to see the lurking arguments:

- The real danger on the highways is speed and the belief that speed is an inherent good.
- American roadways are plagued not so much by particular groups of drivers but by the pace of everyday life.
- Americans' prejudices against one another are dramatized on the highway.
- Americans' strong sense of individuality (which centers on their own homes, their own cars, their own lawnmowers, etc.) makes it difficult for them to share anything—even the highways.

In short, invention gets writers past their initial ideas and propels them beyond their personal opinions. It is the genesis of good writing and powerful argumentation. Because the goal of argument is to reveal a new way of seeing a topic (hence persuading people to rethink their positions and beliefs), good invention strategies are the key to success. Invention is such a key part of good writing and good arguing that Chapters 7–12 in this textbook devote several sections to it. These Invention sections offer series of questions that lead writers to increasingly complex and revelatory ideas.

Activities

1. Closely examine the discussion among Jack, Linda, and Diana. Describe the specific points in the conversation that take the ideas beyond Jack's initial opinion. Describe, in specific terms, how Diana and Linda help Jack go from his initial opinion to a more complex insight.

2. With a small group of peers (in class or online), develop an idea from an initial opinion to a more complex insight (as Jack, Linda, and Diana do on pages 11–12). Keep a running record of the conversation. Try to trace the progression of thought. After the discussion, answer the following:

   a. What new ideas (new ways of thinking about the topic) emerged?

   b. What prompted the new way of thinking—a probing question, a provocative statement, a debate about some particular word or phrase?

3. At the beginning of the chapter, we claim that "American history can be seen, and is often taught, as a series of arguments." Consider this recruitment ad from World War II. How does it, as an artifact of history, make an argument about America, women, gender, or war?

Library of Congress Prints & Photographs Division Washington, DC/ Falter, John Philip, 1910-.[LC-USZC4-1856]

Philippe Lissac/Godong/Encyclopedia/Corbis

2

Claims

WHAT IS A CLAIM?

A **claim** is an argumentative assertion. It is the statement being put forward—the idea that requires support. Complex arguments, like those developed in academic essays, usually have more than one claim: they have a main claim and supporting claims (what we call *premises* in Chapter 3). Such arguments are actually one argument made up of smaller arguments.

Basic Argument	Complex Argument
Claim	Main Claim
Support	*Supporting Claim*
	Support
	Supporting Claim
	Support
	Supporting Claim
	Support
	Supporting Claim
	Support

A main claim can have any number of supporting claims (not just four, as shown in the preceding illustration). For example, in a discussion about where to take a week's vacation, someone might claim, *We should go to Myrtle Beach.* To support this claim, the person would make other claims, such as *Myrtle Beach has one of the finest beaches on the East Coast; Myrtle Beach has over 250 golf courses*; and so on. And those supporting claims can be developed with additional supporting claims. For example, to support *Myrtle Beach has one of the finest beaches on the East Coast,* one might claim that *The Myrtle Beach area includes sixty miles of diverse beaches* or that *The beach includes a new boardwalk with amusements, food, and lots of great people-watching.*

TYPES OF CLAIMS

Main claims, which are sometimes called thesis statements, are the primary assertions about a given topic. Main claims do not merely state what the argument is about; they reveal the arguer's particular stance on a given topic. Some theorists split argumentative claims into three types: fact, value, and policy.

CLAIMS OF FACT argue that a condition exists, has existed, or will exist. This type of claim may be confusing because we often associate fact with truth, but facts themselves are always in dispute. They must be proven or at least supported so that others accept them. The following claims, for example, are not facts but *claims of fact*—statements that call for support:

- The Roman Empire influenced all of Europe.
- CO_2 emissions are impacting temperatures globally.
- The Packers will win the Super Bowl this year.

Claims of fact include those that argue a definition:

- Education is the process of building new concepts and destroying old ones.
- Despite the Democratic Party's stated principles, it can easily be defined as the slightly less corporate wing of the Republican Party.
- Punk is not about a particular fashion but the constant denial of the mainstream, manufactured aesthetic.

Claims of fact also assert cause or effect:

- Teenagers smoke marijuana because it fits into their socioeconomic structure.
- Students procrastinate because the traditional school assignment has taught them to.
- Racial tension in the city lingers because no public official has acknowledged the string of aggressive police actions in recent years.

Scholars in all disciplines make claims of fact. For instance, they claim what exactly happened at the Battle of Wounded Knee, what dark matter is, how feminism evolved into different strands of thought, what caused a plane to disappear, how a new Cold War will likely develop, and so on. Because claims of fact are so important to academic writing, they drive most of the sample essays and articles in this book. The following chapters focus exclusively on claims of fact:

Chapter 6: Analyzing Argument

Chapter 7: Arguing Definitions

Chapter 8: Arguing Causes

Chapter 12: Arguing the Future

CLAIMS OF VALUE argue that something possesses or reflects a particular quality (good, bad, just, unreasonable, practical, unfair, etc.). It may assert approval or disapproval. Any claim that argues worth is a claim of value. An adjective, or what is called a predicate of value, usually can be found in the claim. For instance, *good, underhanded,* and *irresponsible* are all predicates of value in the following:

The Packers are not a very good team this year.

The governor's strategies for getting elected are underhanded.

Because of growing amounts of CO_2 in the atmosphere, it is irresponsible to build high-emission automobiles.

Claims of value generate arguments about the harm or worth of actions, ideas, policies, laws, texts, and even entire academic disciplines. In this chapter, Ryan Brown argues about the harm of automobile culture. And in Chapter 9, Arguing Value, all the essays, activities, and assignments focus directly on claims of value.

CLAIMS OF POLICY argue that some action should be taken or some change made. Claims of policy make a case for a particular behavior, approach, or even attitude.

- The Confederate flag should not be flown above government buildings.
- Voluntary prayer should be allowed in public school.
- The local Humane Society branch should launch an educational campaign about rabies.

With claims of policy, arguers call for something to happen. Granted, at some level, all arguments call for action: they invite others to shift their positions, cling to a stance, or adopt a new one. But a claim of policy makes that call explicit. If policy is the main claim of an essay, then all supporting claims, evidence, examples, and appeals work to develop and substantiate that call.

Even when they are arguing fact or value, writers often end with or suggest a policy claim. For example, in her famous essay about the nature of war, Margaret Mead (page 118) asserts a claim of fact: war is not a biological necessity but an invention of some civilizations. But in her conclusion, Mead makes a case for change:

> There is further needed a belief that social invention is possible and the invention of new methods which will render warfare as out of date as the tractor is making the plough, or the motor car the horse and buggy. A form of behavior becomes out of date only when something else takes its place, and, in order to invent forms of behavior which will make war obsolete, it is a first requirement to believe that an invention is possible.

Like Mead, plenty of writers throughout this book end with a claim of policy. But Chapter 10, Arguing Crisis, focuses exclusively on policy claims.

Activity

The three types of claims (fact, value, and policy) do not belong to any topic or situation. Notice, for instance, how different claims can work in an argument about the past:

Claim of Fact: The failed school levy of 2000 changed the operations of the public schools for the entire decade.

Claim of Value: The voting public was misguided in its decision to vote down the 2000 school levy.

Claim of Policy: The voting public should not have voted against the school levy in 2000, and the community should work to repair the negative impact of that significant year.

As a class, take on one of the following topics and develop three argumentative claims (fact, value, and policy):

- the blurring between news and entertainment
- increasing photo and video capabilities on cell phones
- the price of college tuition

Jerry Seinfeld

Understanding different claims is vital to good argument. In fact, in our everyday lives, we sometimes work hard to manage the way others hear us. We use a standard formula for dispelling any confusion: I'm not saying _____; I'm saying _____. Often, this move is to make sure others understand the nature of our point:

- I'm not saying we should do anything; I'm just saying that the guy is a fake!

- I'm not saying that Martha's parties are boring; I'm saying that I don't want to go tonight.

- I'm not saying that we shouldn't get a dog; I'm saying that it will be hard work.

- I'm not arguing whether or not they won; I'm arguing that they didn't win fairly.

In each case the speaker is clarifying the nature of the claim—saying, in effect, "I am making this type of claim, not one of the others." For *Seinfeld* fans, this potential confusion was played out in an episode in which the main character, Jerry, found himself insisting that he wasn't gay. He said repeatedly, "I'm not gay" (a claim of fact), and then followed each time with "not that there's anything wrong with that" (a claim of value). In other words, he didn't want people to think he was making a value judgment about sexual orientation. He was, instead, making a claim of fact about his own orientation.

Sometimes, different claims work in tandem. For instance, a claim of fact may launch a claim of policy. In the following, the first clause ("Because…") establishes the fact while the second clause calls for action:

- Because the minds of our generation are consumed and distracted by sports, the only alternative is to remove athletics completely from public high schools.

- Because corporate testing services now dictate curriculum while sucking huge amounts of money from public education, teachers and parents must unite and halt the entire system.

A claim of fact may also launch a claim of value. In Charles Nelson's essay "Investing in Futures," he makes a claim of fact about college tuition (that it will likely grow past the worth of some degrees) and then suggests a claim of value about the cultural effects:

> Students are paying the same tuition for different degrees, and some of those degrees will eventually be boxed out of college because students graduating with the degree won't be able to pay back the loans. Unless something gives, when the cost of a college degree hits two or three hundred thousand dollars, colleges may be void of students studying art, poetry, or (in some states) education. If college tuition continues to increase at its present rate (and there's nothing to suggest it will not), higher education might price itself out of teaching literature, humanities, anthropology, sociology, philosophy . . . all the disciplines that explore what it means to be human. From there, it doesn't take a science fiction writer to imagine the ill effects on our little civilization.

We get a better understanding of Nelson's argument when we understand his claims—what he is and isn't arguing. It's important to know he is predicting the future of college costs (making a claim of fact), suggesting some harm (making a claim of value) but not at all arguing that students shouldn't major in the humanities (making a claim of policy). But imagine if someone were to read this passage and claim, "Nelson thinks people shouldn't major in philosophy!" Such a characterization would distort Nelson's argument beyond the point of recognition.

In sound argument, we should work to understand what people are arguing—not only the topic but the type of claim. Sometimes, people intentionally distort the nature of someone else's claim. For example, notice how the following exchange veers away from Senator Green's original claim:

> *Senator Green:* "Our state spends twenty million dollars on employee health care."
>
> *Senator Gray:* "This seems like the right amount to me. We cannot simply go cutting employee health care every time someone mentions the word."

Senator Green originally made a claim of fact. But Senator Gray changed the terms of engagement by pulling the issue into a claim of value (the amount is appropriate) and then a claim of policy (the state should not cut employee health care). When people like Senator Gray thrust the conversation too quickly away from the claim of fact—and into a claim of value or policy—they move the argument prematurely to the realm of judgments and solutions before the audience has a good grasp of the situation.

INVENTING CLAIMS

As you move into later chapters of this book, you will be prompted to invent your own claims. And while each writing project will have its own issues, it's worth considering some general qualities or attributes that make arguments more sophisticated. Powerful arguments develop *focused*, *arguable*, and *revelatory* main claims.

FOCUSED CLAIMS guide the reader's and writer's attention to a particular aspect of an issue. When a claim is focused, the argument gains depth, while a broad claim generates a shallow or incoherent argument. To check for focus, writers examine the main parts of a sentence, the subject and predicate, to see if they can be more specific. Notice the following unfocused claim:

Today's popular music is bad for children.

The subject is only slightly focused. While *popular music* is more focused than *music*, *today's popular music* includes a wide variety of genres and styles, from hip-hop to country. The writer would do well to focus on a particular aspect of popular music—a genre, a particular style, a particular medium, or a particular element of the music world:

fashion trends packaged with today's pop music

lyrics about inflated egos in today's hip-hop music

marketing strategies of today's country music

lack of genuine storytelling in today's rock music

The predicate of the sentence is vague as well. The fact that something *is bad* does not give us any particular insight. The adjective *bad* can be attributed to anything from pneumonia to cookies. Part of the problem stems from the verb *is*, which is a linking verb rather than an action verb. When linking verbs are used as the main verbs in sentences, they work like equals signs:

today's popular music = bad for children

Linking verbs prompt writers to think in vague terms and to use unfocused adjectives such as *bad*. Action verbs can help focus ideas:

deteriorates children's abilities to think critically

directs children to trivial issues

oversimplifies the complexities of urban life

conjures up delusions of self-importance in children

Notice how the verbs (deteriorates, directs, oversimplifies, conjures) create focus.

Activity

Consider how the following unfocused thesis statements could be more focused. Decide if the problem lies in the subject or in the predicate. Create at least two different subjects and two different predicates for each.

1. People should avoid large corporate retailers.
2. *King Lear* is Shakespeare's best work.
3. The settlers were wrong in driving out the Native Americans.
4. There are many good things about public television.

ARGUABLE CLAIMS make assertions that could be challenged on various grounds. In other words, they invite or directly address opposition. Some common problems can keep thesis statements from being arguable.

The Question Problem

A question is not a claim because it offers no stance. People sometimes use questions to imply a stance: *Isn't that the point of democracy? Why can't you be more like your sister?* But this is generally an informal strategy, something done in everyday communication. A formal argumentative stance usually suggests a particular position amid a realm of many others, something that a question does not do.

The Obvious Fact Problem

Good arguments often attempt to overturn common beliefs or things that people presume to be true. For instance, in opposition to the beliefs of his day, the medieval astronomer Copernicus argued that the Earth was not the center of the universe. In contrast, an argument that simply announces a commonly known condition or a widely held belief is no argument at all. Imagine someone arguing: *Many people go to college for their futures; Americans love cars; Space exploration is expensive.* Because they express common beliefs instead of overturning them, such statements function as observations but not argumentative claims.

The Personal Response Problem

Argument depends upon the presence of multiple perspectives peering at the same topic. When writers proclaim a personal response about their tastes, likes, dislikes, or desires, they merely make public their own state of mind. "I really liked the first *Pirates of the Caribbean*" is not an argumentative stance; it is a statement about a person's tastes. But the statement "Johnny Depp's portrayal of a wayward pirate illustrates his superior range as an actor" invites opposition. It goes beyond a personal response, and other positions can then engage the point critically.

Activity

Explain why the following statements are not arguable, and change them to invite opposition:

1. Should people shop at Walmart?
2. Injustice hurts people.
3. The Internet has changed the world.
4. I prefer taking the train to flying.

REVELATORY CLAIMS reveal an unfamiliar topic or a new layer of a familiar one. They challenge something that previously seemed entirely agreeable, or they show a hidden side to an issue. Revelatory claims do more than simply take a stand on an issue; they imply "You may already have an opinion, but . . . have you seen *this* side of the issue?" They tear down the curtains and show who is hiding behind them; they clear away the dirt and reveal the roots. Notice the difference between the following claims:

- Home schooling is good for families.
- Home schooling reconnects home life and formal learning.
- Home schooling reestablishes a key concept that disappeared throughout the twentieth century: that the home is the center of learning, development, and intellectual growth.

While the first claim celebrates home schooling, it does not offer a particular insight about its worth. It is an opinion, but nothing more. The second claim goes further and suggests a particular aspect about home schooling. The third claim goes further still by situating the point in history. The reader of the last two claims, especially the third, has been given a novel insight about home schooling. And the reader is bound to encounter a fresh way of thinking about the topic in the argument that develops. Revelatory claims are more than personal opinion; they are particular and persuasive insights. Revelatory argument depends on fresh perspectives that make an audience reconsider topics.

Activities

1. Consider how the following unfocused thesis statements could be more focused. Decide if the problem lies in the subject or in the predicate. Create at least two different subjects and two different predicates for each.

    A. People should avoid large corporate retailers.

    B. *King Lear* is Shakespeare's best work.

    C. The settlers were wrong in driving out the Native Americans.

    D. There are many good things about public television.

2. Explain why the following statements are not arguable, and change them to invite opposition:

    A. Should people shop at Walmart?

    B. Injustice hurts people.

    C. The Internet has changed the world.

    D. I prefer taking the train to flying.

3. Revelatory claims do not belong exclusively to academic writers. Performers, public figures, and artists often push audiences to reconsider common topics and basic assumptions.

Kevin Winter/Getty Images

Jim Lo Scalzo/epa/Corbis Wire/Corbis

    A. How is Lady Gaga's meat dress a revelatory claim? What does it claim?

    B. What other public figures have urged audiences to reconsider a particular topic or assumption?

    C. Is there a difference between shock and revelation? Or is shock value a part of revelation?

A Community of Cars

RYAN BROWN

Ryan Brown attends Northern Michigan University. In this essay, which he wrote for a college English course, he argues that our overreliance on the automobile diminishes important human needs. And he offers a fresh insight by arguing that fuel-efficient cars actually keep people from seeing the negative effects of an automobile culture.

A small stuffed animal buffalo sits on my bookshelf, a reminder of my childhood and my grandmother. In all her eighty-odd years on this planet my grandmother never once drove a car. Occasionally she would ride the bus, but almost anywhere she went she walked. The sight of her trudging along with her determined nurse's gait in rain, shine, or snow was familiar to many in our town. I remember going shopping with her when she would babysit me. We would walk along tree-lined sidewalks down to the neighborhood grocery store, along the way stopping so I could race sticks and leaves down the creek. The store was worlds removed from modern, antiseptic supermarkets. The old brick building had worn hardwood floors that creaked when you walked across them. The store's specialty was buffalo meat, and the grocer, who knew my grandmother by name, would lift me up on his shoulders so that I could pet the enormous buffalo head mounted on the wall.

The store is gone now, replaced by a modern supermarket outside of town. No doubt business has improved. The new location is more spacious and better lit, with a better selection, and most importantly, much better parking. They even offer a service through which a person can call in their grocery order and simply drive up to have it loaded into their vehicle. All in all, much more convenient. But whenever I see those shelves towering up from the gleaming linoleum floors towards the blinding lights far above I am struck with the thought that

eight brands of canned peas are paltry recompense for the loss of the character in that old wood floor. I can't help but feel that an old friend sold his soul for a parking lot.

How ironic it is that one must drive by the location of the old neighborhood store to reach the new one outside of town. Why is the remote new location more convenient than the old centralized one? Because a person can drive there in the time it took to walk to the old store, and the parking is more than ample.

We are increasingly becoming a drivers' society. "Why walk when you can drive?" seems to have become our creed. We ignore the negative impacts to our environment, our communities, and our own health for the sake of convenience.

The greetings and brief, friendly conversations we used to have when passing an acquaintance while walking have been replaced with honks of a car horn. The friendly banter at a lunch counter has given way to a voice crackling through our car window, "Would you like fries with that?" We are a society of drivers, preferring to drive ten miles over walking two blocks. Downtown areas and neighborhood stores have been pushed aside in the wake of urban-sprawl shopping centers. Ever outwards we expand, paving over forest and farmland. 5

What, in this sprawling world of parking lots, subdivisions, strip malls, and shopping centers, can be defined as a community? A community is a group of interdependent, interrelating people, sharing culture, history, and traditions. Our community is our home. It represents a large part of our identity, who we are, where we came from, what we care about. But in a society built around cars, not the people who drive them, we seem willing to sacrifice *community* for *convenience*.

Along with community, we are also sacrificing the human body, perhaps the most efficient and best-designed mode of transportation known

kilometers each day (the daily exercise regime recommended by the US Institute of Medicine of the National Academies), carbon dioxide emissions would be reduced by eleven percent and the average weight loss would be "enough to virtually eliminate the obesity epidemic" (qtd. in Cohen).

It seems clear that as our driving increases, our health deteriorates. The driver's culture is a sedentary one. Nearly any conceivable product or service can now be found through a drive-through window, making it no longer necessary to exert even the energy to walk across a parking lot. A person can now tend to all daily errands without ever leaving the comfort of the driver's seat. We are increasingly bereft of natural exercise and exposed to harmful pollution and increased stress, so it is no wonder that our health as a nation is deteriorating. "Post-World War II-style suburban planning assumes everyone has a car and wants to use it. This model, some urban planners assume, is what accounts for the growing epidemic of obesity, heart disease and diabetes" (Ryberg). In her article, "Building Illness," Amanda Spake outlines some statistics:

- Since 1960, the number of people commuting to work out of the county they live in jumped by 200 percent. Residential "sprawl" has meant a 250 percent increase in vehicle miles traveled. The average driver spends 443 hours yearly behind the wheel, the equivalent of 11 workweeks.

- Driving displaces other activities, like exercise. "Being in a car doesn't do anything for you in terms of being thin," says Lawrence Frank of the University of British Columbia. "For every additional hour people spend in the car, there's a six percent increase in the likelihood of being obese" (qtd. in Spake 54).

- Increased auto traffic is also a key source of ground-level ozone. Asthma rates among children, who are believed to be particularly sensitive to ozone, more than doubled between 1980 and 1995.

to us. Fueled entirely by a variety of organic, renewable fuels, the human body produces an amount of kinetic energy per calorie input unmatched by any technology we have yet developed. In addition, it suffers from a low instance of mechanical failure, is self-maintaining and repairing, produces only ecologically useful emissions, and, unlike the pollutant effects of automobiles, its use is actually beneficial to human health. Walking truly is the most efficient and ecologically friendly mode of transportation, yet we make every effort to minimize this healthful and sensible activity.

University of California, Berkley, Earth systems scientist Paul Higgins touted increasing walking as a solution both to obesity and global warming. Higgins pointed out that if Americans between the ages of ten and sixty-five substituted driving with walking five kilometers or cycling twenty

- Living in the suburbs is linked to eating more higher-calorie fast food. At least 1 in 4 adults now eats fast food on any given day. For children, 1 of every 3 meals is fast food.

- Childhood obesity has more than doubled in three decades. But the number of kids who walk or bike to school has dropped from nearly half in 1960 to about 1 in 10 today, largely because schools are far from homes.

10 That automobiles are environmentally harmful is unarguable (Harrington and McConnell 6). Emissions from burnt fuel produce greenhouse gases that contribute to global warming, oxides of nitrogen that deplete the ozone layer, sulfides that result in acid rain, and toxic carbon monoxide. Roadways tear up the countryside, destroying wildlife routes and habitats; road and parking lot runoff pollutes watersheds. Increased driving and expansion of vehicle-related infrastructure naturally increases this pollution.

Relatively low fuel prices and high gas mileage keep the cost of driving low, allowing this drivers' society to perpetuate. As fuel economy increases, fuel prices can rise, sprawl can expand further outward, and the consumer can rest easy knowing he is a friend to the environment by virtue of his efficient new vehicle as he shops at the shopping center (formerly pastureland) twenty-five miles from his subdivision home (at one time, forest). Everyone wins, right? Progress at its finest. And never once does the driver of the thirty-six mile-per-gallon ultra-efficient compact car pause to remember how his mother used to walk down to the corner grocery store with her canvas shopping bag for her groceries, or how his grandfather used to drive to town only once a month for whatever supplies were needed on the farm.

We modern Americans think with our wallets. We will take a stand on an issue, if it's not too inconvenient and we can afford it. Perhaps if it costs us a bit more to drive, we would be more conscious of how many miles we drive each day.

This is beginning to happen with the rise in gas prices. Government regulations pushing higher fuel efficiency and keeping fuel prices reasonable keep the consumer happy and spending while paying lip service to environmental causes. Perhaps our efforts would be more wisely focused on development of alternative fuel sources and on the strengthening of communities.

New Urbanism and other social reform movements promise to bring back the days of centralized, walkable communities, incorporating features such as wide sidewalks and narrow streets, neighborhood stores and schools. Proponents claim that these planned neighborhoods make for stronger communities, better health, and are more ecologically friendly. Susan Handy, Associate Professor of Environmental Science at the University of California, Davis, writes, "I strongly believe that as planners we have an obligation to give the residents of our communities choices, in particular, choices that are healthier for us as individuals, for the community as a whole, and for the environment" (10). These ideas seem novel only in light of the sidewalk-less subdivisions and strip malls on the outskirts of town.

The notion of walking any significant distance as a necessary means of transportation seems so alien to us, but the drivers' society is a recent phenomenon. A hundred years ago hardly anyone drove. Suburbia did not exist prior to the Second World War. Fast food dates back to the sixties, strip malls to the seventies. Have the developments of these last few decades really been enough for us to cast aside our relationships with our neighbors for the sake of our conveyance?

Ultimately it is individual choice that will determine if our communities are to become mere pit stops on the highway. We can choose the easy route and drive, or exert a little extra effort for the sake of ourselves, each other, and our Earth.

Perhaps we need to take a step back from 15 our highway-paced lives and slow things down to a gentle stroll. The liberalists of the industrial revolution predicted that technology would free our time so that we might live lives of leisure. Running late and stuck in traffic, I often think back to the days when Grandma and I would spend a whole afternoon just getting groceries. Maybe the only difference between *inconvenience* and *leisure* is mindset.

Works Cited

Cohen, Philip. "To Cool the World Eat Less, Walk More." *New Scientist*, vol. 184, no. 2478, 18 Dec. 2004, p. 17. *Academic Search Elite*, 15501052.

Congress for the New Urbanism. *Charter of the New Urbanism*. Edited by Emily Talen, 2nd ed., McGraw-Hill Education, 2013.

Handy, Susan L. "Questioning Assumptions 1: Do New Urbanists Walk More?" *Planning*, vol. 72, no. 1, American Planning Association, Jan. 2006, pp. 36–37. *Academic Search Elite*, 19691210.

Harrington, Winston, and Virginia McConnell. *Motor Vehicles and the Environment*. Resources for the Future, Apr. 2003, www.rff.org/files/sharepoint/WorkImages/Download/RFF-RPT-carsenviron.pdf.

Hutchinson, Harry. "Easy on the Gas." *Mechanical Engineering*, vol. 128, no. 7, July 2006, pp. 26–33.

Ryberg, Erica. "Building the New Urbanism." *Smithsonian*, 31 July 2006, www.smithsonianmag.com/science-nature/building-the-new-urbanism-126548080/?no-ist.

Spake, Amanda. "Building Illness." *U.S. News & World Report*, vol. 138, no. 23, 20 June 2005, pp. 54–55.

Torma, Tim. "Urban Sprawl and Public Health: Designing, Planning and Building for Healthy Communities." *Journal of the American Planning Association*, vol. 72, no. 1, 2006, pp. 123–24.

United States, Environmental Protection Agency, Office of Transportation and Air Quality. *Towards a Cleaner Future*. 2005, nepis.epa.gov/Exe/ZyNET.exe/20017FRJ.TXT?ZyActionD=ZyDocument&Client=EPA&Index=2000+Thru+2005&Docs=&Query=&Time=&EndTime=&SearchMethod=1&TocRestrict=n&Toc=&TocEntry=&QField=&QFieldYear=&QFieldMonth=&QFieldDay=&IntQFieldOp=0&ExtQFieldOp=0&XmlQuery=&File=D%3A%5Czyfiles%5CIndex%20Data%5C00thru05%5CTxt%5C00000010%5C20017FRJ.txt&User=ANONYMOUS&Password=anonymous&SortMethod=h%7C-&MaximumDocuments=1&FuzzyDegree=0&ImageQuality=r75g8/r75g8/x150y150g16/i425&Display=p%7Cf&DefSeekPage=x&SearchBack=ZyActionL&Back=ZyActionS&BackDesc=Results%20page&MaximumPages=1&ZyEntry=1&SeekPage=x&ZyPURL.

"The US Weighs In." *Tufts University Health & Nutrition Letter*, vol. 24, no. 6, Aug. 2006, p. 3. *Academic Search Elite*, 21820625.

Assignments: Identifying and Describing Claims

1. Categorize the following claims from Brown's essay as fact, value, or policy:

   A. "[W]henever I see those shelves towering up from the gleaming linoleum floors towards the blinding lights far above I am struck with the thought that eight brands of canned peas are paltry recompense for the loss of the character in that old wood floor."

   B. "[I]n a society built around cars, not the people who drive them, we seem willing to sacrifice *community* for *convenience*."

   C. "The greetings and brief, friendly conversations we used to have when passing an acquaintance while walking have been replaced with honks of a car horn."

   D. "New Urbanism and other social reform movements promise to bring back the days of centralized, walkable communities, incorporating features such as wide sidewalks and narrow streets, neighborhood stores and schools."

   E. "Perhaps we as a society need to take a step back from our highway-paced lives and slow things down to a gentle stroll."

2. In a brief passage, state Brown's main claim (or thesis), and identify his main supporting claims.

3. In a small group, write out a simple opinion that is a claim of value (such as *Home schooling is good for families*), and then develop a more revelatory insight (such as *Home schooling reconnects home life and formal learning*). Ask questions about the opinion—about each word in the opinion—until you've opened up new intellectual possibilities. Based on your discussion, write a new claim of value that is more revelatory and focused than the original opinion.

Myopia/Terra/Corbis

3

Support

Sometimes called grounds or proofs, support comes in various forms: authorities, testimony, facts, statistics, allusions, anecdotes, illustrations, scenarios, appeals to logic, appeals to character, appeals to emotion, appeals to need, and appeals to value. Scholars have categorized and recategorized these support strategies for centuries. One long-standing perspective divides them into three main groups:

Evidence: authorities, testimony, facts, statistics

Examples: allusions, anecdotes, illustrations, scenarios

Appeals: to logic, character, emotion, need, value

Certain types of claims may rely more heavily on a particular support category. For instance, a claim of fact may rely more on evidence than appeals. A claim of value may rely on appeals more than evidence. However, most arguments rely on support strategies from all three categories. In everyday life and even in specialized situations, we use a range of appeals, types of evidence, and examples.

EVIDENCE

Evidence is a type of support that already exists, unlike appeals, which are created by a writer. Evidence can be used at any point in an argument: it can support the main claim or a supporting claim. But merely mentioning evidence or providing a fact is not enough. Arguers must explain the relevance of the evidence.

In his essay "Somewhere in the Past" (from Chapter 11), Cameron Johnson refers to facts and authorities and then, at the end of the paragraph, connects the evidence to his main point—that decreased school funding decreases community involvement:

> All across America, local school systems have been facing consistent budget cuts, and as in Clarksville, the cuts impact the delicate layer of social life around the schools: summer school, sports, music, and art programs have consistently been lopped off the agendas. Some districts, such as one in Orange County,

Florida, are considering moving back starting times to 10:30 or 11:00 a.m. (Stover). It is easy to see that budget cuts have made schools shrink inward—balling themselves into smaller space and smaller bits of time. And even when communities pass local levies, they are often not enough to turn the tide. Increased taxes have not always kept up with the rate of inflation. According to the League of Education Voters, in the state of Washington, for example, from 1993 to 1999 state funding per student increased $528. Yet because of inflation, there was actually a decrease—of $527. Even in those few years, the system lost money. And when that loss is projected over decades, it is easy to imagine the economic effect: a consistent reduction of programs and a consistent reduction in the role that schools once played in their communities.

The specific evidence about Orange County is not simply presented to the reader. Instead, Johnson invites the reader to imagine "the economic effect" and to see his argument's relevance.

AUTHORITIES are experts who offer specialized knowledge. These sources are used in arguments to give credibility to a writer's claims, to illustrate outside or opposing perspectives, to help explain a topic, or to give a sense of popular opinion or historical context. In his essay "Shakespeare and Narcotics" (from Chapter 11), David Pinching uses authority to help support his own claims about the past:

> The mindset behind such an outlook is the really depressing thing. People like to imagine Shakespeare freebasing and rolling up joints because they see him as an establishment figure. As such, portraying him as a junkie causes amusement and indignation because of our modern attitude to substances that allows certain kinds of intoxication but not others. Shakespeare would not have understood our simultaneous and hypocritical prudishness and excess. He was, in his time, a radical, a novelty and far more dangerous to the establishment with his damning indictments of royalty in *King Lear, Richard III* and *King John,* among others, than any of our media starlets. The idea that you can be anti-establishment by becoming incapable of think-ing properly is pretty out of date anyway. And, as the worst excesses of post-Sixties fiction, music and art have proved, "mind-altering" does not necessarily mean "art-improving." Ann Donnelly, the curator of the Shakespeare Birthplace Trust, was unimpressed with the evidence from the pipes and claimed that people are always trying to "come up with reasons for saying Shakespeare was not a genius." This may be some-thing of a spoilsport attitude, but it is a fair one.

As Pinching attempts to discredit the claims that Shakespeare used drugs, he brings in a credible voice on the matter, Ann Donnelly. Notice that Pinching states Donnelly's credentials in a phrase (highlighted) directly after he first gives her name. This short phrase, referred to as an *appositive*, helps writers quickly explain their sources' qualifications. Since authorities are a kind of evidence, explaining their qualifica-tions is a way of explaining the relevance of the evidence.

   Authorities, or references to outside sources, can be used in a variety of ways, but they are used most often to give an idea credence or believability. In his essay "Lunar Eclipse," Ed Bell follows up the initial point of his paragraph with a quotation:

> Because of light pollution, some people have never seen a dark sky. "In most cities, there's little point in gazing at the sky—unless you're fascinated by the sight of a few stars and some airplanes against a glowing background," says David Tennebaum, a science, health, and environment writer (for ABCNEWS.com, *Technology Review, Bio-Science, Environmental Health Perspectives, American Health,* and other publications). "If you have not seen a truly dark sky, you may not know that the urban glow conceals a network of uncountable stars in intriguing constellations."

TESTIMONY is an eyewitness or firsthand account. An arguer's personal testimony appeals to readers by inviting them into his or her vision of the world. For example, Ed Bell's essay on light pollution strategically opens with his own testimony:

Jonathan Ernst/Reuters/Corbis

In court cases and Congressional hearings, testimony and authority often blend together.

> The moon is gently orange with a thin, star-white bottom; its dark top disappears into the blackness surrounding it. Thirty-seven miles north, in town, it lacked the magically dull glow it has here eleven miles south of the store and gas station and twenty miles north of the next nearest bright lights. Driving east while it was still light out, I noticed a crescent moon, but knew it was a full-moon night. An eclipse! I watched as the crescent got smaller and smaller; I was hoping to find a dark spot where I could pull off to the side of the road and take in the full beauty of a lunar eclipse. I was approaching town, though.
>
> I grew up in the country, then moved to the city in my early twenties. I must have seen star-filled skies as a child. I don't remember any. After a young adulthood of city lights, I remember the first night I saw the stars again. I was in my mid-thirties, traveling west, and we stopped to camp for the night. The rest of that summer we traveled the West, camping Utah, Oregon, Arizona, pitch-black nights and a billion stars, uncountable, so many that shooting stars were not rare to see and the constellations were so full of other stars I had trouble making them out.

Bell's testimony, a type of evidence, gives a personal angle to the issue. Rather than simply tell the reader "many people are bothered by light pollution," he narrates a personal experience. This testimony establishes Bell's character and helps the reader feel a sense of wonder about the stars.

FACTS are agreed-upon bits of knowledge that do not require further support in an argument. As a type of evidence, facts are verified claims. This is not to say that facts cannot be disputed; they often are. But when arguers use a fact, they assume that it carries its own support. Notice how Laura Tangley uses facts in her article "Natural Passions":

> Even scientists who are most opposed to the idea of animal passion acknowledge that many creatures experience "primary emotions"—-feelings such as aggression and fear that are instinctive and require no conscious thought. Essential to escaping predators and other dangers, fear, in particular—along with predictable freeze, flight or fight responses—seems to be hardwired. A laboratory rat that has never encountered a cat, for example, will still freeze if it is exposed to the smell of this predator.

As readers, we get the sense that Tangley's assertions in this passage can be easily verified, that "primary emotions" in animals are considered a fact among those who study them or observe them casually. This is her starting place. She later goes on to argue that animals feel more than primary emotions, that they experience a complex range of emotions, much like humans. These latter points require other types of evidence beyond a declaration of facts. Like Tangley, many arguers use facts as a starting place and build from what is evident or easily verifiable.

In academic writing, facts that the audience would not otherwise know should be cited, as illustrated in the following excerpt from Charles Nelson's "Investing in Futures: The Cost of College":

> It is widely known that college has been a good investment for students. It has traditionally offered many advantages, the most obvious being that some degrees pay off financially. For example, according to the National Association of Colleges and Employers' 2002 Salary Survey, starting salaries for some majors exceed $50,000—chemical engineering: $50,387; computer science: $50,352; mechanical engineering, management information systems/business data processing, accounting, civil engineering, and economics/finance all start above $40,000 (Geary).

STATISTICS are figures drawn from surveys, experimentation, and data analysis. In her essay "Higher Education through Discombobulation" (from Chapter 9), Betsy Chitwood explains her own learning experience and then offers statistical research to support the idea:

> This learning process, albeit an extreme example, motivated me to take risks and seek ways to succeed in my chosen career. The impact of the disorientation was in direct proportion to the personal growth brought about by my "education" and it definitely shaped who I am today.
>
> Evidence from academic research supports this theory. In a study by Craig and Graesser at the University of Memphis, college students participated in an introduction to computer literacy by using AutoTutor, an intelligence tutoring system (ITS). The study, which tracked the effect of confusion and other emotions on students' responses, showed that a higher percentage (68%) of learning gains were achieved when the students were met with confusion (4).

Or notice Ellen Goodman's strategic use of statistics in her article "Culture in Need of an Extreme Makeover":

> But even after the ban on silicone, women chose to "enhance" or "augment" their breasts, this time using saline implants. The annual number of breast enlargements actually grew, hugely, from 32,607 in 1992 to 225,818 last year.

Like all forms of evidence, statistics can be used dishonestly. For instance, opinion polls are often used as evidence of a particular trend in society. But those polls may be conducted on an unrepresentative section of the population. If someone were to poll viewers of Fox News, for example, the results would be characterized by the ideological leanings (the unstated beliefs and values) of that audience. So imagine that Fox News (or MSNBC or CNN) reported the following:

> According to a recent national poll, 72% of Americans are not overly concerned about honesty in the stock market. This suggests that revamping the role of the Securities and Exchange Commission should not necessarily be a priority.

While the statistic gives some sense of legitimacy to the statement, we do not know if the poll was taken on a representative sample of the U.S. population. Also, we do not know the nature of the survey questions. Many respondents could have said they were "concerned" but not "highly concerned" (as they might have been about terrorism or job security). Statistics can be valuable and add legitimacy to claims, but their origin should be revealed to the audience so that readers know not just the numbers, but the process that gives them meaning. (For more statistics and persuasion, see Julie Burks's essay, "The Patsy: A Story of a Number," pages 334–336.)

Activities

1. In small groups, discuss how a writer might use authorities, testimony, facts, and statistics to support one of the following claims: *College football is more like a professional than an amateur sport. Reality TV shows help teach viewers some important lessons about life. Employers should provide more incentives for workers to bike to work.*

2. Explain a recent instance from everyday life when you used authorities, testimony, facts, or statistics to support a claim.

EXAMPLES

Examples are specific occurrences of a phenomenon. Whenever arguers support a claim with particular versions of a point, they are using examples. For example, in her essay about technological addiction (at the end of this chapter), Lynda Smith gives a range of everyday examples that support her claim about "the desire of instant gratification":

> In this fast-paced society of compacted time restraints, we long for more leisure time. At the same time, we are consumed with the desire for instant gratification. We want immediate access to people, information, and services any time, day or night. We believe that somehow if we do everything faster, we will have more free time. Our lives have become a world filled with services to help us move through life with increased speed. We have drive-thrus for food, banking, even laundry so we don't have to leave our cars. We have u-scan checkouts at grocery stores so we don't have to wait in line. And now, different speeds at which we can choose to move through life. There is high speed, turbo speed, and new elite speeds where you can, without leaving your home, hit speeds up to 6.0 Mbps (AT&T).

ALLUSIONS are references to some public knowledge from history, current events, popular culture, religion, or literature. (For more about literature, see page 33.) Allusions add depth and meaning to an argument. By making connections to culturally shared bits of knowledge, allusions link an argument to the world beyond it. In her essay "No Sex Please, We're Middle Class" (from Chapter 8), Camille Paglia alludes to popular culture to develop her argument:

> In the 1980s, commercial music boasted a beguiling host of sexy pop chicks like Deborah Harry, Belinda Carlisle, Pat Benatar, and a charmingly ripe Madonna. Late Madonna, in contrast, went bourgeois and turned scrawny. Madonna's dance-track acolyte, Lady Gaga, with her compulsive overkill, is a high-concept fabrication without an ounce of genuine eroticism.

By using these allusions, Paglia taps into the readers' collective knowledge about popular culture and links her argument to that knowledge, thus adding power to her ideas. Earlier in the essay, she alludes to the "racy lingerie" of Victoria's Secret, the "blazingly raunchy" scenarios of country music, the "Black rhythm and blues" of the Mississippi Delta, and the "hard rock bands of the '60s." When she alludes to the Rolling Stones' recording of Willie Dixon's "Little Red Rooster," Paglia's *New York Times* readers are likely to hear the Stones' "visceral rawness and seductive sensuality."

ANECDOTES are short accounts of a particular event or incident. They often are given in the form of a brief story that supports an arguer's point. While *testimony*, another form of support, comes from an eyewitness ("I saw the train coming around the mountain. . . ."), an anecdote is told by the arguer as though he or she is an objective reporter of events ("The incident on the train tracks started with the train coming around the mountain. . . ."). The details in an anecdote can provide powerful support: Since anecdotes are examples, they help to draw an audience into a specific scene. However, they should always be relevant to the main idea of the argument.

Imagine that a writer is arguing that the small local farmer has a more positive impact on communities than large corporate farms do. Notice the following two possible anecdotes. Which one seems more relevant to the main claim?

> Martin Grove farmed the fields of Northwestern Ohio for decades, and he bought his supplies locally— everything from basic tools to seed. But last summer, he came into Feed & Supply and made his last purchase: materials for packing up his farm so he could sell it off. In a five-year period, four other local farmers did the same thing, and this year, Feed & Supply has begun laying off employees because the corporate farms that have moved in do not rely as heavily on local business for supplies.

> Martin Grove farmed the fields of Northwestern Ohio for decades. He had fields of corn, wheat, and soybeans, and he developed a healthy orchard of apples—the best around, according to locals. In fact, in the summer of '68, Jerry Foster announced at the town jubilee that, next to Grove's apples, his own apples were fit for birds only. (And some say that the old saying "that's for the birds" comes from Foster's proclamation.)

The details in the first anecdote speak directly to the idea that local farmers support communities more than corporate farms do. The second anecdote, while interesting, is not obviously related to this claim. The writer would have to make that connection for the reader.

ILLUSTRATIONS are graphic descriptions or representations of an idea. Writers may illustrate a point with words alone, carefully describing the details of an idea to create an image in the reader's mind. In

LINES

Representing the Relative Mortality of the Army at Home and of the English Male Population at corresponding Ages

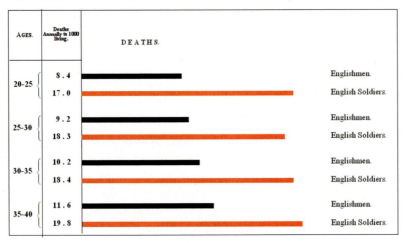

Note   The Mortality of the English Male Population, at the above Ages, is taken from the English Life Table (1849-53)

essence, they are drawing a picture—an example—with words. But illustrations, in the strict sense of the word, use actual graphics. Alone, they can make persuasive points. For instance, Florence Nightingale used graphics to argue about medical conditions. The following commentary, from the Florence Nightingale Museum website, points out significant elements of the illustration:

> The other highly original chart is what I will call the "Lines"—a bar chart showing how soldiers in peacetime, living in their barracks in England, were dying at a faster rate than civilians in the cities around them.
>
> There is a black bar in each of four age ranges, and a longer red bar. The black bar is the number of civilians who die each year, and the red is the number of soldiers. There are a number of curious overtones to this graphic, which may just be a coincidence.
>
> First, the title "Lines" (in ornate script in the original) makes it sound like a poem, as in Lines on the Death of Bismarck. There are four pairs of bars, when actually the message is clear from one pair alone. There seems to be a kind of repetition, as in a chorus. This effect is increased by the words, repeated at the end of each line, English Men, English Soldiers . . . It sounds like a funeral march.
>
> Second, the red bar for the soldiers would certainly make some people think of the "Thin Red Line," which had become famous in the Crimean War when a two-deep row of red-jacketed British infantrymen stopped a Russian heavy cavalry charge, something that was thought to be impossible. The thin red lines on Nightingale's chart represented these same heroic soldiers who were now dying unnecessarily because of bad hygiene in their barracks.

SCENARIOS are fictional or hypothetical examples. As a persuasive tool, they can support nearly any argumentative claim. For example, imagine a writer, Angela, is arguing about grading policies at her college:

> The problem with the four-point system is that it does not present the true variation among students. Imagine three students all achieve a 4.0 in a class. James's final score was 93%, Tonya's 95%, and Will's 100%.

The 4.0 final grade would not reflect the broad range of performance between James and Will. In fact, Will's perfect score is not at all differentiated from a student who balances on the margin of a 4.0 and 3.0.

Although these students are not real people, they put a picture in readers' minds. Scenarios like these help readers to envisage an otherwise abstract point. If the scenario is likely, readers can imagine it actually occurring. If the scenario is detailed enough (and if those details correspond to a possible reality), readers may not make a distinction between what's possible and what has occurred. In Angela's scenario, readers can easily imagine the three students and their grades.

When arguers use scenarios, they should signal the audience that they are in hypothetical territory. This can involve a simple cue such as "Imagine that . . ." or something even subtler, such as verb mood:

> If one student were to score 93%, another 95%, and another 100%, they would all receive a 4.0. However, the final grade would . . .

Or notice Tracy Webster's strategy in his argument, "Big House in the Wilderness." Webster simply asks a set of questions that introduce readers to a possible reality:

> What would happen if Americans could somehow overcome their own selfish and hypocritical desires to overbuild and overdestroy, and instead make *every* effort, not just *some* effort, to peacefully and respectfully co-exist with non-human life? Doing this would require a new sort of vision—seeing all the wildlife that they presently overlook. It would also require a new look at rhetoric, replacing words like "harvest" with "slaughter" and "environment" with "home." What would happen if all new homebuilders saw themselves more as visitors, guests, and newcomers? And better yet, as intruders, conquerors, and imperialists?

Notice that the verb mood often changes in scenarios from the *indicative* ("Americans overcome their own desires") to the *subjunctive* ("Americans could overcome their own desires").

Literary Works

Literary works function uniquely as allusions. Novels, poetry, drama, songs, and short stories speak to broad themes such as government corruption, self-sacrifice for family, institutional oppression of the individual, self-discovery, and so on. Writers often allude to literature because it sheds light on human affairs. In each of the following examples, writers use a literary passage or quotation to give dimension to an idea. Notice how the writers set up the literary work: Before they give the key lines or scene, they first give the author and title. For fiction (novels and short stories), they also give a brief explanation of the overall setting or scene. And they always explain the relevant idea—the point that the reader should take away from the excerpt:

- If we paid attention only to mainstream media and governmental posturing, we might come to see revenge as a simple knee-jerk human response, a reaction that is inherently justified and morally correct. But the path of revenge is difficult, fraught with its own hardships, ambivalences, and self-destruction.

continued

Shakespeare's *Hamlet* embodies the uncertainty; he is caught between the desire to strike out against his father's murderer and a web of other, unspeakable, thoughts:

> To be, or not to be: that is the question:
> Whether 'tis nobler in the mind to suffer
> The slings and arrows of outrageous fortune,
> Or to take arms against a sea of troubles,
> And by opposing end them. (*Ham.* 3.1.56–60)

- Throughout our history of warfare, there has been one constant: It always exceeds our expectations of horror and confusion. Each new war seems to bring about its own particular type of confusions. In *Legends of the Fall,* Jim Harrison tells of World War I, when American soldiers were caught between an old world of physical contact and a new world of technological horror. The scene is a Parisian hospital. The main character, Tristan, has lost his brother to German mustard gas and has gone on a rampage of revenge by scalping numbers of German soldiers. After being subdued by his commanders, Tristan now stands in the main office of a psychiatric ward:

> The doctor so doubted his ability to knit up [the soldiers'] souls that he became almost bored with his patients and did all he could to have them shipped home. Thus he was fascinated with the arrival of Tristan when the ambulance driver advised him that a true "crazy" was waiting to be unloaded. The doctor sent attendants and read the report from Tristan's commander. He felt himself oddly unmoved by the scalpings and was surprised at the commander's horror. How could mustard gas be considered normal warfare and not scalping, in the reaction to the death of a brother? (218)

- The sexuality of young women in small towns is far more complex, and even political, than what polite society normally wants to acknowledge. Barbara Kingsolver's narrator in *The Bean Trees* invites the reader into the lives of several young women whose lives illustrate the deep connections among sexuality, social acceptance, reproduction, and motherhood. Almost immediately in the novel, we hear of Jolene, a small-town Appalachian girl who comes into a medical center with a gunshot wound to the shoulder:

> Jolene was a pie-faced, heavy girl and I always thought she looked like the type to have gone and found trouble just to show you didn't have to be a cheerleader to be fast. The trouble with that is it doesn't get you anywhere, no more than a kid on a bicycle going no hands and no feet up and down past his mother hollering his head off for her to look. She's not going to look till he runs into something and busts his head wide open. (8)

- Americans, say many scholars and thinkers, have always been after something that we destroy by pursuing it. F. Scott Fitzgerald's classic *The Great Gatsby* brings us face to face with a narrator who realizes this at the end of the novel, as he peers over the Eastern coastline:

> And as the moon rose higher the inessential houses began to melt away until gradually I became aware of the old island here that flowered once for Dutch sailors' eyes—a fresh, green breast of the new world. Its vanished trees, the trees that had made way for Gatsby's house, had once pandered in whispers to the last and greatest of all human dreams; for a transitory enchanted moment man must have held his breath in the presence of this continent, compelled into aesthetic contemplation he neither understood nor desired, face to face for the last time in history with something commensurate to his capacity for wonder. (189)

continued

Religious Texts

To many people, religious texts are paths to the truth. But in public argument, in situations that involve diverse audiences, writers cannot simply hold up a particular religious text *as* truth. Because there are so many religious perspectives (Hinduism, Buddhism, Sikhism, Judaism, Christianity, Islam, Shinto, Confucianism, just to name a few), and so many religious texts (the Vedas, the Bhagavad Gita, the Torah, the New Testament, the Koran, the Guru Granth Sahib, and so on) referring to one as the truth is apt to alienate readers. Because most audiences are diverse and cannot be assumed to hold a consensual belief in one religious text, writers must be cautious. (One cannot assume, for instance, that everyone accepts, as fact, that Jesus is the son of God.) But, with that caution in mind, writers can use religious texts. These books have enormous significance in people's minds, whether or not they are followers of a specific faith.

So, how do religious texts function in argument? In the New Testament, Jesus says, "Love your neighbor," and then tells a parable about the Good Samaritan to explain the concept. Whether or not one's reader is a Christian, Jesus's point about love and his supporting parable can be used to develop an argument about personal relationships, national policies, or world affairs. Because the particular religious teaching transcends Christianity, it can be applied to various situations and arguments. The ideas of Buddha, Muhammad, Parsvanatha, and others can be used in the same way—not as unquestionable truths, but as appeals to value. At the very least, these appeals can help writers create common ground with their readers.

APPEALS

Appeals are a major form of support in argumentation. They call on the reader's sense of logic, character, emotion, need, or value. Because the arguer makes a connection between the topic and the reader's consciousness, appeals call for intellectual commitment, both on the part of the arguer and of the audience.

Appeals differ from forms of evidence (statistics, facts, illustrations, etc.) in an important way: While evidence is already formed for the writer, an appeal must be constructed out of logical steps, shared values, beliefs, or needs. The writer must *create* the bridge between the topic and the audience. For this reason, Aristotle called appeals *artistic proofs* and forms of evidence *inartistic proof.*

Appeals constitute most of what we know as argument; without appeals, other types of support such as statistics, examples, and illustrations have little persuasive power. In the hands of a good writer, appeals make all the difference between a flat argument that does not speak to audiences and an engaging argument that calls out audiences' reasoning power, values, beliefs, and needs. Good writers can use appeals to make a topic come to life and enter the lives of their audience.

REUTERS/HO/Landov

Notice how the above leaflets, dropped into Iraq during the first phase of the war in 2003, appeal to values.

Appeals to Logic

In mainstream culture, people believe that something is "true" if it can be substantiated with mounds of data. But in academic writing, it's not the mounds of data but the appeal to logic that matters most. In fact, without a logical framework, statistics and facts can mean nothing—or anything. Writers use an appeal to logic whenever they invite an audience to think through an idea, to walk along an intellectual path. Sometimes, that invitation is direct. Statements like the following show a writer appealing explicitly to readers' logic:

- Let us consider the following reasons . . .
- Because of the stated conditions, we can only conclude that . . .
- Yet another reason to accept the idea . . .
- Given the following rationale, we should dismiss the idea of . . .

Or in the next passage, the writer calls on readers to set aside emotions and investigate the legal issues. This, too, is a direct appeal to logic:

John Metz

Gay marriage in America has become a fairly emotional issue. But we should work around the emotions involved and investigate the issue of rights and state law. It has been established that individual states can define marriage. The question, then, lies in the role of other states: Does every state have to honor a marriage licensed in other states? This, it seems, is merely a matter of constitutional law.

But logical appeals are often more indirect. The writer often establishes a subtle line of reasoning: a series of logical steps (or premises) that lead arguer and audience to a main claim. If the path is well crafted—with few missteps or gaps between premises—readers follow along and become more accepting of the overall argument. Sometimes the line of reasoning is easy to see; it has been made explicit. (Writers may even use cues such as "first" or "the first reason.") But the line of reasoning is usually harder to detect. It works quietly behind the progression of supporting ideas. In the following passage from "Somewhere in the Past" (Chapter 11) Cameron Johnson invites the reader to follow his line of reasoning, to see the links among school budgets, school programs, students, and the surrounding community. Once these logical links are established, Johnson makes the final point that less funding equals less community:

Another example helps illustrate the vital connection between school and community. Many Clarksville citizens grew up in, and have fond memories of, the school's summer recreation program that was cut back steadily each year and finally abandoned in 1996. While this program can be seen as nonessential, it was hardly fluff in the budget. The summer recreation program was an important link between school and community. It not only gave kids something to do, but it helped forge a stronger bond between school and student, and this bond created other bonds: between school and community and between community and student. Because of less funding, schools end up offering less support (for academics) and less attraction (for extracurricular activities). In the long run, schools with less funding become less important to students and less important within the community as a whole. The summer recreation program is just one example of this subtle, or silent, breakdown.

For an argument to be successful, the reader must accept each premise in the line of reasoning—not stumbling, getting off the path, or stopping halfway through. Therefore, the writer has to make certain that each step is supported or made acceptable so the reader can move forward. This is where all the support strategies come into play: personal testimony, allusions, facts, examples, statistics, and primary and secondary sources. Imagine an argument emerging from the following premises:

- Popular culture influences how people think.
- Mainstream popular culture encourages young people to be overly energized and unfocused.
- The lack of focus is one of the main hurdles to educational success—and seems to be increasing in schools and colleges.
- The recent surge in energy drinks increases the problem because they decrease students' ability to maintain focus.
- The energy drink fad adds more twitch to an overly twitchy generation of students.

Each of these premises needs support. For instance, the first premise calls for some examples in the present or past that show a pop culture message influencing the behavior of the masses. The second premise calls for examples of pop culture encouraging people to be unfocused. Specific commercials, messages, products, and fads would illustrate the point. For the third and fourth premises, the writer might search for teachers' testimonies about students. Once all the premises are supported, the final claim can be accepted. (In this way, a line of reasoning can function as the scaffolding of an argument. When a writer thinks through the premises that support the main claim, she can discover a basic structure or support system for the argument.)

TYPES OF REASONING *Deductive reasoning* builds a conclusion from accepted premises or general principles. Often, this means relying on classes (all dogs, all men, all raincoats, all months beginning in J). For example:

- All birds have beaks. (general statement about the class)
- Polly the parrot is a bird. (specific statement that puts Polly in the class)
- Therefore, Polly has a beak. (conclusion built from the premises)

Deduction may also rely on, or build from, a definitional statement—a statement that says what something is:

- Bipeds are animals with two legs.
- Ostriches are two-legged animals.
- Therefore, ostriches are bipeds.

Deductive logic often lurks behind legal or ethical decisions. A general principle or legal definition helps people conclude something about a specific case or situation. In the following passage, the writer makes a deductive case that begins with a constitutional premise and works toward a specific claim about gay rights:

Under the Constitution, people are endowed with equal rights. Throughout history, we have been prompted to act from that fundamental notion despite public opinion about minorities: women, African Americans, Hispanics, and Japanese Americans. Gay and lesbian couples are no different. Their sexuality does not strip them of citizenship, nor exile them from constitutional rights. They should be given the same rights as heterosexual couples despite public or religious opinions to the contrary.

Inductive reasoning builds from specific premises and leads to a general claim. Here's a basic example: *I found a mouse in the toilet last week. I saw a mouse in the kitchen yesterday. Therefore, mice have found a way into the house!* In other words, anytime we make a conclusion based on several specifics, we are doing induction. Of course, the situation can be more sophisticated. In the following line of reasoning, the preliminary steps are specific, and the more general concluding statement is derived from those specifics:

John Metz

What kind of reasoning is operating in this billboard? What are the premises?

- The warmest average annual temperatures recorded have occurred since 1991.
- Throughout the world, most high-temperature records have been set in the past three years.
- On the whole, average winter temperatures have increased in the past fifty years.
- While the average temperature of all regions is increasing, no regions have experienced average decreasing temperatures.
- The Earth is warming.

You are probably familiar with inductive logic. It is the primary engine of scientific argument and of many of the arguments that come from scientific study. Much of what we accept about our food, medicine, even our own health comes from inductive reasoning. Researchers line up tests to prove something occurs not just once but many times under certain conditions. Then they draw a general conclusion about such things as eggs, liver, artificial sweeteners, red wine, and so on. But the conclusion does not always account for other variables. Consider this increasingly common scenario: A pharmacology company is studying a particular kind of pill. The company does many studies, testing the pill on a variety of animals and then people. After hundreds or thousands of tests, the researchers conclude that the pill works to increase bone density. Their logic looks something like this:

The pill increased density in test subject A.

The pill increased density in test subject B.

The pill increased density in test subject C. (And so on.)

Therefore, the pill increases bone density.

The many premises seem to support the conclusion. However, the conclusion is not certain. The researchers may later discover that the studies did not account for a particular age range, particular racial variables, even particular genetic predispositions. Therefore, the company will qualify its conclusion: The pill increases bone density in Caucasian women over 60 with a particular bone loss disease. As this example shows, induction always attempts to outrun the variability of life—all the possibilities that might challenge the conclusion.

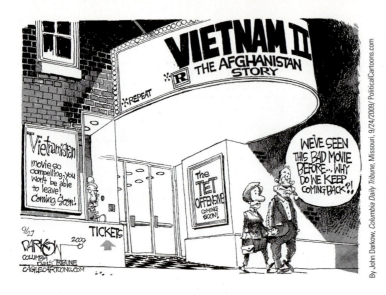

By John Darkow, *Columbia Daily Tribune, Missouri, 9/24/2009/ PoliticalCartoons.com*

Analogical reasoning depends on comparisons (or analogies). The arguer moves from one particular situation or case to another. Comparisons, metaphors, allegories, parables, and examples all have an analogous quality: they argue that if two things are alike in certain respects, they are also alike in other respects. Analogies shed light on something by comparing or contrasting it with something familiar. For example, an analogy can be historical, explaining a present situation by comparing it to a similar situation from the past. Some people have compared the U.S. involvement in Afghanistan to the Vietnam War. Drawing attention to similarities between the two situations (an elusive enemy halfway around the world, a divided nation, a questionable cause, and so on) sheds light on the Iraq war and makes a case for pulling troops out. The line of reasoning is that since key circumstances are similar, the results are likely to be similar.

In everyday life, we often use a form of reasoning called the *enthymeme*, which is a line of reasoning that contains an unstated premise. The unstated premise is so widely accepted that it goes unmentioned. The audience is left to conclude or assume the point. For example, if someone says, *I've received high marks on every assignment thus far, so I'm going to receive a high grade in the course*, she omits a point: high grades on all the assignments will lead to a high grade in the course. This point is so widely assumed that it can safely be left unsaid.

In Stephen Toulmin's model of reasoning, which is discussed more in depth in Chapter 5, the assumption high *grades on all the assignments will lead to a high grade in the course* is called a **warrant**, which is the link between a claim and its grounds (the claim's supporting reason). The warrant (which is sometimes stated, sometimes unstated) expresses why a person would accept a claim based on the grounds.

Grounds: I've received high marks on every assignment thus far. (support for the claim)

Claim: I'm going to receive a high grade in the course. (an assertion that requires support)

Warrant: High grades on all assignments will lead to a high grade in the course. (why the grounds support the claim)

As Chapter 5 explains, unstated premises (or warrant assumptions) constitute a significant part of any argument. Good arguers tap into that quiet part—into the realm of assumptions and values that make arguments acceptable, questionable, or especially heated.

Logical Fallacies

Good logic is critical to sound argument. The tighter the logic, the better the argument. But poor logic often sounds good. Politicians use nice-sounding phrases and reasonable-sounding premises to hide poor logic. If we had no tools for figuring out good versus bad logic, we might simply accept all those nice-sounding arguments. That is why readers and writers of argument study *logical fallacies:* flaws in the structure of an argument that make a claim invalid. A fallacy is a falsehood, so a logical fallacy is a logical falsehood that makes no sense within a given situation. Some of the most common fallacy types are discussed next, but many more types exist.

Ad hominem (Latin for *to the person*) fallacies are personal attacks. Instead of responding to the *ideas* someone has put forth, the arguer attacks the *person* or some quality of the person. In politics, these personal attacks draw attention away from important policy debates and focus instead on character. For example, if one group does not believe in the science that supports global warming, they might make fun of Al Gore, a leading voice on global warming, for having a big house. (The size of Gore's house has nothing to do with the evidence about global warming.) Concerns about someone's character can be relevant to an issue. However, ad hominem attacks focus on character at the expense of the issue at hand.

Strawperson fallacies involve misrepresenting a position and then dismissing it as wrong. In this type of fallacy, an arguer sets up an opposing position (called a *strawperson* or *scarecrow*) that is easy to knock over or beat up. For example, imagine that Molly opposes leash laws. But Tom argues that dogs should be kept on leashes when they are walked through town. Rather than engage Tom's position in a fair manner, Molly responds by saying, "Tom isn't a dog person. He thinks they should always be tied up and *never* allowed to run free." Molly has distorted Tom's position. She has made him seem unreasonable, even mean-spirited, which unfairly bolsters her position.

Post hoc, ergo propter hoc (or faulty cause-effect) fallacies claim that if one thing happened before another, then the first thing must have caused the second. *Post hoc, ergo propter hoc* is Latin for "after this, therefore because of this" (and is often shortened to *post hoc*). Such arguments are false because they confuse sequence with cause. If a rooster crows just before sunrise, that rooster didn't cause daylight. That's easy to conclude. But in public life, things can be more complex. For instance, if a new governor takes office just before the state's economy goes into a recession, the cause might involve a range of complex financial dynamics—and *not* the new governor.

Either/or fallacies oversimplify an issue by claiming that only two options exist when there are more options to choose from. The old slogan "love it or leave it" suggests only two choices. A third (unmentioned) alternative is to stay and work toward changes that will improve the situation. Either/or thinking can transcend particular arguments and seep into the collective state of mind—the national consciousness. For example, in the United States we tend to label political positions as either conservative or liberal.

continued

Hasty generalizations draw conclusions based on too little evidence. For example, generalizing about a city because you drove through it on a Sunday morning can be dangerous because cities are quieter and have less traffic on Sunday mornings. Claiming that Santa Rosa is a sleepy little town, based on one Sunday morning, ignores many other dimensions and possibilities about the town. A generalization based on so little evidence is considered *hasty* or *broad*. This intellectual habit often surfaces in arguments about gender, race, age, sexual orientation, and even vocation—for example, *lawyers are not to be trusted*.

Non sequitur (Latin for *it does not follow*) skips or confuses logical steps. The conclusion cannot logically be arrived at through the premises. Any argument in which the conclusion doesn't follow logically from the premise can be considered a non sequitur. Each of the following conclusions may be true, but they do not follow logically from their premise: Because Bob is smart, he will get a good job. Alphie is honest; therefore, he will lead a happy life. The buildup of nuclear arms in the past twenty-five years was the only thing that kept the United States out of war.

Slippery slope fallacies claim that a certain way of thinking or acting will necessarily lead to more of the same—that once you begin sliding down a slippery slope, you will keep sliding. While one action may in fact lead to similar actions, the slippery slope fallacy appeals to fear by claiming that taking a certain moderate action will lead to more extreme actions: *If we put limitations on the sale of semi-automatic guns, it won't be long until shotguns are illegal, then steak knives.*

Begging the Question (also called *circular reasoning* and, in Latin, *petitio principii*) involves supporting a claim by restating (in different words) the claim itself. No support is provided; the arguer simply repeats the claim. *Tim would be a good president because he is presidential material* is circular reasoning. It is like a dog chasing its own tail. A student who argues that he should not receive a *C* because he is an *A* student is caught up in circular reasoning. Instead, the student must argue that he deserves an *A* because of his quality of work.

Red herring fallacies are deliberate attempts to change the subject. Instead of dealing with the actual argument, the arguer introduces irrelevant points to distract the audience. A red herring is like rattling keys in front of a crying baby: the baby's attention becomes focused on something else—the keys. If a supervisor confronts an employee about being late for work again, and the employee responds that tech support still hasn't solved his computer problem, he is using a red herring to shift attention away from the supervisor's charge.

Bandwagon fallacies claim that because everyone else is doing it, you should, too. They invite people to accept something because it is popular. This is also referred to as *herd mentality*. If a child argues for her right to get a tattoo by pleading, "All of my friends already have one," she is relying on the bandwagon fallacy. Or if a cell phone company urges people to buy its product by proclaiming, "Everyone's coming over to our plan," it is relying on bandwagon logic, which—by the way—tends to work on consumers.

continued

Association fallacies claim that two people or things share a quality just because they are somehow associated, connected, or related. One type of association argument is guilt by association, in which the arguer claims that one person or thing has the same negative characteristics as another because the two are somehow associated. Honor by association is also possible, and can be just as fallacious. A particular type of association fallacy is *reductio ad Hitlerum*. This type of fallacy claims that anything Adolf Hitler (or the Nazi party) did or thought must be evil. (The same false logic could be applied to anything: Republicans, Democrats, the ACLU, Osama bin Laden, and so on.) The logic is that something is evil because it is associated with Hitler. But genocide, for example, is evil on its own merits, not because of Hitler. And Hitler was a vegetarian, but that doesn't make vegetarianism evil.

Golden age fallacies characterize the past as broadly and inherently better. Arguments based on a golden age perspective prompt us to imagine some bygone era as though no crime, no immodesty, no illicit behaviors existed before the present. In the mainstream media and in popular political rhetoric, people often associate the 1950s with purity, simplicity, and easy living. They rely on Hollywood versions of the past and on sanitized memories while ignoring the violence, war, and rampant racism of the era. Certainly, life may have been more innocent or more peaceful for some people at some point in the past. But only lazy arguers imagine that all parts of their civilization were inherently better "back in the day." Such a perspective yields some other fallacies such as appeals to antiquity or appeals to tradition, in which arguers imagine that any values from the past are good simply because they are "tried and true."

Activities

1. Take one of the fallacies listed in this section. In a small group, generate at least two statements that illustrate the particular fallacy. Share the two statements with the rest of the class and explain how they are flawed.

2. Do a Google search for logical fallacies. Find one not listed in this section and report it to others in your class. As you describe the fallacy, invent your own statement that demonstrates the flawed logic. If possible, use a timely political or cultural issue.

Appeals to Character

Appeals to character draw attention to the arguer's (writer/speaker's) personal nature, integrity, experience, wisdom, or personality. They are used to fend off any doubts about the arguer's credibility. Appeals to character are usually a small part of a bigger argument and are used to make the audience comfortable and more apt to accept other claims. They are an explicit strategy for building trust or confidence in the arguer. For instance, imagine that a writer is arguing against increasing standardized testing in elementary education. To create credibility, she draws attention to her own experience:

In my fifteen years as an elementary school teacher, I have watched students' learning time diminish and their test-taking time greatly increase. I have seen first-hand how students leave behind their curiosity and wonder—essential for the development of young minds—and fix their attention on the little circles and blanks on standardized tests.

Politicians often use appeals to character, either to suggest something positive about their own credibility or to make voters doubt the credibility of their opponents. For instance, a presidential candidate may discuss his military duty to show his own patriotism and then point to his opponent's lack of military duty. Even campaign photos of political candidates work as appeals to character.

Appeals to character can be used dishonestly, as a way to avoid focusing on other issues. For instance, if someone asked a politician about the logic of a policy decision and she replied, "Don't question what's in my heart," she would have side-stepped the question and drawn attention to something the audience cannot possibly know anyway: her "heart." Such dishonest rhetorical moves are common in political debate. In the following passage from George Orwell's *Animal Farm*, Squealer, the pig, appeals to character:

> We pigs are brainworkers. The whole management and operation of this farm depend on us. Day and night we are watching over your welfare. It is for your sake that we drink that milk and eat those apples.

Squealer focuses on the pigs' intentions, something his audience cannot possibly know or dispute. The move distracts the animals from asking other questions about the pigs' behavior.

In formal argument, appeals to character should be used with caution. While they can help an arguer create credibility, they should not replace a strong logical argument. Some voters may be swayed by good looks, charismatic gestures, or even a good movie career, but academic readers look for sophisticated logic as the primary attribute of an argument.

Appeals to Emotion

Appeals to emotion draw on the emotions (fears, hopes, sympathies, yearnings) of the audience. In her essay "More Than Cherries" (from Chapter 8), Samantha Tengelitsch appeals to her readers' emotions by describing the illness and death of a local woman:

> Last spring an article ran in the local paper about a young woman running for the prestigious title of National Cherry Queen. It told the story of Lauren Hemming, a twenty-year-old college student, who was raised on a Peninsula Township cherry farm and who was battling non-Hodgkin's lymphoma (a cancer of the lymphatic system) while running for the prestigious title. A photograph included with the article captured Lauren sitting cross-legged in a hammock in front of her home. It was spring and sun shown brightly. At the time of the photograph, Lauren was undergoing chemotherapy for the lymphoma and had lost her hair, but this in no way detracted from her beauty. Her story was inspirational and touched me as I'm sure it touched others.
>
> Unfortunately, Lauren was not able to continue with her bid for Cherry Queen. Instead, she fought bravely to save her own life and the following winter died from the cancer, which had spread to her brain.

Tengelitsch even points to her own emotional state—and attempts to draw readers into a sense of loss. As her argument about cause continues, it depends heavily on forms of evidence, so this initial emotional appeal helps to create an important human element.

Appeals to emotion are sometimes used dishonestly. For instance, notice another set of appeals from George Orwell's *Animal Farm,* in which Squealer tries to convince the other animals that only the pigs should eat the milk and apples:

> "Comrades!" he cried. "You do not imagine, I hope, that we pigs are doing this in a spirit of selfishness and privilege? Many of us actually dislike milk and apples. I dislike them myself. Our sole object in taking these things is to preserve our health. Milk and apples (this has been proven by science, comrades) contain substances absolutely necessary to the well-being of a pig. We pigs are brainworkers. The whole management and operation of this farm depend on us. Day and night we are watching over your welfare. It is for your sake that we drink that milk and eat those apples. Do you know what would happen if we pigs failed in our duty? Jones would come back! Yes, Jones would come back! Surely, comrades," cried Squealer almost pleadingly, skipping from side to side and whisking his tail, "surely there is no one among you who wants to see Jones come back."

Squealer appeals to his audience's sense of fear. Rather than appeal to their logic, which might prompt the other animals to think in more reasonable ways, Squealer blurs the issue with panic. In this case, the dishonest Squealer knows that the other animals' fears will allow him to justify an unreasonable claim.

Appeals to Need

Appeals to need make a connection between the subject and a basic human need (such as food, shelter, belonging, intimacy, self-realization, etc.). Like appeals to value, appeals to need tap into a broad spectrum of human affairs. They try to reach inside an audience, into people's essential requirements for living.

Appeals to need can be highly effective. For instance, if many people are living in poverty, a politician may attempt to connect their basic human needs (food, work, security) to his or her particular goals. The Bolshevik revolution in Imperial Russia, which overthrew the czar and established communist rule for most of the twentieth century, gained momentum by appeals to need. Because so many people were poor and lacked basic elements of survival, the Bolsheviks were able to convince them to join their cause and overthrow the aristocracy. In more recent times, we know that terrorism is bred at least in part out of poverty, out of conditions that leave people in need. When people's basic needs are not met, they are vulnerable; others can appeal to the void in their lives and draw them into behavior they would not otherwise consider.

But appeals to need are not exclusively used for destructive ends. They can be used to make valuable arguments. For instance, political leaders may argue for universal health care as a basic human need, against those who place more importance on profit. In American politics, basic human needs often are pitted against profit or economic growth: basic individual needs versus broader economic goals.

Notice how Samantha Tengelitsch distinguishes between hospital policies and women's needs during the birthing process:

> Women actually experience less pain at home. During labor, oxytocin, the hormone that causes contractions and helps the baby to be born, works in harmony with endorphins—the body's own pain-relieving hormone. During a homebirth, the woman's body will release these hormones according to her needs and she will usually cope well with the sensation of labor.

Appeals to Value

Appeals to value make a connection between the topic and a shared value or principle (such as fairness, equality, honor, kindness, selflessness, duty, responsibility, profit, or practicality). For example, in her essay "In Defense of Darkness" (from Chapter 5), Holly Wren Spaulding links her topic, nighttime darkness, to values such as mystery, enchantment, release, and calm. She even nudges readers to treasure these values, to find them precious in our busy everyday lives:

> It's like this: darkness bleeds the boundaries between myself and that which is just beyond my physical form. It contains unknown depths (the lake is hard to make out as its surface melts into the rest of night), enchantment, and a release from the manners and mannerisms of daytime, circumscribed as it is with routine and work and propriety. Nighttime darkness also bears the prospect of sleep and dreams (increasingly precious in this age of insomnia and sleep disorders), and an unbridling of inhibitions by way a kind of anonymity, if not invisibility. In the dark one finds light-footed walking and slowness; a sense that there is enough time and that rushing is no longer necessary.

Like Spaulding, all good arguers understand that people are moved by their sense of value. Good arguers know how to bring a particular value to the foreground and make it seem pressing. For example, notice how Justin James in "Standardized Testing vs. Education" (from Chapter 7), highlights the value of curiosity over high test scores:

Some situations contain a range of competing values.

The [No Child Left Behind] act has placed an emphasis on accountability, which is being determined by student test results. Test scores might rise. But does that really mean the schools are doing a better job or students are getting a better education? The current emphasis on testing can have harmful results. What's more, the method used to find out the scores teaches students a dangerous definition of *education*.

The emphasis placed on standardized testing teaches students that *education* means getting content from a teacher or getting good at a skill. They come to think *education* means getting a grade on a test, accumulating points, and arriving at an average grade based on those points. But students will benefit more in all aspects of life if they can experience education differently—as having to do more with exploring, discovery, being curious. Standardized testing deprives students from the opportunity to experience an education that values curiosity, and is more valuable than an education consumed with standardized tests.

Appeals to value may be the most intense and abundant appeals in popular arguments. Whenever someone says, "It's not fair!" he or she is appealing to a value (fairness). In fact, any argument based on

Bettmann/CORBIS

equality, justice, duty, responsibility, security, or honesty probably relies on an appeal to value. When arguers can connect a particular point to a broader value, they tap into something beyond their particular argument and call on the belief system of both their audience and the broader public.

Activities

1. For one of the following claims, develop a line of reasoning with at least three steps. Explain what support strategies could be used to develop each premise.

   - Facebook should be used in college classes because it engages students in course material and helps them stay actively involved.
   - Because it is harmful to the environment and consumers, holiday shopping must be reduced.
   - Elementary school classrooms should rely less on computers.
   - Colleges and universities should offer more women's sports.

2. Develop an inductive line of reasoning that supports a claim about the students in one of your classes.

3. As a class, choose a popular political, social, or cultural topic. Then list the appeals to value that are used in the arguments about the topic. (Make sure to explore all the positions toward the topic.)

4. Carefully examine an advertisement and describe how it uses an appeal to character, emotion, need, or value.

Disconnected

LYNDA SMITH

Lynda Smith wrote the following essay for her second-semester college English course. Originally, she used the Arguing Crisis chapter of this book (see Chapter 10) to reveal a critical part of everyday life that people normally take for granted or ignore entirely. In the argument, she uses a wide range of rhetorical strategies.

A jogger runs down the Leelanau Trail talking on a cell phone. A student text-messages while in class. High-speed. Real-time. BlackBerry, Razr, and Firefly. Like it or not, technologically advanced communication devices have taken over our lives. Rapidly reaching epidemic proportions, we have come to accept and rely on them as if our very lives depended on it. But have we slowed down long enough to ask ourselves, is "faster" giving us more time? Are more ways to connect making us more connected? Have we compromised our values for mass produced values?

I admit it! I am a technophobe. Or in technospeak, a P.O.N.A. (acronym for *person of no account*). Yes, I have exercised my right to choose what communication devices I will allow in my world. But, it's hard. Every day, I am bombarded with catchy commercials, communication catalogs, and people who are trying to convince me all of this techno stuff is inevitable, a sign of the times, the way of the world. That "faster" will give me more time and being hyper-connected will fulfill my needs for connecting with friends and loved ones. While I do own a cell phone (it's in my car somewhere) and a computer, I resent the fact that the outside world attempts to persuade me to compromise my values for mass-produced values. I treasure the choice to talk to whom I choose when I choose, time to enjoy a lazy walk in the woods where the only sound is nature, real-time, face-to-face conversations with close friends over a nice dinner and a bottle of wine. Call me old-fashioned, but I'm not convinced all this technology is giving us more time or making us more connected.

Communication technology has been around for a long time. "In point of fact, humans have been creating ways to transmit, store and manipulate information and messages for centuries—if not millennia" (Thurlo et al. 37). Inventions such as the printing press, telegraph, and telephone were exciting, important innovations that for the first time allowed us to "reach out and touch" family and friends in ways that were previously not available. But, with the rapid advancement of present-day technologies, it has become an obsession to be connected with the latest devices.

Advertising for these communication devices is big business. Appealing to our desires for connectedness and more leisure time, communication conglomerates spend billions of dollars on advertising campaigns. Their ads are bigger and more prevalent than ever before. Every day we hear about new inventions that make it easier to stay connected. We are bombarded with catchy commercials and sophisticated ads for high-speed Internet, long-distance calling plans, and cell phones. Infectious phrases such as "Can you hear me now?" saturate our subconscious, silently reinforcing our need for connection. High-speed Internet surfing caters to the rampant desire for instant gratification while quietly leading us to believe faster will give us more time. Visual images lure us in using color, strategically placed props, and text to appeal to our emotions. The omnipresent repetition of these persuasive messages is seducing us into a state of intellectual numbness, making us immune to logical thinking so we will buy their products. In the United States, there are now 194,479,364 cell phone users and 203,824,428 Internet users (United States, Central Intelligence Agency). We can't go anywhere these days without seeing a cell phone attached to someone's ear or pocket. Ask anyone on the street and he or she will tell you they have a cell phone "just in case" someone needs to contact them, or they are "handy to have" because they can do so many things. According to a report by the United States Department of Transportation, cell phone subscriptions rose from 340,213 in 1985 to a whopping 117,000,000 in 2001 (155). These numbers clearly indicate that this subliminal invasion has taken hold.

5 But are technologically advanced communication devices inevitable, or are we allowing huge corporations to lead us blindly from being real-time human beings to virtual puppets?

Human beings are social by nature. We desire heartfelt connections with our families and friends. This desire is exactly what communication conglomerates use in their advertising campaigns to convince us that we need cell phones. This is how it works. First, they fill their ads with lots of pictures. Photos of smiling people talking on cell phones and pictures of the endless variety of wireless devices we can fill our lives with. Next, they bombard us with catchy phrases and text, phrases like "spread the word" and text such as "be connected" and "let's talk." In other words, they use a need to create a need.

Take my friend Randy, for example. When I first met him, his cell phone was his constant companion. He felt that he needed to be available for his family and friends any time day or night. And he was. Barely a minute went by that he was not talking on his phone. After a while, he started to realize the constant connection was taking up more and more of his time and the amount of stress in his life was increasing. What had initially started out as an innocent need to connect had turned into a self-perpetuating cycle. The more time he spent talking on the phone, the less connected he felt to his family and friends. That in turn triggered the need to feel connected, and the cycle would repeat. He came to realize that the phone was preventing him from spending quality face-to-face time with loved ones as well as himself. He has since learned to use his phone in moderation.

Being connected is easier than ever before, but it has allowed us to become "hyper-connected." The time we spend keeping "in touch" is on the rise. Cell phone customers used 1.5 trillion MOU's (minutes of use) in 2005, up 36% from 1.1 trillion in 2004 ("Wireless"). This obsession with our cell phones has become a type of cultural addiction. The *Encyclopedia of Psychology* describes an addiction as an "overpowering desire or need for an . . . action or interaction . . . that produces a psychophysical 'high.' This desire or need is repetitive, impulsive, and compulsive in nature" (Hatterer 16). Our obsession with cell phones is not unlike other addictions that consume our lives—addictions such as working too much, buying too much useless stuff, or even taking drugs.

And the more an addiction takes over, the more our true needs are not being met. While many would insist that talking on their cell phones is synonymous to face-to-face communication, the fact remains that talking on a cell phone can't replace real-time human connection with its eye-to-eye contact, physical touches, and emotional responses.

10 In this fast-paced society of compacted time restraints, we long for more leisure time. At the same time, we are consumed with the desire for instant gratification. We want immediate access to people, information, and services any time, day or night. We believe that somehow if we do everything faster, we will have more free time. Our lives have become a world filled with services to help us move through life with increased speed. We have drive-thrus for food, banking, even laundry so we don't have to leave our cars. We have u-scan checkouts at grocery stores so we don't have to wait in line. And now, different speeds at which we can choose to move through life. There is high speed, turbo speed, and new elite speeds where you can, without leaving your home, hit speeds up to 6.0 Mbps (AT&T). This desire for speed is just one more way that big communication companies can use to draw us in. They appeal to our desire for more time by supplying us with increasingly faster services.

Even though we can connect with the world at faster rates, our whole sense of time gets warped. We get mesmerized by the speed and actually end up with less time. It becomes a self-perpetuating cycle. The faster we go, the more time spent, the less time we have, the greater our needs, the more we crave, and the faster we want to go. AT&T's new slogan promises, "Your world delivered." But is all that speed really giving us the time and connections we desire? Mark Slouka's example in his book *War of the Worlds* says it well:

> As everyone knows, unreality increases with speed. Walking across a landscape at six miles an hour, we experience the particular reality of place: its smells, sounds, colors, textures, and so on. Driving at seventy miles an hour, the experience is very different. The car isolates us, distances us; the world beyond the windshield—whether desert mesa or rolling farmland—seems vaguely unreal. At supersonic speeds, the divorce is complete. A landscape at 30,000 feet is an abstraction, as unlike real life as a painting. (3)

In other words, the further we move away from our basic needs, the more separated from our lives we become.

Technologically advanced communication devices are the guiding force leading us into our own virtual worlds. For example, look at the recent advancements in cell phones. Besides talking on them, we can e-mail, text-message, watch TV, play games, and take pictures. The Samsung Company is now working on developing a cell phone that can "feel, think, evolve, and reproduce" (Maney). That's scary. We already use computers for information, entertainment, companionship, and even love. "Our home computers . . . will soon come with a face capable of responding to our expressions, understanding our gestures, even reading our lips. Its eyes will follow us around the room. We'll be able to talk with it, argue with it, flirt with it. . . . Will it have emotions? You bet" (Slouka 8). That's even scarier!

The acceptance of these technological advances into our lives has propelled us toward a virtual society. What does this mean?

> A culture once based exclusively on physical contact is in the process of being transformed into one where goods and services are accessible without the need for face-to-face contact with other people. Technology has enabled this transformation toward virtual societies. Technology is the glue that makes virtual societies plausible, but technology alone does not guarantee the viability of the virtual society, for the technical power must be used intelligently and deliberately by an informed population. (qtd. in Agres et al.)

With all this talk about cell phone addiction, high-speed Internet surfing, and virtual societies one might believe that I am totally against computers and cell phones. Although I am a self-proclaimed technophobe, I do recognize there are benefits to having both. Having a computer has enabled me to write this paper, and it allows me to keep in contact with friends and family who live far away. And while I have never had to use a cell phone for an emergency, I do believe it is an important reason to have one. More than 224,000 9-1-1 calls are placed each day and many lives have been saved ("Wireless"). But I am still not convinced that all this technology stuff has given me more time or has made me feel more connected. Mark Burch says it best: 15

> To the degree that we cultivate the capacity to enter deeply into the experience of the moment, we also cultivate the experience of joy, plenitude, and well-being in our lives. This requires few things, but the capacity to know and enjoy them with profound intensity. It is a process, finally, of cultivating oneself and one's relationships with others. . . . Mainstream society consists of the exact opposite—ever-briefer and more superficial encounters with ever-larger quantities of goods, services, and people. There

is no pleasure or contact, only the giddy adrena-line-fueled whirl of changing experience without substance, touch without intimacy, information without meaning, company without community. (qtd. in Pierce 305)

Computers and cell phones can benefit our lives, but spending too much time with them can lure us away from real-time experiences, face-to-face interactions, and isolate us from our surroundings. We need to ask ourselves: Are we going to accept these devices as inevitable, a sign of the times, the way of the world? Are we so busy connecting with the outer world that we have forgotten what it feels like to connect with our inner worlds? Have we moved away from our most basic needs? "Within the universe created by Isaac Asimov [a science fiction writer], people slipped unconsciously into a virtual society. The pendulum swung from a physical to a virtual society without any examination or recognition of the changes . . ." (Agres et al.). What will your choice be?

Works Cited

Agres, Carole, et al. "Transformation to Virtual Societies: Forces and Issues." *Information Society*, vol. 14, no. 2, Mar. 1998, pp. 71–82, doi: 10.1080/019722498128881.

AT&T. *Why Just Surf When You Can Fly?* 2006.

Grmoljez, Aimee. "Wireless Industry: Growing and Competitive." Energy and Telecommunications Interim Committee, Helena, 1 May 2008. Presentation.

Hatterer, L. J. "Addictive Process." *Encyclopedia of Psychology*, edited by Raymond J. Corsini, J. Wiley & Sons, 1994.

Maney, Kevin. "Top Popped on What Cell Phone Technology Can Do for Us." *USA Today*, 1 Mar. 2006.

Pierce, Linda Breen. *Choosing Simplicity*. Gallagher Press, 2000.

Slouka, Mark. *War of the Worlds*. Basic Books, 1995.

Thurlo, Crispin, et al. *Computer Mediated Communication: Social Interaction and the Net*. Sage Publications, 2004.

United States, Central Intelligence Agency. *The World Factbook*, 2006.

United States, Dept. of Transportation, Research and Innovative Technology Administration, Bureau of Transportation Statistics. "Cell Phone Service Subscriptions: 1985–July 2001." *Transportation Statistics Annual Report*, 2001.

"Wireless Quick Facts." CTIA, Apr. 2006, files.ctia.org/ pdf/Wireless_Quick_Facts_April_06.pdf.

Assignment: Summarizing Arguments

Summary is a process of abbreviating and rewording the main ideas of a text. If that text is an argument, the main ideas can often be identified by focusing on the line of reasoning. For instance, if we were to identify Ryan Brown's line of reasoning (pp. 21–24), we would work through the essay and find the main statements that lead us to accept his argument about cars.

¶1–2 Intro/background/description.

¶4–5 We are a society of drivers, preferring to drive ten miles over walking two blocks.

¶6 But in a society built around cars, not the people who drive them, we seem willing to sacrifice community for convenience.

¶7 Along with community, we also are sacrificing the human body, perhaps the most efficient and best-designed mode of transportation known to us. Walking truly is the most efficient and ecologically friendly mode of transportation, yet we make every effort to minimize this healthful and sensible activity.

¶9 It seems that as our driving increases, our health deteriorates.

¶10 That automobiles are environmentally unfriendly is unarguable.

¶11 Relatively low fuel prices and high gas mileage keep the cost of driving low, allowing this drivers' society to perpetuate.

¶12 We modern Americans think with our wallets.

¶13 New Urbanism and other social reform movements promise to bring back the days of centralized, walkable communities, incorporating features such as wide sidewalks and narrow streets, neighborhood stores and schools.

¶14 The notion of walking any significant distance as a necessary means of transportation seems so alien to us, but the drivers' society is a recent phenomenon.

¶15 Ultimately it is individual choice that will determine if our communities are to become mere pit stops on the highway.

¶16 Perhaps we as a society need to take a step back from our highway-paced lives and slow things down to a gentle stroll.

Identifying Brown's line of reasoning helps us to see the scaffolding—the basic structure—of his argument. Now, we can develop a thorough and accurate summary by putting Brown's premises into our own words:

> In his essay, "A Community of Cars," Ryan Brown argues that society's reliance on driving instead of walking has sacrificed community, our bodies, and the environment. Our reliance on driving has replaced human inter-action such as friendly conversation with less personal interaction such as honking horns and drive-thru transactions. According to Brown, we have sacrificed community for the convenience of driving—of zooming across town to grab everything at once in one big store.
>
> We have also, he explains, sacrificed our bodies, which are well designed for transportation. They run on organic and renewable fuels, are durable, self-maintaining and self-repairing, and they produce only ecologically useful emissions. Walking is efficient and ecologically friendly, yet we avoid it. And as our driving increases, our health deteriorates. The Post-World War II suburban model has contributed to obesity, heart disease, and diabetes.
>
> Brown also contends that driving harms the environment. Auto emissions produce harmful greenhouse gases, oxides of nitrogen, sulfides, and toxic carbon monoxide. And roads hurt the environment because they destroy wildlife habitat and contribute to runoff that pollutes the water.
>
> Low fuel prices and good gas mileage encourage driving, but even if people drive a vehicle that gets good gas mileage, they are still driving instead of walking. Reform movements like New Urbanism encourage walk-ing, but walking a significant distance is foreign to us now, even though driving is a recent phenomenon.
>
> Whether we drive or walk is a matter of personal choice. And since driving has not provided us with the leisure that was predicted, Brown suggests that we step back and examine the pace of our lives.

This summary follows some basic conventions:

- The title and author of the essay are given in the first paragraph.
- Brown's essay is discussed in present tense ("Brown also contends" rather than "Brown also contended").
- The main points are separated in paragraphs.

Now, try your own summary. In a 250–300 word passage, summarize Lynda Smith's argument in "Disconnected." Start by identifying the premises in the line of reasoning. Then, put those premises in your own words. Make the summary flow. To do this, you may decide to combine sentences, add connecting or transitional words (and, but, on the other hand, etc.), or make other changes in word choice and sentence structure. As you do this, be accurate! Your summary must accurately reflect the meaning of the original. (For more specifics on writing summaries, see pp. 338–340.)

4

Opposition

Argument is not a monologue. It is not one person expressing a solitary, personal opinion. Instead, argument is about engagement, tension, and friction among claims. In academic writing, that engagement is crucial. It must be dramatized and highlighted. Projecting one's opinion is not enough. Writers cannot simply assert a claim and offer support. Instead, they must directly engage other and opposing ideas. They must deal with the friction or overlap between their own claims and those of others. In fact, the most successful arguments are those that deeply engage opposition—that enter into intensive dialogue with other claims and values. Counterargument, concession, and qualifiers bring opposing ideas into contact.

COUNTERARGUMENT

Counterarguments refute claims or positions opposed to those that the writer or speaker is forwarding. Good arguers *counterargue*. They explain how other positions opposed to their own are somehow wrong. Perhaps other positions are unethical, unreasonable, logically flawed, or impractical. Whatever their shortcomings, opposing viewpoints must be addressed head-on. Notice how C.S. Lewis in "The Law of Human Nature" responds to an opposing claim:

> I know that some people say the idea of a Law of Nature or decent behavior known to all men is unsound, because different civilizations and different ages have had quite different moralities.
>
> But this is not true. There have been differences between their moralities, but these have never amounted to anything like a total difference. If anyone will take the trouble to compare the moral teaching of, say, the ancient Egyptians, Babylonians, Hindus, Chinese, Greeks and Romans, what will really strike him will be how very like they are to each other and to our own.

Lewis begins the first paragraph with what "some people say" and then responds to that claim in the next paragraph. He has anticipated the logic of the opposition. Notice, also, that his acknowledgment is not drawn out. He quickly mentions the opposing perspective and then responds with his own reasoning. In other cases, the writer may choose to explain the opposing perspective in more detail, especially if it is complex. Writers may dedicate several paragraphs to an opposing perspective so that they can respond to particular ideas, assumptions, or phrases.

Writers use counterarguments to help the audience understand and possibly accept a claim. But counterargument also generates ideas. In other words, counterargument is an important invention strategy. Before they communicate their thinking, good arguers examine others' positions and try to imagine contrary points. This helps them draw clear boundaries between their positions and others'. Imagine, for instance, a writer asserting a definition of education:

> Education is an exploration of what is possible in any given field.

By imagining how other people might define education (*Education is a process of learning what experts know. Education is the accumulation of knowledge. Education is the process of becoming socialized into a way of thinking and behaving.*), the writer might realize that *an exploration* is starkly different from *an accumulation*—that her way of thinking is, in fact, very different from other ways of thinking. And she might then come to a more intensive position:

> Education is a process of exploring new ground and struggling against conventional modes of thinking.

When counterarguing, writers should be cautious of tossing aside the opposition too quickly. Dismissing opposing positions too easily can strangle or short circuit an argument. Imagine a writer, Sam, is arguing that U.S. corporations should not freely take their operations out of the country. He begins a paragraph by explaining an opposing position:

> The Center for Applied Business argues that American corporations need to take their operations overseas because labor in the United States is too expensive. However, this is just silly. Americans should be paid well because they do a great job.

Sam counterargues by taking on the opposing position of the Center for Applied Business. However, his counterargument misses the mark because it moves too quickly in saying that the center's claim is "just silly." (See "The Personal Response Problem" on page 19.) If Sam wants his readers to share his judgment, he should further analyze that claim. That is, he should more closely examine the layers of the claim and unearth the values beneath it:

> The Center for Applied Business argues that American corporations need to take their operations overseas because labor in the United States is too expensive. This position obviously values the bottom line of business rather than the life of business. The claim comes from a desire to maximize profit at the expense of the people in and of the company itself—and the communities that first gave them their start. The emphasis on cutting labor costs also assumes that the money is simply saved, that moving operations to another country somehow alleviates the strain caused by higher wages demanded in American industry. However, the desire to maximize profit by shrinking labor costs is a never-ending, and often self-defeating, battle.

Sam could then go on to develop his logic and show the specific nature of that self-defeating battle. He not only would make better use of the opposing claim but also would develop a more layered argument.

Write down your position (claim and support) on the following issues, and then for each issue, imagine at least two claims that oppose your own.

1. The government has a right to know what a citizen is smoking.
2. Spam e-mail should be illegal.
3. Spammers should pay a fine and spend at least one year in prison.
4. The school cafeteria should not use Styrofoam plates and cups.

MIGUEL MEDINA/AFP/Getty Images

CONCESSION

While counterargument looks to others and says, "I'm afraid not, and here's why," concession looks to others and says, "Okay. Good point." In short, concession acknowledges or grants value to an opposing claim. Arguers who simply ignore, dismiss, or explain away ideas that challenge their own are simplifying arguments instead of dealing with complexities. Not all opposing positions or accounts should be (or can be) explained away. Conceding certain points and qualifying others are important strategies for strengthening an argument. Some opposing points have value, and good arguers acknowledge those points by conceding them. In a letter to the department store Kohl's, K. T. Glency argues that the store deceives customers into applying for credit cards. However, he does concede several points:

> **I agree with you that people should be able to figure some things out.** Some people will be able to figure out more than others. And some people will be able to figure out very little.

> **Of course Kohl's employees cannot spell out every detail of a situation,** but they should not take any action to purposely deceive. Society has a responsibility to educate people enough so that they can figure things out on their own. And influential executives such as you have a responsibility to *not* purposely deceive the public.

Glency anticipates an opposing claim and concedes to it so that he can make an important distinction between inadvertently misleading people and purposely deceiving them. His concessions do not undermine his argument; instead, they acknowledge common ground and show that he has a reasonable understanding of the situation.

It is easy to become fixated on our own opinions and draw firm boundaries between our perspective and others'. Concessions allow writers to cling less tightly to their own perspectives and invent more nuanced points. This does not mean that *conciliatory* arguments (those that concede points) are wishy-washy. It means that they are engaged with the opinions swirling around in the rhetorical situation. Consider, for instance, how Glency's argument gains important nuance (or dimension) when he concedes that Kohl's cannot "spell out every detail" for its customers. This concession allows him to dig further into the issue—into the kinds of details that retail stores *should* spell out. Because Glency understands an opposing viewpoint, his own argument becomes more sophisticated.

In mainstream political debates, arguers rarely concede. In fact, concessions are often seen as weakness. Even when political candidates are shown to be wrong, they might not acknowledge the value of opposing positions or even undeniable evidence! Consequently, their own arguments become overly simplistic. Public issues like the economy, health care, the environment, immigration, and military deployment are complex, and that complexity demands a certain degree of concession. Without it, arguments turn into boxing matches wherein each side tries to outpunch, rather than out-think, the opposition. Mature debate, the kind that we hope to nurture in academic writing, embraces the real complexity of issues, and concession is one of its key tools.

Activities

1. Choose an argument you strongly disagree with, and then make an important concession to that argument. Explain how your concession makes your response to the argument more persuasive.

2. Watch an interview about a controversial issue—national health care, global warming, deep sea drilling, etc. What concession does the person being interviewed make, or what concession should the person have made? How does the concession strengthen the interviewee's position? If it doesn't, why?

QUALIFIERS

Qualifiers are closely related to concessions, but while concessions focus on others' ideas, qualifiers focus on the arguer's ideas, acknowledging their limitations. We often use qualifiers in everyday conversation: "I'm not saying that all politicians are bad, but many of them seem to distort the truth." "Granted, some country music is good, but a lot of it just rubs me the wrong way." We do this to make our opinions more acceptable.

Imagine a day without qualifiers. We would go around spouting hasty generalizations: *College students are too immature to manage their time. Television is evil. Professors don't care about their students. Teenagers are rotten drivers.* While such claims might work in a small crowd of like-minded friends, they would quickly draw fire from others.

Qualifiers make such claims more reasonable and potentially worthy of public attention: *When distracted by cell phones and stereos, even the most attentive teenager can become a rotten driver.*

In more formal argument, qualifiers prevent arguers from making claims that are too extreme. Tracy Webster uses a qualification in this passage from "Big House in the Wilderness" (in Chapter 10):

> I began by thinking out loud how it seems odd that men come here to hunt deer that you have to try not to hit with your car. The deer aren't hard to find, and when they see you they just stand there, motionless, staring. Of course, you can't shoot the ones standing on the road. You have to drive out a ways, then walk a bit farther, and then shoot one. Back there, in the woods, the deer might have a better chance, by blending in with the trees and hearing or smelling or seeing you before you see them.
>
> But this is not an anti-hunting essay or an anti house-in-the-wilderness essay. It is an anti big-house-in-the-wilderness essay. The big house in the wilderness is more dangerous than any hunter is. It's the big house, the too-big house, that is unjustifiable.

In the second paragraph, Webster qualifies his ideas by making clear that he is not condemning hunters or all houses in the wilderness.

Qualifiers also show up as words that make statements seem less extreme. By qualifying claims, words such as *perhaps, seems, often, some, sometimes, most, certain, occasionally, probably, might* and so on can make an argument appear more careful. Notice the qualifiers John Adams uses in "Evaluation of 'The Education of Ms. Groves'" (from Chapter 9):

> Many people will realize that *Dateline NBC* turned a complex issue into a TV drama like *Desperate Housewives* or *Grey's Anatomy*. It had an attractive leading character, some good drama (even a fight!), and an emotional (uplifting) ending. Unfortunately, though it will entertain, this show will disappoint a curious mind because it reduces a serious issue to a Hallmark card. A lot of dedicated, loving, trick-savvy teachers are probably laughing (though with frustration) at the TV-style docu-drama of American education. While it showed the father in prison, the homeless family, and so on, according to *Dateline NBC,* it can all be over-come (all of American culture can be overcome) if our teachers just know to count backwards. *Supernanny* and *Wife Swap* deal with complexity more than this.

The qualifiers (highlighted) temper Adams's position. While Adams makes some bold claims (*it had an attractive leading character; it reduces a serious issue to a Hallmark card; it can all be overcome;* Supernanny and Wife Swap *deal with complexity more than this*), he tempers other claims with qualifiers (*many* [not all] people will realize; it had *some* [not a lot of] *good drama; teachers are probably* [not definitely] *laughing*). Arguers must decide what ideas to qualify, what ideas not to qualify, and what type of qualifier to use. An unqualified argument can be effective, but such force and certainty requires an argument that makes the readers equally certain. Unless an argument will create certainty for readers, it should allow space for caution, and qualifiers allow that space. While qualifiers are valuable tools for argument, they must be used judiciously. If points are overqualified, arguments lose their intensity and arguers end up backing out of their positions inadvertently.

Activities

1. In groups, generate a list of ways to qualify an idea. Write down words and phrases and any other ideas your group comes up with.

2. As a class, discuss the following: What qualifiers operate in our everyday lives? Consider claims of the college, counselors, professors, government officials, and students. (For instance, what qualifying statements are operating in your course syllabus or textbook?) How do those qualifiers affect your thinking?

3. Consider the following image. How is the flower emerging from the woman's hijab a response to some other position? Does it seem like a counterargument, concession, or qualifier?

Alain Keler/Sygma/Corbis

ROGERIAN ARGUMENT

We are all aware of arguments based on confrontation and hostility. Such arguments are common in popular media where pundits and politicians attack others' views as simply wrong, absurd, or evil. Psychologist Carl Rogers (1902–1987) offered a different approach. Rogers proposed a type of argumentation based on cooperation and understanding.

Rogers is best known for his contributions to psychology and clinical therapy. In his book *Freedom to Learn* (1969), Rogers explains, "The most socially useful learning in the modern world is the learning of the process of learning, a continuing openness to experience and to incorporate into oneself the process of change." His notions about mutual understanding, trust, and supportive rather than competitive rhetoric have become key concepts in argument.

According to Rogerian theory, arguers should first seek to understand opposing views. Once we know the terrain of our opponents, we can build a bridge to it. The goal is not to attack an opponents' thinking, but to discover key similarities between our perspectives and theirs. Only then can we genuinely determine the nature of our own positions and effectively change how we think, which is a key element in Rogerian theory. In "Communication: Its Blocking and Its Facilitation" (printed below), Rogers explains some key concepts of Rogerian argument:

- The "tendency to react to any emotionally meaningful statement by forming an evaluation of it from our own point of view is . . . the major barrier to interpersonal communication."

- "Real communication occurs when . . . we listen with understanding . . . [seeing] the expressed idea and attitude from the other person's point of view, [sensing] how it feels to him, [achieving] his frame of reference in regard to the thing he is talking about."

- "Each person can speak up for himself only when he has first restated the ideas and feelings of the previous speaker accurately, and to that speaker's satisfaction. You see what this would mean. It would simply mean that before presenting your own point of view, it would be necessary for you to really achieve the other speaker's frame of reference to understand his thoughts and feelings so well that you could summarize them for him."

- "[O]nce you have been able to see the other's point of view, your own comments will have to be drastically revised. You will also find the emotion going out of the discussion, the differences being reduced, and those differences which remain being of a rational and understandable sort."

- "If you really understand another person in this way, if you are willing to enter his private world and see the way life appears to him without any attempt to make evaluative judgments, you run the risk of being changed yourself."

When taking a Rogerian approach to argument, you should not simply follow a prescribed format, as if filling in a form. What's important is to understand the basic concept and then make rhetorical decisions to put forth a Rogerian-style argument. Since a Rogerian argument is about finding common ground, its components would likely include:

1. a statement of the problem or issue at hand, including any necessary background information (key information about the particular rhetorical situation) and perhaps the possible effects of the problem or issue

2. an explanation of one of the positions or claims (we might think of this as the opposing position)

3. an explanation of another (or *the* other) position or claim (we might think of this as the writer's position)

4. a fair and reasonable discussion of the pros and cons of each position, comparing/contrasting the two sides to work through and argue for a particular claim the writer would like the reader to accept

5. a conclusion or wrapping up of the main points that lead the reader to understand and accept the writer's main claim.

Communication: Its Blocking and Its Facilitation

CARL R. ROGERS

The text above presents some of Carl Rogers' main points about communication. However, this is like having a friend describe a movie to you. Think Tom Hanks and *Cast Away*. A friend can describe the scene in which Wilson floats out to sea. She can tell you how sad it was. But that is a poor substitute for the real sadness you may feel by watching the movie yourself, not just hearing an explanation of it. As you read Rogers' actual essay, look for new and interesting ideas in addition to the ones discussed above. Then after you read the essay, describe a rhetorical situation in which a Rogerian approach would have led to better results. (Note: *Rhetoric* is the way you communicate an idea; the way you persuade others to think and act differently; and the way you yourself use language to think through issues and come to a particular decision or belief. A *rhetorical situation* is any opportunity to do these things.)

It may seem curious that a person whose whole professional effort is devoted to psychotherapy should be interested in problems of communication. What relationship is there between providing therapeutic help to individuals with emotional maladjustments and the concern of this conference with obstacles to communication? Actually the relationship is very close indeed. The whole task of psychotherapy is the task of dealing with a failure in communication. The emotionally maladjusted person, the "neurotic," is in difficulty first because communication within himself has broken down, and second because as a result of this his communication with others has been damaged. If this sounds somewhat strange, then let me put it in other terms. In the "neurotic" individual, parts of himself which have been termed unconscious, or repressed, or denied to awareness, become blocked off so that they no longer communicate themselves to the conscious or managing part of himself. As long as this is true, there are distortions in the way he communicates himself to others, and so he suffers both within himself and in his interpersonal relations. The task of psychotherapy is to help the person achieve, through a special relationship with a therapist, good communication within himself. Once this is achieved he can communicate more freely and more effectively with others. We may say then that psychotherapy is good communication, within and between men. We may also turn that statement around and it will still be true. Good communication, free communication, within or between men, is always therapeutic.

It is, then, from a background of experience with communication in counseling and psychotherapy that I want to present here two ideas. I wish to state what I believe is one of the major factors in blocking or impeding communication, and then I wish to present what in our experience has proven to be a very important way of improving or facilitating communication.

I would like to propose, as an hypothesis for consideration, that the major barrier to mutual interpersonal communication is our very natural tendency to judge, to evaluate, to approve or disapprove, the statement of the other person, or the other group. Let me illustrate my meaning with some very simple examples. As you leave the meeting tonight, one of the statements you are likely to hear is, "I didn't like that man's talk." Now what do you respond? Almost invariably your reply will be either approval or disapproval of the attitude expressed. Either you respond, "I didn't either. I thought it was terrible," or else you tend to reply, "Oh, I thought it was really good." In other words, your primary reaction is to evaluate what has just been said to you, to evaluate it from your point of view, your own frame of reference.

Or take another example. Suppose I say with some feeling, "I think the Republicans are behaving in ways that show a lot of good sound sense

Carl R. Rogers, "Communication: Its Blocking and Its Facilitation." *Northwestern University Information*, vol. 20, no. 25, 1952, pp. 9–15. Reprinted with permission by the author.

these days," what is the response that arises in your mind as you listen? The overwhelming likelihood is that it will be evaluative. You will find yourself agreeing, or disagreeing, or making some judgment about me such as "He must be a conservative," or "He seems solid in his thinking." Or let us take an illustration from the international scene. Russia says vehemently, "The treaty with Japan is a war plot on the part of the United States." We rise as one person to say "That's a lie!"

5   This last illustration brings in another element connected with my hypothesis. Although the tendency to make evaluations is common in most all interchange of language, it is very much heightened in those situations where feelings and emotions are deeply involved. So the stronger our feelings, the more likely it is that there will be no mutual element in the communication. There will be just two ideas, two feelings, two judgments, missing each other in psychological space. I'm sure you recognize this from your own experience. When you have not been emotionally involved yourself, and have listened to a heated discussion, you often go away thinking, "Well, they actually weren't talking about the same thing." And they were not. Each was making a judgment, an evaluation, from his frame of reference. There was really nothing which could be called communication in any genuine sense. This tendency to react to any emotionally meaningful statement by forming an evaluation of it from our own point of view, is, I repeat, the major barrier to interpersonal communication.

But is there any way of solving this problem, of avoiding this barrier? I feel that we are making exciting progress toward this goal and I would like to present it as simply as I can. Real communication occurs, and this evaluative tendency is avoided, when we listen with understanding. What does that mean? It means to see the expressed idea and attitude from the other person's point of view, to sense how it feels to him, to achieve his frame of reference in regard to the thing he is talking about.

Stated so briefly, this may sound absurdly simple, but it is not. It is an approach which we have found extremely potent in the field of psychotherapy. It is the most effective agent we know for altering the basic personality structure of an individual, and improving his relationships and his communications with others. If I can listen to what he can tell me, if I can understand how it seems to him, if I can see its personal meaning for him, if I can sense the emotional flavor which it has for him, then I will be releasing potent forces of change in him. If I can really understand how he hates his father, or hates the university, or hates communists—if I can catch the flavor of his fear of insanity, or his fear of atom bombs, or of Russia—it will be of the greatest help to him in altering those very hatreds and fears, and in establishing realistic and harmonious relationships with the very people and situations toward which he has felt hatred and fear. We know from our research that such empathic understanding—understanding with a person, not about him—is such an effective approach that it can bring about major changes in personality.

Some of you may be feeling that you listen well to people, and that you have never seen such results. The chances are very great indeed that your listening has not been of the type I have described. Fortunately I can suggest a little laboratory experiment which you can try to test the quality of your understanding. The next time you get into an argument with your wife, or your friend, or with a small group of friends, just stop the discussion for a moment and for an experiment, institute this rule. "Each person can speak up for himself only after he has first restated the ideas and feelings of the previous speaker accurately, and to that speaker's satisfaction." You see what this would mean. It would simply mean that before presenting your own point of view, it would be necessary for you to really achieve the other speaker's frame of reference—to understand his thoughts and feelings so well that you could summarize them for him. Sounds simple doesn't it? But if you try it you will discover it one of the most difficult things you have ever tried to do. However, once you have been able to see the other's point of view, your own comments will have to be drastically revised. You will also find the emotion going out of the discussion, the differences being reduced, and those differences which remain being of a rational and understandable sort.

Can you imagine what this kind of an approach would mean if it were projected into larger areas? What would happen to a labor-management dispute if it was conducted in such a way that labor, without necessarily agreeing, could accurately state management's point of view in a way that management could accept; and management, without approving labor's stand, could state labor's case in a way that labor agreed was accurate? It would mean that real communication was established, and one could practically guarantee that some reasonable solution would be reached.

10   If, then, this way of approach is an effective avenue to good communication and good relationships, as I am quite sure you will agree if you try the experiment I have mentioned, why is it not more widely tried and used? I will try to list the difficulties which keep it from being utilized.

In the first place it takes courage, a quality which is not too widespread. I am indebted to Dr. S. I. Hayakawa, the semanticist, for pointing out that to carry on psychotherapy in this fashion is to take a very real risk, and that courage is required. If you really understand another person in this way, if you are willing to enter his private world and see the way life appears to him, without any attempt to make evaluative judgments, you run the risk of being changed yourself. You might see it his way, you might find yourself influenced in your attitudes or your personality. This risk of being changed is one of the most frightening prospects most of us can face. If I enter, as fully as I am able, into the private world of a neurotic or psychotic individual, isn't there a risk that I might become lost in that world? Most of us are afraid to take that risk. Or if we had a Russian communist speaker here tonight, or Senator Joe McCarthy, how many of us would dare to try to see the world from each of these points of view? The great majority of us could not listen; we would find ourselves compelled to evaluate, because listening would seem too dangerous. So the first requirement is courage, and we do not always have it.

But there is a second obstacle. It is just when emotions are strongest that it is most difficult to achieve the frame of reference of the other person or group. Yet it is the time the attitude is most needed, if communication is to be established. We have not found this to be an insuperable obstacle in our experience in psychotherapy. A third party, who is able to lay aside his own feelings and evaluations, can assist greatly by listening with understanding to each person or group and clarifying the views and attitudes each holds. We have found this very effective in small groups in which contradictory or antagonistic attitudes exist. When the parties to a dispute realize that they are being understood, that someone sees how the situation seems to them, the statements grow less exaggerated and less defensive, and it is no longer necessary to maintain the attitude, "I am 100% right and you are 100% wrong." The influence of such an understanding catalyst in the group permits the members to come closer and closer to the objective truth involved in the relationship. In this way mutual communication is established and some type of agreement becomes much more possible. So we may say that though heightened emotions make it much more difficult to understand with an opponent, our experience makes it clear that a neutral, understanding, catalyst type of leader or therapist can overcome this obstacle in a small group.

This last phrase, however, suggests another obstacle to utilizing the approach I have described. Thus far all our experience has been with small face-to-face groups—groups exhibiting industrial tensions, religious tensions, racial tensions, and therapy groups in which many personal tensions are present. In these small groups our experience, confirmed by a limited amount of research, shows that this basic approach leads to improved communication, to greater acceptance of others and by others, and to attitudes which are more positive and more problem-solving in nature. There is a decrease in defensiveness, in exaggerated statements, in evaluative and critical behavior. But these findings are from small groups. What about trying to achieve understanding between larger groups that are geographically remote? Or between face-to-face groups who are not speaking for themselves, but simply as representatives of others, like the delegates at Kaesong? Frankly we do not know the answers to these questions. I believe the situation might be put this way. As social scientists we have a tentative test-tube solution of the problem of breakdown in communication. But to confirm the validity of this test-tube solution, and to adapt it to the enormous problems of communication-breakdown between classes, groups, and nations, would involve additional funds, much more research, and creative thinking of a high order.

Even with our present limited knowledge we can see some steps which might be taken, even in large groups, to increase the amount of listening with, and to decrease the amount of evaluation about. To be imaginative for a moment, let us suppose that a therapeutically oriented international group went to the Russian leaders and said, "We want to achieve a genuine understanding of your views and even more important, of your attitudes and feelings, toward the United States. We will summarize and resummarize these views and feelings if necessary until you agree that our description represents the situation as it seems to you." Then suppose they did the same thing with the leaders in our own country. If they then gave the widest possible distribution to these two views, with the feelings clearly described but not expressed in name-calling, might not the effect be very great? It would not guarantee the type of understanding I have been describing, but it would make it much more possible. We can understand the feelings of a person who hates us much more readily when his attitudes are accurately described to us by a neutral third party, than we can when he is shaking his fist at us.

But even to describe such a first step is to suggest another obstacle to this approach of understanding. Our civilization does not yet have enough faith in the social sciences to utilize their findings. The opposite is true of the physical sciences. During the war when a test-tube solution was found to the problem of synthetic rubber, millions of dollars and an army of talent were turned loose on the problem of using that finding. If synthetic rubber could be made in milligrams, it could and would be made in the thousands of tons. And it was. But in the social science realm, if a way is found of facilitating communication and mutual understanding in small groups, there is no guarantee that the finding will be utilized. It may be a generation or more before the money and the brains will be turned loose to exploit that finding.

In closing, I would like to summarize this small-scale solution to the problem of barriers in communication, and to point out certain of its characteristics.

I have said that our research and experience to date would make it appear that breakdowns in communication, and the evaluative tendency which is the major barrier to communication, can be avoided. The solution is provided by creating a situation in which each of the different parties come to understand the other from the other's point of view. This has been achieved, in practice, even when feelings run high, by the influence of a person who is willing to understand each point of view empathically, and who thus acts as a catalyst to precipitate further understanding.

This procedure has important characteristics. It can be initiated by one party, without waiting for the other to be ready. It can even be initiated by a neutral third person, providing he can gain a minimum of cooperation from one of the parties.

This procedure can deal with the insincerities, the defensive exaggerations, the lies, the "false fronts" which characterize almost every failure in communication. These defensive distortions drop away with astonishing speed as people find that the only intent is to understand, not judge.

20   This approach leads steadily and rapidly toward the discovery of the truth, toward a realistic appraisal of the objective barriers to communication. The dropping of some defensiveness by one party leads to further dropping of defensiveness by the other party, and truth is thus approached.

This procedure gradually achieves mutual communication. Mutual communication tends to be pointed toward solving a problem rather than toward attacking a person or group. It leads to a situation in which I see the problem appears to you, as well as to me, and you see how it appears to me, as well as to you. Thus accurately and realistically defined, the problem is almost certain to yield to intelligent attack, or if it is in part insoluble, it will be comfortably accepted as such.

This then appears to be a test-tube solution to the breakdown of communication as it occurs in small groups. Can we take this small-scale answer, investigate it further, refine it, develop it and apply it to the tragic and well-nigh fatal failures of communication which threaten the very existence of our modern world? It seems to me that this is a possibility and a challenge which we should explore.

Assignment: Identifying and Summarizing Opposition

Arguments do not exist alone. They exist in a world of other arguments. They emerge from opposing ideas, and they are developed through an ongoing process of examining other, contrary positions. In a brief essay, describe Rogers' (pp. 61–65), Brown's (pp. 21–24), or Smith's (pp. 48–51) argument and focus specifically on counterarguments, concessions, and qualifiers. Use the following questions to help guide your thinking:

1. What is the purpose of the argument? How does the arguer want the audience to think and act differently?

2. What prompted the argument? Why has the author bothered to make it?

3. To what other argument is the author responding? How does the writer analyze opposing or popular positions on the topic?

4. What counterarguments are made? How do they help the audience understand and possibly accept the writer's main claim?

5. What concessions are made? How do they impact the overall argument?

6. What points are qualified? Which qualifiers are most important and why?

Caution

As you develop the essay, avoid getting pulled into the argument. If you agree or disagree with the writer (Rogers, Brown, or Smith), try to remain outside of the fray. Don't attack, defend, or celebrate the writer's position. Instead, imagine that your job is to describe how the writer deals with opposition. Also, concentrate your focus on the essay itself—on the writer's rhetorical moves rather than the writer. In other words, describe the argument, not the arguer.

David Sailors/Terra/Corbis

5

Values and Assumptions

Below the surface of New York City lies a hidden layer that includes thousands of miles of electrical cable, fiber-optic and coaxial cable for telecommunications, water pipes (carrying a billion gallons of water a day), a central steam heating system, gas pipes, air ducts, the subway, sewer pipes, parking garages, and underground foundations. Most people are unaware of what lies beneath the surface of a city—and of what lies beneath the surface of an argument. To read and understand an argument, one must be aware of its hidden layers, where the force of argument lives.

ASSUMPTIONS

An assumption is a logical connection between a claim and its support. Every argument contains an assumption that is crucial to its validity. Assumptions are sometimes stated and sometimes unstated. Unstated assumptions can rest so deeply and quietly in the arguer's mind that he or she may not even recognize it. The following argument contains an unstated assumption:

You should dress nicely for your interview because you want to make a good impression on the employer.

Broken down into claim and support, this is the argument:

Claim: You should dress nicely for your interview.

Support: You want to make a good impression on the employer.

And inside the argument lies an unstated assumption so obvious that it need not be stated:

Assumption: Dressing nicely makes a good impression on potential employers.

The assumption lurks between the claim and support, connecting the two. This assumption is beyond debate, as most people in most situations would not dispute it. However, assumptions are often debatable, even highly questionable, as in the following example:

Claim: We should invade Vietnam before the communists take it over.

Support: The communists will threaten the American way of life.

Inside this argument lies a debatable assumption: *If the communists take over Vietnam, the American way of life will be threatened.* This was the logic that drove the United States into a long and tragic war; when we reveal the assumption, we can see why so many people protested in the late 1960s and '70s. Many Americans could not accept the assumption that a communist takeover in a small Southeast Asian country would ultimately threaten their own way of life. The Johnson and Nixon administrations were hard-pressed to maintain the argument.

British philosopher Stephen Toulmin (1922–2009) developed a system for digging up and evaluating hidden assumptions—or what he called *warrants.* Toulmin analysis, a way of looking at and understanding an argument, divides arguments into six parts. The first three—claim, grounds, warrant—exist in every argument. The second three—backing, rebuttal, qualifier—may or may not exist.

Claim, Grounds, Warrant

Every argument includes a **claim**, which puts forth an assertion; **grounds** to support the claim; and a **warrant**, either stated or unstated, that links the claim and support.

- **claim:** a statement that makes an assertion (The main claim of an essay is the thesis.)
- **grounds:** particular facts (evidence, data, observations) to support a claim
- **warrant:** the link between grounds and claim (The warrant is not always stated.)

The grounds support the claim and the warrant connects the claim and grounds.

Backing, Rebuttal, Qualifier

Some arguments include **backing**, support for the warrant; **rebuttals**, which acknowledge exceptions that might invalidate the claim; and **qualifiers** that modify (*probably, some, most,* etc.) the claim.

- **backing:** support for the warrant
- **rebuttal:** circumstances that could invalidate the claim
- **qualifier:** words that modify (*might, could, sometimes,* etc.) the claim

Sometimes the warrant (why the reader should accept the claim based on the grounds) needs support. The backing supports, or backs up, the warrant. The rebuttal acknowledges circumstances that might invalidate the claim. And the qualifier modifies the claim by using a word such as *some, many, often, sometimes, rarely, always, seems* (instead of *is*), *perhaps, possibly, usually,* and so on.

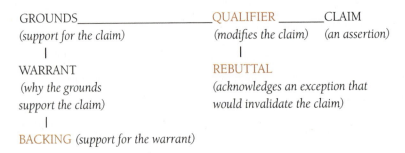

GROUNDS_____QUALIFIER _____CLAIM
(support for the claim)   *(modifies the claim)*   *(an assertion)*
     | |
WARRANT   REBUTTAL
(why the grounds   *(acknowledges an exception that*
support the claim)   *would invalidate the claim)*
     |
BACKING *(support for the warrant)*

Now let's look at an example of how reasoning fits into Toulmin's model. This example (about eating at Taco Time) may seem trivial; however, its purpose is to illustrate the basic way the Toulmin model can be used to analyze or create any argument.

Claim: We should eat at Taco Time.

This is a claim of policy, in which the arguer says what should or should not happen. To make an argument, this claim requires support, which Toulmin calls *grounds*.

Grounds: (We should eat at Taco Time) because Taco Time is inexpensive.

The grounds provide evidence (facts, data, observations) for accepting the claim, in this case *why* we should eat at Taco Time. If we diagram it like this, GROUNDS—CLAIM, by reading left to right, the relationship between the parts is SO; and if read right to left, the relationship is BECAUSE—

Taco Time is inexpensive (grounds) **so** we should eat at Taco Time (claim).
We should eat at Taco Time (claim) **because** Taco Time is inexpensive (grounds).

Warrant: Eating inexpensive food is a desirable thing to do.

Warrants connect the grounds and claim. A warrant (or warranting assumption) is the reason why the reader would be willing to accept the claim based on the grounds provided. This relationship, claim/warrant/grounds, exists in every argument. In this example, the warrant (the assumption or reasoning that connects the grounds and claim) is that eating at an inexpensive restaurant is a desirable thing to do. A person who doesn't agree with this assumption will not accept the claim. For example, someone might respond, "So what it's inexpensive? I don't want to eat at a cheap fast food restaurant. It's our anniversary, so we should eat at Ted's instead."

The warrant is a bridge. Instead of providing more grounds to support a claim, we often need to provide a bridge between the already existing grounds and claim. This bridge answers the question *How do you get there?* or *Why is that?* Often the answer is obvious—already assumed—so it can go unstated. But sometimes the audience requires an answer. For example, our audience probably accepts that Taco Time is inexpensive (more facts about that aren't necessary), but it might wonder how you get from the grounds to the claim—from the cheap prices at Taco Time to the conclusion that we should eat there. If the audience won't accept the claim based on the grounds, we must reinforce the bridge (or warrant) that connects them. The process of reinforcing the warrant is called *backing*.

Notice that grounds are more specific (we can think of them as facts, evidence, observations) and warrants are more general (we can think of them as principles; laws of nature; rules of thumb; appeals to accepted values, customs, and so on). Toulmin likens grounds to *ingredients* and warrants to the *recipe*. The recipe says how you get from ingredients (grounds) to cake (claim). So far the parts of this argument are:

GROUNDS_____ CLAIM
Taco Time is inexpensive.   We should eat at Taco Time.
                                WARRANT
                                Eating inexpensive food is
                                a desirable thing to do.

Keep in mind that an arguer might provide various grounds for eating at Taco Time, not just that it is inexpensive. For example, other reasons might include:

- Taco Time has good food.
- Taco Time is convenient.
- Taco Time is close to work.
- Taco Time has good, quick service.   **So** we should eat at Taco Time.
- Taco Time food is nutritious.
- Taco Time has a 99 cent burrito special.

Each of these reasons would support the claim based on a different warrant. And, an arguer could provide different warrants for the same reason. For example, the warrant above is we should eat inexpensive food *since it is a desirable thing to do*. A different warrant could be that we should eat inexpensive food *since it is a necessity: we only have five dollars*. Another warrant might be that we should eat inexpensive food *since it is good for one's soul*. Each warrant would call for different backing, rebuttals, and qualifiers.

Backing: In economic times like these, we should save money whenever we can.

In our Taco Time argument, the warrant might not require backing. For example, two poor college students without other inexpensive dining options might quickly agree on eating at Taco Time. However, we can imagine a situation where backing up the warrant might be helpful or necessary. Whether to provide backing and what backing to provide depends on the particular situation and factors such as audience. *Eating inexpensive food because it is a desirable thing to do* could require backing such as *in economic times like these, we should save money whenever we can* or *we should save money on food because we want to vacation in Hawaii*.

Rebuttal: Unless we eat at Dairy Queen.

The rebuttal anticipates a challenge to the claim. For example, if Taco Time is next door to Dairy Queen, another inexpensive dining option, a persuasive argument would anticipate and respond to an opposing claim that we should eat at Dairy Queen instead. Here, the arguer might **concede and counter** by acknowledging that Dairy Queen too is inexpensive (concession); however, Taco Time is running an even lower priced 99 cent burrito special, which provides more food per cost than Dairy Queen (counterargument).

The rebuttal leads to more claims and support. For example, as part of the rebuttal, the arguer might introduce additional warrants and/or backing. Yes, Dairy Queen is inexpensive too, but Taco Time has better food. One can see, then, that the Toulmin model not only helps in analyzing and understanding an existing argument; it also helps an arguer invent ideas. It ensures that an arguer is engaging opposition (the ideas of others) and is complicating his or her thinking about the topic.

Qualifier: We should *probably* eat at Taco Time.

Qualifiers modify the claim. Many arguments will not claim something *should* happen or that *everyone* should do something. They will instead qualify the claim by saying it **probably** *should* happen or **most** or **many** or **a few** *people* should do it.

We can think of qualifying claims as the simple act of saying *should*, *definitely should*, or *probably should* or saying *everybody*, *nobody*, or *some people*. However, qualifying claims isn't simple. It requires fine-tuning ideas by thinking through and determining **precisely** what you can **honestly** claim. This determines the range and limitations of the overall argument.

Some Qualifiers

some	quite possibly	at first
many	usually	maybe
often	presumably	should
sometimes	probably	definitely should
rarely	normally	probably should
always	certainly	everybody
seems (instead of is)	necessarily	nobody
perhaps	likely	some people
possibly	plausibly	and so on
very possibly	as far as we can tell	

So far we have been looking at single arguments: one claim, one ground, one warrant, one backing, one rebuttal, one qualifier. In everyday life (at work, home, school, and play), arguments contain these six parts, only more of them. For example, a discussion about where to eat might include *several* grounds for eating at Taco Time, the grounds would include more than one warrant, and backing might involve additional claims, support, and rebuttals. Claims are responses to previous claims, and they prompt subsequent claims. This is the world of ideas in which we swim.

We can sketch a basic argument with one main claim, basic grounds, a simple warrant, backing, and a rebuttal. But practical arguments often include a main claim and various supporting claims, which emerge from the grounds, warrants, backing, and rebuttals. The Toulmin model helps you break down and see how ideas work. However, the basic model is just that—a basic model. In a college essay, a discussion with a friend, a business report, and the thoughts you think through while driving, running, or anything else that most students can imagine themselves doing, you are working through various interacting claims, grounds, warrants, backing, rebuttals, and qualifiers. And these parts can occur in different orders.

Activity

For each of the following, discover the assumption and then decide if it is acceptable or questionable. Explain your decision for each.

Claim: Retirement accounts should be in the hands of private companies and not the federal government.

Support: Private companies can generate more money than government-controlled accounts can.

Claim: Light pollution is a crisis that should be addressed.

Support: Most people cannot see the stars anymore.

Claim: Power companies should not be regulated by the federal government.

Support: Power companies can self-regulate more efficiently.

UNDERLYING VALUES

We are constantly encountering subtle strategies designed to nudge our thinking in a particular direction. Businesses, activists, government offices, and everyday citizens choose language that corresponds to what we value and what we hope for. Many common terms have been carefully selected to replace old terms that did not have the desired effect on the audience. *Anti-abortion* became *pro-life; in favor of lawful abortion* became *pro-choice; global warming* is now *climate change;* and *tax cuts* are called *tax relief.* While businesses, politicians, and activist organizations select words to elicit a particular response, regular people do the same thing, often quite naturally. For example, instead of asking someone out on a "date," a person might ask someone if he or she would like to "get some coffee." Such moves are not necessarily meant to deceive. Instead, they may simply reveal the underlying values between arguers, between arguer and audience, or between two people standing on a sidewalk.

Arguments emerge from value systems, from the collective group of ideals that people quietly cherish. In mainstream modern America, the following values are generally, and automatically, seen as good:

Achievement	Adventure	Affection	Art
Change	Community	Competition	Cooperation
Country	Creativity	Democracy	Efficiency
Excellence	Excitement	Fame	Freedom
Friendships	Harmony	Hard work	Independence
Integrity	Intellect	Honesty	Leadership
Location	Loyalty	Knowledge	Nature
Order	Physicality	Money	Power
Privacy	Public service	Pleasure	Relationships
Religion	Responsibility	Quality	Self-respect
Stability	Status	Security	Wealth
Wisdom	Work	Truth	Youth

For the most part, people do not walk into a room and argue for the worth of friendship, integrity, or wisdom. There are probably very few, if any, *anti-wisdom* groups. Wisdom is simply one of those ideals that most Americans, and others, believe in as an inherent good. And while it may not count as a hot argumentative issue, it underlies—quietly sits beneath—other topics. For instance, when people make an argument that United States presidential candidates should be at least thirty-five years old, they may rely on or tap into that shared belief in wisdom.

Understanding underlying values helps writers invent more convincing arguments. If we know the shared values in a rhetorical situation, we can create better appeals. We can tap into something the audience deeply cherishes. In "Standardized Testing vs. Education" (from Chapter 7), Justin James argues against educational trends that value memorization and rote skills. To move his readers beyond those trends, he taps into the shared value of curiosity. James begins with a reference to a child's sense of discovery:

> It is no wonder my niece says school is boring. When she was younger, she loved it. It was all about discovery; now it's all about tests. Tests can be valuable in education, of course. But they can be hazardous, too. They can hinder learning and teach students and society at large a false definition of education. Standardized tests teach students to *practice and perform,* but education is more about *developing a sense of curiosity.* [. . .]

This reference helps to root James's argument in the underlying shared value—in the belief that curiosity and discovery are inherently good and worth nurturing.

Activities

1. Consider each of the following claims and what value it suggests.

   a. People should not litter.

   b. When you come across other people's litter, you should pick it up.

   c. You should not litter, but you shouldn't feel obligated to pick up other people's litter.

   d. It is wrong to make money off other people's hardship.

   e. It is wrong to make money off other people's ignorance.

   f. It is fair to make money off other people's ignorance.

2. Decide what values are lurking in these bumper stickers.

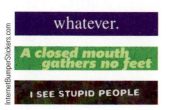

In Defense of Darkness

HOLLY WREN SPAULDING

In this essay, Holly Wren Spaulding shows how quiet ideals, unstated assumptions, learned associations, and unquestioned values impact people's lives and the natural world around us. Spaulding, a poet, essayist, and activist who lives in northwestern Michigan, nudges readers to confront an entire unexamined belief system.

There was the time we climbed atop Sentinel Rock, a massive quartzite granite formation in Joshua Tree National Monument, and looking at the dark sky and the moving lights above us, we wondered about the top secret tests that the military is said to conduct at nearby Area 51. Or the time, in my late teens, when I arrived in Florence in the middle of the night and rather than spend scarce resources on a hostel, camped out in a city park for the final hours of that summer night. My travel companion and I laid our heads on our backpacks when we noticed the many figures murmuring in the shadows. Night travelers—loners, junkies, lovers, and the homeless—were busy living and moving about in the darkness, bursting with what is never imagined during the day.

Or, the June I drifted through layers of warm and cool air as my friend, a composer, sampled lake and air sounds for a piece of electronic music he was writing. I paddled, always aware not to knock the side of the boat for the sake of the recording, and eventually found a rhythm with one stroke for every four or so heartbeats. The sky and shore and water were all one inky darkness though stars sparkled on the watery surface. We were soaked from all directions in night and sky and when the moon rose, full and brilliant, I leaned back against the boat while we coasted, our eyes adjusting so that we could see the shapes of bats, profiles of cedars on the far shore, a single boulder rising out of the lake. I remember how my senses seemed suddenly more alert. Loons yodeled anciently. Cricket hums and owl calls carried across Eagle Lake as we made our way from one side to the other. We were quiet adventurers, rapt and attentive to each ordinary and remarkable thing we encountered. The Milky Way draped itself over our heads like a cosmic veil threaded through with a hundred billion sparkling gems until it disappeared in the fog and we were soon almost invisible to one another, uncertain of where we were on the lake. We barely moved, smitten as we were with the perfection of everything: the lake was ours, the night

Credit Data courtesy Marc Imhoff of NASA GSFC and Christopher Elvidge of NOAA NGDC. Image by Craig Mayhew and Robert Simmon, NASA GSFC.

was ours, and no one knew where we were. We would likely always remember this journey.

...

Meanwhile, darkness is a habitat and it's dwindling. My city friends respond with childlike delight when they visit me at my rural homestead. They stand in the yard pointing and ahhing as if at a performance. Where they live it's never dark, and the stars are actually satellites. Here, the sky is like a museum exhibit, and it's novel and compelling because it stands apart from the familiarity of their usual experience. I enjoy their enthusiasm and their giddiness at seeing something this rare and, indeed, rather magical. As far as I can tell, they accept that urban living means they won't see many stars and instead they enjoy the other amenities of the city and, as any forward thinking urban planner will explain, high density living is in fact the greenest lifestyle choice. So I'm not trying to talk anyone into giving up the city. And yet, I am thinking about the dark; what it might mean to ignore it or lose it or live entirely without the spaces, the habitats—both physical and mental—that it helps to shape; how to make sense of a value that seems otherwise under-appreciated by so many others around me.

Darkness can feel like nothing—like no place, like Nothingness. But it is not nothing. It is alive with insect hum, wind in the trees, warm air rising off the surface of the water. It is one of the places we encounter ourselves in right proportion, or in a more reasonable proportion, to the world around us. Among its many qualities is a spiritual dimension. Beyond what we know about the environmental impacts of light pollution, the carbon footprint, the trouble it makes for astronomers, migrating birds, and nocturnal animals, and beyond the fact that it wastes huge amounts of public and private money, I remain focused on this other, less tangible quality that is lost when our lives are lit from every angle at all times.

5   We modern, industrial, technological Homo sapiens favor light; it is one of the ways we control our environments, both natural and built. Our lives are well lit and we've gotten used to the way things look and feel from this side of darkness. That which is illuminated is regarded as safe, and evidence of progress; it represents human achievement and development. So-called security lights, billboards, communications towers, and decorative lighting (have you been to Las Vegas lately?) are ubiquitous to the point that we mostly take all of it for granted. The infrastructure goes largely unchallenged and so we tacitly accept things as they are. But what is that infrastructure? What are the systems, structures, attitudes and modes of living that result in such a widespread decline of the dark?

Consumer capitalism quietly brands our daily lives with reminder after reminder (made more obvious by spotlights) that *the action is here, this is the thing* to buy, that *we are open for business,* that *this is the way.* All of this light strikes me as a kind of cultural inertia if not outright hostility toward the dark. Whether or not we take action against the creep of light pollution in its many guises, or simply accept all as it is, our indifference is destroying darkness, by which I mean not only those remarkable night skies, but the realm within our minds and the experiences that go with all of it, that are layered with texture and meaning of a darker variety.

John Metz

Perhaps it seems ungenerous or even paranoid to regard the physical, bright-lit world in such a way. I know that it is more common to be surrounded by a gazillion watts of light at night than to spend more than a few minutes in any kind of real darkness each day. In this country, most of us would have to make a considerable effort if we wanted to get anywhere that was not bathed in perpetual light. But why not bask in our remarkable achievement? I can imagine all manner of push-back, devil's advocacy, disagreement or shoulder shrugging dismissal of the idea that darkness matters. Who cares? says the voice. With all of the other things to worry about, speak out for, and take action against, why defend darkness? The answer is fairly straightforward: When we are estranged from the dark, we lose access to vital human emotions and sensual experiences including wonder and awe and humility.

It's like this: darkness bleeds the boundaries between myself and that which is just beyond my physical form. It contains unknown depths (the lake is hard to make out as its surface melts into the rest of night), enchantment, and a release from the manners and mannerisms of daytime, circumscribed as it is with routine and work and propriety. Nighttime darkness also bears the prospect of sleep and dreams (increasingly precious in this age of insomnia and sleep disorders), and an unbridling of inhibitions by way of a kind of anonymity, if not invisibility. In the dark one finds light-footed walking and slowness; a sense that there is enough time and that rushing is no longer necessary. Is there anything about our daylight existence that does all of this? No, because our values have evolved such that speed, availability, exposure and outward interaction are the flavor of the moment. It is harder and harder to come by the circumstances which permit anything but a full-blown light-show in which attention is drawn to our every action, thought or location on the planet (witness the rise of social media and reality television).

This is not a manifesto against light, per se, or against the daytime, which is its own and necessary habitat. I am not an anachronist, though

it is poignant to note how "of another time" my values suddenly seem. But what is at the heart of our neglect, if not disdain, for darkness and the dark? We quickly recognize the ways in which it is associated with crime, danger, clandestinity, and revolt. We freely employ it as a metaphor for the "unknown" and "uncertainty," even as a synonym for ignorance ("he was totally in the dark on the issue"). We have other negative associations as well: dark secrets, going over to the dark side, the dark underbelly; it represents that which is marginal and Other, but also pleasure and vice (women of the night, libertines). We fear it and yet some of us are simultaneously attracted to it, perhaps precisely because we are not entirely at home there.

The dominant religions of the world preach a dualism that pits light against dark, and man against nature; at the heart, or so it seems to me, is a presumed separation between ourselves and the Other (whether that is nature, the divine, each other). It is a deeply entrenched paradigm, a default setting of sorts, and so we go about without realizing some of our prejudices. If I transgress those boundaries and distinctions, even just in my imagination, I already sense a shift in my perception of the world and people and phenomena around me.

So that I am clear: my point is not exclusively about the dark; after all, there are many ideas, sensations, and realms of awareness that we humans veer away from, not wanting to know or to feel what is potentially foreign, other, uncomfortable. Our deep anxiety about our own mortality must be part of that instinct to withdraw; why penetrate that veil any sooner than necessary? Let's close the lid, let's cover the evidence. The prevailing sentiment seems to be that the best possible life is the one in which we proceed with a broad smile and full of hope into the bright day before us.

I recently found myself among a group of writers, discussing a new work of fiction by one of those assembled and in which a character's experience of childhood abuse by a family member is implied, but not explained directly. The reader senses the dark history, but it is a faint mention, and we don't know for certain what happened. And yet we know. One of our group said, "I thought maybe that had happened but I didn't want to go there." In her mind, she was not committing to that interpretation of the story because she "hated to think of it." Another reader said, "I was afraid to ask." Because we were discussing the story with its author, our suspicions were confirmed: indeed, bad things had happened to the character in the story. Initially, and due to an aversion to that side of experience, an essential part of that character's past was being denied by certain readers. It may be a stretch to suggest that those readers were bent on preserving a happier, less flawed view of the world, but I do wonder: is denial of darkness—in this case, the metaphorical version—not at the heart of our history as a nation? At the core of so many of our psychological ailments? Perhaps even an explanation for the kind of distance that can separate people from one another as soon as their differences become evident or suggest anything but an impeccable resume? I think of the soldiers who are returning from the Iraq and Afghan wars these days, the reports of P.T.S.D., and the supreme loneliness that they must feel when it becomes clear that few of us can possibly understand what they've been through, and worse, don't actually want to "go there" in conversation or in our imaginations.

Am I stretching too far? Are fear of the actual dark and our apprehension of the metaphorical dark related?

But of course, there really are dangers that lurk in dark places. During my first year of college in Ann Arbor, female students were cautioned over and over to never to go anywhere alone after dark. A serial rapist had been terrorizing the area and so we got accustomed to carrying mace, walking in pairs, and prevailing upon our male friends to walk us home from the library at night. I was grateful that in general, the streets near my apartment were well lit. Indeed, it is useful and suitable to light our public spaces to ensure safety. But this is not the bone I am trying to pick. There is a difference between light that is useful, suitable, even aesthetic, but must there be light all of the time?

Franz Kafka wrote that we must read the books that are "an ax to the frozen sea inside us" (qtd. in Cixous 7). The poet Emily Dickinson said that she knew she was reading a great poem when it felt as if her head had been blown off. It is a commonplace that great art of all kinds can be profound and affecting, and I have found that the same happens to be true of my encounters with darkness. Sitting on a midnight lake surrounded by mountains and the sky can trigger a similar sense of being transported to awe, and confronted with beauty and strangeness. Faced with an uncompromised night sky, I immerse myself in vastness and take stock of the space around me; I re-situate myself in relation to the other beings and phenomena with which I share the space. A sort of elegant contraction occurs: I shrink in size but in so doing, something in me is enlarged because the ego recedes, as do some of my more mundane discontents, cravings, petty aspirations. I'd like to think I am more fully human at these moments because it is a time when I do feel that I am among (as opposed to "apart from") the multitudes (as Whitman would have said) or as the Buddhists say, interconnected with all beings. "By acknowledging such links between the inner psychological world and the perceptual terrain that surrounds us, we begin to turn inside-out, loosening the psyche from its confinement within a strictly human sphere . . ." says David Abram, a philosopher, cultural ecologist and performance artist (262). It seems true to my experience. Or as the German poet Rainer Maria Rilke wrote:

> Ah, not to be cut off,
> not through the slightest partition
> shut out from the law of the stars.
> The inner—what is it?
> if not intensified sky,
> hurled through
> with birds and deep
> with the winds of homecoming.

Works Consulted

Abram, David. *The Spell of the Sensuous: Perception and Language in a More-Than-Human World.* Vintage Books, 1997.

Cixous, Helene. *Three Steps on the Ladder of Writing.* Translated by Susan Sellers and Sarah Cornell, Columbia UP, 1994.

Kafka, Franz. *Letters to Friends, Family and Editors.* Translated by Richard and Clara Winston, Schocken Books, 1978.

Palmer, Bryan D. *Cultures of Darkness: Night Travels in the Histories of Transgression from Medieval to Modern.* Monthly Review Press, 2000.

Rilke, Rainer Maria. "Ah, not to be cut off." *Ahead of All Parting: The Selected Poetry and Prose of Rainer Maria Rilke,* edited and translated by Stephen Mitchell, Modern Library, 1995, p. 191.

Suzuki, David T. "Forward: Thoughts on Extinction." *Left Bank #2: Extinction,* edited by Linny Stovall, Blue Heron Publishing, 1992.

Works Cited

Abram, David. *The Spell of the Sensuous: Perception and Language in a More-Than-Human World.* Vintage Books, 1997.

Cixous, Helene. *Three Steps on the Ladder of Writing.* Translated by Susan Sellers and Sarah Cornell, Columbia UP, 1994.

Kafka, Franz. *Letters to Friends, Family and Editors.* Translated by Richard and Clara Winston, Schocken Books, 1978.

Rilke, Rainer Maria. "Ah, not to be cut off." *Ahead of All Parting: The Selected Poetry and Prose of Rainer Maria Rilke,* edited and translated by Stephen Mitchell, Modern Library, 1995, p. 191.

Activities

1. In a brief essay, describe how Holly Wren Spaulding argues at the layer of assumptions and values. Point out specific passages and statements. Explain how each takes the reader beyond the surface claims about light pollution, light, darkness, and so on. Describe how Spaulding's line of reasoning delves into the unstated assumptions about the topic.

2. Find an advertisement and identify the value to which it appeals. Explain how the appeal would sway the audience. Why does the appeal seem legitimate or disingenuous?

ARGUMENTS IN DISGUISE

Often, the most persuasive arguments are those in disguise, those that seem like reports, histories, songs, advertisements, or harmless statements. Their persuasive power lies in their silent appeal, their quiet movement into our consciousness. Arguments disguised as something else are hidden. Although indirect and subtle, their claims, appeals, and assumptions still affect audiences. While our intellectual backs are turned, we can be persuaded into consuming a particular view of the world. However, we can raise our awareness and pick out the disguises of argument. We can learn to see through the emotional appeals, to recognize a selective portrayal of facts, and to recognize persuasion even when it is hidden.

The Objectivity Disguise

The objectivity disguise fools the audience into thinking that the presented information is entirely unbiased. An objective statement or text lacks personal opinion or bias; it solely presents facts. However, facts do not appear out of thin air. They exist within a rhetorical situation: someone chose these facts over those, to start with A and not B, to ignore C, to minimize D. All of these decisions or reflexes help to create a particular version of the truth. A news report, for instance, may exclude important facts, oversimplify a complicated situation, or minimize a detail important to another perspective. Consider the following news report:

> Today in Florida, protesters blocked sidewalks and caused undue congestion in downtown Miami. The protesters were demanding a change in voting statewide. When reached for comment, the Miami chief of police said that two people were arrested for blocking the free flow of traffic, and that everything was back to normal by 6:00 p.m.

This report seems like an objective statement of facts; however, it persuades an audience to think a particular way.

- Immediately, we learn about "protesters"—not "concerned citizens" or "voters' rights supporters."
- The first sentence of the report characterizes the protesters as a nuisance. They "blocked" sidewalks and caused "undue congestion."
- The story focuses on (is about) the congestion, not about the political issue that sparked the protest.
- The second sentence characterizes the protesters as insistent and threatening, by describing them as "demanding" change.
- The third sentence reinforces the idea that the protesters are criminals, as the chief of police (a strong symbol of government authority) says "two people were arrested."
- The report ends with everything getting "back to normal" (no protesting).

Such a report subtly urges the audience to see protests as offensive, inherently wrong, and against the best interests of society. It encourages audiences to see quiet streets and unblocked sidewalks as important American values.

How else might the protest be characterized? Consider the following account of the same event:

> Today in Florida, over five thousand protesters assembled in front of the courthouse in Miami to draw attention to the inequity in voting technology across the state. According to organizers, wealthier counties have

Instead of characterizing the protesters as dangerous or threatening, this report explains their message. Instead of casting them as criminals, it humanizes them by including, and ending with, a particular person's words. That person is referred to not as a "protester," but as an "advocate." Both reports present facts. And neither report distorted the facts (or lied about them). But the selection and placement of information forwards a particular way of thinking. By characterizing the issue as it does, the second report prompts the audience to see equality and citizen action as American values.

There are too many facts to mention for any given situation. News organizations and anyone else who makes an argument must choose which facts to include (and where to place them) and which facts to leave out. The arguer's values and beliefs play a major role in determining which facts get mentioned and how. To find arguments disguised as objective information, readers ask, *How might the selection and placement of facts, or apparently objective information, make an argument? What might the selection and placement of facts reveal about the arguer?*

The Personal Taste Disguise

This disguise camouflages an argument as or within an appeal to the audience's personal tastes and desires. While speaking directly to the audience's passion for color, interest in sex, or longing for family fun, for example, the text *conceals* a hidden argument. The argument nestles up against us, makes us feel comfortable, and then delivers a way of thinking about ourselves, others, and the world around us.

The disguise can come in any genre (an essay, song, speech, etc.), but it often comes in the form of advertising. Most ads try to make us believe that they are addressing us personally, that they are reaching out to something we enjoy or desire. They lure us in with colors, images, and words that sit well with our tastes. At the same time, they make arguments about what we should value, what we should long for, what we should eventually possess, whom we should admire, and even whom we should dislike.

Sometimes the appeal to personal taste is obvious. Someone may ask, "Wouldn't you like a greener lawn?" Such a question goes directly to a personal desire, but it may also bring along assumptions and values: a green lawn is good; lawns should be well-manicured, not wild-looking; it is worth a homeowner's time and money to keep a yard (and home) looking a certain way; neighbors may think negatively of the homeowner who doesn't maintain his or her yard; the wildness of nature must be tamed (kill the weeds). The simple question about "a greener lawn" makes sense only because of the assumptions and values that it implies. Whenever someone appeals to our personal desires, we should be aware of the unstated assumptions and values behind the appeal.

It might be easy to dismiss hidden arguments, saying, for instance, that an ad does not make people think a particular way. That is true: a single advertisement (or any one argument) does not *make* an audience behave a certain way or accept a certain value system. However, arguments (including hidden arguments) do help to create a reality that we all inhabit. Through sheer repetition and allure, arguments with the personal taste disguise reinforce beliefs and values. They help to shape what we like and dislike, what we find acceptable and unacceptable, and what we tolerate and dismiss. They eventually can become so pervasive that they become part of our *ideology*: our way of seeing and valuing the world.

Consider images of women's bodies. Eroticized women are used to sell everything, including insurance and bank loans. What's sexy about a bank? Nothing. But when an attractive woman nestles up to the camera and pitches herself to the audience, many viewers are ready to listen. At the most obvious level, such an ad pulls readers in by their attraction to a particular female body. A subtle message is that the bank is available. But such advertising strategies also project an argument about women—that they should be erotic and presented as a service. When ads like this are shown by the thousands every day, they make a powerful argument that women should look and act a particular way. Even if the ads (the arguments) don't persuade you, they persuade others. And when other people adopt particular beliefs, those beliefs create an aspect of the world in which *you* live. You are affected too. To uncover the personal taste disguise, readers ask, *How does this text appeal to the audience's personal tastes or desires? Is the appeal easy or difficult to notice? What argument does it disguise?*

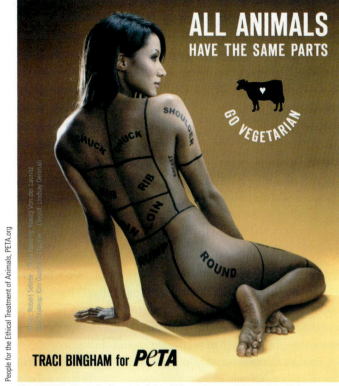

People for the Ethical Treatment of Animals, PETA.org

Photo: Robert Sebree · Prop Stylist: Nancy Von de Launtz · Hair/Makeup: Kim Goodwin Studios · Layout: Lindsay Berman

ALL ANIMALS HAVE THE SAME PARTS

GO VEGETARIAN

TRACI BINGHAM for PeTA

This PETA (People for the Ethical Treatment of Animals) ad featuring Traci Bingham appeared in the July 2002 issue of *Gear* magazine. What is the hidden argument? What particular values, perspectives, or claims are hiding in the text and image?

Spin

Spin is a heavily biased portrayal of information. *Spinning* an event or statement involves turning its obvious or apparent meaning into something else—a meaning that is more favorable to the spinner's cause or position. The term *spin* is most often associated with political discourse, but it is not exclusive to politics. Anyone can spin situations to his or her advantage by making an argument that changes the meaning of an event or statement.

Anyone who pays attention to the arguments of politicians, their advisors, and partisan political analysts is familiar with spin. For example, if a president's approval rating drops significantly, his or her supporters are likely to spin the situation, turning an obviously negative situation into something positive. Spin is an effort to distract people from the real meaning:

> The approval rating actually is higher than it has been at this point in the term for many presidents. We see the slight drop as a sign that the president's policies are taking root and making people's lives significantly better in the long run.

This statement puts a positive spin on a negative situation. But spin involves more than just being positive. Spin is often dishonest and harmful. When public speakers spin every event or statement, public discourse suffers. People must sift through the spin to discover the truth. Instead of argument being a tool for the exploration and discovery of ideas, it becomes a tool for the advancement of a particular ideology at the expense of everything else.

One way spin works to shift meaning is by focusing the audience's attention away from one aspect (the broader picture) and toward a particular aspect the arguer deems worthy. In the following passage from George Orwell's *Animal Farm*, notice how the speaker creates *selective attention*. Here, Squealer the pig is spinning, trying to convince the other animals that the pigs did not break a commandment by sleeping in the house:

> "You have heard then, comrades," he said, "that we pigs now sleep in the beds of the farmhouse? And why not? You did not suppose, surely, that there was ever a ruling against beds? A bed merely means a place to sleep in. A pile of straw in a stall is a bed, properly regarded. The rule was against sheets, which are a human invention. We have removed the sheets from the farmhouse beds, and sleep between blankets. And very comfortable beds they are too! But not more comfortable than we need, I can tell you, comrades, with all the brainwork we have to do nowadays. You would not rob us of our repose, would you, comrades? You would not have us too tired to carry out our duties? Surely none of you wishes to see Jones back?"

Although the commandment says nothing about sheets, Squealer has created a diversion. He also turns the question (Did the pigs break a commandment?) back onto the other animals: *You would not rob us of our repose, would you?* With such a question, Squealer makes the other animals into potential villains who want to rob the pigs of sleep. And he even adds an appeal to emotion (fear) at the end in mentioning Jones, the farmer who had previously owned them.

Orwell's animals illustrate how humans dishonestly use arguments to make one thing mean something else. Orwell's pigs make spin and all other types of argumentative disguises easy to see (unless you are one of the animals in the book). But in everyday life (politics, work, popular culture, schools, etc.), these tactics are often more subtle. To recognize spin, readers ask, *How does the text move attention away from an obvious or apparent meaning and into something else, favorable to the arguer's position? Is the shift in meaning legitimate or deceptive?*

Propaganda

Propaganda is a complex set of strategies used to drive audiences into a uniform way of thinking and feeling (often called a *doctrine*). Propaganda serves to crush differences in thinking, minimize nuances, and squash potential reflection. It works to unite many people into a simple intellectual habit. Propaganda may depend on the objectivity disguise and/or the personal taste disguise to achieve its goal. It may also use any of the following devices:

- Vague or ill-defined words and phrases
- Repetition of simple words and phrases (or slogans)
- Strong appeals to emotions (fear, anger, happiness, regret, etc.)
- Strong appeals to human need (belonging, sexual intimacy, food, safety), etc.
- Strong appeals to character
- Intellectual and moral certainty
- Easy demarcation of groups (Us versus Them)
- Fallacies (hasty generalization, faulty cause-effect, either/or reasoning, etc.)

Notice that the tools of propaganda run counter to sound reasoning. Propaganda deliberately saturates the consciousness with appeals to value, need, emotion, and character *and* with persistent slogans so that sound logic is drowned out. When people are victims of propaganda, they accept a doctrine as unquestionable truth. They are immune to curiosity. And when their doctrines come into question (because of someone else's views), the victims of propaganda defend with intensity what they accept as truth.

Imagine the propaganda necessary to make millions of people buy the same style of jeans. Imagine the language necessary to make millions of people hate millions of other people they have never met. Imagine the repetitive and consistent messages required to make millions of people follow the words of one man. Imagine the disguised argument necessary to make hundreds of millions of people feel like a single team against the rest of the world. Such intellectual obedience requires training—training that is invisible to the uncritical eye and ear. Readers looking for propaganda ask, *How does the text use the tools of propaganda to crush differences in thinking, minimize nuances, and squash potential reflection (to drive all readers into a uniform way of thinking and/or feeling)?*

Activities

1. Examine a news report that appears to be objective, and explain how the selection and placement of information makes an argument.

2. Imagine that you work for a political campaign and that you hope to protect your candidate's character above all else—above honesty, the public good, democratic principles. It's been discovered that your candidate accepts funds from a racist organization. In a small group, write a passage that would spin public attention away from the issue. Use as much subtlety as possible. After all groups have presented their spin, discuss the following: How does spin impact your understanding of national events?

3. Businesses often use spin to fool customers. Describe how you, as an employee, used spin on customers, or how a business used spin on you. How effective was the spin, and why?

4. As a class, discuss the following: Is spin dishonest?

5. What propaganda strategies or devices are used to sell a Big Mac? What strategies are used to sell (or to influence people to think a predetermined way about) a particular fast food chain, a political candidate, a clothing brand, a type of music, a sport or game, a celebrity, a policy, or a way of life? Provide specific examples of the strategies or devices.

Assignment: Identifying and Summarizing Hidden Layers

As you examine the rhetoric of an argument, you will begin to see beneath the surface layer. For this project, read either Ryan Brown's "A Community of Cars" (pp. 21–24) or Lynda Smith's "Disconnected" (pp. 48–51) and summarize the argument's hidden layers. To explore hidden layers as much as possible, use the following questions:

1. How does the writer engage readers' unstated assumptions (about driving, spending money, walking, connecting with others, and so on)?

2. What assumptions are operating in the argument? Are those assumptions acceptable or questionable? If the writer makes a questionable assumption, how does this damage the argument?

3. What values exist beneath the explicit claims and support? How do they create or fail to create a connection between argument and audience?

4. What arguments are in disguise, and how might these hidden arguments influence the audience? (Look for the objectivity disguise, personal taste disguise, spin, and propaganda.) Caution: Do not confuse a strong argument with propaganda. If a writer is calling for change in thinking, that doesn't mean he or she is trying to blur away complexity and establish doctrine.

5. What appeals are disguised, and how might they influence the audience? (Look for appeals to character, emotion, logic, need, and value.)

moodboard/Corbis

Analyzing Argument

Analysis is the act of investigating how something works. It involves seeing how individual parts add up to the whole, how specific aspects figure into the overall operation. If we were to analyze a car engine, we would try to figure out how individual components—the pistons, carburetor, battery, air filter—contribute to the working machine. If we were to analyze a novel, we would ask how characters, plot, setting, and narrative style figure into the whole aesthetic experience. The same goes with analyzing argument. We can ask how specific rhetorical moves work in the overall piece, how the line of reasoning proceeds, how examples support the main claim, how opposition is countered, how underlying values give way to appeals, or how the writer engages the intended audience.

THE ANALYTICAL POSTURE

Analyzing an argument requires reading with a specific goal: to understand how the argument works. Reading analytically calls for a particular posture, one that is different from some of our most basic intellectual reflexes. When we are reading an argument, we may feel the reflex to respond—to seek out points of agreement or disagreement. We might ask ourselves, *Do I agree or disagree? Do I like the point being made or not? Do I like this author or not?* But in analysis, such questions must be put aside. Even if we find ourselves outraged by or in total agreement with the argument, we have to think in analytical terms. After all, an analysis seeks to make claims of fact rather than claims of value.

Sometimes, it's difficult to put aside the basic reflex to agree or disagree, especially if the argument itself is heated. For example, consider the following argumentative passage from Cameron Johnson:

> Facebook is fun. It connects people to old friends and, many would say, it even generates new friendships. But here's a question that's not often asked: so what? Even if we accept the idea that friends confirmed on FB are anything close to real friendship (and only the most giddy among us would), we might ask ourselves if another corporate controlled friend-making device should be so celebrated. While America is well known as a civilization absolutely turned in on itself, unaware of its own history, ignorant of the grisly business just outside its borders,

millions of otherwise savvy thinkers are spending countless hours learning what their e-friends are drinking or feeling after drinking whatever they drank. Certainly, FB fans would say that many users trade important views about war, poverty, history, religion, and so on. But there's nothing about FB itself that urges hard reflection on such matters. In fact, the medium works, primarily, to thrust quick blurby opinions back and forth. From what I've seen in my admittedly limited experience, FB is yet another bourgeois tool for celebrating *me*, my personal thoughts, and my closed bubble of acquaintances. Like an electronic junior high clique, it reinforces a pre-adolescent take on the world. Like *Fox News*, like most morning news programs, like most talk radio, like mainstream sports, FB bolsters the everything-I-like-about-my-life mentality that civilizations, at some point, must evolve beyond.

We might have a range of responses to the passage: *Hell, yes! It's totally true! No way! I love Facebook! What if Facebook has made my life bigger, not smaller? I hate Cameron Johnson!* But such responses veer toward claims of value rather than claims of fact. They fall into the argument about Facebook rather than remaining outside of the argument on analytical ground. To be an analytical reader, we have to ask how the passage works. We have to ask what premises the passage puts forward, how it seeks to convince us of each premise, how it appeals to shared values, how it relies on examples to create a convincing reality.

Analyzing an argument is commonly called *rhetorical analysis* because we are trying to discover the basic rhetorical strategies—those discussed in the previous chapters: Claims, Appeals, Examples, Evidence, Counterarguments, Concessions, Qualifiers, and Assumptions. If we can point to these argumentative moves and understand the intended audience, we are well on the way to analysis. It can be tricky business because these moves are not evident. (Writers do not go out of their way to tell us what they're up to!) But if we can, for example, identify an appeal to value amid a range of other moves, we begin to understand how the argument functions. Here's how we might begin to identify the moves in Johnson's passage about Facebook:

ALLUSIONS:	To *Fox News*, talk radio, mainstream sports
APPEALS TO VALUE:	To the value of world knowledge, history, maturity
APPEAL TO LOGIC:	"Even if we accept the idea that friends confirmed on FB are anything close to real friendship (and only the most giddy among us would), we might ask ourselves if another corporate mediated friend-making device should be so celebrated."
CONCESSION:	"Facebook is fun."
COUNTERARGUMENT:	"But there's nothing about FB itself that urges hard reflection on such matters. In fact, the medium works, primarily, to thrust quick blurby opinions back and forth."
QUALIFIER:	"From what I've seen in my admittedly limited experience, . . ."

Once we've identified these basic rhetorical ingredients, we are on an analytical path. But analysis goes far beyond labeling the parts. Good analysis involves explaining *how* something works, how each part functions in the whole. It is not enough to simply call something an appeal to value and then move on. The following example not only identifies an appeal but also explains *how the appeal works* in Johnson's passage:

> Johnson's argument against Facebook relies on several appeals to value—especially to the concept of world knowledge. Johnson calls on readers to condemn Facebook primarily because it fixes users' concentration on personal, even petty, rather than global issues. The worst parts of American culture,

he argues, are those that turn people's attention inward away from a world of difference. The passage suggests that global consciousness is inherently good while self-involvement is a form of arrested development, a reflex that keeps people and entire civilizations from maturing. The appeal is most apparent in the description of FB users as junior high children who disregard the bigger world beyond their own small social network.

Staying on the analytical path is difficult. But the path does lead to new insights. In fact, the goal of analysis is just that: to discover something about a text—to see some complexity, some underlying connections, some underlying principle. Analysis should lead us to some better, richer understanding of the thing itself. All three sample analyses in this chapter achieve that richer understanding. They each identify rhetorical moves, explain how the moves work, and then articulate some insight about the text being analyzed.

In his analysis of Chief Seattle's speech (pp. 92–94), Andrew Buchner discovers an important layer—something that a quick glance might not reveal. After carefully walking through specific rhetorical strategies in the speech, Buchner finds an interesting and subtle tension within Seattle's concession:

> So, while Seattle's speech can be broadly viewed as a concession, it is a concession *on his own terms*. He hasn't assented to the superiority of the white way of living. He hasn't conceded that he has been beaten by the better opponent. He only concedes to the fact that his wave has crested and spilled onto the shore, whereas the white man's wave may simply be further out at sea.

In her analysis of a Benetton clothing ad, Megan Ward discovers something about the interplay between the ad and its broader context. The ad itself (p. 101) says very little. But through careful analysis, Ward shows that its complexity is bound to the cultural arguments it quietly engages:

> Benetton engages its audience on an "immediate, emotional level" with the bare images of meat so starkly presented. But when we acknowledge the ad's context—all the cultural debates about race, difference and equality—we can see how it argues on a "much broader stage."

And in his analysis of *Avatar* (pp. 104–106), Benjamin Wetherbee discovers a powerful tension in the movie's implied values:

> Here, however, enters *Avatar's* logical contradiction. The movie's explosively violent final act implies what most action films do (e.g., the *Rambo* and *Lethal Weapon* franchises): real results, ultimately, come only from manning up and settling matters through armed conflict. This macho, right-wing truism, popular among American film audiences, appears most transparently in the climactic final battle, wherein Sully expresses unequivocal joy at the chance to fight and kill the merciless colonel who had been his superior officer. The movie glorifies this moment, even as it gainsays the Na'vi wisdom that killing should be only an affair of sad necessity. In its finale, *Avatar* does not bemoan the violence it presents. The violence is meant to be fun. As audiences uncritically tag along on this final explosive ride, they accept its logic; they accept the "git-'er-done" attitude that values decisive, violent action, and rebukes diplomacy and dialogue.

All of these discoveries are the result of powerful analysis—close inspection of the argumentative parts. Each writer (Buchner, Ward, Wetherbee) comes to a new understanding about the original argument.

SUMMARY AND ANALYSIS

To understand how an argument works (analysis), we must understand what it is arguing (summary). The *how* depends upon the *what*. Usually, rhetorical analysis relies on an initial, brief summary. For instance, if we were conducting an analysis of Holly Wren Spaulding's essay, "In Defense of Darkness" (from Chapter 5), we first would need to understand it to accurately portray its claims:

> In her argument, Holly Wren Spaulding celebrates the power of darkness, genuine darkness that is not injured by artificial light. She explains how nighttime gives birth to vital dimensions of life: connectivity to others, an ability to wonder, the reflex to extend outward and feel something other than fear. Part of this celebration involves condemning the increasing drive to illuminate the world. She denounces the uncritical and deeply engrained habit of keeping on the lights.

After we get a good sense of the argument, we can begin to understand how it works, how Spaulding urges readers to believe in something that is different from, even contrary to, mainstream assumptions. Without that initial basic understanding, analysis is nearly impossible.

And even after we summarize, when we enter analytical territory, we still need summary. For instance, notice how the following passage begins with a brief summary statement and then moves to analysis. In this case, summary and analysis work together. The power of the analysis depends upon a close and accurate summary:

> Spaulding begins her fifth paragraph with a general point about modern industrial society. She says that we, in this current age, favor electrical light—that it defines our lives. This characterization puts her argument, and her readers, in time—in the long epic narrative of the human species. She describes herself and readers as "We modern, industrial, technological Homo sapiens," which puts us in proportion within the bigger human story. And this desire for proportion—for understanding ourselves in proper relation with the rest of the world—is a major component of Spaulding's argument.

SUMMARY VERSUS ANALYSIS

While summary is important to good analysis, it can also become a problem. It can overshadow the analytical moves. If we are doing analysis (if analysis is the goal), then we must be careful to keep summary from taking over—from eclipsing our explanation of how the argument works. This can be a difficult path. In the following passages, a writer examines Ryan Brown's essay (from Chapter 2). In the first, the writer strictly summarizes. In the second, the writer identifies Brown's appeal to value but then shifts into summary, merely restating the argument rather than analyzing the appeal. And in the third, the writer genuinely analyzes Brown's argumentative move:

Summary: In his third paragraph, Brown says that we have lost the intimate dialogue that comes from walking in our everyday lives. He goes on to blame cars for pulling us away from downtown communities and to suburban shopping centers.

Almost-Analysis: In Brown's sixth paragraph, he appeals to value. He argues that our communities are our homes. But, he says, we don't treat them as such. Instead, we drive quickly through them for the sake of convenience.

Analysis: In Brown's sixth paragraph, he appeals to value by connecting the over-reliance on cars and the breakdown of community. Brown draws our attention to the inherent good in familiarity, location, and social connectedness. He then shows how car culture undermines those principles—those ideals that people seem to cherish but also ignore on their way to the shopping plaza on the other side of town.

In the following examples, we see the writer summarizing, almost-analyzing, and finally analyzing Holly Wren Spaulding's argument. Notice the critical difference between almost-analysis and analysis:

Summary: In her third paragraph, Spaulding tells about her city friends' awe at the dark skies above her home. She explains that they can hardly believe the beauty of all the stars.

Almost-Analysis: Spaulding appeals to our yearning for calm. She says that our cultural reflex is to brighten up the landscape, to turn away from darkness and watch only what is easily visible. This, she explains, is a result of consumer capitalism.

Analysis: Spaulding appeals to our yearning for calm. In her testimony about the silent canoe ride across the lake, she describes, in lush detail, moments of reflection and discovery. These moments are contrasted by descriptions of fast-paced mainstream life that is lit up, overly bright, and "insomnia-producing." In her personal testimony, the darkness is characterized as inspiring and even curative while everyday mainstream life is characterized by isolation and petty consumer fulfillment.

To accomplish genuine analysis, the writer has to both identify the argumentative move (such as an appeal to value) and then *explain how it works*. If we discover an appeal to value, we have to describe what value, what cherished ideal, the writer appeals to and how that drives the argument forward or how it supports the main claim.

FOUR COMMON PITFALLS

Rhetorical analysis comes with a few unique dangers—four traps to avoid. First, some writers get lured inside the points of the argument they are analyzing, and rather than remain outside of that argument, on solid analytical ground, they begin **making a case** for the argument. In the first passage below, the writer further develops—makes a case for—Brown's idea. It's as if the writer has suddenly been possessed by Brown. In the second passage, the writer analyzes Brown's argument:

Making a Case for Brown: Brown shows why communities in our modern civilization are breaking down. We elect the car over our own feet. And when we get into cars, roll up the windows, turn on the tunes, and drive away, we have little interaction with the people around us. We learn to see the world around us as a blurry landscape on the road to our singular destination.

Analyzing Brown: Brown shows why communities in our modern civilization are breaking down. Through a series of connected premises, he describes a cause/effect relationship between consumer habits, driving patterns, and urban planning. The cause/effect relationship is developed over several paragraphs that detail everyday life for mainstream Americans in typical towns like Brown's.

The second pitfall involves **describing the effect** of the original argument. In this situation, the writer describes how the argument (or a part of it) might affect an audience. This is not inherently wrong. After all, rhetorical analysis does involve an understanding of the argument's impact. But, as you will see, dealing with effect can be tricky. In the following passage, the writer examines Lynda Smith's essay (from Chapter 3) and *appropriately* considers the effect on readers:

Lynda Smith likens technological dependence to drug dependence. She walks through the harmful effects of chemical addiction and compares them to the quieter, but equally ruinous, effects of technological craving.

This comparison appeals to readers' knowledge of drug addiction—its peril, its obvious harm to individuals and communities. It taps into the emotional baggage associated with drugs.

But imagining the effect quickly gets dangerous. After all, we don't know exactly how an audience will respond. We cannot assume that readers or viewers will automatically laugh, think, cry, or get angry. But we can examine how a specific argumentative move corresponds to an audience's characteristics. This is a fine line. The danger is that the original argument (the text being analyzed) gets left behind while the focus shifts to imagined audience responses. The following passage crosses into dangerous territory because it begins to move away from Smith's argument and emphasizes particular audience responses:

> Lynda Smith's argument strikes at the core for many readers who are already leery about the latest cell phone technology. Her claims make us realize that *we are surrounded by a growing and alarmingly powerful wave of technological progress.* Because we cannot, alone, stave off the power of corporate America, *we feel her argument at an emotional level. We become afraid for our own ability to live an independent life.*

While the previous pitfall focuses too much on an imagined audience, the third pitfall involves **describing the author's intent**. This strategy is fraught with problems. Because we cannot genuinely know a writer, advertising agency, or movie director's thoughts, we must be careful not to conjure them based on one argument. In the following example, a writer examining Carl Rogers' essay in Chapter 4 strays from rhetorical analysis into imagining the interior life of the author, suggesting, for example, that he is "deeply troubled":

> Rogers hopes people truly understand the arguments to which they are responding. Because he is a psychologist, he is deeply troubled when someone puts forth an argument without first listening and then accurately restating the original argument. He thinks this shows a lack of personal courage, and he values courage above all else. Rogers wants people to be more courageous which he thinks will lead to everyone getting along better.

Evaluation is the fourth pitfall. In evaluation, we make and defend judgments about the worth of an argument. We condemn it, celebrate it, or explain that it's okay but not great. Analysis does none of that. It avoids judging the success, the worth, the soundness, the acceptability of any of its claims. Analysis avoids taking a side for or against the argument. In the first of the following lists, the statements judge the worth of Brown's, Smith's, or Johnson's argument. They are claims of value. The second list makes analytical points (or claims of fact).

Evaluation (Claims of Value)

Brown does a good job of supporting his main idea.

Smith's ideas are right on target.

Brown effectively convinces me that we are reliant on automobile culture.

I don't accept Smith's claims.

I am suspicious of Johnson's ideas because they seem ungrounded.

Analysis (Claims of Fact)

Brown relies on personal testimony to set up his main idea.

Smith develops an appeal to need with several paragraphs.

Brown directly addresses opposing assumptions about transportation.

Johnson immediately appeals to emotion by connecting the topic, telemarketers, to a predatory economic climate—to the fear and quiet anger associated with corporate power.

Now, let's look at the difference between evaluation and analysis in a full paragraph. In the first passage, the writer openly condemns Johnson's passage about Facebook (pp. 85–86). This passage is clearly evaluative because it judges the soundness of Johnson's points. The second passage is clearly analytical. It avoids judging Johnson's argument and, instead, explains its rhetorical strategies.

Evaluative: Johnson's argument mischaracterizes Facebook users. He suggests that users think primarily about themselves and their own small social circles. But users have lives beyond the website. They heal, govern, administrate, build, preach, sell, and even teach in their everyday lives. While Johnson's claims against the broader popular culture might hold some water, his insistence that all Facebook users think like adolescents ignores their real non-Facebook lives and caricaturizes the reality.

Analytical: Johnson's argument against Facebook relies on several appeals to value—especially to the concept of world knowledge. Johnson calls on readers to condemn Facebook primarily because it fixes users' concentration on personal, even petty, rather than global issues. The worst parts of American culture, he argues, are those that turn people's attention inward, away from a world of difference. The passage suggests that global consciousness is inherently good while self-involvement is a form of arrested development, a reflex that keeps people and entire civilizations from maturing. The appeal is most apparent in the description of FB users as junior high children who disregard the bigger world beyond their own small social network.

Activities

1. Write a short analysis paragraph of the Cameron Johnson argument on pages 85–86. Try to avoid evaluating, agreeing, or disagreeing. Instead, explain how a particular rhetorical strategy works. In other words, make claims of fact about Johnson's argument.

2. Read the following passage from Holly Wren Spaulding's essay, "In Defense of Darkness" (pp. 74–78). Identify the primary rhetorical moves in the passage. In other words, what is the main argumentative strategy here? Then, explain how that move works in Spaulding's overall argument. How does the move work to make her main claim acceptable?

   Perhaps it seems ungenerous or even paranoid to regard the physical, bright-lit world in such a way. I know that it is more common to be surrounded by a gazillion watts of light at night than to spend more than a few minutes in any kind of real darkness each day. In this country, most of us would have to make a considerable effort if we wanted to get anywhere that was not bathed in perpetual light. But why not bask in our remarkable achievement? I can imagine all manner of push-back, devil's advocacy, disagreement or shoulder shrugging dismissal of the idea that darkness matters. *Who cares?* says the voice. With all of the other things to worry about, speak out for, and take action against, why defend darkness? The answer is fairly straightforward: When we are estranged from the dark, we lose access to vital human emotions and sensual experiences including wonder and awe and humility.

3. Read Chief Seattle's speech on the land (pp. 92–94). Decide on his main claim. What is Seattle's main assertion about the land? And what is the main line of reasoning? In other words, what individual statements (premises) build up to his main claim?

4. After reading Chief Seattle, read Andrew Buchner's analysis (pp. 95–96). Buchner identifies Seattle's line of reasoning, a counterargument, a concession, and at least one major appeal to value. Beyond those strategies Buchner identifies, what other important rhetorical strategies does Seattle use?

Chief Seattle's Speech

Chief Seattle (c. 1786–1866) was leader of the Suquamish and Duwamish Native American tribes, in what is now the state of Washington. During treaty negotiations in 1854, he gave a now-famous speech about Native American rights and environmental values. Different versions of his speech exist—all secondhand accounts. This version appeared in the *Seattle Sunday Star* on October 29, 1887, more than thirty years after Chief Seattle gave the speech. It was reconstructed by pioneer Dr. Henry Smith, based on Smith's notes.

Chief Seattle statue in downtown Seattle, Washington.

Yonder sky that has wept tears of compassion on our fathers for centuries untold, and which, to us, looks eternal, may change. Today it is fair, tomorrow it may be overcast with clouds. My words are like the stars that never set. What Seattle says, the great chief, Washington . . . can rely upon, with as much certainty as our pale-face brothers can rely upon the return of the seasons.

The son [a reference to Terr. Gov. Stevens] of the White Chief says his father sends us greetings of friendship and good will. This is kind, for we know he has little need of our friendship in return, because his people are many. They are like the grass that covers the vast prairies, while my people are few, and resemble the scattering trees of a storm-swept plain.

The great, and I presume also good, white chief sends us word that he wants to buy our lands but is willing to allow us to reserve enough to live on comfortably. This indeed appears generous, for the red man no longer has rights that he need respect, and the offer may be wise, also, for we are no longer in need of a great country.

There was a time when our people covered the whole land, as the waves of a wind-ruffled sea cover its shell-paved floor. But that time has long since passed away with the greatness of tribes now almost forgotten. I will not mourn over our untimely decay, nor reproach my pale-face brothers for hastening it, for we, too, may have been somewhat to blame.

When our young men grow angry at some real 5 or imaginary wrong, and disfigure their faces with black paint, their hearts, also, are disfigured and turn black, and then their cruelty is relentless and knows no bounds, and our old men are not able to restrain them.

But let us hope that hostilities between the red-man and his pale-face brothers may never return. We would have everything to lose and nothing to gain.

True it is, that revenge, with our young braves, is considered gain, even at the cost of their own lives, but old men who stay at home in times of war, and old women, who have sons to lose, know better.

George Rose/Getty Images

Our great father Washington, for I presume he is now our father, as well as yours, since George [a reference to King George III, i.e., Great Britain] has moved his boundaries to the north; our great and good father, I say, sends us word by his son, who, no doubt, is a great chief among his people, that if we do as he desires, he will protect us. His brave armies will be to us a bristling wall of strength, and his great ships of war will fill our harbors so that our ancient enemies far to the northward, the Simsiams [Tsimshian] and Hydas [Haidas], will no longer frighten our women and old men. Then he will be our father and we will be his children.

But can this ever be? Your God loves your people and hates mine; he folds his strong arms lovingly around the white man and leads him as a father leads his infant son, but he has forsaken his red children; he makes your people wax strong every day, and soon they will fill the land; while my people are ebbing away like a fast-receding tide, that will never flow again. The white man's God cannot love his red children or he would protect them. They seem to be orphans who can look nowhere for help. How then can we become brothers? How can your father become our father and bring us prosperity and awaken in us dreams of returning greatness?

10   Your God seems to us to be partial. He came to the white man. We never saw Him; never even heard His voice; He gave the white man laws but He had no word for His red children whose teeming millions filled this vast continent as the stars fill the firmament. No, we are two distinct races and must remain ever so. There is little in common between us. The ashes of our ancestors are sacred and their final resting place is hallowed ground, while you wander away from the tombs of your fathers seemingly without regret.

Your religion was written on tables of stone by the iron finger of an angry God, lest you might forget it. The red man could never remember nor comprehend it.

Our religion is the traditions of our ancestors, the dreams of our old men, given them by the great Spirit, and the visions of our sachems, and is written in the hearts of our people.

Your dead cease to love you and the homes of their nativity as soon as they pass the portals of the tomb. They wander far off beyond the stars, are soon forgotten, and never return. Our dead never forget the beautiful world that gave them being. They still love its winding rivers, its great mountains and its sequestered vales, and they ever yearn in tenderest affection over the lonely hearted living and often return to visit and comfort them.

Day and night cannot dwell together. The red man has ever fled the approach of the white man, as the changing mists on the mountain side flee before the blazing morning sun.

However, your proposition seems a just one, 15 and I think my folks will accept it and will retire to the reservation you offer them, and we will dwell apart and in peace, for the words of the great white chief seem to be the voice of nature speaking to my people out of the thick darkness that is fast gathering around them like a dense fog floating inward from a midnight sea.

It matters but little where we pass the remainder of our days.

They are not many. The Indian's night promises to be dark. No bright star hovers above the horizon. Sad-voiced winds moan in the distance. Some grim Nemesis of our race is on the red man's trail, and wherever he goes he will still hear the sure approaching footsteps of the fell destroyer and prepare to meet his doom, as does the wounded doe that hears the approaching footsteps of the hunter. A few more moons, a few more winters, and not one of all the mighty hosts that once filled this broad land or that now roam in fragmentary bands through these vast solitudes will remain to weep over the tombs of a people once as powerful and as hopeful as your own.

But why should we repine? Why should I murmur at the fate of my people? Tribes are made up of individuals and are no better than they. Men come and go like the waves of a sea. A tear, a *tamanawus,* a dirge, and they are gone from our longing eyes forever. Even the white man, whose God walked and talked with him, as friend to friend, is not exempt from the common destiny. We *may* be brothers after all. We shall see.

We will ponder your proposition, and when we have decided we will tell you. But should we accept it, I here and now make this the first condition: That we will not be denied the privilege, without molestation, of visiting at will the graves of our ancestors and friends. Every part of this country is sacred to my people. Every hill-side, every valley, every plain and grove has been hallowed by some fond memory or some sad experience of my tribe.

20   Even the rocks that seem to lie dumb as they swelter in the sun along the silent seashore in solemn grandeur thrill with memories of past events connected with the fate of my people, and the very dust under your feet responds more lovingly to our footsteps than to yours, because it is the ashes of our ancestors, and our bare feet are conscious of the sympathetic touch, for the soil is rich with the life of our kindred.

The sable braves, and fond mothers, and glad-hearted maidens, and the little children who lived and rejoiced here, and whose very names are now forgotten, still love these solitudes, and their deep fastnesses at eventide grow shadowy with the presence of dusky spirits. And when the last red man shall have perished from the earth and his memory among white men shall have become a myth, these shores shall swarm with the invisible dead of my tribe, and when your children's children shall think themselves alone in the field, the store, the shop, upon the highway or in the silence of the woods they will not be alone. In all the earth there is no place dedicated to solitude. At night, when the streets of your cities and villages shall be silent, and you think them deserted, they will throng with the returning hosts that once filled and still love this beautiful land. The white man will never be alone. Let him be just and deal kindly with my people, for the dead are not altogether powerless.

Seattle's Rhetoric

ANDREW BUCHNER

Chief Seattle's speech on the land is read widely. There are many interesting layers to consider. Andrew Buchner focuses on Seattle's main line of reasoning—and a consistent tension between Seattle's religion and the religion of white man. Andrew Buchner has a BA in English from Western Michigan University and an MA in English from Miami University.

In his speech on the land, Seattle opens with a major premise in his line of reasoning: that which seems eternal will change according to the dictates of nature. He contrasts this state of change with the strength of his words, which, he claims, are as reliable as the stars in the sky. With these introductory statements, Seattle situates himself as a reliable person and puts the weight of his character behind the speech itself. He also establishes that his claims will remain true and accurate regardless of the passage of time.

In the third paragraph, Seattle acknowledges the American president's good will in allowing the Native-Americans to retain some land. Then, he provides personal testimony about the decline of his people. He openly accepts this fate, and his acceptance echoes the reasoning of his speech. He views his people's passing as analogous to the changing weather or other natural phenomena indifferent to the will of anyone under their power.

He then contrasts his own stoicism with that of the young people in his tribe, who are enraged at the present state, and who, against the advice of the elders, go to war against the white man. This contrast between stoicism and rage borrows a shared assumption—one that may even transcend the divide between Native American and European American cultures: that older men are wiser than younger men because younger men tend to be rash and foolhardy.

Seattle then offers a scenario wherein his people accept the American government's offer and are protected from their enemies by the American navy and army. But the next paragraph begins a strong counterargument to this proposed scenario. This counterargument takes the form of an appeal to authority. Seattle argues that while the American government may promise to provide protection to his people, the white man's god will not offer the same protection. He is essentially going over the US government's head and arguing that a higher power will prevent it from keeping its promise.

Seattle uses an allusion to the Ten Command- 5 ments to further highlight the irreconcilable differences between the whites' god and the religion of the indigenous people: Christianity, he suggests, primarily stresses the afterlife and an escape from this world, while his religious beliefs are tied to this world. In Seattle's belief system, his people will not end up in Heaven but will, instead, choose to remain with the world they love. Seattle frames these differences within the main line of reasoning. He notes that "the red man has ever fled the approach of the white man, as the changing mists on the mountainside flee before the blazing morning sun." This comparison echoes the opening lines of the speech where he shows the indifferent and Protean character of the natural world, a comparison which again highlights the fact that everyone is subject to the dictates of nature.

This main line of reasoning also contains an unstated premise—one that haunts the argument and acts as a counterargument. He does not accept the white man's religious worldview, nor does he believe that white dominance is proof of an inherent superiority. Instead, he explains the current state of white dominion as one more caprice of nature. As he puts it, "men come and go like the waves of the sea." This leads to an inevitable, but unstated, point: the fate of his people will be the fate of white men, and so one day "they may be brothers after all." Such a statement reads like an expression of Seattle's spiritualism. But it is also an intense counter to the white man's belief in himself, in his rightful place as the dominant force on the continent. If white men are bound to the same destiny as the native population, then his god will have failed him. The impending doom of the white man would mean he was subject to the same principles of nature as anyone else and that his god does not offer him any special protection. It would also mean that Seattle's conception of the world is the correct one.

So, while Seattle's speech can be viewed as a concession, it is a concession *on his own terms.* He has not assented to the superiority of the white way of living. He has not conceded that he has been beaten by the better opponent. He only concedes to the fact that his wave has crested and spilled onto the shore, whereas the white man's wave may simply be further out at sea. The one qualifier Seattle adds further cements this position. Seattle claims he will only agree to the terms set forth if the American government allows his people to visit the graves of their ancestors. This qualification confirms Seattle's commitment to uphold the underlying values of his people, even in the face of his tribe's destruction.

The two closing paragraphs further affirm this commitment and bring the main line of reasoning to its conclusion. In these final paragraphs, Seattle reaffirms his people's special connection with the land. He argues that this connection will keep them residing on this earth even after they are dead, even after their lives are but myths on the tongues of the whites. Finally, he explains that white man's children will never be truly alone, that they will also be surrounded by the native dead. Thus, even if Seattle's people are destroyed in their material form, their spiritual form will eventually, again, take sole possession of the land that was once theirs.

ANALYZING VISUAL ARGUMENTS

Written language is not the only argumentative force in our lives. We are surrounded by arguments. Films, images, photographs, songs, and art of all genres make arguments. They make claims and appeals, they use examples, they employ evidence, they engage opposition, and they even tap into cultural assumptions and values. Consider this historically important painting, *George Washington Crossing the Delaware* by Emanuel Leutze:

Many details in the painting make a point about Washington's—and America's—strength. Consider the placement of Washington in the boat, his height, his posture, the lighting, the colors, the position of his boat in comparison to others. These details add up to a claim. While they may not make a direct line of reasoning, they still function inductively. They accumulate visually and lead the viewer to a conclusion about General Washington.

Bettmann/Corbis

Or consider the following two pictures of President Obama. Both were taken by professional photographers and selected for the White House gallery. In other words, like in the painting of Washington, the elements are not accidental. The composition, lighting, angle, and overall tone of each picture were considered—and they all add up to different claims about the president's character.

Official White House Photo by Pete Souza

Official White House Photo by Pete Souza

GRAND CANYON N.P. NPS PHOTO

GRAND CANYON N.P. NPS PHOTO

God Bless America!

Of course, not every image is an argument. Alone, and without some context or language, an image may not make a focused and readily apparent argument—one that can be experienced or discussed publicly. Consider the following image of the Grand Canyon. Does it, alone, make an argument? Maybe. But the possibilities are so broad, so varied, so vague, that it would be difficult to decide. People would first have to answer some basic questions and come to shared conclusions. Is the argument about beauty, nature, the West, serenity, unity? It's hard to say. Nothing in the image itself dictates the focus of the would-be argument.

But if a few words are added, everything changes. With a short statement, the image suddenly takes on argumentative force. Now, the image functions as a kind of appeal. The grandeur and magnitude of the land supports an unstated claim about the magnitude of a country. The image can be seen as a premise in a line of reasoning about America.

Advertising

In advertising, images and words are meticulously crafted to form intensive arguments. The lines of reasoning are simple and usually lead to some form of the claim: *buy this product!* But the support strategies can be wildly complex and subtle. Sometimes they involve a list of the product's attributes: it will get your toughest stains out! Sometimes they involve appeals to values, such as cleanliness: it will keep grime out of your life for good! Or they may go beyond the product and argue something about the consumer: You don't want to be a disorganized mess, right?

As many historians have explained, advertising took a dramatic turn in the latter half of the twentieth century. The majority of ad makers realized that arguments about the consumer's values, fears, and hopes were far more powerful than arguments about the product. For example, which of the following passages, A or B, would have more impact on someone's behavior?

A. Our Super Round tires are very strong, with steel-belted reinforcements. They have complex and tested traction patterns for maximum stopping power. Make sure you consider Super Rounds.

B. Your family puts their trust in you. When you drive, their well-being—their collective future—is entirely in your hands. Your driving ability depends on the quality of your tires. Make sure you consider Super Rounds, the best choice for your family's future.

As it turns out, the appeals to family, responsibility, safety, duty, honor, attractiveness (indeed, the whole range of human needs and hopes) are far more powerful than facts about the product. When advertisers link their brands with shared principles, values, hopes, and fears, the buying public responds. In short, version B works. And as the last several decades prove, it works really well. Millions of perfectly intelligent and reasonable people respond immediately to advertising campaigns that appeal to values, character, need, and emotion. (For more on appeals, see pages 35–53.)

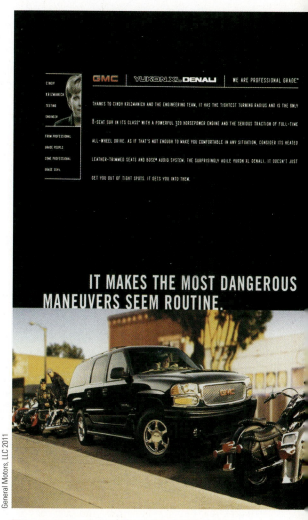

General Motors, LLC 2011

And as imaging software has evolved, those appeals have become more visually layered. Words and images are married to create the maximum effect. In this ad for a GMC truck, the image and words function together. The main text simply states, "Makes the most dangerous maneuvers seem routine." But the statement takes on more meaning because of the photograph: As the bikers closely watch the woman pull around their motorcycles, the GMC truck appears huge. It is a wall of steel that surrounds the lone woman and separates her from the two men. (Notice that she is outnumbered.) The photograph gives particular meaning to the broader term *dangerous,* and it even establishes an unstated premise, which is something like, *The GMC truck will protect you from dangerous people.* And we could go even further. Together, the image and the words distinguish between the types of people who are dangerous and the types of people who are worth protecting. In other words, *the type of woman who drives this truck should be protected from the type of people who drive motorcycles.*

This magazine ad, part of a national advertising campaign, appeared in 2004. What is the hidden argument? What particular values, perspectives, or claims are hiding in the text and image?

The Hearts of Argument: Benetton's Advertising Appeal

MEGAN WARD

Advertising taps into broader cultural conversations. The images and words are often chosen specifically to echo present debates, jokes, concerns, crises, even other ad campaigns. So doing rhetorical analysis of an ad involves some awareness of the social context. In this analysis, Megan Ward explains how the broader social context can figure into one ad's persuasive elements. Ward is the Writing Center Director at Northwestern Michigan College.

In 1996, United Colors of Benetton, a clothing company based in Italy, created an advertisement that shows three human hearts with the labels: *white, black,* and *yellow,* respectively. The type is bold and black on a stark white background. The only colors present within the ad are the vivid, wet, fleshy browns and reds of the hearts and a green box on the right side that reads "United Colors of Benetton." With that, the ad is complete. However, beneath the surface, an entire argument takes place, one that engages shared assumptions and cultural values.

With the visual interplay of the hearts and the three labels, the ad asserts a claim of fact about human identity: when stripped of superficial identifiers, we are all the same. And with the hearts, as opposed to lungs or livers or kidneys (which also could have been used), the ad's argument goes further than same-ness. The heart represents humanity. It is a symbol of love, caring, generosity, and spirituality. Art, cinema, literature, and everyday mainstream language consistently celebrate the heart as the center of human life. When we are devastated, our hearts are broken; when we forgive, we have heart; when we love, we give our hearts away; when

we have found truth, we are at the heart of it all. Such common phrases illustrate how much we use the heart as a representation of who we are and what we assume about identity. Benetton uses this powerful symbol, and what it means within culture, to say that we share a basic "human-ness" beneath visible, political, ethnic differences.

While the ad asserts a singular claim of fact, it is also participating in a broader conversation about race. In a sense, it is a counterargument. It speaks back to common assertions about difference—to claims about heritage and descent. One common argument about race is that we can take difference and make it into something positive. Difference, say many, is real. It should not be ignored but embraced and used for better understanding. However, the Benetton ad obliterates the idea of difference. The visual impact of three human hearts pushes against the words, the labels, the very notion of Caucasian (white), African (black), and Asian (yellow) descent. In this sense, Benetton uses the more striking feature (extracted human organs) to trump the less striking feature (plain black words). In Benetton's argument, identifiers are useless—not worthy of attention. There is no acknowledgment of historical complexity, political oppression, slavery, or genocide. These are conspicuously absent.

Benetton's ad was featured on billboards in France and other countries as part of World Anti-Racism Day ("United Colors"). As in many fashion ads, Benetton does not outwardly define its products, but expects the audience to fill in the details about the product and the company. These billboards were in European cities, where the public would likely be aware of United Colors of Benetton and its usual risqué advertising moves, which draw attention to the brand's character or attitude rather than its product. The ad does not argue that people should buy Benetton's clothing. Instead, it implies a broader point about the company's character—that it cares about social issues, that it is in touch with the things that

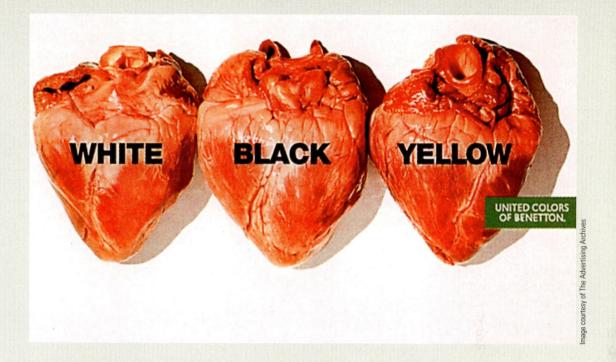

WHITE BLACK YELLOW

UNITED COLORS
OF BENETTON.

Image courtesy of The Advertising Archives

matter. And beyond that, the ad suggests something about the character of Benetton's consumers: people who buy from Benetton are people who care deeply about important issues.

5   As a visual argument, especially one placed on such a large scale, the ad's complexity cannot be overlooked. Benetton uses shock value, acting on the audience's visceral, and perhaps emotional, response at seeing internal organs. The startling image calls on audiences to pay attention, to feel something intense, and may even draw on people's beliefs about "acceptable" material for a billboard. Benetton then uses the emotional effect to push its assertion about human identity, equality and homogeny.

      J. Francis Davis says, in an article discussing images and their power, "Pictures have become tools used to elicit specific and planned emotional reactions in the people who see them." Benetton made a specific choice in using such imagery in its advertisement. Davis points out two main ways that images are utilized today: "First there is the immediate, emotional level on which we recognize the flag or

the sexy body and react in a way that taps our inner stories or emotions. But second, there is a much broader stage on which we can step back and look at one image in context with hundreds of others." Benetton engages its audience on an "immediate, emotional level" with the bare images of meat so starkly presented. But when we acknowledge the ad's context—all the cultural debates about race, difference and equality—we can see how it argues on a "much broader stage."

Works Cited

Davis, J. Francis. "Power of Images: Creating the Myths of Our Time." *Center for Media Literacy*, no. 57, 1992, www.medialit.org/reading-room/power-images-creating-myths-our-time.

"United Colors of Benetton Celebrates World Anti-Racism Day with MTV and Liberation." *Press Area: Press Releases – 1996*, United Colors of Benetton, 1996, www.benettongroup.com/media-press/press-releases-and-statements/united-colors-of-benetton-celebrates-world-anti-racism-day-with-mtv-and-liberation/.

Film

Popular movies often make arguments about love, war, government, freedom, history, crime, and religion—just to name a few. The *Da Vinci Code,* for example, makes a heated argument about the Catholic Church's control over history. It makes its point through a wide range of rhetorical moves: the protagonist himself appeals to viewers' beliefs in honesty and truth. He also appeals to viewers' emotional comfort. Tom Hanks, after all, has a familiar, common face for mainstream white viewers. The antagonists (enemies) reinforce the opposite. The menacing albino monk functions as an opposing force, an opposing ethos. In this way, popular movies often assert arguments—about who or what is good, who or what is bad. And these arguments often correspond to mainstream biases and assumptions. For instance, Arabic men are often cast as villains in modern American movies. Fat or obese people are often cast as bumbling fools—comic relief characters who have little sense of right and wrong. The government is often drawn as quietly evil, plotting, dangerous. The single hero (usually thin and muscular) saves the day, the world, or the universe.

Mainstream movies often use these biases and assumptions. Because they are so widely and quietly accepted as normal, they support the movie's claims about good and bad, right and wrong. Some movies, however, challenge mainstream assumptions. The hero, for instance, may be a very pregnant folksy sheriff—as in the movie *Fargo.*

Consider how your favorite movie ends. Who wins? Who doesn't? What does the plot invite you to dread, believe in, and hope for? What kind of person gets celebrated? What kind of person gets demonized? What behavior has consequences? What behaviors have none? Answers to these questions reveal the subtle (sometimes not-so-subtle) arguments of that movie. If a character wins in the end, we might conclude that the movie makes an argument for that person's behaviors and worldview. When Luke Skywalker finally defeats Darth Vader, *Star Wars* concludes its argument: the allure of power and domination can, in fact, be denied. The prevailing question recurs throughout the six episodes: Can people resist the drive to rule the universe? Or is the lust for power really too overwhelming? As viewers, we are made to sympathize with Luke. We don't want him to become his father. Of course, the opposing forces line up against us: Darth Vader, the Emperor, Count Dooku, Jabba the Hutt, and so on. All these characters embody the lust for absolute power. They are the opposition. On our side are Luke, Leia, Yoda, Obi Wan. They make the film's primary argument. As it turns out, Darth Vader was wrong: the dark side isn't all that powerful.

But figuring out a movie's primary argument is not as simple as describing the characters' fates. Often, sympathetic characters (those with whom we are supposed to share hopes) die in the end. When Thelma and Louise drive off the cliff, viewers do not cheer. Thelma and Louise are, after all, not the villains of the movie. Their apparent suicide makes a point about the overwhelming power of men's rules. When Jack dies in *Brokeback Mountain,* we understand this as mainstream society's condemnation of gay men. And as Ben Wetherbee explains, the death of the Na'vi chief (in *Avatar*) makes a point about imperialism.

Analyzing movies can quickly become perilous work. It's easy to drift into movie review territory—a form that blends analysis and evaluation. The goal of a review is to share judgments about the movie's worth. But a movie analysis focuses strictly on how the movie works. And specifically, for our purposes, such an analysis focuses on how its elements work together to make a claim about the world and support it.

Activities

1. Find an image that doesn't already have text attached to it. Add a single statement that gives the image argumentative force. Share your image and statement with the class and explain the relationship between the image and the statement. How do they relate? Does the image suggest a claim? Or does the image function as some kind of support? Or maybe even a counterargument?

2. Choose an online or print ad. Closely examine the images and text. What is the main claim in the ad? (It's likely related to the product or service.) How does the ad support its claim? To what common values does the ad appeal? What common assumptions (about identity, happiness, technology, progress, superiority, exclusion, freedom) does the ad rely on? Is there a subtle line of reasoning? What premises (stated or unstated) would the audience have to accept before accepting the main claim?

3. In a small group, focus on a popular movie—one that all members have seen. Consider the following questions: In the end, who wins? Who doesn't? What does the plot invite you to dread, believe in, and hope for? What kind of person gets celebrated? What kind of person gets demonized? What behavior has consequences? What behaviors have none? How might all of these elements lead to some overall claim? What is that claim?

Progressive Profiteering: The Appeal and Argumentation of *Avatar*

BEN WETHERBEE

As Ben Wetherbee shows, mainstream films often make overt arguments. And if a claim about the world is asserted and supported, it can be analyzed. In this concise essay, Wetherbee avoids arguing for the film's worth and, instead, shows how it makes and supports a particular claim. Wetherbee is completing a PhD in English, specializing in the rhetoric of film.

In December 2009, director/screenwriter James Cameron's sci-fi epic *Avatar* swept American cineplexes like a gale. Amid vast critical praise, the film grossed nearly 749 million dollars, a record in the United States, besting *Titanic, The Dark Knight* and *Star Wars* on the list of the nation's all-time top box-office draws ("All-Time"). Clearly, the film struck a certain chord with American audiences, but to what, exactly, do we owe the monolithic financial and critical success of *Avatar*? One might highlight Cameron's Hollywood savvy, the spectacular CGI jungle serving as the film's setting, the steady action, the familiar storyline, or any number of other facets. Most scholars of film or rhetoric, though, would quickly rebuke the oversimplification. *Avatar's* appeal comes from its fusion of standard Hollywood action movie features and the specific time of its release.

One avenue worth exploring is the movie's social-political consciousness. I recall a friend of mine who loved *Avatar*. "It's the perfect movie for a liberal," he said, a claim that is perhaps problematic but also understandable. It isn't difficult to imagine why *Avatar* might fare better among moderates and left-wingers than conservatives. Entwined in no subtle terms into the film's plot is a message of environmentalism and anti-imperialism that seems particularly deliberate and timely—coming off the heels of George W. Bush's administration. Contrary to most other sci-fi films dealing with extraterrestrial life (including Cameron's own *Aliens)*, *Avatar* vilifies humankind, illustrating a scenario wherein the technologically superior humans seek to exploit and devastate the home of the Na'vi, a race of 12-foot blue-skinned humanoids with feline lineaments, for its natural resources. Moreover, the film evinces a distinct allusion to contemporary American politics; as critic J. Hoberman points out, "The rampaging Sky People are heavy-handedly associated with the Bush administration. They chortle over the failure of diplomacy, wage what is referred to as 'some sort of shock-and-awe campaign' against the Na'vis, and goad each other with Cheney one-liners. . . ." Cameron's screenplay, then, succeeds in landing immediate appeal by grounding its fantastic story in the actual. Viewers who might have dismissed *Avatar* as a fine-looking fairy tale are invited to consider the film as something weightier. Whether this consideration takes the form of applause or indignation might very well depend on the political ideology the viewer takes into the theater, but either way, the movie assumes an air of importance.

Social relevance alone, however, cannot guarantee box-office success. *Avatar* would have had meager success were the viewer unable to establish an emotional bond with the characters. In asking American audiences to identify with the Na'vi, Cameron pulls a textbook Hollywood maneuver that echoes the likes of *Dances with Wolves, Last of the Mohicans* and *The Last Samurai*. In each of these titles, the "good guys" are not, as they are in most Hollywood fare, the Anglo-Saxon Americans. These films employ white males—the characters of Kevin Costner, Daniel Day-Lewis and Tom Cruise, respectively—as conduits into the "foreign" cultures with which the audience is meant to identify. The main character is not Native American

Reprinted with permission from Benjamin Wetherbee.

or Japanese, but white. In *Avatar*, Sam Worthington's character, the paraplegic marine Jake Sully, fills the same role; he is the white male whose consciousness is inserted into a Na'vi body—his "avatar." The movie thus establishes a small chain of emotional appeals: viewers identify with Jake Sully, the archetypal white, male American hero (and wounded veteran, to boot), and, then, after Sully has assimilated into the Na'vi, "learned their ways," and fallen in love with a Na'vi woman, *Avatar* invites viewers to emotionally invest themselves in and cheer for the blue alien "good guys." Cameron, one might infer, concluded before writing his screenplay that American audiences are unready to identify with a group of non-white (indeed, non-*human*, here) "others" without a "normal" protagonist to introduce the group.

While technically non-human, though, the Na'vi are hardly unfamiliar to American audiences. Their culture comprises a cliché-heavy amalgam of Native American philosophies and religious tenets— or simplistic pop-cultural perversions thereof—that abound in other Hollywood films, *Dances with Wolves* and *Last of the Mohicans* included, that attempt to treat Native Americans sympathetically. The artificial culture Hollywood concocts for these natives incorporates such teachings and assumptions as, one should only kill out of need, one finds happiness in simplicity, God—or The Great Spirit—is found in nature, and happiness, harmony and truth lie in oneness with nature. The common Hollywood representation is that of a simple, self-sustaining and naïve people who are, barring the azure skin and catlike features, the spitting image of the Na'vi. Such beliefs are those exactly of the Na'vi, and these alien natives speak and dress just like stereotypical Hollywood Native Americans. Their chief, to cap off the comparison, is played and voiced by Wes Studi, a full-blooded Cherokee.

5   Such Native American pseudo-culture and its assumed wisdom becomes the scaffold upon which Cameron hangs his environmentalist argument. It is interesting to note, here, the lack of a renowned star—a Tom Cruise or Daniel Day-Lewis—to fill

Avatar's primary role. Worthington, like most of the film's actors, is a B-list Hollywood name; Sigourney Weaver is the only exception, playing an important but decidedly secondary role. *Avatar*'s "star," then, its true selling point, is not the cast but the CGI world, Pandora—complete with sky-eclipsing foliage, trees 40 stories high, phosphorescent airborne jellyfish, dragons and floating rocks. Drowning in this ceaseless computer-rendered spectacle, the viewer is meant to develop an awe-induced emotional connection to Pandora, whose beauty towers above and beyond the run-of-the-mill screenplay and performances. The logic that the movie creates, furthermore, reaffirms that true power comes from oneness with nature. Only by praying to Eywa, the Na'vi's equivalent of "The Great Spirit," is Sully able to harness Pandora's natural power on behalf of the Na'vi and defeat the rampaging humans. Nature trumps technology, the argument goes.

Here, however, enters *Avatar*'s logical contradiction. The movie's explosively violent final act implies what most action films do (e.g., the *Rambo* and *Lethal Weapon* franchises): real results, ultimately, come only from manning up and settling matters through armed conflict. This macho, rightwing truism, popular among American film audiences, appears most transparently in the climactic final battle, wherein Sully expresses unequivocal joy at the chance to fight and kill the merciless colonel who had been his superior officer. The movie glorifies this moment, even as it gainsays the Na'vi wisdom that killing should be only an affair of sad necessity. In its finale, *Avatar* does not bemoan the violence it presents. The violence is meant to be fun. As audiences uncritically tag along on this final explosive ride, they accept its logic; they accept the "git-'er-done" attitude that values decisive, violent action, and rebukes diplomacy and dialogue.

The movie exploits its conflicting arguments for several purposes: the cultural teachings that Hollywood fabricates for its Native Americans and the Na'vi, on one hand, serves the purpose of making *Avatar* a "serious" film with "something to say" about the real-world issues of environmental destruction and the American propensity to meddle with cultures it doesn't understand. The second set of arguments—the "any means necessary" attitude of valorized militarism—satisfies the simple expectation of fighting, explosions and a decisively happy ending that American audiences bring to a sci-fi epic. Logically, these arguments do *not* add up, but a quick glance toward *Avatar's* box-office numbers, and toward the enthusiasm that buzzed around its theatrical and DVD releases, indicates that they do financially.

Works Cited

"All-Time Box Office: Domestic Grosses." *Box Office Mojo*, IMDb, www.boxofficemojo.com/alltime/domestic.htm. Accessed 7 Apr. 2016.

Avatar. Directed by James Cameron, performances by Sam Worthington, Sigourney Weaver, Twentieth Century Fox, 2009.

Hoberman, J. "*Avatar's* Sticker Shock (and Awe)." *The Village Voice*, 15 Dec. 2009, www.villagevoice.com/film/avatars-sticker-shock-and-awe-6394499.

Assignment: Inventing a Rhetorical Analysis

As the essays in this chapter show, nearly any text, image, or artifact from popular culture can be analyzed. If it works to address or attract an audience, if it appeals to people's sensibilities, if it makes an argument (for itself or about anything in the world), then it has rhetorical dimensions. As writers and thinkers, we are free to explore how those dimensions work. For your own analysis, take on one of the following: a written essay (from this book or elsewhere, such as a magazine or blog), an image, an advertisement, or even a film. Examine the text closely—with a particular posture toward analysis. Consider the main argumentative moves and apply the following questions:

1. **Audience/Rhetorical Situation:** Who is the audience? Can you tell? If it's not clear by the language and nature of the argument, consider the publication. Where was it published? What organization wrote, supports, or sponsors the publication?

2. **Claim:** What is the main claim (or thesis)? What type of claim is it? In other words, what is the argument working toward? Does it seek to make the audience evaluate the worth of something (claim of value); believe in a past, present, or future condition (fact); or want to do something (claim of policy)?

3. **Line of Reasoning:** Every argument has some line of reasoning—premises that walk the audience toward the main claim. What individual premises are asserted? How do they lead to the main claim? What premises are unstated? What points does the reader fill in?

4. **Other Appeals:** How does the argument tap into shared values (courage, peace, honor, trust, personal responsibility, knowledge)? How does the argument prompt a certain feeling (fear, anger, hope, regret)? How does the argument call on basic human needs (safety, belonging, actualization)? How does the argument refer directly to the writer's own experience or wisdom?

5. **Examples and Evidence:** How does the argument rely on allusions, scenarios, illustrations, anecdotes, personal testimony, facts, or statistics? How do the specific forms of example or evidence function in the overall argument? How do they support the main claim or serve within an appeal?

6. **Opposition:** In what ways does the argument engage opposition? Or how does opposition shape the premises of the argument? Does the argument engage one major opposing position or does it take on several? Does the argument dismantle the assumptions or values operating in an opposing position? Or does it just refute some factual claim? Does the argument grant value to another position? Does it qualify its own claims?

7. **Values and Assumptions:** What assumptions do you detect? What does the argument assume, but not necessarily state, about the topic—or about people, institutions, life, social norms, and so on? Do those assumptions point to any underlying values? Does the argument, for instance, rest on the notion that progress, or freedom, or creativity, or responsibility, or equality, is inherently good? (For more shared ideals, see page 72.)

How Should I Arrange the Analysis?

There are two common structures for arranging a rhetorical analysis: rhetorical and sequential. In *rhetorical arrangement,* the writer focuses on individual elements separately. For instance, you might begin by describing the type of claim, and then move to supporting appeals, and then to supporting examples, and then to forms of evidence, and then to counterargument, and so on. The idea here is to thoroughly describe each major rhetorical move before moving to the next:

- Brief, one paragraph summary of the argument or argumentative situation
- Analysis of the line of reasoning
- Analysis of other appeals
- Analysis of evidence and example
- Analysis of counterargument, concession, qualifiers
- Analysis of unstated or hidden layers
- Articulation of new insights gained from analysis

In *sequential arrangement,* the writer simply walks through the original text passage by passage, or element by element. The writer uses the structure of that text to organize the analysis.

- Analysis of the introductory rhetorical moves
- Separate analytical paragraph for each segment (paragraph, feature, or image)
- Articulation of new insights gained from analysis

As you can see in the sample analyses, the writers in this chapter illustrate the two general strategies detailed here. Andrew Buchner's analysis of Chief Seattle proceeds sequentially. He walks through the main sections of the speech and explains the major rhetorical moves. Notice that he does not describe each individual sentence—or even each individual paragraph. Instead, as he proceeds through the speech, he finds the major moves (which may involve two or more paragraphs).

Wetherbee's analysis uses rhetorical arrangement. Rather than walking through the movie chronologically, he deals with rhetorical issues separately. In each paragraph, Wetherbee focuses attention on distinct dimensions—regardless of when/where they show up in the movie:

¶1 Description of the rhetorical situation

¶2 Explanation of the hidden political argument

¶3 Analysis of appeals

¶4 Analysis of allusions

¶5 Analysis of the movie's logic

¶6–7 Analysis of the logical tension and the new insight

Ward's analysis also uses rhetorical arrangement:

¶1 Summary of the ad

¶2 Analysis of the hidden argument

¶3 Analysis of the opposition (on the broader cultural stage)

¶4 Analysis of value and logical appeals

¶5 Analysis of emotional appeals

¶6 Analysis of the rhetorical situation and the new insight

Of course, these strategies can be combined, parsed out, and re-mixed. But generally, the writer benefits from having a general plan for arranging ideas.

PART TWO

Inventing Argument

Jonathan Poore/Cengage Learning

The willingness to genuinely explore nuances creates an engaging argument.

Stockexchange

7

Arguing Definitions

WHAT IS IT?

When you think of the term *argument*, you might imagine people debating an issue that has already been defined: *Should abortion be legal? Should the death penalty be eliminated? Should the drinking age be lowered? Should states legalize gay marriage?* Such arguments usually play out according to pre-established positions, with people lining up on one side or the other. But beneath such typical arguments lurks a layer of questions (and possible arguments) such as *What is guilt? What is innocence? What is responsibility? What is marriage? What is love?* Such questions get to our basic assumptions. They prompt us to examine and defend definitions that operate undetected beneath everyday life. Consider, for instance, the various ways we might define *love:* a chemical attraction, a social declaration, an interpersonal commitment, an emotional feeling, a gift from God, a state of selflessness, a highly evolved psychological attribute. Each definition has profound significance for how one might live and think—and how one might argue about issues like marriage.

In short, definitions have power. This is not to suggest that definitions make everyone think in a particular way, but they do suggest a mental framework, and once that framework is in place, ignoring it becomes difficult. Consider this: If a forested area is called *undeveloped,* people may imagine it as empty space to build on; if it is called *virgin timber,* people may think of it as wood; if it is called *wildlife habitat,* people are apt to imagine it as a place already occupied. And once people imagine the forest in a particular way, they respond to it accordingly. An *undeveloped* piece of land is apt to be built on, whereas a *wildlife habitat* is more likely to be preserved.

In short, what we call something matters. And definitions enable us to make other arguments. For instance, those who characterize terrain as a wasteland may hope to conjure a picture of useless space. Those who characterize it as a vital ecology may hope to create the idea of its worth within a larger environmental cycle. Or consider how one might define *patriotism*. If we argue that patriotism involves supporting all the policies of one's country, right or wrong, then we can say that the Nazis were good patriots and Martin Luther King Jr. was not. If we argue that patriotism involves guiding and correcting the policies of one's country, then we would say the opposite about Nazis and King.

Unclear or slippery definitions can drive arguments. Debates might arise because of competing definitions of an unclear term or phrase. For example, a professor might explain that a student's project illustrates "good writing." But when the student receives the final grade, he is surprised to see a *B* rather than an *A*. The student and professor then debate the grade, but beneath their debate is a slippery concept: *good writing*. If the phrase had not been defined formally in the course, the professor and student may each carry their own definitions, which are associated with different grades. Not until they reach a shared understanding of *good writing* will the professor and student come to an understanding about the grade.

Often, a particular situation will prompt an argument over definitions. Someone may ask if a particular event or thing fits into a broader category. This is the case in court trials, when the jury must decide if a particular event fits into a definition that has already been outlined. Was it murder or manslaughter? Was the driver reckless or merely careless? Was the bar patron disorderly or annoying? Is this copyright infringement or artistic license? In such cases, the definition already exists and the lawyers debate the specifics, trying to contrast or compare them with the definition. But this type of argument doesn't belong solely to court proceedings. Consider some important political debates from recent history: Is oral sex "real" sex? Is hooding a prisoner and shocking him with electrodes a form of torture? Is bailing out the nation's big banks a form of socialism or federalism? Is a lone terrorist truly a terrorist?

Arguments over definitions may arise because a subject has so many dimensions. Words like *science, God, love, marriage, economy, war,* and *peace* evoke a huge number of possible definitions. And people across nations, cultures, towns, or even within a single classroom are likely to hold different definitions. *Science* to one group of people might be *mythology* to another. *War* to one group might be *terrorism* to another. In all these cases, people debate a word that seems obvious or self-evident to someone else.

It may be easy to disregard all this potential diversity of thought, to simply announce, "One person's trash is another person's treasure," but people who share a world, a democracy, an environment, a community, a workplace, or a classroom must have some shared definitions. They must have a common understanding of certain concepts; otherwise, decisions about public affairs are nearly impossible. Arguing definitions is more than wordplay. Those who define terms in any situation define the intellectual landscape. Those who know how to argue definitions are those who define the starting points of other debates—and even shape policy in the long run. As you read the essays and images for this chapter, notice how the authors forward a narrow definition of their topics. Either directly or subtly, they make a case for a particular way of seeing.

Much of the argument in academic disciplines focuses on definitions:

- Each discipline defines *human* in a particular way: as a tool-using animal, as a symbol user, as a spiritually motivated being, as a conscious dreamer, and so on.
- Each discipline debates the definition of its own work: Geographers always redefine the nature of their field; psychologists constantly reshape the boundaries of their study; historians take on increasingly more diverse questions about human affairs.

- Higher education itself wrestles with its identity: an institution that creates new knowledge, a tradition that dispenses what is already known, a community of scholars that questions what is already known, or even a service that enables people to enter the workforce.

Activity

In small groups, write a definition for *love*. Share your definitions with the class, and then answer the following questions:

1. Which definitions are most similar? What particular concepts do they share?
2. Which definitions are most dissimilar? Try to specify exactly where and how they differ.
3. What does each definition assume about human emotions, about people's wants or needs? How do the groups' assumptions differ or relate?

What's the Economy for, Anyway?

JOHN DE GRAAF

A definitional argument might involve a basic question of purpose: *What is X for?* In this essay, de Graaf argues that we should ask this basic question about the economy—that the question itself would reveal something critical about our collective situation. John de Graaf is the national coordinator of the Take Back Your Time campaign, coauthor of *Affluenza: The All-Consuming Epidemic* (2002), and editor of *Take Back Your Time: Fighting Overwork and Time Poverty in America* (2003). He is also a film-maker and recently coproduced *The Motherhood Manifesto* (2006).

> **"If they can get you asking the wrong question, they don't have to worry about the answers."**
>
> **—Thomas Pynchon,**
> ***Gravity's Rainbow***

Suggest any alternative to the status quo these days—greater environmental protection, for example, or shorter working hours—and the first question reporters are likely to ask is, "But what will that do to the economy?" Immediately, advocates must try to prove that their suggestions will not adversely affect economic growth or the Dow Jones industrial average.

It's long past time for a new framing offensive, one that turns the obligatory question on its head and shifts the burden of proof to those who resist change. Imagine bumper stickers, posters, Internet messages, a thousand inquiries visible everywhere, asking a different question:

"What's the Economy for, Anyway?"

It's time to demand that champions of the status quo defend their implicit answer to that question. Do they actually believe that the purpose of the economy is to achieve the grossest domestic product and allow the richest among us to multiply their treasures without limits?

For in practice, that really is their answer.

But what if we answer the question differently, 5 perhaps as Gifford Pinchot, the first Chief of the U.S. Forest Service, did a century ago? His answer was, "The greatest good for the greatest number over the long run."

In that light, economic success cannot be measured by Gross Domestic Product (GDP) or stock prices alone. It must take into account the other values that constitute the greatest good—health, happiness, knowledge, kindness—for the greatest number—equality, access to opportunity—over the long run—in a healthy democracy and sustainable environment.

Historical Background

It's time to set America back on course.

After increasing social equality and greatly improving health and other quality-of-life measures (including major increases in leisure time) from World War II until the mid-1970s, the United States abruptly changed its economic trajectory.

"It will be a hard pill for many Americans to swallow," *Business Week* predicted in October 1974, "—the idea of doing with less so that big business can have more. Nothing that this nation or any other nation has done in modern history compares in difficulty with the selling job that must now be done to make people accept the new reality."

Emboldened by Richard Nixon's landslide 1972 10 victory, extreme conservatives moved to reduce the responsibilities (and increase the wealth) of wealthy Americans, while cutting back on public services for the poor and average working Americans.

These policies accelerated during the 1980s and early 1990s and are now enshrined in the "you're on your ownership" attitude of the present federal policies.

John de Graaf, "What's the Economy for, Anyway?" from www.newdream.org/newsletter/economy_for.php. Reprinted with the permission of the author.

Meanwhile, Western European nations took a different course, maintaining their social contracts and at least modestly improving their safety nets for the poor. Their provision of more public goods—healthcare, education, transportation, common space, etc.—supported by higher and more progressive taxation measures than in the United States—reduced the need (or desire) of individuals to maximize their own incomes.

So What Happened?

First, in terms of productivity per worker hour, Western Europeans nearly closed the gap with the United States. They were producing, on average, 65 percent as much as Americans produced per hour in 1970. By 2000, their productivity was 95 percent that of Americans.

But on the other hand, their consumption of goods and services, measured in GDP per capita, remained where it was in 1970—roughly 70 percent that of Americans.

15 There is a simple explanation for this seeming anomaly: European working hours, which in 1970 were slightly longer than those of Americans, dropped to about 80 percent of U.S. hours.

We could say that Europeans traded major portions of their productivity increases for free time instead of money, while Americans—consciously or otherwise—put all their gains into increasing their per capita GDP.

Pose the question, "What did that do to the economy?" and the answer appears clear—Americans, with a much bigger GDP, are the obvious winners.

But ask instead, "What is the economy for, anyway?" and a different answer emerges.

For most of the final quarter of the 20th century, Europeans improved their quality of life relative to Americans in almost every measure.

Health

20 While American health has improved in absolute terms since the 1970s, the United States once ranked near the top in terms of overall health. It now rates below that of every other industrial country, despite spending by far the highest percentage of GDP on health care.

Equality

If one looks at equality, a similar pattern emerges. America, which was about at the median among industrial countries in terms of economic equality in 1974, now has the widest gap between rich and poor.

Savings

Savings are a key indicator of security for many people. While American personal savings rates (10 percent) were slightly higher than those of Europeans in 1970, they have dropped to negative numbers (−1.6 percent last year), while EU citizens now save an average of 12 percent of their incomes.

Sustainability

European progress has also come at a lower cost to the environment. While EU nations were choosing more leisure time rather than working harder to close the consumer gap with Americans, they also took greater steps toward sustainability.

The result is that EU countries require only half the energy consumption per capita as that of Americans, while producing 70 percent as many goods and services. The average American has an ecological footprint (the productive land and water necessary to produce his or her lifestyle) of 24 acres; for Europeans, the average is 12 acres.

One can find similar results in many other areas 25 of quality of life, including: levels of trust, crime, incarceration, family breakdown, literacy, happiness indicators, preschool education, and even access to information technologies.

Tellingly, the Genuine Progress Indicator—an alternative to the GDP developed by Redefining Progress that measures 24 quality-of-life indices—shows a fairly consistent decline in well-being in the United States since a peak in 1973. Similar indices for Europe show consistent improvement in most areas of life, even if increases are sometimes slow or spotty.

Meeting Our Needs

One model for judging the success of the economy is to see how well it allows citizens to meet their needs as outlined by psychologist Abraham Maslow. In his often-cited hierarchy of needs theory, Maslow suggested that humans must first adequately satisfy such basic needs as food, shelter, health and safety, and "belongingness" before moving on to what he called "higher" or "meta" needs.

In the early 1970s, Maslow suggested that as a society the United States had met nearly all its citizens' physiological and safety needs and was moving to satisfy higher needs as well. Ironically, by such a standard, we have lost ground rather than gaining it—we have more citizens living in poverty and a much greater overall sense of insecurity today than we did then, despite more than a 60 percent increase in real per capita GDP.

Most Americans know intrinsically that increases in GDP do not mean economic success if health outcomes and social connections continue to decline relative to other countries.

30   This is why we must raise the question "What is the economy for, anyway?" to a crescendo that cannot be ignored by the media or our political leaders. Only when we begin to ask the right question can we hope to find answers that can improve our quality of life.

We must then ask, "What roles do the market, the state, nongovernmental organizations, and our common wealth respectively have to play in achieving the greatest good for the greatest number over the long run?"

Inevitably, even sympathetic reporters and others will ask us, "Can we change the economy in the ways the Europeans have and still compete in the global economy?"

The answer, quite simply, is yes.

According to the World Economic Forum, the United States ranks second in world economic competitiveness. So it's possible to do things our way—reducing government, slashing taxes, cutting the safety net, and widening the divide between rich and poor—and be competitive.

But is it necessary? Consider that the other four 35 most competitive nations are Finland (ranked first), Sweden, Denmark, and Norway. In fact, European nations make up most of the top 10. All these nations are far more globalized and far more subject to international competitive pressures than we are and have been for many years.

And all of them are far more egalitarian than the United States. Finland has, in fact, the smallest gap between rich and poor of any nation. The Finnish social safety net is a generous one and workers enjoy a great deal of leisure time—an average of 30 days of paid vacation. The story is similar in other European countries. Clearly, it is possible to have a more just and people-friendly economy and compete globally.

Imagine seeing our simple question: "What's the economy for, anyway?" everywhere—in print, posters, on bumper stickers, on websites—or hearing it asked over and over on TV, radio, and in forums and debates. It might be seen as a Trojan horse, seemingly innocent, but remarkably subversive.

The point of all this is not simply to change this or that specific policy, but to create a different thought context by which we might begin to change the entire trend toward privatization and inequality. The point is to show that current "common sense" about economics is "non-sense" if our goal is a better quality of life that is sustainable over the long run.

When we forget to ask, "What is the economy for, anyway?" we leave ourselves open to the GDP worship of so many of our leaders. When we ask the question over and over and demand answers, we open possibilities for a new and better world.

Analyzing Argument

1. What claim or position is de Graaf countering? What passages best illustrate his counterargument?

2. According to de Graaf, what is wrong with the current frame we have for looking at the economy, and how should the issue be reframed?

3. How does de Graaf support his claim that "Europeans improved their quality of life relative to Americans"? Why is or isn't his support persuasive?

4. What competing assumptions and values are at the root of de Graaf's argument?

5. Why do so many Americans accept the "common sense" about economics without question?

Warfare: An Invention—Not a Biological Necessity

MARGARET MEAD

Margaret Mead (1901–78) was a highly acclaimed, and sometimes controversial, anthropologist and writer. In her long career, she served as president of various organizations, including the American Anthropological Association, and she counseled several U.S. presidents on ecological and domestic affairs. Her studies of world cultures and shrewd insights on contemporary issues prompted *Time* magazine to call her "Mother of the World" in 1969. In the following argument, published in 1940, before the United States entered World War II, she illustrates her well-known strategy: discovering and debunking a widely held assumption.

Is war a biological necessity, a sociological inevitability, or just a bad invention? Those who argue for the first view endow man with such pugnacious instincts that some outlet in aggressive behavior is necessary if man is to reach full human stature. It was this point of view which lay back of William James's famous essay, "The Moral Equivalent of War," in which he tried to retain the warlike virtues and channel them in new directions. A similar point of view has lain behind the Soviet Union's attempt to make competition between groups rather than between individuals. A basic, competitive, aggressive, warring human nature is assumed, and those who wish to outlaw war or outlaw competitiveness merely try to find new and less socially destructive ways in which these biologically given aspects of man's nature can find expression. Then there are those who take the second view: warfare is the inevitable concomitant of the development of the state, the struggle for land and natural resources, of class societies springing not from the nature of man, but, from the nature of history. War is nevertheless inevitable unless we change our social system and outlaw classes, the struggle for power, and possessions; and in the event of our success warfare would disappear, as a symptom vanishes when the disease is cured.

One may hold a sort of compromise position between these two extremes; one may claim that all aggression springs from the frustration of man's biologically determined drives and that, since all forms of culture are frustrating, it is certain each new generation will be aggressive and the aggression will find its natural and inevitable expression in race war, class war, nationalistic war, and so on. All three of these positions are very popular today among those who think seriously about the problems of war and its possible prevention, but I wish to urge another point of view, less defeatist, perhaps, than the first and third and more accurate than the second: that is, that warfare, by which I mean recognized conflict between two groups as groups, in which each group puts an army (even if the army is only fifteen pygmies) into the field to fight and kill, if possible, some of the members of the army of the other group—that warfare of this sort is an invention like any other of the inventions in terms of which we order our lives, such as writing, marriage, cooking our food instead of eating it raw, trial by jury, or burial of the dead, and so on. Some of this list anyone will grant are inventions: trial by jury is confined to very limited portions of the globe; we know that there are tribes that do not bury their dead but instead expose or cremate them; and we know that only part of the human race has had the knowledge of writing as its cultural inheritance. But, whenever a way of doing things is found universally, such as the use of fire or the practice of some form of marriage, we tend to think at once that it is not an invention at all but an attribute of humanity itself. And yet even such universals as marriage and the use of fire are inventions like the rest, very basic

Margaret Mead, "Warfare: An Invention . . . Not a Biological Necessity" from Asia 40, 1940, pp. 402–405. Reproduced by permission of the American Anthropological Association. Not for sale or further reproduction.

ones, inventions which were, perhaps, necessary if human history was to take the turn that it has taken, but nevertheless inventions. At some point in his social development man was undoubtedly without the institution of marriage or the knowledge of the use of fire.

The case for warfare is much clearer because there are peoples even today who have no warfare. Of these the Eskimos are perhaps the most conspicuous examples, but the Lepchas of Sikkim described by Geoffrey Gorer in *Himalayan Village* are as good. Neither of these peoples understands war, not even defensive warfare. The idea of warfare is lacking, and this idea is as essential to really carrying on war as an alphabet or a syllabary is to writing. But, whereas the Lepchas are a gentle, unquarrelsome people, and the advocates of other points of view might argue that they are not full human beings or that they had never been frustrated and so had no aggression to expand in warfare, the Eskimo case gives no such possibility of interpretation. The Eskimos are not a mild and meek people; many of them are turbulent and troublesome. Fights, theft of wives, murder, cannibalism occur among them— all outbursts of passionate men goaded by desire or intolerable circumstance. Here are men faced with hunger, men faced with loss of their wives, men faced with the threat of extermination by other men, and here are orphan children, growing up miserably with no one to care for them, mocked and neglected by those about them. The personality necessary for war, the circumstances necessary to goad men to desperation are present, but there is no war. When a traveling Eskimo entered a settlement, he might have to fight the strongest man in the settlement to establish his position among them, but this was a test of strength and bravery, not war. The idea of warfare, of one group organizing against another group to maim and wound and kill them was absent. And, without that idea, passions might rage but there was no war.

But, it may be argued, is not this because the Eskimos have such a low and undeveloped form of social organization? They own no land, they move from place to place, camping, it is true, season after season on the same site, but this is not something to fight for as the modern nations of the world fight for land and raw materials. They have no permanent possessions that can be looted, no towns that can be burned. They have no social classes to produce stress and strains within the society which might force it to go to war outside. Does not the absence of war among the Eskimos, while disproving the biological necessity of war, just go to confirm the point that it is the state of development of the society which accounts for war and nothing else?

We find the answer among the pygmy peoples 5 of the Andaman Islands in the Bay of Bengal. The Andamans also represent an exceedingly low level of society; they are a hunting and food-gathering people; they live in tiny hordes without any class stratification; their houses are simpler than the snow houses of the Eskimo. But they knew about warfare. The army might contain only fifteen determined pygmies marching in a straight line, but it was the real thing none the less. Tiny army met tiny army in open battle, blows were exchanged, casualties suffered, and the state of warfare could only be concluded by a peacemaking ceremony.

Similarly, among the Australian aborigines, who built no permanent dwellings but wandered from water hole to water hole over their almost desert country, warfare—and rules of "international law"—were highly developed. The student of social evolution will seek in vain for his obvious causes of war, struggle for lands, struggle for power of one group over another, expansion of population, need to divert the minds of a populace restive under tyranny, or even the ambition of a successful leader to enhance his own prestige. All are absent, but warfare as a practice remained, and men engaged in it and killed one another in the course of a war because killing is what is done in wars.

From instances like these it becomes apparent that an inquiry into the causes of war misses the fundamental point as completely as does an insistence upon the biological necessity of war. If a people have an idea of going to war and the idea that war is the way in which certain situations, defined within their society, are to be handled, they will sometimes go to war. If they are a mild and unaggressive people, like the Pueblo Indians, they may limit themselves to defensive warfare, but they will be forced to think in terms of war because there are peoples near them who have warfare as a pattern, and offensive, raiding, pillaging warfare at that. When the pattern of warfare is known, people like the Pueblo Indians will defend themselves, taking advantage of their natural defences, the mesa village site, and people like the Lepchas, having no natural defences and no idea of warfare, will merely submit to the invader. But the essential point remains the same. There is a way of behaving which is known to a given people and labeled as an appropriate form of behavior; a bold and warlike people like the Sioux or the Maori may label warfare as desirable as well as possible, a mild people like the Pueblo Indians may label warfare as undesirable, but to the minds of both peoples the possibility of warfare is present. Their thoughts, their hopes, their plans are oriented about this idea—that warfare may be selected as the way to meet some situation.

So simple peoples and civilized peoples, mild peoples and violent, assertive peoples, will all go to war if they have the invention, just as those peoples who have the custom of dueling will have duels and peoples who have the pattern of vendetta will indulge in vendetta. And, conversely, peoples who do not know of dueling will not fight duels, even though their wives are seduced and their daughters ravished; they may on occasion commit murder but they will not fight duels. Cultures which lack the idea of the vendetta will not meet every quarrel in this way. A people can use only the forms it has. So the Balinese have their special way of dealing with a quarrel between two individuals: if the two feel that the causes of quarrel are heavy, they may go and register their quarrel in the temple before the gods, and, making offerings, they may swear never to have anything to do with each other again. . . . But in other societies, although individuals might feel as full of animosity and as unwilling to have any further contact as do the Balinese, they cannot register their quarrel with the gods and go on quietly about their business because registering quarrels with the gods is not an invention of which they know.

Yet, if it be granted that warfare is, after all, an invention, it may nevertheless be an invention that lends itself to certain types of personality, to the exigent needs of autocrats, to the expansionist desires of crowded peoples, to the desire for plunder and rape and loot which is engendered by a dull and frustrating life. What, then, can we say of this congruence between warfare and its uses? If it is a form which fits so well, is not this congruence the essential point? But even here the primitive material causes us to wonder, because there are tribes who go to war merely for glory, having no quarrel with the enemy, suffering from no tyrant within their boundaries, anxious neither for land nor loot nor women, but merely anxious to win prestige which within that tribe has been declared obtainable only by war and without which no young man can hope to win his sweetheart's smile of approval. But if, as was the case with the Bush Negroes of Dutch Guiana, it is artistic ability which is necessary to win a girl's approval, the same young man would have to be carving rather than going out on a war party.

10   In many parts of the world, war is a game in which the individual can win counters—counters which bring him prestige in the eyes of his own sex or of the opposite sex; he plays for these counters as he might, in our society, strive for a tennis championship. Warfare is a frame for such prestige-seeking merely because it calls for the display of certain skills and certain virtues; all of these skills—riding straight, shooting straight, dodging the missiles of the enemy and sending one's own straight to the mark—can be equally well exercised in some other framework and, equally, the virtues endurance, bravery, loyalty, steadfastness can be displayed in other contexts. The tie-up between proving oneself a man and proving this by a success in organized killing is due to a definition which many societies have made of manliness. And often, even in those societies which counted success in warfare a proof of human worth, strange turns were given to the idea, as when the plains Indians gave their highest awards to the man who touched a live enemy rather than to the man who brought in a scalp—from a dead enemy—because the latter was less risky. Warfare is just an invention known to the majority of human societies by which they permit their young men either to accumulate prestige or avenge their honor or acquire loot or wives or slaves or sago lands or cattle or appease the blood lust of their gods or the restless souls of the recently dead. It is just an invention, older and more widespread than the jury system, but none the less an invention.

But, once we have said this, have we said anything at all? Despite a few stances, dear to the instances of controversialist, of the loss of the useful arts, once an invention is made which proves congruent with human needs or social forms, it tends to persist. Grant that war is an invention, that it is not a biological necessity nor the outcome of certain special types of social forms, still once the invention is made, what are we to do about it? The Indian who had been subsisting on the buffalo for generations because with his primitive weapons he could slaughter only a limited number of buffalo did not return to his primitive weapons when he saw that the white man's more efficient weapons were exterminating the buffalo. A desire for the white man's cloth may mortgage the South Sea Islander to the white man's plantation, but he does not return to making bark cloth, which would have left him free. Once an invention is known and accepted, men do not easily relinquish it. The skilled workers may smash the first steam looms which they feel are to be their undoing, but they accept them in the end, and no movement which has insisted upon the mere abandonment of usable inventions has ever had much success. Warfare is here, as part of our thought; the deeds of warriors are immortalized in the words of our poets, the toys of our children are modeled upon the weapons of the soldier, the frame of reference within which our statesmen and our diplomats work always contains war. If we know that it is not inevitable, that it is due to historical accident that warfare is one of the ways in which we think of behaving, are we given any hope by that? What hope is there of persuading nations to abandon war, nations so thoroughly imbued with the idea that resort to war is, if not actually desirable and noble, at least inevitable whenever certain defined circumstances arise?

In answer to this question I think we might turn to the history of other social inventions, and inventions which must once have seemed as finally entrenched as warfare. Take the methods of trial which preceded the jury system: ordeal and trial by combat. Unfair, capricious, alien as they are to our feeling today, they were once the only methods open to individuals accused of some offense. The invention of trial by jury gradually replaced these methods until only witches, and finally not even witches, had to resort to the ordeal. And for a long time the jury system seemed the best and finest method of settling legal disputes, but today new inventions, trial before judges only or before commissions, are replacing the jury system. In each case the old method was replaced by a new social invention. The ordeal did not go out because people thought it unjust or wrong; it went out because a method more congruent with the institutions and feelings of the period was invented. And, if we despair over the way in which war seems such an ingrained habit of most of the human race, we can take comfort from the fact that a poor invention will usually give place to a better invention.

For this, two conditions, at least, are necessary. The people must recognize the defects of the old invention, and someone must make a new one. Propaganda against warfare, documentation of its terrible cost in human suffering and social waste, these prepare the ground by teaching people to feel that warfare is a defective social institution. There is further needed a belief that social invention is possible and the invention of new methods which will render warfare as out of date as the tractor is making the plough, or the motor car the horse and buggy. A form of behavior becomes out of date only when something else takes its place, and, in order to invent forms of behavior which will make war obsolete, it is a first requirement to believe that an invention is possible.

Analyzing Argument

1. In Mead's view, what is wrong with the three most popular conceptions of warfare?

2. As Chapter 3 explains, analogical reasoning depends on comparisons (or analogies). Comparisons, metaphors, allegories, parables, and examples all have an analogous quality: they argue that if two things are alike in certain respects, they are also alike in other respects. Analogies shed light on something by comparing or contrasting it with something familiar. Examine the logic in paragraph two and write out the line of reasoning. (Be especially mindful of the analogous reasoning.)

3. How does Mead deal with the opposing claim outlined in paragraph four? In what passages does she counterargue this claim?

4. Examine the logic in paragraph ten and write out the line of reasoning. How important is this paragraph to the overall argument?

5. Although the argument primarily focuses on redefining warfare, Mead also urges readers to see a purpose for a new definition. In your words, what is the reason she offers? Why should we begin to imagine warfare as invention?

The Fashion Punk Paradox

ANDREW HYDE

For years, Andrew Hyde was interested in punk, and a college English assignment was an opportunity to explore the idea. Hyde saw a problem with the way punk was being defined in mainstream fashion, and so developed the following argument. Although mainstream fashion was not deliberately or explicitly defining punk, Hyde saw the quiet suggestions (the unstated definitions) being asserted in advertising. His argument, written in 2006, is a response to those unstated definitions.

Andrew Holbrooke/Corbis

When most folks consider the word "punk," two ideas come to mind: a troublesome youngster with funny hair, or the dry and crumbly innards of an old log. Probably more accurate is an anonymous submission to Urbandictionary.com. The writer explains punk with an anecdote: "A guy walks up to me and asks, 'What's Punk?' So I kick over a garbage can and say, 'That's punk!' So he kicks over the garbage can and says, 'That's Punk?' and I say, 'No, that's trendy!'" (loserksjfdfds). Nonconformity has always been key in the punk subculture, and yet conformity is taking over in the form of fashion. Now, the real punks and fashion punks battle over the term itself.

The connotation of punk as a musical genre and fashion style has roughly a thirty-year history. There is much debate over when and where it began. Some would say punk began with the Rolling Stones, the Beatles, or Iggy Pop and the Stooges. A few would even proclaim that the attitude was born with stars such as Johnny Cash or Bob Dylan. Although these artists earned large sums of money, they still had a hatred for the popular music industry. The songs were written for personal satisfaction, and money was a bonus. Regardless of attitude, punk music made a definitive entrance to popular culture in 1976. This occurred with the nearly simultaneous introduction of the Ramones in New York and the Sex Pistols in Great Britain. Punk music was defined by simple and fast-paced chord progressions, and the lyrics were rebellious and often had a political theme.

Fashion styles also began to differ drastically in the punk scene from disco and the leftover hippies. Clothing became dark, ragged, and often brandished hand-sewn patches and safety pins. Facial piercing and wild hairstyles came about. Dick Hebdige's *Style in Revolt: Revolting Style* describes punk fashion as correlating with the artistic Dada movement of the 1910s and '20s, and specifically Marcel Duchamp's "ready-mades." Hebdige explains how punks used similar items for the same purpose: "The most unremarkable and inappropriate items—a pin, a plastic clothes peg, a television component, a razor blade, a tampon—could be brought within the province of punk (un)fashion" (107). Not only did punks draw fashion ideas from Dada, but political and social views as well. The Dada movement was a response to the Great War. Artists were disgusted with the events of the time, and made a statement by proclaiming insignificance. Dadaists describe themselves as nihilists, as believers in nothing:

> Dada knows everything. Dada spits on everything. Dada says "knowthing." Dada has no fixed ideas. Dada does not catch flies. Dada is bitterness laughing at everything that has been accomplished, sanctified. . . . Like everything in life, Dada is useless, everything happens in a completely idiotic way. . . . We are incapable of treating seriously any subject whatsoever, let alone this subject: ourselves. (Kleiner and Mamiya 754–55)

Although the punks have not directly attributed much to Dada, the connection is almost lucid. Punk is not simply a subculture of rebellious kids with nothing better to do than dress up in costumes and listen to loud music. Anarchy became more effective than nihilism, but the intent remained the same as Dada: to ridicule government policy and attack the flaws of society.

5   Through the 1980s, punk became even more political. With bands like T.S.O.L., Social Distortion, and Operation Ivy, the movement focused on social issues that were not being acknowledged by the Reagan administration. Tax codes were changed in a way to benefit the rich, while social policy moved away from helping the poor. And punk bands responded with a litany of album titles, song titles, and lyrics, for example, the Dead Kennedys released "Kill the Poor" in 1980 on the album *Fresh Fruit for Rotting Vegetables*. Punk became a mindset rather than a statement. The increasingly thoughtful political awareness continued into the 1990s, until a series of events significantly changed punk. Bands like Green Day, the Offspring, and Rancid were getting attention. Songs were heard on the radio, and videos seen on MTV. Punk went pop. My middle school years put me right in the middle of this musical transformation. Specifically, in seventh grade, Katie (one of the popular girls in my class) asked

what I was listening to on my Walkman. I took out the dirty, overplayed cassette tape to show her Green Day's 1994 release of *Dookie*. Of course I was teased for my musical taste that differed from the Gin Blossoms, or whatever was popular at the time. Less than a few weeks later, I saw Katie listening to the compact disc version of *Dookie*, singing along to "When I Come Around." The song had become a hit on Rick Dees's weekly top 40.

Through the late '90s and the first few years of the new millennium, many have said that punk is officially dead. While the movement may not be entirely dead, thirty years since the beginning, punk ideologies have changed. Clothing styles of modern-day punk still embrace the roots of the movement, but have become a target for fashion companies to market as a popular trend. The music is still fast and simple. Unfortunately, it has almost completely lost the political aspect it once had. Both bands and fans reject being labeled as "punks" yet hold onto many of the characteristics that have been around since the 1970s. This fashion-based genre known as "emo" is becoming increasingly popular. Teens relate with bands through lyrics describing failed relationships, depression, and lack of attention from parents. Personal-identity politics and clothing are the foci rather than current political issues, with kids spending large amounts of money in order to separate themselves from other styles in pop culture. In this sense, punk has transformed—from kicking over the can to dressing it in particular clothes.

> With bands like T.S.O.L., Social Distortion, and Operation Ivy, the movement focused on social issues that were not being acknowledged by the Reagan administration.

One aspect of online teen culture closely associated with emo is the Internet fad called MySpace. The site allows anyone to build a simple Web page, which allows the user to easily connect with any of the 50 million other users (McDermott). A website for teens to chat may not seem like such a bad thing. It allows them to meet new people, hear about other parts of the country and world, and maybe even discuss political issues. The original intent of MySpace was to allow up-and-coming bands to stream music, allowing more people to hear them. This should allow for a diverse music collection among teens, right? Spend just a few minutes surfing the site, and you will see that almost all bands sound very similar. Of course, they focus on emo points of view in order to attract more listeners. Instead of discussing socio-political issues, users spend time rating the attractiveness of fellow members' photographs. Many schools have banned students from accessing MySpace from school computers, as well as many similar sites such as Xanga or Facebook (McDermott). This banning apparently hasn't fazed teens, as MySpace is expected to make over $200 million this year.

MySpace is not the only company capitalizing on the emo fad. The chain store Hot Topic is rapidly spreading through the malls of the United States. Hot Topic markets the punk fashion trend to the kids who resist (but ironically promote) conformity, and is making money hand over fist. Not only does Hot Topic market this trend, it attempts to create a new image of punk rock, with no respect for the values that punk originally created. Hot Topic encourages anyone interested in the punk scene to spend money on its products. Unfortunately the company is putting a fashion mask over the face of punk, and not only hiding but also obliterating the defining quality of punk. By creating a slickly manufactured image of punk, Hot Topic takes a movement that previously rejected conformity, and twists it into a fashion trend. Just when true punk was beginning to scratch the surface of the mainstream, it was buried by the music that goes along with this fashionably slanted image of punk.

Hot Topic and similar corporations seem to enjoy keeping America's youth in check in order to further manipulate fashion trends and make another buck. It would seem that punks would rise up and simply boycott the store, putting them out of business. However, the punks who would be willing to boycott the store already avoid it at all costs. Luckily for Hot Topic, the target market consists of kids who have no interest in punk's deeply rooted anti-capitalist ideals.

> It would seem that punks would rise up and simply boycott the store, putting them out of business. However, the punks who would be willing to boycott the store already avoid it at all costs.

Punks would gladly put many corporations under by means of boycott if they existed in a large enough population. Unfortunately, punks make up a rather small part of America's youth. Even smaller yet is the portion of punks that aren't infatuated with tight clothing and makeup. What about the rest of the youth in America? Regardless of choice in music, teens are losing interest in important issues across the country. What was once the politically active pop music of Creedence Clearwater Revival, Neil Young, or even the Grateful Dead has become Ashlee Simpson and Kelly Clarkson. Country was once very socially minded with the lyrics of Johnny Cash and Willie Nelson, but is now interested in beer and women. Hip-hop used to consist of NWA and the Beastie Boys, who both spoke up for civil rights. Rap has now become obsessed with money, demonstrated by 50 Cent's new movie, *Get Rich or Die Tryin'*.

10 I spent a year living in Midland, Texas, during the 2004 presidential election. At the same time, Green Day's new album *American Idiot* was released. While riding my motorcycle on a hot summer day, I was stopped at a traffic light next to a man in his early twenties. For the next 40 seconds, all I heard was his voice over a radio blaring "American Idiot."

For a moment I was relieved. As I listened to the lyrics questioning and rejecting dominant political, cultural, and consumerist messages, I thought that maybe people were catching on to current issues and possibly even thinking for themselves. My moment was over as I realized the context of the situation. The young man was sitting in a jacked-up two-wheel-drive truck, wearing a cowboy hat. The truck brandished stickers and magnets pledging allegiance to President Bush, and promising to support our troops. More stickers explained that marriage belongs between only a man and a woman, and that abortion is a mortal sin. The vehicle and driver seemed to be a rolling contradiction.

This is not to say that people cannot listen to Green Day if they do not agree with the message. In fact, it is a wonderful feeling to continue to enjoy something that conflicts with your own beliefs. This is also by no means to say that all music must be politically minded. In fact, not all "real" punk music is politically minded. Punk makes a simple statement by questioning authority and not accepting the status quo. And even with that consistent principle, punk is always changing. According to John Goshert:

> The call for an absolutely correct definition of punk will always miss the point, for the stable form of genre or fashion is always subject either to appropriation by the flattening forces of the entertainment industry, or to transformation by punks themselves. Instead, punk is better seen as a series of performative traces [that]

will never serve as hardened constraints of its definition.[1]

As popular culture changes, punk consciousness will also transform. Large companies will move away from punk to support something else—or the watered-down version of something else—with the intent of making a few dollars and keeping America's youth brainwashed enough to purchase overpriced items. And beneath the fashion parades, the real punks will be chafing against and kicking over whatever is hailed as lovely, admirable, and attractive. And maybe there is one thing we can say for sure: whatever punk is or will be, it sure as hell won't be pretty.

Works Cited

Goshert, John. "Punk after the Pistols: American Music, Economics, and Politics in the 1980s and 1990s." *Popular Music and Society*, vol. 24, no. 1, 2000, p. 85, doi: 10.1080/03007760008591760.

Hebdige, Dick. "Style in Revolt; Revolting Style." *Subculture: The Meaning of Style*, Routledge, 1981, pp. 106–12.

Heisel, Scott. "Your Antidote for Apathy." *Alternative Press*, 15 Oct. 2005.

Kleiner, Fred S., and Christin J. Mamiya. *Gardner's Art through the Ages: The Western Perspective*. 12th ed., Thomson, 2006.

McDermott, Irene. "I Need MySpace." *Searcher*, vol. 14, no. 4, Apr. 2006, pp. 22–25. *Academic Search Elite*, 20493968.

loserksjfdfds. "Punk." Urban *Dictionary*, www.urbandictionary.com/define.php?term=punk. Accessed 27 Apr. 2006.

Works Consulted

Hansell, Saul. "New MySpace Goal: Profit, Not Just Friends." *The New York Times*, 23 Apr. 2006, www.nytimes.com/2006/04/23/technology/23iht-myspace24.html?pagewanted=all&_r=0.

Operation Ivy. "Unity." *Energy*, Lookout!, 1989.

---

[1]Goshert, John. "Punk after the Pistols: American Music, Economics, and Politics in the 1980s and 1990s." *Popular Music and Society*, vol. 24, no. 1, 2000, p. 85, doi: 10.1080/03007760008591760.

Analyzing Argument

1. How is Hyde's notion of punk fundamentally opposed to mainstream messages about punk? Why is that difference important?

2. Allusions are a key part of Hyde's argument. Choose one cultural allusion, and explain how it functions in the overall line of reasoning.

3. What values lurk beneath the explicit claims about original punk culture? (In other words, what principles or qualities must a reader value to accept Hyde's argument?)

4. Describe Hyde's use of counterargument. Point to a particular passage and explain how it works as counterargument—and how it helps to develop Hyde's overall point.

5. Take a close look at Hyde's Works Cited and Works Consulted lists. Based on this list, how would you define "authority" in academic argument?

Standardized Testing vs. Education

JUSTIN JAMES

James wrote the following essay for a college English assignment. His goal was to argue a definition of education as it applies to today's schools. While standardized testing was the starting place for James's argument, he discovers an underlying tension—one of competing definitions.

In three sentences, a personal example introduces the main issue.

It is no wonder my niece says school is boring. When she was younger, she loved it. It was all about discovery; now it's all about tests. Tests can be valuable in education, of course. But they can be hazardous, too. They can hinder learning and teach students and society at large a false definition of education. Standardized tests teach students to *practice and perform*, but education is more about *developing a sense of curiosity*. Practice and perform actually discourages curiosity: All the practicing and performing takes time, which takes time away from activities that might encourage a more curious mind. Standardized testing ends up sending a wrong message: It tells students and society that *education* is a quantity to be consumed and measured.

The introduction provides an overview of the problem with standardized esting.

Appeal to logic: Students, like humans in any situation, respond to cues they are given.

Students, like humans in any situation, respond to cues they are given. If they are not taught to be curious, if they are prompted toward other modes of thought and behavior, they will act accordingly. In short, standardized testing takes the curiosity out of students. Standardized tests don't engage students' sense of curiosity. Instead, school becomes drudgery. And now more than ever, despite these effects, standardized tests are being touted as the saving grace to failing schools. The No Child Left Behind Act of 2001 was well intended, perhaps. Signed by President George W. Bush on January 8, 2001, the act "gives our schools and our country groundbreaking educational reform, based on the following ideals: stronger accountability for results, more freedom for states and communities, encouraging proven education methods, more choice for parents" (United States, Congress). The act has placed an emphasis on accountability, which is being determined by student test results. Test scores might rise. But does that really mean the schools are doing a better job or students are getting a better education? The current emphasis on testing can have harmful results. What's more, the method used to find out the scores teaches students a dangerous definition of *education*.

Reference to the No Child Left Behind Act helps to emphasize the relevance of the argument.

The first two sentences explain how education comes to be defined a certain way.

The emphasis placed on standardized testing teaches students that *education* means getting content from a teacher or getting good at a skill.

Justin James, "Standardized Testing vs. Education." Reprinted with permission.

They come to think *education* means getting a grade on a test, accumulating points, and arriving at an average grade based on those points. But students will benefit more in all aspects of life if they can experience education differently—as having to do more with exploring, discovery, being curious. Standardized testing deprives students of the opportunity to experience an education that values curiosity, and is more valuable than an education consumed with standardized tests.

Beginning with "But," James provides an alternative definition of education.

In 2001, Donald Perl, a middle school teacher in Greeley, Colorado, refused to administer a standardized test. Perl, who said he "anguished" over the decision, believed "the test cultivates competition instead of cooperation and test-taking skills over 'true stimulation of our children's curiosity'" (qtd. in Ednalino). Many teachers, like Perl, have doubts about the side effects of standardized testing. Ann Lahrson Fisher, in "Side Effects of Standardized Testing," compiles an interesting list of more than thirty side effects. She argues that tests teach students, in subtle ways, ideas such as:

When quoting, James provides name (Donald Perl), context (who Perl is), and only as much quoted material as necessary.

Support from an authority is introduced and listed.

- Someone else knows what you should know better than you do.

- Learning is an absolute that can be measured.

- Your interests are not important.

- The subject areas being evaluated on the test are the only things that are important to know.

- Thinking is not valued; getting the "right" answer is the only goal.

- The answer (to any question) is readily available, indisputable, and it's one of these four or five answers here; there's no need to look deeper or dwell on the question.

Fisher's long list of side effects suggest it is at least possible that standardized tests define education for students: "Reliance on standardized test scores reduces initiative, independence, creativity, and willingness to take risks in learning situations." Fisher explains that "test scores become the goal of student work (extrinsic reward) rather than the sense of satisfaction and wonder that naturally follows discovery of something new (intrinsic reward)." Should the goal of education be test scores, or should students experience a sense of satisfaction and wonder? Should students discover something new, or prep for tests?

James shows how Fisher's points support his argument.

As students in American public schools get older, they don't necessarily encounter increasingly intense opportunities to explore intellectually. But they should. If they don't get this opportunity, they'll get bored—not because education is boring, but because what students have been exposed

James explains the negative consequences of a false definition of education: Students will think education is boring.

Appeal to value: Exploring motivations and discovering connections is more educationally valuable than memorizing facts.

to as *education* is an absence of *education,* and that is boring. If students aren't having fun, it's because they're not encouraged to be curious. When we focus so much on standardized tests, we ask students to leave their curiosity behind and start down the practice-and-perform path. Like a magician, the tests misdirect everyone's attention, and students, based on their educational experiences, develop a false belief. For example, a student who is taught to explore the meaning of revolutions, to imagine the connection between the Revolutionary War and the Civil War, will ultimately have a deeper understanding of history than the student who is asked to memorize the dates of the decisive battles in each war. When a student is asked "Why did people in both wars want to free themselves from another government?" she is given an opportunity to think about the motivations of real people and to discover connections. But under the yoke of standardized tests, teachers are obliged to pump students full of facts and then move to test-taking (performance) strategies. The students, then, reach the easy conclusion that *education* equals memorize and then test.

The concluding paragraph qualifies an important point: Opponents of standardized testing are not for throwing standards out the window. This clarifies the writer's position and strengthens the argument by pointing out common ground with those who might disagree.

Today's No Child Left Behind testing is redefining *education*. This new definition is harmful. People are coming to believe that education is primarily about practicing and performing on exams—not about developing curiosity and exploring vast possibilities. But in an environment (a definition) where they can explore, students thrive; teachers thrive; learning thrives. Standardized tests squelch all that. They should be used modestly. It is not that opponents of standardized testing are for throwing standards out the window. And it's not that they think all testing is bad. They simply believe the more valuable definition of *education* promotes curiosity, not practice and perform.

Works Cited

Ednalino, Percy. "Teacher Won't Administer CSAP Tests." *The Denver Post,* 27 Jan. 2001, p. A1.

Fisher, Ann Lahrson. "Side Effects of Standardized Testing." *National Home Education Network,* 2004. Accessed 8 July 2004.

United States, Congress. *No Child Left Behind Act of 2001.* Government Printing Office, 8 Jan. 2002. 107th Congress, Public Law 107–10, 115 Stat. 1425.

Analyzing Argument

1. According to James, how does standardized testing define education?

2. What is James's line of reasoning? What basic premises must you follow before you accept his main claim? (Are any of those premises unstated in James's essay?)

3. Discuss how the following sentence makes an appeal to values:

> Standardized testing ends up sending a wrong message: It tells students and society that education is a quantity to be consumed and measured (paragraph 1).

Then find another sentence in the essay and explain how it appeals to a value.

4. Explain how the testimony from teachers works in the argument. What premise do they help to support?

5. How do counterarguments and concessions function in the argument? What additional counterarguments or concessions could have been helpful?

This bumper sticker was on a truck in Livingston, Montana.

Analyzing Argument

1. What does the bumper sticker argue?

2. Explain the logic behind the bumper sticker. Is it sound or flawed logic?

3. How are the pink and blue footprints behind the text part of the bumper sticker's argument?

JIM BOURG/Reuters/Corbis

Analyzing Argument

1. What is the line of reasoning in the sign? Consider the unstated premises between the assertion to preserve marriage and the man's definition of marriage.

2. If this sign is a counterargument, what is the original argument? To what is the man responding?

EXPLORING FOR TOPICS

In this chapter, you will argue for a particular definition. The goal is to draw clear boundaries—to argue for what a thing *is* and *is not.* As you consider possible topics, dig into common situations. Any situation, an everyday occurrence or a special event, can help us to rethink the very essence of things. Imagine a World Wrestling Entertainment match: If we are watching a 300-pound man in a yellow leotard stomp around a wrestling ring, we might think about the nature of entertainment. We might ask ourselves, "What exactly *is* entertainment?" Once the question is asked, it can be answered in a number of ways. Every situation holds potential for digging up basic definitions. But we must be willing to ask questions that normally do not get asked. Following are possible starting places for an argument about a definition:

Focus on a specific situation or thing—and ask whether it falls within or outside of a particular definition.

- **Popular culture:** Is *American Idol* a reality show or something else? Is *Dateline* a news program? Is the "No Spin Zone" really a no spin zone? Is your local news program really *news,* or is there a more accurate word? Is *Adult Swim* really for adults? Can WWE competitions be defined as *wrestling,* or are they some kind of muscle-bound ballet?

- **Politics:** Is the United States government really a democracy? Is the current administration liberal? Is the Tea Party really conservative?

- **School:** Is business an academic discipline? Are you a college student in the traditional sense? How would you define your instructors? Are they professors, instructors, teachers, or lecturers?

- **Work:** Do you have a job or a career? In what sense are you a laborer? Could someone say that you're part of a team? (Or is it a team only in name?)

- **Choose a reading or image from this chapter:**
  Enter the argument by raising a new way of seeing the disputed term.

Focus on a term—and argue for a specific definition.

- What term do people misunderstand or misapply?

- In your eyes, what is the most important debate currently being waged in your community? What definition is at the root of the debate? (Even though people might not label the debate as one about definitions, what word are they disagreeing about?) For example, a debate about which farmers have the right to sell their produce at the local farmer's market might ultimately hinge on the definition of "local" (or even "produce").

WHAT IS IT?

Life is DoWntown

To view this video, visit the English CourseMate at CengageBrain.com.

Top to bottom: Madhouse; Jim Wehtje/Getty Images; xandert/morguefi le.com; John Metz; John Metz; From CourseMate video (BBC: Same Sex Marriage)

- Focus on an important cultural or national debate. At the heart of the debate, beneath all the fervor, what word seems undefined or misunderstood? For example, what is liberalism? What is fascism? What is conservative? Fundamentalism? Transsexuality?

Focus on an unstated definitional argument that lurks in a common practice.

- Justin James argues that standardized tests teach students to define *education* as practice and perform. What other common academic practices make subtle definitional arguments? How does the standard classroom arrangement define *education*? How does a syllabus define *education*?

Focus on the visual.

- How does the appearance and design of a course textbook define *college*? How does your campus geography or architecture define *college*?
- How does a particular fashion trend define *woman* or *man*?
- How does your current hairstyle define your gender?
- Look for visual arguments about definitions where you work. Even landscaping or the interior of a building could be arguing a definition.

Invention Workshop

For each category on the previous page, develop more questions. Consider both cultural situations, such as the Super Bowl or Christmas, and professional situations, such as a business meeting. Then generate questions to highlight potential arguments of definition. Generate as many examples as possible—and consider even the most eccentric or seemingly insignificant ideas.

There are two general approaches to arguing definitions: (1) examining a specific subject and arguing that it fits or does not fit into a category, and (2) examining a term and arguing for or against an accepted definition. If you start with a specific subject (for example, a classroom, a television program, an image), then it will be helpful to inspect its particulars. For instance, imagine that a writer is examining *American Idol*. She wonders if it fits into the reality show category. First, she might list qualities of the show itself:

- The contestants are ordinary people, not professional actors.
- Judges and producers whittle down the contestants according to their own tastes and understanding of the audience.
- As the judges eliminate contestants, a select few are given air time, mini-biographies, that showcase their stories.
- The mini-bios are heavily produced and characterize the contestants in a particular way.
- As the competition progresses, the finalists perform in Hollywood for the judges, a live audience, and the television viewers.
- The viewers vote on winners—but only after the judges give official commentary.

The writer could go on listing qualities or elements of the show: advertisers, stage production, contestant guidelines, and so on. Then she might find a definition of *reality show* and compare the definition with her specific notes. In this early phase, she might find that some of the show's qualities match that definition while others seem to oppose it.

If you begin with a specific subject, consider the following invention questions:

▶ What are the particular qualities of the situation or thing?
▶ How do those qualities match up with an agreed-upon definition?
▶ How do those qualities oppose or stretch an agreed-upon definition?

If you begin with a general term (such as education or entertainment), consider the following invention questions:

▶ What specific behaviors, attitudes, values, policies, or qualities does the term involve?
▶ What specific qualities differentiate it from other like things?
▶ What is its opposite? (Does it have an opposite?)
▶ Under what conditions does it thrive or suffer?

INVENTING A CLAIM

Because any argument exists within a context of public opinion, good arguers plan how they will engage other positions and insights. To engage those other positions, research common understanding about your subject. Consider conducting an informal survey about your subject (see pages 320–321) or exploring your library's periodical databases, which contain journal and magazine articles that can help uncover many layers of a topic. Scholarly, or peer-reviewed, journal articles can be especially helpful in an argument about definitions because much academic research seeks to define terms. Scholars are constantly making arguments about the nature of things: *psychology is . . . ; life is . . . ; American currency is . . . ; the human mind is. . . .* Even a basic Internet search can reveal some common thinking about the topic—everything from informal rants to official government studies. Using the same noun strings as you used in the periodical databases, search Google or another major search engine. As you search, be open to opinions and associations. The goal is not to find sources that agree with your initial position but to explore *what's out there*, to see what has been said.

Answers to the following questions will help you to craft a specific position in relation to others.

What Do Others Claim?

• What do people normally think of when they hear the word?
• What do specific sources say about the subject or the word itself?
• Why might reasonable people disagree about or argue over the word?

What Do I Claim?

• What important aspect or layer do others overlook?
• Why is it important that the topic be defined correctly?
• What specific notion or understanding can you correct or clarify?

If you can answer the last question, you are well on your way to developing a main argumentative claim. Remember that definitional arguments are driven by *claims of fact*. For this project, then, you will argue about the basic nature or properties of a topic—not about the effect or worth. Your argument might do one of the following:

- Argue that a particular (situation, event, show, etc.) does or does not match a definition:
    - Because a few powerful corporations, rather than civic groups and people, make policy in America, we are closer to an oligarchy than a democracy.
    - Although *American Idol* often gets lumped in with other reality shows, the tightly controlled contestant selection makes it more of a slick national talent show.
    - The standard classroom layout and overreliance on big-screen technology suggest propaganda rather than education.
- Argue that a common term is often misapplied or entirely misunderstood:
    - Higher education is not about job training or occupational retrenchment; it's about the development of intellectual possibilities beyond any particular job.
    - Punk is not about a particular fashion but the constant denial of the mainstream, manufactured aesthetic.
    - Liberalism is not hell-bent on killing God, disbanding the military, and putting white men at the bottom of the food chain; instead, liberalism hopes for the democratization of knowledge and power.

Such finely tuned statements do not fall from the sky; they must undergo some tinkering and shaping. Notice how Justin James's claim evolved. The first statement is merely a broad response to a situation. His final claim is more than just a position—and it is more than a simple definition. It is a statement that promotes a new way of thinking about education.

- Standardized tests are ruining education.
- Education is about discovery, not performance.
- While standardized tests teach students that education is a practice-and-perform process, education is actually a discovery process.
- While standardized tests teach students to practice and perform, education is actually about developing a sense of discovery in each subject.

More Sample Claims

Popular Culture

- Popular culture in mainstream America is actually popular *anti*-culture.
- The product sold on television is the viewing audience.

Politics

- While nations are defined by borders, a nation can also be defined as a group of people engaged in argument about common issues.

- A strong economy cannot be determined by the stock market, new housing starts, or automobile sales; instead, one must examine the financial circumstances of middle- and lower-class citizens.
- Despite the Democratic Party's stated principles, it can easily be defined as the slightly less corporate wing of the Republican Party.

School

- While training is the process of acquiring skills, it should not be confused with education, which is the active process of uncovering ideas.
- Education is the process of personal intellectual restructuring.
- Education is the deliberate escape from boredom.
- Education is the process of building new concepts and destroying old ones.

Work

- Comfort is an illusion unless it is achieved through perseverance and struggle.
- Work should be considered a spiritual dimension of one's life, not merely an economic necessity.
- Teaching is not part of the new "service industry"; if anything, it resembles politics because of its role in maintaining, or vitalizing, popular consciousness.

Activity

In small groups, share your main claims. Evaluate the claim of each group member and help each to evolve in the same way as James's did. Apply the following questions:

- Is it a claim of fact? Does it deal with the basic properties or nature of the topic?
- Is the claim arguable? Could it be more arguable by referring to an opposing idea?
- How could the claim be more focused? What words could be more precise?
- How could the claim be more revelatory? How could the definition suggest something unique or surprising?

INVENTING SUPPORT

While many other support strategies can be applied to this project, the following forms of evidence and appeal are commonly used. (For a more complete explanation of the support strategies listed in this section, see Chapter 3.)

LINES OF REASONING call on the audience to make logical connections between points or ideas. In an argument of definition, the arguer hopes to lead readers to a particular definition—to believe that a particular definition is the most correct or most applicable to a situation. This involves more than simply stating the definition. Often, the arguer has to convince the audience that several premises are true. For example, consider the following definitions of education:

A. Education is the process of making people better thinkers.

B. Education is the process of changing the brain.

Readers are not likely to accept each definition without some reasoning or premises that lead to the idea. Therefore, the arguers would need to walk readers through a line of reasoning:

A. Education is the process of making people better thinkers.

- Humans are natural thinkers.
- Humans are naturally *bad* thinkers (predisposed to prejudice, egocentrism, superficiality, vagueness, etc.).
- No occupation or discipline values bad (egocentric, superficial, vague, narrow-minded, prejudicial, imprecise) thinking.
- We must train people in explicit ways to become better thinkers.
- Therefore, education is the process of making people better thinkers.

B. Education is the process of changing the brain.

- Learning prompts the brain to take on increasingly challenging stimuli.
- The brain changes to accommodate new stimuli.
- The act of learning actually changes the brain's structure—how the brain works.
- Therefore, education is the process of changing the brain.

Each premise may require support of its own, such as examples, analogies, statistics, scenarios, and so on. The arguments, then, would move slowly, treating each premise as a mini-argument. Without some development of these premises, the arguments would likely fail. Readers wouldn't see the rationale for accepting the definitions.

ANALOGICAL REASONING allows writers to compare two things, to argue that if those two things are alike in certain respects, they are also alike in other respects. In his essay, Andrew Hyde works to define punk. In the following passage, he borrows some analogical reasoning from a source:

> Dick Hebdige's *Style in Revolt: Revolting Style* describes punk fashion as correlating with the artistic Dada movement of the 1910s and '20s, and specifically Marcel Duchamp's "ready-mades." Hebdige explains how punks used similar items for the same purpose: "The most unremarkable and inappropriate items—a pin, a plastic clothes peg, a television component, a razor blade, a tampon—could be brought within the province of punk (un)fashion" (107). Not only did punks draw fashion ideas from Dada, but political and social views as well. The Dada movement was a response to the Great War. Artists were disgusted with the events of the time, and made a statement by proclaiming insignificance.

This is an important move in Hyde's essay. The comparison to Dadaism allows him to articulate the political dimension of punk. Even though the Dadaist movement occurred decades before punk rock, it shares a number of social and aesthetic qualities. Hyde goes on to make the case that understanding Dadaism is a key to understanding punk.

APPEALS TO VALUE make a connection between the topic and a value such as fairness, equality, duty, or responsibility. Although the appeal to value is more often used in arguments of value or crisis, it can promote or give urgency to a definition; it can prompt people to see why a particular definition *should be* accepted. For example, Margaret Mead's argument urges readers to see the moral benefits to accepting her definition of warfare:

There is further needed a belief that social invention is possible and the invention of new methods which will render warfare as out of date as the tractor is making the plough, or the motor car the horse and buggy. A form of behavior becomes out of date only when something else takes its place, and, in order to invent forms of behavior which will make war obsolete, it is a first requirement to believe that an invention is possible.

Mead attaches an important value to her definition. Likewise, Andrew Hyde attaches a positive value to the original notion of punk and a negative value to its corporate-sponsored notions. For Hyde, the corporate-sponsored version of punk misses an important social quality: the denial of manipulation and conformity:

By creating a slickly manufactured image of punk, Hot Topic takes a movement that previously rejected conformity, and twists it into a fashion trend. Just when true punk was beginning to scratch the surface of the mainstream, it was buried by the music that goes along with this fashionably slanted image of punk. Hot Topic and similar corporations seem to enjoy keeping America's youth in check in order to further manipulate fashion trends and make another buck. It would seem that punks would rise up and simply boycott the store, putting them out of business. However, the punks who would be willing to boycott the store already avoid it at all costs. Luckily for Hot Topic, the target market consists of kids who have no interest in punk's deeply rooted anti-capitalist ideals.

EXAMPLES, specific cases or illustrations of phenomena, may be the most valuable support strategy in this project. Directing attention to particular examples can help show important aspects of your definition. Margaret Mead, for instance, relies on two particular examples:

The case for warfare is much clearer because there are peoples even today who have no warfare. Of these the Eskimos are perhaps the most conspicuous examples, but the Lepchas of Sikkim . . . are as good. Neither of these peoples understands war, not even defensive warfare.

Mead then goes on to detail the Eskimo and Lepcha cultures, further explaining how they support the idea that war is a human invention, not a universal trait.

SCENARIOS, hypothetical or fictional accounts, can help illustrate important layers of your definition. Writers often invite readers to imagine situations that focus attention on particularly relevant information. For instance, notice how James constructs a scenario to support his take on *education:*

For example, a student who is taught to explore the meaning of revolutions, to imagine the connection between the Revolutionary War and the Civil War, will ultimately have a deeper understanding of history than the student who is asked to memorize the dates of the decisive battles in each war. When a student is asked "Why did people in both wars want to free themselves from another government?" she is given an opportunity to think about the motivations of real people and to discover connections. But under the yoke of standardized tests, teachers are obliged to pump students full of facts and then move to test-taking (performance) strategies.

Notice that James does more than describe the scenario; he also relates it to the standardized test problem, which gives his argument some context. Because scenarios are entirely created by the writer, they can be very persuasive. With a scenario, a writer can focus readers' attention on a particular situation that illustrates the exact nature of the point.

ALLUSIONS are references to bits of public knowledge (from history, current events, popular culture, religion, or literature). They invite an audience to consider a commonly known reference and see its relevance to the argument. Allusions are persuasive because audiences feel like they are reminded of something that they have held in the backs of their minds; when an arguer makes a connection to a familiar point in history, a line in a song, or a scene from a movie, the audience is apt to follow along with the thinking. In his essay on punk, Andrew Hyde relies heavily on pop culture allusions:

> Regardless of choice in music, teens are losing interest in important issues across the country. What was once the politically active pop music of Creedence Clearwater Revival, Neil Young, or even the Grateful Dead has become Ashlee Simpson and Kelly Clarkson. Country was once very socially minded with the lyrics of Johnny Cash and Willie Nelson, but is now interested in beer and women. Hip-hop used to consist of NWA and the Beastie Boys, who both spoke up for civil rights. Rap has now become obsessed with money, demonstrated by 50 Cent's new movie, *Get Rich or Die Tryin'*.

Hyde assumes his readers know the difference between Neil Young and Ashlee Simpson—between a politically outspoken songwriter and a mainstream pop singer. He assumes that readers understand how Young represents one way of thinking and Simpson another, so he does not give details about their songs.

LITERARY WORKS are a particular type of allusion. Writers often borrow the words of poets, songwriters, playwrights, and fiction writers to lend heft and credibility to their own ideas. Sometimes, the words are directly related to the writer's argument as in Andrew Hyde's essay. The song lyrics he gives directly support his main claim about the nature of punk. Notice how Hyde first sets up the lyrics by explaining their significance:

> Through the 1980s, punk became even more political. With bands like T.S.O.L., Social Distortion, and Operation Ivy, the movement focused on social issues that were not being acknowledged by the Reagan administration. Tax codes were changed in a way to benefit the rich, while social policy moved away from helping the poor. This hate for Republican conservatism may have been expressed best by the Dead Kennedys:
>
> The sun beams down on a brand new day
> No more welfare tax to pay
> Unsightly slums gone up in flashing light
> Jobless millions whisked away
> At last we have more room to play
> All systems go to kill the poor tonight

Most often literary works are used more indirectly—not to show the particular sentiments of a decade but to orient the reader's thoughts. And one of the common applications is the epigraph: a short quoted passage that occurs before an essay. The epigraph floats above the argument and functions like a sign to readers: before entering the argument, consider this broader point. For example, in his essay about the economy, John de Graaf begins with an epigraph from a contemporary novel:

> "If they can get you asking the wrong question, they don't have to worry about the answers." —Thomas Pynchon, *Gravity's Rainbow*

The quotation from *Gravity's Rainbow* says nothing directly about de Graaf's topic. But it helps to establish a broader point in de Graaf's argument: that most people have been duped into thinking the wrong thing about the economy.

As you consider your topic, use the following questions to help create support:

▶ What line of reasoning must people follow to accept this definition?

▶ What examples best illustrate my understanding of the topic?

▶ What hypothetical situations can I create to illustrate my point?

▶ What other real situations might make useful comparisons to my topic? What references to history, literature, nature, current events, or popular culture help to illustrate something important about the topic?

▶ How might a literary passage illustrate the point or function as an epigraph to orient the reader's thinking?

▶ Why is it important (good, fair, practical, fulfilling, honest, moral) to accept this definition?

ARRANGEMENT

WHERE SHOULD I GIVE MY DEFINITION? Your definition might appear early and then get developed throughout the rest of your argument. This direct approach can help the reader more easily understand the support that comes later. But the direct approach is not always preferable. Some situations might call for the new definition to come later, after the reader has been introduced to some key ideas or even an entire line of reasoning. For instance, Andrew Hyde uses most of his argument to explain the seemingly inexplicable nature of punk. He details the differences between the past political movements and the recent fashion trends. He even argues that the nature of punk cannot be packaged and easily consumed. And toward the end of his argument, only after he has complicated the readers' thinking, he firms up the idea:

> Punk makes a simple statement by questioning authority and not accepting the status quo.

And in his final paragraph, he goes one step further toward concretizing the abstraction:

> And beneath the fashion parades, the real punks will be chafing against and kicking over whatever is hailed as lovely, admirable, and attractive. And maybe there is one thing we can say for sure: whatever punk is or will be, it sure as hell won't be pretty.

Hyde's essay illustrates the point that a main claim—in this case, a -definition—should come only when readers are ready for it.

HOW SHOULD I COUNTER OPPOSING DEFINITIONS? Any term can be defined in various ways, and a sound argument will counter(argue) or refute opposing definitions. As in most arguments, the opposition can be dealt with in a number of ways, even at the beginning of the essay. For example, Margaret Mead begins her essay with three views of warfare. Her first two paragraphs detail the logic of those views, and then she offers a counter:

All three of these positions are very popular today among those who think seriously about the problems of war and its possible prevention, but I wish to urge another point of view, less defeatist, perhaps, than the first and third and more accurate than the second. . . .

Mead then goes on to develop her definition against others' logic. She pushes off against them into her own argument. This is a standard, and powerful, move in all forms of argument.

DOES A CONCESSION OR QUALIFIER HAVE TO GO IN EVERY ARGUMENT? Conceding and qualifying are valuable argumentative strategies: they show readers that a writer is listening and dealing with the complexities of an issue instead of oversimplifying it. Most credible arguments acknowledge their own weaknesses as well as the validity of certain opposing views. As Andrew Hyde shows, even an essay about punk can concede points. Although Hyde laments the loss of political edge in popular music, he concedes some ground:

> This is not to say that people cannot listen to Green Day if they do not agree with the message. In fact, it is a wonderful feeling to continue to enjoy something that conflicts with your own beliefs. This is also by no means to say that all music must be politically minded. In fact, not all "real" punk music is politically minded. Punk makes a simple statement by questioning authority and not accepting the status quo. And even with that consistent principle, punk is always changing.

Concessions (and counterarguments) reveal a writer who is engaging other points of view and therefore interacting with readers, not just speaking at them. While concessions are not always required, and making unimportant concessions can be a harmful distraction, writers should explore what concessions they might make in order to strengthen their argument. Not conceding points that should be conceded weakens an argument.

HOW MANY OTHER DEFINITIONS SHOULD I INCLUDE? You may include just one or several other definitions in your argument. To decide, reflect on your reason for writing. If you are arguing for a particular definition, then you are responding to some other definition(s). Mead, for example, sees a need to push against three popular definitions, or "positions," for the basis of warfare. As you develop your own argument, consider other, perhaps flawed, definitions or ways of thinking, and address them in your argument. While you might respond only to one main definition, you might respond to several other definitions as well. For your own topic, ask the following questions:

- ▶ What do readers need to know before getting my definition?
- ▶ Do readers need to hear about a particular situation before they understand the nature of my argument?
- ▶ If I start with someone else's definition (or way of thinking about the topic), what will that show? Good thinking? Bad thinking?

AUDIENCE AND VOICE

Unless it's a part of some daring writing strategy, be careful not to offend the reader. The way you say it is as important as what you say. Identify words, phrases, and sentences that may sound rude or insulting. Be confident but not overbearing. Remember, you are arguing to persuade, to influence the reader's way of thinking. Readers nearly always tune out a harsh or insensitive voice, and they are less likely to be influenced by an insecure or wishy-washy one.

The language you choose can influence how your readers feel as they move through your argument. Imagine your audience—specific people, with particular beliefs and opinions. And imagine how they might come to your argument: bored, uninterested, focused, unfocused, skeptical, hopeful. Following are a few strategies to consider:

FORMALITY Depending on your readers and their relationship with the topic, formality can elevate the reading experience and make the topic itself feel important and worthy of serious attention. Formality can be created by careful word choice. Notice the difference between these two sentences:

> For this, two things have to happen.

> For this, two conditions, at least, are necessary. (Margaret Mead)

The difference between the words themselves can create a subtle shift in formality. However, more formal writing does not always depend on sophisticated vocabulary. Ornate language can over-formalize a text and render it weak. Imagine a comparison to clothing: A suit and tie are more formal than blue jeans and a T-shirt. But a suit and tie, with a sparkling silver top hat, a golden cape, and a jewel-studded walking cane is, in most situations, overly dramatic, and therefore less appropriate. Like a person, language can be overdressed, even gaudy.

Formal writing avoids slang or excessive figurative language—phrases that draw attention to themselves or go beyond literal meaning:

> After emerging from the primordial goo, humans were probably not marrying each other or singing songs around a fire.

> At some point in his social development man was undoubtedly without the institution of marriage or the knowledge of the use of fire. (Margaret Mead)

The first sentence uses a particularly vivid image, "primordial goo," to communicate an idea. The phrase itself lends a kind of informality to the point. The second sentence, from Mead's essay, makes a similar point but does so with more restrained and formal language.

INFORMALITY As you might infer from the preceding passages, informal writing may employ street language, slang, and everyday figurative language. Informality can also be created with attention to the writer and to the writer's own thinking, as in this passage from Andrew Hyde's essay:

> I spent a year living in Midland, Texas, during the 2004 presidential election. At the same time, Green Day's new album *American Idiot* was released. While riding my motorcycle on a hot summer day, I was stopped at a traffic light next to a man in his early twenties. For the next 40 seconds, all I heard was his voice over a radio blaring Green Day's title track from the most recent album: . . .
>
> For a moment I was relieved. I thought that maybe people were catching on to current issues and possibly even thinking for themselves. My moment was over as I realized the context of the situation. The young man was sitting in a jacked-up two-wheel-drive truck, wearing a cowboy hat. The truck brandished stickers and magnets pledging allegiance to President Bush, and promising to support our troops. More stickers explained that marriage belongs between only a man and a woman, and that abortion is a mortal sin. The vehicle and driver seemed to be a rolling contradiction.

The personal testimony helps support Hyde's premise about punk, but it also establishes an informal voice, which works with the nature of Hyde's topic and position.

INFORMALITY/FORMALITY Writers are always creating voices; they tweak word choice, sentence structure, and figurative language to account for the particular situation. Even the most zany writer can (and should!) heed formal expectations when the situation calls for it. Most academic writers walk a middle road between formal and informal. They want to keep important ideas elevated with formal moves, but also keep readers awake with subtle cues and nudges. Justin James's essay walks this fine line. He maintains a sober and serious tone; he keeps metaphors to a minimum; and he draws little attention to his own presence. But he also keeps sentences varied and lively:

> Today's No Child Left Behind testing is redefining *education*. This new definition is harmful. People are coming to believe that education is primarily about practicing and performing on exams—not about developing curiosity and exploring vast possibilities. But in an environment (a definition) where they can explore, students thrive; teachers thrive; learning thrives. Standardized tests squelch all that. They should be used modestly. It is not that opponents of standardized testing are for throwing standards out the window. And it's not that they think all testing is bad. They simply believe the more valuable definition of *education* promotes curiosity, not practice and perform.

REVISION

Inventing claims and support involves hard mental work. As you prepare your draft for Peer Review, return to the Invention questions and respond more fully. This can be a valuable way to fill in gaps, or to see some aspect of your thinking in a different way. Remember, as you responded to these questions earlier, you were thinking about them for the first time. Now that you have developed your thinking, you can return to those same questions and explore them from a different, more informed, point of view.

RESEARCH AND REVISION: If you used outside sources, consider the following questions. As you revise, refer to the corresponding pages in Chapters 13 and 14:

- Have you used research as means of discovery? (pp. 309–328)
- Have you evaluated sources for ideology, reliability, relevance, timeliness, and diversity? (pp. 329–338)
- Are the ideas from outside sources integrated smoothly into your ideas? (pp. 338–349)
- Are the sources documented appropriately (with in-text and end citations)? (pp. 350–375)

Peer Review

Exchange drafts with at least one other writer. (If time allows, exchange with two or three writers to gather a range of perspectives or comments.) Use the following questions to generate specific constructive comments about others' drafts:

1. Does the argument focus on a definition? Does it get to the defining characteristics of the topic—and avoid slipping into an argument about its value?

2. Identify the writer's claim. Can it be further narrowed and more revelatory? Does it offer a clear way of seeing the topic?

3. What is the most supportive passage in the argument? Describe why it works well in the argument.

4. Examine the logic of the argument. A successful argument will establish distinct qualities or defining characteristics for the topic (for example, education is X, Y, Z—not Q, R, S). These characteristics will then be illustrated in some particular fashion. Does the writer give specific qualities or defining characteristics that support the claim?

5. Look out for vague or overly general passages. Where could the writer use more allusions, examples, scenarios, or testimony to illustrate specific points? For example, rather than a broad phrase ("reality shows are about uncertainty"), could the writer describe how uncertainty plays into the specific components of a show?

6. The writer should have already engaged opposing perspectives, other opinions about the definition. But what other opposing points could the writer address? Can you imagine further objections to the argument?

7. Should the writer concede or qualify any points? Do you sense any passages that make the writer's argument seem too unwavering and narrow-minded? How would a concession or qualifier help that passage?

8. Rewrite the introduction to the argument. Even if the present introduction seems appropriate, write a totally new paragraph that demands attention while also bringing the reader into the argument's particular logic. (This rewrite may then prompt the writer to try something equally engaging and fresh.)

9. Check for paragraph coherence: Identify any paragraphs that seem to shift focus or take on too many separate points without a clear line of reasoning.

10. Are sources integrated smoothly, rather than being forced into passages? Explain any gaps between the writer's line of reasoning and the ideas from an outside source. (See pp. 338–349.)

Enigma/Alamy

8

Arguing Causes

Why Did This Happen?

Asking *Why?* is fundamental to human existence. Why does lightning strike? Why do hurricanes hit during a particular time of year? Why are school shootings on the rise? Why do bad things happen to good people? Answers to these questions are a form of argument. They are assertions about causes, and different perspectives will generate different answers to the question *Why did this happen?*

We can look back through history and see a range of interesting causal arguments:

- Lightning strikes because God is angry.
- Women aren't as educated as men because they have smaller brains.
- People get sick because their humors are out of balance.
- The crops failed because a witch lives among the villagers.

Today, we realize the deeply flawed logic in such claims. But even contemporary arguments about causes can be suspicious. What caused the attacks on 9/11? Consider some of the following answers: God was punishing our culture for promoting feminism and homosexuality; the terrorists hate freedom; the U.S. government wanted a reason to increase its military presence in the Middle East. Political commentators, religious figures, bloggers, and even politicians have forwarded these arguments. Of course, the real causes are far more complex—and we have probably not yet heard all the political and cultural factors that led to the attacks.

In any career, probing for causes is critical to success. People at the top of business organizations constantly make causal arguments: they try to discover the cause of decreased sales, increased sales, increased competition, consumer behavior, and so on. And then they have to persuade others that X, not Y, caused sales to shoot downward. In short, the executive is paid to find out why things happen, to persuade others of certain causes, and to direct his or her organization to benefit from those causes. Arguments about causes constitute everyday work across career fields and academic disciplines:

- Business executives meet at the beginning of the quarter and ask: *Why are we suddenly losing market share?*
- A group of political scientists probe the reasons behind the rise of the Tea Party movement.
- Environmental scientists pile up evidence showing that fossil fuel emissions and deforestation are the primary causes of global warming.
- Cultural theorists and sociologists ask, *Why do so many Americans dismiss or ignore the claims of science?*
- A group of psychologists probe for the cause of school shootings.

Sometimes, the most obvious causal arguments are the most flawed: The student failed because she didn't work hard enough; the candidate lost because people didn't like his policies; the company failed because it lacked focus. While such statements have a ring of truth, they may conceal more important causes. The student may have failed because she didn't know how to work hard; the candidate may have lost because voters were distracted by mischaracterizations and phony appeals; the company may have failed because it miscalculated the power of transnational competitors. In any organization, academic discipline, or public situation, the most valuable contributions often come from those who can look beyond the obvious causes and make a case for some lurking cause, some factor that others might overlook. Such contributions take inventive thinking and well-wrought arguments.

No Sex Please, We're Middle Class

CAMILLE PAGLIA

We may have a range of gut reactions to a product like Viagra for women. We might judge its worth, necessity, potential effectiveness. But Camille Paglia goes causal. She inspects the reasons for decreased female libido. Rather than think in medical terms, Paglia explores the material conditions, the everyday lives, of middle-class women. She builds up a forceful argument about the real causes—those that are beyond the reach of medical science.

Will women soon have a Viagra of their own? Although a Food and Drug Administration advisory panel recently rejected an application to market the drug flibanserin in the United States for women with low libido, it endorsed the potential benefits and urged further research. Several pharmaceutical companies are reported to be well along in the search for such a drug.

The implication is that a new pill, despite its unforeseen side effects, is necessary to cure the sexual malaise that appears to have sunk over the country. But to what extent do these complaints about sexual apathy reflect a medical reality, and how much do they actually emanate from the anxious, overachieving, white upper middle class?

In the 1950s, female "frigidity" was attributed to social conformism and religious puritanism. But since the sexual revolution of the 1960s, American society has become increasingly secular, with a media environment drenched in sex.

The real culprit, originating in the 19th century, is bourgeois propriety. As respectability became the central middle-class value, censorship and repression became the norm. Victorian prudery ended the humorous sexual candor of both men and women during the agrarian era, a ribaldry chronicled from Shakespeare's plays to the 18th-century novel. The

priggish 1950s, which erased the liberated flappers of the Jazz Age from cultural memory, were simply a return to the norm.

Only the diffuse New Age movement, inspired by nature-keyed Asian practices, has preserved the radical vision of the modern sexual revolution. But concrete power resides in America's careerist technocracy, for which the elite schools, with their ideological view of gender as a social construct, are feeder cells.

In the discreet white-collar realm, men and women are interchangeable, doing the same, mind-based work. Physicality is suppressed; voices are lowered and gestures curtailed in sanitized office space. Men must neuter themselves, while ambitious women postpone procreation. Androgyny is bewitching in art, but in real life it can lead to stagnation and boredom, which no pill can cure.

Meanwhile, family life has put middle-class men in a bind; they are simply cogs in a domestic machine commanded by women. Contemporary moms have become virtuoso super-managers of a complex operation focused on the care and transport of children. But it's not so easy to snap over from Apollonian control to Dionysian delirium.

Nor are husbands offering much stimulation in the male display department: visually, American men remain perpetual boys, as shown by the bulky T-shirts, loose shorts and sneakers they wear from preschool through midlife. The sexes, which used to occupy intriguingly separate worlds, are suffering from over-familiarity, a curse of the mundane. There's no mystery left.

The elemental power of sexuality has also waned in American popular culture. Under the much-maligned studio production code, Hollywood made movies sizzling with flirtation and romance. But from the early '70s on, nudity was in, and steamy build-up was out. A generation of filmmakers lost the skill of sophisticated innuendo. The situation worsened in the '90s, when Hollywood pirated video games to turn women into cartoonishly pneumatic superheroines and sci-fi androids, fantasy figures without psychological complexity or the erotic needs of real women.

10   Furthermore, thanks to a bourgeois white culture that values efficient bodies over voluptuous ones, American actresses have desexualized themselves, confusing sterile athleticism with female power. Their current Pilates-honed look is taut and tense—a boy's thin limbs and narrow hips combined with amplified breasts. Contrast that with Latino and African-American taste, which runs toward the healthy silhouette of the bootylicious Beyoncé.

A class issue in sexual energy may be suggested by the apparent striking popularity of Victoria's Secret and its racy lingerie among multiracial lower-middle-class and working-class patrons, even in suburban shopping malls, which otherwise trend toward the white middle class. Country music, with its history in the rural South and Southwest, is still filled with blazingly raunchy scenarios, where the sexes remain dynamically polarized in the old-fashioned way.

On the other hand, rock music, once sexually pioneering, is in the dumps. Black rhythm and blues, born in the Mississippi Delta, was the driving force behind the great hard rock bands of the '60s, whose cover versions of blues songs were filled with electrifying sexual imagery. The Rolling Stones' hypnotic recording of Willie Dixon's "Little Red Rooster," with its titillating phallic exhibitionism, throbs and shimmers with sultry heat.

But with the huge commercial success of rock, the blues receded as a direct influence on young musicians, who simply imitated the white guitar gods without exploring their roots. Step by step, rock lost its visceral rawness and seductive sensuality.

Big-ticket rock, with its well-heeled middle-class audience, is now all superego and no id.

In the 1980s, commercial music boasted a beguiling host of sexy pop chicks like Deborah Harry, Belinda Carlisle, Pat Benatar, and a charmingly ripe Madonna. Late Madonna, in contrast, went bourgeois and turned scrawny. Madonna's dance-track acolyte, Lady Gaga, with her compulsive overkill, is a high-concept fabrication without an ounce of genuine eroticism.

Pharmaceutical companies will never find the 15 holy grail of a female Viagra—not in this culture driven and drained by middle-class values. Inhibitions are stubbornly internal. And lust is too fiery to be left to the pharmacist.

Analyzing Argument

1. What is Paglia's main claim? And how does her line of reasoning support that claim?

2. How is Paglia doing more than arguing cause? How is she making subtle judgments (claims of value) about the cause of women's decreased libido? Point to a particular passage where she condemns, even in subtle terms, the lives of middle-class women.

3. How do the allusions to rock music figure into Paglia's argument? What is their purpose? What point (premise) do they support?

4. How does Paglia engage opposition? To answer this, you might first decide on the opposition. What perspective or claims does Paglia seem to be opposing? How does she counter or concede or qualify?

5. What does Paglia mean by a "culture drained by middle-class values," and why is such a phrase important to her argument?

Disparities Demystified

PEDRO A. NOGUERA AND ANTWI AKOM

The following argument first appeared in *The Nation*, a political magazine, in June of 2000. As Noguera and Akom explain, their argument emerged from an ongoing set of events: Standardized tests consistently revealed an achievement gap between ethnic groups, despite national programs to address this gap. In a time of heated debates about affirmative action and college enrollment policies, the authors try to cut through the argumentative fog and explain the causes behind the persistent achievement gap.

Once again national attention is focused on the racial gap in academic achievement, thanks in part to the high-stakes tests now in vogue across the nation. The appearance of this racial gap is by no means a new development. For years, African-American, Latino, and Native American students have lagged far behind their white and Asian peers on most standardized tests. The gap is also present in graduation and dropout rates, grades, and most other measures of student performance. The consistency of such patterns in almost every school and district in the country has the effect of reinforcing well-established assumptions regarding the relationship between race, academic ability, and intelligence.

More often than not, explanations for the achievement gap focus on deficiencies among parents and students. Dysfunctional families, lazy and unmotivated students, and the "culture of poverty" in inner-city neighborhoods are all frequently cited as causes of the gap. Left overlooked and unaddressed are the conditions under which children are educated and the quality of schools they attend. Since popular explanations often determine the types of remedies that are pursued, it is not surprising that the renewed attention directed toward the racial gap in academic achievement has not led to calls to address the real problem: inequality in education.

First, it's important to recognize that achievement test results reflect more than just racial disparities. An analysis of test scores also reveals a close correspondence between the scores children obtain and broader patterns of social inequality. With few exceptions, children of the affluent outperform children of the poor. Explaining why poor children of color perform comparatively less well in school is relatively easy: Consistently, such children are educated in schools that are woefully inadequate on most measures of quality and funding. This is particularly true in economically depressed urban areas, where bad schools are just one of many obstacles with which poor people must contend. Parents often perceive inner-city public schools as hopeless and unresponsive to their needs, prompting those who can to opt for private schools. Many have also actively sought alternatives through vouchers and various privatization schemes.

Yet what makes the racial gap uniquely paradoxical is the fact that the benefits typically associated with middle-class status don't accrue to African-American and, in many cases, Latino students. In many school districts, children of color from middle-class, college-educated families lag significantly behind white students in most achievement measures. The performance of these relatively privileged students has brought renewed attention to the relationship between race and educational performance. This is the issue that has prompted fifteen racially integrated, affluent school districts to form a consortium called the Minority Student Achievement Network. With the support of researchers assembled by the College Board, the network, comprising districts in such communities as White Plains, New York, Ann Arbor, Michigan, and Berkeley, California, seeks to understand the causes of the racial achievement gap and to devise solutions for reversing it.

On the face of it, the potential for success in 5 reducing the gap in these districts would seem high.

All fifteen school districts in the network have a track record of sending large numbers of affluent white students to the best colleges and universities in the country. Additionally, unlike schools in high-poverty areas, funding is largely not a major obstacle to reform. Each district is located in an affluent community with a highly educated population known for its commitment to liberal political and social values. Yet in all fifteen districts there is a persistent, deeply ingrained sense that even this ambitious and well-intentioned effort will fail to alter student outcomes.

The pessimism in these districts, and in others that have launched efforts to overcome the racial achievement gap, must be understood in historical context. In many areas greater emphasis has been placed on how to achieve racial integration in schools than on how to serve the educational needs of a diverse student population. Even in the liberal districts in the Minority Student Achievement Network, some of which were among the first in the nation to voluntarily desegregate, the arrival of significant numbers of students of color in the late sixties and early seventies met with considerable opposition. From the very beginning, the presence of African-American children, especially those from low-income families, was perceived as an intrusion, and because the children were perceived

as disadvantaged and deficient in comparison with their white schoolmates, educating them has always been regarded as a challenge. Since students of color were framed as "problems" and "challenges" from the very start, it is hardly surprising that they would continue to be treated as a problem requiring special intervention years later.

Moreover, educational practices often have the effect of favoring white students and hindering the educational opportunities of African-Americans and Latinos. This is particularly true when it comes to tracking and sorting students on the basis of ability. A large body of research has shown that students of color are more likely to be excluded from classes for those deemed gifted in primary school, and from honors and Advanced Placement (AP) courses in high school. The Education Trust has shown, through its research on science and math education, that even students of color who meet the criteria for access to advanced courses are more likely to be turned away based on the recommendation of a counselor or teacher. They are also more likely to be placed in remedial and special-education classes, and to be subject to varying forms of school discipline.

A close examination of access to AP courses in California reveals how certain educational practices contribute to the maintenance of the racial achievement gap. Since the mid-eighties, the number of AP courses available to students at high schools in California has tripled. This increase has been attributed to a 1984 decision by the University of California to give greater weight to the grades earned by students who enroll in AP courses. However, AP courses are not uniformly available to students. At some inner-city and rural schools, few if any such courses are offered, while at private and affluent suburban schools, it is not uncommon for students to have access to fifteen or more AP courses. Moreover, our own research at Berkeley High School has shown that even when minority students are enrolled at schools that do offer a large number of AP courses, they are more likely to be actively discouraged from taking them by teachers and counselors.

© Cengage Learning®

Beyond the policies and practices that contribute to the achievement gap, a number of complex cultural factors are also important. Missing from the research and policy debates is an understanding of the ways in which children come to perceive the relationship between their racial identity and what they believe they can do academically. For many children, schools play an important role in shaping their racial identities because they are one of the few social settings where kids interact with people from different backgrounds. To the extent that a school's sorting processes disproportionately relegate black and brown children to spaces within schools that are perceived as negative and marginal, it is likely that children of color will come to perceive certain activities and courses as either suitable or off-limits for them.

10   In schools where few minority students are enrolled in AP courses, even students who meet the criteria for enrollment may refuse to take such courses out of concern that they will become isolated from their peers. The same is true for the school band, newspaper, debating team, or honor society. When these activities are seen as the domain of white students, nonwhite students are less likely to join. Peer groups play a large role in determining the academic orientation of students, not to mention their style of clothes, manner of speech, and future career aspirations. For middle-class African-American and Latino students, this means that despite receiving encouragement from their parents to do well in school, the peer group with whom they identify may push them in a different direction.

There are also cultural factors related to the attitudes and behaviors of students and the childrearing practices of parents that influence student performance. Several studies, for example, have indicated that middle-class African-American and Latino students spend less time on homework and study in less effective ways than middle-class white and Asian students. Also, despite the visibility of African-American students in sports such as football and basketball, research shows that these students are less likely to be involved in other extracurricular activities (which are shown to positively influence achievement), and in their responses to surveys they are more likely to emphasize the importance of being popular among friends than doing well in school.

Finally, images rooted in racial stereotypes that permeate American society limit the aspirations of African-American and Latino students. Despite the daunting odds of success in professional sports and entertainment, many young people of color believe they have a greater chance of becoming a highly paid athlete or hip-hop artist than an engineer, doctor, or software programmer. And with the rollback of affirmative action at colleges and universities, there is little doubt that students who possess entertainment value to universities, who can slam-dunk or score touchdowns, will be admitted regardless of their academic performance, even as aspiring doctors and lawyers are turned away.

When placed within the broader context of race relations in American society, the causes of the racial achievement gap appear less complex and mysterious; the gap is merely another reflection of the disparities in experience and life chances for individuals from different racial groups. In fact, given the history of racism in the United States and the ongoing reality of racial discrimination, it would be more surprising if an achievement gap did not exist. If the children of those who are most likely to be incarcerated, denied housing and employment, passed over for promotions, or harassed by the police did just as well in school as those whose lives are largely free of such encumbrances, that would truly be remarkable news.

Lest recognition of the racial achievement gap drive us into greater despair about the prospects for eliminating racial inequality in America, we must also recognize that to the extent change is possible, it is more likely to occur in education than in any other sector. This is because despite its faults, public education remains the most democratic and accessible institution in the country. In fact, in the post–welfare reform period, it is virtually all that remains of the social safety net for poor children.

15   Moreover, there are schools where no achievement gap exists, and there are students who achieve at high levels despite the incredible odds facing them. These bright spots of success reveal what might be possible if we lived in a society that truly valued children and was genuinely committed to equity and high-quality education for all.

Realizing such an ideal would require a comprehensive effort to reverse the effects of racial and economic inequality in the classroom, but it might begin with a few basic, though costly, measures: (1) significantly raising salaries so that teaching would be an attractive career for the best college graduates; (2) ensuring that poor children have access to well-qualified teachers from diverse racial and ethnic backgrounds, and to schools with adequate resources; and (3) providing parents in low-income areas with the means to exert greater influence over the schools their children attend. These are not radical measures. Indeed, they are already features of schools in most middle-class suburban communities. But bringing them to low-income areas would require states to address the huge disparities in funding that arise from the way schools are financed throughout the country. Since the electoral defeat of former New Jersey governor Jim Florio in 1993—the last major elected official to make a serious attempt to address such inequities—few have been willing to take on this critical issue.

Despite the defeats such measures have suffered in the courts and at the polls, politicians do recognize that the public is deeply concerned about improving the quality of education, and as they clamor to position themselves as friends and supporters of education we must demand that they address questions of equity. For those of us who believe that public education can serve as a source of hope and opportunity, the time is ripe for making our voices heard so this historic opportunity is not missed.

Analyzing Argument

1. What is Noguera and Akom's main claim?

2. How do Noguera and Akom address other perspectives and claims on this topic? Choose two passages in which they directly take on other views and describe their strategy. In the face of opposition, are they counterarguing, conceding, or qualifying their own claims?

3. How does Noguera and Akom's assertion relate to mainstream views on this topic? How do they address any differences or gaps between their assertions and mainstream views?

4. What is the most persuasive support strategy in the argument? Why? (Consider different appeals, different forms of evidence and examples.)

5. Examine paragraphs three through six. What is the line of reasoning in those paragraphs? Try to summarize each paragraph in a single sentence and then detect how the logic builds from paragraph to paragraph.

More Than Cherries

SAMANTHA TENGELITSCH

Samantha Tengelitsch lives in the top cherry-producing region in the United States. As an ecologically minded writer, mother, and community member, she wondered about the connection between agricultural chemicals and human health. After a local woman was diagnosed with cancer, Tengelitsch began researching that connection. She originally wrote this essay for her college English class. The following semester, the project won first place in the Michigan Liberal Arts Network for Development (LAND) essay contest. A year after researching and writing this project, Tengelitsch herself was diagnosed with non-Hodgkin's lymphoma. After intensive treatments, she is doing well.

I must find a man who still loves the soil
Walk by his side unseen, pour in his mind
What I loved when I lived until he builds
Sows, reaps, and covers these hill pastures here
With sheep and cattle, mows the meadowland
Grafts the old orchard again, makes it bear again
Knowing that we are lost if the land does not yield.
— *Jeanne Robert Foster*

Each year, an estimated 500,000 people pass through Traverse City, Michigan, for the annual National Cherry Festival. They come here for the pristine national lakeshore, to explore and hike the sand dunes, to taste wine at the local vineyards, and to see our native wildlife. They come for the serenity of a region tucked away in the northern Lower Peninsula, to escape the rigor of their daily lives. And in July they come for the world's largest celebration of cherries, the National Cherry Festival.

What began in the 1920s as a "Blessing of the Blossoms" has grown into a multimillion-dollar event. Last year alone, the National Cherry Festival is said to have contributed over 26 million dollars to the area's revenue (Rodgers). According to Susan Olson, Media Relations Director for the National Cherry Festival, over 40,000 pounds of cherries are sold during the week-long festival and local growers account for 75% of tart cherries grown around the world, just a few of many reasons Traverse City is known as the "Cherry Capital of the World." However, three of the last twelve festivals have not sold local products (Olson). The festival is held the first week of July, to coincide with 4th of July weekend and local cherries are not always ready in time. In those years when there is a delay in production, the cherries must be imported from Washington state and other regions.

While on the surface the cherry festival is about cherries, it was once about something more: the families who worked to produce these cherries and the community where the cherries are grown. Some feel our local festival has outgrown the area. A recent editorial that ran in the Traverse City *Record Eagle* points out: "[L]ots of people have advocated returning to a smaller, less grandiose effort that more closely reflects the festivals they remember. . . ." ("C-Fest"). The festival no longer caters to local residents and growers, but instead focuses on larger crowds and higher revenues. And with this, the demand on farmers for cherries is great. This increase in demand has fostered an environment where farmers have grown dependent on chemical pesticides and fertilizers. And an increase in the use of pesticides and other toxic chemicals has left our once small farming community vulnerable to the dangers of exposure to these harsh chemicals.

It was the cherry festival that highlighted for me, not the pride we might feel in being well known for our cherry production, but the unrealistic expectations we have placed on local farmers. I began to look beyond revenue at the impacts of agriculture, and in particular cherry farming, on our region.

Last spring an article ran in the local paper about a young woman running for the prestigious title of National Cherry Queen. It told the story of Lauren Hemming, a twenty-year-old college student, who was raised on a Peninsula Township cherry farm and who was battling non-Hodgkin's lymphoma (a cancer of the lymphatic system) while running for the prestigious title. A photograph included with the article captured Lauren sitting cross-legged in a hammock in front of her home. It was spring and sun shown brightly. At the time of the photograph, Lauren was undergoing chemotherapy for the lymphoma and had lost her hair, but this in no way detracted from her beauty. Her story was inspirational and touched me as I'm sure it touched others.

Unfortunately, Lauren was not able to continue with her bid for Cherry Queen. Instead, she fought bravely to save her own life and the following winter died from the cancer, which had spread to her brain. I read her obituary and felt a deep sense of loss, not just for the young woman and her family, but also for our community. I questioned the origin of her illness and I began to wonder whether or not it was possible Lauren's illness might have been impacted by the use of chemical pesticides and fertilizers on and around her family farm. I decided to run a query of medical journals and websites to see whether a link existed between the lymphatic cancer and pesticides and was surprised at what I found.

According to the Pesticide Education Center website, non-Hodgkin's lymphoma is the cancer "most frequently associated with pesticide exposure and is now one of the most studied cancers in agriculture" (Moses). The Lymphoma Research Foundation says people exposed to chemicals such as pesticides or fertilizers are at higher risk for non-Hodgkin's lymphoma, or NHL. Over the last twenty-five years, the foundation reports, "new cases of NHL seen each year escalated almost 83%, among the highest increases of any cancer" ("Non-Hodgkin Lymphoma"). Twenty years earlier, agricultural communities like ours saw a parallel increase in the use of chemical pesticides and fertilizers. This corresponding increase caught the attention of researchers who began to question whether or not there existed a significant association between NHL and agricultural families.

A population-based, incidence case-control study which evaluated pesticide product use and the risk of non-Hodgkin's lymphoma in women addresses this correlation: "NHL has received research attention because the recent rapid increase in its incidence parallels an exponential growth in pesticide use with a few decades of lag" (Kato et al.). Researchers investigated other "high-risk" groups as well and found some correlation between these groups and NHL, but the most significant association was found in agricultural families. As one study reports:

> With increasing cumulative number of hours exposed to pesticides at these jobs other than farming, there was a marginal increasing trend in risk of NHL. When farming and other jobs associated with pesticide exposure were combined, the total duration at any of these jobs was significantly positively associated with the risk of NHL. (Kato et al.)

While pesticides sold in the United States must first be registered with the Environmental Protection Agency (EPA) and additionally in the states where they are being distributed for use, an EPA label does not in any way imply the product is safe for human exposure. The label discloses vital information about how the user might limit his or her exposure to the chemicals, directions for physicians treating people who have had significant exposure, and warnings of the environmental impact of each product. All pesticides must be labeled for legal sale disclosing the level of toxicity for humans (Smith), but the EPA does not require that pesticide manufacturers list the re-entry periods, or the amount of time that must pass before people can re-enter a treated area (Rindels-Larsen).

Children, as a result, may be more vulnerable 10 to exposure as they may unwittingly enter a treated area too early or because the residue of sprays may be present on the clothing or boots of family members. This factor may make children one of the most pesticide-exposed subgroups in the United States ("Trouble"). The National Institutes of Health (NIH), a government agency, conducted a study to evaluate risk factors for cancer in children exposed to pesticides. They released their findings last year, cautioning: "Identification of excess lymphoma risk suggests that farm exposures including pesticides may play a role in the etiology of childhood cancers" (Flower 631).

Organophosphates are found in pesticides commonly used by farmers today (Elsner). The Natural Resources Defense Council website reports: "Metabolites of organophosphates pesticides used only in agriculture were detectable in the urine of two out of every three children of agricultural workers and in four out of every ten children who simply live in an agricultural region" ("Trouble").

The Hemmings live in the heart of cherry country, Peninsula Township. The township was home to the region's first cherry farm one hundred and

Patti Adair/stockxchng.com

fifty years earlier, but with an increase in demand for cherries, farming techniques have changed since then. The land is weakening with this increase in demand and nutrients must be supplemented with chemical fertilizers. Pests are not controlled, but rather eliminated with insecticides that are harmful to people and to the environment. And while the orchard is an enticing place in the springtime for children, a time when the trees are in bloom and when workers are getting ready for the upcoming summer harvest, it can also present danger of exposure to these toxic compounds. Children playing outside the orchards may still be exposed to the residue of pesticides that may have drifted into their play area.

Organophosphates may vary in toxicity relative to exposure, but children exposed to organophosphates are at a particularly high risk as their livers are immature and unable to detoxify the poisonous compounds. Dr. Michael Collins of the Grand Traverse Health Department explains: "Since the child's liver will [detoxify] less effectively than an adult's, the result is that the chemical will stay in the body, in unaltered form, for a longer time than would be true for an adult. Thus whatever type of damage the chemical may do, it has more opportunity to do it." Most testing done today assesses the risk for adults, so little is known about long-term pesticide exposure in children.

In addition to chemical pesticides, orchards have become increasingly reliant on chemical fertilizers. These chemical fertilizers combined with run-off wastes from livestock and septic systems all contribute to higher levels of nitrogen in the ground. Nitrogen converts into nitrates, which pass through our permeable soil into the water table. An executive summary posted on the EPA website addressing nitrate pollution in groundwater reveals, "EPA found that nitrate is the most widespread agricultural contaminant in drinking water wells, and estimates that 4.5 million people are exposed to elevated nitrate levels from drinking water wells" ("Consumer Factsheet").

15   While some nitrates are naturally occurring and may be harmless, elevated levels may make people sick. As Leah Halfon writes, "Numerous epidemiological studies have shown higher nitrate concentrations to be associated with hyperthyroidism, non-Hodgkin's lymphoma, reproductive and developmental disorders, gastric cancer, neuropathy, and morbidity and mortality due to several other cancers."

    Nitrate levels that exceed the United States Environmental Protection Agency's 10 milligrams per liter may result in illness ("Consumer Factsheet"). Recently, a study was released from the Department of Environmental Quality (DEQ) to the (Grand Traverse) County Health Department that contained historical nitrate data for Grand Traverse County taken from between 1983 and 2003. According to Tom Buss, head of the Environmental Health Division for Grand Traverse County, "Our county equalization department printed a map of the county showing areas of nitrates in 'ranges.' The map does show the highest concentrations of nitrates in Peninsula Township, which has been heavily agricultural throughout the years." In more than one area on the peninsula, nitrate levels not only reached the EPA's warning level of 10 milligrams per liter, but in multiple areas levels exceeded 20 mg/L.

    Non-Hodgkin's lymphoma is one of many adverse health conditions associated with exposure to dangerous compounds like the ones mentioned previously. Various forms of cancer, neurological disorders, reproductive problems, birth defects, and spontaneous abortions have all been linked to long-term pesticide exposure (Moses) and elevated nitrate levels in groundwater. I chose to research non-Hodgkin's lymphoma and its link to agriculture because of a photograph of a Cherry Festival contestant; a young woman who grew up on a cherry farm in the heart of cherry country who died last winter from cancer. Did Lauren Hemming die from high nitrate levels or pesticide exposure in her youth? It is impossible for me to say with any certainty. Yet her story was the catalyst for my research; it inspired me to look further and in doing so, I discovered the true irony of her death.

    A new look at the local festival that has "blossomed" into a multimillion-dollar mega-event complete with corporate sponsors will reveal the real problem. We have created a large demand on local growers to produce a flawless product at a relatively low cost to consumers. In doing so, we have overused the land and weakened our soil and, in trying to supplement nutrients naturally found in healthy soil, we have poisoned our water and indirectly we may be poisoning ourselves.

    Bill McKibben, in his book *The Age of Missing Information*, writes that while it is said we are living in the Information Age, "we also live at a moment of deep ignorance, when vital knowledge that humans have always possessed about who we are and where we live seems beyond our reach. An Unenlightenment" (9). This "unenlightenment" has spilled over into our agricultural practices. Farms today are so heavily reliant on chemical pesticides and fertilizers that a basic knowledge of farming techniques comes second to a good understanding of the periodic table. Sarcasm aside, farmers today probably know less about traditional farming methods than they did a century ago. And that ignorance has come at a great cost to our health and well-being.

    Yet, all hope is not lost. Many farmers are aware 20 of the negative impact that chemical pesticides and fertilizers have had and will have on our environment and, with help from the federal government, are moving to techniques that reduce the usage of these chemicals, according to the Natural Resources Conservation Service website. These techniques include reducing human exposure through groundwater contamination by building Agrichemical Containment Facilities, known as ACFs, designed with an impervious floor and a sump pump to collect run-off. While the use of ACFs is not required, they are growing in popularity among local growers.

    I spoke with Tom Adams of the National Resources Defense Council office in Traverse City, who said there is a "huge interest in moving from organophosphates to softer chemicals or pesticides." EQIP aids farmers in identifying and targeting specific pests present in their orchards, resulting in the use of more timely, specific pesticide applications. Some of the newer sprayers even utilize "smart spray" technology, in which the sprayers detect the branches of fruit trees and spray only within a certain distance of the tree, reducing pesticide "drift" to other parts of the orchard. This results in fewer contaminants making their way into our drinking water.

A few farmers in the Grand Traverse region have done away with chemical pesticides altogether. Alan and Cheryl Kobernik own and operate North Star Organics, one of the region's first organic cherry farms. The Koberniks were once conventional farmers who utilized the same farming techniques other area farmers have employed over the last half-century, but the farm was not economically viable.

Their first motivation to making the switch to organic farming practices, they admit, was money. On forty acres, it was difficult for the Koberniks to compete with so many area farms already producing sweet and tart cherries. Over time, however, their attitude toward organic growing has shifted. They have seen their land in the last seven years flourish. In a phone interview, Cheryl expressed her enthusiasm about the change in the soil. She explained that in place of traditional herbicides used to keep the weeds at bay between trees, they now use mulch and shredded newspaper. In the early days of their transition, the ground was dead—the result of years of poisons and chemical fertilizers. But today the ground is alive with microorganisms that now devour this material in the course of a few days. These microorganisms are vital to the sustainability of the orchard. They are part of a food chain, or a nutrient cycle that exists normally uninhibited in nature. With the orchard chemical-free, Cheryl's children can now lie in the grass between rows, and in fun she warns them not to stay in the orchard too long, or the ground may absorb them as well.

American poet Wendell Berry wrote, "To cherish what remains of the Earth and to foster its renewal is our only legitimate hope of survival." This community is about something more than cherries. Farmers today are rethinking what goes into producing their product. A handful, like the Koberniks, have traded pesticides for peace of mind and gone organic. Others are participating in government subsidies to reduce their dependence on toxic chemicals. And in recent years, efforts like Community Supported Agriculture (CSA) have grown in popularity among local farmers.

A CSA connects farmers with the public, who pay a membership fee in exchange for produce. Some CSAs employ community members and encourage a lasting relationship between the farm and the consumer. CSAs may be one way to reconnect community members with the farmers who sustain them.

I asked Duke Elsner of the MSU Extension Office in Traverse City whether or not he believed farmers were making a switch to less dangerous pesticides because they care and want to or because of EPA regulations banning the more dangerous chemicals. He said he thought it was a mix of both. For some, it's about production and profit to preserve the farm. For others, who look beyond the boundaries of their own farmland, it's about farming today, tomorrow and well into the future; a preservation of thought that the land is not something we own, but rather something we are borrowing from the future.

Works Cited

Berry, Wendell. *Gift of Good Land*. North Point Press, 1982.

"C-Fest Continues March to Bigger-Is-Better Tune." Editorial. *Record-Eagle* [Traverse City], Community Newspaper Holdings, 22 Mar. 2005, static.record-eagle.com/2005/mar/22edit.htm.

Elsner, Duke. Personal interview. 7 Mar. 2014.

Flower, Kori B., et al. "Cancer Risk and Parental Pesticide Application in Children of Agriculture Health Study Participants." *Environmental Health Perspectives*, vol. 112, no. 5, Apr. 2004, pp. 631–35, www.ncbi.nlm.nih.gov/pmc/articles/PMC1241933/pdf/ehp0112-000631.pdf.

Halfon, Leah. "Ground Water." *Virginia Environmental Quality Index*, Center for Environmental Studies, Virginia Commonwealth U, 2000, www.veqi.vcu.edu/gw_indic.htm.

Kato, Ikuko, et al. "Pesticide Product Use and Risk of Non-Hodgkin Lymphoma in Women." *Environmental Health Perspectives*, vol. 112, no.13, Sep. 2004, pp. 1275–81, doi: 10.1289/ehp.7070.

McKibben, Bill. *Age of Missing Information.* Penguin, 1993.

Moses, Marion. "Cancer in Adults and Pesticide Exposure." *Pesticide Education Center*, Nov. 2002, www.yumpu.com/en/document/view/40041845/cancer-in-adults-and-pesticide-exposure-pesticide-education-center.

"Non-Hodgkin Lymphoma." *Lymphoma Research Foundation*, www.lymphoma.org/site/pp.asp?c=bkLTKaOQLmK8E&b=6292453. Accessed 7 Mar. 2014.

Quintana, Penelope, et al. "Adipose Tissue Levels of Organochlorine Pesticides and Polychlorinated Biphenyls and Risk of Non-Hodgkin's Lymphoma." *Environmental Health Perspectives*, vol. 112, no.18, June 2004, pp. 854–861, www.ncbi.nlm.nih.gov/pmc/articles/PMC1242012/.

Rindels-Larsen, Sherry. "Understanding Pesticides." *Integrated Pest Management at Iowa State University*, Dept. of Horticulture, Iowa State U, 17 June 1997.

Rogers, W. Bruce. "Festival Is Vital to Community." *Record-Eagle* [Traverse City], Community Newspaper Holdings, 27 Feb. 2005, archives.record-eagle.com/2005/feb/27forum.htm.

Smith, William. "Pesticide Labels." Pesticide Management Education Program, Cornell U, 10 Dec. 2004, psep.cce.cornell.edu/Tutorials/pesticide_labels.aspx.

"Trouble on the Farm." *National Resources Defense Council*, wcachildren.org/national-resources-defense-council-report-trouble-on-the-farm.

United States, Dept. of Agriculture, Natural Resources Conservation Service. *Environmental Quality Incentives Program.* www.nrcs.usda.gov/wps/portal/nrcs/main/national/programs/financial/eqip/.

---, Environmental Protection Agency. "Consumer Factsheet on: Nitrates/Nitrites." *Ground Water and Drinking Water*, 22 May 2007, archive.epa.gov/water/archive/web/pdf/archived-consumer-fact-sheet-on-nitrates-and-or-nitrites.pdf.

---, ---. "Feedlots Point Source Category Study: Preliminary Data Summary." *Effluent Guidelines*, 6 Mar. 2012.

Analyzing Argument

1. Summarize the series of causes in Tengelitsch's argument.

2. Describe the use of appeals in the essay. Point out particular passages in which Tengelitsch relies on logic, value, character, emotion, or need.

3. How does the author's presence (the "I") function in this argument? While the "I" could have been omitted from the essay, Tengelitsch includes it at key points. What is the effect?

4. Compared to other essays in this chapter, Tengelitsch's topic seems uncommon. Tengelitsch does not have to contend directly with many opposing claims. Nevertheless, she does have to consider mainstream values and assumptions about farming, chemicals, and cancer. Describe how she deals with common ways of thinking about these issues. How do common values and assumptions figure into her argument?

5. What is the most persuasive passage in this argument? Why?

All for a Virtual Cause: The Reasons Behind MMORPG Success

J. NOEL TRAPP

J. Noel Trapp, owner of Noel's Restoratives, became an online gamer in his late 20s. Shortly after discovering City of Heroes, he realized the immense popularity and lurking appeal of the game. He asked an important question: *Why is this game such a huge success?* He developed the following argument by using the prompts in this chapter. He goes beyond more obvious reasons (that the game itself is exciting, that the graphics pull people in, and so on) and discovers a set of causes in the real world—the one outside of virtual reality.

In the 1970s, we played Pong where one pixilated ball was bounced between two bars. In the 1980s, we evolved into Atari. We one-upped with Mario and the generation of Nintendo. By the mid-1990s gaming consoles such as Nintendo and Sega had become a strong cultural component of middle-class America. Recently, the gaming world leapt ahead, leaving the isolated, individual Nintendo player a century behind. Rather than bonk a ball back and forth or run perpetually across the screen dodging barrels and angry pixilated snakes, gamers now live out elaborate, collective schemes. The advent and growth of MMORPGs (Massive Multiplayer Online Role-Playing Games) has drastically shaped the landscape of the gaming world, and reshaped our cultural roles within such a world. Though the initial success of these games was founded on revolutionary technological qualities, something else is behind their continued and extraordinary success. Something beyond the technological wonders of the games themselves drives thousands of players to their computers and into virtual space.

> The cultural allusions help place the reader within the world of gaming. And they make MMORPGs part of a history rather than an isolated phenomenon.

> Mentions a more obvious cause but suggests a lurking, more hidden, cause.

Psychologically, the impacts and effects of video games have been quite easy to observe. In the original role-playing games of the late 1990s, people were allowed into a virtual realm, no longer as spectators, but as active participants making decisions in realities they could not achieve (or were not possible) in the physical world around them. Fantasy, imagination, and escapist tendencies were all fueled by the increasing number of games, whether a player was the star quarterback of a famous football team, or a mage fighting off the demons of some unknown underworld. This diversity was one cause of initial successes, while another rested on better technologies which allowed these alternate video-based realities to become more lifelike, colorful, and revolve around new engines,

> Explains one cause of the early fantasy games' success.

which would support worldly (and otherworldly) physics and animations. Gamers could escape much more completely into their fantasies, immersed by better graphics, audio, and options among games. Yet, for all the media hype and increasing number, the gamers were still, essentially, isolated in their individual fantasies, communicating with only the artificial intelligence (A.I.) of the game, which, despite great strides, always became predictable.

The updates and continuing improvements of the Internet and wider bandwidths allowed the video game industry an entirely new frontier. Until fast enough access to centralized gaming servers, computer games themselves were no different than video games; both were escapist hobbies allowing the user to interact only with A.I. Once fast and sophisticated enough, centralized gaming servers allowed gamers to face each other in a digital world, where they would be able to interact with both A.I. and H.I. (human intelligence). The results were fantastic. By allowing users the freedoms found in the past along with the infinite new number of variables supplied by other human players, the gaming industry flourished in its new online environment, and the gamers, in turn, began to reap more rewards beyond mere escapism.

Currently, one of the most successful MMORPGs on the market is City of Heroes, by NCsoft. On its website, the company invites users to "live the story" in an "online world that's home to an entire universe of heroes, where you and thousands of other players take on the roles of super-powered heroes." The question of why a user may want to do such a thing is answered with the simple statement: "You are a hero." With hundreds of character options and an advanced graphics component, City of Heroes has won numerous awards in its several years on the market. Players can form supergroups with other members, fight side by side or against each other, hunt for badges (a hobby within a hobby), or simply use the game as a glorified chat room for casual or serious discussion. In addition to simple escapism, this online environment allows people to feel real senses of accomplishment, through feats in the game, in both their own eyes and the eyes of their peers.

In their non-virtual lives, many players are involved in business and the military. They are often separated from loved ones or just insulated within their own busy-ness. Other players are stricken with one illness or another that makes "normal" face-to-face interactions difficult. But in their virtual lives, where no one is ever ill, where everyone has more than human strengths, players share collective achievements, victories, and struggles.

More and more people are finding themselves in this collective space, where they fulfill basic psychological needs. The Hamidon Raid, in City of Heroes, illustrates the desire for collective achievement. The raid is an event scheduled by players, in which over eighty heroes battle a large beast, simply for the satisfaction of beating it together, as well as the game rewards that come with it. Teams are drawn up simply to heal, others to do damage, while a primary "targeter" hero calls out where everyone needs to aim. It is an exercise in teamwork, orchestrated and carried out by huge groups—sometimes over 100 different players simultaneously. The accomplishment and gratification in this case is immediate and shared.

"Collective achievement" is tied to the success of the games.

In addition to such collective gaming moments, relationships can develop online, resulting in at least one publicly observed virtual wedding, in which two people were wedded by an actual preacher in a digital world. Other events are much more somber, such as when a player died in real life, and a memorial service was held in a central location in the game. The more active the player, the higher the social and emotional stakes, and simple actions result in all the normal psychological ways: heartbreak, joy, grief, and so on. From friendships to funerals, badges to high-level heroes, the impacts of this online community are far reaching and have implications in the real world as well as the digital one.

Specific details of the game reinforce the point about collectivity and belonging.

Examples of deeper human connections among the gamers further reinforce the point.

The aims of the gaming industry to entice people into using their product have never been so successful as with MMORPGs such as City of Heroes. In addition to the initial forty-dollar cost of the game, users pay a monthly subscription fee of fifteen dollars per account. Some of the avid gamers may hold up to ten accounts at a time in order to have room to create more and more heroes on any particular server. This means that every year, single players are spending at least $180 in subscription fees alone for a single account, and in return, they are given access to a world where their superhuman characteristics can be employed, their valor unleashed, and their needs for gratification, interaction, and accomplishment sated by an invented reality that often supersedes the reality of the actual physical world around them.

Articulates all the qualities (human needs) associated with MMORPG success.

Without the incredible and increasing depersonalization of the workplace, the decentralization and dismissal of local communities, such games may not enjoy the kind of success that they have, and remain relegated to the fringes of an industry. However, they have become a financial staple of the gaming industry, as well as a social staple for the lives of many of their players. Regardless of the state of the actual physical world a player experiences, the virtual world meets some basic psychological

Reinforces the driving force behind the games' success.

The conclusion briefly encapsulates the line of reasoning in the argument (and the evolution of the games).

needs: for intense social interaction, visible and collective accomplishment, and the recognition of individual accomplishment.

MMORPGs have allowed an incredible avenue for such needs to be fulfilled, not necessarily in the healthiest of fashions, but an outlet nonetheless. These games, which once relied solely on better technology and inventive storylines, have become more and more reliant on the social aspects of gaming to ensure their continued success. Having been in existence for at least a decade, the continued success of MMORPGs rests on their rhetoric more than their creativity—on their appeals to fundamental psychology. By offering a virtual world in which a true community can exist, they offer more than a virtual challenge, but rather a full ensemble of potentially sated human needs.

Work Cited

City of Heroes. NCsoft, 28 Apr. 2004.

Analyzing Argument

1. What is behind MMORPGs' success? Point out particular passages in Trapp's argument that support your answer.

2. What is the most persuasive support for Trapp's argument? Consider specific appeals, examples, and forms of evidence.

3. Try to summarize Trapp's line of reasoning. What premises must we believe before we accept his claim about the cause of MMORPGs' success?

4. In his conclusion, Trapp argues, "Having been in existence for at least a decade, the continued success of MMORPGs rests on their rhetoric more than their creativity. . . ." How does this distinction (rhetoric versus creativity) support Trapp's overall argument about the causes of MMORPGs' success?

5. Toward the end of his essay, Trapp argues, "Without the incredible and increasing depersonalization of the workplace, the decentralization and dismissal of local communities, such games may not enjoy the kind of success that they have, and remain relegated to the fringes of an industry." How does this point support his argument?

Protesters in Pakistan Chant Anti-American Slogans during a Protest in Islamabad, September 17, 2001.

Analyzing Argument

1. How is this image a counterargument?

2. How is this image an argument about cause?

EXPLORING FOR TOPICS

Why do people argue about causes? Why not simply react or respond to each situation as it arises? Why all the debate? Most public situations worth responding to (from school shootings to forest fires, from grade inflation to political upheaval) are worth careful analysis. History shows that responding to the wrong cause is often more dangerous than not responding at all. So discovering the real cause of a phenomenon—and convincing others of that cause—is often vital.

Good writers often recognize a rhetorical need: Something is misunderstood; something has happened and needs careful analysis; people keep forwarding the wrong set of causes and someone needs to help clarify the situation. Or perhaps some phenomenon keeps occurring despite attempts to address it. For instance, school violence continues to escalate despite "zero tolerance" policies. In this case, a writer may seek to get beyond the conventional responses—the public hand-wringing and political noise. Good writers see an intellectual gap that needs to be filled with new insights. They seek out those topics that seem incomplete, ignored, or entirely misunderstood. As you search for possible topics, consider the following situations:

- **A local event or situation:** Something has happened, and the cause needs to be figured out: Why did the community vote down the recent school levy? Why are there still deep racial divisions between the downtown neighborhoods and the city police force?

- **A particular behavior or trend in college life:** What are the real reasons that students drop out of classes after the semester has begun? Why do students binge drink? What is the cause of procrastination? (Why don't students start their English assignments sooner?!)

- **A particular political phenomenon:** What's behind the upswing in religiously motivated voters? What caused the Tea Party movement? Why didn't it happen ten years earlier?

- **A social phenomenon:** Despite all the public outcries and open forums, why do school shootings continue? What's the real cause behind teenage marijuana use? Despite some attempts to address gender disparity, why do more males than females go into the sciences?

- **A popular culture phenomenon:** Despite a mountain of arguments against super-thin models, why do models continue to resemble wire hangers? Why the huge success of food-related television shows? Why the success of online video games? Why isn't PBS

To view this video, visit the English CourseMate at CengageBrain.com.

more popular? If PCs are so prone to viruses, why has Mac not converted more PC users? Despite all the arguments against Walmart, Best Buy, and other big box stores, why do shoppers continue to support them at the expense of smaller, local stores?

- **A situation in your academic discipline or career field:** Consider major changes in your discipline or career field. What has caused recent layoffs or upswings in employment?

Remember that any phenomenon—whether a social event, a cultural trend, or a physical occurrence—has many possible causes. Beyond the most obvious cause are a number of situational or environmental factors that give rise to the phenomenon. For instance, if a writer is researching school violence and trying to understand the cause of recent shootings across the country, she might begin by listing all the possible factors:

- **Personal:** The perpetrators of school shootings often carry around feelings of isolation, loneliness, fear, anxiety.
- **Social:** School violence often comes as a result of bullying. Weaker students feel victimized and long to lash out. In high school, the popular cliques learn to perform hostile actions toward or publicly humiliate those who don't fit the popularized norm. And college culture can be lonely and alienating.
- **Cultural:** Movies, video games, and prime-time television dramas feature and glorify violence. A long list of prime-time, crime-based dramas make a consistent point about shooting, blasting, or forcing your way to a victorious conclusion. That's the thesis of every single night on television.
- **Political:** War. We cannot deny the big political message of our day: Getting things done in the world requires a gun. If our politicians make that point on a daily basis—if they constantly justify the need to shoot other people—we have to acknowledge the presence of that logic in kids' lives.

Some of these factors are more abstract or indirect than others. Bullying, for instance, is more direct, more immediate than the political climate. Still, at this early phase, a writer benefits from such expansive and open thinking. Even if she doesn't argue for all of these causes, she has broadened her understanding of the situation.

Use the following invention questions to explore the less obvious causes of your topic:

▶ What are the most direct causes?

▶ What economic or business conditions may have figured in?

▶ What attitudes, fears, or values may have initiated it or indirectly supported it?

▶ What people, organizations, or institutions were directly or indirectly involved?

▶ Might some basic human need or fundamental physical principle have played a part?

Invention Workshop

In a small group, share topic ideas and then walk through the following steps:

1. Apply at least three of the preceding invention questions to each topic. Focus on one topic at a time and collectively try to dig up a range of causal factors for each topic—not simply the obvious physical factors but also the quieter cultural factors.

2. Before moving to the next writer's topic, decide what factors the writer might explore through secondary research. What theories, facts, or statistics might the writer want to know?

3. If the writer should conduct secondary research for the topic, suggest a particular type of source; for example, academic journals, popular magazines, a particular government website. (See more about secondary research on pages 321–328, and web searches on pages 326–328.)

Deeply Rooted Cause or Just an Excuse?

In popular culture, good analysis sometimes is short-circuited by the simplistic statement, "That sounds like an excuse!" People might stop thinking about causes because they imagine that discovering a deeply rooted cause somehow excuses behavior. For example, someone might say, "Blaming prime-time television for school shootings excuses the act." However, rigorous analysis of bad behavior doesn't mean an acceptance of that behavior. Academic writers can try to discover why something happens, beyond the quick reflexes of popular culture. Discovering a deeply rooted cause does not justify or excuse an act or behavior. It does, however, help us to understand why things happen.

INVENTING A CLAIM

Some topics are highly debated: Some people argue X while others argue Y, and both groups try to disprove the other. For example, some high school administrators, parent groups, and school boards blame pop culture influences (like rock music, movies, Goth apparel, unconventional hairstyles) for school shootings. To address these supposed causes, they have enacted "no tolerance" policies that disallow for any visible signs of tension in the student body. Others argue that music and fashion, no matter what type, do not contribute to school shootings. Instead, they claim that teens feel increasingly isolated in their everyday lives—shunned by mainstream high school culture, isolated from neighbors, distanced from their own families. If a writer were researching this topic, she would likely find heated debates. These debates, then, would impact her claims.

Other topics are not so heated. But less heated topics are not less interesting. In fact, a topic that has not already been over-analyzed, mis-analyzed, and screamed to death can be a writer's opportunity. The argument may focus on revealing a new insight about a cause, as if to say, "I bet no one realized the cause of this!" Either way, it is essential to understand what others have said or not even imagined about your topic.

What Do Others Claim?

- What main causes do other writers put forward?
- What causes have other writers not considered?
- If you have a particular source, what does the author assume (but not necessarily state) about the topic?

What Do I Claim?

- How do my assumptions differ from or overlap with others'?
- What cause or set of causes do I think is most critical?

Answers to these questions might shed light on the way people think about your topic—which can make all the difference in determining an argumentative strategy. Because any argument exists within a context of public opinion, because it rests up against a landscape of other positions and insights, good arguers plan how they will engage those other positions and insights.

As you consider your topic and all the possible causes, look back over your notes, especially at your responses to the invention questions, and generate a focused claim of fact. Your project might do one of the following:

CLAIM A SINGLE CAUSE Almost every phenomenon has many pre-conditions—many physical, cultural, political, or natural factors that play an indirect part. But writers may still want to clear the air of those preconditions and point to a single cause:

- The levy failed because the town's population is aging and those who don't have children at home feel no attachment to the schools.
- Students procrastinate because the traditional school assignment has taught them to.

The benefit of the single-cause claim is that the argument gains focus and intensity. The difficulty, however, is that a writer must hold that particular factor well above the list of preconditions. The writer must make a clear and strong connection between that one factor and the phenomenon itself—and explain why other factors are inconsequential.

CLAIM MULTIPLE CAUSES Some arguments have too many influencing factors to argue for only one. Claiming that various factors figure into a phenomenon is not necessarily copping out. Pointing to several causes, instead of one, can make for a sophisticated argument:

- More voters are religiously motivated because of several recent religious-themed movies and political rhetoric that frames all cultural issues in Judeo-Christian metaphors.
- Teenagers smoke marijuana because it fits into their socioeconomic structure: it's relatively cheap, easy to obtain, and easy to transport.

The benefit of the multiple-causes claim is that the argument may gain some interesting layers and sophistication. The danger is that the argument could lose intensity and could even become a laundry list of factors. In short, it could turn into no argument at all. To offset this danger, consider forming a counterargument (pages 54–56).

TRANSCEND COMMON WISDOM Most topics have a common understanding or a widely held view. People generally don't question or argue about why kids hate homework, why people like dogs, why Americans are getting fatter. But the lack of debate doesn't mean lack of opportunity—just the opposite. An uninspected topic can make for the most exciting argument because the writer can open up new logic:

- The loathing for homework comes from popular and wrong-headed notions about home, not from the general dislike of work.

- People want dogs not for companionship but for routine. Since dogs are highly routinized creatures, they provide flesh-and-blood regularity to increasingly chaotic lifestyles.

These two examples show how a writer can dig up common wisdom and then assert a contrary point. The benefit of an uncommon or anti-conventional claim is that the argument has a built-in sense of revelation: it invites the readers (and writer!) to rethink an issue from the start. The difficulty is that the writer is pretty much on his or her own and must build an argument from unlikely sources and support. (But—as with most writing projects—the difficulty also becomes an opportunity.)

More Sample Claims

Local Situations

- The growth and development issues affecting Crawford City are not the fault of the city manager, but of individual citizens vying for their own financial gain.

- Racial tension in the city lingers because no public official has acknowledged the string of aggressive police actions in recent years.

College Trends or Situations

- The "sophomore slump" comes not so much from harder second-year courses but from the social demands of fraternities and sororities.

- College students tend to migrate away from their religious upbringing because academic life introduces new social and philosophical questions.

Political Phenomena

- Presidential candidates are not elected by voters on Election Day, but by financial contributors more than a year before Election Day.

- Young voters are dissuaded—or turned off from politics—by the exaggerated claims from both the right and left wing.

- A major cause of exorbitant health care costs is lack of government oversight.

Social Phenomena

- Many Americans struggle financially not because of poor education or low income but because financial institutions have loaned them money they cannot afford to pay back.

- While many factors, such as international crises and weather events, contribute to the increase in gasoline prices, the underlying factor is Americans' continual and excessive use of gasoline.

- People consider traditional news sources to be either liberal or conservative based not simply on the bias of the news source but on their own biases.
- People shop at big box stores for a simple reason: in most towns, there are few viable alternatives.

Professional or Career Trends

- More women are entering medical school because they were encouraged, in their formative years, to study and succeed in the sciences.
- More and more companies are shifting to virtual offices because technology continues to make working off-site easier and more economical.

Activities

1. In groups, narrow and intensify the following broad claims:
   - Ignorance is the cause of racism.
   - School dropout rates increase because of poverty.
   - Higher grades lead to better jobs.

   Share your revised claims with the class, and then discuss exactly how your group proceeded through the task. That is, what phrases or words did you target as you approached the claims?

2. In small groups, choose one claim from this sample list, and describe the opposing positions that the writer would have to address in an argument.

INVENTING SUPPORT

LINE OF REASONING When developing a causal argument, writers need to make a clear connection between potential causes and their effects, especially if those factors are indirectly related. In her argument, Samantha Tengelitsch sets up a complex, but tightly knitted, line of causes:

> While on the surface the cherry festival is about cherries, it was once about something more: the families who worked to produce these cherries and the community where the cherries are grown. Some feel our local festival has outgrown the area. A recent editorial that ran in the Traverse City *Record Eagle* points out: "[L]ots of people have advocated returning to a smaller, less grandiose effort that more closely reflects the festivals they remember. . . ." ("C-Fest"). The festival no longer caters to local residents and growers, but instead focuses on larger crowds and higher revenues. And with this, the demand on farmers for cherries is great. This increase in demand has fostered an environment where farmers have grown dependent on chemical pesticides and fertilizers. And an increase in the use of pesticides and other toxic chemicals has left our once small farming community vulnerable to the dangers of exposure to these harsh chemicals.

After Tengelitsch links the heavy demand for cherries to a change in farming strategies, she links particular pesticides and fertilizers to a deadly form of cancer. Her line of reasoning, which takes up most of her essay, develops according to these steps:

- Over the years, the cherry festival has created a higher demand for cherries.
- That demand has prompted heavy use of dangerous pesticides and fertilizers.

- Those chemicals significantly increase the risk of cancer, especially in children.
- Because a young woman grew up in this area of heavy chemical use, she developed non-Hodgkin's lymphoma.

Tengelitsch devotes several paragraphs to the third step (the connection between chemicals and the risk of cancer). Because it is the most unexpected, and most important, premise of her argument, she carefully builds up evidence (statistics and scientific authorities) to support it.

LOCAL AUTHORITIES We should not assume authorities must be distant, published voices that we find on a database or in a book. Often, the most authoritative voices live in our own communities—those who are deeply involved with an issue. Tengelitsch strategically integrates insights from local farmers:

> In a phone interview, Cheryl expressed her enthusiasm about the change in the soil. She explained that in place of traditional herbicides used to keep the weeds at bay between trees, they now use mulch and shredded newspaper. In the early days of their transition, the ground was dead—the result of years of poisons and chemical fertilizers. But today the ground is alive with microorganisms that now devour this material in the course of a few days.

HIDDEN LAYERS Academic readers value new understanding. They want to be given a new perspective. Therefore, successful academic writers try to reveal the unseen layers of a topic. They go beneath the surface or most direct and obvious points. Camille Paglia's entire argument emerges from an insight about the hidden layers of the topic. If the effect is decreased libido, then she explores the quiet realm of diligence, decorum, and propriety that have defined mainstream Western life for centuries:

> The real culprit, originating in the 19th century, is bourgeois propriety. As respectability became the central middle-class value, censorship and repression became the norm. Victorian prudery ended the humorous sexual candor of both men and women during the agrarian era, a ribaldry chronicled from Shakespeare's plays to the 18th-century novel. The priggish 1950s, which erased the liberated flappers of the Jazz Age from cultural memory, were simply a return to the norm.

Paglia digs deep. But she cannot merely toss out these broad historical statements. She has to give specifics throughout her argument and let them build persuasively throughout. She describes office life, domestic life, popular movies, and popular music all as a way to illustrate an undeniable force of desexualization.

And in the following passage, Noguera and Akom point to the surface—the most obvious assumption people may have about the topic—and then reveal a less obvious layer:

> On the face of it, the potential for success in reducing the gap in these districts would seem high. All fifteen school districts in the network have a track record of sending large numbers of affluent white students to the best colleges and universities in the country. Additionally, unlike schools in high-poverty areas, funding is largely not a major obstacle to reform. Each district is located in an affluent community with a highly educated population known for its commitment to liberal political and social values. Yet in all fifteen districts there is a persistent, deeply ingrained sense that even this ambitious and well-intentioned effort will fail to alter student outcomes.

The final sentence of the paragraph suggests that the causes of the achievement gap lurk in a complex set of forces. As their argument continues, the writers explain those forces more specifically.

LITERARY WORKS Poems, novels, plays, songs and short stories are often included in arguments to connect the specific topic to a broader human condition, hope, tension, or principle. In her essay, Samantha Tengelitsch uses a Wendell Berry line to connect contemporary farming techniques and the broader hope for human survival:

> American poet Wendell Berry wrote, "To cherish what remains of the Earth and to foster its renewal is our only legitimate hope of survival." This community is about something more than cherries. Farmers today are rethinking what goes into producing their product. A handful, like the Koberniks, have traded pesticides for peace of mind and gone organic. Others are participating in government subsidies to reduce their dependence on toxic chemicals. And in recent years, efforts like Community Supported Agriculture (CSA) have grown in popularity among local farmers.

As you consider your own argument, use the following questions to develop both evidence and appeals.

- ▶ What line of reasoning must I establish? How can I support each premise?
- ▶ What historical or current events or figures illustrate something about my topic?
- ▶ What local authority might help reveal something about the topic?
- ▶ What are the logical causes (direct and indirect) of the topic on a surrounding community—or the broader society?
- ▶ What hidden, or indirect, factors can I describe?
- ▶ How might a literary passage help to illustrate a broader point or principle?

Invention Workshop

Form a group with two or three other writers. After sharing main claims, help each writer develop possible support strategies by collectively answering at least two of the preceding invention questions.

ARRANGEMENT

WHERE SHOULD I INCLUDE MY MAIN CLAIM? A main claim or thesis can be *implied* (suggested by the details of the essay but not directly stated) or *explicit* (directly stated). There is no universal rule for placement of an explicit main claim. Contrary to some high school teaching, the main claim (or thesis statement) of an essay does not have to go at the end of the first paragraph. In fact, the first paragraph in many academic and professional essays is reserved for introducing the reader to the complexities of the issue or getting beyond some common assumptions. In his introduction, J. Noel Trapp gives some basic history about technological development in video games, but he ends the first paragraph by setting up the main argument, the "something else" that he will develop as the essay rolls along:

> The advent and growth of MMORPGs (Massive Multiplayer Online Role-Playing Games) has drastically shaped the landscape of the gaming world, and reshaped our cultural roles within such a world. Though the initial success of these games was founded on revolutionary technological qualities, something else is behind their continued and extraordinary success. Something beyond the technological wonders of the games themselves drives thousands of players to their computers and into virtual space.

Trapp, then, fully describes that "something else" throughout his essay. In his conclusion, we get a complete sense of the idea:

> Having been in existence for at least a decade, the continued success of MMORPGs rests on their rhetoric more than their creativity—on their appeals to fundamental psychology. By offering a virtual world in which a true community can exist, they offer more than a virtual challenge, but rather a full ensemble of potentially sated human needs.

Noguera and Akom's main claim comes toward the end of their essay, after several causes have been explained:

> When placed within the broader context of race relations in American society, the causes of the racial achievement gap appear less complex and mysterious; the gap is merely another reflection of the disparities in experience and life chances for individuals from different racial groups.

WHERE SHOULD I DEAL WITH OPPOSITION? This depends on the number and intensity of opposing claims. When writers have one primary opposing force, they often begin their argument there—explaining what others believe and detailing the logic of that belief. Then, they begin their argument against that belief. In this sense, the opposition acts as a springboard into the writer's main claim and line of reasoning. In the following example, the writer uses opposition as a springboard to start her essay:

> Political leaders often claim that school shootings are caused by an infection in teenage culture, specifically first-person shooter video games and hard core music. They see a direct cause/effect relationship between entertainment and horrifying outbursts of violence. They imagine that the way teenagers escape from reality directly impacts how they deal with the frustrations of everyday life. Such a simplistic understanding of cause/effect ignores the more complex, but far more powerful, factors that surround teenagers and incite them toward violence. As it turns out, the most direct factors are not at all part of some adolescent subculture. They are core parts of mainstream American life.

HOW SHOULD I WORK SCIENTIFIC RESEARCH INTO THE ARGUMENT? Scientific research can provide powerful support, but it comes with a potential hazard: Readers can easily become overwhelmed by unfamiliar terms or too much jargon. Therefore, good writers briefly explain (or set up) scientific findings or conclusions before they give data or dense quotations. In her essay, which relies heavily on scientific conclusions, Samantha Tengelitsch works to set up those conclusions for the reader. In the following passage, she gives two quotations, and before each she explains the significance of the point:

> A population-based, incidence case-control study which evaluated pesticide product use and the risk of non-Hodgkin's lymphoma in women addresses this correlation: "NHL has received research attention because the recent rapid increase in its incidence parallels an exponential growth in pesticide use with a few decades of lag" (Kato et al.). Researchers investigated other "high-risk" groups as well and found some correlation between these groups and NHL, but the most significant association was found in agricultural families. As one study reports:
>
>> With increasing cumulative number of hours exposed to pesticides at these jobs other than farming, there was a marginal increasing trend in risk of NHL. When farming and other jobs associated with pesticide exposure were combined, the total duration at any of these jobs was significantly positively associated with the risk of NHL. (Kato et al.)

HOW SHOULD I DEAL WITH MULTIPLE CAUSES? If you are developing a multiple-cause argument, you can use paragraphs to separate and detail each cause. Pedro A. Noguera and Antwi Akom use paragraphs to separate the causes of the achievement gap. In the following, they begin a new paragraph to shift from more direct to less direct (or cultural) factors:

> Beyond the policies and practices that contribute to the achievement gap, a number of complex cultural factors are also important. Missing from the research and policy debates is an understanding of the ways in which children come to perceive the relationship between their racial identity and what they believe they can do academically. For many children, schools play an important role in shaping their racial identities because they are one of the few social settings where kids interact with people from different backgrounds. To the extent that a school's sorting processes disproportionately relegate black and brown children to spaces within schools that are perceived as negative and marginal, it is likely that children of color will come to perceive certain activities and courses as either suitable or off-limits for them.

Similarly, Tengelitsch shifts paragraphs to move from one type of hazard (pesticides) to another (fertilizer):

> In addition to chemical pesticides, orchards have become increasingly reliant on chemical fertilizers. These chemical fertilizers combined with run-off wastes from livestock and septic systems all contribute to higher levels of nitrogen in the ground. Nitrogen converts into nitrates, which pass through our permeable soil into the water table.

The idea here is to use paragraphs as basic organizational units. Even though your argument may grow in complexity—dealing with multiple causes, various hidden layers, different appeals, opposing positions, and several support strategies—the paragraphs can keep those elements from getting too entangled.

AUDIENCE AND VOICE

Voice is key to academic argument. Even when the writing is highly formal, it has a voice. And the writer controls the nature of that voice with each sentence, phrase, and word. Although voice involves a broad range of issues and strategies, this section offers advice on two key issues: sentence variety and pronoun use.

VOICE AND SENTENCE VARIETY Since writers cannot use volume, they must rely on other means to make their voices lively. Sentence length is equivalent to pitch and volume in writing. When sentences are generally the same length, the voice seems flat and monotonous, but when sentences are varied in length (moving from long to short), the voice breaks out of flatness, and readers experience a tug and pull on their minds. In short, sentence length matters. (Big time.) In her essay, Camille Paglia pulls the reader into complex ideas (with complex sentences) and then punctuates the intellectual experience with a short, powerful assertion:

> Nor are husbands offering much stimulation in the male display department: visually, American men remain perpetual boys, as shown by the bulky T-shirts, loose shorts and sneakers they wear from preschool through midlife. The sexes, which used to occupy intriguingly separate worlds, are suffering from over-familiarity, a curse of the mundane. There's no mystery left.

Like Paglia, all good writers try to accent or emphasize ideas with shorter sentences—especially after longer, more nuanced, sentences. Noguera and Akom apply the same strategy:

A close examination of access to AP courses in California reveals how certain educational practices contribute to the maintenance of the racial achievement gap. Since the mid-eighties, the number of AP courses available to students at high schools in California has tripled. This increase has been attributed to a 1984 decision by the University of California to give greater weight to the grades earned by students who enroll in AP courses. However, AP courses are not uniformly available to students. At some inner-city and rural schools, few if any such courses are offered, while at private and affluent suburban schools, it is not uncommon for students to have access to fifteen or more AP courses (see Alan Jenkins, "Leveling the Playing Field," March 6).

VOICE AND PRONOUNS Pronouns are tricky business in academic writing. Particularly, the first-person pronoun "I" raises concerns for many readers because it draws attention to the writer rather than the subject under consideration. Notice the difference between the following statements:

- It is my opinion that the elemental power of sexuality has also waned in American popular culture.
- The elemental power of sexuality has also waned in American popular culture.

The first statement draws attention, first, to the writer's opinion. The power of sexuality is, literally, subordinated to the writer. But in the second sentence (taken from Paglia's essay), the subject matter (sex) is at the front of the sentence. It's the first thing the reader sees. In other words, the second sentence is more intense, more direct.

The point here is a caution about phrases such as "I think that" or "In my opinion." They are unnecessary unless the writer needs to make a distinction between his or her own ideas and those of an outside source.

However, even in the most formal essays, writers sometimes draw attention to their own thinking, to their own experience, to their presence in the text. They do this intentionally to shift attention to their own thinking or writing process—and even to humanize part of an argument. For example, in her essay, Samantha Tengelitsch uses "I" in the middle of a lengthy scientific explanation of pesticides:

> Various forms of cancer, neurological disorders, reproductive problems, birth defects, and spontaneous abortions have all been linked to long-term pesticide exposure (Moses) and elevated nitrate levels in groundwater. I chose to research non-Hodgkin's lymphoma and its link to agriculture because of a photograph of a Cherry Festival contestant; a young woman who grew up on a cherry farm in the heart of cherry country who died last winter from cancer. Did Lauren Hemming die from high nitrate levels or pesticide exposure in her youth? It is impossible for me to say with any certainty. Yet her story was the catalyst for my research; it inspired me to look further and in doing so, I discovered the true irony of her death.

Second-person pronouns (*you, your*) address the reader directly. Such pronouns can be rhetorically effective. But just as using the first person can draw attention away from the subject and to the writer, using the second person can draw it away from the subject and to the reader. Consistent use of third person (*they, he, she, it*) helps focus attention on the subject of the writing, not the writer or the reader.

Another problem with second-person pronouns is that they can actually be third- person references in disguise. This pronoun confusion can be cleared up by changing the second-person references to third-person. Consider the following examples:

- Psychologically, the impacts and effects of video games have been quite easy to observe. In the original role-playing games of the late 1990s, you were allowed into a virtual realm, no longer as a spectator, but as an active participant making decisions in realities you could not achieve (or were not possible) in the physical world around you.

- Psychologically, the impacts and effects of video games have been quite easy to observe. In the original role-playing games of the late 1990s, people were allowed into a virtual realm, no longer as spectators, but as active participants making decisions in realities they could not achieve (or were not possible) in the physical world around them.

The first example unnecessarily involves the reader: The writer doesn't mean when *the reader* was allowed into a virtual realm. The pronoun reference, although understandable, is not accurate. Such unfocused references can draw the reader's attention away from the subject matter and even make inaccurate (and unintentional) statements about the reader. The second sentence, from J. Noel Trapp's essay, maintains focus on gamers—and does not suggest that the reader (*you*) is part of that group. Trapp's strategy represents most academic and professional writing.

Using "I" in Your Writing

Writing instructors sometimes require students to avoid the first-person pronoun in writing. This is to help students develop a more academic writing style. But as you can see, many academic writers use the first-person pronoun even in very formal situations. The prohibition of the first-person often emerges from the hope that students will not rely on—or hide behind—the "I" when pressed to make intensive claims. As you consider your own writing, discuss the issue with your instructor.

REVISION

Revision requires both distance and proximity. A writer must pull away from the text and imagine its qualities from a reader's perspective, but also get up close enough to inspect particular claims, sentences, and word choice. Perhaps the biggest mistake that writers make is focusing only on editing at the sentence level. (The harder part, of course, is backing up and asking questions about the project's overall worth.)

Above all else, academic readers value *revelation*—arguments that reveal something beyond common thinking. The argument should argue for a cause that readers might not consider, or a cause that readers may have dismissed.

Ask yourself the following questions:

- In what way is this argument revelatory? (How does it help readers to re-see the topic or discover something?)
- If the argument focuses on a common topic, does it offer some new complexity?
- Does the main claim rely on a variety of support strategies (appeals, examples, and evidence)?
- Does the argument genuinely address opposition—and concede when appropriate?

RESEARCH AND REVISION: If you used outside sources, consider the following questions. As you revise, refer to the corresponding pages in Chapters 13 and 14:

- Have you used research as means of discovery? (pages 309–328)
- Have you evaluated sources for ideology, reliability, relevance, timeliness, and diversity? (pages 329–338)
- Are the ideas from the outside sources integrated smoothly into your ideas? (pages 338–349)
- Are the sources documented appropriately (with in-text and end citation)? (pages 350–375)

Peer Review

Exchange drafts with at least one other writer. (If time allows, exchange with two or three writers to gather a range of perspectives or comments.) Use the following questions to generate specific constructive comments about others' drafts:

1. Does the argument answer the basic question: Why did this happen?

2. Identify the writer's main claim. How can it be more focused on a particular cause?

3. What is the most supportive passage? Describe why it works well in the argument.

4. How is this argument revelatory? (What genuinely new perspective does it offer? How does it help us to re-see the topic?)

5. How could the writer use more allusions, examples, scenarios, or testimony to illustrate specific points?

6. The writer should have engaged opposing perspectives. What additional opposing points could the writer address? Can you imagine other objections to the argument? What points might the writer concede or qualify?

7. What phrases or passages could be more focused, more specific? Comment on any phrases, sentences, or passages that speak broadly about the topic and lack specific explanation or a detailed support strategy.

8. Check for paragraph coherence: Identify any paragraphs that seem to shift focus or take on too many separate points without a clear line of reasoning.

9. Are sources integrated smoothly, and not forced into passages? Explain any gaps between the writer's line of reasoning and the ideas from an outside source. (See pages 338–349.)

John Metz

9

Arguing Value

What Good Is This?

We are often told to avoid judging others. But the advice to "judge not" can easily turn into a kind of avoidance—a perspective that sees no distinctions between that which is harmful and that which is helpful. It would be reckless, and probably impossible, to live without judging the world around us, without making distinctions between the dangerous and the valuable. We must engage in complex judgments; we must think actively and speak publicly about people, policies, behaviors, laws, products, and even attitudes: Is the new policy on overtime hurtful to the staff? Is the local curfew good for teenagers? In these situations, we do more than react at a gut level. We weigh arguments, analyze the layers of the issue, and ultimately act—for instance, by protesting a new overtime policy or voting against a local proposal. We make reasoned decisions about how to act on a personal level.

In academic, civic, and professional settings, evaluations are not personal. They are important to a larger situation—and it is the individual's job to convince others of a particular way of seeing:

- A scientist must convince her colleagues that a proposed research program is unfocused.
- The faculty at an elementary school must convince the principal and ultimately the school board that a testing program is unsuccessful and counterproductive.
- A magazine publisher must persuade two major advertisers that the cover story of a particular issue is not potentially offensive to a politically conservative audience.
- A basketball coaching staff argues about the value of a potential player: to justify the player's potential salary, the coaches must convince team owners of the player's worth.

In these situations, the topic is in plain view. However, in other cases, people have to argue about the *hidden* value of something. Imagine a doctor who has detected a flaw not only in a surgical procedure but also in the broader approach to diagnosing potential surgery patients or a citizen who sees the harm caused by a long-standing tradition in her community. People are often in such situations, noticing aspects of something that others do not see, and so they must do more than argue an opinion; they must use argument to reveal the issue.

Whenever writers argue value, they are in difficult territory. They are not merely expressing a personal opinion: they are working to shape others' responses to something—to make others see the same qualities or dimensions as they do. This is no small task, especially in America, where we believe that people have their "own opinions." The writer has several big jobs: to understand the topic itself, to detect what readers value in relation to that topic, and to change what readers value so they see the topic differently. In rhetorical terms, the writer has to research the topic, understand the rhetorical situation, assert and support a way of seeing, and counterargue. Counterarguing is especially difficult with arguments of value because people keep their values protected. They defend any hint of a challenge with learned phrases: "Everyone's entitled to his opinion," "Beauty is in the eye of the beholder," "I like what I like," and so on. Writers must work around or through those intellectual walls.

The readings in this chapter reveal something new to readers and then call on some shared values, inviting readers into a way of thinking and evaluating. They go far beyond saying that something is simply bad, good, evil, wrong; they seek to show their readers *how* something harms or helps people. As with all academic writing, the goal is to reveal something (some new point, some layer of meaning, some hidden element) so that readers rethink the topic.

Activities

1. Generate a list of prevailing attitudes or behaviors that cause harm to a community or people. Try to focus on widespread attitudes or behaviors that seem totally acceptable to most people. For each, explain the harm it causes and why people tend to ignore or overlook the harm.

2. In small groups, take a stance on this question: *What is the value of the automobile to American culture?* Share responses with other groups in the class:

   - Which groups have the most similar stances?
   - Which groups have the most competing or different stances?
   - What basic values and beliefs underlie the stances in each group?
   - Beneath the groups' stated positions, what values and beliefs do they share? What values and beliefs collide?

Evaluations

Evaluation is another term for an argument of value. But it usually refers to a particular type of text—a particular situation or convention. Evaluations come in many guises, ranging in levels of formality: movie reviews, music reviews, book reviews, restaurant reviews, employee evaluations, teacher evaluations, and so on. Each of these categories has a set of stated or unstated rules. Readers of movie reviews, for instance, expect to see a brief summary of the movie, a description of its genre (comedy, horror, action), a list of key actors, a statement about expectations, and a judgment about the movie's ability to meet those expectations.

The particular context (an institution, a media outlet, a company) helps to define expectations. For example, a positive movie review on Rotten Tomatoes.com is marked with a fresh, red tomato icon, and a bad review with a smashed, rotten tomato icon. Evaluations are very much defined by particular institutional or audience expectations. The argument emerges from a prescribed, established situation (an assignment, an annual program review, a new fiscal year, an entertainment section in a magazine) rather than an unscripted social situation.

For this chapter, we use the phrase "argument of value" to cast a category that is broader than any particular type of evaluation. With this phrase, we hope to promote the idea that people often begin arguing outside of prescripted situations. They see something in the world around them—within or beyond specific institutional situations—and recognize a need to call it out, make people aware of it, ring the alarm bell, or defend it . . . whatever the case may be. But every evaluation—whether it closely follows certain conventions or not—consistently addresses the following two questions, either explicitly or implicitly:

- What are the criteria for judgment? In other words, what does a good example of this (teacher, comedic movie, novel, budget, etc.) do or possess?
- How well does the subject under consideration fulfill those criteria?

If you are asked to write an evaluation, your instructor probably has particular conventions in mind. Regardless of formatting and arrangement issues, you can assume that the preceding two questions will be necessary. Additionally, you can use the sections in this chapter to create a more sophisticated argument with a revelatory and focused main claim.

Evaluation of "The Education of Ms. Groves"

JOHN ADAMS

John Adams teaches college writing. He wrote the following argument after seeing a *Dateline NBC* episode that aired in 2006. As many good arguers do, Adams saw past the apparent message of the television program. While *Dateline* intended to offer an informative report on education in America, Adams realized the subtle and deeply flawed assumptions at work. He saw how those assumptions quietly support an inaccurate and injurious mode of thinking. Like many academic arguments, Adams's argument tries to dig up and reveal the dangerous assumptions that people would otherwise gladly accept.

Dateline NBC is one of those TV shows that blurs the line between news and entertainment. The show's website says the show "bring[s] viewers compelling investigative reports and personal stories." "The Education of Ms. Groves," which recently aired on *Dateline NBC*, illustrates the dangers of mixing news and entertainment, investigative reporting and storytelling. The show engages its audience through classic storytelling techniques, beginning with the likeable and attractive Ms. Groves. She is an optimistic first-year teacher, quickly faced with many challenges. Every engaging story has a crisis to be resolved, and it remains suspensefully unclear up until the end whether or not Ms. Groves will resolve hers.

There are five parts to a plot line (exposition, rising action, climax, falling action, and resolution), and *Dateline NBC* employs them dutifully. While their storytelling technique keeps the viewer tuned in, their oversimplification of the complexities of education do a disservice to teachers and students and communities at large. "The Education of Ms. Groves" ends up being like a sitcom or a cheesy TV drama, not an insightful look at a troubled American education system. In the first half of the program, Ms. Groves has lots of problems; then in the last half, the crisis is simply resolved, as if teaching and learning is just that easy. While NBC claims to be "chronicling a new teacher's first year," it edits and oversimplifies in a way that reinforces harmful misconceptions about teaching and learning.

Of course the crisis is that Ms. Groves is having a hard time getting through to her students. They are unruly and, what's worse (according to the show), doing poorly on tests. How was the crisis resolved? Ms. Groves (who was underprepared as a teacher) learns a few tricks. She counts 3, 2, 1 and her previously unruly students become silent. She posts grades publicly and everyone, it seems, gets focused and motivated. (We see students eagerly rushing up to see their scores, then working harder than they were before.) The show suggests that had Ms. Groves simply done these things at first, she wouldn't have had any problems. *Her* foolish mistake was not to know these *simple* tricks of the trade. The show suggests that anyone can and should learn these things in college before entering the classroom as a teacher. (Ms. Groves was not an education major in college, but chose to join Teach for America, an organization that recruits outstanding college graduates to teach in low-income communities. Ms. Groves's father wanted her to go to law school.)

Certainly, tricks (techniques or strategies) help immensely in any profession, but the show oversimplified the messy issue of education—of teaching and of learning. And the degree to which it oversimplified something so complex, ongoing, and lifelong is what's stunning. The show told Americans frustrated with their education system that education is easy: Teachers simply need to be dedicated, love their students, and learn a couple nifty tricks. From the show, Americans are to conclude that students

John Adams, "The Education of Ms. Groves." Reprinted with permission.

fail for one reason: because of bad teachers (because the teacher failed the student, the parent, and the country).

According to the show, a good teacher simply overcomes the rest of American culture. Of course a father must get out of prison (all's well when he does) and a homeless family needs a house (once in it, problem solved). But in "The Education of Ms. Groves," other complex factors such as media, consumerism, or diet simply don't exist. The show makes two big mistakes: (1) It oversimplifies what it does talk about, and (2) it doesn't mention some other very messy contributing factors.

5   Of course, a one-hour TV show can't cover everything. Producers must select and edit to put forth a certain argument, but the *Dateline NBC* argument is logically flawed. It relies, for example, on a strawperson fallacy—by flattening out and oversimplifying the qualities of the people and their situation: The show sets up at the beginning that Ms. Groves has had only five weeks of teacher training. So her first term is unsuccessful, why? Because of her lack of knowledge about teaching. But she perseveres; she doesn't quit. She gets the magic tips from the principal, and then she succeeds. Eureka, within the first year! Anyone thinking on this simplistic level would quickly conclude: Why not train the teacher a little better up front (tell her the tricks, stupid)? Or, one might conclude: Things worked out in the end, so there's no real harm. It's like a *Three's Company* episode. If Jack had simply taken out the garbage like Crissy told him to, there wouldn't have been any misunderstanding, and all the wacky shenanigans would not have ensued.

Dateline NBC would have served viewers better by doing some in-depth analysis of this complex issue. Instead, they misrepresented and oversimplified, as they do with other issues (presidential elections, the environment, war). One consequence, whether positive or negative, of the show's "logic" may be that it motivates some people to try teaching. Golly, it looks so easy: All a teacher needs to do is get the tricks of the trade from the principal

first, then he or she can avoid all the problems that Ms. Groves encountered. Of course, anyone who thinks this way isn't really thinking much. Many people will realize that the show ignored complexities (the way a politician does when he says the economy's good because more Americans own homes than ever before).

Many people will realize that *Dateline NBC* turned a complex issue into a TV drama like *Desperate Housewives* or *Grey's Anatomy.* It had an attractive leading character, some good drama (even a fight!), and an emotional (uplifting) ending. Unfortunately, though it will entertain, this show will disappoint a curious mind because it reduces a serious issue to a Hallmark card. A lot of dedicated, loving, trick-savvy teachers are probably laughing (though with frustration) at the TV-style docu-drama of American education. While it showed the father in prison, the homeless family, and so on, according to *Dateline NBC,* it can all be overcome (all of American culture can be overcome) if our teachers just know to count backwards. *Supernanny* and *Wife Swap* deal with complexity more than this.

Many of the cultural problems educators are up against are created, reinforced, and spread by American media. American children grow up immersed in a loud, often stupid, world of media and consumption (the two are really the same).

Today's children and many adults are not comfortable with quiet. They're bombarded with noise; there is always something to watch, listen to, and do. They're not permitted (or subjected to) a moment of peace and quiet so that they can learn to explore their own thoughts. Then we expect them to have completely different minds once they enter a classroom. "The Education of Ms. Groves" suggests that Ms. Groves overcomes all this somewhat magically, by counting backwards, 3, 2, 1, problem solved. (There's no place like home. There's no place like home. There's no place like home.)

NBC (and its brother, sister, and parent companies) creates a lot of that noise; thus, it has helped to create elementary schools full of restless consumers. "The Education of Ms. Groves" suggests that none of that matters. Instead, the problem is prison, homelessness, undertrained teachers. In the show, the media never looks at the media. It is apparently unable to see its own role in the culture that it reports on.

10   Ms. Groves had only five weeks of teacher training. And her first term as a teacher didn't go well. We know this, according to the show, because of students' test scores. This is another unfortunate oversimplification and misrepresentation. *Dateline NBC* simply bought into the idea that tests and scores measure learning, that they *make* learning, that they *are* learning. And it passed this assumption on to its viewers, unquestioned. After four months of experience and a little talking to the principal (him giving her the magic pill), all is well. This leads viewers to believe that the failures of the American education system (and there are many and they are complex) are because of one simple thing: bad teachers. The show claims that good teachers can overcome everything, if they care and love and know a few simple tricks. Apparently, according to the show, most American teachers don't do this. As *Dateline NBC* tells it, all it takes is a semester of teaching and some talks with a principal to correct a wrong answer.

Analyzing Argument

1. What is Adams's main claim about "The Education of Ms. Groves"?

2. According to this argument, what should an investigative news program do for viewers? Why does this particular *Dateline* episode fall short?

3. Chart out Adams's main line of reasoning. What are the stated and unstated premises that a reader must follow before accepting the argument's main claim?

4. Where does Adams qualify or concede points? How are those qualifiers or concessions important to the overall argument? How do they relate to Adams's voice?

5. Adams alludes to several television dramas and sitcoms. How do they make a point about an investigative report on *Dateline*?

6. Explain how Adams uses an understanding of logical fallacies. Why are logical fallacies important to this argument?

Adventure Is Calling

MICHAEL C. HILLIARD

Essays about video games, like essays about any topic, run the risk of being mundane. For example, they often make the same old points about video games leading (or not leading) to violent behavior. In "Adventure Is Calling," Michael C. Hilliard goes beyond the typical argument. He shares an insight about the nature of video games and how they compare to classic literary adventure stories.

I have always loved adventure stories. As I was growing up homeschooled, my mother imparted a love of reading early on in my life, first reading to me and my sisters, then encouraging us to read on our own as we grew older. The library was a favorite destination and we would often vacation there for hours at a time, getting to know Mrs. Bert, the children's librarian, discovering new books, and taking far too many back home with us. Getting our own personal library cards was a significant milestone in our lives and we were quite proud of the privilege—better still, now we could take out even more books.

Adventure and fantasy stories were my favorites. I couldn't tell how many times I've pored over tales of *Narnia, Middle Earth* and *Wonderland,* making dear friends of elves, dwarves, dragons, Hobbits who lived in holes, and a little girl who fell down another sort of hole entirely; not to mention all of the wonderful wizards, fauns and other manner of talking beasts along the way.

Introduces the topic of books, and then adventure and fantasy stories.

But it wasn't all fun and games or pleasant walks in the woods. Quite the contrary, the stories were filled with peril: Savage beasts, fearsome swordfights, and terrifying villains always seemed to lurk in the path of my beloved heroes, and their noble quests often seemed doomed to fail. And yet, no matter how dire the situation, no matter how impossible the odds or frightening the villain, the heroes would press on, even when they had the chance to run away. Choosing what was right instead of what was easy, they persevered and won the day.

Narrows the focus to peril and the importance of pressing on, choosing what was right instead of what was easy.

Adventure stories have always played a major role in the growth and development of a society. Instinctively, it seems, people crave stories of heroes and villains, strange lands and daring quests. Although we could venture an in-depth psychological analysis to attempt to identify just what it is that people love about adventure stories, I think the answer is simple: we need inspiration. As the heroes in our stories make brave choices and remain steadfast, we identify with them, making them role

Connects adventure stories to the growth and development of society.

Reprinted with permission from Michael Hilliard.

models for our own lives. In a world that often seems lost and broken—where monsters take the form of terrorist bombings and school shootings, when the princess in need of rescue is a family member struggling with addiction, or a friend dealing with emotional abuse—we need stories of hope and determination, stories that inspire us to face the adversity head on, even when hope seems lost.

Until recently, books were the primary method for delivering adventure stories to the masses, but such is becoming a thing of the past; now, movies and video games are the media of choice. Video games in particular seem to be taking over the adventure market in recent years. Rarely do kids clutch a book to their chest; instead, they carry miniaturized video game systems ablaze with explosions of light and sound. And not just kids, either. As a matter of fact, the Entertainment Software Association reports that the average gamer is 35 years old, and there are more women over the age of 18 playing video or computer games than boys aged 17 or younger. A few short years ago, hardly anyone living in the sunlight knew what *WoW* referred to, but now it's safe to say that at least one person you know is playing *World of Warcraft* on a regular basis—heck, even Mr. T. of '80s *A-Team* fame is now appearing in TV commercials for the game. Skepticism has existed in equal measure—you hear complaints that video games are rotting the minds children, that people should read more, or that video game violence might be linked with cases of real-world violence—but in popular practice these arguments don't seem to have much effect, judging by the meteoric rise the video game industry has experienced over the past decade (NPD Group).

Evidence that video games are replacing books as a primary method for delivering adventure stories.

Joerg Carstensen/Corbis Wire/epa/Corbis

At the Gamescom trade fair in Cologne, Germany, two women dressed as video game characters

As video games become one of the dominant forces for providing society with tales of adventure, it should give us pause to wonder if they are up to the task. All too often the fantasy worlds in which we attempt to immerse ourselves through graphic game play prove too shallow to offer any in-depth character or story development, which is essential for good adventure stories. Certainly, books are just as capable of failing in this regard. Poor writing can infect any mode of communication. However, a video game is all too often handicapped by conventions that detract from the storytelling. Instead of encouraging players to grapple with difficult circumstances in their lives, video games all too often distract us with illusions of adventure, action, amusement and escapism.

Question of value about video games versus books when it comes to delivering adventure stories to the masses.

Genuine storytelling depends on some key elements. For one, any good adventure story will have a compelling crisis. In *Alice in Wonderland,* it started as little more than a dreary day; but, as the story progressed and down the rabbit hole we traveled, solving riddles, drinking potions, and avoiding the wrath of a head-hunting queen all became a part of Alice's crisis before the day was out. In perhaps one of the greatest fantasy adventure stories ever written, J.R.R. Tolkien's *Lord of the Rings,* a motley crew of characters must cross an entire continent, battling legions of powerful and deadly foes on a quest to destroy a powerful magical object upon which the fate of the world precariously hangs. Adventures thrive on dangerous quests with impossible odds. It is the very act of overcoming adversity that changes someone from ordinary to extraordinary, from "zero to hero" as the bard might say.

Specific examples of books and crisis (*Alice in Wonderland; Lord of the Rings*).

Video games often present the player with a crisis, typically developed through a series of cut-scenes interspersed at regular intervals throughout the game. But how often do these brief scenes of exposition transcend the 30-second cut-scene to provide real depth of meaning for the much more dominant action sequences where players spend the vast majority of their time? In writing a good adventure story, an author is able to concern herself entirely with the workings of the story, the development of the characters and the crises they face. In writing a good video game, the studio's primary goal is to create a game that is enjoyable to play, because otherwise no one would buy it.

Video games don't provide the depth of meaning books do when it comes to crisis

Don't get me wrong. Book-publishers want to sell books just as much as game developers want to sell games, but one is successful through talented writing and a good story, while the other succeeds primarily if it is fun to play. In a normal adventure story, action scenes (battles and the like) are tools for the development of the story. In a video game, however, the story generally serves as the requisite base for developing the action scenes: fighting the *Balrog* isn't necessary so that the Fellowship will be

Further explanation of how video games treat crisis differently than books.

forced to deal with the loss of the wise and knowing Gandalf when he falls into the abyss after fighting the demon; instead, it's just another boss fight at the end of a level.

To work within the framework of game conventions based on character progression, plot development is boiled down to a series of required objectives or tasks the player must complete, but in this they become tasks of compulsion rather than tasks of purpose: the hero saves the princess because he must to get to the next level, not because of any sense of honor, love, or moral duty. For the player, actions performed become a matter of skill at operating a game controller rather than a question of perseverance in the face of fear or impossible odds. The traditional roles are reversed. In place of action and adventure as catalysts for character development, character development becomes a compulsory base for the—much more important—action sequences. Focus shifts from inspiration, imagination and learning to simple amusement.

I'm not arguing that video games never present interesting moral dilemmas or opportunities for learning. In his book *The Ethics of Computer Games*, Miguel Sicart attempts a thorough exploration of the many facets of ethics pertaining to society's interaction with video games. His case study of the 2007 release *Bioshock* tells of both the successes and failures present in video games as they attempt to provide a meaningful moral experience for players. In his review, Sicart praises the unique narrative development of *Bioshock*, where a final revelation in the plot forces players to reflect critically on the morality of their previous actions in the game. Indeed, video games rarely encourage moral reflections from players, and *Bioshock*'s unique plot twist represents a refreshing shift in game design. However, Sicart also criticizes several other aspects of *Bioshock*'s game play, particularly the very elements for which it was purported to present players with meaningful ethical dilemmas. In the supposed ethical exigencies, players of *Bioshock* are routinely presented with the choice of either killing or "saving" computer-controlled characters. The situation might be considered morally challenging, Sicart argues, except that the choice is deprived of meaningful consequences because game play and progression is not significantly altered based on either decision (151–63). *Bioshock* and many games like it fail to be compelling morally because developers don't want to create a game in which the consequences of a player's actions could prevent or inhibit their progression through the game. After all, who would want to play a game that would send you to jail and keep you from playing until you've served your time? In the end, although Sicart finds that many games do present interesting aspects of

In video games, unlike books, the "focus shifts from inspiration, imagination, and learning to simple amusement." Concession that video games do sometimes present interesting moral dilemmas and opportunities for learning. An authority, Miguel Sicart, is used to help the reader understand and accept the main claim, that though video games amuse, they often fail to inspire.

ethical design, he believes the industry on the whole cares very little, if at all, about creating ethical games (229).

I like video games. Starting back when all we had was a monochromatic green-screen computer, playing knock-off versions of *Space Invaders* or *Pong* on giant five-and-a-quarter inch floppy disks, to more recent times with games like *Star Wars: Knights of the Old Republic* on a PC, or *Fable* on the *Xbox,* I've happily whiled away many hours beating up bad guys and vying for high scores. After a long day at school or at work, I've often relaxed into a game's easy pleasure. I'm certainly not one to make the argument that video game entertainment is all wrong. But, as a dominant force in providing tales of adventure to our society, video games too often amuse rather than inspire.

Acknowledges the positive value, yet limitation, of video games.

Works Cited

Entertainment Software Association. "Industry Facts." 2015, www.theesa.com/about-esa/industry-facts/.

The NPD Group. "2009 U.S. Video Game Industry and PC Game Software Retail Sales Reach $20.2 Billion." 14 Jan. 2010, www.npd.com/wps/portal/npd/us/news/press-releases/pr_100114/.

Sicart, Miguel. *The Ethics of Computer Games*. MIT Press, 2009.

Analyzing Argument

1. What difference between adventure stories and video games does Hilliard draw the reader's attention to?

2. How does Hilliard use opposition to develop his argument?

3. What main criterion does Hilliard use to evaluate video games?

4. Identify a place where Hilliard carefully guides the reader from one idea to another. Explain his strategy.

5. What value is at the root of Hilliard's argument?

Higher Education through Discombobulation

BETSY CHITWOOD

In "'Have It Your Way': Consumerism and Education," Simon Benlow explains the important difference between a customer and a student. For example, he writes, "When I think back to the best teachers and professors in my education, I recall those who demanded everything contrary to the consumerist mentality. They insisted on active students; they made us read staggering amounts of material and then actively put that material to use; they prompted us into confusion and disorientation; they made us uncomfortable, and then, sometimes, offered paths to clarity." After reading Benlow's argument in her second-semester college writing course, Betsy Chitwood wrote the following essay in which she supports Benlow's point by arguing for the value of confusion in the learning process.

I have fond memories of my mother saying, "I'm all discombobulated!" It's really just an interesting way of saying you're confused or disoriented. Of course she said it to make me laugh and so I didn't see confusion as a negative aspect of life. But neither did I realize that confusion is an important element to learning. Confusion and disorientation are important in the learning process because these emotions force us to go beyond what we know in search of answers. Also called cognitive disequilibrium, confusion and disorientation create a motivating challenge to students to explore and take risks as they step out—or are pushed out—of their comfort zone.

My own experience is offered in support of this learning process. Stepping out from my familiar surroundings and entering the military brought about a disorientation that remains unmatched to this date. Military training included: becoming a member of a new culture, long hours of study, physical training,

adhering to a regimented lifestyle, no personal time and all this (and more) on very little or no sleep. This learning process, albeit an extreme example, motivated me to take risks and seek ways to succeed in my chosen career. The impact of the disorientation was in direct proportion to the personal growth brought about by my "education" and it definitely shaped who I am today.

Evidence from academic research supports this theory. In a study by Craig and Graesser at the University of Memphis, college students participated in an introduction to computer literacy by using AutoTutor, an intelligence tutoring system (ITS). The study, which tracked the effect of confusion and other emotions on students' responses, showed that a higher percentage (68%) of learning gains were achieved when the students were met with confusion (4). Researchers Dalton and Crosby, in their study of cognitive or psychological disequilibrium, note its usefulness in gaining higher understanding and personal growth. And developmental psychologist Erik Erikson used the concept of "crisis" to describe the experience of reaching the point where you wrestle with confusion to reach the higher ground of understanding (qtd. in Dalton and Crosby 2). Students who are reluctant to take on the challenge will find their learning experience stifled and their education slow, but those who meet the challenge will realize a higher level of knowledge and self awareness. American psychologist Lawrence Kohlberg refers to disequilibrium as a means to improve understanding concerning moral and ethical situations stating, "Without such conflict and struggle moral reasoning can become stuck at conventional and conformist levels of thinking" (qtd. in Dalton and Crosby 2). Psychologist and educator Nevitt Sanford suggests experiences of psychological discord produce internal conflict. This conflict pushes students to go beyond their inner limits and enter into new understanding, joining their previous knowledge with a new level of knowing (Dalton and Crosby 1).

Reprinted with permission from the author.

memory banks, we will be confused. Confusion won't last long if we realize that it is a means to an end. We need to think it through, find answers—or whatever is required—and gain understanding to go on. Each time we find success, we can draw on this experience to take on the next challenge. If we are not willing to use confusion to our advantage as an educational tool, we may feel frustrated and not know where to turn. If this continues we may become discouraged in our education, lose motivation, and give up or struggle along while we seek ways to alleviate these feelings.

In his essay "'Have It Your Way': Consumerism Invades Education," Simon Benlow states, "the best teachers . . . prompted us into confusion and disorientation . . . and then, sometimes, offered paths to clarity" (131). Paths to clarity must be found as we seek to restore an inner harmony. Students who search out their own paths will find these paths lead not only to higher understanding, but more importantly, they are building character, confidence and producing the content of who they are becoming.

Confusion and disorientation, appearing to some as negative, unwelcome intruders, are actually the seeds of personal growth and higher understanding. If we see these emotions as seeds of opportunity, and not something to be avoided or anesthetized, we will find that we have the fortitude to face them head on. If we take what knowledge we have and add what we can acquire, we will reach higher awareness on an educational and personal level.

Some may disagree with the use of confusion as a tool in the learning process, stating that students may remain at a standstill if the confusion or challenge is too great. Since we are not all alike, not all techniques will have the same effect. Although students may be motivated by a challenge, some may need support in order to step into learning. Finding balance between challenge and support is the key. From parent to professor, a teacher needs an awareness of a student's ability to meet challenges *and* their need for support. Chickering suggests that an optimum learning climate uses a balance of challenge and support appropriate for each student's educational level (qtd. in Dalton and Crosby 1).

5   We must all face confusion at times. Anytime we encounter something we don't understand, and knowledge is required that is not stored in our

Works Cited

Benlow, Simon. "'Have It Your Way': Consumerism Invades Education." *The Composition of Everyday Life: A Guide to Writing*, by John Mauk and John Metz, 4th ed., Wadsworth, 2013, pp. 130–32.

Craig, S. D., and A. C. Graesser. "Why Am I Confused: An Exploratory Look into the Role of Affect in Learning." *Advances in Technology-Based Education: Towards a Knowledge-Based Society*, edited by A. Méndez-Vilas and J. A. Mesa Gonzalez, vol. 3, Junta De Extremadura, 2003, pp. 1903–1906.

Dalton, Jon, and Pamela Crosby. "Challenging College Students to Learn in Campus Cultures of Comfort, Convenience and Complacency." *Journal of College & Character*, vol. 9, no. 3, 2008, pp. 1–5, doi: 10.2202/1940-1639.1112.

Analyzing Argument

1. What is the essay's main claim?

2. What argument is the essay a response to?

3. What support strategies help the reader accept Chitwood's claims?

4. What additional support strategy might Chitwood use and why?

5. How does Chitwood's voice help the reader understand and accept her position? Use excerpts from the essay to support your claim.

6. How could Chitwood make her argument more insightful by introducing more opposition?

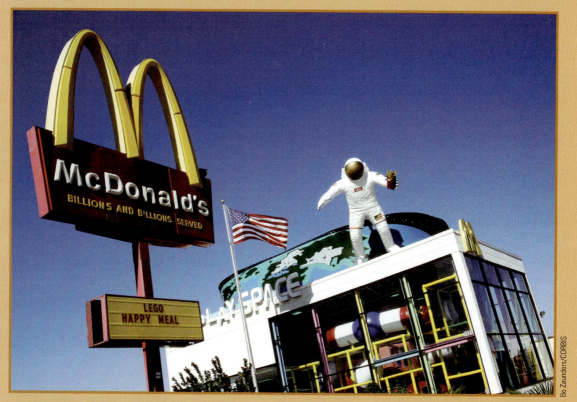

Bo Zaunders/CORBIS

What is the value of a Happy Meal?

Analyzing Argument

1. Make a list of details from the McDonald's photograph (Lego, Happy Meal, American flag, and so on). How does each detail appeal to the customer? How does the detail appeal to adults? How does it appeal to children?

2. Beyond this photograph, how does McDonald's appeal to logic, emotions, values, need?

3. Make a list of the positive and negative consequences of eating at McDonald's and other fast-food restaurants. What is the positive value of a Happy Meal, of McDonald's, of fast food in general? What is the negative value?

4. What do children gain from eating at McDonald's? What do they lose?

EXPLORING FOR TOPICS

While some things are obviously harmful and others are obviously good, this chapter focuses on topics about which people may disagree. As the chapter readings illustrate, good argument involves more than announcing opinions. It seeks to reveal a new way of thinking so that readers are jolted (or lulled) into re-seeing the topic. Using the following sections, explore a topic that might otherwise go unnoticed, or draw out unseen layers of a familiar topic. Then develop an insightful argument about that topic's value. Go beyond finding fault or giving unqualified praise and discover how a topic impacts the world around it: how does it affect a community, the environment, an organization, a business, animals, children, family members? Ask yourself: *How is this thing valuable or perilous?*

- On your college campus, examine a placement policy, absenteeism, student medical benefits, grading standards, the physical campus itself, administrator salaries, student dress, faculty dress, buildings.

- At an organization or corporation, evaluate a marketing campaign, staffing policies, slogans, individual products or product lines, individual services, sales strategies, mergers.

- In popular culture, defend a public figure or policy against popular sentiment.

- In the media, examine people or things that *seem* harmless but that actually influence the world negatively. Alternatively, examine people or things that *seem* harmful but actually have a positive role.

- At a sporting event or concert, consider a team's or a player's performance, audience behavior, facilities, staff.

- Closely examine an element of popular or consumer culture: a consumer trend, a musical genre, a news channel, a specific program, a newspaper article, a slogan, credit cards, a new look.

- Look into politics. Examine a particular policy, a campaign ad, a particular speech, anti-terrorism policies, an education reform bill, a health care approach, military strategy, a proposed solution.

What good is this?

To view this video, visit the English CourseMate at CengageBrain.com.

Top to bottom: © Madhouse; © Cengage Learning®; © Cengage Learning®; © Cengage Learning®; From CourseMate video (BBC: Arranged Marriage)

Activity

In groups, generate several responses for the following statements

1. ___ seems harmless, but actually, he/she/it ___.
2. ___ seems negative, but actually, he/she/it ___.

Try to generate topics that other groups may not consider—policies, attitudes, products, or services that normally get overlooked, but that need a close examination.

Arguments that point out the obvious or express often-stated opinions are not valued in academic writing, or in most other writing. Academic audiences value arguments that *reveal* something new—in this case, the deeply harmful or beneficial qualities of a subject. Such arguments evolve over time, beginning with an initial but thorough analysis. Use the following invention questions to launch your thinking:

► Who or what does the topic harm?
► Who or what does it benefit or help?
► Does the topic promote a particular kind of behavior, thought process, or attitude?
► What is its purpose or intent? (Is that purpose a good one? Why or why not?)
► Despite its intent, what are its hidden effects? (How does it impose on others, impede future action, oversimplify thinking, slow action, create frenzy, undermine principles, support core principles, enrich lives, free people, facilitate action?)

The most powerful insights lie beyond initial responses as you stretch the limits of what you normally think. Notice how John Adams develops his ideas about a TV program:

► Despite its intent, what are its hidden effects?

The show told the story of a first-year teacher having problems in the classroom: her students are unruly and they're not doing well on tests. After it shows the problems she's having, the show moves into the solution phase. It's somewhat suspenseful, just like the typical entertainment program on TV. You wonder if Ms. Groves is going to give up or persevere, if she's going to get through to her students or not. And just like the typical entertainment programs, there's a happy ending. But, what's the hidden effect of this? The program treats a complex issue with a basic plot—exposition, rising action, climax, falling action, resolution. This could be informative and instructive. But is it? Does the American TV viewer learn something important and valuable about education? Or does the viewer get an oversimplistic misunderstanding? Certainly, young teachers probably struggle, learn, improve, and become more effective. But the way *Dateline* presents the situation is too simple. It gives the viewer a harmful impression about education. It makes it seem simple and easy, and it suggests to Americans who are concerned about problems with public education that complex issues can be solved by learning a few basic tricks.

Adams uses this invention writing to move beyond his initial, gut reaction. His first few sentences are a summary that helps him eventually think more analytically and begin to work toward discovering an evaluative insight.

Invention Workshop

With one or two other writers, answer the preceding invention questions for your topic. Go beyond the initial answers for each. For instance, if someone suggests that an organization is harmful because it is dishonest, probe further, not only revealing the specifics of the dishonesty but also tracing the aftereffects of dishonesty. Use the discussion as a tool for *finding out*, for exploring layers beyond your group's initial preconceptions. During the discussion, record the evolution of ideas by taking notes.

Research

Although they may already have a sense of their position on a topic, before taking a firm stance, arguers use primary and secondary research to explore other positions. Surveys, a type of primary research, collect three layers of information: people's knowledge about, experience with, and opinions on the subject. Even if a survey has a small number of respondents, it can yield valuable insights. For instance, an arguer focusing on online courses could develop a short survey and use questions like the following:

- Have you ever taken a course online? How many?
- What influenced your decision to choose an online course?
- If given the choice between taking a course in person or online, which would you choose?
- What are the main reasons you would take an online course?
- What are the main reasons you would avoid taking an online course?

Depending on the answers, the researcher might get a deeper understanding of the topic. Respondents might explain that they took an online course because they thought it would be easier and less time consuming, yet it turned out to be the opposite, and this information might give a writer a sense of direction or purpose.

Arguers use electronic databases to find published discussions, a type of secondary research, about a subject. Keyword searches that allow you to enter various nouns connected by Boolean operators such as *and* provide good starting places. The trick is to explore various combinations of words. Too few words can yield too many sources to search through, and the wrong words can yield little or nothing. A careful search will yield a manageable and readable list of sources.

Activities

1. You can survey members of your class or a range of people outside of class. Ask respondents if they know about your topic, then delve into their opinions with specific questions. Be careful to gather information without leading the respondents to your position, and record their responses so you can return to them later. (See more about conducting surveys on pages 320–321.)

2. In groups, suggest various words and word combinations for searching each person's topic. For example, if researching the value of computers in education, one keyword search might be "computers *and* education." Then group members might suggest "online courses," "children *and* computers," "learning *and* technology," and so on.

> An argument that does not deal with the world of thought surrounding the topic is merely an island of opinion.

INVENTING A CLAIM

Since arguments exist within a context of public opinion, good arguers must know what others have said about a topic. Then they can engage other positions and put forth a persuasive argument. Answers to the following invention questions will shed light on the way people think about the topic and help you to develop a claim of value.

What Do Others Claim?

- What do others think about it, and why do they hold their opinions?
- If you have a particular source, what does the author of the source value? What does he or she assume (but not state) about the topic?
- Beyond explicit statements, how might people express their opinions about the subject (by passive acceptance, votes, active public support, purchasing a product or service)?
- What situations, media, traditions, policies, behaviors, or attitudes have kept people from evaluating the topic?

What Do I Claim?

- How do my views on the topic relate to others' views?
- What values and assumptions do I share with others?
- How do my values and assumptions differ from others'?

It is easy to characterize a topic as bad, evil, great, or interesting, but a main claim should do more. It will *reveal* something unique and particular about the subject. For instance, the first of the following statements is flat, uninteresting, and pretty obvious, but the second reveals a particular negative aspect:

Dateline NBC is wrong about education in America.

Dateline NBC oversimplifies the many complicated problems plaguing the American education system and leads us to the dangerous conclusion that bad teachers are simply to blame for the system's failures.

In the first statement, *wrong* can mean many things. It is a vague adjective that could be applied to nearly any subject. (Lying is wrong. You dialed the wrong number.) Adjectives like *bad, unfair, evil, odd, great,* and *wrong* do little more than share a general feeling about a topic. They do not focus an argument on a particular aspect or point, so they limit the intensity of a claim. In the preceding examples the first statement also contains a linking verb: *is.* Verbs such as *is, am, are, was, were* simply link the parts of the sentence that come before and after them: *Dateline NBC* = wrong about education in America. Linking verbs limit what a sentence can do. They can even encourage writers to use broad adjectives such as *bad, unfair, evil.* But when a writer uses an active verb, such as *oversimplifies* or *leads,* the sentence gains potential and the writer is able to see further possibilities for the argument. The words a writer uses actually impact the writer's own thinking, and bland words create bland thinking.

Good arguers watch out for words and phrases that work against the goal of developing a narrow and intense point. The following words and phrases can dull your thought:

> *Linking Verbs:* is, are, was, were, be, have been, etc.
>
> *Vague Adjectives:* bad, unfair, mean, broken, ridiculous, stupid, wrong, awful, interesting, etc.

To generate more intensive focus, writers changed the following flat statements into revelatory alternatives by changing linking verbs and vague adjectives.

Typical Flat Statements

- The parking situation on campus is unfair to students.
- High school education focuses too much on standardized tests.
- College classes outside student majors are unnecessary.
- Energy drinks are bad for today's kids.

Revelatory Alternatives

- The campus parking lots breed panic and competitive hostility in students—even before they get to class.
- Our culture's over-reliance on cars, rather than mass transportation, causes individual students undue anxiety.
- The campus parking lots demonstrate an uncomfortable truth: America's car culture has grown beyond convenience.
- Standardized tests have transformed students into budgetary items.
- The language surrounding standardized tests has made students see themselves as cash cows for their schools.
- The rhetoric justifying standardized tests has ruined the meaning and purpose of public education.
- Required college composition courses have made writing into a laborious performance rather than an intellectual tool.
- Red Bull and its weird chemical cousins provide more twitch to an already twitchy generation.

More Sample Claims

Politics

- Despite the open hostility against political campaign ads, they do force candidates to consider their constituents beyond the usual financial supporters.
- The lack of a viable third party in American politics diminishes real debate about the environment.

Education

- Despite teachers' grumpiness about text messaging, it does not diminish the English language.
- When students are comfortable, college has failed.
- Struggling to word the main idea of an argument in one clear and concise claim statement helps a writer to explore the complexities of an idea and develop critical thinking skills.

Popular Culture

- The icons and eye candy encircling the television screen on major networks distracts viewers from any one particular news story.
- While steering consumers away from harmful junk foods, the low-carb diet craze has also diminished our collective joy in comfort food.
- The sex appeal sold on *American Idol* overshadows the nuances of live vocal performance.
- Microbrews have saved beer throughout the country by ending the reign of awful corporate beer and its dim-witted culture.

Professional Life

- Massage therapy, once thought a bourgeois luxury, rescues everyday people from heavy dosages of synthetic and quietly harmful prescription drugs.
- Contrary to popular opinion, an organization with many supporters and few members works more effectively than one with many members.

Activities

1. In small groups, add one claim of value to each category: Politics, Education, Popular Culture, Professional Life.

2. As you consider your argument, look back over your notes, especially at your responses to the invention questions so far, and try to make a specific and revealing claim of value that goes beyond a bald statement. (You may find that changing linking verbs to active verbs helps in this process.)

3. In groups, narrow and intensify the following broad main claims:
   - Too much money in politics is bad.
   - The current college football playoff system leaves something to be desired.
   - Restaurant chains are rotten places to eat.
   - The college's new registration policies are unfair.

   Share your revised claims with the class, and then discuss how your group proceeded through the task. What phrases or words did you target as you approached the statements?

INVENTING SUPPORT

It is easy to pass off responsibility in an argument by saying that people should decide for themselves if something is good or bad. But the responsibility of an arguer is to convince people to see a topic a particular way—in this case, to see that something has a particular value. The goal is not to convince others to like or dislike something, but to convince them that something is just or unjust, ethical or unethical, manageable or unmanageable, practical or unpractical, prophetic or short-sighted, and so forth.

CRITERIA Nothing can be evaluated without criteria, or standards of judgment. Without a set of principles beyond our own opinions, an evaluation becomes a mere projection of personal likes and dislikes. The criteria for evaluating a restaurant might include the food quality, cost, service, atmosphere. The criteria for evaluating a movie might include the plot, acting, cinematography, special effects. An important aspect of any evaluation is deciding on appropriate criteria. For example, an evaluation of a romantic comedy might not speak to special effects, which might be an important criterion for evaluating an action-adventure movie.

John Adams gives a specific criterion in his evaluation of a *Dateline NBC* show: *News programs and investigative reports should not oversimplify complex social issues.* Although not stated directly, it is a key part of the argument:

> Many people will realize that *Dateline NBC* turned a complex issue into a TV drama like *Desperate Housewives* or *Grey's Anatomy*. It had an attractive leading character, some good drama (even a fight!), and an emotional (uplifting) ending. Unfortunately, though it will entertain, this show will disappoint a curious mind because it reduces a serious issue to a Hallmark card. A lot of dedicated, loving, trick-savvy teachers are probably laughing (though with frustration) at the TV-style docu-drama of American education. While it showed the father in prison, the homeless family, and so on, according to *Dateline NBC,* it can all be overcome (all of American culture can be overcome) if our teachers just know to count backwards. *Supernanny* and *Wife Swap* deal with complexity more than this.

ANALOGICAL REASONING Showing similarities to other subjects can add a powerful layer to an argument. An analogy can be explicit, drawing out many similar qualities between one thing and another and taking several paragraphs or pages to develop. Or a writer can make brief and more indirect comparisons to reinforce a key point. In "Adventure Is Calling," Michael Hilliard compares and contrasts adventure stories and video games. For example, after a paragraph explaining how overcoming adversity is key to an adventure story, Hilliard explains how overcoming adversity is also key to video games, but that video games lack the same depth of meaning:

> Video games often present the player with a crisis, typically developed through a series of cut-scenes interspersed at regular intervals throughout the game. But how often do these brief scenes of exposition transcend the 30-second cut-scene to provide real depth of meaning for the much more dominant action sequences where players spend the vast majority of their time? In writing a good adventure story, an author is able to concern herself entirely with the workings of the story, the development of the characters and the crises they face. In writing a good video game, the studio's primary goal is to create a game that is enjoyable to play, because otherwise no one would buy it.

TESTIMONY Even in the most formal argumentative essays, writers may rely on personal experiences to support claims. While Betsy Chitwood provides support from researched, secondary sources, she also develops her argument with testimony. This testimony is an effective support strategy because Chitwood also uses researched sources, and her personal experience fits into an overall line of reasoning:

> My own experience is offered in support of this learning process. Stepping out from my familiar surroundings and entering the military brought about a disorientation that remains unmatched to this date. Military training included: becoming a member of a new culture, long hours of study, physical training, adhering to a regimented lifestyle, no personal time and all this (and more) on very little or no sleep. This learning process, albeit an extreme example, motivated me to take risks and seek ways to succeed in my chosen career. The impact of the disorientation was in direct proportion to the personal growth brought about by my "education" and it definitely shaped who I am today.

Hilliard also uses personal experience, but in a different way. The bulk of Hilliard's argument avoids personal testimony and the first-person pronoun "I." But Hilliard uses testimony in his first two paragraphs to move into his argument, and in the last paragraph to move out of it.

LITERARY WORKS One way writers help readers understand and accept claims is by alluding to literary works. In "Adventure Is Calling," to help the reader understand a key difference between video games and stories, Hilliard refers to *Alice in Wonderland* and *Lord of the Rings*. Notice how he introduces the literary works, summarizes the relevant information, and connects it to the claim the reader should accept:

> Genuine storytelling depends on some key elements. For one, any good adventure story will have a compelling crisis. In *Alice in Wonderland,* it started as little more than a dreary day; but, as the story progressed and down the rabbit hole we traveled, solving riddles, drinking potions, and avoiding the wrath of a head-hunting queen all became a part of Alice's crisis before the day was out. In perhaps one of the greatest fantasy adventure stories ever written, J.R.R. Tolkien's *Lord of the Rings,* a motley crew of characters must cross an entire continent, battling legions of powerful and deadly foes on a quest to destroy a powerful magical object upon which the fate of the world precariously hangs. Adventures thrive on dangerous quests with impossible odds. It is the very act of overcoming adversity that changes someone from ordinary to extraordinary, from "zero to hero" as the bard might say.

APPEALS TO LOGIC As we explain in Chapter 3, appeals to logic or lines of reasoning lead readers through a series of claims that ultimately support the main argumentative claim. Lines of reasoning are intellectual pathways, logical progressions that may develop over the course of an entire essay.

For example, Michael Hilliard's line of reasoning walks the reader methodically through his essay and toward his main point about video games. In its most basic form, his line of reasoning looks like this:

- Adventure stories inspire people to grapple with complex circumstances in their lives.
- Video games are a new and popular form of adventure story.
- Video game story lines sacrifice complexity for the sake of action.
- Video games, then, lack sufficient complexity to help people grapple with the circumstances in their lives.

The following claims (pulled directly from Hilliard's essay) are more elaborate than our boiled down version, but his line of reasoning is still detectable:

- Adventure stories have always played a major role in the growth and development of a society.

- We need stories of hope and determination, stories that inspire us to face the adversity in our lives head on with courage, even when hope seems lost.

- Until recently, books were the primary method for delivering adventure stories to the masses.

- Now, movies and video games are the media of choice.

- Instead of encouraging players to grapple with difficult circumstances [to face adversity] in their lives, video games all too often distract us with illusions of adventure, action, amusement and escapism.

- Unlike an adventure story, video games don't present a crisis with depth of meaning.

- As a dominant force in providing tales of adventure to our society, video games too often amuse rather than inspire.

As we explain in Chapter 3, each step (or premise) in a line of reasoning may require support. It's not enough to state each claim and then move on. As Hilliard's essay illustrates, some claims in a line of reasoning may require explanation, background, evidence, and examples. It all depends on the premise and audience: if the audience is likely to accept a premise, writers can move quickly to the next logical step, but if the audience is less likely to understand or accept a premise, writers have to provide support in whatever form they can.

APPEALS TO VALUE When writers appeal to value, they show how a topic is either in or out of tune with shared values such as equality, fairness, honor, and so on. For example, in "Evaluation of 'The Education of Ms. Groves,'" Adams shows that *Dateline* oversimplifies a complex issue. He argues that a news program should value critical thinking, not just entertainment.

> Certainly, tricks (techniques or strategies) help immensely in any profession, but the show oversimplified the messy issue of education—of teaching and of learning. And the degree to which it oversimplified something so complex, ongoing, and lifelong is what's stunning. The show told Americans frustrated with their education system that education is easy: Teachers simply need to be dedicated, love their students, and learn a couple nifty tricks. From the show, Americans are to conclude that students fail for one reason: because of bad teachers (because the teacher failed the student, the parent, and the country).

Throughout his argument, Adams reminds the reader of this appeal. For example,

- But in "The Education of Ms. Groves," other complex factors such as media, consumerism, or diet simply don't exist. The show makes two big mistakes: (1) It oversimplifies what it does talk about, and (2) it doesn't mention some other very messy contributing factors. [paragraph 5]

- *Dateline NBC* would have served viewers better by doing some in-depth analysis of this complex issue. Instead, they misrepresented and oversimplified, as they do with other issues (presidential elections, the environment, war). [paragraph 7]

In his essay, Hilliard appeals to values of hope, determination, and inspiration. For example,

> As the heroes in our stories make brave choices and remain steadfast, we identify with them, making them role models for our own lives. In a world that often seems lost and broken—where monsters take the form of terrorist bombings and school shootings, when the princess in need of rescue is a family member struggling with addiction, or a friend dealing with emotional abuse—we need stories of hope and determination, stories that inspire us to face the adversity in our lives head on with courage, even when hope seems lost.

Use the following invention questions to develop both evidence and appeals for your argument:

- ▶ What criteria should I use to evaluate the topic?
- ▶ How can I compare or contrast my topic to something else? To what situation, person, or thing does my topic relate? What qualities do they share? How can I use those shared qualities to support my point?
- ▶ Have I experienced something that might reveal an important aspect of this topic? How could it fit into the argument?
- ▶ What claims will create a line of reasoning that leads the audience to my conclusion?
- ▶ What values does the subject compromise or challenge?

ARRANGEMENT

HOW SHOULD I BEGIN? Writers often begin with a short introduction that leads up to the main claim. (See Chitwood's essay in this chapter.)

This strategy helps take the reader from the outside world into the world of the essay; it walks the reader up to the main idea that the rest of the essay will support. But arguers don't always state the main claim in the first paragraph. For example, Adams and Hilliard spend several paragraphs establishing important background and building a line of reasoning that leads to a statement of the main claim later in the argument.

HOW DO I LEAD THE READER FROM ONE IDEA TO THE NEXT? Good arguments flow smoothly from one idea to the next. One claim in a line of reasoning follows logically from a previous claim, and arguers connect claims and support. Notice how Hilliard walks the reader from one idea in the line of reasoning (Adventure stories were often filled with peril.) to the next (Choosing what was right instead of what was easy, they persevered and won the day.):

> But it wasn't all fun and games or pleasant walks in the woods. Quite the contrary, the stories were often filled with peril. Savage beasts, fearsome swordfights, and terrifying villains always seemed to lurk in the path of my beloved heroes, and their noble quests often seemed doomed to fail. And yet, no matter how dire the situation, no matter how impossible the odds or frightening the villain, the heroes would press on, even when they had the chance to run away. Choosing what was right instead of what was easy, they persevered and won the day.

Once Hilliard has taken the reader to a new point, he is ready to make the next point: *Adventure stories have always played a major role in the growth and development of a society. . . .* While the content of Hilliard's paragraph carries the reader from one idea to the next, arguers also use transitional sentences, phrases, (such as *however, but, and*) so that readers don't get lost. In the preceding example, Hilliard uses *But, Quite the contrary,* and *And yet* to lead the reader from idea to idea.

AUDIENCE AND VOICE

CONCESSIONS AND QUALIFIERS When arguers use concessions and qualifiers to acknowledge the validity of opposition, their arguments become more sophisticated and more appealing to a broader audience. *Concessions* are statements that acknowledge the value of an opposing claim, and *qualifiers* acknowledge limits on the writer's own claims.

When the argumentative stance is intense because the arguer is making heated points, concessions and qualifiers are especially valuable. Adams concedes two points in his essay. In the first concession, he admits that a single news program has certain limitations that can't be overcome:

> Of course a one-hour TV show can't cover everything. Producers must select and edit to put forth a certain argument, but the Dateline NBC argument is logically flawed.

In another paragraph, while he seems to oppose the notion of teacher tricks, he acknowledges they have some value:

> Certainly, tricks (techniques or strategies) help immensely in any profession, but the show oversimplified the messy issue of education—of teaching and of learning. And the degree to which it oversimplified something so complex, ongoing, and lifelong is what's stunning.

These concessions enhance Adams's voice by acknowledging other views. Without concessions and qualifiers, Adams would appear unaware of complexity, and the strength of his argument would suffer.

ASIDES (PARENTHETICAL COMMENTS) The aside or parenthetical comment allows writers a virtual space to stretch out and give the reader slightly more. Although the parenthetical comment is used for a broad range of purposes, three uses are dominant: (1) to give more detailed information; (2) to add an informal and often more opinionated assertion; (3) to emphasize or extend a point. In the following passage, John Adams uses asides (ideas placed within parentheses) for all three reasons. For example, in the first paragraph below, the aside "(presidential elections, the environment, war)" gives more detailed information about the "other issues":

> *Dateline NBC* would have served viewers better by doing some in-depth analysis of this complex issue. Instead, they misrepresented and oversimplified, as they do with other issues (presidential elections, the environment, war). One consequence, whether positive or negative, of the show's "logic" may be that it motivates some people to try teaching. Golly, it looks so easy: All a teacher needs to do is get the tricks of the trade from the principal first, then he or she can avoid all the problems that Ms. Groves encountered. Of course, anyone who thinks this way isn't really thinking much.
>
> Many people will realize that the show ignored complexities (the way a politician does when he says the economy's good because more Americans own homes than ever before). Many people will realize that *Dateline NBC* turned a complex issue into a TV drama like *Desperate Housewives* or *Grey's Anatomy.* It had an attractive leading character, some good drama (even a fight!), and an emotional (uplifting) ending. Unfortunately, though it will entertain, this show will disappoint a curious mind because it reduces a serious issue to a Hallmark card. A lot of dedicated, loving, trick-savvy teachers are probably laughing (though with frustration) at the TV-style docu-drama of American education. While it showed the father in prison, the

homeless family, and so on, according to *Dateline NBC,* it can all be overcome (all of American culture can be overcome) if our teachers just know to count backwards. *Supernanny* and *Wife Swap* deal with complexity more than this.

Many of the cultural problems educators are up against are created, reinforced, and spread by American media. American children grow up immersed in a loud, often stupid, world of media and consumption (the two are really the same).

Activity

Several asides appear in the paragraphs above:

- (the way a politician does when he says the economy's good because more Americans own homes than ever before)
- (even a fight!)
- (uplifting)
- (though with frustration)
- (all of American culture can be overcome)
- (the two are really the same)

For each aside, does it (1) give more detailed information, (2) add an informal and more opinionated assertion, (3) emphasize or extend a point?

REVISION

To revise, begin with the larger questions. You can find these global concerns by reviewing the chapter introduction, which emphasizes important general points when it comes to arguing about value. For example,

- What important idea—about something that is harmful or helpful, dangerous or valuable, and so on—does the essay communicate to the reader?
- How does the argument go beyond your gut reaction? How does it carefully weigh an issue or situation, analyze its layers, and claim something revelatory?
- What hidden value does it bring to light?
- Why is it important to help others accept the main claim and act accordingly?

RESEARCH AND REVISION: If you used outside sources, consider the following questions. As you revise, refer to the corresponding pages in Chapters 13 and 14:

- Have you used research as means of discovery? (pages 309–328)
- Have you evaluated sources for ideology, reliability, relevance, timeliness, and diversity? (pages 329–338)
- Are the ideas from the outside sources integrated smoothly into your ideas? (pages 338–349)
- Are the sources documented appropriately (with in-text and end citation)? (pages 350–375)

Peer Review

Exchange drafts with at least one other writer. (If time allows, exchange with two or three writers to gather a range of perspectives or comments.) Use the following questions to generate specific constructive comments about others' drafts:

1. How does the argument answer this basic question: *What is the value of the topic?*

2. What is the argument's main claim? If it depends on linking verbs and general adjectives—"College athletics are unfair," "Liberals don't have a clue," "Required courses are unnecessary"—how can it be more focused on a particular aspect or point?

3. What is the most supportive passage? Describe why it works well in the argument. What passage might the arguer delete and why?

4. How is this argument *revelatory*? (What genuinely new perspective does it offer? How does it help us to re-see the topic?)

5. How could the writer use more allusions, examples, scenarios, or testimony to illustrate specific points?

6. How does the argument respond to opposition? What counterarguments does the writer make? What points might the writer concede or qualify?

7. What phrases or passages could be more focused, more specific? Comment on any phrases, sentences, or passages that speak broadly about the topic and lack a specific explanation or detailed support strategy.

8. Check for paragraph coherence: What paragraphs shift focus or take on too many separate points without a clear line of reasoning?

9. Are sources integrated smoothly, not forced into passages? Explain any gaps between the writer's line of reasoning and the ideas from an outside source. (See pages 338–349.)

John Metz

10

Arguing Crisis

What Are We Going To Do?

Rhetoricians in ancient Greece and Rome taught students about argument by using examples of crises. They would place students in hypothetical situations: *The barbarians are coming over the hill and attacking the city; what should we do?* Their students would create arguments that addressed the complexities of the situation. Such lessons were important because they illustrated the vital role of argument in everyday life. Public crises almost always give way to arguments, and the most persuasive arguments have dictated the direction of local, national, and international policies in all civilizations.

Saul David Alinsky, a Chicago community organizer, said, "When written in Chinese, the word 'crisis' is composed of two characters—one represents danger, and the other represents opportunity." From a rhetorical perspective, crises are opportunities to think differently, to act differently, to develop new ideas. In fact, in a crisis situation, thinking in the same old ways can lead nowhere. (The status quo can be downright dangerous!) Good arguers know how to bring their audiences out of intellectual, social, political, economic, and spiritual crises.

Crises loom in nearly every situation, whether social, institutional, professional, or political. Something unsavory that no one predicted is bound to happen. And once something does go awry, the arguments begin: Should we sell the company, downsize, or retool the inventory? Should we call a plumber or fix it ourselves? Should we run for the hills or stay here and fight? Should we start driving cars with better gas mileage or revamp the public transportation system in this country? Should we make friends with these pale-skinned settlers, drive them back to their boats, or ignore them and hope they go away?

Any one crisis prompts a huge variety of possible responses. But those often get whittled down to two options, and advocates of either side A or B argue over the worth of one response while tearing apart the other. This focus on only two options, however, blurs other possibilities. During the Cold War, for example, many people in the Soviet Union and the United States imagined that one side would attack the other: "It's either them or us." But a third course of events took place: the Soviet economy slowly caved in, and the standoff between the two nations faded into history.

Insightful thinkers try to see through the crossfire, beyond the two common possibilities. Imagine the following: A group of managers at a small company are faced with a dilemma. The materials they use for shipping and packaging have not arrived, and they need to ship their product to a customer who needs it on time. One manager suggests calling the customer and breaking the news but also giving a discount on the product. Another manager argues that they should ship the product without the proper packaging so the order arrives on time. While the managers debate the value of those two options, someone raises a third option: They could buy a limited amount of material from a nearby packaging service so a portion of the shipment could be sent and then wait to ship the remainder. The third, slightly more involved, option would probably best address the crisis. Like this situation, most crises can be handled in a variety of ways, but the realm of possibility may lie hidden behind a wall of common practices, traditional perspectives, or a perceived either/or choice.

A crisis is a crucial or decisive situation in which things are about to change with potentially severe or intense consequences. Experts in all fields and academic disciplines must deal with crises:

- Engineers scramble to develop new plans for a bridge that must account for new information about the shifting sediment on the river's flood plain.
- A nursing staff must respond to increased patient care demands and a projected decline in hiring.
- A council for regional artists must address an anticipated cut in funding for the National Endowment for the Arts.
- Because a local school tax levy failed, teachers must figure out how they will staff an important after-school program for junior high students.

Regardless of the particular situation, those who react to crises and propose the best possible solutions (the most manageable, ethical, practical, economic, far-reaching, etc.) are often the most valuable individuals in a given situation. They can see hidden implications, blurred boundaries, and potential consequences.

Arguments about crisis involve two layers: (1) the crisis, and (2) possible solutions. The essays in this chapter spend more time developing the first layer—attempting to persuade readers that a particular crisis exists. Tracy Webster, Amber Edmondson, and Laurie Schutza focus on crises related to homes, consumer behavior, and hoarding. Their essays focus primarily on the crises and not so much on solutions. Because readers may not see the urgency of each situation, these writers devote most of their arguments to the crisis layer. Curtis White takes a slightly different approach by focusing on the complex cause of the crisis. He claims that the environmental crisis continues because mainstream society is too weak to acknowledge it and because environmental activism is incapable of addressing its real origins. Curtis argues that solutions become possible only if we understand the complexity of the crisis. As these arguments illustrate, the emphasis on crisis or solution depends on the topic, the opposing voices, and even previous solutions.

Proposals

A proposal is an argument that calls for a particular course of action. Proposals are one type of argument that emerges from a critical social situation—a situation that warrants collective or public action. They take many forms. Business proposals, course proposals, and congressional or legislative proposals are more formal types, which require specific formatting conventions. But proposals also come in more generic and informal arguments. In fact, the proposal essay is a common form, and it usually contains the following elements:

- **Description of the situation that warrants action (the crisis):** a claim of fact about the situation and evidence to support it.
- **Counterarguments:** why people should accept the situation as warranting action, despite other portrayals of the situation.
- **Description of the proposed solution:** how it would address the situation, how life would look once it is implemented.
- **Support (evidence and appeals) for the solution:** why it should be implemented or at least attempted.
- **Counterarguments against other solutions:** how other solutions (beyond the writer's) might fall short.
- **Concession about other solutions:** how other solutions (beyond the writer's) might be of value.

The proposal argument has no universal formula. Its elements change depending on the situation. For instance, if a writer is addressing a relatively common crisis, something that many other people have acknowledged as important, then he will spend less time describing that crisis but more time dealing with other solutions. If a writer is taking on a relatively new crisis, something readers have not generally acknowledged, then she would spend more time on the description and little or no time discussing other solutions. But despite the potential difference, one quality remains consistent: The proposal writer foregrounds or prioritizes the action to be taken—or the claims of policy. While some arguments prioritize the crisis itself (getting readers to believe that a particular crisis exists), proposals spend more energy on asserting and defending the steps to address the crisis or a plan of action.

The invention work throughout this chapter will generate important rhetorical strategies for a proposal argument. Specifically, the following questions should be considered for a successful argument:

- **The crisis:** What is the critical situation? Do readers need to be introduced to it and convinced that action should be taken? Why might people dismiss the situation? What reasons would they give for dismissing it? Can you address those reasons?
- **The solution:** What particular strategy can you assert? How will your solution address specific elements or causes of the crisis? How is your solution particularly practical, logical, manageable, ethical, humane, or economical?
- **Other solutions:** What else has been tried or proposed? Why might your solution be more practical, manageable, logical, ethical, cost-effective, or necessary?

The Idols of Environmentalism

CURTIS WHITE

I n this essay, White makes a powerful move: he explains how the environmental crisis continues despite, and even because of, environmentalists' arguments. While many essays about the environment blame particular people or policies for ongoing destruction, White walks readers toward increasingly subtle layers of cause and effect. For him, the crisis lingers in the very language most people use to discuss the crisis. In this sense, White argues about the nature of the argument. The article was first published in *Orion Magazine* in 2007.

Environmental destruction proceeds apace in spite of all the warnings, the good science, the 501(c)3 organizations with their memberships in the millions, the poll results, and the martyrs perched high in the branches of sequoias or shot dead in the Amazon. This is so not because of a power, a strength out there that we must resist. It is because we are weak and fearful. Only a weak and fearful society could invest so much desperate energy in protecting activities that are the equivalent of suicide.

For instance, trading carbon emission credits and creating markets in greenhouse gases as a means of controlling global warming is not a way of saying we're so confident in the strength of the free market system that we can even trust it to fix the problems it creates. No, it's a way of saying that we are so frightened by the prospect of stepping outside of the market system on which we depend for our national wealth, our jobs, and our sense of normalcy that we will let the logic of that system try to correct its own excesses even when we know we're just kidding ourselves. This delusional strategy is embedded in the Kyoto agreement, which is little more than a complex scheme to create a giant international market in pollution. Even Kyoto, of which we speak

longingly—"Oh, if only we would join it!"—is not an answer to our problem but a capitulation to it, so concerned is it to protect what it calls "economic growth and development." Kyoto is just a form of whistling past the graveyard. And it is not just international corporations who do this whistling; we all have our own little stake in the world capitalism has made and so we all do the whistling.

The problem for even the best-intentioned environmental activism is that it imagines that it can confront a problem external to itself. Confront the bulldozers. Confront the chainsaws. Confront Monsanto. Fight the power. What the environmental movement is not very good at is acknowledging that something in the very fabric of our daily life is deeply anti-nature as well as anti-human. It inhabits not just bad-guy CEOs at Monsanto and Weyerhaeuser but nearly every working American, environmentalists included.

It is true that there are CEO-types, few in number, who are indifferent to everything except money, who are cruel and greedy, and so the North Atlantic gets stripped of cod and any number of other species are taken incidentally in what is the factory trawler's wet version of a scorched-earth policy. Or some junk bond maven buys up a section of old-growth redwoods and "harvests" it without hesitation when his fund is in sudden need of "liquidity." Nevertheless, all that we perceive to be the destructiveness of corporate culture in relation to nature is not the consequence of its power, or its capacity for dominating nature ("taming," as it was once put, as if what we were dealing with was the lion act at the circus). Believing in powerful corporate evildoers as the primary source of our problems forces us to think in cartoons.

5   Besides, corporations are really powerless to be anything other than what they are. I suspect that, far from being perverse merchants of greed hell-bent on destruction, these corporate entities are as bewildered as we are. Capitalism—especially

subject to. There is an idol even in the language we use to account for our problems. Our primary dependence on the scientific language of "environment," "ecology," "diversity," "habitat," and "ecosystem" is a way of acknowledging the superiority of the very kind of rationality that serves not only the Sierra Club but corporate capitalism as well. For instance:

- "You can pump this many tons of greenhouse gases into the atmosphere without disturbing the major climatic systems."

- "This much contiguous habitat is necessary to sustain a population allowing for a survivable gene pool for this species."

- "We'll keep a list, a running tally of endangered species (as we'll call these animals), and we'll monitor their numbers, and when that number hits a specified threshold we'll say they are 'healthy,' or we'll say they are 'extinct.' All this is to be done by bureaucratic fiat."

I am not speaking here of all the notorious problems associated with proving scientifically the significance of environmental destruction. My concern is with the wisdom of using as our primary weapon the rhetoric and logic of the very entities we suspect of causing our problems in the first place. Perhaps we support legalistic responses to problems, with all their technoscientific descriptors, out of a sense that this is the best we can do for the moment. But the danger is always that eventually we come to believe this language and its mindset ourselves. This mind-set is generally called "quantitative reasoning," and it is second nature to Anglo-Americans. Corporate execs are perfectly comfortable with it, and corporate philanthropists give their dough to environmental organizations that speak it. Unfortunately, it also has the consequence of turning environmentalists into quislings, collaborators, and virtuous practitioners of a cost-benefit logic figured in songbirds. It is because we have accepted this rationalist logos as the only legitimate means of debate that we are willing to think that what we need is a balance

in its corporate incarnation—has a logos, a way of reasoning. Capitalism is in the position of the notorious scorpion who persuades the fox to ferry him across a river, arguing that he won't sting the fox because it wouldn't be in his interest to do so, since he'd drown along with the fox. But when in spite of this logic he stings the fox anyway, all he can offer in explanation is "I did it because it is in my nature." In the same way, it's not as if businessmen perversely seek to destroy their own world. They have vacation homes in the Rockies or New England and enjoy walks in the forest, too. They simply have other priorities which are to them a duty.

The idea that we have powerful corporate villains to thank for the sorry state of the natural world is what Francis Bacon called an "idol of the tribe." According to Bacon, an idol is a truth based on insufficient evidence but maintained by constant affirmation within the tribe of believers. In spite of this insufficiency, idols do not fall easily or often. Tribes are capable of exerting will based on principles, but they are capable only with the greatest difficulty of willing the destruction of their own principles. It's as if they feel that it is better to stagger from frustration to frustration than to return honestly to the question, does what we believe actually make sense? The idea of fallen idols always suggests tragic disillusionment, but this is in fact a good thing. If they don't fall, there is no hope for discovering the real problems and the best and truest response to them. All environmentalists understand that the global crisis we are experiencing requires urgent action, but not everyone understands that if our activism is driven by idols we can exhaust ourselves with effort while having very little effect on the crisis. Most frighteningly, it is even possible that our efforts can sustain the crisis. The question the environmental tribe must ask is, do our mistaken assumptions actually cause us to conspire against our own interests?

The belief that corporate power is the unique source of our problems is not the only idol we are between the requirements of human economies and the "needs" of the natural world. Its as if we were negotiating a trade agreement with the animals and trees unlucky enough to have to share space with us. What do you need? we ask them. What are your minimum requirements? We need to know the minimum because we're not likely to leave you more than that. We're going to consume any "excess." And then it occurs to us to add, unless of course you taste good. There is always room for an animal that tastes good.

We use our most basic vocabulary, words like "ecosystem," with a complete innocence, as if we couldn't imagine that there might be something perilous in it. What if such language were actually the announcement of the defeat of what we claim to want? That's the worm at the heart of the rose of the "ecologist." It is something that environmentalism has never come to terms with because the very advocates for environmental health are most comfortable with the logic of science. never mind what else that logic may be doing for the military and industry. Would people and foundations be as willing to send contributions to The Nature Conservancy or the Sierra Club if the leading logic of the organization were not "ecosystems," but "respect for life" or "reverence for creation"? Such notions are, for many of us, compromised by associations with the Catholic Church and evangelicalism, and they don't loosen the purse strings of philanthropy. "Let's keep a nice, clean scientific edge between us and religion," we protest. In the end, environmental science criticizes not only corporate destructiveness but (as it has always done) more spiritual notions of nature as well.

Environmentalism seems to conclude that the best thing it can do for nature is make a case for it, as if it were always making a summative argument before a jury with the backing of the best science. Good children of the Enlightenment, we keep expecting Reason to prevail (and in a perverse and destructive way, it does prevail). It is the language of "system" (nature as a kind of complicated machine)

that allows most of us to feel comfortable with working for or giving money to environmental organizations. We even seem to think that the natural system should work in consort with our economic system. Why, we argue, that rainforest might contain the cure for cancer. By which we also mean that it could provide profitable products for the pharmaceutical industry and local economies. (God help the doomed indigenous culture once the West decides that it has an economy that needs assistance.) Al Gore's An Inconvenient Truth may have distressing things to say about global warming, but subconsciously it is an extended apology for scientific rationality, the free market, and our utterly corrupted democracy. Gore doesn't have to defend these things directly; he merely has to pretend that nothing else exists. Even the awe of Immanuel Kant's famous "starry skies above" is lost to modern environmentalism, so obsessed is it with what data, graphs, and a good PowerPoint presentation can show.

In short, there would be nothing inappropriate or undesirable were we to understand our relation to nature in spiritual terms or poetic terms or, with Emerson and Thoreau, in good old American transcendental terms, but there is no broadly shared language in which to do this. So we are forced to resort to what is in fact a lower common denominator: the languages of science and bureaucracy. These languages have broad legitimacy in our culture, a legitimacy they possess largely because of the thoroughness with which they discredited Christian religious discourse in the eighteenth and nineteenth centuries. But many babies went out with the bath water of Christian dogma and superstition. One of those was morality. Even now, science can't say why we ought not to harm the environment except to say that we shouldn't be self-destructive. Another of these lost spiritual children was our very relation as human beings to the mystery of Being as such. As the philosopher G. W. Leibniz famously wondered, "Why is there something rather than nothing?" For St. Thomas Aquinas, this was the fundamental religious question. In the place of a relation to the world that was founded on this mystery, we have a relation that is objective and data driven. We no longer have a forest; we have "board feet." We no longer have a landscape, a world that is our own; we have "valuable natural resources." Even avowed Christians have been slow to recall this spiritualized relationship to the world. For example, only recently have American evangelicals begun thinking of the environment in terms of what they call "creation care." We don't have to be born again to agree with evangelicals that one of the most powerful arguments missing from the environmentalist's case is reverence for what simply is. One of the heroes of Goethe's *Faust* was a character called Care (Sorge), who showed to Faust the unscrupulousness of his actions and led him to salvation. Environmentalism has made a Faustian pact with quantitative reasoning; science has given it power but it cannot provide deliverance. If environmentalism truly wishes, as it claims, to want to "save" something—the planet, a species, itself—it needs to rediscover a common language of Care.

The lessons of our idols come to this: you cannot defeat something that you imagine to be an external threat to you when it is in fact internal to you, when its life is your life. And even if it were external to you, you cannot defeat an enemy by thinking in the terms it chooses, and by doing only those things that not only don't harm it but with which it is perfectly comfortable. The truth is, our idols are actually a great convenience to us. It is convenient that we can imagine a power beyond us because that means we don't have to spend much time examining our own lives. And it is very convenient that we can hand the hard work of resistance over to scientists, our designated national problem solvers.

We cannot march forth, confront, and definitively defeat the Monsantos of the world, especially not with science (which, it should go without saying, Monsanto has plenty of). We can, however, look at ourselves and see all of the ways that we conspire against what we imagine to be our own most urgent interests. Perhaps the most powerful

way in which we conspire against ourselves is the simple fact that we have jobs. We are willingly part of a world designed for the convenience of what Shakespeare called "the visible God": money. When I say we have jobs, I mean that we find in them our home, our sense of being grounded in the world, grounded in a vast social and economic order. It is a spectacularly complex, even breathtaking, order, and it has two enormous and related problems. First, it seems to be largely responsible for the destruction of the natural world. Second, it has the strong tendency to reduce the human beings inhabiting it to two functions, working and consuming. It tends to hollow us out. It creates a hole in our sense of ourselves and of this country, and it leaves us with few alternatives but to try to fill that hole with money and the things money buys. We are not free to dismiss money because we fear that we'd disappear, we'd be nothing at all without it. Money is, in the words of Buddhist writer David Loy, "the flight from emptiness that makes life empty."

15   Needless to say, many people with environmental sympathies will easily agree with what I've just said and imagine that in fact they do what they can to resist work and consumption, to resist the world as arranged for the convenience of money. But here again I suspect we are kidding ourselves. Rather

than taking the risk of challenging the roles money and work play in all of our lives by actually taking the responsibility for reordering our lives, the most prominent strategy of environmentalists seems to be to "give back" to nature through the bequests, the annuities, the Working Assets credit cards and long distance telephone schemes, and the socially responsible mutual funds advertised in Sierra and proliferating across the environmental movement. Such giving may make us feel better, but it will never be enough. Face it, we all have a bit of the robber baron turned philanthropist in us. We're willing to be generous in order to "save the world" but not before we've insured our own survival in the reigning system. It's not even clear that this philanthropy is a pure expression of generosity since the bequest and annuity programs are carefully measured to provide attractive tax benefits and appealing rates of return.

Even when we are trying to aid the environment, we are not willing as individuals to leave the system that we know in our heart of hearts is the cause of our problems. We are even further from knowing how to take the collective risk of leaving this system entirely and ordering our societies differently. We are not ready. Not yet, at least.

Analyzing Argument

1. Summarize White's argument in one or two sentences. Try not to lose the complexity of his main claim.

2. White makes many claims in the essay, but what are his most important claims? In other words, what are the main premises (steps in his line of reasoning)? What logical steps must you, as a reader, make to accept his point about the crisis?

3. How does White use appeals to value? Point to one passage that relies on an appeal to value and explain its role in the overall argument.

4. How does counterargument work in White's essay? Focus on one passage and explain how it takes on (pushes against, refutes, or overturns) an opposing position.

5. Do you detect a solution in White's argument? If so, what kind of solution does he suggest?

6. Describe White's voice in this argument. Point to a particular passage that illustrates your understanding of his voice.

RMBrown/Alamy

Big House in the Wilderness: Moratoriums on Building and Individual Irresponsibility

TRACY WEBSTER

Tracy Webster developed this argument after reading Anna Quindlen's 2003 *Newsweek* article, "A Shock to the System," which proposes a moratorium on building permits. Webster seems to understand what he's up against: an ideology of self-righteousness and privilege. He knows that most readers feel entitled to do, buy, and build whatever they please. It's the American way. Therefore, he takes on that ideology directly and figures it into his argument for a radical solution. Webster's response also illustrates one way an outside source can be used in an argument: as a springboard into one's own set of assertions.

It's hunting season. I hear guns. Where I live, you can't drive home at night without stopping for a deer in the road, an elk, or even a moose. A bear ran alongside my car one night, and in the same place a few months later, one chased a jogger. What a great place this must be to hunt. In October, when it snows in the mountains, wild animals come down into the valley, and hunters shoot them. Even buffalo are in danger. They call it "harvesting" buffalo, and when the great bovines wander down into the lower elevations and cross a certain line (thus, "leaving the park"), hunters are there, to harvest them. The ranchers like this because they are afraid that the buffalo will infect their cattle with brucellosis, a bovine disease that the buffalo carry. No record of buffalo infecting cattle exists.

This is not an anti-hunting essay, though. Where I live, people build houses where buffalo live. They like it here. So they see a nice spot, a 20-acre parcel; deer graze on it and perhaps an eagle nests high in a tree. And the people build a 3,000- or 4,000- or 5,000-square-foot home, right there where the wild animals used to live. The people are proud of their homes. They show them off to their friends. Their homes make them feel good about themselves. If you live in such a home, you are no doubt successful. No doubt. But the deer eat their saplings and the mud swallows make nests in their eaves. And it's off: the battle between the homeowner and the nuisance, wildlife. So, the homebuilders are as big a threat to the wildlife as are the hunters. A bigger threat, really.

In "A Shock to the System," *Newsweek* essayist Anna Quindlen says that "no one seems to have considered the obvious alternative: instead of issuing hunting permits, call a moratorium on building permits. Permanently." (She's referring to hunting permits in New Jersey, for bear.) To some, Quindlen's argument may seem extreme, unnecessary, and perhaps un-American, taking away honest, hardworking Americans' rights to "life, liberty, and the pursuit of happiness." If they have, or can borrow, the money to buy property and build a home, don't they as Americans have the right (the freedom) to build as large a home as they individually choose to build anywhere they can buy to build it? It is, after all, their money, their home, their inalienable right, isn't it?

A moratorium on building, at this time, anywhere, seems unlikely. With the current American mindset, it is more likely that a building permit will be granted for yet another big home building supply store, one of those massive cathedrals to home building which helps make it cheaper and easier to conquer and destroy nature through construction. But are moratoriums on building permits, as Quindlen suggests, really necessary?

5 One question is: Can't individual Americans simply build differently? (Are moratoriums necessary?) Of course, to pursue this question (this line of thinking), the reader must accept the premise that Americans are overbuilding, and that by overbuilding, Americans are foolishly and unnecessarily overdestroying nature, the environment, wildlife. They have to accept the premise that current building practices are somehow harmful. Some Americans, to be certain, don't accept this premise. Here's why they should:

As Americans, we must walk a narrow path. The cities are dirty and crowded and dangerous. The countryside, the mountains, the wilderness are clean and peaceful. Who can blame someone for fleeing the city—or, even more, for fleeing the suburbs? What an awful place suburbia can be. It's thick with traffic and littered with strip malls. If it's all you know, it's not that bad; but to the more rural-minded, it can be quite offensive. And as millions of suburbanites and city dwellers discover the pain and misery and hell of their lives, they dream of getting out. And some do.

But Americans, perhaps more than any other people who have ever lived, are terrible at walking narrow paths. They cannot just move to the wilderness and live. They must pound the wilderness to death. They must beat it to hell. They must drive gas-guzzling, polluting, school-bus-sized SUVs a hundred miles to work and back. They must build huge homes, large enough to be small hotels.

Anna Quindlen says that according to the National Association of Home Builders, "the average American home has doubled in size in the past century." Some see this, no doubt, as a great achievement—a sign of their own and their country's success and prosperity. But family size hasn't doubled; it has decreased. Americans have come to simply want, expect, and possess *more stuff*. And along with this, they cannot merely displace a few animals and live in relative peace with the rest. Instead, they see it as their right to destroy the homes—and what have been the homes for centuries—of more wildlife than a thousand humans have any acceptable reason to destroy, simply because they'd like to have a large and impressive home in a pretty place. Sadly, this is why Quindlen's proposed moratorium is necessary, and why it is the only solution.

Americans, left alone, will not build smaller or smarter or more compassionately. Instead, a few concerned activists, those who truly see the issue, must build a coalition to force others, through government action (a moratorium on building permits) to live more responsibly.

10   I began this essay by thinking out loud how it seems odd that men come here to hunt deer that you have to try not to hit with your car. The deer aren't hard to find, and when they see you they just stand there, motionless, staring. Of course, you can't shoot the ones standing on the road. You have to drive out a ways, then walk a bit farther, and then shoot one. Back there, in the woods, the deer might have a better chance, by blending in with the trees and hearing or smelling or seeing you before you see them.

But this is not an anti-hunting essay or an anti-house-in-the-wilderness essay. It is an anti-big-house-in-the-wilderness essay. The big house in the wilderness is more dangerous than any hunter is. It's the big house, the too-big house, that is unjustifiable. Quindlen compares the way that Americans act with their animal counterparts today to the way our ancestors once acted toward Native American people: We are willing to "tolerate" them as long as "they don't demand to share." She says, "If they don't cooperate, we slaughter them." We "harvest" them, she means. She is right to make connections between the past and the present, and between building permits and hunting permits: *Homebuilders are slaughtering buffalo.*

Moratoriums on building permits would not be necessary if individual homebuilders acted more responsibly, but how in our present culture could Americans ever bring themselves to act more responsibly? Some do, of course. But most can't. They simply see it as their right to do whatever they feel like doing. They see anything else as an infringement on their freedom, a personal insult, and a public injustice. Quindlen's suggestion requires collective, or government, action—a more extreme measure that must be taken to prevent individual freedom-loving Americans from eating the whole pie, instead of having just one piece. As more and more Americans, attracted to a beautiful life among wildlife, build homes in deserts and forests and fields, their own sensitivity and integrity is at stake. We would all benefit if individual homebuilders had in the past considered, *or would in the future consider*, a few hard questions before changing the landscape so drastically:

- How large a home should I build? How destructive to the plants and animals should it be? How important or necessary is it that I build such a large home where animals once lived, and won't be able to live anymore?

- What, honestly, is my relationship to nature? Am I mostly appreciating it, or am I mostly torturing it?

- How might I build differently out of respect for what I claim to value and love—wildlife?

What would happen if Americans could somehow overcome their own selfish and hypocritical desires to overbuild and overdestroy, and instead make *every* effort, not just *some* effort, to peacefully and respectfully coexist with nonhuman life? Doing this would require a new sort of vision—seeing all the wildlife that they presently overlook. It would also require a new look at rhetoric, replacing words like "harvest" with "slaughter" and "environment" with "home." What would happen if all new homebuilders saw themselves more as visitors, guests, and newcomers? And better yet, as intruders, conquerors, and imperialists?

If Quindlen's proposal seems extreme, it is because in American society where narrow paths have become unimaginable to many, individual freedom allows for, and encourages, individual irresponsibility. As long as Americans are free to build obscenely large houses, to destroy acres of wildlife habitat, to pollute the air and rivers, many Americans are going to do exactly that. Why? Because they see it as their right, because they are free, because they are Americans. Quindlen is right: Moratoriums on building permits are the obvious alternative.

Analyzing Argument

1. Why does Webster connect hunting and home building? How is that connection important to his line of reasoning?

2. In paragraph 4, Webster says, "With the current American mindset, it is more likely that a building permit will be granted for yet another big home building supply store. . . ." To what mindset does Webster refer?

3. Describe Webster's use of counterargument, concession, and qualifier. How do they function in his argument? Which does he rely on most?

4. As a secondary source, Quindlen's argument is vital to Webster. In your own words, how would you describe the relationship between Quindlen's and Webster's arguments?

5. Webster says, "*Homebuilders are slaughtering buffalo*" (paragraph 11). What is the effect of this phrase on readers? What is the effect of the italics?

The Pack Rat Among Us

LAURIE SCHUTZA

Laurie Schutza developed the following argument over several weeks in her English composition course. As with many good academic arguments, Schutza's began with a personal problem—one that worked quietly in her own life. She even wondered if it was appropriate for the public context of academic argument. But as she invented layers of her initial thoughts and researched others' struggles with hoarding, she realized the significance of the topic. Her argument, then, attempts to drag this quiet crisis into the light of day.

I look up at the house on the hill. Situated in a relatively affluent neighborhood, overlooking the ocean, it looks like a normal, well-maintained home from street level, but as I walk up the driveway and it comes into full view, the reality of the situation hits me like a stack of old newspapers. There is no doubt this is the home of compulsive hoarders. It is also the home of people I love.

The contents of the garage, filled with unpacked moving boxes of twenty years, unfinished projects, and every tool known to mankind are spilling onto the driveway. There is an old Chevy van with peeling paint that has been sitting up for years. Several working refrigerators and freezers filled with food that will spoil before eaten line the narrow pathway to the front door. Along this obstacle course, I must watch my step, for there are many tripping hazards. A tangle of old hoses and extension cords roam and twist like snakes along the trail. Mountains of long-forgotten objects peek from under tattered tarps overgrown with ivy. I walk past old tires, car parts, construction materials, broken-down appliances, and old machinery in need of repair. Standing water, fallen leaves, moss, and lichen form the frosting on top of the layers of debris. The front porch is lined with boxes and bags of unknown contents.

As I enter the front door, I am greeted with disorganized heaps and stacks of papers, plastic bags, more cardboard boxes, and various junk drawers. Finding a place to sit becomes a scavenger hunt. If I investigate further, I can see the sofas, chairs, tables, antiques, and decorations that furnished what was once a tasteful living room, now made unlivable by the clutter. The dining room is covered with piles of paper. Family meals at the table are nonexistent. Junk mail, newspapers, magazines, videotapes, vitamin supplements, dishes, and stockpiles of food and paper products fill the kitchen counter space. Even the stove is unusable unless one moves the piles. Empty milk jugs, cans, containers, and general trash line the kitchen floor.

The rest of the house is no better. I squeeze myself through cramped paths where cobwebs drape from the ceiling and a thick veil of dust covers everything. The closets are full to capacity and are spilling into every bedroom. Clothes, books, knickknacks, brand-new electronic equipment never even taken out of their boxes, and more magazines and paper fill every nook and cranny. Items such as food, batteries, flashlights, tools, work gloves, and office supplies are stashed and stockpiled "just in case." Family treasures, mementos, and heirlooms languish under the junk like relics waiting to be discovered. It's impossible to find anything when needed, time is wasted, and important things get lost. There is no space to work, play, sit, eat, or even sleep. No longer can any of the rooms be used for their intended purpose. As I maneuver my way through the house, I feel like the walls are swallowing me: "I'm suffocating," I think to myself. How has this happened? How has the house on the hill become such an insurmountable nightmare?

To many observers this is certainly an extreme situation, but the inhabitants of this house did not start out this way. It was a slow process of accumulation over years. These family members are not idle or lazy, but hard-working, well-educated individuals. To the outside world, they seem perfectly normal and no one would ever suspect. But they are experts at hiding their secret life, never inviting guests in and only meeting friends in places other than their chaotic home. Hoarders are generally misunderstood by the public and are jokingly referred to as "pack rats." Most of us would be appalled and say, "Why don't they just clean up the junk?" But hoarders have extreme difficulty giving up their possessions and become emotionally attached to everything they own. They don't like living this way and would like to change, but the task seems too overwhelming, the clutter so pervasive that they can't figure out where to begin. Living in fear, embarrassment, and shame, they have built a fortress of stuff that isolates them from the outside world. Feeling out of control, they can eventually give up.

Why do hoarders attach themselves to things? Is it because of fear and what are they afraid of? Have they been adding things to their existence to fill an emptiness or void? Are they hiding within the walls, battling the inevitable realities of life such as new relationships, careers, and even death? The fortress of stuff may be a defense against fear. Like a security blanket giving them a layer of comfort that insulates them from the outside world, their possessions may help them to feel safe and secure. Maybe by attaching themselves to things, they are fulfilling a need for security.

Many people are happy to be considered pack rats, collecting items and storing them until needed. Our homes may even have one of those junk rooms, hidden behind closed doors that we would rather forget about. But when this mentality is taken to an extreme, and every room is crammed with large disorderly quantities of things, the home can become dangerous and unlivable. This condition is known as compulsive hoarding. It is a debilitating mental illness related to obsessive-compulsive disorder (OCD). And more common than one might think: "2.5 percent of Americans suffer from OCD, which translates into approximately seven million people or roughly one out of every forty adults . . . between one-quarter to one-third of those with OCD also have hoarding symptoms" (Neziroglu et al. 2). Researchers say this estimate may be low because of the secretive nature of the hoarder. According to The Children of Hoarders, a support group devoted to helping those with this disorder, "more than 1.4 million homes in the United States alone are . . . hoard homes" (Children of Hoarders). There are even studies showing that hoarding can be genetic. One such study "found that 84% of compulsive hoarders reported a family history of hoarding behaviors in at least one first-degree relative" (qtd. in Saxena and Maidment 1144). There are numerous motivations behind hoarding, and even though the volume of items differentiates us from the hoarders, we may recognize some of these tendencies in ourselves.

What is the fundamental reason behind hoarding and collecting stuff? Humans developed approximately 100,000 years ago as hunter/gatherers. To survive brutal winters, drought, and famine, our ancestors were genetically programmed to eat and store calories when food was abundant. Likewise, they learned it was to their advantage to save and store anything that was important for survival. But what else motivated them to save? According to the authors of the book *Overcoming Compulsive Hoarding*, "fear is the basic reason behind the drive to save. . . . If you think about the bare essentials for human survival, food and shelter are crucial. . . . [Hoarders] may have learned to temporarily avoid feeling fear by feeling secure and safe with [their] possessions" (Neziroglu et al. 31).

To acquire more and save is fundamentally human. No wonder the tendency to stockpile and hoard is affecting our daily lives. As Mary Duenwald writes in her article for *Discovery*, "That compulsion, scientists now theorize, is a natural and adaptive instinct gone amok" (30). Whereas at one time, only royalty and the wealthy could afford material extravagances, the Industrial Revolution and mass production created a middle class that could finally enjoy affordable goods. Now that food and material things are plentiful, we have developed problems of overindulgence.

10   But what motivates hoarders to amass huge quantities of stuff? The reasons vary, but the fear of being without is the common thread that runs through the compulsion. They are afraid to discard anything that might be useful some day, so they decide to keep everything. The "just in case" scenario comes into play (Neziroglu et al. 133). Hoarders live in fear of being unprotected if anything goes wrong. They acquire junk as insurance against any conceivable future need. They feel their very survival depends on it. (And many elderly hoarders are products of the Great Depression where they were taught to save everything or the Cold War where they were taught to stockpile and always be prepared.)

Every item seems unique and therefore irreplaceable. Hoarders tend to keep what many may consider useless items such as empty food containers or cardboard boxes. They may even place the same importance on items like empty milk jugs, light bulbs, or a gold necklace. One may find all three of these items in one of the many piles of a hoarder. They have difficulty categorizing so everything ends up in disorganized heaps. Printed information such as newspapers and magazines are not thrown out until they are read and understood (Neziroglu et al. 35). They actually fear losing information that may change their lives for the better. The amount of paper coming into all our homes is staggering. Tons of junk mail, magazines, and newspapers worm their way in, and if one doesn't stay on top of the paper flow, it can stack up fast. Reading it all can become a monumental task. Unread reading material is one of the most common items kept by hoarders. They think, one of these days they will read it all. But that day never comes.

Hoarding can actually replace spending time with loved ones. Hoarded objects fill the emptiness and loneliness. Empty nesters replace their grown children, retired people replace a lost career, and a widow replaces a deceased spouse.

Inability to prioritize and indecisiveness is perhaps the most pervasive problem facing the hoarder. Having to decide what to get rid of, they begin to feel anxious and uncomfortable (Neziroglu et al. 36). They over-think every item, so they end up keeping it all. A phenomenon called "churning" may occur (qtd. in Neziroglu et al. 38) when one tries to clean one pile and it is intermixed with another. Things get lost, creating more disorder, and piles never leave the house.

Hoarders tend to have many interests and can be quite creative, seeing the potential in everything. They want to do it all themselves at their own pace, considering it an extravagance or a sign of weakness to enlist the help of others. In reality they think no one else can do the job to their standards. Having big, ambitious ideas, they may decide to start several projects all at once, but they bounce back and forth between the tasks and cannot seem to follow through. There is an inclination to avoid the task because everything they do becomes tedious and overwhelming. This difficulty to prioritize can lead to procrastination. Hoarders have this utopian vision that one day there will be enough time to finish all they plan to do, including cleaning up the mess. The problem is there's never enough time and in actuality, they would need several lifetimes to accomplish all they set out to do. This way of thinking may even be their defense against the inevitabilities of life and death; their way of displaying their invincibility. As long as these ongoing works in progress are alive and well, they are too. Unfortunately, time marches on all too quickly, and all the items bought and saved, with the best of intentions, are just added to the other piles of grand dreams.

These are some of the more common traits of   15
the hoarder. They may sound extreme, but how far removed are we, the consumers, from this tendency to collect and save? Are we just a few steps

away from extreme hoarding? Do *we really need* everything we buy and save? Although the hoarder's behavior is taken to a pathological extreme, we all seem to share the same basic tendency to avoid fear by acquiring and collecting possessions that create that feeling, or at least impression, of safety and security. And maybe the pathology is somewhat collective. America has become a nation of mass consumers. We are encouraged to be good shoppers and it's our obligation as citizens to buy, because it fuels greater productivity, creating more jobs that lead to more wealth for consumers to buy more stuff. It's the American way. Life might be just a little more perfect if we just had that new television, computer, or car. We are constant upgraders and are driven to buy the newest, up-to-date gadget proclaiming, "Just get rid of the old model," creating our so-called "throwaway" society. The problem is, hoarders don't throw anything away and consider themselves resourceful recyclers. In the past thirty years, we've gone from records, reel-to-reel, eight-track, cassettes, compact discs, and now MP-3 players all in a blink of an eye. Every year the technology gets smaller, sleeker, and faster. Consumers want "it" and have to have "it" now (whatever "it" may be). The whole system is geared to help us acquire all that we desire, but the hawkers of products haven't addressed how to rid ourselves of these things when they become undesirable.

Advertising is built around and for consumption. We are constantly being force-fed stuff—and the need for more stuff. We can't escape the barrage. According to University of Victoria Professor Daniel Laskarin:

> We live in a culture of consumption. . . . Many of us sacrifice more than half of our lives doing things we don't enjoy to buy things we don't need. We have plenty, yet feel dissatisfied. . . . The only way out is to stop and ask what we really want instead of letting the media and big business tell us (qtd. in Gibson 61).

Television commercials try to convince us that our dreams will come true if we buy their products. Celebrities promote spending money to achieve a certain look. Newspapers are full of shopping "bargains" we can't resist. They lure us in with early-bird specials and enticing coupons. Holiday advertising encourages us to buy gifts to show our love for one another. But stores can actually create a sense of urgency unleashing shopping frenzies turning violent and ugly, where people fight over merchandise and possibly get trampled in the process. The ads can convince us to buy things we didn't even know we needed.

There are more and more ways to acquire things. Department, specialty, and discount stores are old reliables. The arrival of online shopping and television shopping channels has made purchasing even more accessible. Items can be ordered without having to leave home or interact with people, creating more separation from the outside world. And now popular warehouse stores such as Sam's Club and Costco encourage us to stockpile. Garage sales, resale shops, flea markets, and antique malls are favorite places to find bargains. Television shows like *Antiques Roadshow* give us false hope that our treasures will become valuable someday. This encourages us to save items that maybe we shouldn't. Some of these treasures may end up on eBay and the cycle goes on. Compulsive shopping is now a common form of shopping. It sends millions of "average" consumers spiraling into debt. Meanwhile, the average home becomes a warehouse for all the stuff. Junk drawers spill over to kitchen counters and tables. Closets, attics, and basements overflow into bedrooms. Crammed garages lead to storage rentals. Our possessions elbow us into bigger homes so we can fill more rooms with even more stuff. According to Anna Quindlen, "the average American home has doubled in size in the past century" (qtd. in Webster 302). Tracy Webster continues, "Some see this, no doubt, as a great achievement—a sign of their own and their country's success and prosperity. But family size hasn't doubled; it has decreased. Americans have come to simply want,

Kathy Bishop/morguefile.com

from letting anything new into our lives. We may miss out on blossoming relationships, fascinating careers, or exciting trips if we continue to dwell in the past. The key is "to stop saving memories and start making them" (Children of Hoarders).

If possessions get too out of hand, they can cre- 20 ate dangerous health risks, including tripping and fire hazards and allergies due to molds and dusts. Many hoarders are elderly with health problems such as osteoporosis or blindness. Just one fall can send them to the hospital, never to return home. There are even instances where people have been buried alive by their own junk. The most legendary is the case of two hoarding brothers, Homer and Langley Collyer. They were discovered dead in their New York City mansion in 1947 buried under tons of debris collected over a forty-year period (Duenwald 30).

Clutter can put a strain on relationships. Our neighbors don't appreciate junked-up houses in their communities. Homes that are overflowing, spilling into driveways and yards are unsightly and may cause property values to lower in the neighborhood. There are cases where the stuff gets so out of hand that either neighborhood associations or the public health department must step in. Friends stop coming over or calling. Wives have given husbands ultimatums: "Clean it up or I'm leaving you." It's difficult for family members to visit when the stuff becomes the main focus. It's a huge distraction, making it impossible to relax and converse. Tension builds up, tempers flare, and feelings get hurt. It can literally tear families apart. This burden, this legacy of stuff, will eventually be handed down to the next generation to deal with.

I would like to save the people that live in the house on the hill, but it is an imposing job. I have attempted to tackle a closet or a room, but to my dismay, any empty space that I create is immediately filled. Sometimes it seems hopeless. Their things seem to come first, because they are so emotionally tied to them. The stuff keeps them occupied, but they miss out on new opportunities. These new situations can be scary, but they use their possessions as an excuse to further separate themselves

expect, and possess more stuff" (302). As comedian George Carlin once quipped, "Your house is just a pile of stuff with a cover on it . . . a place to keep your stuff while you go out and get more stuff."

Our homes can become museums of our own personal artifacts. Souvenirs from every trip we took over the years, programs from every event we've attended, and boxes stuffed with childhood memories. Sometimes these things can keep us living in the past. Memories are attached to objects and in turn we attach ourselves to those objects. We may feel if the item is discarded, we are somehow throwing a part of ourselves away with it. Some things are important to keep such as photos, letters, and mementos of very special occasions. But when we keep too many of these things, it can become a compulsion and we can't let go. If we keep a whole lifetime's worth of possessions, they can prevent us from society. They feel safe and secure in their own little world they have created: this *fortress of isolation*. If I could break through those walls, I would, but it's an arduous task to try to change people so set in their ways. As much as I want to alter their behavior, hoarders can't bear to part with their stuff.

I look at myself and wonder: Do I have these tendencies? Am I destined to become a pack rat? I look in my closets crowded with clothes and shoes, much I don't wear. Stacks of mail that I keep saying I'm going to sort and read are piled up around my house. My grown kid's artwork, clothing, and toys fill the attic, but I can't part with so much of it for sentimental reasons. Who among us can say we have none of the characteristics of the hoarder? Haven't we all taken pleasure from buying and owning things? The motivation to collect and store is powerful. Our ancestors used this survival technique to their advantage, but today, "living in a land of wants, not needs, creates its own dilemmas" (Vanderbilt). Do we buy it or not . . . do we keep it or throw it out? That's the big question. There are so many choices; maybe too many. Most of us can make these decisions efficiently, but the hoarder agonizes over each and every item and ends up keeping it all. But aren't we all attached to our possessions to a certain extent? We like our things until they threaten to control us. That need to feel safe and secure to avoid feeling fear is what links all of us to the hoarder. Even the most organized and efficient among us must admit to feeling a bit overwhelmed by the volume of stuff and junk we possess, accumulate, and think we need. In our quest to acquire and attach ourselves to things, are we just a few steps away from the inhabitants of the house on the hill? Perhaps a little "pack rat" resides in all of us.

Works Cited

Children of Hoarders. *Can't Let Anyone in Your House?* 2013, www.childrenofhoarders.com/files/Hoarder_color_june1406.pdf.

Duenwald, Mary. "The Psychology of . . . Hoarding." *Discover*, Oct. 2004, pp. 30–31.

Gibson, Katherine. *Unclutter Your Life: Transforming Your Physical, Mental, and Emotional Space*. Beyond Words, 2004.

Neziroglu, Fugen, et al. *Overcoming Compulsive Hoarding: Why You Save and How You Can Stop*. New Harbinger Publications, 2004.

Saxena, Sanjaya, and Karron M. Maidment. "Treatment of Compulsive Hoarding." *Journal of Clinical Psychology*, vol. 60, no. 11, Nov. 2004, pp. 1143–54, doi: 10.1002/jclp.20079.

Vanderbilt, Tom. "Self-Storage Nation." *Slate*, 18 July 2005, www.slate.com/articles/arts/culturebox/2005/07/selfstorage_nation.html.

Webster, Tracy. "Big House in the Wilderness: Moratoriums on Building and Individual Responsibility." *Inventing Arguments*, by John Mauk and John Metz, 2nd ed., Wadsworth-Cengage, 2009, pp. 301–03.

Analyzing Argument

1. What is the most important appeal in this argument? What passage best illustrates that appeal?

2. Schutza does not develop an explicit solution to hoarding. Although she implies a set of personal goals or hopes, she does not explain them and call for a particular policy or action. Why might this particular topic, at this particular point in time, lack a direct and collective solution?

3. In several passages, Schutza blurs the line between hoarders and the average consumer. How does this affect the argument? As you read, how did it affect you?

4. Examine Schutza's use of secondary sources. Choose a particular quotation and explain how the quoted source functions in the argument— for example, as part of an appeal, concession, counterargument, or evidence.

5. What values or assumptions does Schutza share with the other writers in this chapter (White, Webster, and Edmondson)?

Citizens and Consumers

AMBER EDMONDSON

Amber Edmondson argues about a crisis in community. It is not merely the crisis of big box stores in small towns, but the loss of culture in those towns. While her argument uses secondary research, her starting place and most of her examples come from the real geography of Edmondson's life. She wrote this essay for the final research project in her first-year college writing course and used the invention tools in this chapter.

Scottville, my hometown, consisted of two blocks of commercial Main Street—and it really was called "Main Street"—surrounded by sightless miles of plowed fields. The downtown was small, housing a handful of the necessities: a hardware store, a grocery store, a tractor supplier, whose titles were each preceded by a family name. Schoenberger's Market, Frosty's Flicks, Cox's Sales and Service. But Scottville always seemed to be more than a tumbleweed-infested one-horse farm town. Instead, the downtown was blocked off every autumn and hosted the Harvest Festival that crowned the Asparagus Queen. Through all seasons, the Scottville Clown Band serenaded the town, led then by the mayor and sheriff. Every winter, an arts and craft show was held at the middle school. Even as the big box stores moved into neighboring Ludington, family-run businesses dominated Scottville.

> Introduction paints a picture of Scottville, which faces a crisis.

Growing up in a small farming community can have a profound effect. While my family did not farm, reverence for the land was instilled at an early age. When we bought our groceries, we knew that all the produce had been sown and harvested nearby. The citizens were very resourceful and self-reliant. No Walmarts or Meijers came to town, nor did the people ever see the need for any. This resourcefulness was particularly evident to my family, whose breadwinner was a hairdresser trying to make money in a town that cut its own hair. We eventually packed up and moved north to Cadillac where people, I would discover, were much more dependent.

> Description of the people of Scottville.

Cadillac's boundaries stretched farther than Scottville's and were teeming with streets and buildings and cars, yet seemed much emptier. The town showed irreparable scars from the hard fist of corporate power, having seemingly allowed the big box stores in during economic hard times. They promised jobs and price-lowering competition and quickly put the downtown shops out of business. No longer was it sensible for consumers to venture downtown for trips to the grocery, a shoe store, and the pharmacy when they could simply get it all in one place. The slogan for their newest welcomed big box is "A million reasons, a single store." One by one, letters fell from the downtown marquees and windows became cloudy and dark on the main street. But the growing north end glowed and pulsed with neon excess. It became apparent that this excess, this growing corporate presence, was making itself the economic and cultural center of town, while Cadillac neglected to preserve its culture, its own unique intellectual and artistic tastes.

Appeal to value: culture should be preserved.

While it may seem that the Walmarts and Meijers of the world bring variety to their host towns, thereby adding to the local culture, these giants truly have the opposite effect. Instead of joining the existing culture, big box stores work independently to duplicate their product line and game plan. They decide what books, music, and films get stocked as well as what fashions are peddled. Walmart HQ doesn't know or care about the Scottville Clown Band or Elk Rapids poet Terry Wooten. Instead, Britney Spears and *Chicken Soup for the (fill in the blank) Soul* are imported into towns across the nation. These decisions are made in remote boardrooms "where the values and needs of the local community carry little or no weight," according to Stacy Mitchell of the New Rules Project in Minneapolis (qtd. in "New" 25). This homogenization of regional cultures makes it easier for citizens to let go of their downtowns—nay, for citizens to even be unaware of the existence of downtown at all—at the beck and call of a mega-chain store.

Responds to claim that box stores are good for the community.

Local culture, however, is not the only aspect of a community that these corporations affect. Economically, allowing chain stores into a town would seem like a sound game plan. They offer jobs, cheaper products, and perhaps the security that comes along with national brand recognition. However, the money grossed at these stores does not stay in the community, save the meager employee paychecks. Often, these stores offer no benefits to employees and "[give] very little back to the community," according to We're Against the WAL campaign organizer Albert Norman (418).

Transition from culture to economics.

And it is shortsighted to say that the products are cheaper even if the price tag displays a smaller number. If the health of downtown is taken into account, the price is rather quite high. Local businesses cannot compete with the low prices available to larger corporations and many are forced to close their doors for good, putting an end to a possible family legacy. Instead of becoming the sun they promised to be at the center of a community, these chain stores turn into black holes, slurping a town's money "somewhere else."

Counterargument anticipates the argument that products are cheaper.

According to economic development consultant Donovan D. Rypkema in "The Importance of Downtown in the 21st Century," not only are these chains harming our downtowns economically and artistically, they are also threatening the social communities in which they feed. Rypkema describes downtown as the gathering place of citizens and as the center of local culture (10). Once people are relegated to the outskirts of town to work in large chain stores and factories, social bonds begin to deteriorate. When people work at corporate department stores, they are often paid just enough to get by, making it difficult to achieve personal happiness. Psychologist Abraham Maslow's hierarchy of needs places physiological, then psychological, security at the very base of his pyramid (Gwynne). Before moving up to the next level, love and belongingness, one must first be able to eat, have shelter, and be mentally and emotionally sound. When people are just scraping by, they don't have time to worry about being part of a community. This, however, is in keeping with the entrepreneurial every-man-for-himself spirit of the capitalist system.

Refers to an authority for support

This economic system is a fairly young experiment that seems to contradict our natural tendencies toward community. When citizens in a community become simply consumers in an economy, they forget how to operate as a cooperative and the benefits of doing so. When local restaurants bow out to more expensive, more upscale operations like Ruby Tuesday, "regulars" disappear and servers lose that bond with their customers and their connection to the community. When local farmers are forced out of work by corporate farms and chain stores that stock food from unknown origins, communities lose a source of local food and quickly forget that food comes from anywhere but the supermarket.

A gentleman I was speaking to recently explained that less than twenty years ago, he could walk down the road to buy his eggs, milk, and meat for a wholesale price from a local farmer. His farming neighbor made a living off these transactions and the money stayed in the community, while the gentleman retained the peace of mind that comes along with knowing where your food is coming from and knowing where your money is going. After a while, with corporate farms shipping food into the new corporate supermarkets, the farmer could no longer make ends meet and was forced to sell his farm and work in a factory. Both the gentleman and the farmer now get their food at a higher cost from Meijer and eat strawberries that have traveled countless miles, while the farmer, left with no skills applicable to the influx of corporate jobs, has lost forty years of his life and his occupation.

Personal testimony used for support.

Personal testimony used for support.

This assault on independence and self-reliance is perhaps the most destructive threat to our communities by these corporations. When the leaders of a town become focused on economic growth while ignoring social growth, businesses most often win out in the end, and they have very different goals and needs than the average citizen. It may seem, then, that little difference exists between small local businesses and the department store giants. However, while local businesses can still affect town leaders' decisions, the added profits that are gained as a result stay within the community. When Walmart influences town decisions in its favor, the money it makes is shipped out to Walmart headquarters states away. Also, notes Mitchell, "large corporations are required by law to maximize returns to shareholders, [while] locally owned businesses can be guided by other values besides the bottom line" (qtd. in "New" 25). When control over the economic forces of small towns is taken away from citizens—business owners included—people can easily forget what it means to help out locally if there is no such thing as "local."

Suggests solution to crisis.

There can exist a middle ground, however, between "local" and "corporate." After fleeing Cadillac to pursue a college degree in Traverse City, I expected little more than another version of Cadillac, merely with a mall and more square miles of neon. I did find those elements, but I also found a surprisingly well-developed downtown. It stretched for several blocks, spilling onto perpendicular streets off the main drag, and incorporated shops frivolous and necessary, cultural and touristy. It appears that while Traverse City allowed in the big boys, it also nurtured the business district that formed the town and, while citizens may not go downtown for all of their basic shopping needs, Front Street remains a cultural center of the town. The Cherry Festival, Friday Night Live, and the Open Space are all guests of and products of the downtown, offering artistic and intellectual gatherings throughout the year.

Along with the seasonal events held downtown, Front Street also offers many unique shops owned and operated by local citizens. It may be more convenient and perhaps cheaper to shop at a big box store for these specialty wares, but a consumer might only be skimming the top of a particular hobby or interest such as beading. While most anything that could be bought downtown can also be bought in bland, generic form at Walmart or Meijer, the downtown specialty shops offer higher quality goods, often made right in town or perhaps only as far away as Leelanau County.

As well as helping the community as a whole, the downtown shops offer benefits to individual community members. Instead of going to work at Walmart, people can be employed at these locally owned stores and have much more access to the intricacies of operating a business. Employees also get to learn more about the specialties of these stores, be it beading, crystal meditation, brewing specialty espresso drinks, or making fudge. As a Walmart employee, one merely learns to run a cash register, to put boxes on a shelf, and to get paid very little. So, while these megastores may hire several hundred people in the community, these people—largely adults—are merely focused on getting by and not on bettering themselves.

Is Edmondson's description of working at locally owned stores or at Walmart effective?

What is more disturbing than even the personal deterioration of individuals occurring today is the possibility of their communities becoming a Cadillac tomorrow. In his "Apology to Future Generations," Simon Benlow suggests that people no longer see themselves as part of society as a whole but instead are focused on their own selfish desires and instant gratification. While it may seem better for people to choose today to discard their membership to a community and allow themselves to operate solely as a consumer, that course leaves the children of tomorrow without the option of simply being a citizen. When local businesses cannot succeed and citizens cannot offer their own unique skills to a community, children have only the choices of submitting to lifelong employment at Walmart or having to leave their community in search of another where their skills have a chance of contributing. While Benlow talks about consumerist tendencies in general, much of his essay can be applied to what people have done to their communities: "As [consumerism] came through every town, no one could resist it. It banged and clamored and woke everyone from dreamy isolation, and so even the most ascetic types played along in some small way" (416). Benlow makes it clear that while consumerism and the corporations that encourage such behaviors deteriorate communities, citizens are the ones with the power to decide how far the destruction will go.

Uses Benlow to explain how consumerism is harmful.

Citizens must resist being reduced to merely consumers if they are to preserve their communities. In Albert Camus's "The Myth of Sisyphus," the protagonist learns after being tethered to an eternity of futile labor that people may not have control over their situation, but they do have control over their behavior within that situation. It seems to be taking a while for most of America to realize not only how much power they have but also that something is wrong. Instead of turning away in droves once Walmart was discovered to have been employing illegal immigrants, consumers caused the megastore's stock to rise three-quarters of a percent that day ("Moyers"). When people should have been appalled at the store's behavior, they were reminded of "always low prices, always Walmart" and started Christmas shopping a bit early.

But citizens are starting to stand up to the corporations that threaten their areas, seemingly as a direct result of the strength of their communities. While the one political action undertaken by Cadillac citizens was a poorly planned and executed protest against a tire-burning plant, Traverse City is a hotbed of grassroots action, most likely due to the focus on community development, which allows for personal development. Recently, a group advocating local currency has formed, the local food cooperative is flourishing, various peace groups meet frequently and march periodically, and the local bookstore hosts local musicians as well as philosophy and Green Party meetings. The local Sweetwater Alliance has taken extensive action with some success against a water-bottling factory that had moved into the local area to filter not just money from the region, but to remove the community's resources as well. This seeking out of like-minded others is the level after security in Maslow's hierarchy of needs and can be found in its truest sense in our local communities.

Provides examples of what can be done.

This belonging is perhaps the most important element offered by our communities, and it may be the element most likely to save them. In Traverse City, this seeking out of the like-minded led to the formation of the Traverse Area Community Currency Initiative (TACCI), whose goal is to create a local currency for the area. Modeling their system after that which is succeeding in Toronto and Madison, TACCI is one of many groups working toward similar causes. These groups will someday achieve great change for their areas, but they would not have formed without an already strong community. Cadillac may be many years away from forming its own version of TACCI, and Scottville may never need that, but it all comes back to community.

Scottville is strong because of its community and its reverence of its culture. Cadillac, on the other hand, has a very weak culture but could make the shift to improving it. Before any of this can happen, however, the citizens must acknowledge this importance of community through a concerted educational effort by those in charge. Citizens must also reject the big box stores that threaten their economies and must weigh the importance of convenience versus community. This addiction to convenience needs to be stopped before our communities can again be strong. We need to emphasize our own local cultures and again become citizens instead of consumers.

Works Cited

Benlow, Simon. "An Apology to Future Generations." *The Composition of Everyday Life: A Guide to Writing*, by John Mauk and John Metz, 4th ed., Wadsworth-Cengage, 2014, pp. 389–94.

Camus, Albert. "The Myth of Sisyphus." *The Mercury Reader*, edited by Maurice Scharton et al., Pearson Custom Publishing, 2001.

Gwynne, Robert. *Maslow's Hierarchy of Needs*. U of Tennessee, Knoxville, 1997.

"Moyers and Brancaccio Track the News." *NOW with Bill Moyers*, PBS, 7 Nov. 2003.

"New Rules for the New Localism: Favoring Communities, Deterring Corporate Chains (an Interview with Stacy Mitchell)." *Multinational Monitor*, vol. 23, no. 10, Oct.–Nov. 2002, pp. 25–29, www.multinationalmonitor.org/mm2002/102002/interview-mitchell.html.

Norman, Albert. "Eight Ways to Stop the Store: Up against Wal-Mart." *The Nation*, vol. 258, no. 12, 28 Mar. 1994, p. 418.

Rypkema, Donovan D. "The Importance of Downtown in the 21st Century." *Journal of the American Planning Association*, vol. 69, no. 1, 2003, pp. 9–15, doi: 10.1080/01944360308976290.

Analyzing Argument

1. Explain how Edmondson responds to opposing positions or perspectives. Describe specific passages in which she counters or concedes.

2. According to Edmondson, why are "big box stores" so popular? What does their popularity tell us about American values?

3. Choose four statements from Edmondson's essay that you consider premises in her line of reasoning. Explain how each statement functions as a premise in her argument.

4. How does Edmondson use Scottville and Cadillac to develop her argument?

5. What values underlie Edmondson's statement: "It became apparent that this excess, this growing corporate presence was making itself the economic and cultural center of town, while Cadillac neglected to preserve its culture, its own unique intellectual and artistic tastes" (paragraph 3)? Choose another key sentence from Edmondson's argument, and explain the underlying values.

6. Edmondson uses sources throughout her argument. Which ones are most effective? Why?

Is bottled water a crisis?

Analyzing Argument

1. What arguments have you heard for and against bottled water?

2. How does bottled water pose a threat to the public? How does this image make a case for or against bottled water?

EXPLORING FOR TOPICS

A crisis is more than a rupture in the flow of normal events. It is a crucial or decisive situation. In a crisis, severe or intense consequences are at stake; things are teetering on a line between beneficial and disastrous outcomes. A crisis also can occur when something goes totally awry, when an expected outcome or routine is nowhere in sight, when systems and organizations break down just when they are needed most. As you scan your environment for possible topics, look for critical situations, those on the brink of drastic change. The following strategies can help you focus on a specific crisis.

- In a local, college, or national newspaper, look for crises in any of the following: school budgets, city government, labor, transportation, health care, environment, entertainment, energy, or day care.

- In your town or neighborhood, look for crises with security, equality, zoning, sprawl, policing, agriculture, traffic, or safety.

- Check out school-sponsored documents (posters, fliers, signs, letters, websites, and so on). Does your school claim that any crises exist? If so, how are those crises characterized? Would you characterize them differently?

- Tune in to a political talk show. Listen for social and political crises such as military conflict, terrorism, trade disputes, state budgets, the Medicare budget, or corporate fraud.

- Use the following prompt to explore for crises that usually go unnoticed: While people go on with their everyday lives, they do not recognize _____ and its looming threat.

- Investigate your academic major. Speak with a professor or read a journal in your field and search for crises involving labor, research strategies, funding, the environment, big business, assessment, control, salaries, reporting, and so on. What crisis affects the most people? What crisis affects you?

- With a group of peers, examine the world around you and ask questions about social problems. Be adventurous: *What will we do with all the used tires? How can so many people vote against their own best interests? Doesn't anyone care that prime-time television shows are ruining people's ability to think clearly? What social crises do graffiti artists point out?*

- Focus on a crisis described in one of the chapter readings, but try to see the crisis from a different perspective and characterize it in your own words.

The first move of any good writer is some basic detective work—to look closely and see what others might overlook. Use the following invention

To view this video, visit the English CourseMate at CengageBrain.com.

questions to help probe the particulars of the situation. Make certain to focus on particulars. Be careful not to simply answer the questions; rather, use the questions to *explore* the real complexities of the issue:

- ▶ What makes the situation a crisis? (How is it a critical turning point?)
- ▶ What is being threatened—what cherished thing, value, principle, resource?
- ▶ What is the threat? A way of thinking? A behavior? Something else?
- ▶ Who or what caused the crisis? How did the situation evolve into a crisis?
- ▶ When might it climax (or go to the point of no return)?
- ▶ What can be done to resolve the crisis?

Invention Workshop

With one or two other writers, answer the preceding invention questions for your topic. Let the ideas evolve. For instance, if someone explains the cause of a crisis, ask whether it may have begun before that, in some less obvious way. Use the discussion as a tool not simply for *talking about* the topic, but for *finding out* more—for exploring layers beyond your group's initial preconceptions. As the discussion evolves, record the ideas by taking ample notes.

Hint: Keep asking questions about the situation to discover the most basic cause of the crisis. For instance, you might ask: *What basic human need is not being addressed? What oversight put things in motion? What misunderstanding or natural occurrence cultivated the crisis?* Try to discover what the people involved do not see because they are too close to the events or blinded by their own biases or perceptions.

INVENTING A CLAIM

In addition to a close examination of the topic itself, writers should know what opinions are circulating—how people characterize the crisis or if they even acknowledge it at all. Writers sometimes discover voices that oppose their initial thoughts on a topic. Such discoveries can be of great value. They can help a writer to build a bridge, to shape an argument so that doubtful or even hostile readers will consider new ideas.

As in Tracy Webster's case, writers may find sources that completely coincide with their own point of view or extend that point of view. But finding these connections is not easy. Writers must be able to see past the surface of articles—past titles, main claims, or even the primary focus. Often, the deepest and most helpful connections lie in the underbrush. For example, Tracy Webster's argument focuses on big houses in the wilderness. His main source, Anna Quindlen's article, is titled "A Shock to the System." The "shock" refers to a regional power outage in the Northeast. A novice researcher may have overlooked Quindlen's article, dismissing it because the title has nothing to do with Webster's main focus. But Webster sees past the surface difference (between his topic and Quindlen's article) and finds a shared set of values and beliefs.

Webster's topic: Big houses in the wilderness.

Quindlen's title: "A Shock to the System."

Webster's focus: Big houses that destroy natural habitat.

Quindlen's focus: Power outage and bear hunting in the Northeast.

Webster's assumption: Humans should live in harmony with their surroundings.

Quindlen's assumption: Humans should live in harmony with their surroundings.

Had Webster skipped over Quindlen's article, he would have missed a supporting voice. Even though their essays emerge from different situations, Webster and Quindlen share important values and assumptions. As you scan databases or the Internet for sources, keep Webster's discovery in mind: Often, the most helpful source looks very different once you get past the title and initial claims.

Using your library's periodical databases or the Internet, find published discussions about the crisis you have chosen. If the crisis is fairly recent (in the past few months), you will probably have success finding related newspaper articles rather than journal articles. If the crisis is very local, like the strike at a local factory, you may find articles in local newspapers. You could also extend the search to find how people tend to argue about your topic. (For more on finding and integrating outside written sources, see pages 321–349.)

Although you may not find people arguing about your particular crisis, you can use other arguments to understand related values and claims. After collecting outside opinions on the situation (through surveys, secondary research, or both), use the following questions to explore the various possible positions related to the crisis:

What Do Others Claim?

- How do other people or sources characterize the crisis?
- What possible actions or solutions are put forth?
- What do other arguments seem to value (money, progress, children, equality)?
- If solutions have been suggested, how thorough are they? (What details do they omit? What significant factors do they ignore?)

What Do I Claim?

- How do I see the crisis differently from others?
- What values and assumptions do I share with others?
- Based on my values and assumptions, I believe the crisis can be addressed by_____.

Of course, there are limitless ways to approach a crisis. But it may help to apply some common strategies. Consider the following formula. Even though you may not maintain the exact structure, these sentence patterns can generate an initial path for your argument. The first two patterns (A and B) would keep you focused on a claim of fact. You would not argue for a solution but try to persuade readers about the nature of the crisis. The latter two patterns (C and D) would set you up to argue for a solution. You would make the case about the crisis (a claim of fact) and then propose a strategy for solving it (a claim of policy):

A. Because _____ is _____, there is no stopping it.

B. The _____ crisis continues primarily because _____ do not recognize _____.

C. Because _____, we should _____.

D. To address the current _____, we should _____.

More Sample Main Claims

Politics

- Because the United States has strategic and economic interests in Afghanistan, there is no stopping the ongoing war.
- Because corporate lobbyists now control politics in Washington, DC, states must begin taking back governmental control.
- To end the constant "pork" projects in federal government, public citizens must call for strict term limits for members of Congress.

Popular Culture

- The corporate news networks have created a citizenry that is dangerously close to losing control of, or happily letting go of, its democracy.
- Hard-hitting, impolite, and shrewd comedy is necessary in a free society, which is why comedy should be studied and discussed more often in humanities courses.
- Because of the toxic chemicals released during the manufacturing and discarding of plastic bottles, bottled water should be taxed to reduce its popularity.

Education

- Because the minds of our generation are consumed and distracted by sports, the only alternative is to remove athletics completely from public high schools.
- Because corporate testing services now dictate curriculum while sucking huge amounts of money from public education, teachers and parents must unite and halt the entire system.
- College curricula continue to shape students into consumers and button-pushers, which means that yet another generation will go into the workforce and the voting booths without critical literacy.

Town and Community

- The disappearance of senior citizens from the center of civic life has created a psychological void.
- Because township officials have allowed low-end national food and hotel chains to colonize the beaches, we are in danger of losing the most unique qualities of our area.

Activity

Which is the most insightful claim in the preceding list? Why?

INVENTING SUPPORT

LINES OF REASONING A crisis may seem like chaos, so a good argument provides a logical path away from the crisis. When writers develop a set of connected premises, they establish that path. Sometimes, writers even draw attention to each premise. Notice how Tracy Webster directly discusses an important premise:

> One question is: Can't individual Americans simply build differently? (Are moratoriums necessary?) Of course, to pursue this question (this line of thinking), the reader must accept the premise that Americans are overbuilding, and that by overbuilding, Americans are foolishly and unnecessarily overdestroying nature, the environment, wildlife. They have to accept the premise that current building practices are somehow harmful. Some Americans, to be certain, don't accept this premise. Here's why they should:

Webster then goes on to develop his line of reasoning and support the premise that Americans are overbuilding and destroying nature.

An argument about a crisis may have several layers of cause and effect. And writers often need to argue that particular behaviors, ideas, or practices created the crisis. In his argument about the environment, Curtis White walks readers through complex layers. For him, the crisis is not simply about pollution, degradation of resources, or even evil corporate executives. The crisis is hidden in the actual language about the environment. White's courageous argument takes readers, one step at a time, into deeper and deeper layers:

> Perhaps we support legalistic responses to problems, with all their technoscientific descriptors, out of a sense that this is the best we can do for the moment. But the danger is always that eventually we come to believe this language and its mindset ourselves. This mindset is generally called "quantitative reasoning," and it is second nature to Anglo-Americans. Corporate execs are perfectly comfortable with it, and corporate philanthropists give their dough to environmental organizations that speak it. Unfortunately, it also has the consequence of turning environmentalists into quislings, collaborators, and virtuous practitioners of a cost-benefit logic figured in songbirds.

APPEALS TO VALUE Many arguments about crisis call readers to act—or at least to imagine the best action possible. And an appeal to value is a powerful tool for motivating action. Notice Webster's argument, which subtly calls on the audience's sense of responsibility:

> But Americans, perhaps more than any other people who have ever lived, are terrible at walking narrow paths. They cannot just move to the wilderness and live. They must pound the wilderness to death. They must beat it to hell. They must drive gas-guzzling, polluting, school-bus-sized SUVs a hundred miles to work and back. They must build huge homes, large enough to be small hotels.

Later in the argument, Webster goes even further with the appeal, and makes it more explicit:

> Moratoriums on building permits would not be necessary if individual homebuilders acted more responsibly, but how in our present culture could Americans ever bring themselves to act more responsibly? Some do, of course. But most can't. They simply see it as their right to do whatever they feel like doing. They see anything else as an infringement on their freedom, a personal insult and a public injustice. Quindlen's suggestion requires collective, or government, action—a more extreme measure that must be taken to prevent individual freedom-loving Americans from eating the whole pie, instead of having just one piece.

AUTHORITIES Consider the various possible ways that outside sources can help develop your ideas:

- To help explain the nature of the crisis
- To help explain a solution
- To integrate an opposing perspective on the crisis or a solution
- To explain a related value or way of thinking

Remember that helpful authorities are sometimes voices from the past. Philosophers, writers, scholars, scientists, and thinkers from history can give much to a current argument. In his essay, Curtis White borrows statements from philosophers of the past to explain a way of thinking. While the philosophers were not speaking about White's topic (the environmental crisis), their perspectives support one of White's key premises:

> Even now, science can't say why we ought not to harm the environment except to say that we shouldn't be self-destructive. Another of these lost spiritual children was our very relation as human beings to the mystery of Being as such. As the philosopher G. W. Leibniz famously wondered, "Why is there something rather than nothing?" For St. Thomas Aquinas, this was the fundamental religious question. In the place of a relation to the world that was founded on this mystery, we have a relation that is objective and data driven. We no longer have a forest; we have "board feet." We no longer have a landscape, a world that is our own; we have "valuable natural resources."

As this example shows, authorities need not match your position exactly. They often help give dimension to an argument by reinforcing a broader concept, a way of conceiving an issue, even a way of seeing the world.

TESTIMONY When a writer shares something personal, the argument itself becomes more human and more immediate. Testimony brings a topic into the real (even intimate) dialogue between writer and audience.

> I look up at the house on the hill. Situated in a relatively affluent neighborhood, overlooking the ocean, it looks like a normal, well-maintained home from street level, but as I walk up the driveway and it comes into full view, the reality of the situation hits me like a stack of old newspapers. There is no doubt this is the home of compulsive hoarders. It is also the home of people I love.

Schutza's experience does more than suggest, "This happened to me." Rather, it humanizes a potentially distant topic, hoarding, and brings it closer. But her argument does not rely exclusively on the personal. Her own experience is rounded out with a variety of other support strategies.

LITERARY WORKS Fiction, poetry, and drama often speak to the human foibles that create and sustain crises. In fact, some see this as literature's power: it shows us the effects of our weird moral, social, and psychological hiccups. In his argument about the environment, White alludes to the fictional character Faust, who makes a deal with the devil. In White's argument, the devil is quantitative reasoning:

> We don't have to be born again to agree with evangelicals that one of the most powerful arguments missing from the environmentalist's case is reverence for what simply is. One of the heroes of Goethe's *Faust* was a character called Care (Sorge), who showed to Faust the unscrupulousness of his actions and led him to salvation. Environmentalism has made a Faustian pact with quantitative reasoning; science has given it power but it cannot provide deliverance. If environmentalism truly wishes, as it claims, to want to "save" something—the planet, a species, itself—it needs to rediscover a common language of Care.

As White's move illustrates, integrating a literary work requires some imaginative analysis. We have to think beyond the specific crisis and inspect the deeper sources of tension—people's greed, ignorance, fear, detachment, and so on. Then, we can try to recall works that explore those tensions. To develop support for your argument, use the following questions to explore possibilities:

▶ What logical appeals are necessary for my argument? (What line of reasoning do I want my audience to follow?)

▶ What authorities can I use? What philosophers, novelists, poets, or thinkers from the past uphold a way of thinking that might help make my case about the current crisis?

▶ What personal situations can I use? (What situations from my life reveal something important about the nature of the crisis or the solution?)

▶ What appeals to value can I make? (What values are tucked inside my argument? Can I call on the audience's sense of duty, justice, family, personal responsibility, or something else?)

ARRANGEMENT

WHERE SHOULD I DISTINGUISH BETWEEN THE CRISIS AND THE SOLUTION? Each argument is different from the next. While some arguments about crisis focus significant attention on solutions, others attempt only to draw out the nature of the crisis and characterize it as worthy of attention. Still others may explain the nature of the crisis and then counterargue the worth of others' proposed solutions. While the arguments in this chapter vary significantly in their emphases, they all share some common ingredients:

- Description of the crisis
- Description of life without the crisis
- Evidence or appeals about the crisis
- Counterarguments
- Description of the solution
- Support (evidence and appeals) for the solution
- Counterarguments of other solutions
- Concession about other solutions

Notice the arrangement of Webster's essay:

Paragraphs 1–2	Description of the crisis (or the starting place)
Paragraph 2	Qualifier (describing the specific nature of the crisis)
Paragraphs 3–4	Authority (Quindlen) and a proposed solution
Paragraphs 5–9	Counterargument (and appeal to logic in support of the solution)
Paragraphs 10–11	Qualifier (reinforcing the specific nature of the crisis)
Paragraphs 12–14	Appeal to logic in support of the solution

What's important is that the basic ingredients of an argument can be arranged in an unlimited number of ways, depending on the nature of the crisis and the stance of the writer.

HOW SHOULD I BEGIN? In any argument, introductions vary depending on the nature of the topic, the nature of the writer's voice, and the nature of the audience. An informal strategy might involve a personal narrative (as in Laurie Schutza's essay). A more formal approach may give a less personal report on the crisis. In his essay, White begins broadly. But he does not say what his readers already know (that environmental destruction is bad, that it is increasing, that it hurts us all). Instead, he begins his analysis of cause:

> Environmental destruction proceeds apace in spite of all the warnings, the good science, the 501(c)3 organizations with their memberships in the millions, the poll results, and the martyrs perched high in the branches of sequoias or shot dead in the Amazon. This is so not because of a power, a strength out there that we must resist. It is because we are weak and fearful. Only a weak and fearful society could invest so much desperate energy in protecting activities that are the equivalent of suicide.

Despite different approaches, one quality is consistent in good argumentative essays: they avoid squeezing in too much information in the introduction, such as a description of the crisis and an articulation of the solution. Instead, they attempt, simply, to introduce a crisis.

HOW SHOULD I INCLUDE COUNTERARGUMENTS, CONCESSIONS, OR QUALIFIERS? Doing counterargument involves challenging other positions—and showing why any opposing claims are not as reasonable as one's own. Other opinions must be addressed, even confronted directly. Confronting other opinions, or counterarguing, helps create sophisticated and more persuasive arguments. In an argument about crisis, opposition to your main idea might arise at two primary places: at your characterization of the crisis, and at your solution. In other words, people might disagree with the way you portray a critical situation, and they might also disagree with the effectiveness of your solution (if you propose one). It might help to consider all the possible opposing views and then respond directly to each—or to the most important.

Your portrayal of the situation	*Possible opposing views:*
	"It's not as bad as you suggest."
	"It's much worse than you suggest."
	"Your description is short-sighted."
	"Your understanding of the cause/effect is wrong."
Your proposed solution	*Possible opposing views:*
	"It won't work."
	"It's too dangerous, unethical, unmanageable, costly, unpopular, etc."

Of course, opposition can come in many other places in an argument. (Generally, people can disagree with any claim made.) However, be especially cognizant of these two important layers.

AUDIENCE AND VOICE

Arguers use various strategies to get an audience involved in a crisis. Some create a voice of urgency; others project calmness. And even though writers do not benefit from using the sound of their voices (with changes in pitch and volume), they can use a variety of tools for attracting readers.

INFORMALITY An informal voice can be an asset—even in formal academic argument. Strategies for developing an informal voice include strategically placed slang or idiosyncratic phrasing. Webster creates informality by linking words together in an unorthodox manner:

> But this is not an anti-hunting essay or an anti-house-in-the-wilderness essay. It is an anti-big-house-in-the-wilderness essay. The big house in the wilderness is more dangerous than any hunter is. It's the big house, the too-big house, that is unjustifiable.

Informality is also created with certain pronouns, specifically, by drawing attention to "you" and "I." For instance, Laurie Schutza begins with personal testimony and returns to it at key points in the essay. And her conclusion reinforces her personal connection, in part by cataloguing her own collection of saved items:

> I look at myself and wonder: Do I have these tendencies? Am I destined to become a pack rat? I look in my closets crowded with clothes and shoes, much I don't wear. Stacks of mail that I keep saying I'm going to sort and read are piled up around my house.
> My grown kid's artwork, clothing, and toys fill the attic, but I can't part with so much of it for sentimental reasons. Who among us can say we have none of the characteristics of the hoarder?

FORMALITY Formality in writing is the degree to which the features correspond to standard conventions or expectations. In formal academic settings, readers expect to encounter writing that does not veer too far off course and does not draw attention to itself or to the writer's emotions. Notice, for example, Amber Edmondson's final paragraph. Although it makes a strong appeal, it also refrains from sounding too plaintive or accusatory:

> Scottville is strong because of its community and its reverence of its culture. Cadillac, on the other hand, has a very weak culture but could make the shift to improving it. Before any of this can happen, however, the citizens must acknowledge this importance of community through a concerted educational effort by those in charge. Citizens must also reject the big box stores that threaten their economies and must weigh the importance of convenience versus community. This addiction to convenience needs to be stopped before our communities can again be strong. We need to emphasize our own local cultures and again become citizens instead of consumers.

Edmondson could have easily drawn attention to her own anger or frustration. Instead, this passage reinforces key points of her argument without turning overly emotional.

ACCUSATION A strong stance on a topic often comes along with a stern voice, and sometimes the arguer wants to create a voice that targets another position. Notice Webster's accusation of particular homebuilders:

> If Quindlen's proposal seems extreme, it is because in American society where narrow paths have become unimaginable to many, individual freedom allows for, and encourages, individual irresponsibility. As long as Americans are free to build obscenely large houses, to destroy acres of wildlife habitat, to pollute the air and rivers, many Americans are going to do exactly that. Why? Because they see it as their right, because

they are free, because they are Americans. Quindlen is right: Moratoriums on building permits are the obvious alternative.

In these passages, the voice of accusation is concise. It depends upon short and clean phrasing that draws attention away from the writer and toward the culprits. For your own argument, consider the following:

▶ Is the argument too informal or formal? How can I create a formal, but engaging, academic voice?

▶ How can allusions help to create the most appropriate voice?

▶ Is there someone to blame for the crisis? If so, can I accuse him or her without sounding too harsh?

REVISION

Revision—or re-seeing—involves evaluating one's own work: identifying its strengths and weaknesses and making effective changes. Rethink your essay by reconsidering the chapter introduction:

- "Insightful thinkers often see through the crossfire, beyond the two common possibilities." How does the essay get readers beyond common possibilities?

- "Regardless of the particular situation, those who react to crises and propose the best possible solutions (the most manageable, ethical, practical, economic, far-reaching, etc.) are often the most valuable individuals in a given situation." How does your argument propose the best way out?

- "The emphasis on crisis or solution depends on the topic, the opposing voices, and even previous solutions." If you do not propose a direct solution, why? Does the argument do something equally important?

RESEARCH AND REVISION: If you used outside sources, consider the following questions. As you revise, refer to the corresponding pages in Chapters 13 and 14:

- Have you used research as means of discovery? (pages 309–328)

- Have you evaluated sources for ideology, reliability, relevance, timeliness, and diversity? (pages 329–338)

- Are the ideas from the outside sources integrated smoothly into your ideas? (pages 338–349)

- Are the sources documented appropriately (with in-text and end citation)? (pages 350–375)

Peer Review

In peer review, writers have an opportunity to understand how their ideas influence others—not simply if their ideas are wrong or right, if the spelling is good and the grammar correct. The process can actually make an argument come to life. If the reviewers read closely and offer focused comments, they can help to add new dimensions to the argument. Notice that the following questions do not focus on editing (or correctness and grammar rules). Rather, they focus on the argumentative moves in the essay—on intensifying the claims and support strategies where possible.

Exchange drafts with at least one other writer. (If time allows, exchange with two or three writers to gather a range of perspectives or comments.) Use the following questions to generate specific constructive comments about others' drafts:

Main Claim

1. Does the argument focus your attention on a specific crisis? Are you convinced that it is a crisis worthy of public attention? If not, what could the writer do to convince you?

2. How does the essay go beyond discussing obvious possibilities? Could the writer go further in suggesting a way out of the crisis?

Support

3. What support strategy is most effective? What support strategy could be deleted without weakening the argument?

4. Identify appeals to logic in the essay. Explain how the writer could further develop a specific logical appeal so that you better understand the nature of the crisis or the validity of the proposed solution.

5. Identify an appeal to value, and explain how it figures into the argument. How, for example, does the essay call on the reader's sense of fairness, justice, honor, or duty? Explain how the writer could further develop the appeal. How might the writer draw more attention to the shared value?

6. Consider outside sources. How do they help support the writer's claims? Do outside sources take over any portions of the argument? Do they overwhelm the writer's voice?

Counterarguments/Concessions/Qualifiers

7. Consider counterarguments. How might a reader remain unconvinced because the essay did not anticipate and respond to some other valid viewpoint? What additional counterarguments would be helpful?

8. Should the writer concede or qualify any points to help strengthen the argument?

Arrangement

9. How might the argument be more engaging if ideas were arranged differently?
For example, should the crisis be described sooner, or more quickly? Should long sections of narrative (or storytelling) be helped along with connections to the essay's main idea?

Audience and Voice

10. What makes the writer sound fair and informed? What focuses too much on personal feelings, attacks, and accusations?

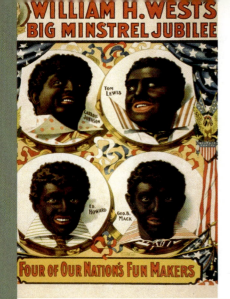

WILLIAM H. WEST'S
BIG MINSTREL JUBILEE

TOM
LEWIS

CARROLL
JOHNSON

ED.
HOWARD

GEO.B.
MACK

FOUR OF OUR NATION'S FUN MAKERS

Library of Congress Prints and Photographs Online
Collection LC-USZ62-26078

11

Arguing the Past

What Happened?

P eople are prone to repetition. Companies continue policies (which may or may not work well); countries keep laws on the books (which may or may not coincide with core national principles); and, of course, individuals knowingly continue bad habits (which may hurt them or others around them). In short, we are willing to base the present on the past—unless an argument about the past changes our perspective. Imagine, for instance, a large company that keeps a particular sales policy in place for years because it assumes the policy has been successful. Then a manager argues in a detailed report that the policy has actually added unnecessary costs throughout the years. If this new argument is persuasive enough, it may cause the company to restructure its sales policy entirely.

Such arguments regularly occur in professional life. In fact, many organizations hire people whose sole job is to study and make arguments about past actions and policies. Colleges hire institutional researchers to examine the success of past hiring practices; businesses of all types hire accountants to examine their economic histories and make recommendations based on those histories; institutions hire quality control officers to not only examine present operations but also scrutinize past operations; and huge organizations (from NASA to the Environmental Protection Agency) hire specialists in many different fields to examine their history and make suggestions about present and future action.

Arguments about the past occur in almost all aspects of life. People argue about the justice or injustice of past action, debating, for instance, if the purchase of Manhattan from the Native Americans was fair or, more recently, if the North American Free Trade Agreement (NAFTA) has benefited or hurt U.S. workers. Politicians argue over the country's past condition: Was it a good year for manufacturing, or was it bad? Was it a successful or unsuccessful economic policy? Was it a justified or unjustified military action? Depending on the answers (the arguments) to such questions, people make decisions about the future (whom to vote for, which policy to support, and so on).

All of this assumes that the past is important—it is not dead. And anyone bound for serious study of the present and future must first understand the link to the past. History itself is a collective debate about what happened, who was involved, and who was responsible. As you examine the readings in this chapter, notice how the arguments, regardless of their specific position or focus, make an important link between the past and the present. They each argue for a different way of seeing the past.

Activities

1. Think of a moment from history when new evidence prompted people to rethink a past event or historical figure. What specific evidence prompted the rethinking? Specifically how did people's thinking change? What conflicting views still exist?

2. Humans are part of history; each person has a past that is connected to other people's pasts. What histories are you a part of? Search through a school yearbook, family photos, a stack of old family letters, a town history. Look for a connection to the past that you haven't thought about before. For example, how might something about your school, classmates, grandparents, or town history have influenced your current interests, values, struggles, or psychoses?

3. People in all walks of life and in all academic disciplines return to the past to discover if present versions of the past accurately portray reality. For example:

   - Psychologists argue over the influence Freud had on clinical practices.

   - Art historians debate the role of political influence on particular artists or even entire movements.

   - Nursing professionals argue about the wisdom of past hiring practices, which have led to present staffing shortages.

   - Geographers argue about the role the Appalachian Mountains played in the development of the American frontier.

   Add two examples to this list—one related to a particular career or field of study.

Shakespeare and Narcotics

DAVID PINCHING

Steven Vidler/Eurasia Press/Corbis

When the Shakespeare Birthplace Trust in Stratford-upon-Avon permitted researchers to perform chemical tests on twenty-four pipe fragments from Shakespeare's house and nearby sites, two of the pipes showed traces of cocaine and hallucinogenic drugs. The findings were reported in the *South African Journal of Science* in 2001. "Shakespeare and Narcotics" was published on www.Bibliomania.com in response to reaction to the findings.

The recent discovery of a drug-tainted clay pipe in Stratford-upon-Avon, home of Shakespeare, has caused some fervent discussion on the topic of the Bard's possible cocaine usage. In early March of this year, some South African researchers explained that their chemical analysis of seventeenth-century pipes had revealed traces of cocaine, compounds created by the burning of cannabis, and hallucinogenic substances. Apparently, then, Shakespeare and his contemporaries had access to a number of narcotics. Naturally, tabloids and websites alike responded by claiming that Shakespeare was inspired by drugs. A few choice headlines include everything from "Drugs Clue to Shakespeare's Genius" and "Did Shakespeare Seek Inspiration in Cocaine?" to the less subtle "Shakespeare's 'Cannabis Sonnet'" and "Shakespeare May Have Been Stoned on Pot." Every academic who could be bothered to dip into the mire of such shock journalism shrieked back that there was no proof that Shakespeare took the substances and that, crucially, he was a genius regardless of his lifestyle. In the lather of spurious information from the drug lobby, entirely innocuous phrases such as "noted weed" and "compounds strange" were cited as proof that the writer of *Much Ado About Nothing* and *Romeo and Juliet* was drugged up to the ruff.

Actually, in the relevant context, "noted weed" means "famous type of clothing" and a "compound strange" is nothing more exciting than an unusual word construction.

Oddly, in all the desperate kafuffle to find some loose reference to narcotics that could appear in a twenty-line tabloid article, journalists failed to note more suspect goings-on in the plays themselves. Was it not Macbeth who saw a dagger floating in the air in front of him, Hamlet who ran about murderously after being visited by his father's ghost, and Othello who babbled incoherently about "goats and monkeys"? Almost the entire cast of *A Midsummer Night's Dream* are given drugs and sleeping potions at some point and one is entirely convinced that he is a wall (actually, he is one of the few not drugged, but the point holds). The fact that the journalists and academics alike seemed to avoid studiously was that there was nothing remotely illegal about the drugs found in the pipes in Shakespeare's day. As most people are aware, Queen Victoria herself took cannabis for the relief of period pains and every poet worth his or her salt in the nineteenth century ingested enough laudanum and opium to make the Beatles blush. The fact that we seem to want Shakespeare to have taken drugs for sensational value says more about our age of celebrity than it does about the great playwright. Those who like to degrade the great and promote the sensational would like to imagine Shakespeare, spliff in mouth like the ridiculous and once ubiquitous "psychedelic" poster of the *Mona Lisa*. It is a lot easier to debunk something than to create something worthwhile oneself.

The mindset behind such an outlook is the really depressing thing. People like to imagine Shakespeare freebasing and rolling up joints because they see him as an establishment figure. As such, portraying him as a junkie causes amusement and indignation because of our modern attitude to substances that allows certain kinds of intoxication but not others. Shakespeare would not have understood our simultaneous and hypocritical prudishness and excess. He was, in his time, a radical, a novelty, and far more dangerous to the establishment with his damning indictments of royalty in *King Lear, Richard III,* and *King John,* among others, than any of our media starlets. The idea that you can be anti-establishment by becoming incapable of thinking properly is pretty out of date anyway. And, as the worst excesses of post-Sixties fiction, music, and art have proved, "mind-altering" does not necessarily mean "art-improving." Ann Donnelly, the curator of the Shakespeare Birthplace Trust, was unimpressed with the evidence from the pipes and claimed that people are always trying to "come up with reasons for saying Shakespeare was not a genius." This may be something of a spoilsport attitude, but it is a fair one. Everyone in England is forced to read Shakespeare at school, and plenty of other countries have a similar policy regardless of the fact that Shakespeare is hardly the easiest entry point into the English language. However, one suspects that if cream buns and Britney Spears were forced on pupils as Shakespeare is, they too would become distrusted at an early age. As such, Ms. Donnelly is right in saying that people often look for a way to knock Shakespeare off his high

horse. There was the school of thought that said that Shakespeare was not even the author of the plays published under his name but that, in fact, an aristocrat wrote them. Others have claimed that Ben Johnson and other worthies of the age were responsible. Generally, it seems that people have a problem accepting that one man wrote so much, let alone so much great literature. What we are effectively saying in insisting that Shakespeare probably smoked drugs is that given the task of trying to write all the plays Shakespeare did we would probably turn to narcotics. The fact is that reading the Bard's works or going to see a good production of one of his plays is infinitely more rewarding than taking drugs. Thankfully, Shakespeare's plays are also cheaper and more freely available. Read them all on Bibliomania.

Analyzing Argument

1. What basic principle, issue, or value is at the root of the argument?

2. What is the main claim? Is it a claim of fact, value, or policy?

3. What values are at play in the following statements?

   It is a lot easier to debunk something than to create something worthwhile oneself. (paragraph 2)

   People like to imagine Shakespeare freebasing and rolling up joints because they see him as an establishment figure. (paragraph 3)

   The fact is that reading the Bard's works or going to see a good production of one of his plays is infinitely more rewarding than taking drugs. (paragraph 3)

4. What other values (in addition to the ones from question 3 above) are important to Pinching's argument?

5. How does Pinching connect the past to a larger point about contemporary Western culture?

A Nation Made of Poetry

JOANNIE FISCHER

When the U.S. National Archives and Records Administration compiled a list of 100 milestone documents in U.S. history from 1776 to 1965, Joannie Fischer, a contributing editor for *U.S. News and World Report,* responded by exploring the role of unofficial documents (speeches, songs, novels, and so on) in American history. The official documents are available at www.ourdocuments.gov.

The official documents now on display in Washington, D.C., offer one version of America's story. It's an authorized biography of sorts, screened and sanctioned. But the beauty of words in a democracy is that anyone can offer them up, and they live or die not by a ruler's dictate, but by their ability to permeate hearts and minds, to ignite passions, and to provoke action. Throughout our history, we have learned that words with enough resonance—whether from a slave, a student, or a songwriter—can change history as dramatically as any decree.

In fact, for every official document marking our nation's progress, there are countless others that have steered events, whether by inciting, critiquing, warning, encouraging, cajoling, enraging, or inspiring. Sometimes the words in these unofficial manifestos are so powerful that they still echo through time, blending with other potent phrases from other outspoken souls to form a grand montage of ideas and urgings, odes and rants, tall tales and truthful testimonies. This "unauthorized" biography of our nation is scrawled in letters and diaries, in pamphlets and propaganda, in poems and rock concerts, in novels and essays. From the whole, vast array, we each pick and choose those lines that move us most, and piece together our own story of what it really means to be an American.

To be sure, without some of these scripts, key moments in U.S. history might never even have taken place. Without Thomas Paine's elegant and angry prose, for example, we might not even exist as an independent country today. In 1775, Colonial leaders were torn by warring views about how to deal with mother England. Then, in January 1776, Paine's pamphlet *Common Sense* was published in Philadelphia, opening with the legendary phrase, "These are the times that try men's souls." It argued forcefully for the necessity of revolution and sold 150,000 copies overnight. It's widely credited with overcoming dissenters' qualms and unifying opinion enough to make the Declaration of Independence possible. "Without the pen of Paine," said John Adams, "the sword of Washington would have been wielded in vain."

So, too, was the Civil War sparked not by the flare of a cannon but by a flair for language. Although slavery had been controversial for 100 years, and tensions between the North and South ran strong and deep, it took novelist Harriet Beecher Stowe's *Uncle Tom's Cabin* to convey in intimate detail the horrors of slavery and galvanize the abolitionist movement. In 1851 and 1852, roughly 10 years before the siege of Fort Sumter, some 300,000 people had devoured her tome, published in weekly installments in a magazine and ending with this exhortation: "On the shores of our free states are emerging the poor, shattered, broken remnants of families. . . . They come to seek a refuge among you." Stowe so famously fueled fevers that Abraham Lincoln, upon meeting her in 1862, is said to have declared, "So you are the little woman who wrote the book that started this great war!"

And, ironically, if not for a letter signed by 5 the great pacifist Albert Einstein, we might never have dropped atomic bombs on Hiroshima and Nagasaki, plunging the world into the nuclear age. In 1939, when physicists found a way to split uranium atoms and release immense amounts of energy, the American press was abuzz with the expert opinion that such energy would never be harnessed into a bomb—a claim that the U.S. government bought into. But Einstein, a refugee from Nazi Germany, became convinced by colleagues not only that a bomb was scientifically feasible but that if the United States didn't build one first, the Nazis would, thereby gaining an unbeatable advantage over the rest of the world. On Aug. 2, 1939, he signed a letter to President Roosevelt advising him the atomic bomb was not only possible but imminent. The letter also warned that Germany had commandeered Czechoslovak uranium mines and halted further sales of the ore. To ward off disaster, he urged the president to sponsor a fast-moving U.S. atomic project. Einstein's letter launched the Manhattan Project and the nuclear arms race, which led six years later to the devastation of Hiroshima and Nagasaki. Toward the end of his life, Einstein said that sending the letter was "the greatest mistake" he ever made.

At times in our history, laws on the books had declared an issue resolved, a case closed, but informal voices sprang up and forced us as a people to reconsider. In 1963, for example, decades after a constitutional amendment gave women the vote and supposed equality, Betty Friedan wrote in her book *The Feminine Mystique* about "the problem that has no name." As she described it, "Each suburban wife struggled with it alone. As she made the beds, shopped for groceries, matched slipcover material . . . chauffeured Cub Scouts and Brownies, lay beside her husband at night—she was afraid to ask even of herself the silent question—'Is this all?'" With these words, Friedan awakened women of the "silent generation" and spawned a movement for women's rights that continues even today.

And in the same year, a century after the Emancipation Proclamation and years after the official end of racial segregation, Martin Luther King Jr. reminded the country: "We must face the tragic fact that the Negro is still not free." His words were epic: "When the architects of our republic wrote the magnificent words of the Constitution and the Declaration of Independence, they were signing a promissory note," King said. "It is obvious today that America has defaulted . . . insofar as her citizens of color are concerned." The force and eloquence of his words emboldened crusaders, and within two years both the Civil Rights Act and the Voting Rights Act were enacted. To this day, his words challenge each American to answer whether our black citizens can truly say, "Free at last! Free at last! Thank God Almighty, we are free at last!"

No matter what the time or place, our unofficial scribes have helped us to define our national character. Acting as mentors, they have fostered traits such as our famous individualism. Ralph Waldo Emerson did this when he wrote in *Self-Reliance:* "Whoso would be a man must be a nonconformist." And Henry David Thoreau echoed that sentiment in a personal diary that's been as influential in American culture as many archived documents: "I went to the woods because I wished to live deliberately . . . and not, when I came to die, discover that I had not lived." These philosophers and essayists have held up models for us to emulate, with stories of strong heroes like Paul Bunyan and courageous pioneers like Davy Crockett. And they have encouraged our world-renowned work ethic, as in Walt Whitman's celebration of carpenters and mechanics and shoemakers in *I Hear America Singing,* or more recently Woody Guthrie's and Bob Dylan's and Bruce Springsteen's paeans to American folklife and the nobility of labor.

Yet we often stumble into virtually irreconcilable tensions in trying to derive solidarity and community from millions of ambitious individualists. Indeed, our wordsmiths have often warned us when we have tipped too far off balance. Robert Frost was cautioning the nation when he wrote, "Something there is that doesn't love a wall . . . before I built a wall I'd ask to know what I was walling in or walling out." (Yet so wed are we to the values of freedom and solitude that we tend to skip over Frost's intended irony and quote his final phrase as words to live by: "Good fences make good neighbors.")

10   It took an outsider, the French social critic Alexis de Tocqueville, to alert early Americans to the "restlessness in the midst of their prosperity." Indeed, he chastised Americans for their "taste for physical gratifications," for "brooding over advantages they do not possess," and for the "vague dread that constantly torments them lest they should not have chosen the shortest path" to success. Writing in 1835, he concluded: "It is impossible to spend more effort in the pursuit of happiness."

In the almost two centuries since *Democracy in America* appeared, countless homegrown sages have tried to warn us of the deceptive lure of the pot at the end of the rainbow. There was the folktale of John Henry, who out of pride worked himself to death in order to beat a steam engine blasting holes through a mountain. There was F. Scott Fitzgerald's tragic Gatsby, doomed by his materialistic appetites, and at the opposite pole, John Steinbeck's hardworking but lost families in *The Grapes of Wrath,* cast into wretchedness by forces beyond their control. The folk duo Simon and Garfunkel sang cautionary rhymes about a fraudulent "big, bright green pleasure machine" and about the superficially successful Richard Cory—first the subject of an 1897 Edwin Arlington Robinson poem—who despite all his worldly riches and power was so miserable as to put a bullet through his own head.

Some influential writers have gone so far as to reject our capitalist ways altogether. In his 1906 polemic *The Jungle,* socialist Upton Sinclair argued: "There is one kind of prison where the man is behind bars, and everything that he desires is outside; and there is another kind where the things are behind the bars, and the man is outside." Half a century after Sinclair was writing, a new generation of young socialists would spark the wave of 1960s protests. "The American political system is not the democratic model of which its glorifiers speak," declared the Port Huron Statement, the manifesto of Students for a Democratic Society. "In actuality it frustrates democracy by confusing the individual citizen, paralyzing policy discussion, and consolidating the irresponsible power of military and business interests." One 1960s peace activists' motto—"make love, not war"—still reverberates today, and more recent counterparts of the antiwar activists have added "no blood for oil" to the unofficial national lexicon.

To its credit, America has always shown a great measure of tolerance for such self-criticism. Indeed, even when we have disagreed most vehemently, Americans have tended to agree on basic principles like the right to disagree. Again, Emerson's words have guided us: "Nothing is at last sacred but the integrity of your own mind." Others have created icons of integrity, such as Harper Lee's character Atticus Finch, a southern lawyer who in *To Kill a Mockingbird* defends a black man whom everyone else would scapegoat. Such high principle may be best portrayed by the ultimate American hero, the scrappy Huck Finn, who after much soul-searching decides that the right course of action is to defy all authority and help the runaway slave, Jim, to escape to freedom.

Freedom: the term Americans say best defines our nation. It's the juncture at which all of our most defining documents—both official and unofficial—always intersect. Our government proclaims freedom as a God-given right, and our songs chime "let freedom ring." Our activists protest freedoms still denied, and our sages remind us time and again that freedom is only truly worthwhile when we use it to "do the right thing." Perhaps that is why, indelibly engraved into our collective conscience, are not only the words "land of the free" but also "home of the brave."

Analyzing Argument

1. What basic assumption or shared value is at the root of Fischer's argument?

2. What is Fischer's main claim? Is it a claim of fact or value?

3. How does Fischer's argument rely on shared values? Point to specific passages to support your answer.

4. How does Fischer engage opposition? Where does she counter, concede, or qualify her own claims? Explain how that move (or moves) functions in her argument.

5. How could Fischer's claim be more focused and revelatory?

Red (White and Blue) Scare

STEPHEN PELL

Stephen Pell developed this argument in his second-semester college English course, using ideas about spin and propaganda from essays in the previous edition of *Inventing Arguments*. Pell's argument not only sheds light on the past, but it also reveals a connection between past and current events.

After World War II, after the Nazis had been pushed back into Germany, after Hiroshima and Nagasaki, a new power threatened our way of life: its name, communism. Josef Stalin reigned supreme over the Soviet Union. He had killed and imprisoned numerous citizens of his own country during now infamous purges, and ruled his country with an unflinching iron fist, oppressing his citizens with sheer brutality and show of force. The Russian poet Anna Akhmatova, whose poetry inspired many of her countrymen during these dark times, describes, in haunting verse, the horror that was impressed upon the population by Stalin's atrocities. Akhmatova herself had been an unintentional victim of the Stalinist purges; her husband and son were both imprisoned. The poem, often considered her most famous piece, is entitled "Requiem." In one passage, she remembers those who stood beside her outside the prison walls, waiting in futility, "The fading smiles upon submissive lips, / The trembling fear inside a hollow laugh. / That's why I pray not for myself / But all of you who stood there with me / Through fiercest cold and scorching July heat / Under a towering, completely blind red wall" (Akhmatova).

This terrifying account is the communism Americans knew and feared. Fear of "Reds" was palpable throughout the country. As Michael Barson and Steven Heller point out, the angst towards communism boils to the surface in Steinbeck's classic, *The Grapes of Wrath:* "A red is any son of a bitch that wants thirty cents when we're paying twenty-five" (qtd. in Barson and Heller 8).

The "Red" threat wasn't completely illegitimate. The purges that took place under Stalin certainly warranted a fair amount of opposition, and the Cuban missile crisis was nothing to sneeze at. To be fair to the American public living through these dark times, communism, as they knew it, was a serious concern to the way in which they lived. The problem, however, was that communism itself became synonymous with Stalin. This correlation had already embedded itself deep within the public psyche, making it easy for the government to capitalize on the public's premonitions. Continued use of the public's own fear of communism allowed the government to justify aggression against communist states such as Cuba, Guatemala, and Korea.

The Guatemalan conflict was relatively short compared to other anti-communist military actions of the time period, such as Korea and Vietnam, but it was well publicized. In June 1954, *Time* took a close look at the Guatemalan civil war. As expected of an article featured in a popular American magazine during the Cold War, sensationalism of glorious triumph over the "Reds" nearly oozes from the pages ("Guatemala"). The author of the article has the uncanny ability to present a gray situation, like a civil war, in such a fashion that the gray areas seem to fade away, leaving a defined line between black and white. The communist president of Guatemala, the enemy, is portrayed as a backstabbing, bloodthirsty madman. Throughout the article, the ideal of communism is presented as though it is a lesser form of government, as "rudimentary." This and other articles in popular magazines became some of the strongest forms of propaganda available to the masses.

Stephen Pell, "Red (White and Blue) Scare." Reprinted with the permission of the author.

5   The U.S. government was not only waging the war abroad, but back home as well. Paired with the national media, the government controlled its own people, not with guns, but with words. Americans were being attacked on all fronts with anticommunist propaganda: everything from movies to posters to public service announcements, speeches, articles in magazines, books, and even real-life world events. These world events often centered around military or paramilitary action towards a select group of communists or a country, usually ending with the communist forces being crushed to illustrate the superiority of capitalism.

Naturally, the dirty details of these paramilitary operations were never divulged to the American public until many years after the fact, making these operations a form of intense propaganda, in many ways more effective than conventional forms of propaganda. A government could *claim* that a rival nation's economy was failing. They could say that a nation's leader was an evil madman who violently oppressed his people. Posters could be pasted on the sides of buildings; radio waves could be broadcast to the masses; schools could be required to educate on the dangers of a communist government; but nothing convinces the population of a truth better than creating the truth firsthand.

Anti-communist advocates argue that the communist system of government was overtly oppressive and vastly inferior to capitalism. They may cite the economic instability in countries such as the Soviet Union and Cuba. However, it was not revealed until later that one of the biggest contributors to the instabilities of these countries was none other than our own CIA. These events of sabotage were planned as full-scale paramilitary operations, the most notable being "Operation Mongoose," which was primarily designed to cripple Cuba's economy and incite an uprising from within the country. Author James W. Symington writes in his article for the *National Review*:

In sum, if the intent of the past two generations of U.S. policy towards Cuba has been to render its economy comatose—energy consumption cut in half, vehicular travel horse- and mule-drawn or fixed in time to the 1950s, agricultural production inadequate, diet restricted, plumbing and street lamps non-operational, professional classes earning less than busboys in the gleaming Veradero tourist hotels, and too many of her fairest daughters walkers of the night streets—I would have to pronounce the policy an unqualified success. (37)

Symington's article is calling for the stoppage of America's trade embargo of Cuba, an embargo started during the Kennedy administration, that is only hurting an already economically battered country.

How did they do it? How could a nation's government convince an entire population to think the same way about an issue without tanks rumbling through the streets or by leveling the business end of a rifle at the collective mass? Propaganda.

10   America had had a history of utilizing propaganda to either stir up the masses or subdue them. "Loose talk" was a common issue addressed in American propaganda during World War II and the years following. One poster in particular illustrates how much America emphasized the value of keeping quiet. The poster bears the image of a GI helmet draped over a white cross with the words: "A careless word . . . another cross." Still another poster bears the image of a housewife and the ridiculous claim that her "loose talk" cost lives. What information could she possibly know?

This theme trickled beyond issues of national security and into everyday life. Americans were warned of "petty squabbles" among coworkers. A piece of propaganda during the early '40s features a bird's head and these words: "IF you MUST TALK about your boss or the person working alongside (*squawk squawk*) wait till the war is over. Office and factory politics and jealousies are destroyers of production. Chew a piece of gum instead" ("Petty Squabbles").

Propaganda during the Cold War took on many forms. It was a poster plastered to the side of a building, reminding the American public of the dangers the communists posed. It came in the form of blockbuster Hollywood hits like *I Married a Communist, The Red Menace,* and of course, every James Bond film up until the collapse of the Soviet Union. Articles detailed nightmare scenarios, such as communist guerillas taking over Detroit. *Look* magazine became the premiere periodical for sensationalized articles intent on stirring up the American public's anti-communist imagination. *Look* even featured a helpful template to be used to identify American communists with greater ease.

Americans faced propaganda from all angles during the Cold War. Not even the children were safe from the onslaught of anti-communism. Comic books of the time featured subtle and not-so-subtle undertones of capitalism, in the form of their favorite superhero vanquishing an ominous villain, clearly representing the Soviet Union. Bubble gum contained "Children's Crusade Against Communism" cards in every pack. Instead of the pictures of their favorite ballplayers, children were greeted with the wrinkled face of Josef Stalin or an artist's interpretation of what New York City *would* look like in the aftermath of a nuclear attack.

These appeals to everyday Americans' logic were by no means lofty. The propaganda was directed squarely at the middle class, which was not likely to dissect the hidden arguments lacing each and every propaganda poster. This attack on a specific class is a proven and effective method in the art of propaganda. Hitler states that "[for the intellectual class], propaganda is not suited. . . . All propaganda must be presented in a popular form and must fix its intellectual level so as not to be above the heads of the least intellectual of those to whom it is directed." Propaganda posters were often bright and colorful, with few words. The posters presented their ideas

and hidden ideas quickly and easily. However, when text was necessary to convey the complete argument against communism, it was often in the form of an article in a popular magazine, circulated throughout the middle classes. There was no escaping it. The "Red Scare" seeped its way into every form of media available to the masses. Everyday life became saturated with the appeals against communism.

The threat of communism was taken very seriously during the Cold War era. The Soviet threat became an excuse to take drastic measures against countries that posed no real danger to our way of life. Such was the case in Guatemala, when our nation's government justified to the American public that serious action against Guatemala was imperative, simply by scaring them with the "monster" that was communism. Noam Chomsky, a well-known and often controversial voice when it comes to America's foreign relations, writes in his book *Hegemony or Survival*, "The Soviet threat was routinely invoked, abetted by Guatemala's appeal to the Soviet bloc for arms after the U.S. had threatened attack and cut off other sources of supply. The result was a half-century of horror, even worse than the U.S.-backed tyranny that came before."

Hegemony. A thousand times more effective than the physical display of power, hegemony is power internalized within the very psyche of a group of people, altering how they think, directing who they associate themselves with, and making its presence known whenever a tough decision should arise. The government's control over information was the equivalent of covering up all but a small portion of a painting. The public wasn't getting the whole picture. Thus, the government had great leverage in establishing what the public *should* think about communism. Presenting only one side of communism, the dark side, the American government was able to simultaneously encourage hostility towards the Soviets while winning the trust of the American public.

Americans were living in a bubble. Petrified of the outside world of "Reds" and rebels and dictators,

15

Americans clung ever tighter to Uncle Sam, if only to protect themselves from impending doom. Thomas Hobbes' 17th-century book, *Leviathan*, describes the motives behind the formation of the first commonwealths:

> [The commonwealth] is the foresight of their own preservation, and of a more contented life thereby; that is to say, of getting themselves out from that miserable condition of war which is necessarily consequent, as hath been shown, to the natural passions of men when there is no visible power to keep them in awe, and tie them by fear of punishment to the performance of their covenants, and observation of those laws of nature.

The first governments were founded on the idea that an individual could not withstand the tumult of the outside world alone. The only safety came in groups. A commonwealth of individuals banded together to establish a larger body, a stronger body, one that could keep them safe from surrounding barbarism. In the case of the United States during the Cold War, the barbarism was replaced by communism, and Americans, driven by fear, voluntarily sacrificed their freedoms for security, positioning themselves further under the wing of the Republic, allowing the roots of hegemony to penetrate free thought.

The notion of a people sacrificing individuality and imagination for alleged security and blissful ignorance vaguely resembles the predictions found in Aldous Huxley's dystopic future in *Brave New World*. Characters are described as "bottled" from the outside world, and from themselves. The term "bottled" is used as a euphemism for *intoxicated* on the drug of choice, *soma*. In the novel, soma, along with years of subliminal conditioning, allows the government to maintain order among a society ranging in the billions. However, while the soma brings peace, it strips its users of freedom, rational thought, and individuality altogether. Users (everyone) stumble about in a dazed state, delightfully unaware of their surroundings. This is how propaganda leaves the average

citizen. It is the opiate of the masses, the intellectual assault that makes hegemony within our society a very real, past and present danger.

Hegemony is so powerful because it targets 20 the mind. A physical show of force, such as armed guards stationed on every corner or the threat of imprisonment for any suspicious activity against the government, is an effective method of controlling a population, but it has its downside. A select few will always fight against such obvious power, and though their bodies are being oppressed, their minds are free to think, free to reason, and free to conceive plots of a revolution. Hegemony attacks the mind, smothering the fires of change before they have a chance to ignite. Its effectiveness lies in its subtlety. A hegemonic authority can implement fear and sensationalism to convince the public that a certain choice is more acceptable or inherently right. Adolf Hitler himself addressed this potency: "Here the art of propaganda consists in putting a matter so clearly and forcibly before the minds of the people as to create a general conviction regarding the reality of a certain fact, the necessity of certain things and the just character of something that is essential."

Hegemony is still present today. Communism is certainly still unwelcome in this country, but now there is a new threat to our culture: terrorism. In the months following the attacks of September 11th, an

Communist Controlled Countries - 1980

Ambrose Video

all-out war on terror was declared while we continued to ponder the motives behind the attacks. During these initial months, any questioning of the government's actions in dealing with this new threat was enough to get oneself alienated from society. It was a vulnerable point in our nation's history. Trust in the government was high, as well as fear of the outside world. The masses could be easily swayed with a dramatic speech or sensationalized news piece. A unified mindset could be sensed throughout the majority of the population. The mere hint of hostile countries possessing weapons of mass destruction was enough to send people into a panic. We were afraid of another September 11th, as illustrated by the hasty creation and ratification of the Patriot Act, an act that trades freedom for security. Most Americans were unfazed. They had come to believe that it was the right thing to do. The painful memories of 9/11 swarmed in the back of their minds, memories that could be harnessed.

Hegemony and democracy cannot coexist. Anti-communist propaganda during the Cold War presented a one-sided view of communism, instilling fear in the population and restricting rational thought. This blatant bid for total thought control reveals the hidden motives of those in power, those who wish to control rather than to sustain freedom, those who wish to present a black-and-white description of what is right and what is wrong. Though such a tightly controlled view of the world promises unity, it comes at the price of truth and intellectual liberty.

Works Cited

Akhmatova, Anna. "Requiem." *PoemHunter*, www.poemhunter.com/poem/requiem.

Barson, Michael, and Steven Heller. *Red Scared! The Commie Menace in Propaganda and Popular Culture.* Chronicle Books, 2001.

Chomsky, Noam. "Cuba in the Cross-Hairs: A Near Half-Century of Terror." *Hegemony or Survival*, Metropolitan Books, 2003, chomsky.info/hegemony02/.

"Guatemala: Battle of the Backyard." *Time*, vol. 63, no. 26, 28 June 1954, content.time.com/time/magazine/article/0,9171,860889,00.html.

Hitler, Adolf. "Mein Kampf." 1925. *The Noontide Press, Books Online*, www.angelfire.com/folk/bigbaldbob88/MeinKampf.pdf.

Hobbes, Thomas. "Of the Causes, Generation, and Definition of a Commonwealth." *The Leviathan*, London, 1651.

Huxley, Aldous. *Brave New World*. 1932. Perennial Classics, 1998.

"Petty Squabbles." McGovern-Anderson, 1942. *UMedia Archive*, U of Minnesota, umedia.lib.umn.edu/node/42380.

Symington, James W. "Into Cuba." *National Review*, 10 Nov. 2003, pp. 36–38.

Analyzing Argument

1. According to Pell, what happened?

2. How does the argument connect the Red scare of the past to the reader's life today? How important is the connection?

3. What types of support are used, and how? Consider evidence, examples, and appeals.

   Evidence: authorities, testimony, facts, statistics

   Examples: allusion, anecdote, illustration, scenario

   Appeals: to logic, emotion, character, value, need

4. Academic audiences look at the inner workings of an argument. To examine Pell's argument more carefully, ask:

   • What does the argument assume about readers' values?

   • What assumption (from the previous question) might a reader object to? Make an argument in support of the assumption. That is, argue for why the reader should accept the assumption.

   • For what assumptions might Pell have offered more support (backing)?

Somewhere in the Past: Clarksville's School and Community Life

CAMERON JOHNSON

Using the invention prompts in this chapter, Cameron Johnson explored the complexities of a common topic: school funding. While Johnson concedes that class size has remained consistent and school buildings have been well-maintained, he unearths a less obvious and extremely important consequence of budget cuts, and he cautions the citizens of Clarksville (and other communities) that such cuts extend beyond school and into the very life of the community.

School funding has been steadily decreasing in the Clarksville Area School district for the past decade. While the district has managed to keep the schools running, providing lunches, busing, and textbooks, cuts in funding have hurt Clarksville Schools and Clarksville, the community, in subtle and important ways. When school funding does not keep up with the growing needs of students, the whole community pays the price.

Some influential community leaders have argued for years that schools, like all companies, organizations, and households, should "tighten their belts" in times of economic woe. And, for years, that is what our schools (and most others around the country) have been doing. So while those community leaders can applaud the school board, superintendent, teachers, and students for getting by on less, citizens of Clarksville should be cautious about their optimism. While class size has remained consistent and school buildings are well maintained, lack of funding has hit the schools and our community in other places.

> Appeal to value. (The passage engages the values of those who prefer spending less on schools.)

Deceptively important academic programs and extracurricular activities have been cut. A 1990 *Oracle*, the school's yearbook, includes photographs of several groups and clubs that no longer exist: perhaps most notably, the Junior High Drama Club and the Senior High Thespians, but also the Jazz Ensemble, Sundancers, Future Business Leaders, and more. None of these losses alone is devastating, yet many Clarksville citizens have fond memories of high school musicals, such as *Guys and Dolls* and *Bye-Bye Birdie*, musicals replaced now by an evening watching TV or a movie at the local cinema. High school musicals, and other extracurricular events, help to connect school, student, and community, not just the night of the event, but for years to come.

> "Deceptively" = there is more going on with these programs than meets the eye.

> This is the main idea of the argument.

Cameron Johnson, "Somewhere in the Past: Clarksville's Schools and Community Life." Reprinted by permission of the author.

Another example helps illustrate the vital connection between school and community. Many Clarksville citizens grew up in, and have fond memories of, the school's summer recreation program that was cut back steadily each year and finally abandoned in 1996. While this program can be seen as nonessential, it was hardly fluff in the budget. The summer recreation program was an important link between school and community. It not only gave kids something to do, but it helped forge a stronger bond between school and student, and this bond created other bonds: between school and community and between community and student. Because of less funding, schools end up offering less support (for academics) and less attraction (for extracurricular activities). In the long run, schools with less funding become less important to students and less important within the community as a whole. The summer recreation program is just one example of this subtle, or silent, breakdown.

All across America, local school systems have been facing consistent budget cuts, and as in Clarksville, the cuts impact the delicate layer of social life around the schools: summer school, sports, music, and art programs have consistently been lopped off the agendas. Some districts, such as one in Orange County, Florida, are considering moving back starting times to 10:30 or 11:00 a.m. (Stover). It is easy to see that budget cuts have made schools shrink inward—balling themselves into smaller space and smaller bits of time. And even when communities pass local levies, they are often not enough to turn the tide. Increased taxes have not always kept up with the rate of inflation. According to the organization Funding Washington Schools, for example, the purchasing power for education in the state of Washington has actually decreased 33% since 1992 because of inflation (Shutz and Billinghurst). And when that loss is projected over the coming decades, it is easy to imagine the economic effect: a consistent reduction of programs and a consistent reduction in the role that schools once played in their communities.

In previous generations in America, the people of small towns convened—perhaps at the church, a town hall, a school, or all of these. Some institution served as an assembly place. But now, American communities are less communal than they have ever been. According to sociologist Robert D. Putnam, "There is striking evidence . . . that the vibrancy of American civil society has notably declined over the past several decades" (65). Putnam's important essay, "Bowling Alone: America's Declining Social Capital," details a range of individual and collective behavior that illustrates diminishing civic engagement in American towns:

Addresses potential opposing position—that only essential programs should be funded.

The series of points is an appeal to logic. Here we see the line of reasoning at the heart of the argument.

This is a more generalized expression of the claim.

The secondary sources show that Clarksville's funding issues are common throughout the country. (The information about other schools reinforces the point about Clarksville.)

Before we move into Putnam's points, the writer sets up the points and creates appropriate context for the quotations.

A series of identical questions posed by the Roper Organization to national samples ten times each year over the last two decades reveals that since 1973 the number of Americans who report that "in the past year" they have "attended a public meeting on town or school affairs" has fallen by more than a third (from 22 percent in 1973 to 13 percent in 1993). By almost every measure, Americans' direct engagement in politics and government has fallen steadily and sharply over the last generation, despite the fact that average levels of education—the best individual-level predictor of political participation—have risen sharply throughout this period. Every year over the last decade or two, millions more have withdrawn from the affairs of their communities. (68)

Although the quotation is lengthy, all the information is relevant to the argument. It reinforces Johnson's key point: that public interaction is shrinking in communities like Clarksville.

In other words, people may be getting more schooling (graduating from high school, going to college), but they are doing so in a more private manner. Their educational experiences are more divorced from their community experiences—and so the whole purpose of education seems more wrapped in individual private success. Even parental involvement has waned:

Johnson follows up the quotation and makes it feel even more relevant to the argument.

The parent-teacher association (PTA) has been an especially important form of civic engagement in twentieth-century America because parental involvement in the educational process represents a particularly productive form of social capital. It is, therefore, dismaying to discover that participation in parent-teacher organizations has dropped drastically over the last generation, from more than 12 million in 1964 to barely 5 million in 1982 before recovering to approximately 7 million now. (Putnam 69)

This is not to say that parents are generally less engaged in their children's schooling. They may, in fact, be more engaged than before. But if they are, it is a private engagement, one not dramatized in public life.

Here's another follow-up. Johnson qualifies the point of the quotation.

Putnam's study corresponds to my own experiences. In the 1970s and 1980s, when I was coming through the public schools, they were more central to town life than they are now. I remember huge turnouts for a wide range of school-sponsored events (even beyond the Friday night football games): ice-cream socials, plays, orchestra concerts, spelling bees, even marching band *practice*. But something has changed fundamentally.

A transition from the outside source to Johnson's personal testimony.

Somewhere in the past is the community of Clarksville. Certainly, it is still a town. But it is slightly less alive than it was. It may have a strip mall and two more fast-food establishments than it did ten years ago, but

Johnson returns to the specific focus on Clarksville. He is careful to qualify the claims.

it is less involved in its own affairs. The public schools were a key part of a past vitality. But as funding has been cut, extracurricular programs, the ones that created an intensive social life around the schools, have also been cut. We have let something important, something about our community, fade into history.

Works Cited

Putnam, Robert D. "Bowling Alone: America's Declining Social Capital." *Journal of Democracy*, vol. 6, no.1, Jan.1995, pp. 65–78.

Shutz, Byron and Barb Billinghurst. "School Funding Facts." *Funding Washington Schools*, www.fundingwaschools.org/index_files/FundingStats_Funding_WA_K12_Schools.htm.

Stover, Del. "Stretching the Incredible Shrinking School Budget." *Education Digest*, vol. 69, no. 1, Sept. 2003, p. 59.

Analyzing Argument

1. What basic assumption or shared value is at the root of Johnson's argument?

2. Does the argument convince the reader of its main point? In other words, is anything left hanging that might call the argument into question?

3. What logical appeal is important to the argument, and how?

4. Review the section on Toulminian Argument in Chapter Five, and then fill in the following:
   Main Claim:
   Unstated Assumption(s):
   Support:

5. In groups, identify several unstated assumptions that are crucial to Johnson's argument. How might Johnson have argued for the validity of the unstated assumption?

6. What attempt does the argument make to connect with the audience? Does the argument concede, qualify, or counterargue? Does the language or voice engage people with a different position or perspective?

Apache Children

From the 1880s to the mid-1900s, the U.S. government used schools outside Indian reservations, such as the Carlisle School (a boarding school for Native Americans), to teach Indian children American ways of thinking and living. School administrators often took "before" and "after" photographs.

Apache children on arrival at the Carlisle Indian School in Pennsylvania.

Apache children four months after arrival at the Carlisle Indian School in Pennsylvania.

Analyzing Argument

1. What do the images show about past or present attitudes or values?

2. How do these images argue about the past?

3. Besides Native Americans attending U.S. government-sponsored boarding schools, to what broader issues do the images speak? How might those issues involve arguments about the past?

Carr Fork Canyon, Utah (circa 1939–1945)

Analyzing Argument

1. What does the photograph say about the past?

2. What does it tell us about ourselves?

EXPLORING FOR TOPICS

Arguments often emerge from conflicting perspectives about the past. A topic might involve a highly debatable issue such as the circumstantial evidence used to convict or set free someone accused of a crime. But a topic need not concern an event already surrounded by debate. Some of the most engaging arguments involve topics that at first seem beyond argument. As you examine the world around you, pay attention to how the past has been described and look for any discrepancy between your perspective and others'. Or look for tension among different accounts of the past. If you discover tension in the way someone has been characterized, something has been defined, or something has been sequenced, you may have a topic that will develop into an argument. Use the following prompts to find topics and begin developing your own argument:

- Consider past national or world events: a military action, governmental election, political scandal, economic crisis, marketing campaign, political protest.
- Read about an era or time: prewar Europe, the Jazz Age, the golden age of Greece, the Reagan years, the Clinton years, the Cold War, the Beat Generation.
- Recall a past local event: an election, high school sporting event, political scandal, industrial accident, schoolyard mishap, business deal, violent crime, festival, parade.
- Read an old magazine or newspaper and look for behaviors, trends, or fashions from the past: architectural trends, gender roles in the workforce or at home, educational practices, work schedules, standards of beauty, hairstyles.
- Visit a place that characterizes the past: a museum, national monument, historical landmark, amusement park, corporate headquarters.
- Explore your academic major: browse through a related textbook or journal, or ask someone involved in the field (a professor or even a student who has taken several classes) about the history and development of the discipline. The following questions may be helpful: What particular past events are still being debated in the discipline? Is there debate about the cause of any trends, situations, or events in the discipline? Is research in the field or discipline on the right track? Why or why not?

We should never have made cars so affordable to the masses.

WHAT HAPPENED?

Real family entertainment died with *The Waltons* and *Little House on the Prairie*

To view this video, visit the English CourseMate at CengageBrain.com.

Top to bottom: Madhouse; Library of Congress; Madhouse; © Cengage Learning®. From CourseMate video (BBC: Civil Rights March)

- Consider the opening image for this chapter: What does it suggest about America's past? What does it say about fun, entertainment, American spirit, or race relations?
- Consider the readings and images from this chapter: Which makes you want to speak out? What point is not resolved in your mind? From your perspective, which raises an especially important topic?
- What song or songs argue about the past? What version of the past does the song argue for? Do most people accept that version of the past?

To fully explore the past, arguers go beneath the obvious information and examine details, acting like detectives collecting clues. From these clues, they build and argue for a valid account of events. Use the following invention questions to explore your topic. While it may be tempting to answer quickly and move on, the insights you are seeking lie beyond the first, quick response:

▶ Who was involved? Explain their influence.
▶ What factors (natural, political, etc.) were involved, and what was their influence?
▶ How were institutions or policies involved?
▶ What were the consequences of the event or behavior in question?
▶ How were people's lives directly or indirectly affected?
▶ Might other effects become clear at some point in the future?
▶ What are the hidden effects (the layers no one can actually see)?

Now, notice how Cameron Johnson takes one of the questions and explores:

▶ How were people's lives directly or indirectly affected?

> When school funding does not keep up with the growing needs of students and teachers, the whole community pays the price—not financially, but in other ways. When schools can't afford to pay for after-school programs, clubs, and teacher assistants (the kind of things that are the first to go when funding gets low), the schools become less of a center for student life. The schools shrink inward and involve fewer people. The schools offer less support (for academics) and less attraction (for extracurricular activities). In the long run, schools with less funding become less important to students—and within the community as a whole. And when that happens, ironically, the communities go downhill (slowly but surely). And when communities go downhill, property values go downhill (slowly but surely). This is what has happened in Clarksville. School funding has slowly been decreasing over the years. As a result, the public schools have shrunk away from the community.

Johnson's invention writing explores the direct, and also the indirect and subtle, effects of the situation. Now he might look for additional effects by asking, *So what if the public schools shrink away from the community? Who or what might be affected? What problem(s), if any, might arise?*

Invention Workshop

For your topic, with one or two other writers answer the invention question, "How were people's lives directly or indirectly affected?" Then identify an indirect or subtle effect that more people should be aware of.

EXPLORING FOR PRINCIPLES AND PRECEDENT Good arguers go beyond a topic's specific details to discover relevant principles (standard rules that govern behavior) and precedents (cases that came before). Johnson's topic, Clarksville public school funding, relates to general principles about school funding and the general relationship between communities and schools. During invention, he writes:

> In the long run, schools with less funding become less important to students—and within the community as a whole. And when that happens, ironically, the communities go downhill (slowly but surely). And when communities go downhill, property values go downhill (slowly but surely).

Here we see Johnson making a general claim about the school/community relationship, pointing to a principle beyond Clarksville, and applying it to the specific topic:

> This is what has happened in Clarksville. School funding has slowly been decreasing over the past fourteen years. As a result, the public schools have shrunk away from the community.

Johnson could go even further and investigate the relationship between public institutions and communities:

> Communities are better off when they nurture their public institutions. From libraries to city park services, public institutions make a community better. When those institutions are developed with care and proper funding (with sustained attention), they give back to the community in many unseen ways—in essence, they offer a huge financial, cultural, and civic return.

Johnson's exploration transcends the particulars of Clarksville. This exploration pays off because the broader principles can be applied to the specific case. Johnson could also explore precedent (similar cases that have occurred) by asking, *How has public school funding worked in America? How have most public schools fared under decreasing tax dollars?* In general, these questions ask: *What has happened before?* As you consider your own topic, ask yourself the following:

▶ What bigger principles, issues, or values are involved?

▶ What other situations are like this? What has happened in these other situations?

COLLECTING OPINIONS Answers to survey questions can help writers understand conventional views and imagine some unconventional or peculiar ones. But informal surveys rarely yield highly credible support. The responses do not amount to a collective truth about the topic; instead, they reveal patterns of perception in particular communities. Claims from surveys should be used accordingly—not as ultimate grounds for claims, but as tools of exploration.

CONDUCTING SECONDARY RESEARCH Writers use secondary sources (articles, books, websites, and so on) to find out what has already been said and to develop a sense of their own position. If little has been said directly about a topic and published arguments are hard to find, this does not mean all hope is lost. On the contrary, it means you have some open argumentative terrain.

Because every topic is related to broader principles and precedents, research can take many different paths. For instance, Johnson's focus on Clarksville relates to the broader relationship between communities and public institutions. So a range of relevant information could emerge from a database search of the following keyword combinations: *school funding and property value; public institutions and funding; public institutions and funding and communities.* These searches could lead to sources that address broader issues such as the general decline in civic engagement or the national trends in school funding, and these sources would shed light on the particular situation in Clarksville. Research includes different layers—both particular details and broader principles. While researchers sometimes pursue a particular fact or statistic to support their position, they also look for theories and arguments that help them see the topic in a new way. This is the heart of inventive research.

Activities

1. As a class, discuss what types of sources may best develop arguments about the past—or which ones might help you to see the past in a new way. Consider the following source types:

Primary Sources	Secondary Sources	
Interviews	Books (nonfiction)	Government documents
Surveys	Newspapers	Pamphlets
Literary works	Magazines	Speeches
Novels	Journals	Performances
Short stories	Online periodicals	Films, television, music
Poetry	Websites	Posters
Religious texts	E-mails	

2. Survey at least five students from your class and at least five people not in your class. First ask if they know of the event or situation you have chosen. Then ask them to give their accounts. Do not lead them to an answer, but ask for their opinions of what happened and how they characterize the events. Listen for descriptive words such as *terrible, excellent, proud, guilty, surprising, irresponsible, brave, correct*. Record the responses and look for how others perceive the topic, what patterns exist, and any unconventional ways of thinking.

INVENTING A CLAIM

To make a persuasive argument about the past, arguers must first become aware of other versions or accounts. Only then can they plan an effective argumentative strategy. Use the following questions to examine possible arguments about your topic.

What Do Others Claim?

- What is the mainstream or official account? (What do most people say happened?)
- How is the event or situation characterized or defined? (What key descriptive words or adjectives do people use?)
- What are the marginalized accounts (those that are rarely mentioned)?

What Do I Claim?

- Do you agree or disagree with any accounts you have heard or read?
- How is your own perspective different from or similar to others'?

For any one situation or event, an unlimited number of points can be argued. For example, you may argue that something caused an event, that a past behavior was warranted or unwarranted, that a past situation is deeply misunderstood, or that someone was guilty or innocent. The following are standard types of arguments about the past, focused in different ways:

CAUSE/EFFECT ARGUMENTS Cause/effect arguments assert claims of fact. They make a case for or against a particular cause:

- The freedom of the Jazz Age was, in part, a response to the tightly controlled behavior of the preceding decades.
- The rawness of the grunge sound was a backlash against the slick fashions of mainstream 1980s music.
- The train collision last month occurred because Westway Railroad refused to address major mechanical deterioration.

DEFINITION ARGUMENTS Definition arguments also assert claims of fact. They argue about the nature or basic properties of a subject:

- The Jazz Age was more about sexuality than jazz.
- Grunge was not necessarily the music of a generation.
- Last month's railway collision was a classic example of corporate irresponsibility.

EVALUATION ARGUMENTS These arguments assert a claim of value (that some event or situation was good/bad, wrong/right, misguided/appropriate, and so on):

- Jazz was America's most important cultural discovery.
- The grunge sound of the early 1990s saved the music industry from an insipid direction.
- Westway Railroad Company was grossly negligent in last month's train collision.

Now that you have a topic in mind, choose an argumentative path. Ask yourself:

▶ What exactly can be argued about the topic?

▶ What path do I want to take?

▶ Is the tension based on the cause or sequence of events, the characterization of people or things, or the evaluation of something or someone?

You might begin this process with a broad claim. But as you research and invent support, try to narrow your focus. Generally, the more precise the point, the more intense the argument. Notice the difference between the following statements—how the second and third claims get more focused and more intense:

• Music of the 1960s was better than the music of today.

• The rock music of the 1960s opened people's hearts to important issues.

• The civic unrest of the late 1960s gave rock-and-roll music a social urgency.

The first statement has a broad subject, and the verb *was* does not focus the reader on a particular quality or issue. The statement does not reveal an insight, but flatly states a broad opinion ("better" in what way?). The second and third statements go further and invite readers to see a particular aspect about popular music in the 1960s. As you develop your claim, consider the subject and verb: Are they specific enough? If the subject of the sentence is not specific, how can you better focus your thoughts? Does the verb direct attention to a particular quality or action?

A CAUTION ABOUT CLICHÉS Clichés, worn-out expressions that people use in everyday conversation, should be avoided in formal arguments. Even though cliché phrases sound engaging at first, they create mental roadblocks for writers and readers. For example, the second claim about 1960s music relies on a vague and unarguable phrase (*opened people's hearts*). Like most clichés, the phrase doesn't reveal anything specific about the topic and would be difficult—if not impossible—to support. Often, as in this example, clichés come up early in the invention process when writers are grappling with ideas. But good writers push past the clichés and try to generate fresh claims . . .

More Sample Claims

Politics

• As the Clinton era illustrated, federal fiscal discipline, once a trademark of the Republican Party, has been taken over by the Democrats.

• Contrary to modern romantic notions, Native Americans were often territorial and fought to defend or occupy new land before European settlers brought their notion of war to this continent.

Community Issues

• Had the township elected not to allow big box stores to take over the outskirts of the city in the early 1990s, the downtown, and perhaps the outlying region, would still be thriving today.

• Like many small towns in America, Coventry emerged only because of the farming that surrounds it.

Popular Culture

- Commercials are not getting less sophisticated. Since the beginning of television, they have been insufferably dim-witted, aimed at the lowest possible level of consciousness and self-awareness.

- The hope of the hippy era faded into history because, like any mass movement in America, its collective energy focused on fashion and image, not real political change.

Environment

- When it comes to the health of the environment, the "scientific community" has always been dismissed by the masses, and—as history shows—the masses have consistently been wrong.

- The attempts to clean up the Great Lakes in the 1970s and 1980s were met with derision and contempt, showing that mainstream political ideology has valued the right to poisonous living conditions for decades.

INVENTING SUPPORT

Building an argument is not simply a matter of saying what you think. It is a process of supporting a debatable claim or set of claims. Writers develop arguments with various support strategies.

TESTIMONY Testimony is an individual's personal portrayal or understanding of events. In an argument about the past, testimony can be especially persuasive. Firsthand testimony can be used to capture the details or emotion of a past situation, or to show a particular account:

> In the 1980s, the standardized test craze was just beginning to enter public schools. Certainly, students had been taking standardized tests, such as the California Achievement Test, for years, but in the '80s, the once-a-year testing sessions started to climb. In fact, my memories of the sixth grade are filled with hours of the fill-in-the-bubble, number-2-pencil-only tests, the names of which I do not recall. Nor do I recall receiving anything back about my scores.

Arguers can also use the testimony of others:

> Some historians with an ax to grind are quick to dismiss Woodstock as a mere incident—as something that had little meaning outside of the drug culture of the era. However, the drug culture was only a single layer of Woodstock, and many participants still explain that they were very much aware of the significance of the event. According to Bill Crandle, the meaning was palpable in the air: "We all knew that it was something special, and that history would remember us. People even talked about it, saying things like 'people won't ever forget it.'"

EXAMPLES Examples are specific cases or illustrations of phenomena. They help to make an abstract point clearer or more concrete. Examples also can help narrow down generalizations or broad claims. In her article "A Nation Made of Poetry," Joannie Fischer argues that America's past is built on great poetic texts, and most of her article offers examples through history:

> To be sure, without some of these scripts, key moments in U.S. history might never even have taken place. Without Thomas Paine's elegant and angry prose, for example, we might not even exist as an independent country today. In 1775, Colonial leaders were torn by warring views about how to deal with mother England. Then, in January 1776, Paine's pamphlet *Common Sense* was published in Philadelphia, opening with the legendary phrase, "These are the times that try men's souls."

AUTHORITIES Authorities are sources or people who can substantiate points based on their research or professional qualifications. Authorities are important to use when offering specialized information (anything that might require focused research or experimentation). Notice how Johnson uses an organization as a source:

> It is easy to see that budget cuts have made schools shrink inward—balling themselves into smaller space and smaller bits of time. And even when communities pass local levies, they are often not enough to turn the tide. Increased taxes have not always kept up with the rate of inflation. According to the organization Funding Washington Schools, for example, the purchasing power for education in the state of Washington has actually decreased 33% since 1992 because of inflation (Shutz and Billinghurst).

Johnson uses the source to show historical precedent and explain a dimension of public school funding. The sentence immediately following brings the reader back to his main point:

> And when that loss is projected over the coming decades, it is easy to imagine the economic effect: a consistent reduction of programs and a consistent reduction in the role that schools once played in their communities.

ANALOGIES To draw an analogy is to draw out the similarities between two different phenomena or situations. This is often done in arguments about the past. If someone wants to prove something about past event A, he or she may show how it is like event B:

> In some ways, the search for the source of the river Nile was like the search for the fountain of youth: European explorers plunging into foreign (and conquerable) lands to gain notoriety, to gain immortality.

Analogies are often used to discuss past political affairs:

> Only twice in American history have we had father/son presidents: the Adams and the Bush families. In some ways, the families are much alike. Both had immense power in the country, which enabled the sons to be channeled into the positions. The difference, however, lies in the nature and use of that power.

LITERARY WORKS Literary works such as novels, poetry, drama, and short stories can be used in various ways to support a writer's claims. In "Red (White and Blue) Scare," Pell uses Aldous Huxley's novel *Brave New World* to help the reader understand his claim that "people [sacrifice] individuality and imagination for alleged security and blissful ignorance." Pell states his claim, introduces Huxley's novel, makes specific references to the novel, and connects those references to the larger points of his argument about propaganda and hegemony:

The notion of a people sacrificing individuality and imagination for alleged security and blissful ignorance vaguely resembles the predictions found in Aldous Huxley's dystopic future in *Brave New World*. Characters are described as "bottled" from the outside world, and from themselves.

> The term "bottled" is used as a euphemism for *intoxicated* on the drug of choice, *soma*. In the novel, soma, along with years of subliminal conditioning, allows the government to maintain order among a society ranging in the billions. However, while the soma brings peace, it strips its users of freedom, rational thought, and individuality altogether. Users (everyone) stumble about in a dazed state, delightfully unaware of their surroundings. This is how propaganda leaves the average citizen. It is the opiate of the masses, the intellectual assault that makes hegemony within our society a very real, past and present danger.

APPEALS TO LOGIC This type of appeal calls on the audience to follow a line of reasoning. In an argument about the past, the logical appeal often is based on cause and effect: the arguer would like the audience to see a reasonable relationship between an action and a reaction. For example, notice Johnson's final paragraph:

> Somewhere in the past is the community of Clarksville. Certainly, it is still a town. But it is slightly less alive than it was. It may have a strip mall and two more fast-food establishments than it did ten years ago, but it is less involved in its own affairs. The public schools were a key part of a past vitality. But as funding has been cut, extracurricular programs, the ones that created an intensive social life around the schools, have also been cut. We have let something important, something about our community, fade into history.

Johnson's argument provides a direct connection between the cause (funding cuts in the school district) and the effect (loss of community). The passage invites readers to understand that one impacted the other.

APPEALS TO VALUE Appeals to value make a connection between the topic and a value such as fairness, equality, duty, or responsibility. Sometimes, writers use a shared value to drive their own claims. Other times, they examine the values of their opposition and try to use those to build common ground. In his essay, Johnson engages the value of thrift or frugality. He knows that people in his community have argued for spending as little as possible on schools. And so he takes on that argument and even adopts its underlying value:

> Some influential community leaders have argued for years that schools, like all companies, organizations, and households, should "tighten their belts" in times of economic woe. And, for years, that is what our schools (and most others around the country) have been doing. So while those community leaders can applaud the school board, superintendent, teachers, and students for getting by on less, citizens of Clarksville should be cautious about their optimism. While class size has remained consistent and school buildings are well maintained, lack of funding has hit the schools and our community in other places.

For your own topic, use the following invention questions to develop support:

- ▶ What specific situations show my point about the past?
- ▶ What people or events from history, popular culture, or literature show my point?
- ▶ What line of reasoning should the reader follow to understand my point? (How can I best walk the reader through that line of reasoning?)
- ▶ What emotions can I evoke in the reader? How will those help the reader understand my position?
- ▶ What values underlie my position? How can I invite the reader to share those values?
- ▶ What literary works help to illustrate my point about the past?

Invention Workshop

With one or two other writers, answer the preceding invention questions for your topic. See how many types of support you can find for each topic.

Types of Support

Evidence: authorities, testimony, facts, statistics

Examples: allusion, anecdote, illustration, scenario

Appeals: to logic, emotion, character, value, need

ARRANGEMENT

Arranging an argument means arranging how the reader will experience the issue. In this case, the arrangement will determine how the reader returns to the past, experiences particular claims and details, and then returns to the present. The writer is a guide to the past, taking the reader on a persuasive tour, and the arrangement of a text is the path the reader takes.

HOW SHOULD I BEGIN? Arguments about the past can begin with a current event that prompted the argument. For example, in "A Nation Made of Poetry" Joannie Fischer begins her argument by referring to official documents now on display.

> The official documents now on display in Washington, D.C., offer one version of America's story. It's an authorized biography of sorts, screened and sanctioned. But the beauty of words in a democracy is that anyone can offer them up, and they live or die not by a ruler's dictate, but by their ability to permeate hearts and minds, to ignite passions, and to provoke action. Throughout our history, we have learned that words with enough resonance—whether from a slave, a student, or a songwriter—can change history as dramatically as any decree.

In "Shakespeare and Narcotics," David Pinching uses the same strategy, starting with a current event:

> The recent discovery of a drug-tainted clay pipe in Stratford-upon-Avon, home of Shakespeare, has caused some fervent discussion on the topic of the Bard's possible cocaine usage.

In "Somewhere in the Past: Clarksville's Schools and Community Life," Johnson begins by illustrating what happened in the past:

> School funding has been steadily decreasing in the Clarksville Area School district for the past decade. While the district has managed to keep the schools running, providing lunches, bussing, and textbooks, cuts in funding have hurt Clarksville Schools and Clarksville, the community, in subtle and important ways. When school funding does not keep up with the growing needs of students, the whole community pays the price.

Johnson's first sentence illustrates the past (what has been happening); the second sentence asserts a problem (cuts in funding have hurt the school *and* the community); the third sentence transcends the particulars of Clarksville and points to a principle (the importance of schools to the community). The rest of the essay develops Johnson's claim "When school funding does not keep up with the growing needs of students, the whole community pays the price."

WHERE SHOULD I DETAIL THE PAST? Joannie Fischer details the past throughout most of her essay, always connecting past details with their significance to the present:

> To be sure, without some of these scripts, the key moments in history might never even have taken place. Without Thomas Paine's elegant and angry prose, for example, we might not even exist as an independent country today. In 1775, Colonial leaders were torn by warring views about how to deal with mother England. Then, in January 1776, Paine's pamphlet *Common Sense* was published in Philadelphia, opening with the legendary phrase, "These are the times that try men's souls." It argued forcefully for the necessity of revolution and sold 150,000 copies overnight. It's widely credited with overcoming dissenters' qualms and unifying opinion enough to make the Declaration of Independence possible. "Without the pen of Paine," said John Adams, "the sword of Washington would have been wielded in vain."

Like Fischer, the other writers in this chapter detail the past throughout their essays. Pell focuses on the past for eighteen paragraphs, then changes focus to the present:

> Hegemony is still present today. Communism is certainly still unwelcome in this country, but now there is a new threat to our culture: terrorism. . . .

HOW CAN I BRIEFLY EXPLAIN ACCOUNTS OF THE PAST? While accounts of the past are sometimes explained at length (a chapter or even an entire book can explain an account of the past), accounts are often explained briefly and then responded to. Notice how Johnson creates an account of the past in his first two sentences, and then develops how and why that account has changed:

> In previous generations in America, the people of small towns convened—perhaps at the church, a town hall, a school, or all of these. Some institutions served as an assembly place. But now, American communities are less communal than they have ever been. According to sociologist Robert D. Putnam, "There is striking evidence . . . that the vibrancy of American civil society has notably declined over the past several decades" (65). Putnam's important essay, "Bowling Alone: America's Declining Social Capital," details a range of individual and collective behavior that illustrates diminishing civic engagement in American towns. . . .

Invention Workshop

With one or two others, discuss how you might explain accounts of the past in your essay.

1. How many accounts of the past will you explain and why?
2. How much detail is necessary to bring the reader's thinking in line with your own?
3. What details would take away from the argument's intensity?
4. Will you explain an account at length, or can you sum it up in a sentence or two?
5. Will you explain an account by correcting some other account, as Pinching does?

Activity

For practice in describing the past, and to help figure out how you might describe the past for your argument essay, describe your version of the past in two pithy sentences, then describe it in a paragraph or more.

AUDIENCE AND VOICE

BRIDGING VALUES Writers use their understanding of the audience to find common ground and bridge values. Building a bridge to the values of one's opponents is an especially powerful argument strategy. As Fischer argues the importance of unofficial documents in American history, she connects individual voices and documents to American values such as *individualism and hard work:*

> No matter what the time or place, our unofficial scribes have helped us to define our national character. Acting as mentors, they have fostered traits such as our famous individualism. Ralph Waldo Emerson did this when he wrote in *Self-Reliance:* "Whoso would be a man must be a nonconformist."

And Henry David Thoreau echoed that sentiment in a personal diary that's been as influential in American culture as many archived documents: "I went to the woods because I wished to live deliberately . . . and not, when I came to die, discover that I had not lived." These philosophers and essayists have held up models for us to emulate, with stories of strong heroes like Paul Bunyan and courageous pioneers like Davy Crocket. And they have encouraged our world-renowned work ethic, as in Walt Whitman's celebration of carpenters and mechanics and shoemakers in *I Hear America Singing,* or more recently Woody Guthrie's and Bob Dylan's and Bruce Springsteen's paeans to American folklife and the nobility of labor.

While Fischer connects Emerson, Thoreau, Bunyan, Crocket, Whitman, Guthrie, Dylan, and Springsteen to individualism and hard work, she connects other voices to *self-criticism,* another important American value:

In the almost two centuries since *Democracy in America* appeared, countless homegrown sages have tried to warn us of the deceptive lure of the pot at the end of the rainbow. There was the folktale of John Henry, who out of pride worked himself to death in order to beat a steam engine blasting holes through a mountain. There was F. Scott Fitzgerald's tragic Gatsby, doomed by his materialistic appetites, and at the opposite pole, John Steinbeck's hardworking but lost families in *The Grapes of Wrath,* cast into wretchedness by forces beyond their control. The folk duo Simon and Garfunkel sang cautionary rhymes about a fraudulent "big, bright green pleasure machine" and about the superficially successful Richard Cory—first the subject of an 1897 Edwin Arlington Robinson poem—who despite all his worldly riches and power was so miserable as to put a bullet through his own head.

Fischer's many examples help the reader accept her account of the past in which unofficial documents resonate and steer history.

For your own topic, use the following invention questions to build bridges to opposing viewpoints:

- ▶ When you picture yourself arguing this topic, who is on the receiving end?
- ▶ What values do you share with that audience?
- ▶ What values might you not share? (Do you, for instance, value individual rights more than your audience does or vice versa?)
- ▶ What connections can you make between your values and the values of those who might disagree with you?

COUNTERARGUMENTS, CONCESSIONS, AND QUALIFIERS Another way writers connect with their audience is through counterarguments, concessions, and qualifiers. Notice how Cameron Johnson explains and then refutes an opposing position:

Some influential community leaders have argued for years that schools, like all companies, organizations, and households, should "tighten their belts" in times of economic woe. And, for years, that is what our schools (and most others around the country) have been doing. So while those community leaders can applaud the school board, superintendent, teachers, and students for getting by on less, citizens of Clarksville should be cautious about their optimism. While class size has remained consistent and school buildings are well maintained, lack of funding has hit the schools and our community in other places.

Not all opposing positions can be explained away. Some have value, and good arguments acknowledge that value by conceding opposing points or by qualifying their own points. Notice how Johnson acknowledges an opposing view and then responds:

> Another example helps illustrate the vital connection between school and community. Many Clarksville citizens grew up in, and have fond memories of, the school's summer recreation program that was cut back steadily each year and finally abandoned in 1996. While this program can be seen as nonessential, it was hardly fluff in the budget. The summer recreation program was an important link between school and community. It not only gave kids something to do, but it helped forge a stronger bond between school and student, and this bond created other bonds: between school and community and between community and student.

Johnson concedes that the summer recreation program can be seen as nonessential. Then he counters that position by arguing the summer program had value as an important link between school and community ("it was hardly fluff").

AUTHORITY One strategy for building authority is to project a voice that is more discerning than popular opinion. Notice how David Pinching corrects an opposing, popular view and creates a sense of authority:

> In the lather of spurious information from the drug lobby, entirely innocuous phrases such as "noted weed" and "compounds strange" were cited as proof that the writer of *Much Ado About Nothing* and *Romeo and Juliet* was drugged up to the ruff. Actually, in the relevant context, "noted weed" means "famous type of clothing" and a "compound strange" is nothing more exciting than an unusual word construction.

Whenever writers can legitimately correct opposing views, or even point out a fact that others ignore, they indirectly build authority, which then gives credence to their other claims.

Activity

Ask two peers to read your essay, and then discuss the following audience and voice issues: How does the argument build a bridge to shared values? How does it connect with readers through counterarguments, concessions, and qualifiers? How does the writer establish authority? How might the argument do these things more effectively?

REVISION

During revision, writers see their argument with more clarity and get their most powerful ideas. Good revision requires two things: the willingness to step back from one's work and see it from a new perspective, and the willingness to make significant changes. As you respond to the following revision questions, refer to the relevant sections of this chapter. Rereading the discussions and responding again to the invention questions will help you explore ideas further and develop new, more persuasive support.

Claim

1. What is the main claim about the past? Could any clichés be replaced with specific language? How could the main claim be more precise and intense?

Support

2. What principle or shared value is at the root of the argument? How could it be brought more to the foreground?

3. How does the argument convince the reader? Is anything left hanging that might call the argument into question?

4. Is the past event or situation explained sufficiently? Where and how would more detail help persuade readers to accept the main claim?

5. Is the past event or situation explained in too much detail? Which details could be deleted without weakening the argument?

6. Does the argument depend too much on one kind of support? If so, which support is overused, and what other strategies might be employed instead?

7. How does the argument respond to opposing positions? What counterarguments, concessions, and qualifiers could strengthen the argument?

Arrangement

8. How does arrangement keep the argument interesting? How might ideas be rearranged, or even deleted, to give the argument more momentum?

Audience and Voice

9. How does the language or writer's voice invite people with a different perspective into the argument?

10. Is the argument lively and intense enough? How could it be more so?

Sources

11. If you used outside sources, consider the following:

- Have you used research as a means of discovery? (pages 309–328)
- Have you evaluated sources for ideology, reliability, relevance, credibility, timeliness, diversity? (pages 329–338)
- Are the ideas from the outside sources integrated smoothly into your ideas? (pages 338–349)
- Are the sources documented appropriately with in-text and end citations? (pages 350–375)

Peer Review

In a group of four, take turns workshopping one essay at a time:

1. One writer reads his or her essay to the group.

2. Other group members write down their initial ideas about the essay.

3. The writer reads his or her essay again, and group members write down more specific comments. (To generate specific comments, use the preceding Revision Questions.)

4. Each group member shares his or her comments with the writer, as the writer takes notes.

Group members will be tempted to discuss ideas, but this method of peer review discourages discussion. Instead, it is designed to provide four writers with feedback from three readers in a short period of time.

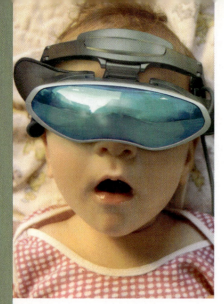

Comstock/PhotoLibrary

12

Arguing the Future

What Is Going to Happen?

No one can be certain of the future. However, popular culture offers a constant stream of prophetic visions. Films *(Planet of the Apes, The Matrix* trilogy, *The Day After Tomorrow)*, novels *(Brave New World)*, and short stories ("There Will Come Soft Rains") have attempted to warn us of an impending, perilous future. Meanwhile, swarms of advertisements try to convince us that the future will be full of more and better conveniences, products, and services. From the most sophisticated literary work to the most simplistic ads, many texts in our daily lives make bold assertions about the future. They shape how we imagine ourselves, our civilization, our species, and our planet in coming years.

But the future is not written only by fiction writers, Hollywood directors, and marketers. Every day, we make personal decisions based on our assumptions about the future. We sign apartment leases and assume that our financial situations will remain stable; we buy a week's worth of food and assume that the electricity will continue powering our refrigerators; we store our personal money in banks and assume that the institutions will remain solvent. And we often have to argue about the way we see the future. Business leaders, for example, must make their peers believe in or doubt the staying power of current trends. Imagine a sales executive for a major automaker arguing that the company should maintain its SUV output because, she argues, the price of oil will eventually stabilize and then decrease as tensions in the Middle East are resolved. Another executive argues that gas prices are certain to increase as Russia gains power. Depending on the most acceptable view of the future, the automaker will make a decision on SUV production.

Arguments about the future are always based on the past and present. Therefore, convincing arguments about the future depend on existing knowledge. They are connected to what people already know about past behavior and/or present trends:

- Having traced the past migratory patterns of butterflies, a scientist argues that certain species will continue to move northward.

- Based on past findings about children's television viewing habits and the link to attention deficit disorder, a psychological study predicts that American children will become less able to focus in formal academic settings.
- Pointing to the population shifts of the twentieth century, a sociologist argues that the twenty-first century will challenge major metropolitan areas to invent new modes of transportation.
- Basing its conclusions on trends from the past 100 years, a committee of climatologists argues that average global temperatures will continue to increase in the next century.

But an argument about the future can diverge from the past: someone might argue that the future will look radically different from the past and present. That person must argue especially well to make the future seem plausible. Imagine a writer who focuses on the future of higher education. Although the latter half of the twentieth century saw increasing access to higher education, he argues that college will become *less* accessible to the middle and working classes. Because this claim counters the past trend, the writer must provide reasoning for this shift, arguing, for instance, that several factors (global markets, political access, changing political ideology) will establish new conditions. (See Charles Nelson's essay, "Investing in Futures: The Cost of College," in this chapter.)

The future is open to interpretation. When we argue about the future, we must take into account not only what has happened and what is likely to happen, but also what could possibly happen. We must imagine a realm of scenarios—and then convince others that one particular path, out of unlimited possibilities, is the most likely. As you examine the following readings, notice how the authors present a possible (or even likely) future based on the trends of the present.

Live Forever

RAYMOND KURZWEIL

Not long ago, most people could not imagine personal computers, satellites, or cell phones. In this essay, Ray Kurzweil suggests a version of the future unimaginable to most people today—a version in which humans merge with the technology they have created and then live forever. Kurzweil is an inventor, author, and editor of KurzweilAI.net, a website that "features the big thoughts of today's big thinkers examining the confluence of accelerating revolutions that are shaping our future world." "Live Forever" was first published in *Psychology Today* magazine in 2000.

Thought to Implant 4: OnNet, please.

Hundreds of shimmering thumbnail images mist into view, spread fairly evenly across the entire field of pseudovision.

Thought: Zoom upper left, higher, into Winston's image.

Transmit: It's Nellie. Let's connect and chat over croissants. Rue des Enfants, Paris in the spring, our favorite table, yes?

5   Four-second pause.

Background thought: Damn it. What's taking him so long?

Receive: I'm here, ma chère, I'm here! Let's do it!

The thumbnail field mists away, and a cafe scene swirls into place. Scent of honeysuckle. Paté. Wine. Light breeze. Nellie is seated at a quaint table with a plain white tablecloth. An image of Winston looking 20 and buff mists in across from her. Message thumbnails occasionally blink against the sky.

Winston: It's so good to see you again, ma chère! It's been months! And what a gorgeous choice of bodies! The eyes are a dead giveaway, though. You always pick those raspberry eyes. Très bold, Nellita. So what's the occasion? Part of me is in the middle of a business meeting in Chicago, so I can't dally.

Nellie: Why do you always put on that muscleman body, Winston? You know how much I like your real one.   10

Winston morphs into a man in his early 50s, still overly muscular.

Winston: (laughing) My real body? How droll! No one but my neurotechnician has seen it for years! Believe me, that's not what you want. I can do much better! He fans rapidly through a thousand images, and Nellie grimaces.

Nellie: Damn it! You're just one of Winston's MI's! Where is the real Winston? I know I used the right connection!

Winston: Nellie, I'm sorry to have to tell you this. There was a transporter accident a few weeks ago in Evanston, and . . . well, I'm lucky they got to me in time for the full upload. I'm all of Winston that's left. The body's gone.

When Nellie contacts her friend Winston   15 through the Internet connection in her brain, he is already, biologically speaking, dead. It is his electronic mind double, a virtual reality twin, that greets Nellie in their virtual Parisian cafe. What's surprising here is not so much the notion that human minds may someday live on inside computers after their bodies have expired. It's the fact that this vignette is closer at hand than most people realize. Within 30 years, the minds in those computers may just be our own.

The history of technology has shown over and over that as one mode of technology exhausts its potential, a new, more sophisticated paradigm emerges to keep us moving at an exponential pace. Between 1910 and 1950, computer technology doubled in power every three years; between 1950 and 1966, it doubled every two years; and it has recently been doubling every year.

By the year 2020, your $1,000 personal computer will have the processing power of the human brain—20 million billion calculations per second (100 billion neurons times 1,000 connections per neuron times 200 calculations per second per connection). By 2030, it will take a village of human brains to match a $1,000 computer. By 2050, $1,000 worth of computing will equal the processing power of all human brains on Earth.

Of course, achieving the processing power of the human brain is necessary but not sufficient for creating human-level intelligence in a machine. But by 2030, we'll have the means to scan the human brain and re-create its design electronically.

Most people don't realize the revolutionary impact of that. The development of computers that match and vastly exceed the capabilities of the human brain will be no less important than the evolution of human intelligence itself some thousands of generations ago. Current predictions overlook the imminence of a world in which machines become more like humans—programmed with replicated brain synapses that re-create the ability to respond appropriately to human emotion, and humans become more like machines—our biological bodies and brains enhanced with billions of "nanobots," swarms of microscopic robots transporting us in and out of virtual reality. We have already started down this road: Human and machine have already begun to meld.

20   It starts with uploading, or scanning the brain into a computer. One scenario is invasive: One very thin slice at a time, scientists input a brain of choice—having been frozen just slightly before it was going to die—at an extremely high speed. This way, they can easily see every neuron, every connection, and every neurotransmitter concentration represented in each synapse-thin layer.

Seven years ago, a condemned killer allowed his brain and body to be scanned in this way, and you can access all 10 billion bytes of him on the Internet. You can see for yourself every bone, muscle, and section of gray matter in his body. But the scan is not yet at a high enough resolution to re-create the interneuronal connections, synapses, and neurotransmitter concentrations that are the key to capturing the individuality within a human brain.

Our scanning machines today can clearly capture neural features as long as the scanner is very close to the source. Within 30 years, however, we will be able to send billions of nanobots—blood cell-size scanning machines—through every capillary of the brain to create a complete noninvasive scan of every neural feature. A shot full of nanobots will someday allow the most subtle details of our knowledge, skills, and personalities to be copied into a file and stored in a computer.

We can touch and feel this technology today. We just can't make the nanobots small enough, not yet anyway. But miniaturization is another one of those accelerating technology trends. We're currently shrinking the size of technology by a factor of 5.6 per linear dimension per decade, so it is conservative to say that this scenario will be feasible in a few decades. The nanobots will capture the locations, interconnections, and contents of all the nerve cell bodies, axons, dendrites, presynaptic vesicles, neurotransmitter concentrations, and other relevant neural components. Using high-speed wireless communication, the nanobots will then communicate with each other and with other computers that are compiling the brain-scan database.

If this seems daunting, another scanning project, that of the human genome, was also considered ambitious when it was first introduced 12 years ago. At the time, skeptics said the task would take thousands of years, given current scanning capabilities. But the project is finishing on time nevertheless because the speed with which we can sequence DNA has grown exponentially.

Brain scanning is a prerequisite to Winston and   25 Nellie's virtual life—and apparent immortality.

In 2029, we will swallow or inject billions of nanobots into our veins to enter a three-dimensional cyberspace—a virtual reality environment. Already, neural implants are used to counteract tremors from Parkinson's disease as well as multiple sclerosis. I have a deaf friend who can now hear what I'm saying because of his cochlear implant. Under development is a retinal implant that will perform a similar function for blind people, basically replacing certain visual processing circuits of the brain. Recently,

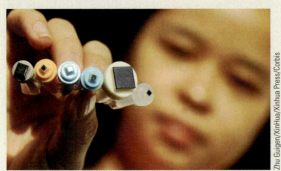

Drug delivery tools made with nano-technology.

scientists from Emory University placed a chip in the brain of a paralyzed stroke victim, who can now begin to communicate and control his environment directly from his brain.

But while a surgically introduced neural implant can be placed in only one or at most a few locations, nanobots can take up billions or trillions of positions throughout the brain. We already have electronic devices called neuron transistors that, noninvasively, allow communication between electronics and biological neurons. Using this technology, developed at Germany's Max Planck Institute of Biochemistry, scientists were recently able to control from their computer the movements of a living leech.

By taking up positions next to specific neurons, the nanobots will be able to detect and control their activity. For virtual reality applications, the nanobots will take up positions next to every nerve fiber coming from all five of our senses. When we want to enter a specific virtual environment, the nanobots will suppress the signals coming from our real senses and replace them with new, virtual ones. We can then cause our virtual body to move, speak, and otherwise interact in the virtual environment. The nanobots would prevent our real bodies from moving; instead, we would have a virtual body in a virtual environment, which need not be the same as our real body.

Like the experiences Winston and Nellie enjoyed, this technology will enable us to have virtual interactions with other people—or simulated people—without requiring any equipment not already in our heads. And virtual reality will not be as crude as what you experience in today's arcade games. It will be as detailed and subtle as real life. So instead of just phoning a friend, you can meet in a virtual Italian bistro or stroll down a virtual tropical beach, and it will all seem real. People will be able to share any type of experience—business, social, romantic, or sexual—regardless of physical proximity.

The trip to virtual reality will be readily reversible since, with your thoughts alone, you will be able to shut the nanobots off, or even direct them to leave your body. Nanobots are programmable, in that they can provide virtual reality one minute and a variety of brain extensions the next. They can change their configuration, and even alter their software.

While the combination of human-level intelligence in a machine and a computer's inherent superiority in the speed, accuracy, and sharing ability of its memory will be formidable—this is not an alien invasion. It is emerging from within our human-machine civilization.

But will virtual life and its promise of immortality obviate the fear of death? Once we upload our knowledge, memories, and insights into a computer, will we have acquired eternal life? First we must determine what human life is. What is consciousness anyway? If my thoughts, knowledge, experience, skills, and memories achieve eternal life without me, what does that mean for me?

Consciousness—a seemingly basic tenet of "living"—is perplexing and reflects issues that have been debated since the Platonic dialogues. We assume, for instance, that other humans are conscious, but when we consider the possibility that nonhuman animals may be conscious, our understanding of consciousness is called into question.

The issue of consciousness will become even more contentious in the 21st century because non-biological entities—read: machines—will be able to

30

convince most of us that they are conscious. They will master all the subtle cues that we now use to determine that humans are conscious. And they will get mad if we refute their claims.

35   Consider this: If we scan me, for example, and record the exact state, level, and position of my every neurotransmitter, synapse, neural connection, and other relevant details, and then reinstantiate this massive database into a neural computer, then who is the real me? If you ask the machine, it will vehemently claim to be the original Ray. Since it will have all of my memories, it will say, "I grew up in Queens, New York, went to college at MIT, stayed in the Boston area, sold a few artificial intelligence companies, walked into a scanner there, and woke up in the machine here. Hey, this technology really works."

But there are strong arguments that this is really a different person. For one thing, old biological Ray (that's me) still exists. I'll still be here in my carbon, cell-based brain. Alas, I (the old biological Ray) will have to sit back and watch the new Ray succeed in endeavors that I could only dream of. But New Ray will have some strong claims as well. He will say that while he is not absolutely identical to Old Ray, neither is the current version of Old Ray, since the particles making up my biological brain and body are constantly changing. It is the patterns of matter and energy that are semipermanent (that is, changing only gradually), while the actual material content changes constantly and very quickly.

Viewed in this way, my identity is rather like the pattern that water makes when rushing around a rock in a stream. The pattern remains relatively unchanged for hours, even years, while the actual material constituting the pattern—the water—is replaced in milliseconds.

This idea is consistent with the philosophical notion that we should not associate our fundamental identity with a set of particles, but rather with the pattern of matter and energy that we represent. In other words, if we change our definition of consciousness to value patterns over particles, then

New Ray may have an equal claim to be the continuation of Old Ray.

One could scan my brain and reinstantiate the new Ray while I was sleeping, and I would not necessarily even know about it. If you then came to me, and said, "Good news, Ray, we've successfully reinstantiated your mind file so we won't be needing your old body and brain anymore," I may quickly realize the philosophical flaw in the argument that New Ray is a continuation of my consciousness. I may wish New Ray well, and realize that he shares my pattern, but I would nonetheless conclude that he is not me, because I'm still here.

Wherever you wind up on this debate, it is 40 worth noting that data do not necessarily last forever. The longevity of information depends on its relevance, utility, and accessibility. If you've ever tried to retrieve information from an obsolete form of data storage in an old obscure format (e.g., a reel of magnetic tape from a 1970s minicomputer), you understand the challenge of keeping software viable. But if we are diligent in maintaining our mind file, keeping current backups and porting to the latest formats and mediums, then at least a crucial aspect of who we are will attain a longevity independent of our bodies.

What does this super technological intelligence mean for the future? There will certainly be grave dangers associated with 21st-century technologies. Consider unrestrained nanobot replication. The technology requires billions or trillions of nanobots in order to be useful, and the most cost-effective way to reach such levels is through self-replication, essentially the same approach used in the biological world, by bacteria, for example. So in the same way that biological self-replication gone awry (i.e., cancer) results in biological destruction, a defect in the mechanism curtailing nanobot self-replication would endanger all physical entities, biological or otherwise.

Other salient questions are: Who is controlling the nanobots? Who else might the nanobots be talking to?

Organizations, including governments, extremist groups, or even a clever individual, could put trillions of undetectable nanobots in the water or food supply of an entire population. These "spy" nanobots could then monitor, influence, and even control our thoughts and actions. In addition, authorized nanobots could be influenced by software viruses and other hacking techniques. Just as technology poses dangers today, there will be a panoply of risks in the decades ahead.

On a personal level, I am an optimist, and I expect that the creative and constructive applications of this technology will persevere, as I believe they do today. But there will be a valuable and increasingly vocal role for a concerned movement of Luddites—those anti-technologists inspired by early 19th-century weavers who in protest destroyed machinery that was threatening their livelihood.

45   Still, I regard the freeing of the human mind from its severe physical limitations as a necessary next step in evolution. Evolution, in my view, is the purpose of life, meaning that the purpose of life—and of our lives—is to evolve.

What does it mean to evolve? Evolution moves toward greater complexity, elegance, intelligence, beauty, creativity, and love. And God has been called all these things, only without any limitation, infinite. While evolution never reaches an infinite level, it advances exponentially, certainly moving in that direction. Technological evolution, therefore, moves us inexorably closer to becoming like God. And the freeing of our thinking from the severe limitations of our biological form may be regarded as an essential spiritual quest.

By the close of the next century, nonbiological intelligence will be ubiquitous. There will be few humans without some form of artificial intelligence, which is growing at a double exponential rate, whereas biological intelligence is basically at a standstill. Nonbiological thinking will be trillions of trillions of times more powerful than that of its biological progenitors, although it will be still of human origin.

Ultimately, however, the Earth's technology-creating species will merge with its own computational technology. After all, what is the difference between a human brain enhanced a trillion-fold by nanobot-based implants, and a computer whose design is based on high-resolution scans of the human brain, and then extended a trillion-fold?

This may be the ominous, existential question that our own children, certainly our grandchildren, will face. But at this point, there's no turning back. And there's no slowing down.

Analyzing Argument

1. What assumptions are important to Kurzweil's argument? That is, what must the reader assume in order to accept his version of the future?

2. How does Kurzweil attempt to bring the reader from the present to the future? Describe how specific passages serve in his line of reasoning.

3. What is Kurzweil's main claim?

4. Explain how the opening scenario figures into Kurzweil's argument.

5. How does Kurzweil engage the opposition? How does he address potential doubters?

6. Why might the reader have trouble accepting this view of the future? What changes might help the reader accept the view?

The End of the Handshake

JOEL COLLINS

Good writers examine the habits and reflexes of everyday life. They imagine quiet trends and subtle changes. In the following essay, Joel Collins considers a widely used social convention—and he points to the signs of its demise. Collins wrote the essay for his second-semester English composition course.

The handshake is everywhere. Hands connect after football games, when a guest comes out on a talk show, and when the president meets with diplomats. The gesture occurs on a private scale when a teenage boy meets his girlfriend's father, when a woman greets a potential boss at a job interview, or when a principal congratulates a student for good marks. Over many years, the handshake has become a symbol of courtesy and the go-to move for anyone trying to make a good impression. It is as common as any other greeting, but despite its popularity, the handshake is about to be no more. As people become more germophobic and technologically advanced, the handshake will disappear from our customs.

The origins of the handshake are still uncertain, but there is no denying that the gesture has been around for a long time. Some speculate that handshakes actually originated with chimpanzees as a way for them to calm each other (Bering). Others say that humans started the handshake as a "demonstration of helplessness" upon meeting a superior (Bering). Despite its beginnings, it stuck, and it has become a staple of any meeting between two individuals. However, over the years, the handshake has undergone plenty of change. People have tried for years to come up with unique ways to greet one another. Simple waves, hugs, head nods, and the relatively new fist bump have all arisen as popular greetings in America. As a society, we have always wanted the newest and the best, whether in transportation, media, medicine, or anything else. If there is something new we can have or do, we do our best to get it. Our value in all things new will not skip over ways of greeting one another. Granted, we also place great importance on tradition and familiarity, but those values can blend with our drive to change. The tradition of people greeting one another will remain, but the handshake, in its traditional form, will fade. Be it the fist bump or some new greeting that has not yet come about, something less involved, less intimate will make it irrelevant.

In addition to the importance we put on finding newer and better things, modernized countries value reaching out, bridging distances. With the invention of ships and airplanes and the internet, we have connected all corners of the world. A person in New York can do business with a Japanese firm which had gotten some of its materials from France. People of different cultures are increasingly interacting with one another. With those interactions comes a blending of cultures. The American may want to greet her Japanese partner with a handshake while the Japanese woman will be more likely to bow. If the French man comes to the meeting, he will be used to greeting people with a kiss on the cheek. As globalization continues to unite different regions of the world, cultures will continue to meet and, in some instances, clash. For example, Michelle Obama recently went to Indonesia, and on her trip she shook hands with an Indonesian official. It turns out that in their society, men are not supposed to have physical contact with women that are not a member of their family, so that man came under intense criticism ("Minister Admits"). Although American culture has a vast impact on the rest of the world, we are not influential enough to change long-established religious customs wherever we want to. The Muslim faith is deeply rooted in the Middle East and

Southeast Asia, places where we have great economic interest, and we won't be able to change their customs. Muslim culture has been able resist American influence thus far, as shown by artifacts such as hijabs, which women must wear to cover their hair.

And it's not simply a matter of custom. With every handshake comes an opportunity for bacteria to move from one host to another. Each person carries nearly 5,000 different species of bacteria and countless amounts of each species just on the palms of their hands, and they are all looking to spread to new areas ("The Irresistible Rise"). With new diseases that threaten to reach pandemic levels seemingly every year, people are starting to take strides to clean up and get healthier. We have been scared by swine flu, bird flu, SARS, the West Nile Virus, MRSA, mad cow disease, and an array of other diseases, many of which are not even able to spread from person to person. These diseases did provide a real threat, but their seriousness was exaggerated by mass hysteria and media hype. The news claimed that it might not be safe to go to work, the airport, or the shopping center because disease was sure to strike. Americans increased their fixation on hygiene.

5   In recent years, a whole new industry has popped up with hand sanitizers being available everywhere. There are cleaners at grocery stores to swab down shopping carts, hand sanitizer pumps at the entrances to restaurants, and even mini tubes of hand cleaner that millions of people carry around in their purses or pockets. Clean hands have come to the forefront of American values. Given this new health kick, it makes perfect sense that handshake will be on its way out in coming years. People do not want extended contact with others, especially with strangers. (Who knows where those hands have been, if that person has been sick, and how many harmful bacteria that person is carrying on the palms?)

Some may argue that the handshake will stick around because of our need for physical contact—the basic emotional need to engage in with others. Certainly, people need the touch of others for emotional comfort and strength; however, that does not include handshakes. Hugging or holding hands with a loved one is vital to human life, but shaking the hand of a stranger or even a friendly acquaintance does not fill the same need. There is very little true emotion behind most handshakes; they are a social convention, not a sign of deep care or intimacy. The drive to avoid contaminants will trump the convention.

Since we no longer live in a time when it is common for people to carry firearms when they travel, the handshake is no longer necessary as a safety precaution. It lingers still because it is now considered a polite greeting, something that people do to gain respect, trust, and compassion from others. However, we live in a world fixed upon what is quick, easy, and necessary. Fast food, texting, and YouTube have replaced sit down dinners, long conversations, and to some extent, movie going. We like to get straight to the point now and cut through the fluff, so what is keeping handshakes alive now? They waste time before the meaty part of a meeting. Since we care less and less about niceties and because efficiency weighs heavier than courtesy, the handshake is on the verge of nonexistence.

In the future, technology will continue to make communication between people even easier. With Skype and other instant video tools, people currently meet across long distances. Technology is even in the works to have 3-D replicas of people beamed to wherever they are needed. Japan, if awarded the right to host the 2022 World Cup, has promised 3-D hologram broadcasts of every game that can be displayed on soccer fields in stadiums throughout the world as if the games were actually taking place in those stadiums (Neild). In time, that same technology will be able to put business people in any meeting room desired without leaving the comfort of their own offices. In this hologram and digitized world, the handshake will become irrelevant.

Almost all aspects of the world we live in are changing, including the ways humans greet each other. As the world advances and becomes more focused on health, convenience, and technology, the handshake will lose its place as a customary greeting and will no longer be used at all.

Works Cited

Bering, Jesse. "Bering in Mind: Limp Wrists and Tight Fists: What Your Handshake Says about You." *Scientific American*, 18 Feb. 2010, blogs. scientificamerican.com/bering-in-mind/limp-wrists-and-tight-fists-what-your-handshake-says-about-you/.

"Minister Admits Reluctant Michelle Obama Handshake." The Associated Press, 9 Nov. 2010. *CTV News*, www.ctvnews.ca/minister-admits-reluctant-michelle-obama-handshake-1.572329.

Neild, Barry. "Can Japan Deliver a Holographic World Cup?" *CNN*, 30 Nov. 2010, www.cnn.com/2010/TECH/innovation/11/30/japan.world.cup.bid/.

"The Irresistible Rise of the Hand Bacteria." *New Scientist*, vol. 199, no. 2681, Nov. 2008, p. 17. *Academic SearchElite*, 35270409.

Analyzing Argument

1. Collins points to specific signs (specific indicators) of the handshake's demise. Which seem the most telling? Which situations or trends seem most indicative of the future he envisions?

2. How does Collins use his understanding of basic human needs or reflexes in his argument?

3. An argument about the future relies on a line of reasoning that begins in the past or present. Explain how Collins walks the reader forward through time. How does he, for instance, bring the reader from a current trend to a future condition?

4. How does Collins engage opposing positions or doubt about his vision of the future?

Investing in Futures: The Cost of College

CHARLES NELSON

In this essay Charles Nelson responds to a college writing assignment to explore the future viability of college. Specifically he focuses on increasing college tuition costs and their effect on lower-paying vocations. He shows how a present trend will project into the future and how that trend will directly impact career choice. Notice that his line of reasoning relies on some simple calculations.

It is widely known that college has been a good investment for students. It has traditionally of-fered many advantages the most obvious being that some degrees pay off financially. For example, ac-cording to the National Association of Colleges and Employers' 2002 Salary Survey, starting salaries for some majors exceed $50,000—chemical engineering: $51,254; electrical/electronics and computer engineer-ing: $50,387; computer science: $50,352; mechanical engineering, management information sys-tems/business data processing, accounting, civil engi-neering, and economics/finance all start above $40,000 (Geary). Students in these majors lay down twenty or forty or eighty thousand dollars, then after several years of schooling land a fine-paying job. The school loan can be paid off in a reasonable time while the graduate earns, and spends, and enjoys a rewarding career.

Explains the financial payoff of a college education

Degrees pay off in other ways too: College exposes students to new issues and subject areas; it helps students to consider the value of things that might otherwise seem pointless; college graduates may lead more rewarding lives, being more mentally engaged by their surroundings. According to *Preparing Your Child for College* a United States Department of Education resource book for parents, reasons to attend college include greater knowledge, more money, greater potential, and more job oppor-tunities. The Department of Education report explains that "a college education will increase your child's ability to understand developments in science and in society, to think abstractly and critically, to express thoughts clearly in speech and in writing, and to make wise decisions. These skills are useful both on and off the job." The Department of Edu-cation report continues: "a college education can help increase your child's understanding of the community, the Nation, and the world—as he or she explores interests, discovers new areas of knowledge, considers lifelong goals, and becomes a responsible citizen."

Explains the nonfinancial rewards of a college education.

Reprinted by permission of Charles Nelson

But if college costs continue to rise at recent rates, in a few years graduates will have spent two or three hundred thousand dollars for a college education. Sound crazy? According to data collected in the College Board's Annual Survey of Colleges, 2003–2004, college tuition increased 14.1 percent over the past year at four-year public institutions, 6 percent at private ones, and 13.8 percent at two-year public institutions, and at four-year public institutions, tuition, fees, room, and board averaged $10,636; at private ones, $26,854 (*Tuition Levels Rise*). If college expenses increase 15 percent a year again and again, an annual tuition of $10,000 becomes $11,500 the next year, $13,225 the year after that, and $15,209 the year after that. The student whose first year costs $10,000 pays a total of $49,934 for all four years. If a bachelor's degree ends up taking that student five, not four, years, make that $67,424.

Introduces a possible future—one that is based on the present.

The math becomes daunting. Simply adding 15 percent each year to a student's tuition and fees raises the future cost of college to a spectacular amount. $15,209 plus 15% equals $17,490. $17,490 plus 15% equals $20,114. $20,114 plus 15% equals $23,131. $23,131 plus 15% equals $26,601. In just eight years, one year of college has increased $16,601—from $10,000 (which doesn't sound like much) to $26,601. The student who begins college at $26,601 a year will end up paying $26,601 + $30,591 + $35,180 + $40,457, equaling $132,829. If it takes that student a fifth year to get a degree, add $46,526 for the extra year, and the cost will be $179,355.

The math works to reinforce the line of reasoning—and the projection about the future

But doesn't college tuition increase at roughly the rate of inflation? Doesn't it all even out? No. College tuition since the 1980s has increased at twice the rate of inflation, with no sign of slowing down. As Scott Ross, the executive director of the Florida Student Association, puts it, the tuition button is stuck in the "up-fast" position (qtd. in Clayton). And while some jobs—chemical engineering, electrical/electronics and computer engineering, and so on—keep pace with college tuition, others can't. So, which majors are we willing to delete?

Quotes an authority.

Unless they can earn back significantly more than they invest, students will be faced with some serious questions: Is learning to think better worth the cost? Can't I expose myself to new issues and subject areas *without college?* What is the value of a $200,000 college degree? Many potential graduates are bound to decide that college, unfortunately, just isn't worth it.

The next step in the line of reasoning: if college costs do increase as above, formal education will become obsolete.

Perhaps educators, politicians, and banks will find ways to keep college costs down, especially for those students who major in the financially less lucrative fields. For example, because a history degree pays less

| | in the marketplace than an engineering degree, a history major might pay less. Of course there's no way to accurately predict a student's future earnings based on his or her major (or based on anything else). A philosophy major could somehow earn millions, while an engineering major may be unable to hold down a steady job. Still, the general concept applies: Students are paying the same tuition for different degrees, and some of those degrees will eventually be boxed out of college because students graduating with the degree won't be able to pay back the loans. Unless something gives, when the cost of a college degree hits two or three hundred thousand dollars, colleges may be void of students studying art, poetry, or (in some states) education. If college tuition continues to increase at its present rate (and there's nothing to suggest it will not), higher education might price itself out of teaching literature, humanities, anthropology, sociology, philosophy . . . all the disciplines that explore what it means to be human. From there, it doesn't take a science fiction writer to imagine the ill effects on our little civilization. |

Offers a slight concession—that the future is impossible to predict exactly.

Appeal to value: exploring "what it means to be human" is a worthy practice.

Leaves the reader considering serious consequences.

Works Cited

Clayton, Mark. "Backlash Brews over Rising Cost of College." *The Christian Science Monitor*, 17 June 2003, www.csmonitor.com/2003/0617/p15s01-lehl.html.

Geary, Leslie Haggin. "Highest Paying College Degrees." *CNN/Money*, 13 May 2002, money.cnn.com/2002/04/03/pf/college/q_hotdiploma/.

Tuition Levels Rise but Many Students Pay Significantly Less than Published Rates. College Board, 21 Oct. 2003, www.pressreleasepoint.com/tuition-levels-rise-many-students-pay-significantly-less-published-rates-0.

United States, Dept. of Education, Office of the Under Secretary, Planning and Evaluation Service. *Preparing Your Child for College: A Resource Book for Parents.* 2000, www2.ed.gov/pubs/Prepare/index.html.

Analyzing Argument

1. According to Nelson, what is going to happen?

2. What are the most effective support strategies in the essay? Consider specific appeals, examples, and evidence.

3. How does Nelson engage opposition or doubt? How does he counter or concede to outside perspectives?

4. How do Nelson's calculations (in paragraphs 3 and 4) help to develop his line of reasoning?

5. Explain the rhetorical effect of Nelson's last statement—about "the ill effects on our little civilization."

Around the Table in Traverse City

JOEL PAPCUN

Making broad claims about the future can be perilous. A claim about the future of all food, for example, would be almost impossible to support. Because communities, states, entire regions evolve (or devolve) in different ways, more focused claims are safer bets. It's more reasonable to imagine the future of one area than the future of all places. Joel Papcun, a culinary arts instructor at Northwestern Michigan College, makes a focused claim about the future of food in his specific region. He supports his vision of the future with specific local trends.

As folks drive through the Grand Traverse region, it is impossible not to recognize the familiar signs of corporate, upscale-casual, family-friendly restaurants that line the busiest corners. The marketing gurus of these corporate giants have long known the formula for successfully luring the tourist and, to some extent, the local patron into their well-placed eateries. Red Lobster, Applebee's, Outback Steakhouse and Hooters to mention a few, the names read like a "who's who" list of fun, entertaining venues that offer everything from soup to nuts. Everything except nutritionally sound food, that is.

Inside these colorful, media-energized dining rooms, patrons' senses are aroused by chemically enhanced aromas emanating from the modern kitchen that lay hidden behind traditional swinging doors. Almost all these restaurants provide local appeal by including locally themed menus highlighted with regionally noteworthy products (which are not necessarily obtained from regional farms). For the educated local diner, the enchantment often wears off after a visit or two, as the flavors seem to blend into a salty, sugary, fatty combination of highly processed foodstuffs.

Almost any region in the country can be found to support a similar cultural attitude. The big brand name restaurants provide a familiar facade to the droves of tourists looking to sate the need of food during their journey. The Grand Traverse region, although still affected by the corporate eating culture of the nation, is different. While we are home to a range of big brand restaurants, a strong cultural drive for "all-things local" resides and thrives here. Local farmers' markets abound during the growing and harvest seasons. Indoor markets pop-up as the winter season bears down on the region. The Grand Traverse area is also home to several newer companies that work to provide a connection between local farmers and the region's stores, restaurants and food processors. The finer restaurants seek out local products before looking to the commercial variety that is easily had through mega-suppliers. Local companies such as "American Spoon" and "Food For Thought" minimally process and can regional food products for year-round consumption.

We have a diverse population, if not by ethnicity, by age group and income. Having been named the eighth best city of the nation in which to retire ("25 Best"), Traverse City continues to lure baby boomers looking to relocate or build a second home in the area. These boomers, many of whom makeup the demographic of well-educated, healthy, culturally aware folks, take the meaning of fitness to heart. Seeking quality of life that is inclusive of the area's offerings, food, nutrition, and dining play a considerable part in their quest for vitality. Twenty- and thirty-somethings, of which there is a growing number, make up the demographic that is ever-increasingly aware of environmental concerns and their effects on everyday life.

Although the State of Michigan as a whole is 5 experiencing financial troubles and a population exodus as never seen before, the Grand Traverse region continues to grow both in population and industry base. The area's open spaces, wildlife, and opportunity for healthy activity continue to create a quality of life environment that is sought

Reprinted with permission from Joel Papcun.

after. Tourists in search of an "active" vacation may seek out one of the area's many wineries, equestrian ranches, or community supported agriculture (CSA) farms. Increasingly popular, agritourism accounts for a growing segment of the area's revenue. In ten short years, the number of CSA farms has more than quadrupled, growing from nearly 400 to more than 1,800 nationally (Gogoi 3). Farmland preservation, benefiting directly from the agricultural interest created by this segment of the tourism industry, resonates with the stewardship-minded. Consequently, the client base for quality food will expand to the far reaches of the region as the area continues to cultivate agritourism and the dollars that come along with it.

Desiring to produce the best quality food possible, several area chefs have led the way to a "locavore" mentality that is spreading through the region. Seeking all things locally produced, raised and grown, these chefs are creating a "foodie Mecca." Local wineries, breweries and distilleries all add to the expanding food culture of the region. Recently asked to cook at the prestigious Beard House in New York City, local chef Myles Anton of Trattoria Stella is a dominant force in the Grand Traverse "locavore" movement. His reliance on regional products to reproduce the ethnically themed menu at Stella's is proof that the area supports a variety of crops and products worthy of national attention.

In addition to the local restaurant and hospitality offerings, the region is home to a state-of-the-art culinary school that draws would-be chefs from around the multi-state region. Placing an emphasis on local, seasonal, and sustainable foods, the Great Lakes Culinary Institute is a valuable and lasting force on the food culture of the area. Many culinary students explore the region's offerings; often deciding to stay in the area after their training has been completed, thus extending the local, sustainable mindset of the area. The local community college is also the Midwest home of the annual Bioneers Conference. This national conference focuses on sustaining the earth's resources through natural bioengineering, organic farming, and sustainable growing and living practices. A co-sponsor of the Bioneers Conference, the Oryana Natural Foods Cooperative located in Traverse City is a conduit for the sustainable food and living culture found here. This locally owned co-op has undergone considerable growth in the last decade.

Local projects continue to play a part in the natural food culture as well. "Taste the Local Difference" and the "Fresh Food Initiative" are two such projects. Bolstering "real food" awareness and providing education to those who are not versed in scratch cooking, or who are part of the non-cooking portion of society, these organizations provide the basic lessons that may transcend the marketing onslaught of the commercial food conglomerates and bring the cooking of whole foods back into the limelight.

Eating local, sustainable foods can, at times, be more expensive than the mass-produced varieties found in large discount grocery stores. While this factor may deter some lower-income families from the nutritional benefits of a potato less traveled, it will not thwart folks determined to find healthy alternatives through a "local" diet. Assistant professor of Health and Wellness at the University of North Carolina at Ashville, Amy Lanou claims, "[local] meat producers . . . can't keep up with demand even though their product costs $1 more per pound than meat in the supermarket" (qtd. in Taylor).

The drive for local food is aided, at least in 10 part, by the desire to maintain the look and feel of the area. Here in Northern Michigan, farmland and open space are important to the overall feel of the region. The sustainability of the soil and ground water is also important to the local communities. Michigan is surrounded by the world's largest fresh water supply. Seemingly pristine, the Great Lakes are still recovering from over a century of ecological abuse that a fledgling, industrialized nation threw at them. Preservation of the Great Lakes is part of being better stewards of the natural resources to which we have been entrusted. To that end, Traverse

City is home to the Water Studies Institute. Situated at the south end of West Grand Traverse Bay, the institute is the first to offer an Associate in Science and Arts Degree for Freshwater Studies in the United States. Continued regional efforts to maintain quality fresh water resources will benefit the area and the nation for years to come.

Another spoke in the wheel of the "real food" bandwagon is the recent enactment of a law allowing the raising of chickens for food or eggs within the Traverse City limits. The ability, or more importantly, the *right* to provide a nutritionally sound, sustainably raised, and economical alternative to mass-produced foodstuffs was confirmed in a majority vote of the local city commission. Due in part to the community voice being heard, this change reinforces the local mentality of self-reliance often found in thriving areas around the country.

The local projects and environmental interest currently seen will continue to prod the communities of the greater Grand Traverse region toward sustainable, natural foods that are grown without the carbon footprint of the resource-gulping factory farms used to produce the worlds Frankenfood supply. The desire to enjoy food, as it was intended, flavorful and full of rich nutrients, will continue to influence the local restaurant menu. In fact, if trends are an indicator, the majority of restaurants will succumb to the demands of an educated, foodies-dominated patronage and provide mostly local, mostly natural and sustainable menu items.

A generation from now, there will surely be those who disregard the social call for personal responsibility, for healthy choices and natural diets full of real, whole, foods. The non-foodie or uninformed consumer, a diminishing demographic of society in the Grand Traverse region, will still make poor choices in food selection, whether in a grocery store or a restaurant. Continued growth of the locavore movement will likely limit the opportunity for such poor choices. Local, sustainable, and natural foods have so much to offer, the extraordinary will become the norm in the next few decades.

Works Cited

Connell, David J. "On the Challenge of Creating Sustainable Food Systems." *Environments Journal*, vol. 36, no.1, Aug. 2008, pp. 75–77, www.thefreelibrary.com/On+the+challenge+of+creating+sustainable+food+systems.-a0203421716.

Gogoi, Pallavi. "The Rise of the 'Locavore.'" *BusinessWeek*, Bloomburg, 20 May 2008, www.bloomberg.com/news/articles/2008-05-20/the-rise-of-the-locavorebusinessweek-business-news-stock-market-and-financial-advice.

Taylor, David A. "Does One Size Fit All? Small Farms and U.S. Meat Regulations." *Environmental Health Perspectives*, vol. 116, no.12, Dec. 2008, pp. A528–531, www.ncbi.nlm.nih.gov/pmc/articles/PMC2599784/.

"25 Best Places to Retire." *CNNMoney*, Cable News Network/Time Warner, 12 Dec. 2012. *Daily Finance*, www.dailyfinance.com/2012/10/16/best-places-to-retire-cnnmoney/.

Analyzing Argument

1. Papcun points to several demographic trends that will lead to increased locavore culture. In your own words, explain how those demographic trends allow for Papcun's vision of the future.

2. All arguments about the future rely on some assumptions about continued collective behavior. Explain how Papcun's argument relies on specific assumptions. Are his assumptions acceptable? Why or why not?

3. How does Papcun engage opposition? Where does he counter, concede, or qualify?

4. What is the most effective supporting passage? What kind of support is Papcun using? A type of appeal? Evidence? Example? Perhaps a combination?

5. Arguments for this chapter assert and defend claims of fact. For the most part, they veer away from value judgments. However, some hint of value does inevitably slip into the arguments. Where do you find value operating in Papcun's argument? Does it help or hurt his case?

A smart car parked beside a Hummer.

Analyzing Argument

1. What does the juxtaposition of the Humvee and the smart car suggest about the past, present, and future?

2. The future does not simply arrive. Technologies, customs, conventions, and habits have to be changed. How does the smart car represent the tension that is always at work in projections about the future?

EXPLORING FOR TOPICS

Robert G. Ingersoll, American politician, abolitionist, and lecturer, said, "The present is the necessary product of all the past, the necessary cause of all the future." Ingersoll prompts us to see a deep connection among the past, present, and future. Whenever people argue about the future, they must keep the past and present in mind—because the future does not emerge from thin air but from real material conditions and real human attitudes. Writers who take on the future must also take on the biases, prejudices, fears, values, beliefs, and assumptions of their present readers.

This chapter is about inventing a particular view of the future. Your readers must believe that a present situation is leading toward a particular future. They must be able to see how the present will evolve, devolve, or in some sense, stay the same. Ultimately, the argument you generate will invite readers to participate in an imagined world—one that does not yet exist.

It would be impossible (or at least unhelpful) to make an argument about "the future" in its entirety. To generate a reasonable argument, we must focus on a particular topic that is set in the future. As in all argumentative situations, the more focused and narrow the topic, the more intensive and engaging the writing process. Use the following prompts to explore for possible topics and begin developing your own argument:

- What particular change in the future will impact your life or your readers' lives?

- What changes do you see as inevitable? Will gay marriage be legal across the United States? Will all employers provide health care for significant others, regardless of gender or marital status? Will only the wealthiest citizens be serious candidates for president? Will women hold fifty percent of Congressional and Senate seats?

- Imagine possibilities and fill in the blanks in the following statement: Most people assume that _____ will continue as is; however, _____.

- Watch a futuristic or science fiction movie, such as *Fahrenheit 451, Gattaca, Idiocracy,* or *The Matrix.* According to the movie, what will the future hold for _____? (Consider particular topics such as the state of technology, the role of law enforcement, the relationships between men and women, the character of government, the relationship between nations.)

- Consider your academic major. How long will it survive as an academic focus? How will economic, demographic, or environmental trends impact it? How will technology impact its future?

To view this video, visit the English CourseMate at CengageBrain.com.

Top to bottom: US Army Soldier Systems Center; Steve Mockensturm Madhouse; Hemera Photo Objects/Cengage Learning; From CourseMate video (BBC: Economics and Education)

- What topic interests you? Imagine how it will look in the future. Consider specifics: a musical genre, college athletics, a political party, the gender ratio in a particular career, megastores, a health care policy, cell phones, online gaming, traditional marriage, profanity, body piercing, religious divisions, comedy films, romance novels, CO_2 emissions, college grades, and so on.
- Closely examine a reading from this chapter. How might the future be different from what is portrayed in the reading? What else can you imagine about the future of that particular topic?
- With a group of peers, think of several futuristic or science fiction movies. Choose one movie that everyone has seen. List the topics that the movie suggests through characters, action, plot, and setting. Then discuss what argument the movie makes.

Activity

1. With a group of peers, continue adding ideas to your lists of topics. Continue until each group member has accumulated several possible topics of interest.
2. As a group, discuss one of the topic ideas from above. Imagine how it might be different in the future. Consider social customs, emotional responses, and even legal issues. How might they all impact the topic?

To understand how something might fare in the future, we must first understand how it functions in the present and what factors (internal and external) are likely to influence it. We must also qualify the vague phrase *the future*. It might mean tomorrow or thousands of years from now. The meaning depends upon the topic and the nature of the argument. For some topics, such as the preservation of species or space travel, *the future* means hundreds, even thousands, of years. For other topics, such as access to higher education, *the future* might mean five, ten, or twenty years.

Decide how far into the future you want to look, and then apply the following invention questions to your topic:

▶ What factors presently influence the topic?
▶ How has it evolved or developed?
▶ What influential factors are likely to change in the future? What effect will those changes have?
▶ What political, social, cultural, environmental, and global factors will influence the future of this topic?
▶ How will the near future differ from the distant future?

INVENTING A CLAIM

Writers arguing about the future must explore the common (and uncommon) opinions surrounding the topic. For this chapter, exploring opinions may be a tricky process. Rather than finding direct assertions about the future, you may find only hopes mixed with present attitudes and behaviors. You may have to infer what people think or fill in the gaps between people's hopes and beliefs.

You can monitor opinion on your topic by browsing the Internet. Search for your topic and seek out personal, professional, nonprofit, governmental, and educational sites. Scan through the sites and read for opinions or characterizations of the topic. You might also take a more focused and intensive research approach, and examine periodical databases.

Charles Nelson discovered specifics by reading published research on funding in higher education. He sought out trends in funding, average college costs, and average increases. He also tried to find the average student loan debt in the country and researched the economic factors that play into college tuition. He used several periodical database searches with the following keywords:

college and tuition and state and funding

college or university and tuition and state and funding

higher and education and funding and state

student and loans and cost and trends

student and college and loans and debt

student and loan and average and debt

Not all of these searches were fruitful; some simply gave too many results. But others helped Nelson find trends in loans, debt, and college tuition.

Despite your particular research requirements, it is crucial to understand how others imagine the future. As you read through potential sources, use the following questions to distinguish between your vision and others' stated or unstated notions.

What Do Others Claim?

- What do people normally think of when they imagine the future of your particular topic? What do they think is going to happen?
- What is the time frame that other people work with? That is, *when* do they think something is going to happen? (Next week? Next month? In the next century?)
- Why do they believe in that particular version? To accept their version of the future, what do they have to assume, value, or believe?
- What do experts in the field believe will happen in the near future? The distant future?

What Do I Claim?

- How is my vision of the future different from the common vision or from expert projections?
- What assumptions (about the topic, about social change, about people, about institutions) underlie my vision of the future?
- What do others not see or consider when they imagine the future of this topic?

Anyone can look forward and imagine the future. But a good argument about the future focuses on some specific condition or situation. We should be cautious of generalized statements that make safe and uncontestable claims. For instance, imagine if Nelson argued the following: *College tuition will be too high for most people in the future.* The claim is safe; it is hardly arguable and contains vague generalities such as "too high" and "most people." Nelson is better off thinking of specific effects of high college costs. Notice how his main idea evolved into increasingly sharper statements:

- College tuition will be too high for most people in the future.
- College tuition will eventually go beyond what the middle class can afford.

- The cost of college education will eventually transcend its earning value.
- In the coming decades, perhaps within the next generation, the cost of college education will transcend its earning value.

Nelson's claim goes beyond broad descriptors (such as "too high") and, instead, offers a particular future condition.

To sharpen your focus, consider the following questions:

▶ What are the possible specific outcomes for this topic?

▶ What is the single most important or significant outcome?

▶ What is not apparent now that will become apparent in the future?

Finally, as you work toward a focused idea, remember that claims of fact drive the arguments for this chapter. Your mission is to make a case about a future condition—not to argue what you *want* to happen or what you think *should* happen. In fact, as with Charles Nelson's essay, you might argue for a future that you don't hope for or desire.

More Sample Claims

Technology

- As the world becomes reliant on digital technologies, more government regulation will be necessary for the protection of all citizens, even those who oppose increased regulation.
- As TV programs like *CSI* suggest, crime fighting in the near future will be characterized not by bullets and badges but by science and forensic technology.

Education

- Because memorization of content lies at the center of American education, standardized testing will likely become the primary mode of teaching and learning.
- If the United States remains a viable democratic nation in this century, its citizens will look back on this era and scoff at the college degree mills now infecting higher education.

Popular Culture

- Based on current trends, the future half-hour sitcom will soon be half commercial and half sitcom. In other words, the *com* will stand for *commercial*.
- In the near future, the American consumer will shift away from the programmed reflex of buying "name brands" and seek out local food that is safer, healthier, and less expensive in the long run.
- The antivaccination movement in the United States will usher in a new era: one that includes periodic outbreaks of communicable disease and higher child mortality rates.

Politics

- In the next election cycle, the Tea Party will overtake the Republican Party as the reigning conservative force across the country.
- Before the next national election, the Tea Party will further alienate itself from mainstream views on taxes and gun laws.
- After the Baby Boomers finally relinquish political control, it will take the next generation only a few political cycles to rid the country of the irrational fear of marijuana and legalize its recreational use.

- In thirty years, mainstream America will look back with horror and disgust at the homophobic propaganda of today's politicians, just as we now look at the chest-beating and banner-waving racism in 1950s and '60s political campaigns.

Invention Workshop

This project calls for a claim of fact. As you develop your argument, try to steer clear of value and policy claims. To that end, apply the following question to your topic: *Given past or present trends, what is likely to happen in the future?* Your response to the question can serve as your main claim—at least your first attempt at it.

1. Write out your main claim about the future, and share it with several other writers. As a group, examine each claim and make sure that each addresses the key question: *Given past or present trends, what is likely to happen in the future?*

2. Next, try to sharpen the focus of each claim. As a group, suggest how broad words and phrases could be more specific.

INVENTING SUPPORT

Supporting an argument about the future (something that has not yet happened) can be tricky. It involves establishing logical connections between what has happened, what tends to happen, and what you think will happen. In other words, it depends on logical appeals. But you are not limited to logical appeals. Explore all the following possible strategies.

ALLUSIONS Because you cannot point directly at the future to support your points, you will have to depend on past and present trends or events. For example, in "Live Forever," Raymond Kurzweil alludes to the human genome project to support his version of the future. After describing a future in which billions of nanobots enter the bloodstream and scan the brain so that it can be re-created, Kurzweil says,

> If this seems daunting, another scanning project, that of the human genome, was also considered ambitious when it was first introduced twelve years ago. At the time, skeptics said the task would take thousands of years, given current scanning capabilities. But the project is finishing on time nevertheless because the speed with which we can sequence DNA has grown exponentially.

Readers who doubt Kurzweil's claims (about scanning machines the size of blood cells) must think again because of his allusion to the success of the human genome project.

LITERARY WORKS Remember that novels, poems, plays, and songs can help give form to your vision of the future. Because literary works deal with some fundamental questions, tensions, and assumptions about our world, they can help to establish what may or may not change in the future. The literary work need not be set in the future. In fact, it may even take place long ago. In his argument, Ray Kurzweil deals with some fundamental assumptions about human identity—assumptions that have been debated for millennia. In alluding to ancient Greek thought, Kurzweil shows the significance of the issue:

> Consciousness—a seemingly basic tenet of "living"—is perplexing and reflects issues that have been debated since the Platonic dialogues. We assume, for instance, that other humans are conscious, but

when we consider the possibility that nonhuman animals may be conscious, our understanding of consciousness is called into question.

FACTS Although facts about the past and present can be disputed, they are necessary for an argument about the future. *What will be* emerges out of *what is,* so a good argument carefully describes the relevant aspects of the present. Notice how Kurzweil always grounds his projections in the certainty of the present. Consistently, he makes clear that we are "already" on the way to his vision:

> In 2029, we will swallow or inject billions of nanobots into our veins to enter a three-dimensional cyberspace—a virtual environment. Already, neural implants are used to counteract tremors from Parkinson's disease as well as multiple sclerosis. I have a deaf friend who can now hear what I'm saying because of his cochlear implant. Under development is a retinal implant that will perform a similar function for blind people, basically replacing certain visual processing circuts of the brain. Recently, scientists from Emory University placed a chip in the brain of a paralyzed stroke victim, who can now begin to communicate and control his environment directly from his brain.

The established fact that neural implants are already used to treat disease helps the reader accept Kurzweil's vision that we will someday swallow or inject billions of nanobots. The paragraph communicates facts that create a logical line of reasoning:

Present Facts

   – Neural implants are already used to counteract tremors.

   – A deaf friend has a cochlear implant, and a similar retinal implant is under development.

   – A chip has recently been placed in a stroke victim's brain.

Future Condition

   – We will someday swallow or inject nanobots.

The facts that Kurzweil provides do not prove him right. Instead, they make his case stronger and more believable. They make it easier for the reader to accept.

STATISTICS/AUTHORITIES Statistics can be compelling because they help paint a picture of reality. But they should always be used as part of a larger argumentative strategy. In Charles Nelson's argument, numbers from the past and present help him to build a case about the future:

> If college expenses increase 15 percent a year again and again, an annual tuition of $10,000 becomes $11,500 the next year, $13,225 the year after that, and $15,209 the year after that. The student whose first year costs $10,000 pays a total of $49,934 for all four years. If a bachelor's degree ends up taking that student five, not four, years, make that $67,424.

But the numbers themselves do not mean anything unless we accept his other points and assumptions about the nature of college, the nature of mainstream culture, the continuation of middle-class life. These statistics are a compelling part of Nelson's argument, but they make sense only because of his broader line of reasoning.

In his essay, Joel Papcun integrates some important statistics to help establish a current trend. The passage is only one, but an important, step in his overall line of reasoning:

> Increasingly popular, agritourism accounts for a growing segment of the area's revenue. In ten short years, the number of CSA farms has more than quadrupled, growing from nearly 400 to more than 1,800 nationally (Gogoi 3). Farmland preservation, benefiting directly from the agricultural interest created by this segment of the tourism industry, resonates with the stewardship-minded. Consequently, the client base for

quality food will expand to the far reaches of the region as the area continues to cultivate agritourism and the dollars that come along with it.

APPEALS TO LOGIC Like all arguments, those about the future are supported by various forms of evidence. Perhaps most significant here is the logical appeal, or a line of reasoning that moves readers from the past and present to the future. For example:

Premise: Because A has happened,

Premise: Because conditions are favorable for A to happen again,

Conclusion: A will probably happen again.

Premise: Because B has been increasing/decreasing,

Premise: Because conditions allow for B to continue increasing/decreasing,

Conclusion: B will continue to increase/decrease.

In "Investing in Futures: The Cost of College," Charles Nelson's argument depends upon a line of reasoning. First, he establishes the trend:

> According to data collected in the College Board's Annual Survey of Colleges, 2003–2004, college tuition increased 14.1 percent over the past year at four-year public institutions, 6 percent at private ones, and 13.8 percent at two-year public institutions, and at four-year public institutions, tuition, fees, room, and board averaged $10,636; at private ones, $26,854 (*Tuition Levels Rise*).

Then, in the same paragraph, Nelson explains how the trend may continue.

Although Nelson takes several paragraphs to develop the point, we can abbreviate his line of reasoning to the following:

Premise: College tuition has increased 15 percent each year.

Premise: This trend is likely to continue.

Conclusion: College tuition will continue to increase 15 percent each year.

Each step in this line of reasoning requires some support, and each step comes with its own set of concerns and opposing points. Notice how Nelson deals with the second premise:

> But doesn't college tuition increase at roughly the rate of inflation? Doesn't it all even out? No. College tuition since the 1980s has increased at twice the rate of inflation, with no sign of slowing down. As Scott Ross, the executive director of the Florida Student Association, puts it, the tuition button is stuck in the "up-fast" position (Clayton).

Once he has established the nature of the trend and its future direction, he argues its likely effect on college programs. Over several paragraphs, Nelson develops another line of reasoning based on the first:

Premise: College will continue to increase 15 percent each year.

Premise: Most post-college careers will not pay enough to cover the cost of a college degree.

Conclusion: The degrees associated with those careers will become too costly for students to consider.

Or, as he explains in his concluding paragraph:

> Unless something gives, when the cost of a college degree hits two or three hundred thousand dollars, colleges may be void of students studying art, poetry, or (in some states) education. If college tuition

continues to increase at its present rate (and there's nothing to suggest it will not), higher education might price itself out of teaching literature, humanities, anthropology, sociology, philosophy . . . all the disciplines that explore what it means to be human.

Like any writer, Nelson must convince his readers that each premise is acceptable and that each one leads to his conclusion. He cannot simply state each premise: He must use a variety of support strategies to make each premise acceptable. Nelson's argument illustrates the way in which appeals involve, and sometimes depend on, other forms of support. (For more on appeals to logic see Chapter 3.)

As you consider your own argument, use the following questions to develop appeals and evidence:

▶ What line of reasoning do I want my readers to accept? (What premises about the past, present, and future must readers accept?)

▶ What novels, films, television shows, or poems have suggested a future that relates to my argument?

▶ What other behaviors, policies, situations, animals, institutions, laws, and so forth relate, in some surprising way, to my topic?

▶ How do authorities or statistics support or oppose my argument?

▶ What historical trends, human behaviors, or natural/physical laws suggest that my vision of the future is reasonable or possible?

Activity

Construct two premises that lead to each conclusion:

1. Standardized testing services will eventually control curriculum in public schools
2. Standardized testing services will eventually be driven out of public schools.
3. The record industry will succeed in closing down online music services.
4. Most new music will be consumed through online services.

ARRANGEMENT

HOW DO I ESTABLISH A PRESENT TREND? Before zooming into the future, some of the writers in this chapter work to establish a present trend. For example, Charles Nelson begins with a widely accepted notion—that college has traditionally been a good investment. He spends two paragraphs describing the relationship between college cost and its rewards. Then he takes the reader to a future in which a college education costs a staggering amount:

> But if college costs continue to rise at recent rates, in a few years graduates will have spent two or three hundred thousand dollars for a college education. Sound crazy?

In "The End of the Handshake," Joel Collins consistently describes the relevant trend before he makes a claim about the future. Whether he is detailing a trend in technology, business affairs, or hygiene, he first focuses on the present:

> In recent years, a whole new industry has popped up with hand sanitizers being available everywhere. There are cleaners at grocery stores to swab down shopping carts, hand sanitizer pumps at the entrances to restaurants, and even mini tubes of hand cleaner that millions of people carry around in their purses or

pockets. Clean hands have come to the forefront of American values. Given this new health kick, it makes perfect sense that handshake will be on its way out in coming years.

In his essay, Joel Papcun devotes several paragraphs to present trends—initiatives, events, and growing organizations that signal a particular kind of future. He uses paragraphs to focus on a community initiative, event, or a growing organization. And, as in the following passage, he makes sure to show how the trend is rooted in the culture—that it's not going away any time soon:

> In addition to the local restaurant and hospitality offerings, the region is home to a state-of-the-art culinary school that draws would-be chefs from around the multi-state region. Placing an emphasis on local, seasonal, and sustainable foods, the Great Lakes Culinary Institute is a valuable and lasting force on the food culture of the area. Many culinary students explore the region's offerings; often deciding to stay in the area after their training has been completed, thus extending the local, sustainable mindset of the area.

HOW SHOULD I CONNECT THE PAST/PRESENT AND FUTURE? An argument builds a version of the future from the pieces and parts of the past and/or the present. Notice how Raymond Kurzweil makes claims about the future, and then supports them by referencing the past:

> But while a surgically introduced neural implant can be placed in only one or at most a few locations, nanobots can take up billions or trillions of positions throughout the brain. We already have electronic devices called neuron transistors that, noninvasively, allow communication between electronics and biological neurons. Using this technology, developed at Germany's Max Planck Institute of Biochemistry, scientists were recently able to control from their computer the movements of a living leech. Charles Nelson uses the particulars of the present to project a version of the future: The math becomes daunting. Simply adding 15 percent each year to a student's tuition and fees raises the future cost of college to a spectacular amount. $15,209 plus 15% equals $17,490. $17,490 plus 15% equals $20,114. $20,114 plus 15% equals $23,131. $23,131 plus 15% equals $26,601. In just eight years, one year of college has increased $16,601—from $10,000 (which doesn't sound like much) to $26,601. The student who begins college at $26,601 a year will end up paying $26,601 + $30,591 + $35,180 + $40,457, equaling $132,829. If it takes that student a fifth year to get a degree, add $46,526 for the extra year, and the cost will be $179,355.

Activity

Write two introductions for your argument. One should take the reader from a common meeting space to a new version of the future. The other should immediately take the reader to the new version of the future—without establishing common ground.

AUDIENCE AND VOICE

Whenever writers assert anything about the future, they tap into a long tradition: from astrologers, palm readers, and fortune cookies to prophets, visionaries, and shamans. From the mundane to the exotic, from the informal to the ritualistic, people who ask others to envision a future are working in a rich tradition and a potentially powerful situation. An argument about the future thus can be an opportunity to explore voice. The situation might call for a somber and grave voice warning of coming peril; it might call for a voice projecting wonder or curiosity; it might even call for an informal, comedic voice.

QUESTION/ANSWER Why ask questions while making an argument? How do questions affect the writer's voice? And can one ask too many questions? Writers ask questions for different reasons. For example, rhetorical questions are more like statements: they assert something and are not meant to be answered. *How many times do I have to tell you to shut the door?* really means *I've told you to shut the door several times. I'm getting tired of telling* you. *PLEASE, shut the door next time.* At the end of a paragraph discussing the popularity of hand sanitizers, Collins uses a common question to voice the kind of concern people often have about germs:

> People do not want extended contact with others, especially with strangers. (Who knows where those hands have been, if that person has been sick, and how many harmful bacteria that person is carrying on the palms?)

In addition to rhetorical questions, writers sometimes ask questions they don't have answers to. While an arguer should make and support claims, this doesn't mean every question can be answered—that every suggestion can be tightly packaged and necessarily concluded. Sometimes it is fair (and even necessary) to leave the reader with unanswered questions. Notice how Raymond Kurzweil asks and answers a question in first paragraph below, and then asks two additional questions in the second paragraph below. Kurzweil does not answer the last two questions because he doesn't know the answers; one might argue that those questions are unanswerable but important to consider:

> What does this super technological intelligence mean for the future? There will certainly be grave dangers associated with 21st-century technologies. Consider unrestrained nanobot replication. The technology requires billions or trillions of nanobots in order to be useful, and the most cost-effective way to reach such levels is through self-replication, essentially the same approach used in the biological world, by bacteria, for example. So in the same way that biological self-replication gone awry (i.e., cancer) results in biological destruction, a defect in the mechanism curtailing nanobot self-replication would endanger all physical entities, biological or otherwise.
>
> Other salient questions are: Who is controlling the nanobots? Who else might the nanobots be talking to?

Writers often ask questions and then answer them, as Nelson does:

> But doesn't college tuition increase at roughly the rate of inflation? Doesn't it all even out? No. College tuition since the 1980s has increased at twice the rate of inflation, with no sign of slowing down.

Nelson could have forgone the question/answer approach, conveying the same idea with only the assertion: *College tuition since the 1980s has increased at twice the rate of inflation.* While the questions do not provide the reader with more information, they do affect Nelson's voice and audience. The questions slow the pace of his argument, and they act as a common ground where writer and reader can meet up before moving on to an important point.

However, writers must be careful not to ask too many questions. Some essays can be effectively arranged based on a question/answer approach, and a paragraph full of questions can be effective in some cases. But too many questions can create a frustratingly slow read. In some cases, the reader may even feel talked down to.

CREDIBILITY While writers may generate intrigue and curiosity, they must also appear credible. The voice coming at the reader needs to sound insightful but not divorced from a reality that the writer and reader both share. Of course, credibility comes from a reasonable argument, one with adequate support and logical claims. But voice is also vital. In fact, no amount of support can help a voice that sounds noncredible.

A credible-sounding voice in an argument about the future invites the reader into a logical perspective and helps establish a reasonable and believable vision. In the following passage, Charles Nelson suggests a negative effect of increasing college costs:

> Unless something gives, when the cost of a college degree hits two or three hundred thousand dollars, colleges may be void of students studying art, poetry, or (in some states) education. If college tuition continues to increase at its present rate (and there's nothing to suggest it will not), higher education might price itself out of teaching literature, humanities, anthropology, sociology, philosophy . . . all the disciplines that explore what it means to be human. From there, it doesn't take a science fiction writer to imagine the ill effects on our little civilization.

Nelson is careful not to project outlandish consequences. Rather, he leaves the reader to imagine. He might have gone further:

> If college tuition continues to increase at its present rate (and there's nothing to suggest it will not), higher education might price itself out of teaching literature, humanities, anthropology, sociology, philosophy . . . all the disciplines that explore what it means to be human. From there, our civilization is likely to forget the more reflective pursuits. We will be in danger of losing our already tenuous understanding of human complexity. We will have more difficulty understanding each others' hearts and minds. We may even become less inclined to ask the big questions than we are now.

These musings are interesting, but perilous. Not only are they logically unsound (bordering on slippery slope and non sequitur), but they also create a voice that seems detached and overly insistent. While writers should appear intense and focused, they should also appear clear-headed. Nelson's strategy, in the original passage, adeptly gets readers to more grounded and insightful points.

> No amount of support can help a voice that sounds noncredible.

REVISION

Intensity is the result of intensive invention. Assuming you have explored your ideas thoroughly, now you can revise to make your argument more forceful and engaging.

1. In the introduction, delete any sentences that do not provide new and important information.

2. Sharpen the opening sentence by eliminating unnecessary words or expressions.

3. Now go through the other sentences in the essay, doing the same as above. What can be deleted? Consider entire paragraphs, sentences, phrases, and words. Avoid cutting out ideas and specific examples; rather, focus on shaving off vague statements, clichés, expletives (*there are, it is*), wordy phrases, and unnecessary attention to yourself as a writer (*I think that . . . , It is my belief that . . .*).

Peer Review

Exchange drafts with at least one other writer. (If time allows, exchange with two or three writers to gather a range of perspectives or comments.) Use the following questions to generate specific constructive comments about others' drafts:

1. Is the argument a claim of fact? Does it answer this question: Given past or present trends, what is likely to happen in the future?

2. What are the most effective support strategies in the essay? What additional support strategies could help to persuade the reader? (What allusions, examples, or scenarios might help create the connection between a present trend and a future reality?)

3. What assumptions might the audience reject? How can questionable assumptions be supported?

4. How does a connection between the past/present and the future help the reader to accept the argument? What other connections between past/present and the future might help a reader to accept the argument?

5. Why might the reader have trouble accepting this view of the future? What changes might help the reader accept the view?

6. When writers conjure visions of the future, they may fall into the slippery slope fallacy—arguing that all will be lost if we continue down a particular path. If writers claim that a catastrophic end will come, for instance, they must provide logical steps to that end. (Readers cannot be expected to accept an extreme picture of the future without the logical steps to get there.) Has the writer provided those necessary logical steps? Has the writer avoided the slippery slope fallacy?

7. If the writer used outside sources, do they seem reliable, relevant, credible, timely, and diverse? Do you have any reason to question the sources? If so, how might the writer address your doubts?

8. Are the ideas from the outside sources integrated smoothly into the ideas?

9. Are the sources documented appropriately (with in-text and end citations)?

Revising in the Future

Perhaps the real value of revising your essay is applying what you have learned through revision to future writing projects. Consider the following questions about revision, and discuss your responses with others:

- What is the most notable improvement in your essay as a result of revision?

- What was most difficult about revising your essay, and how might you cope with this difficulty in the future?

- How, specifically, did revision help to intensify your argument?

PART THREE

Research

Jonathan Poore/Cengage Learning

Research can be seen as an intensely interactive process in which the researcher is engaging with a huge number of other lives.

Jonathan Poore/Cengage Learning

13

The Research Path

When we take a trip, we may follow busy highways that a million others have taken. We may stop at the same places along the way and see the same sights as countless others. We may pay the same tolls, eat the same types of food, travel at the same pace, and make the same turns as those around us. And sometimes, we diverge from the main highways, take smaller roads, and drive through small towns. But even if we travel along with others, our journey will be unique. Ultimately, all travelers end up diverging from others—taking an exit where others stay on the highway, taking a left while others take a right, pulling into a side street while others stay on the main road.

Likewise, a researcher often begins with questions that have been asked countless times before. He or she goes to sources that many others have sought out, and may even take away the same key ideas from those sources. However, as a researcher moves from source to source and generates ideas from each, his or her path starts to become unique. The more the researcher actively reads and generates ideas, the more those ideas start to take on particular nuances. And as the path becomes unique, the insights it generates do as well.

Research is a path filled with twists, turns, and surprises. Like any journey, a particular research path can start in one place, move through several stages, and take the researcher to totally new ground. No matter where it leads, a research path should be seen as a continuous intellectual journey.

INVENTIVE RESEARCH

If researching is like traveling, then inventive researchers are like adventurous travelers. They take back roads; they visit small towns. They may depend on interstates at times, but they also explore two-lane country roads and city neighborhoods. And in those small towns and city side streets, they are bound to see life beyond the repetitive march of fast-food joints and green highway signs.

Rather than reading only the most accessible source (say, the first listed on a database), inventive researchers also read others that may seem irrelevant at first. Rather than seeking only those sources in line with their initial thinking, inventive researchers explore articles that seem opposed to their original positions. They go after essays with strange titles; they crack open dusty books and review obscure websites. Inventive researchers take a particular posture as they encounter sources. They do more than simply read or listen. They also:

- **Look into the meaning of each keyword or phrase.** Inventive researchers see key terms and phrases as opportunities for more exploration. They assume that a word or phrase might generate new ideas. For instance, imagine that a writer is researching labor strikes. Rather than seeking out information only on *strikes,* she thinks about *labor.* She explores the word itself and discovers that philosophers and economists have defined the word according to different views of economy. Suddenly, her way of thinking about labor strikes connects with broader economic theories.

- **Go back in history to find the origin of words, attitudes, and beliefs related to the topic.** For example, imagine a writer is exploring sources for an essay on minstrel shows of the nineteenth century. While he initially believes that they were racist and demeaning to African Americans, he also wants to explore how audiences received them. He looks up "minstrel," which leads him to "blackface" performances. He discovers that the shows climaxed in popularity after the Civil War. He then continues by examining attitudes toward African Americans in the postwar years.

- **Look for principles and precedents.** Every topic connects to general principles (standard rules that tend to govern behavior) or precedents (previous cases). So, beyond their particular focus, inventive researchers imagine how their topics resonate with some broader set of rules or earlier cases.

- **Imagine analogies.** Making comparisons while reading and researching helps writers to see new layers of a topic. A well-crafted comparison may lay the foundation for an argument and create an interesting direction for research. Imagine an argument about the U.S. military action in Afghanistan. A writer may see a connection between it and the Vietnam War. This comparison may become a springboard to further research. For instance, the writer might explore the difference between troop numbers in Afghanistan and Vietnam.

- **Read for underlying values.** All arguments reflect values or assumptions that lie beneath the surface. This layer of an argument can be as important as, if not more important than, the surface statements. The inventive researcher seeks out this layer and asks important questions for further research: What are the arguer's assumptions? How does the presentation of information impact the meaning? What is the reader prompted to value? What fundamental values (related to duty, country, progress, community, family) does the text project? What people or groups share these values? The answers to such questions might prompt the researcher to explore further, to look beyond the main topic and to investigate the value or belief systems beneath it.

For more on hidden arguments and assumptions, see Chapter 5: Values and Assumptions.

SEEKING RESEARCH

Not all research is exploratory. Researchers sometimes need to find particular information, such as data, a specific historical account, or examples to support a claim. They need to find a direct path to particular information, to go from point A to point B. They are tracking down something they assume has been formulated by someone else, and they want to find the best route to that information. They should first evaluate their needs by asking some basic questions:

- What type of information do I need? (Consider theories, historical dates, conclusions from laboratory experiments, demographic information, public opinion, historical precedent, famous quotations, biographical specifics, etc.)
- What discipline or field of study (history, philosophy, economics, etc.) has explored this issue?
- What type of publication is likely to offer such information (journals, magazines, theoretical books, etc.)?
- What is the best way to access that publication (periodical database, website, library shelves, etc.)?

Writers should proceed with caution when looking for particular information: The most prevalent mistake for beginning researchers is assuming that they should do seeking research when they actually need inventive research.

CONDUCTING PRIMARY RESEARCH

Academic writers do both *primary* and *secondary* research. In primary research, information is gathered firsthand by the researcher. A writer doing primary, or field, research makes observations or does experiments, interviews, and surveys. He or she participates in the original actions of gathering data or making conclusions. The writer/researcher is "in the field," collecting opinions, interpreting experiment results, and gaining insights from interviews. Such work allows the researcher to experience events and issues without the influence of someone else's interpretation.

Beyond these physical activities, in which the researcher actively collects or generates information, some texts are considered primary sources. Literary and religious texts are primary sources because the researcher is not *gathering* others' conclusions but is responsible for *making meaning* out of texts. In other words, when researchers use literature or religious texts, they must shape the text's possible meaning and make it relevant to a particular argument. (For more on literary and religious works, see Chapter 3, pages 33–35.)

Primary Sources

- Interviews
- Surveys
- Literary Works
- Religious Texts
- Autobiographies

Secondary Sources

- Books (nonfiction)
- Newspapers
- Magazines
- Journals
- Government Documents
- Reference Books
- Websites
- Blogs/Chats
- Visual Media

The distinction between secondary and primary sources sometimes blurs. For instance, although news articles are usually considered secondary, a researcher arguing about news articles, as a topic, might treat them as primary sources, inspecting them as one might inspect a literary work. The categorizations *secondary* vs. *primary,* then, can depend on how the source is used.

Interviews

At a basic level, interviewing involves gathering information from a single person. But it can mean a great deal more. A good interview, like a good essay, goes beyond basic knowledge and provides insight. Good interviewers seek to engage interviewees in intensive conversations; they probe for knowledge and ideas, but they also allow interviewees to explore and develop ideas. The goal of an interview is not simply to record someone's opinion; rather, it is to prompt someone with particular experiences and insights to reveal something new and valuable.

INTERVIEW QUESTIONS Good interview questions create focus, yet allow interviewees to explore. Although they may seek out specific information, such as facts and dates, interview questions should go beyond collecting basic knowledge. In fact, asking interviewees basic information that can be retrieved through other sources undermines the interview process and wastes both parties' time. A more valuable strategy is to prompt interviewees to reflect on the meaning of issues or to make connections between ideas. Notice the difference between the following:

> What's it like being a doctor?

> How has working in the medical field influenced your personal life?

The first question does not focus attention on any particular issue; the interviewee could talk about anything related to the medical profession. The second question, however, draws attention to a particular issue and asks the interviewee to consider a particular relationship. It is more specific than the first question and still calls for a certain degree of exploration.

FOLLOW-UP QUESTIONS Following up on answers is the interviewer's most powerful research tool. A survey asks a list of preformulated questions, but an interview can follow a line of thought that comes from someone's response. Imagine the following scenario, in which a researcher is interviewing a civil engineer:

INTERVIEWER:	Is being a civil engineer interesting?
ENGINEER:	Sure. I get to deal with all kinds of people and very real situations.
INTERVIEWER:	Is being a civil engineer hard?
ENGINEER:	Well, some of the work can be difficult. Trying to figure in all the variables in a given project can be a mathematical nightmare.
INTERVIEWER:	What would you tell someone who wants to become a civil engineer?

Here, the interviewer comes up short in several ways. First, the questions are too general to yield focused and insightful answers. They prompt the engineer to respond in equally general terms. They are surface questions (the kind one might ask at a party) that invite short and uncomplicated answers. Second, the interviewer misses opportunities to follow up. After the engineer's responses, the interviewer could have asked about the "very real situations" or the "mathematical nightmare" but ignores both ideas and, instead, moves to the next question. This interview does not probe for insight or engage the thoughts of the interviewee. Notice the following example, which evolves within the space of only a few questions:

INTERVIEWER:	How is a civil engineer important to society?
ENGINEER:	Well, civil engineers conceptualize living space for the public. They envision what it might be like to live in a particular place, say, a downtown area, and then lay out plans to make a park, an intersection, even an entire downtown livable—and they do it all while considering how an area will grow and how people's needs may change.
INTERVIEWER:	So civil engineers have to be visionaries?
ENGINEER:	Yes! They are not simply figuring out formulas about buildings and zones and land; they are imagining what it might be like to live and work within a given area in the present and future.
INTERVIEWER:	And they do all this while accommodating the demands of city officials?

Here, the interviewer starts with a more insightful question. While the first interviewer depends on a vague concept ("interesting"), the second interviewer seeks out the meaning of a potential relationship (between civil engineers and society) and consequently receives an insightful response. Also, the interviewer in the second scenario springboards from the engineer's answers ("So, civil engineers have to be visionaries?"), thereby extending the initial thoughts.

PLANNING AN INTERVIEW When setting up an interview, be sure to respect the position and accommodate the schedule of the interviewee. Researchers should never impose themselves on potential interviewees. Use the following tips and strategies:

- Always request an interview well in advance of your own deadlines so that you can accommodate the interviewee's schedule.

- When making a request, introduce yourself and the reason for the interview: Explain the nature of your research and how the interview will be integrated into it.

- Beforehand, negotiate a reasonable amount of time for the interview (such as thirty minutes) and stick to it so as not to impose on the interviewee's time.

- Plan out your method of recording responses—writing, audiotaping, or videotaping. Ask the interviewee if his or her answers can be recorded and if his or her name can be used in the final work.

- At the end of the interview, thank the interviewee for his or her time, and leave promptly.

USING INTERVIEWS An interview can be used to support claims made in argument, to help explain an idea, or even to help explain the history or significance of a topic. In the following example, the writer is trying to persuade readers that the water treatment system in her town is inadequate. The claim made by the interviewee supports the writer's idea:

> Most often the water sewers can withstand the runoff from storms, but the past season has illustrated the inadequacy of the current sewer system. According to Harold Johnston, director of town utilities, the sewer system was overwhelmed twice in the past three and a half months, and the result was that untreated sewage flowed out into Silver Lake. When an overflow occurs and untreated water spills into the natural water system, the high amounts of bacteria affect the wildlife and jeopardize the health of swimmers and water enthusiasts. In essence, anyone or anything in the lake for days after an overflow is swimming in sewage.

Although the writer probably collected extensive information about the treatment system during her interview, she used only one particular point in this paragraph because it directly supports the main idea. (Other information might be used in later passages.)

The Letter Interview and the Research Process

GARYN G. ROBERTS

Garyn G. Roberts is an award-winning author. His most celebrated works include *Dick Tracy and American Culture: Morality and Mythology, Text and Context* (1994), which was nominated for the Mystery Writers of America Edgar Allan Poe Award, and *The Prentice Hall Anthology of Science Fiction and Fantasy* (2001), which he edited and which won the National Popular Culture Book Award. Roberts is authoring a bio-bibliographical history of Chester Gould and Dick Tracy. Much of his scholarly work through the years has depended upon primary research—specifically, the letter interview.

There exists a number of "truths" and generalizations about writing and the writing process. For example, in the strictest sense, all writing, at least on some level, is autobiography, metaphor, and fiction. But, this statement is not the focus here. In general, people are most successful as writers when they write about subjects in that they are not only interested, but also passionate. Though this may seem pedestrian and obvious on the face of it, we write best about subjects and topics that we already know to an extent and/or which we are willing to fanatically pursue. In addition, as clichéd as it may seem, the research process is a grand treasure hunt and the ensuing written product is a treasure realized at the end of the successful hunt. The research process often yields many "doubloons" and "pieces of eight." An essential tool or method used in much of my quest for treasure is oral history, and more specifically the personal interview, and by extension the letter and email interview. Letter and email interviews as research tools are the focus here.

In December 1965, as a first grader, I wrote President Lyndon Baines Johnson. President Johnson responded to my letter and sent photos of his family for my school. A couple of years later, I read my first series of *Dick Tracy* newspaper comic strips by Chester Gould (1900–1985) and I wrote Mr. Gould at the *Chicago Tribune*. We were friends and pen pals from that time into my graduate school years and until the time of his passing more than fifteen years later in 1985. I have interviewed many famous writers by mail and in person, and I did a great deal of marketing research for university business classes via interviews during my undergraduate education in the late 1970s and early 1980s.

It has been my privilege to have met famous people through the interview process (written and oral), and I am very fortunate to know and count some of the world's most famous authors as my friends. In a public presentation he did with me Spring 2003 celebrating the fiftieth anniversary of his novel *Fahrenheit 451*, Ray Bradbury stopped his part of the program to publicly thank me for my friendship and my years of work on his behalf.

Some of my favorite stories of interviews and oral histories, and subsequent research writing success, have come from my students, who have used letter and email interview techniques taught to me in the 1970s by Chester Gould.

Though maybe not thoroughly profound, the format for that letter interview (and now email interview) is based on sound reasoning and common sense, and invariably yields tremendous results. Mr. Gould laid it out for me this way, and I have used this method and taught my students the same for more than twenty-five years.

The philosophy of this type of interview is multifaceted, and designed to create a highly professional, trusting and friendly relationship between interviewer and interviewee. This letter and electronic format establishes the credibility of the writer/researcher, delineates the already existing knowledge and honorable intent of that person, and elicits detailed and important information from the uniquely informed interviewee.

5

Garyn Roberts, "The Letter Interview and the Research Process." Reprinted with permission of Garyn Roberts, Ph.D.

This form of interview facilitates the interviewee's "buy-in" to the efforts of the researcher, and also opens the door for further communication between the writer and receiver of the interview. (It often leads to additional written communications, personal interviews, and enduring professional relationships and friendships.) And, this format politely creates a "contract" between the researcher and that person interviewed.

Amazingly simple in some ways, the letter interview begins with a neatly typed and specifically addressed envelope in which the letter will be sent. Next, and here is where the "contract" is established, a self-addressed stamped envelope is included for the return of written responses made to questions posed. The SASE makes the responder's efforts easier than they might be otherwise. In addition, few people want to ignore and waste the unused stamp on that return address.

In the case of the email interview, the principal is the same—without the stamp. Again, the writer of the interview seeks to establish a bond or even a "contract" of sorts with the interviewee. The sender of the email interview must, like the letter interview writer, remain vigilant when it comes to matters of formality, form, and grammar. It is important to get a sense of the interviewee's preferences. Some may prefer and might only respond to paper letters sent through the U.S. Postal Service; others may prefer and be tolerant of the electronic form. As with the letter interview, the goal of the electronic interview is to make the process as attractive and as comfortable for the interviewee as possible.

10   Use of appropriate letterhead is helpful, but not necessary, in the case of the letter interview. The letter or email itself begins with relevant inside addresses and date. After an appropriate salutary greeting such as "Dear Mrs. . . ." or "Dear Dr. . . . ," the first paragraph—concise but detailed and carefully worded—introduces the researcher/writer to the person addressed. Credibility and dedication to the topic at hand are critical, and are established here. As a student (high school, college,

university or otherwise), you, the researcher, are already stereotyped in a universally positive way. Identify yourself as a student working on a research paper for an English, Sociology, History or (fill in the blank) course. Presented correctly, students are revered in our culture, and people want to advance education of these fine people.

That first paragraph is also where the researcher acknowledges the expertise of the person who receives the letter interview. Always being genuine (not artificial and overly flattering), the researcher pays tribute to the person addressed, and briefly showcases what he/she already knows about that person and the subject at hand. Be polite and unassuming, and after identifying yourself, turn your focus to the person interviewed and topic at hand. This all contributes to matters of credibility, trust, and intent. And, it occurs in an introductory paragraph of five to seven well-conceived sentences.

Conclude that first paragraph by stating that you have some questions you would like to ask, and have included these questions in this very letter. In the last sentences of that paragraph, state, "I have included a few questions here, and would greatly appreciate your responses. If it most convenient for you, please answer these on this letter or in this email, right after each question, and mail these responses back to me in the SASE or at my email address." If you are sending an email, make sure that your interviewee can both open your message with the computer software they have available to them, and can easily respond to that message.

Wishing to avoid overtaxing your respondent, keep these questions to about five or six in number. With this relatively small number of questions, make each question count. Avoid the obvious and questions that can be answered by other general resources. This whole process is designed to celebrate the expertise of the person receiving the letter interview and to facilitate information.

The quality of answers you will receive is directly dependent on the quality of questions posed. Here, again, you are interested in politely, discretely, and without a great deal of fanfare, showcasing your knowledge of the subject already. The kinds of question you ask contribute directly to this goal.

15 Next, after that introductory paragraph, list those five or six questions. On a paper letter, leave ten to fifteen lines between questions so that your respondent can provide answers right after each question. (The interviewee does not have to go to any extra effort to answer your questions—you have made things as easy as possible for that person.)

The concluding paragraph does three things. First, it emphatically but evenly thanks the interviewee for his/her time. Second—optional but recommended—it asks if the interviewee would like a copy of your final research project. (A little extra work on your part, this gesture reassures that your intentions are genuine and your final writing is open to scrutiny. Trust is further strengthened.) Third, it asks one last question and makes one last statement: "May I approach you with follow-up questions as they arise? Thank you again."

This written interview is closed "Sincerely, . . ." and provides contact information—address, telephone, FAX, email, and related and potentially useful information.

Some final words of advice: Send this letter interview, or email interview, at least three to five weeks before the information is needed. Send these interviews to more than one expert. While the return rate on this particular letter interview process is quite high—in the case of the letter interview you sent that stamp and politely foisted off an obligation in your letter—you are not guaranteed a quality response. Your chances are good, and you have helped make these better with a professional and personal written interview, but you never know. Besides, more than one expert has never compromised a research project and related treasure hunt.

Through the years, I have received responses to such written interviews from people after their deaths (sent just before they died, or by their estates after they passed on). Such was the case with Dick Moores (1909–1986), Chester Gould's first assistant on *Dick Tracy* in the early 1930s and famous Walt Disney Studios artist. My dear friend Robert Bloch (1917–1994), famed author of short stories, novels—including *Psycho* (1959)—radio plays, screenplays, teleplays—including three episodes of the original *Star Trek* (1960s)—writers' writer, and mentor to contemporary authors—including Stephen King, dying of cancer, sent me material (including permissions and photos from Hollywood) for his biography he wanted only me to have. He wrote the introduction to that book, "knowing that he would not live to see it in print." Great fun, heavy responsibility, and a way to contribute meaningfully to the heritage and culture that is ours.

Sample Interview Letter

Dear *Formal Name of Interviewee:*

Mrs. Jean Gould O'Connell and I are working on two book-length projects on the life and career of her father, Chester Gould. In doing so, we are most interested in the insights and inputs of people who knew and were closest to Chester and Edna Gould. Could I trouble you to answer the following questions and relate any stories you think might be of importance, then send your responses back to me? Feel free to write your responses on this and other paper. Please be as detailed in your responses as you like. (What might seem unimportant may very well be important. So, please provide as much detail as you can.) Enclosed is a self-addressed stamped envelope for your convenience. All unique ideas and direct quotes will be appropriately credited and documented in our book projects. If you have any questions about this or any other matters, please let me know. Thank you in advance for your time and efforts.

1. How and when did you know Chester and Edna Gould?

2. Do you remember any specific events or people from Chester and Edna's lives that were reflected in Chester's famous comic strip *Dick Tracy?* What and who were these?

3. What memories do you have regarding Chester and Edna helping other people? Please explain.

4. Did Mr. Gould ever relate stories about . . .

    A. His youth in Oklahoma? What were these?

    B. His early years in the Chicago area (1921–1935)? What were these?

    C. His years at Bull Valley (near Woodstock, 1935–1985)? What were these?

5. Do have any stories you can relate regarding Chester's parents (Gilbert and Alice)? Or about his brother Ray and sister Helen? Please explain.

6. Do you remember any special stories about Edna (Mrs. Gould)? Please explain.

7. Is there anything you would like to add? What do think should be said in biographies of Chester Gould?

8. Can you provide me with any names and addresses of people you think I should contact regarding their knowledge of, professional relationships with, and friendship with Chester Gould and his family?

9. Are there any photographs you would like to share for this project? All appropriate credits would be provided for such pictures. (Original copies would be returned.)

This summer, during Dick Tracy Days in Woodstock, Illinois, I will be interviewing people in person regarding their memories of the Goulds and *Dick Tracy.* If you would be willing or would like to meet with me at that time to further discuss your memories and talk about these projects, please let me know. May I send you a second set of follow-up questions?

Thank you again for all your time and efforts. If it has not yet been stated directly here, it is important for you to know that we are interested in paying tribute to Chester and Edna Gould, *Dick Tracy,* and the many important friends and relatives that were part of their lives. We are very excited about these projects and you sharing your stories with us.

Sincerely,

Garyn G. Roberts

Surveys

While an interview is based on an individual's ideas and knowledge, a survey attempts to find public opinion on a topic. An interview is driven, in part, by the interviewee; his or her insights can influence the direction or emphasis of the interview. In surveys, by contrast, the researcher prearranges the direction and emphasis with carefully formulated questions.

GENERATING QUESTIONS In generating survey questions, a researcher should consider three points.

1. Survey questions seek to find out—not *influence*—people's thinking. For example, a question that draws attention to a president's "wealth and privilege" may lead respondents toward a specific response. Instead, the question should be phrased objectively, not leading the respondent in any particular direction.

   Leading Question: Because of his enormous wealth and privileged upbringing, is the president out of touch with labor issues affecting average hardworking Americans?

   Objective Question: Is the president in touch or out of touch with labor issues in the United States?

2. Just as they should not influence the respondents' thinking on an issue, good survey questions should focus on a specific topic.

   Less Focused Question: Do you like our current president?

   More Focused Question: Do you approve of the president's current policies on education funding?

3. Questions should use common, nonspecialized language (unless you are surveying only specialists in a particular field, such as doctors or engineers). Because survey respondents may come from different walks of life, survey questions should avoid technical jargon or specialized terminology.

   Technical Question: Given recent research by CERRIE on genomic instability and mutations in mini-satellites, do you feel that radiation exposure guidelines should be revised?

   Nontechnical Question: Given recent research about the long-term effects of low-level radiation, do you feel that radiation exposure guidelines should be revised?

CHOOSING RESPONDENTS Surveyors must consider the demographics (or characteristics of specific populations) of their potential respondents. A well-designed general survey should include a representative cross-section of the population. Consider the following:

- What is the age range in the respondent group?
- What is the racial makeup of the respondent group?
- What is the gender makeup of the respondent group?
- What is the occupational makeup of the respondent group?
- What is the geographical origin of the respondent group?

RECORDING RESPONSES Responses can be recorded in various ways. Perhaps the easiest means is to elicit written responses by asking the respondents to write or check off their answers. But if that is not possible, the researcher must do the recording by writing or taping. (If you plan to tape answers, either on video or audio equipment, you should always obtain the respondents' permission in advance.)

USING RESPONSES Survey responses are most often used to show public opinion about a topic. Although a survey may collect many different opinions (and opinions about a variety of issues), the results are often boiled down to a particular issue. In other words, the survey generates a particular insight that the researcher presents to the audience. For example, notice how the following paragraph presents a particular insight that was generated by a survey:

> Gone are the days when the average college student dedicates most of his or her time to study. Now, college students are increasingly apt to work. They hold part-time jobs, where they work a few hours per week, and full-time high-stress positions, where they work forty-plus hours per week. At Bay College, nearly 80% of surveyed students said they have some kind of outside employment. And 40% of those work more than thirty hours per week ("Campus Study" 4). Such figures correspond to a growing trend across the country.

CONDUCTING SECONDARY RESEARCH

In contrast to primary research, secondary research is the examination of others' theories, conclusions, and ideas. Secondary sources (such as books, articles, and websites) help researchers to understand the history of a topic, to comprehend what has been said and what else can be said. Secondary sources also help writers get acquainted with others' values and assumptions and with the precedents of a particular field of study or discipline.

Regardless of the topic or discipline, every good researcher benefits from a wide understanding of and familiarity with that field's sources of information. Each type of source represents a possible research direction. And when researchers are familiar with many possible directions, they are bound to discover more than if they were stuck in a singular rut.

Books (Nonfiction)

Nonfiction books can be valuable secondary sources. Although their information may not be as up to date as some other types of sources, such as journals, they can be excellent resources for an in-depth understanding of your topic. There are six main categories of books that will help you in your research.

THEORETICAL BOOKS, which are common in academia, explore ideas. The main goal of theoretical works, in any field, is to reinvent (or help to reinvent) how people think about an issue. Theoretical books are usually aimed at a specialized audience, people who already know something about the subject and who have some sense of other texts written on the matter. Notice the titles of some theoretical books on rhetoric and writing:

Rhetoric and Reality

Fragments of Rationality

The Methodical Memory

Textual Carnivals

Even though theoretical books can be tough going at first, they can help expand your topic. Because they work at the conceptual level and usually aim to redefine something in a field of study, they can generate new (often revelatory!) ways of thinking.

HISTORICAL ANALYSES focus on specific issues or particular historic periods. They involve significant research from authors and usually give surprising and detailed bits of information. Notice, for example, this passage from David Russell's *Writing in the Academic Disciplines, 1870–1990*:

> But the transition from oral to written requirements [at Harvard] was not easy to make, for the new university was no longer a single discourse community with a single curriculum. Even in the early 1870s, the struggle to find a place for writing in an increasingly elective and departmentalized curriculum was already in evidence. Shortly after Eliot became president, students were no longer required to read their compositions aloud. (52)

Historical analyses like Russell's make claims about the nature of events in the past, and they provide ample, detailed evidence that illustrates and supports those claims. (There are even history books about history. These highly theoretical texts, called *historiographies,* usually examine how history has been told.)

EDITED (THEMATIC) COLLECTIONS are groups of essays that focus on one topic. The essays may have been published elsewhere prior to their appearance in the collection. An editor or group of editors selects the essays, arranges them in the book, and usually provides some introduction to the whole collection that explains the nature of the topic. For example, *Women and Power in Native North America* was edited by Laura F. Klein and Lillian A. Ackerman. The editors provide a brief introduction (thirteen pages) that gives a broad overview. Each chapter is an essay from an individual author, and each focuses on slightly different aspects of the broader topic. Notice the titles of the first several chapters:

Women and Power in Native North America

1. "Introduction," Laura F. Klein and Lillian A. Ackerman
2. "Gender in Inuit Society," Lee Guemple
3. "Mother as Clanswoman: Rank and Gender in Tlingit Society," Laura F. Klein
4. "Asymmetric Equals: Women and Men Among the Chipewyan," Henry S. Sharp

Edited collections like this are valuable finds for researchers. They can be used in several ways:

1. The introductions or final chapters (which may also be written by the book's editors) often make general claims about the topic at hand. These sections might characterize the history or future direction of a topic and thus help a researcher to get a handle on some of the more significant events, theories, or approaches to the topic.
2. Each chapter in an edited collection can be read as a separate article—its own statement about a given topic.
3. Several chapters in an edited collection can provide a range of perspectives (and sometimes contradictory opinions) about a topic. In this sense, collections can help a researcher see an ongoing debate and understand competing assumptions, values, and claims.
4. Edited collections usually provide thorough lists of sources, either at the end of each chapter or at the end of the book itself. These lists can be used as starting places for further research.

TEXTBOOKS aim to introduce readers (usually students in a specific course) to a discipline or field of study. They assume that readers need many terms defined, and they present information in digestible units or sections. A reader can examine a chunk of information from the middle of the text without having to read everything before it. Textbooks are also relatively user-friendly: information is presented in various ways, so readers can conceptualize, rather than just consume.

It is important to note that textbooks explain theories or principles but do not seek to *create* new theories. For instance, a psychology textbook is apt to discuss important figures such as Freud, Skinner, and Milgram, but it will not seek to transform how people think of those figures.

BIOGRAPHIES cover the life of an individual, as told by someone else. Most often, a biographer attempts to reveal hidden layers of someone's life and to show something intimate or especially significant about that person. David McCullough's biography of President John Adams, for instance, delves into the character traits of the president and shows how those traits corresponded to his life in office.

AUTOBIOGRAPHIES are personal narratives; they cover the life of the writer. For instance, in his 2004 release, *My Life*, former U.S. president Bill Clinton tells his own story.

Newspapers

Newspapers cover a broad range of topics. They are most valuable for highly publicized topics, such as political events, controversial public figures, national or local disasters, and significant cultural events. National newspapers, such as the *New York Times* or the *Washington Post*, also offer lengthy and in-depth analyses. In a sense, newspapers represent collective responses to the political and cultural events of the day.

Most academic and public libraries have newspaper databases and access to past editions. Practically all newspapers also have websites. And while city newspapers feature local issues, the following cover a range of national and global events: *Afro American Newspaper, American Banker, Atlanta Journal-Constitution, The Boston Globe, Chicago Tribune, The Christian Science Monitor, Denver Post, Detroit News, Houston Chronicle, Los Angeles Times, The New York Times, San Francisco Chronicle, Los Angeles Sentinel, St. Louis Post-Dispatch,* [New Orleans] *Times-Picayune, USA Today, The Wall Street Journal, The Washington Post.*

Magazines

Magazines are for general or casual readers, people who are not specialists in a given field. They range dramatically in style, subject matter, and editorial policy. There is a magazine for every conceivable layer of personal and public life: from gardening to bow hunting, from stamp collecting to hiking, from political intrigue to Hollywood gossip. Some magazines are more news oriented than others. *Newsweek* or *Time,* for instance, is more concerned with delivering world and national news than *People* or *Better Homes and Gardens.* But all magazines have the same goals: to make a profit and to stay in business.

Ultimately, magazines must appeal to two groups: their advertisers and their subscribers (in that order). Without advertising money, magazine budgets would run dry. Therefore, the stories and coverage in magazines rarely run contrary to the values of their advertisers. For instance, a general-interest magazine with major advertising from a car company is not apt to run a story that connects car exhaust to asthma. This is not to say that magazines are entirely controlled by their advertisers' values, but readers should know that choosing magazine content is a highly political process. Magazine editors must consider the financial impact of their decisions.

Look through a magazine. Based on its articles, advertisements, and images, explain its ideology, the hidden values that underlie the content and appeal to readers.

Magazines also cannot afford to alienate readers. Information is the product in a magazine, and if that product is distasteful in any way, readers simply may not buy it. Therefore, magazines tend not to sell information that might offend their readers, even if that information is credible and reliable. Magazine articles, then, are apt to engage the values their readers share. The information will likely resonate with a particular ideology. This is not to say that magazine articles are bound to lack reliability or credibility. But researchers should always be aware of the broader, business-related purpose of magazine articles and look for their underlying ideology and warranting assumptions.

Journals

In contrast to magazines, journals are written for a specialized audience in a particular field of study or discipline. They feature an array of articles by different authors, as magazines do, but differ in key aspects from magazines. Journals explore matters within a specialized field. They are often associated with academic disciplines:

Quarterly Journal of Speech

Management International Review

Mathematics of Computation

Journal of Materials Chemistry

College English

Nurse Researcher

Environmental History

Each discipline has many related journals, each with a specific focus. For instance, notice these chemistry-related journals found in one college library:

Chemical Business	*Chemical Specialties*
Chemical Business Newsbase	*Chemical Week*
Chemical Equipment	*Chemical Week Asia*
Chemical Market Reporter	*Chemical Week Internet Focus*
Chemical Monitor	*Chemical and Industry*
Chemical News and Intelligence	*Chemistry Review*

Another important difference between magazines and journals is in the nature of the articles. Magazines primarily set out to inform readers (give information), but journals set out to argue for new ways of thinking. Journal articles work to transform theories, practices, and policies within a field. Additionally, journals are generally nonprofit, often run by a nonprofit organization. Therefore, they lack advertisements or keep them isolated to the front and back pages. (The few advertisements, like all the content in journals, tend to be black and white—not replete with flashy colors and attention-grabbing devices.)

Journal articles are judged (or "refereed") by anonymous scholars before they are published. For instance, consider this typical scenario: An economist discovers a growing trend in personal debt among consumers. She writes a lengthy essay explaining the nature of the trend and what it may mean for the country and its future, according to a specific school of economic theory. Before the essay is accepted for publication in an economics journal, the editor sends it to several economics scholars throughout the country, perhaps even throughout the world. These scholars examine the research, judge the logic of the claims, recommend changes, and then recommend that the essay be published or rejected. Only after this intensive process (which may repeat several times) does an essay become a journal article. These rounds of judging help to ensure the information in the article is accurate.

Journal articles can be powerful research tools. They are generally available on research databases (such as InfoTrac® College Edition or Academic Search Elite), and they are highly focused, offering specific conclusions, theories, and information. Like theoretical books, journal articles can be filled with technical jargon and dense language. They are not for casual readers. But they often feature a short abstract or concluding section that summarizes the main points.

Journal articles are written when a scholar:

- Applies an ongoing theory to a particular situation.
- Discovers a likely cause or effect that has not previously been imagined.
- Redraws the boundaries of a given discipline or practice.
- Expands or rethinks a previously accepted theory.
- Discovers something previously overlooked in the history of the field.

IS IT A JOURNAL OR A MAGAZINE? At first glance, journals and magazines may look a lot alike. But closer inspection will reveal significant differences. Generally, journals are written for academic or highly specialized readers, and the articles put forward new theories or practices in a particular field of study (sociology, psychology, nursing, English, chemistry, history, etc.). Magazines are written for general readers, who may have a particular interest (cycling, running, gardening, etc.). If you are not certain what kind of periodical you have, use the following criteria:

Journals

- Seek to advance knowledge in a field of study.
- Deal with principles, theories, or core practices in an academic discipline.
- Are associated with a particular discipline or field of academic study.
- Have few advertisements, which usually appear only at the beginning and end (not between or among articles).
- Have few colors and flashy pictures (unless they are related to a study or article).

Magazines

- Report information and news or offer advice.
- Offer the latest technique in a hobby or sport.

- May appeal to readers with a particular interest.
- Have advertisements throughout the pages, even interrupting articles.
- Tend to use lots of color and pictures.

Activity

In groups, decide whether a journal or a magazine probably published the following articles. As a class, discuss the reasoning behind your decisions:

"Make Way for the Cherry Festival!"

"The End of Humanism: An Examination of Postmodern Thought"

"Angina and the Elderly"

"Are the National Parks in Trouble?"

"Climatic Change and Insect Migration"

Government Documents

Government documents include reports, transcripts, pamphlets, articles, speeches, books, maps, films, and more. While the U.S. government is the nation's largest publisher, state and city governments also publish documents. They can be of great value in one's research, and can be found online using keyword searches, going to the website of the relevant agency, or going directly to the Government Publishing Office (GPO) website at www.access.gpo.gov.

Reference Books

Reference books, such as dictionaries, encyclopedias, and almanacs, can be helpful, but they should not be relied upon as the only sources for a college research paper. Using only reference books for research suggests that a researcher was unable or unwilling to find a range of sources, which in turn suggests a lack of depth in the exploration and discovery of ideas. Reference materials are usually found in a library's reference room (or in smaller libraries, a reference area) and cannot be checked out. They can be located, as with other library materials, by searching the library's catalog of holdings.

Websites

Websites are as diverse as the people who create them. (And everyone from a fourth-grader in rural Montana to a senior advisor to the president can create a website.) As most people know, the World Wide Web is a lively, confusing, and enormously diverse space. It contains nearly every type of information, theory, law, policy, reference, and idea imaginable.

For more specific advice on evaluating websites, see page pages 329–338.

The value of the web is fairly obvious to anyone who has spent a few minutes using any search engine: you quickly find vast amounts of information on anything from monkey droppings to Olympic history archives. The downside of the web is fairly obvious as well: the information may be questionable or only slightly relevant to your topic. Although it is easy to find general information on a topic, it is more difficult to find specific theories, conclusions, and data. Also, the web is populated with two significant annoyances: sales pitches and pornography. It is a playground for people selling junk and hawking porn. A serious researcher has to navigate his or her way through advertisements, posters, pop-ups, and "opportunities" of all kinds. However, despite these difficulties, focused web searches can generate interesting results and can function as valuable inventive research.

Blogs/Chats

Blogs (web logs) and Internet chat rooms feature personal and largely informal postings. Although a writer should not rely on blogs and chat rooms for reliable information, these sources can be valuable stops along the research path, revealing new ways of thinking and new directions for further exploration. Ideas gleaned from these sources should be evaluated, integrated, and documented, just as ideas from websites and reference books should be. Because they are not edited by outside parties, these sources should be seen and used as personal statements rather than as proof for any claim.

Visual Media

Visual media include film, digital video, posters, photography, graphics, maps, and so on. Like articles or books, visual media can make arguments. For example, a poster, illustration, or map can assert an important political position or aesthetic judgment: Consider Edward Tufte's visual argument against a popular software program.

Edward R. Tufte

The Cognitive Style of PowerPoint

Military parade, Stalin Square, Budapest, April 4, 1956.
Copyright © 2003 by Edward R. Tufte   November 2004
Published by Graphics Press LLC   P. O. Box 430   Cheshire, Connecticut 06410   www.edwardtufte.com

AP Images. Reprinted by permission, from Edward R. Tufte, The Cognitive Style of Powerpoint (Graphics Press, 2003)

Even if visual media do not argue directly, they function within an argument. A visual source of any kind is an artifact of a culture—a representation of certain values and collective assumptions. A film might reveal something about the attitudes of a particular time and place; a poster or advertisement may show what people value or how they think.

Searching the Library

Books, periodicals, newspapers, government documents, reference books, audiovisual materials, and websites can all be valuable sources of information. All of these sources can be found by searching a library's catalog of holdings and/or the Internet. Knowing how to navigate library catalogs and cyberspace is the first step in finding valuable sources. You might begin by getting familiar with your library's website. The website will explain all the library's resources, and it may provide links to other useful websites and databases.

When searching your library's catalog, you may be given the option of doing an author search, a title search, a subject search, or a keyword search. Do an author search if looking for works by a particular author; do a title search if you already know the title of the specific work. Subject searches are organized by headings (such as "agriculture," "government," "gender") and will usually produce many sources for a particular topic. Keyword searches can be used to focus the research process. For example, a slightly different keyword search produces widely varying numbers of entries:

Keyword Search	Entries Produced
weight	804
weight *and* body	146
weight *or* body	3,993
body weight	93
bodyweight	0

Searches can be made more efficient by using the following words (called *Boolean operators*):

- Using *and* between words narrows a search by finding documents containing multiple words—*weight and body.*
- Using *or* between words broadens a search by finding documents with either word in a multiword search—*weight or body.*
- Using *and not* between words finds documents excluding the word or phrase following "and not"—*weight and not body.*
- Using *near* between words finds documents containing both words or phrases that are near, but not necessarily next to, each other—*weight near body.*

EVALUATING SOURCES

Good researchers always evaluate the nature of their sources. They look closely at the source, the argument it offers, and its hidden arguments. They do not ask if the source agrees with their own way of thinking. Evaluating a source has little or nothing to do with agreeing or disagreeing with it. (In other words, a source is not good because you agree with it or bad because you disagree.) Sources should be evaluated according to their adherence to specific criteria, such as those outlined in this section.

Evaluating sources keeps researchers agile, able to do more than simply ingest facts and fit them into their arguments. The following criteria (relevance, reliability, credibility, timeliness, diversity, the nature of underlying values) can be used to evaluate any source.

Relevance

Relevance refers to the relationship between the source and the writer's topic and particular stance. A source that is relevant is appropriately related to the writer's argument. Perhaps the first inclination regarding relevance is to find those sources that directly support a main claim—sources that specifically speak about the writer's particular subject and espouse his or her particular stance on it. However, this is very limiting, especially since the research process might (and should!) develop or change how a writer thinks about a subject. Sources do much more than back up a writer's opinion. They can help to explain the subject's complexities, explain its history, explain the writer's position, support the writer's position, show claims that oppose the writer's, or show claims that are different from the writer's.

Because sources can be used in a variety of ways, a source that seems only remotely related to your project might be valuable in the long run. Consider the following example: A writer is researching voting practices in his community and wants to make a claim about low voter turnouts in recent elections. He finds a newspaper article about a local school scheduled for demolition that previously had been used as a voting location.

This article might seem irrelevant at first. After all, how does this particular school relate to voting trends in the community? But it actually may suggest a great deal about voting. One factor in voter turnout is proximity to voting locations. This article might show a trend of declining number of voting locations. The same writer might find a government web page about the history of voting in his state. At first, this source may not seem valuable because the writer is primarily concerned with recent voter activity. However, the history may provide some clues about the system itself, about the reasons for establishing Tuesdays as election days, or about the number of constituents in a given area, all of which are potentially valuable factors in understanding the complexities of recent voter turnout.

Use the following questions to weigh the relevance of sources you find:

- How does the source support or oppose my own opinions or hunches about the topic?
- How does the source help to explain something about the topic (its history, its evolution, its nature, etc.)?
- How does the source help to shape the values beneath my opinions?

Reliability

Reliability refers to the quality of information in the source. A reliable source documents the information it offers or proves that its claims can align with others' arguments. It documents claims involving statistics or data and offers paths to other research that supports the main argument. It makes a clear connection to a body of knowledge, to other scholars, thinkers, and researchers who have explored the issue at hand. The most obvious way to make this connection is with formal documentation (in-text citation and a bibliographical list). In effect, formal documentation says to readers, "Here is the path to other relevant research."

For journal articles, reliability may not be a problem because such sources endure a process of critical peer review. However, other publications do not have peer reviews. And magazines and newspapers do not have room to include formal documentation; their editorial policies exclude in-text documentation and Works Cited lists. But there are other ways for writers to signal reliability, such as an appositive phrase:

> **Deirdre Mahoney,** *a professor of writing at Northwestern Michigan College and a scholar of rhetoric,* **argues that online courses are significantly more challenging for college students than traditional face-to-face courses.**

Notice that the information after the name indicates the source's credentials. When a formal Works Cited list is not possible, writers use such phrases to document the reliability of their sources.

Consider the following questions for each source you find:

- Does the source offer formal documentation? Do other sources check out? Are they available?
- If there is no formal documentation, does the source acknowledge others with related credentials or qualifications?
- What about the source itself? Is it published by a reputable organization?

Credibility

Credibility refers to the internal logic and validity of the information presented in the source. While a *reliable* source resonates with other research or corresponds to a body of knowledge, *credibility* is all

In academic writing, previous publications and research credentials act as appeals to character. See pages 43–44.

about the source itself. A credible source is free of logical fallacies. And it does not attempt to hide its biases or its argument. It makes logical claims and helps the reader to follow its logic. If the source offers an argument, it makes its position clear and reveals its biases. (In other words, perfectly credible sources can be biased. They can offer arguments in favor of a position. The problem comes when sources attempt to hide their biases—when they espouse a position or spin information while portraying themselves as neutral.)

Credibility may also involve the author of a source. Some authors have more credentials than others. However, a book or article by a well-known author should not automatically outweigh one by a less familiar writer. Many academic and professional writers are not big names in popular media but are well respected within small communities because they have spent years researching a particularly focused issue. For instance, Patricia Limerick, a highly respected history scholar, has written a great deal about the American West. Although her name is not recognizable to the general public, it is often noted in history scholarship. It is relatively easy to research authors' credentials. Use the following questions to check the credibility of sources you find:

- Are the argument's claims well supported and well reasoned?
- Do you sense any logical fallacies?
- Does the source attempt to "spin" information or conceal its biases?
- Do you have reason to question the author's credibility? (If so, do a quick web or database search to see if he or she has written previously or is referenced in other publications.)

See Logical Fallacies in Chapter 3, pages 41–43. See Spin in Chapter 5, pages 81–82.

For more specific information on credibility and statistics, see Julie Burks's essay on pp. 334–336.

Timeliness

Timeliness refers to the appropriate relationship between the source's publication date and its content. A significant concern in academic research is the date of the sources. It is important that claims are supported with sources that are not obsolete or outdated. But this criterion depends upon the issue and the claim being made. Some claims require very current sources; for example, a writer making a claim about the state of cloning in the United States would be wise to consider sources published only within two to three years of her research. (Because the science of biotechnology evolves so rapidly and because each new advancement prompts significant public debate, claims that are ten years old probably would be antiquated.) However, that same writer might also want to discuss the role of science in human development, and discover a valuable text by a nineteenth-century philosopher who speaks about the role of machines in the evolution of the modern consciousness. In this case, the writer could use current texts to support claims about time-sensitive topics and refer to an older source to express an issue that stretches beyond a particular era.

The focus of certain topics can change because of events in popular culture, politics, and everyday life. Certainly the terrorist attacks of September 11, 2001, changed the way people think about a host of issues. *The 9/11 Commission Report,* released in July 2004, impacted policy decisions in government. Such events create a before-and-after gap, so certain information that would otherwise be considered relatively current might suddenly become outdated.

Although current information is important, the most valuable source is not necessarily the most recent. For some topics, writers may find value in older sources that have had significant impact on writers and researchers. For instance, a writer focusing on contemporary political protests would certainly discover recent sources about protests against the World Trade Organization. However, he might also find texts by Henry David Thoreau, Martin Luther King Jr., or Mahatma Gandhi to be of value. Although such sources are significantly older than a recent article on the Internet, they would provide depth to any discussion about political protests. Of course, a hundred-year-old text would be used differently than a contemporary text: The writer might use Thoreau to explain the importance of civic action as a general principle and turn to a recent source to articulate the present condition of political protest groups. Use the following questions to help you weigh the timeliness of sources:

- Is the information time-sensitive? Is the topic apt to change dramatically from year to year?
- If the information is time-sensitive, is the source current?
- Has anything significant occurred in the field of study (or in everyday life) that may have changed or influenced the information in the source or the nature of the topic?
- If the source is not current, does it help to illustrate something that is timeless (some human, natural, or physical trait)?

Diversity

Here, diversity refers to the variety of sources a writer uses. Writers develop their views on a subject from different sources, much in the same way as people develop their views on religion or marriage or education from taking in and making sense of information from various sources. For example, our social values may have been influenced primarily by our parents; but other sources, such as childhood friends, books, movies, and music, also influenced us. Even views that oppose our own are important because they help us to define the borders of our beliefs. This process of making our own sense out of various pieces of information is called *synthesis*. It is what writers do when researching their topics. Writers need to consider and synthesize various sources about their topics; otherwise, their perspectives and, ultimately, their positions will be limited.

This does not mean that every research project must consult websites, journals, books, and newspapers. A perfectly sound project can emerge from a focus on the journals in a given field. It does mean, however, that writers should be cautious of depending on information from only one publication. If a writer made several claims about the state of American foreign policy, all based on *Newsweek* articles, some important perspectives would be missing. Or if a writer relied heavily on unaffiliated websites (those not associated with a professional organization or institution), the information could have significant gaps.

Underlying Values

Beneath the most objective looking source, there lies a layer of shared values and hidden assumptions. From heated argumentative essays to brief factual news articles, the claims emerge from and rely on some unstated ideas and shared beliefs about the world. This does not mean that a secret agenda, or subliminal message, lurks beneath our sources—or that the government is trying to brainwash us. It simply means that information grows out of what people value. A simple news article, for instance, might report on some "promising new technology" that will help American car companies to increase fuel efficiency. The article may not explain that fuel efficiency is inherently good, that saving money on gasoline is good, that diminishing our collective impact on the environment is good. Such value claims would go unstated and readers would likely accept them as part of the article itself. (For more on underlying values, see page 72 in Chapter 5.)

When we read sources, we should acknowledge the quiet and shared values that may come along beneath the obvious claims and information. Quite often, we will discover some obvious and widely accepted notions about the world—about good/bad, right/wrong. Sometimes, we might discover some complexity, a school of thought, a hope, a yearning, a fear, or a principle that is not so easily accepted. Use the following questions to consider the underlying values beneath the surface of a source:

- What is the reader prompted or invited to value? (What ideas, people, attitudes, policies, or behaviors are held in high regard?)
- What broader set of beliefs or perspectives relates to those values?
- What assumptions can you detect in the argument?
- How are the main issues framed? That is, how does the writer characterize issues to be relevant in people's minds?
- What group, organization, or institution published the source? Might the values of that group influence the information offered?

The Patsy: A Story of a Number

JULIE BURKS

When evaluating a source, we should not be swayed too easily by numbers. Statistics can make a source seem instantly credible—more logical, less biased. But as Julie Burks, an accountant and auditor, explains, statistics themselves are fraught with potential shortcomings. Like any form of support, statistics can be tweaked and framed according to particular biases. This does not mean we should automatically toss out numerical support, but that we should not automatically accept it as beyond bias, beyond accident, beyond opinion.

Believers of statistics beware! Persuading an audience with a statistical analysis is an easy tactic. The reason: Numbers don't lie. However, the data behind the numbers, behind conclusions, behind completed reports, are like any part of human communication: full of potential flaws and misuse. In short, a responsible audience should practice some healthy skepticism when confronted with the mighty statistic.

Statistics are developed from testing samples of a population. The population is comprised of individuals. To most people, *individual* usually means human; but, to a statistician, individuals can also include animals and things. So when a study suggests that 8 out of 9 individuals prefer beef over tofu, it might be wise for the study's interpreter to know if the population being tested was a pack of Golden Retrievers or selection of human beings. Further, if the study focused on human responses, who were the humans? What demographic? Were they specifically selected McDonald's shareholders or randomly selected from cities in multiple states?

Even the timing of a survey can have dramatic effects. For instance, consider the outcome of a survey asking a sample population: Are American office workers subjected to weight-gain due to sedentary activities in the workplace? A survey such as this might bear differing conclusions if asked before or after lunch. Placing blame on externalities (such as the situational activities in the workplace) might come easy once the deep-fried Monte Cristo sandwich, followed by the hard-to-resist blueberry cheesecake, rests in the participant's belly after lunch hour. Conversely, if asked before lunch, the participant may conclude that one's diet and exercise routine has a greater impact on weight control than does the normal course of the work day.

Trusting the source of data often begins with the level of trust an audience has with the spokesperson. When Drew Barrymore lets a crowd in on a little secret about the "number one launch" mascara that doubles lash length, who wouldn't want to "join the six million and counting" (Cover Girl)? Cover Girl cosmetics selected Barrymore for her celebrity. Compound celebrity with statistics and cha-ching: Lash Blast mascara theoretically becomes an instant success. But what does the six million represent? Were these individuals independent consumers, Cover Girl employees, or artificial test eyelashes in the research and development laboratories? Is it the number one launch of all make-up companies world-wide? Or is the number one launch just for Cover Girl that year in America alone?

Another variable that can influence conclusions drawn from data is the scope of the data selected. Many savvy investors lost millions of dollars in the stock market in the late 2000's. After the peak of the housing bubble, investors started becoming wary and losing trust in financial markets. Scare tactics were flowing through various media channels disclosing short-term data (such as that shown on the following graph for the years 2006–2009) which was suggesting that the floor was going to fall out from under the feet of America. Everybody wanted out. The numbers become the scapegoat, the fall guy, the patsy, for

Reprinted by permission of Julia Burks.

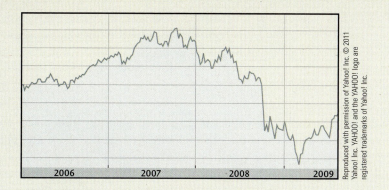

irrational decisions and sporadic impulse. "People get scared in crowds; their confidence comes back one at a time," says Warren Buffet, one of the world's wealthiest investors and philanthropists.

The truth is revealed, however, when one observes the Dow Jones over a longer term (see the following graph). Even shortly after the bubble burst, this particular index is still better off than it was fifteen years prior. So what happened? Did investors neglect to look at the bigger picture? Were they relying on statistics from sources who had unidentified motives? Were the sources of this information jumping to conclusions before analyzing all the data? Regardless of the answers, such questions reveal possible biases or innocent inaccuracies.

Depending on who comprised the tested population, rhetoric within a survey can generate a preferred response for an intended audience. In fact, the entire study could be deliberately formulated to sway respondents. For example, if a group of American teens were asked whether or not they enjoy pâté, most participants would respond unfavorably. However, if the teens were asked if they enjoy meatloaf, the results would tilt in an entirely different direction.

Another concept in uncovering the misleading notions within data is manipulating statistical terminology. Much confusion arises (is created) from two statistical terms: *mean* and *median*. The terms both describe the center of a distribution but in different ways. The median is the number that sits perfectly in the middle of the distribution. The mean is the average of all values. For example, let's say we have the following values: 0, 2, 4, 7, 211. The median is 4 (sits perfectly in the middle) and the mean is 44.8

Top graph: Depicting a significant decline in the Dow Jones Industrial Average from the beginning of 2006 to mid-2009. Bottom graph: Depicts the Dow Jones Industrial Average but extends the scope by 36 years (to 1970) to show larger trends.

(the average: 0+2+4+7+211 divided by 5). These values also have what's called an *outlier*—an observation that is numerically distant from the rest of the data. In this case, the outlier is 211.

Let's say the example in the preceding paragraph was a test in which one table at Applebee's was selected. There were five individuals (humans in this instance) at the table, and these individuals were asked, "How many times do you use your cell phone in a day, whether calling or texting?" Wouldn't it be advantageous for a cell phone company to report that individuals with a median age of 67-years are texting on average 44.8 times per day? But let's look at our Applebee's table again. The ages of these fictitious individuals are 98-years, 68-years, 67-years, 14-years, and 6-years. The average age of this group is 16.4 years less than the median age. Including the outlier as a true representative of this population can lead to questionable results.

Age	# of Calls/Texts per Day
98	1
68	7
67	2
14	211
6	4

As with any argument, a responsibility rests 10 on the interpreter/reader to question the underlying biases: Who is the source? Who is the intended audience? Who comprised the tested population? Is the test or study planned based upon desired results? Now, when persuasive, yet questionable, results emerge from a new study, one might inquire: "Where was the study conducted—a dog park?" The patsy, yet again: an innocent number.

Works Cited

Buffett, Warren. "Warren Buffet on the Economy, the Deficit, LeBron James and BP." *Huffington Post*, interview by Willow Bay, 8 July 2010, www.huffingtonpost.com/2010/07/08/warren-buffet-on-the-econ_n_639165.html.

Cover Girl. *Covergirl Drew Barrymore's Lashblast Mascara Commercial*. Procter & Gamble, 2008. YouTube, www.youtube.com/watch?v=zILszWDXaYs. Accessed 20 July 2010.

Works Consulted

Moore, David S. *The Basic Practice of Statistics*. W.H. Freeman and Company, 2004.

Evaluating Electronic Sources

Writers should be especially careful about the information on websites because anyone with access to a computer can publish one and make any claim he or she wishes. Much information on the World Wide Web is thus potentially bogus. Bias must also be considered. The purpose of many sites is to sell something; therefore, the information may be slanted. Of course, bias is not inherently bad. It is only negative when it is concealed—or pitched as unbiased truth. How do you separate the bogus from the useful on the web? Try applying the following questions when considering websites:

- Who sponsors this site, and what credibility do they have for posting the information?
- Is the site attempting to sell something? If so, how might that impact the nature of the information?
- Does the site ask for personal information? (Does it state the purpose of this request?)
- Are statistics and data supported with appropriately documented sources?
- Is the information up to date? (Is the site updated consistently?)

Evaluating Sources: In Brief

Evaluating sources depends on the application of key principles:

Relevance: the relationship between the source and the writer's topic and particular stance

Reliability: the quality of information in the source

Credibility: the internal logic and validity of the information presented in the source

Timeliness: the appropriate relationship between the source's publication date and its content

Diversity: the variety of sources a writer uses

Underlying Values: the collection of shared values and principles that rest beneath the claims

---

Activity

Wikipedia can be used for three types of research: preliminary survey of the topic, inventive research, and seeking research. To become more familiar with Wikipedia, use a topic you are currently researching or select one of these topics: No Child Left Behind Act, propaganda, Islam, credit cards, rhetoric, consumerism, marketing. Then answer the following questions:

- **Preliminary Research:** What important issues or aspects of the topic did you find out about through Wikipedia? Why should they be explored in your inventive research?
- **Inventive Research:** How did your thinking on a particular issue become more complicated because of the Wikipedia article? What source(s), besides Wikipedia, might you use to explore the issue further?
- **Seeking Research:** What facts from Wikipedia might be important to your argument, and what source(s) might you use to corroborate those facts?

WIKIPEDIA In general, encyclopedias, including Wikipedia, are best used for initial research, to survey the broad territory of a topic before beginning inventive research. This preliminary research then leads to books, articles, and other sources that provide more detailed information that can be used for inventive and seeking research (see pp. 309–311). Wikipedia says,

> As with any source, especially one of unknown authorship, you should be wary and independently verify the accuracy of Wikipedia information if possible. For many purposes, but particularly in academia, Wikipedia may not be considered an acceptable source; indeed, some professors and teachers may throw Wikipedia-sourced material away out of hand. This is especially true when it is used uncorroborated. We advise special caution when using Wikipedia as a source for research projects.

(en.wikipedia.org/wiki/Citing_Wikipedia)

If used for inventive research, Wikipedia should not be used exclusively, since it is not exhaustive. Other key sources that are not mentioned in Wikipedia should be sought out as well. Nonetheless, by following links within articles and external links listed at the end of articles, writers can extend and transform their ideas. While it can also be used to find particular information such as a date (see "Seeking Research," p. 311), Wikipedia is not just a place to locate facts but a place to explore possibilities.

INTEGRATING SOURCES

Once writers have begun to work with other texts, or sources, they must integrate those texts into their own writing. Whether they are building bridges between positions, finding quiet connections, or counterarguing, they have to deal directly with others' words. They have to accurately portray what others have said and then work those ideas into coherent passages that explain their own position. (Some instructors consider this to be among the most difficult rhetorical work for writers!) Whether information is summarized, paraphrased, or directly quoted, it should be blended smoothly into the text so that the reader (1) understands its relationship to the writer's own ideas and (2) knows where the information came from. The challenge is to maintain coherence and flow while integrating others' voices and opinions.

Summary

As Chapter 6 explains, summary is expressing ideas from a source in your own words. Unlike a paraphrase (see pages 341–342), summary removes much of the detail from the original passage. The goal in summary is to abbreviate and reword the original text. In this sense, summary is a tool. It allows writers to place otherwise lengthy sources directly into their own arguments to support a claim of their own, to illustrate a point from an opposing position, or to help explain the topic itself. In other words, summary often serves a bigger purpose. It is also adaptable. A writer can shrink a mammoth Victorian novel into a few pages or a few sentences. Likewise, a ten-page article can be summarized in a page or a paragraph. It all depends on the writer's purpose. If a writer is using a source as one example among others, the summary of that source may be brief. But if the source is being used to illustrate a complex idea, the summary may be longer and more involved.

> Chapter 6, pages 88–89, explains steps for creating an accurate stand-alone summary. This section, however, shows how summary functions in a broader argument—how to summarize a source within an ongoing argumentative essay.

Summary walks a fine line between sufficient and excessive detail. The amount of detail always depends on the use of the source. Writers can ask the following questions when determining how best to summarize:

- What is the role of the source in my argument?
  - One example among many other examples?
  - An important tool for helping readers to think a particular way?
  - An illustration of a complex idea?
- How much detail would best illustrate my point?
- How much detail would distract the reader away from my main point or derail the forward movement of my argument?

Notice how Joannie Fischer, in her essay "A Nation Made of Poetry" (pages 248–251), briefly summarizes lengthy literary works to illustrate her points:

> To its credit, America has always shown a great measure of tolerance for such self-criticism. Indeed, even when we have disagreed most vehemently, Americans have tended to agree on basic principles like the right to disagree. Again, Emerson's words have guided us: "Nothing is at last sacred but the integrity of your own mind." Others have created icons of integrity, such as Harper Lee's character Atticus Finch, a southern lawyer who in *To Kill a Mockingbird* defends a black man whom everyone else would scapegoat. Such high principle may be best portrayed by the ultimate American hero, the scrappy Huck Finn, who after much soul-searching decides that the right course of action is to defy all authority and help the runaway slave, Jim, to escape to freedom.

Two novels are boiled down to key statements that fit into Fischer's broader argument. The very short summaries leave out enormous amounts of plot and character detail. But this is appropriate for Fischer's purpose. Had she included further plot summary, her paragraphs would lose focus, and the reader would find it difficult to stay on the track of her main argument.

EXAMPLE SUMMARIES The length of a summary depends upon a writer's purpose. Most often, academic writers summarize in short-passages—boiling down an entire article or book chapter into a paragraph or sentence. Because they want to maintain the forward momentum of their own arguments, they summarize sources quickly. But if a source is critical to the writer's argument, she may slow down and develop a longer summary, detailing key points from the source. The following summaries of Margaret Mead's essay "Warfare: An Invention—Not a Biological Necessity" (pages 118–122) illustrate three possible strategies:

- **Brief Summaries** give a concise rendering of the main idea:

  Margaret Mead argues that warfare is not a biological necessity or a sociological inevitability as some people believe. Instead, it is an invention, like writing or marriage.

- **Longer Summaries** give the main idea of the source and the most important reasoning:

  According to Margaret Mead, warfare, an organized conflict in which members of two groups fight and try to kill opposing members, is not a biological necessity or a sociological inevitability as some people believe. Instead, it is an invention, like writing or marriage. Some societies don't have warfare because they don't have the idea of it. And without the idea, they cannot have the thing.

Ultimately, people go to war not because of particular causes: disputes over land, struggle for power, or the attempt of a leader to gain prestige. They go to war because the idea of war exists in their culture.

Once an invention becomes known and accepted, people resist giving it up. But poor inventions do give way to better ones. First, people must recognize the defects of the old invention; then they must invent something better. Propaganda against warfare and documentation of its costs encourages people to see that warfare is a defective invention. And this allows people to believe that something better is possible.

- **Lengthy Summaries** give the main idea and supporting examples, reasoning, or evidence within the source:

> In her essay, Margaret Mead explains that warfare, an organized conflict in which members of two groups fight and try to kill opposing members, is not a biological necessity or a sociological inevitability as some people believe. Instead, it is an invention, just as writing, marriage, cooking, trial by jury, using fire, or burial is an invention. People tend to think of these universal practices as necessary characteristics of humanity. But they are, in fact, inventions that can be replaced by better inventions that are more in accordance with the feelings and institutions of the times.
>
> According to Mead, some societies don't have warfare, because they don't have the idea of it. Without the idea, they cannot have the thing. Eskimos, for example, have the personality and circumstances that could lead to war: They are simply not mild or meek people; they have fights, murder, and even cannibalism. Yet, they have no warfare. Ultimately, people go to war not because of particular causes: disputes over land, struggle for power, or the attempt of a leader to gain prestige. Instead, they go to war because war exists in their culture. Some might argue that warfare is absent among Eskimos because they have a low and undeveloped form of social organization. But the Pygmy peoples of the Andaman Islands in the Bay of Bengal and the Australian aborigines had a level of social organization similar to the Eskimos, and these two groups did have war simply because the idea of warfare was present.
>
> Once an invention becomes known and accepted, people resist giving it up. But Mead argues that poor inventions do give way to better ones. First, people must recognize the defects of the old invention; then they must propose, or invent, something better. Public arguments against warfare and documentation of its costs encourage people to see that warfare is a defective invention. And this allows people to believe that something better is possible.

Identify which of the following summaries is best (1, 2, or 3), and explain the problems with the other choices.

Original

Organizing a text with sources may seem more difficult than organizing a text that is based exclusively on personal insights. However, the same principles apply: Paragraphs must be coherent, and transitions must be made between points. Whether information is paraphrased, summarized, or directly quoted, it should be blended smoothly into the text so that the reader (1) understands its relationship to the writer's own ideas and (2) knows where the information came from.

1. Organizing a text with sources is more difficult than organizing a text without sources, even though similar rules apply.

2. The same principles apply to organizing a text with or without sources: coherence and transitions are key. Source information should blend smoothly into the writer's ideas.

3. Although organizing a text with sources may seem more difficult than organizing one without sources, the same principles apply. Paragraphs must be coherent. Transitions must exist between points. Paraphrased, summarized, or directly quoted information must be blended smoothly into the writer's text so that the reader can understand its relationship to the writer's ideas and be able to see where the information originally came from.

Paraphrase

Paraphrase is a rewording of the original source using your own words and expressions. Unlike summary, paraphrase covers the detail and complexity of the original text. Following is a passage from Laura Tangley's article "Natural Passions":

> There is "hard" scientific evidence for animal emotions as well. Neuroscientists who study the biology of emotions, a discipline still in its infancy, have discovered key similarities between the brains of humans and other animals. In all species studied so far, including our own, emotions seem to arise from long-evolved parts of the brain—particularly the amygdala, an almond-shaped structure in the brain's center. Working with rats, they have found that stimulating one part of the amygdala invariably induces a state of intense fear. Rats with damaged amygdalae exhibit neither normal behavioral responses to danger (such as freezing or running) nor the physiological changes associated with fear (such as higher heart rate and blood pressure).

A paraphrase of this passage might read:

> Laura Tangley argues that laboratory experiments prove the existence of complex animal emotions. Some neuroscientists have recently begun studying the "biology of emotions" (120) and have found that human and animal brains are very much alike. According to the experiments, emotions come from parts of the brain that evolved long ago and that humans share with many other species. One such part is the amygdala, which rests in the center of the brain. Scientists found they could produce fear in the rats by stimulating parts of the amygdala. But rats with damage to that specific part of the brain lacked the normal range of responses to danger.

The paraphrase restates Tangley's ideas but does so in new language. In such a paraphrase, a writer might find a particular phrase important and quotable (such as "biology of emotions"), but the passage overall is rephrased and slightly summarized. A paraphrase is generally used because a writer wants to share the nuances of the original source but does not want the tone of the original to interfere with or take over his or her own text.

> **Paraphrasing is not merely changing a word or two, or shifting around sentence arts. Paraphrase demands a total rewording of the original source.**

Activity

Identify which of the following paraphrases is best (1, 2, or 3), and explain the problems with the other choices.

Original

Organizing a text with sources may seem more difficult than organizing a text that is based exclusively on personal insights. However, the same principles apply: Paragraphs must be coherent, and transitions must be made between points. Whether information is paraphrased, summarized, or directly quoted, it should be blended smoothly into the text so that the reader (1) understands its relationship to the writer's own ideas and (2) knows where the information came from.

1. Arranging an essay with outside sources is similar to organizing one without sources. For example, paragraphs should be coherent, and transitions should connect ideas. Information from sources (whether paraphrased, summarized, or quoted) must be integrated smoothly into the text so that readers understand how it fits in with the writer's ideas and know where the information came from.

2. Organizing a text with sources may seem harder than organizing one based only on personal insights. But the same guidelines apply: paragraphs have to be coherent, and transitions must exist between points. Whether information is paraphrased, summarized, or directly quoted, it should blend smoothly into the text so that the reader can understand its relationship to the writer's own ideas and know where it came from.

3. Organizing a text with sources is more difficult than organizing one without sources. The same rules apply, though. In both cases, paragraphs have to be coherent, transitions are essential, and information from sources must blend in with your own ideas.

Plagiarism

In short, plagiarism is the act of using other writers' words or ideas without attribution. It is stealing others' ideas in large chunks (entire essays or passages) or in small bits (a sentence or phrase). Whether in small or large chunks, stolen ideas are stolen ideas. To avoid plagiarism, writers must acknowledge their sources (also referred to as "citing" or "crediting" the source) whenever expressing someone else's idea or whenever providing information, such as a fact or statistic, that is not common knowledge. If writers use a source's exact words, they must put those words within quotation marks and credit the source (quotation marks alone are not crediting the source). If the information from the source is rephrased (paraphrased or summarized), it does not require quotation marks but does still require citation.

Most instructors recognize two different types of plagiarism: (1) sloppy paraphrase and (2) intentional theft.

PLAGIARISM TYPE A: SLOPPY PARAPHRASE PLAGIARISM can occur because writers simply do not go far enough in their paraphrasing. That is, they do not sufficiently reword the ideas from the original source. Rather than reword the ideas of the source, they take a phrase here and there, or mimic the sentence structure while changing only a few words. For example, notice the similar phrases and word choice between Tangley's original and the passage after it. The writer does not rephrase Tangley's ideas but merely shifts words around and replaces others.

> **Original** There is "hard" scientific evidence for animal emotions as well. Neuroscientists who study the biology of emotions, a discipline still in its infancy, have discovered key similarities between the brains of humans and other animals. In all species studied so far, including our own, emotions seem to arise from long-evolved parts of the brain—particularly the amygdala, an almond-shaped structure in the brain's center. Working with rats, they have found that stimulating one part of the amygdala invariably induces a state of intense fear. Rats with damaged amygdalae exhibit neither normal behavioral responses to danger (such as freezing or running) nor the physiological changes associated with fear (such as higher heart rate and blood pressure).

> **Sloppy Paraphrase (Plagiarism Type A)** According to Laura Tangley, there is certain scientific evidence for animal emotions. Neuroscientists, who study the biology of emotions, have found important similarities between the brains of humans and other animals. In all species studied, including humans, emotions arise from long-evolved parts of the brain—particularly the amygdala, an almond-shaped piece at the center of the brain. Working with rats, these scientists discovered that stimulating one part of the amygdala induces intense fear. Rats with damaged amygdalae show neither normal behavioral responses to danger (freezing or running) nor physiological changes associated with fear (higher heart rate and blood pressure).

Activity

What punishment is appropriate for intentional theft of others' ideas? As a class, debate this question. As you develop reasoning, consider the following: In a Rutgers survey, over one-quarter of college students admitted to plagiarizing an essay—and nearly 90 percent admitted to cheating on a test or quiz.

The writer of the second passage has only substituted some words and omitted others. This is not paraphrasing at all because the text retains the original flavor and expression of the author. Although the writer mentions Tangley's name, the passage masquerades as the writer's language. Quotation marks are not used, so it suggests that the writer has rephrased the ideas. While it may not seem like an egregious error, the writer has effectively stolen Tangley's language—and academic readers consider this plagiarism.

A paraphrase avoids using the same subjects and verbs as the original text. A good way to do this is to read the original passage carefully, set it aside, and restate the ideas in your own words. Remember that any one idea can be phrased in infinite ways.

PLAGIARISM TYPE B: INTENTIONAL THEFT Writers sometimes plagiarize intentionally because they are desperate to complete an assignment or pass a class. They set out to steal or buy others' ideas. In this age of technology, students can easily download text from an online source or buy essays online. However, such essays are prepackaged, the topics are generalized, and the writing mediocre. Essentially, they are the opposite of what most college instructors want and are contrary to the invention strategies suggested throughout this book. As websites featuring prewritten essays increase, so does the ability of instructors to detect plagiarism.

Remember, the consequences for students caught plagiarizing are severe: Many colleges have campuswide policies that punish intentional plagiarism with course failure, a permanent mark that denotes plagiarism, and expulsion. Such policies make a point: that academia values the honest work of the individual scholar and condemns any attempt to undermine that value system.

Quotation

Quotation, using the exact words of a source, allows writers to add an especially important phrase or passage to their own writing. Quotations can add flair and intensity to an argument. When an argument includes others' language, it suddenly becomes multi-voiced. You might imagine an academic essay like a dramatic reading, with the writer on a stage, speaking to the audience. Occasionally, the writer may step aside momentarily and bring on another speaker to express a particular point, thereby suggesting to readers, "This passage is so important that it should be given center stage." The key is to carefully select what ideas and manner of expression are worth quoting. Generally, writers do not allow quotations to take up more than fifteen percent of their texts, although certain situations may call for more.

When working with others' language, always quote sparingly—and focus on only the most striking parts. Follow these guidelines when using quotations:

- Choose only the most striking or revelatory passages.
- Cut out unnecessary or irrelevant information from the quote (using ellipses if necessary).
- Prune passages. Whenever possible, quote a sentence rather than a paragraph; quote a phrase rather than a full sentence.

Notice how a writer might pull only the most striking phrasing from a passage by Martin Luther King Jr.:

> In his "Letter from Birmingham Jail," Martin Luther King suggests that "human progress never rolls in on wheels of inevitability" (130).

QUOTATION MARKS ONLY When the quoted matter blends directly into your sentence without a speaking verb (*says, exclaims, proclaims, states,* etc.), no punctuation is required before the quotation. The sentence can be punctuated just as it would be if there were no quotation marks:

> We can then see what some more astute and careful readers of Housman's work have seen: namely, that "the undermining of romantic illusions yields first an appalling vision of death's reality which then creates a renewed appreciation of life in all its varied imperfections" (Lindsay 340).

> Quindlen compares the way that Americans act with their animal counterparts today to the way our ancestors once acted toward Native American people. We are willing to "tolerate" them as long as "they don't demand to share" (68).

SPEAKING VERB FOLLOWED OR PRECEDED BY A COMMA Speaking verbs (*say, says, said, exclaims, states,* etc.) indicate a shift from your voice to the voice of your source. In the second example below, *explains* tells the reader that the text is going to shift from the writer's voice to the voice of the source. A comma separates the quotation from the rest of the sentence:

> "Man is primarily an imagemaker," writes James Hillman, "and our psychic substance consists of images; our being is imaginal, an existence in imagination" (qtd. in *Re-Visioning Psychology* 23).

As Martin Luther King Jr. explains in his "Letter from a Birmingham Jail," "One day the South will know that when these disinherited children of God sat down at lunch counters, they were in reality standing up for what is best in the American dream" (43).

A speaking verb combined with a noun creates an attributive phrase that can be placed at the beginning, in the middle, or at the end of a sentence. Quoting involves carefully crafting sentences to create clear and natural-sounding connections between the writer's own ideas and the words of the source. Here are some standard strategies:

Quotation at the Beginning of a Sentence

"All voting is a sort of gaming, like checkers or backgammon, with a slight moral tinge to it," explains Henry David Thoreau (56).

Quotation in the Middle of a Sentence

As Thoreau points out, "all voting is a sort of gaming, like checkers or backgammon, with a slight moral tinge to it" (56), and it is this moral issue that is often overemphasized on ballots.

Quotation at the End of a Sentence

Henry David Thoreau claims that "all voting is a sort of gaming, like checkers or backgammon, with a slight moral tinge to it" (56).

Quotation Divided by Your Own Words

"All voting," explains Thoreau, "is a sort of gaming . . ." (56).

SENTENCE FOLLOWED BY A COLON The colon sets up or introduces the quotation. It tells a reader, "Here comes the quotation." The colon also allows the writer to explain the significance of the quotation beforehand:

One solution, according to Tenenbaum, is pretty simple: "Avoid making excess light, and use reflectors and shields to direct light toward the ground."

As George Williams notes, protection of white privilege is critical to patterns of discrimination: "Whenever a number of persons within a society have enjoyed for a considerable period of time certain opportunities for getting wealth, for exercising power and authority, and for successfully claiming prestige and social deference, there is strong tendency for these people to feel that these benefits are theirs by 'right'" (727).

OMITTING WORDS Occasionally, writers want to quote a passage but leave out words or phrases. This is done by using ellipsis points (three consecutive periods). This construction tells the reader that words have been taken out of the original passage.

Original

When the leaders of a town become focused on economic growth while ignoring social growth, businesses most often win out in the end, and they have very different goals and needs than the average citizen.

Quotation

According to Amber Edmondson, "When the leaders of a town become focused on economic growth . . . businesses most often win out in the end, and they have very different goals and needs than the average citizen" (qtd. in *Inventing Arguments* 312).

The ellipsis indicates the missing phrase. The same strategy can be applied when cutting any amount of text from a quotation. For instance, notice how a whole sentence is removed from Laura Tangley's original passage. In this case, the ellipsis follows a period:

Original

Even scientists who are most opposed to the idea of animal passion acknowledge that many creatures experience "primary emotions"—feelings such as aggression and fear that are instinctive and require no conscious thought. Essential to escaping predators and other dangers, fear, in particular—along with predictable freeze, flight, or fight responses—seems to be hardwired. A laboratory rat that has never encountered a cat, for example, will still freeze if it is exposed to the smell of this predator.

Quotation

As Laura Tangley explains, "Even scientists who are most opposed to the idea of animal passion acknowledge that many creatures experience 'primary emotions'—feelings such as aggression and fear that are instinctive and require no conscious thought. . . . A laboratory rat that has never encountered a cat, for example, will still freeze if it is exposed to the smell of this predator" (118).

ADDING WORDS It is occasionally helpful to add a note or comment within a quote. In this case, writers use square brackets to offset their own words. For example, a writer may insert a word in a quoted passage to clarify a vague pronoun or to give a brief explanation. In the following, the writer substitutes the actual noun for the pronoun "they." Without the noun, the reader may not understand the meaning of the quotation. As in this example, inserting bracketed comments within quotes can clear up any potentially vague information within a quote while maintaining the flow of the sentence:

Original

After months of exhausting research, they had finally come to understand the problem with their design.

Quotation

"After months of exhausting research, [the nuclear scientists] had finally come to understand the problem with their design" (Smith 82).

NOTING AN ERROR If a quotation is grammatically or syntactically flawed, a writer cannot change it. In such cases, the quotation must remain intact, and the writer must use square brackets and the three-letter word *sic* to acknowledge the error. A reader might otherwise assume that the error is on the part of the writer:

But the political party strategist saw things differently: "Even if we had waited on the Senate Arms Committee to release its findings, our move still would of [*sic*] been perceived as political" ("Politics of the Senate" 73).

USING LENGTHY QUOTES When writers quote more than four lines, they must use a block quote. As in this passage from an essay by Jay Harrington, writers often use a colon before block quotes:

> As Pat Blashill notes in *Noise from the Underground:*
>
>> Alternative culture wasn't invented by Nirvana in 1992. They just brought an anthem of disaffection and anger to the top of the charts, to the malls, to the army bases, and into the living rooms of a nation that had spent most of the eighties trying to convince itself that it was a kind and gentle place. . . . America was all about shiny surfaces, and mainstream culture was about as deep as Bobby McFerrin's 1988 hit song, "Don't Worry, Be Happy." . . . Hollywood was again becoming a factory for empty escapism. The bestseller lists were rocked by *Slaves of New York, Less Than Zero,* and *Bright Lights, Big City,* three very hip novels about people with nice clothes, cocaine, and hardly anything to say. (16)

USING DOUBLE QUOTES Occasionally, writers quote a passage that contains a quotation. In this case, single quotation marks are used inside the double quotation marks:

> As Maria Gallagher has argued, "It is time that we turn the corner on the road of national energy policies and begin to take 'alternative energy' seriously" (23).

Blending Information from a Source

Good writers use sources to forward their own arguments. They stay in control of their own writing. They frame the information from the source with their own language and provide commentary about that information. In the following, Tracy Webster refers to the source, gives a main idea from the source, and provides his own commentary on the idea:

> Anna Quindlen says that according to the National Association of Home Builders, "the average American home has doubled in size in the past century." Some see this, no doubt, as a great achievement—a sign of their own and their country's success and prosperity. But family size hasn't doubled; it has decreased. Americans have come to simply want, expect, and possess *more stuff.* And along with this, they cannot merely displace a few animals and live in relative peace with the rest. Instead, they see it as their right to destroy the homes—and what have been the homes for centuries—of more wildlife than a thousand humans have any acceptable reason to destroy, simply because they'd like to have a large and impressive home in a pretty place. Sadly, this is why Quindlen's proposed moratorium is necessary, and why it is the only solution.

In the following passage*, Jennifer Worley sets up a main idea, gives background about a source, refers to the source, gives information from the source, and returns to her main idea:

> Idealization of women is nothing new. Nathaniel Hawthorne's 1846 short story "The Birthmark" illustrated the tragedy of seeking ideal beauty. In the story, a scientist attempts to remove a birthmark from his wife's face in order to perfect her appearance. Although he is successful at ridding the mark, the process kills her. In a recent essay, Chester McCovey discusses "The Birthmark" and its relevance to our own culture:
>
>> As for physical imperfection in the twenty-first century, it seems odd that on one level we promote respect for all sorts of human "imperfections," yet on the another level, we strive as we do to eliminate them whenever we can. It seems odd because so many times they are not imperfections at all. (613)

---

*From Jennifer Worley, "Fantastic Ideals." Reprinted with the permission of the author.

In other words, what we consider imperfections are also what make us unique, which we are told is important. Still, we make great effort to get rid of imperfections so we get closer to the ideal.

Webster and Worley both frame their sources' information and stay in control of the ideas.

Counterarguing Sources

As we explain in Chapter 4, opposition generates argument. Opposing claims, assumptions, and values help writers to invent new points—reasons, counterarguments, concessions, and qualifiers. If they are fortunate (and good researchers), writers can find sources that oppose their own claims. In other words, they can integrate specific language from a source and then counter that language directly.

There are two common strategies for countering sources. First is the *turnabout paragraph*: The writer refers to the source (summarizing, paraphrasing, or quoting), provides some commentary or explanation for the information, and then counters. For example, in his essay (from Chapter 7), Justin James argues against standardized testing. He uses an opposing source, the No Child Left Behind Act. In the following passage, he gives a specific quotation from the Act, provides commentary, and then counters the idea:

> The No Child Left Behind Act of 2001 was well intended, perhaps. Signed by President George W. Bush on January 8, 2001, the act "gives our schools and our country groundbreaking educational reform, based on the following ideals: stronger accountability for results, more freedom for states and communities, encouraging proven education methods, more choice for parents" (United States, Congress). The act has placed an emphasis on accountability, which is being determined by student test results. Test scores might rise. But does that really mean the schools are doing a better job or students are getting a better education? The current emphasis on testing can have harmful results. What's more, the method used to find out the scores teaches students a dangerous definition of *education*.

Another common strategy is to shift paragraphs for the counterargument. In this case, the writer devotes an entire paragraph (sometimes more) to the opposing source. The counterargument, then, comes separately. For example, James could have extended his commentary and then shifted to counterargument in a separate paragraph:

> The No Child Left Behind Act of 2001 was well intended, perhaps. Signed by President George W. Bush on January 8, 2001, the act "gives our schools and our country groundbreaking educational reform, based on the following ideals: stronger accountability for results, more freedom for states and communities, encouraging proven education methods, more choice for parents" (United States, Congress). The act has placed an emphasis on accountability, which is being determined by student test results. Test scores might rise. All the classroom attention, administrative support, and even parent participation might drive performance upward.
>
> But do better standardized tests scores really mean that schools are doing a better job or that students are getting a better education? The answer might be: no, absolutely not. In fact, test scores might only show that students are better (more obedient, more efficient) test-takers. The whole system gets caught up in the process and that process teaches a dangerous definition of *education*, one that students learn whether they know it or not.

Both strategies—keeping the counterargument in the same paragraph or breaking it into a separate paragraph—can be valuable. The decision may come down to how much commentary and counterargument the writer hopes to develop.

Using Textual Cues

Whatever organizational strategy you use, make certain that you distinguish your ideas and claims from those of others. The reader must be able to tell whose ideas are being explained or asserted. Also, make certain you show the relationships between and among sources. In other words, make certain that you use appropriate *textual cues* (sentences, words, and phrases that explain the relationship between ideas, sources, or points in the paper) for the reader.

> Most music critics, *such as Smith, Castella, and Sanchez,* see the latest alternative genres as a collective response to the grunge scene of the early '90s.

The critics listed here have been discussed prior to this sentence, and the writer simply reminds the reader about these voices and how they relate to the present point being made. Simple phrases (like *such as*) cue the reader to make connections between passages in the text.

> Jones's ideas are often seen as radical. Alberta Slavik, *for example,* casts Jones aside as a "hyper-liberal" journalist: "William Jones has gone too far, simply parading his politics at the cost of facts" (76).

The short phrase *for example* helps the reader keep track of the names. The phrase tells the reader, even before the quotation, that Slavik sees Jones's ideas as radical. Textual cues become increasingly important as writers add names and sources to their texts.

Using Paragraph Transitions

Integrating outside sources can make a text more sophisticated, but it can create confusion if the writer does not make clear connections between points. Because outside sources often increase the complexity of a text, paragraph transitions (sentences and phrases that join the content of paragraphs and show the logical connections) become vital to a coherent paper. Transition statements usually begin paragraphs and act as bridges from one paragraph to the next. The following sentences, which all begin paragraphs, act as bridges from previous points. Notice the key transitional words in each sentence: *however, despite, but, because of:*

- Not all farmers, however, agree with Johnson's strategy.
- Despite this overwhelming amount of evidence, some teachers refuse to acknowledge the way gender and race figure into the classroom.
- But all of the discussion on war distracts voters from significant domestic issues that will impact everyday life in the present and future.
- Because of Smith's recent book, many researchers have begun focusing their attention on the ways technology will change our ability to communicate.

John Mauk

14

Documenting Sources

Documenting sources is more than a formatting game. It is a process of sharing one's research path and leaving a trail for readers to follow. Good documentation shows how knowledge works—how ideas get borrowed, built upon, challenged, extended, and questioned. It also shows readers that a writer has conscientiously researched the subject.

In academia, writers must document all information that they gather from an identifiable source. In other words, if the information was found somewhere (anywhere), it must be cited. Academic writers also cite information that is not commonly known. *Common* may be a difficult concept to grasp. But think of common facts as those that could be heard from various sources at any given time. For instance, most people following mainstream news understand that BP owned the oil well that leaked into the Gulf of Mexico in 2010. The basic information is commonly known. But specific dates about the event or specific details about the leak (such as gallons of oil per day) are not commonly known. If such specific information were used in an academic essay, it would need to be cited. And even when academic writers know specialized or detailed information, they cite it. The citation has rhetorical force. It shows that the information can be examined on its own, beyond the framework of the project at hand. The citation also gives readers a place to find out more.

To Cite or Not to Cite: For each statement, decide if the information warrants a formal citation or if it can be considered common knowledge. Also, describe the reason for your answer:

1. The American Civil War divided the country into the Union states and the Confederacy.

2. It is well known that Michael Jackson's *Thriller* has been one of the most "culturally significant" records in history—selling more than 45 million copies throughout the world.

3. In the past ten years, Americans more than tripled their consumption of bottled water.

4. NASA is in charge of space shuttle missions.

5. In the coming week, NASA technicians will replace the shuttle's power drive unit (PDU), which will take up to three days.

6. The American Civil War claimed between 62,000 and 70,000 lives.

7. Michael Jackson, often referred to as the "king of pop," changed mainstream music with his ground-breaking record, *Thriller*.

8. The Onion began its hilarious parodies of American culture in 1988.

Because so many writers and thinkers participate in ongoing scholarly discussions, they need some agreed-upon conventions for sharing information. They need a standardized means of communicating where information has come from, where it is stored, and how it can be retrieved. Think of formal documentation, then, as a set of conventions—a style for sharing information. Like texting, like Morse code, like graffiti, like smoke signals, documentation styles are merely agreed-upon symbols for communicating across time and space.

The two most common documentation styles in academia are MLA (Modern Language Association) and APA (American Psychological Association). Regardless of the particular style of documentation, the basic concepts are the same. After learning the basic concepts, you can quickly learn the specific variations of a style when called upon to use it. Both styles depend on two basic components: (1) an in-text citation of a work and (2) a list of works at the end of the text (called Works Cited in MLA style and References in APA).

> Think of formal documentation as symbols that communicate through time and space.

MLA DOCUMENTATION STYLE

The Modern Language Association documentation style is used in English studies, humanities, and related fields. Each source requires two parts: an in-text citation and a Works Cited entry.

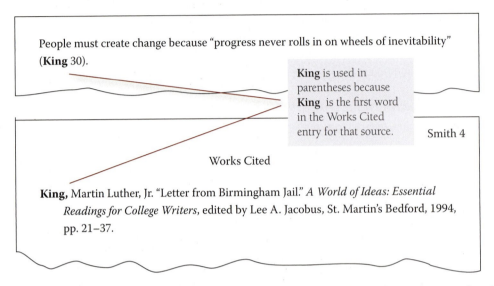

People must create change because "progress never rolls in on wheels of inevitability" (**King** 30).

King is used in parentheses because **King** is the first word in the Works Cited entry for that source.

Smith 4

Works Cited

King, Martin Luther, Jr. "Letter from Birmingham Jail." *A World of Ideas: Essential Readings for College Writers*, edited by Lee A. Jacobus, St. Martin's Bedford, 1994, pp. 21–37.

IN-TEXT CITATION An in-text citation involves referencing the original text in parentheses within the actual sentences of your text. Because the citation uses parentheses, it is sometimes called a *parenthetical citation.* An in-text citation must occur whenever a writer:

- Quotes directly from a source.
- Paraphrases ideas from a source.
- Summarizes ideas from a source.
- References statistics or data from a source.

The basic in-text citation includes the author's (or authors') last name (unless it is given within the sentence) followed by the page number of the source from which the cited material is taken (unless the source is electronic and lacks page numbers):

> A revolution in medieval English poetry was "the gradual detaching of the lyric from music" (Lewis 3).

The end punctuation comes after the citation. Only a space separates the name and the page number.

If the author is referred to in the sentence, the author's name is omitted from the citation:

> Emphasizing her point, Miller demands that "it is now time for something drastic to change here on campus" (43).

If the source has no author, use the first word or phrase of the source's title and punctuate accordingly (quotation marks for articles and italics for books):

> The oil had spread over much of the shoreline and had "already begun its death grip on a vast array of wildlife" ("Black Death" 86).

If the source has two authors, use the last name of both authors:

> (Lunsford and Ede 158)

If the source has more than two authors, use the last name of the first author followed by "et.al." (abbreviation for the Latin *et alii,* "and others"):

> (Margolis et al. 94)

If you have more than one work by the same author, insert a shortened title of the work after the author's name and before the page number:

> (Faigley, *Fragments of Rationality* 43)

If you are citing material that is quoted in the source, cite the source in which you found the quotation and add *qtd. in* before the author name or title:

> (qtd. in Smith 82)

If you want to acknowledge more than one source for the same information, use a semicolon between citations within one set of parentheses:

> (Lunsford and Ede 158; Smith 82)

If you have an electronic source with no page numbers, simply exclude the page number from the citation. Do not add page numbers, and do not use those that a computer printer assigns.

> According to Martha Smith, "untold numbers of children are negatively affected by the proficiency test craze."

WORKS CITED pages list the sources that are directly cited in the text. (Works Consulted pages, on the other hand, list all the sources that a writer has read and digested in the process of researching the project.) The first piece of information in each Works Cited entry should correspond to the in-text citation. In other words, the in-text citation and Works Cited entry should function together to form a trail for the reader to follow. For example, notice the relationship between the in-text citation for King and the entire bibliographic information in the Works Cited, as shown on page 352.

Entries in Works Cited pages must follow strict formatting guidelines, but the process is easy if you know the formulas involved. Although it may not appear so, documentation does follow a pattern. Despite the differences between sources, all entries give the same type of information in the same order, through nine core elements.

The Core Elements

Every source contains some combination of the core elements, but not necessarily all of them. After an overview of the elements, the sections that follow will examine how to identify and format these elements for specific source types.

1. Author.

The person or people who wrote or otherwise created the source—or whose work on the source you are choosing to emphasize. This could be an author, an editor, a director, a composer, a performer, or a narrator. It will usually be a full name but could also be a pseudonym, such as a Twitter handle. Author names are inverted. For two authors, the second author name is not inverted and is listed directly after the first author. List the authors in the order they appear on the title page, not in alphabetical order. For more than two authors, simply add *et al.* after the first name.

- **One author:** Smith, Lynda.
- **Two authors:** Henderson, James, and Willa Henderson.
- **Three or more authors:** Johansen, Sturla, et al.

2. Title of source.

The title of the specific source you are citing. This could be a whole book or a short poem within it, if your focus is on that poem. This could be a specific blog entry or an entire album. Works that are part of a larger whole—for instance, an article within a newspaper—usually use quotation marks, while stand-alone works are set in italics. Titles always come directly after author names, unless no author appears on the source. In this case, the citation begins with the title. The beginning letters of all words are capitalized, except articles, prepositions, coordinating conjunctions, and *to* in infinitives.

- **Article:** "Making Sense of a Sense of Place."
- **Television episode:** "A Streetcar Named Marge."
- **Play:** *The Tragedy of Hamlet, Prince of Denmark.*
- **Book:** *Behavior Disorders of Childhood.*

3. Title of container,

A larger source containing the source you are citing. When you are citing an essay within a book, the container is the book. For an episode of a television show, the container is the series title. An article's container is the title of the periodical or Web site where it appeared. Italicize most container titles.

- **Book:** *Postmodernism: A Reader,*
- **Television show:** *The Simpsons,*
- **Website:** *Poets.org,*

4. Other contributors,

Noteworthy contributors to the work not listed in element one. These may include editors, translators, performers, and so on. Introduce each name (or set of names) with a description of the role played. If listed after element two, capitalize the description; if listed after element three, do not.

- edited by Thomas Docherty,
- performance by Graham Greene and Nicolas van Burek,
- Translated by Caryl Emerson,

5. Version,

Description of a source that appears in more than one version. This element appears most frequently for books that appear in multiple editions. Note that while most books' editions are numbered, some are indicated merely by a descriptor such as "revised" or "expanded." It may also apply to the "director's cut" of a film or a version of software.

- director's cut,
- 15th ed.,
- updated ed.,

6. Number,

Number indicating a source's place in a sequence. This could refer to the volume number of a book that appears in multiple volumes, to the volume and issue numbers of a journal, or to the season and episode numbers for a television show.

- **Television episode:** season 2, episode 1,
- **Book:** vol. 6,
- **Journal Article:** vol. 119, no. 3,

7. Publisher,

Organization that delivers the source to the public. Publishers should be listed for books, films, television shows, and most Web sites, but *not* for periodicals, works published directly by their authors or editors, Web sites for which the publisher's name is the same as the title, or Web sites that do not produce the works they house (such as *YouTube or WordPress*).

- Columbia UP,
- Metropolitan Museum of Art,
- Lucasfilm,

8. Publication date,

When the source was made available to the public. This could mean when a work was published or republished in print or online, or when it was released in theaters or on iTunes, broadcast on television, or performed live. It might be a year, a month, a specific date, or even a specific time.

- 2014,
- Spring 2016,
- 24 Mar. 2015,
- 10 Jan. 2016, 9:30 p.m.,

9. Location.

Where to find the specific source. For a print source, specify location by a page number or page range. For an online source, provide a URL or DOI. (If a DOI is available, you should cite it in preference to a URL. Do not use a URL shortening service such as bit.ly.) This is also the place to record the location of a live performance, the disc number of a work in a DVD set, or another identifier specific to its source type.

- pp. 30–36.
- www.poets.org/poetsorg/text/tell-all-truth-tell-it-slant-first-person-usage-poetry.
- doi:10.1002/cplx.21590.
- Sheraton Hotel, New Orleans.

Finding Source Information

All of the necessary information for books can usually be found on the title and copyright pages.

Inventing Arguments

Version ———— **FOURTH EDITION**

Title of source

John Mauk
Miami University

Author names

John Metz
Kent State University at Geauga

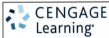 CENGAGE
Learning®

Publisher

Australia • Brazil • Mexico • Singapore • United Kingdom • United States

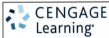 CENGAGE
Learning®

**Inventing Arguments,
Fourth Edition**
John Mauk, John Metz

© 2016, 2013, 2009 Cengage Learning ———— Publication date

WCN: 01-100-101

ALL RIGHTS RESERVED. No part of this work covered by the copyright herein may

Remember that not all sources contain all of the nine core elements, and some of them contain additional or optional elements, which you will learn about in the sections that follow.

Containers within Containers

Some sources are housed in containers within larger containers. For instance, if you cite an article (source) from a journal (container #1) that you accessed through a service like *ProQuest* (container #2), or if you discuss an episode (source) of a television show (container #1) that you accessed on a service like *Netflix* (container #2), then you must include information about that larger container. This will help readers retrace your steps.

To create a works cited entry for a source found in a container within a container, do the following:

- List core elements 1 (author) and 2 (title of source).
- List core elements 3–9 for the first container.
- List core elements 3–9 for the second container.

In the following example, a writer has identified and ordered source information for a television episode using the core elements. She used this process to create a works cited entry.

SOURCE

1.	Author.	Dan Nowak.
2.	Title of source.	"Unraveling."

CONTAINER 1

3.	Title of container,	*The Killing*,
4.	Other contributors,	directed by Lodge Kerrigan,
5.	Version,	
6.	Number,	season 4, episode 2,
7.	Publisher,	AMC,
8.	Publication date,	1 Aug. 2014.
9.	Location.	

CONTAINER 2

3.	Title of container,	*Netflix*,
4.	Other contributors,	
5.	Version,	
6.	Number,	
7.	Publisher,	

8. Publication date,

9. Location.   www.netflix.com/watch/70306003.

WORKS CITED ENTRY

Dan Nowak. "Unraveling." *The Killing,* directed by Lodge Kerrigan, season 4, episode 2, AMC, 1 Aug. 2014. *Netflix,* www.netflix.com/watch/70306003.

Practice Template for MLA Entries

1. Author.

2. Title of source.

CONTAINER I

3. Title of container,

4. Other contributors,

5. Version,

6. Number,

7. Publisher,

8. Publication date,

9. Location.

CONTAINER 2

3. Title of container,

4. Other contributors,

5. Version,

6. Number,

7. Publisher,

8. Publication date,

9. Location.

Optional Elements

- **Date of original publication.** This may be useful as it provides your reader with historical context and shows where the work stands in relation to other published works. In this case, insert the original publication date after the title, followed by a period, and then give the recent publisher and date.

Tolkien, J. R. R. The Hobbit. 1937. Ballantine Books, 1982.

- **City of publication**. While the city of publication is no longer a standard element of MLA citation, it can occasionally be of use to your readers. A publisher with offices in more than one country may release more than one version of a book—for instance, a British version and an American version, using different spelling and vocabulary. In this case, listing the city of publication will help readers identify the source. The city of publication is listed before the publisher and is followed by a comma.

Rowling, J.K. *Harry Potter and the Philosopher's Stone*. London, Bloomsbury, 1997.

- **Date of access**. The date of access can be important when an online source has no publication date, is likely to be changed over time (such as a wiki entry), or is likely to be removed (e.g., a television episode temporarily available through a service such as *Hulu*). The date of access is listed at the end of an entry, in the format "Accessed 29 March 2016."
- **Series name**. If a book is part of a named series, it may be significant for your readers to understand that context. After the location, include the series name and the series number (if any) followed by a period.

Vance, John A. *Joseph and Thomas Warton*. Edited by Sarah Smith, Twayne-Hall, 1983. Twayne English Authors Series 380.

- **Other optional elements**. Other useful elements could include a work's prior publication history or a description of its type when that type might be unexpected (e.g., lecture, transcript). A particular works cited entry may benefit from another element not discussed here. You must use your judgment in determining which information would be useful to your readers.

Citations beyond the Research Paper

Your work throughout college may take other forms than the research paper. Here are some guidelines to citing your sources in other formats. Though there may be more than one correct way to document sources, your goal is always to provide information that is useful to your readers, enabling them to find the sources that underlie your work.

- **Video**. In a video, you can give a brief identification of a source as a text overlay at the bottom of the screen, before including full documentation in your closing credits. For example, the overlay might give the name of an interview subject or the director and title of a video clip.
- **Slide-based presentation**. When making a presentation using software such as *PowerPoint* or *Keynote*, you can give a shortened citation on each slide to identify any borrowed material. Then you

can include a complete works cited list on the concluding slide. To ensure the audience has further access to your works cited list, you might provide a printed handout or the URL link to an online posting.

- **Web projects.** In an interactive Web project, you can link any citation of online materials directly to their original sources. It is recommended that you still include a works cited list at the end of your project.

Sample Works Cited Entries

Author Title of source

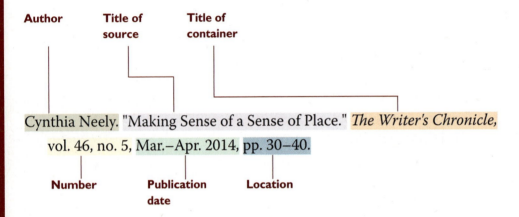

WORK WITH AUTHOR

Palmeri, Jason. *Remixing Composition: A History of Multimodal Writing Pedagogy.* Southern Illinois UP, 2012.

The author name is inverted.

WORK WITH AUTHOR AND ADDITIONAL CONTRIBUTOR

Busch, Frederick. *The Stories of Frederick Busch.* Edited by Elizabeth Strout, Norton, 2014.

Bakhtin, Mikhail. *Problems of Dostoevsky's Poetics.* Translated by Caryl Emerson, U of Minnesota P, 1998.

The names of other contributors are not inverted.

Tour Book: New Jersey and Pennsylvania. American Automobile Association, 2001.

United States, Department of Labor, Bureau of Labor Statistics. *Nontraditional Education: Alternative Ways to Earn Your Credentials.* Government Publishing Office, 2003.

When the author and publisher are separate organizations, list both. When they are the same, use the name of the corporation as the publisher name, omitting the author element. For government publications, list the name of the government first, followed by the agency. Many federal publications are published by the Government Publishing Office.

Wicks-Nelson, Rita, and Allen C. Israel. *Behavior Disorders of Childhood.* 4th ed., Prentice, 2007.

Find the edition information on the title page of the book. Use the abbreviations *2nd ed., 3rd ed.,* and so on, or *Revised ed.* for "Revised edition," depending on what the title page says.

McCreight, M. I. *Chief Flying Hawk's Tales: The True Story of Custer's Last Fight.* Alliance Press, 1936. *The Online Books Page,* edited by John Mark Ockerbloom, U of Pennsylvania, onlinebooks.library.upenn.edu/webbin/book/lookupid?key=olbp17194.

If the book is part of an online scholarly project, which is often the case, include the sponsoring institution.

Docherty, Thomas, editor. *Postmodernism: A Reader.* Columbia UP, 1993.

If you are citing the entire anthology, begin with the name of the editor or editors and then give all the usual information for a book.

CHAPTER FROM AN ANTHOLOGY

Laclau, Ernesto. "Politics and the Limits of Modernity." *Postmodernism: A Reader*, edited by Thomas Docherty, Columbia UP, 1993, pp. 329–43.

If you are only citing a chapter from an anthology, begin with the author and title of the chapter. Then give the title of the container (the book) and other relevant elements, including the page range of the chapter as its location.

ARTICLE IN A NEWSPAPER OR MAGAZINE

Gabriel, Trip. "Learning in Dorm, Because Class Is on the Web." *The New York Times*, 4 Nov. 2010, pp. A1+, www.nytimes.com/2010/11/05/us/05college.html?_r=0.

Stanglin, Douglas, and Amy Bernstein. "Making the Grade." *U.S. News and World Report*, vol. 121, no. 18, 4 Nov. 1996, p. 18.

Add the city name in square brackets if it does not appear in the title of the newspaper and the newspaper is local. Add section letters before the page numbers. If the page numbers are not consecutive, list the first page number, immediately followed by a plus sign.

ARTICLE IN A JOURNAL

Leonard, Rebecca Lorimer. "Multilingual Writing as Rhetorical Attunement." *College English*, vol. 76, no. 3, Jan. 2014, pp. 227–47.

Ryu, Dongwan. "Play to Learn, Learn to Play: Language Learning through Gaming Culture." *Recall*, vol. 25, no. 2, May 2013, pp. 286–301, doi: 10.1017/S0958344013000050.

Silva, Mary Cipriano, and Ruth Ludwick. "Interstate Nursing Practice and Regulation: Ethical Issues for the 21st Century." *Online Journal of Issues in Nursing*, vol. 5, no. 3, 2 July 1999, www.nursingworld.org/MainMenuCategories/ANAMarketplace/ANAPeriodicals/OJIN/Columns/Ethics/InterstateNursingPracticeandRegulation.html.

If an academic journal provides both the volume and issue numbers, provide both in your citation. Otherwise, simply provide the volume number.

ABSTRACT

Zsolnai, Laszlo. "Honesty versus Cooperation: A Reinterpretation of the Moral Behavior of Economics Students." Abstract. *The American Journal of Economics and Sociology,* vol. 62, no. 4, Oct. 2003, pp. 707–12. *JSTOR,* www.jstor.org/stable/3487759.

Include the information for the source in the appropriate format. Add the description Abstract following the source title.

ARTICLE REPRINTED IN AN ANTHOLOGY (CONTAINER WITHIN A CONTAINER)

Faigley, Lester. "Judging Writing, Judging Selves." *College Composition and Communication,* vol. 40, no. 4, Dec. 1989, pp. 395–412. *Landmark Essays on Voice and Writing,* edited by Peter Elbow, Hermagoras Press, 1994, pp. 107–20.

First use the basic article format with the information of the original publication in a periodical—the first container. Then add the information for the anthology—the second container.

ENCYCLOPEDIA ARTICLE

"Writing." *Encyclopaedia Britannica,* 15th ed., 2005.

Begin with an author name (inverted) if one is given. (Check for author names at the beginning or end of the article.) Put the title of the article in quotation marks, and italicize the encyclopedia title.

PAMPHLET

Masonic Information Center. *A Response to Critics of Freemasonry.* Masonic Services Association.

Give information in the same format as a book or other source.

PERSONAL INTERVIEW

Wells, Carson. Personal interview. 4 Mar. 2014.

Begin with the name of the interviewee, inverted. End with the interview date.

PERSONAL LETTER OR MEMO

Shimerda, Antonia. Letter to the Author. 15 Nov. 2013.

Like all sources, begin with the author name (inverted). Then give the title or description of the letter.

PUBLISHED LETTER

Tolkien, J. R. R. "To Christopher Tolkien." 18 Jan. 1944. *The Letters of J. R. R. Tolkien*, edited by Humphrey Carpenter and Christopher Tolkien, Houghton Mifflin, 2000, pp. 67–68.

List the information of the source in which the letter was published, according to the correct format for the source. (In the example above, the container is a book.)

E-MAIL

Miller, Maria. "Changes to Physics Dept." Received by Dennis John, 23 Nov. 2013.

Begin with the author of the e-mail. Then list the title (in quotation marks) that appears in the subject line of the e-mail, the name of the recipient, and the date the e-mail was sent.

TELEVISION PROGRAM

"A Streetcar Named Marge." *The Simpsons*, directed by Rich Moore, season 4, episode 2, FOX, 1 Oct. 1992.

Begin with the title of the episode or segment (in quotation marks). Italicize the title of the program. Name the creator, producer, director, narrator, performer, or writer, depending on whose contributions are most pertinent to your focus.

FILM

Monty Python's The Meaning of Life. Directed by Terry Jones and Terry Gilliam, Universal Pictures, 1983.

Films are often produced and distributed by more than one company. Cite the principal distributor with overall responsibility for the film.

SOUND RECORDING

Griffin, Patty. "Trapeze." *Children Running Through*, ATO Records, 2007.

Begin with the artist's name. Then list the title of a particular song or section (in quotation marks), the collection title (italicized), the recording company, and the year of release. All of this information is available on the product sleeve or insert.

LECTURE OR SPEECH

Pamuk, Orhan. "My Father's Suitcase." Swedish Academy, 7 Dec. 2006, Stockholm. Nobel lecture.

End the citation with a descriptive label (such as *Address* or *Lecture*).

ADVERTISEMENT

Horseshoe Casino. Advertisement. *Cincinnati Magazine*, Sept. 2013, p. 19.

Begin with the company or product name, followed by *Advertisement*. Then list the relevant publication information.

WORK OF ART (PAINTING, SCULPTURE, PHOTOGRAPH)

O'Keefe, Georgia. *Evening Star No. VI.* 1917, Georgia O'Keefe Museum, Santa Fe.

Include the artist's name (inverted), the title of the work (italicized), the date of composition, the collector or institution that houses it, and the city where it is held. (Omit the city if it is part of the institution's name.)

PERFORMANCE

Steinbeck, John. *Of Mice and Men.* Directed by Martha Henry, performances by Graham Greene and Nicolas van Burek, 21 June 2007, Tom Patterson Theatre, Stratford.

Give the date and the site of the performance.

WEBSITE

Bioneers. Collective Heritage Institute, 2015, www.bioneers.org.

McNair, Patricia. *Things Writerly and Readerly.* 2011–2016, patriciaannmcnair.com.

The title of the site is italicized. If the site has no title, offer a description, such as *Home page* (not italicized) in its place. The publisher is often a sponsoring or supporting institution or organization. Omit the publisher if it is essentially the same as the site title.

BLOG OR PAGE FROM A WEBSITE

Marvin, Cate. "'Tell All the Truth but Tell It Slant': First-Person Usage in Poetry." *Poets.org*, Academy of American Poets, 21 Feb. 2005, www.poets.org/poetsorg/text/tell-all-truth-tell-it-slant-first-person-usage-poetry.

Brown, Fleda. "My Wobbly Bicycle, 68." *Fleda Brown*, 9 Apr. 2014, fledabrown.com/2014/04/my-wobbly-bicycle-68.

Begin with the author (if available) or, if unavailable, the title of the article. Next, give the name of the website.

ONLINE PRESENTATION OR VIDEO

Denton, Crystal. "WeVideo Sample." *Vimeo*, 21 Aug. 2012,
vimeo.com/47979624.

Groshelle, Zane. "Visualizing Your Pitch." *Prezi*, 19 Feb. 2015, prezi.com/
oerqtrj5ie3y/visualizing-your-pitch.

"Julia Louis-Dreyfus and Joe Biden: White House Correspondents'
Dinner 2014." HBO, 3 May 2014. *YouTube*, www.youtube.com/
watch?v=da5tjfpKyac. Accessed 13 April 2016.

Give the date of access if the work is likely to be changed or removed.

The information in the in-text citation should correspond directly with the References page (the APA equivalent of a Works Cited page).

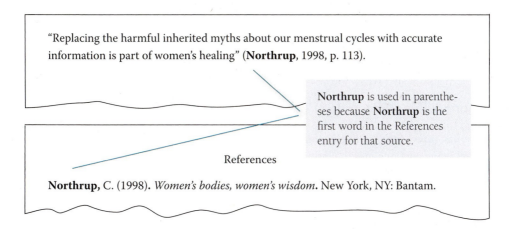

"Replacing the harmful inherited myths about our menstrual cycles with accurate information is part of women's healing" (**Northrup**, 1998, p. 113).

Northrup is used in parentheses because **Northrup** is the first word in the References entry for that source.

References

Northrup, C. (1998). *Women's bodies, women's wisdom.* New York, NY: Bantam.

IN-TEXT CITATION In-text documentation for APA involves referencing the original text in parentheses within the actual sentences of your text. An in-text citation must occur whenever a writer:

- Quotes directly from a source.
- Paraphrases ideas from a source.
- Summarizes ideas from a source.
- References statistics or data from a source.

For direct quotes, APA in-text citations should include the author's name, date (year only) of the source, and page number from which the cited material is taken. Unless an electronic source is based on a print source (as in a PDF), omit page numbers from the in-text citation when not given online. Include the author's name in the citation unless it is given within the sentence.

> "After months of exhausting research, they had finally come to understand the problem with their design" (Smith, 1998, p. 82).

Commas separate elements within the parentheses. The abbreviation *p.* ("page") or *pp.* ("pages") comes before the actual page number(s). End punctuation comes after the parenthetical citation.

Writers using APA style often include the date directly after the author's name in the sentence because timeliness is so important to researchers in the social sciences and other fields that use APA style.

> Emphasizing her point, Miller (2000) demands that "it is now ti.me for something drastic to change here on campus" (p. 43).

If the source has no author, use the first words of the source title and punctuate the title accordingly (either with quotation marks or italics).

> "Even though most of the nation's coastal shorelines can no longer sustain a full range of sea life, the vast majority of Americans seem unconcerned" ("Dead Seas," 2001, p. 27).

If the source has two authors, use the last name of both authors. Notice that APA style uses an ampersand (&) instead of the word *and* in parenthetical citations.

> (Lunsford & Ede, 1994, p. 158)

If the source has three, four, or five authors, use the last name of all authors in your first parenthetical citation. In following citations, use the last name of the first author, followed by *et al.* and the year.

> (Sanger, Cunningham, & Toy, 2003, p. 46)

> (Sanger et al., 2003, p. 46)

If the cited material is quoted in another source, cite the source in which you found the quotation and add *as cited in* before the author name or title:

> (as cited in Smith, 2014, p. 82)

If you want to acknowledge more than one source for the same information, use a semicolon between citations within one set of parentheses. List the authors alphabetically. If you are citing more than one work by the same author, list the citations by date, separated by commas:

> (Lunsford & Ede, 2003; Smith, 2014)

> (Parkinson, 2013, 2002)

REFERENCES The reference list includes the sources that are directly cited in the text. (A bibliography, on the other hand, lists all the sources that a writer has read and digested in the process of researching the project.) The first piece of information in each References entry should correspond to the in-text citation. For example, on page 367, notice the relationship between the in-text citation for Northrup and the entire bibliographic information in the References list.

Entries in a References list must follow strict formatting guidelines, but the process is easy if you know the formulas involved. Despite the differences between sources, all entries give the same type of information in the same order:

1. Author name
2. Date of publication
3. Title of the work

4. Title of the bigger work (book, magazine, newspaper, etc.), if applicable

5. Page numbers, if applicable

6. Place of publication or distribution

7. Publishing or broadcasting company

8. For electronic sources: Retrieval date (if source is likely to change) and DOI (digital object locator) or homepage URL

Each type of source (book, journal article, online magazine, etc.) may require some slight changes in the formula, but the order of information always follows the above pattern. Also, all entries (regardless of the source) adhere to a definite format.

- **Author names, inverted, come first.** First and middle names are always indicated with initials only. Unlike MLA style, all author names are inverted.

- **Dates come in parentheses directly after the author name.** If no author appears on the source, the title comes first.

- **Title of the work comes directly after the date.** Article titles are always in regular type without quotation marks, while the sources in which they appear—newspapers, books, magazines, and journals—are italicized. Only the first letter of the title is capitalized in article and book titles except for proper nouns. For newspaper, magazine, and journal titles, capitalize all words longer than three letters.

- **Publication information follows the title of the source.**

- **If the source is a print article, page numbers come last.** If the source is electronic, the date of access (if needed) and DOI or URL come last.

Printed Books

All of the necessary information for books can usually be found on the title and copyright pages, which are inside the front cover.

GENERAL FORMAT

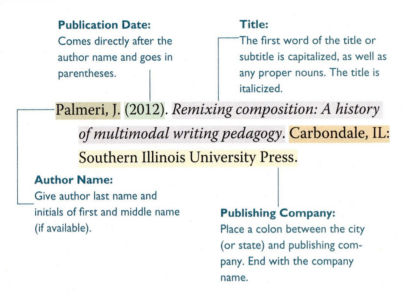

Publication Date:
Comes directly after the author name and goes in parentheses.

Title:
The first word of the title or subtitle is capitalized, as well as any proper nouns. The title is italicized.

Palmeri, J. (2012). *Remixing composition: A history of multimodal writing pedagogy.* Carbondale, IL: Southern Illinois University Press.

Author Name:
Give author last name and initials of first and middle name (if available).

Publishing Company:
Place a colon between the city (or state) and publishing company. End with the company name.

TWO OR MORE AUTHORS

McKee, H. A., & Porter, J. E. (2009). *The ethics of Internet research: A rhetorical, case-based approach.* New York, NY: Peter Lang Press.

Add any additional author names, also inverted, before the title.

CORPORATE AUTHOR

Federation of U.S. Midwives. (2001). *Listening to the mother.* Heathrow, FL: Author.

Use the name of the corporation for the author name. If the corporate author also published the text, write *Author* for the publisher.

SUBSEQUENT EDITIONS

Lauwers, J., & Swisher, A. (2010). *Counseling the nursing mother* (5th ed.). Sudbury, MA: Jones and Bartlett.

Find the edition information on the title page of the book, and write the information in the entry directly after the title. Use abbreviations *2nd ed., 3rd ed.,* and so on, or *Rev. ed.* for "Revised edition."

Beer, M. B., & Nohria, N. S. (Eds.). (2000). *Breaking the code of change.* Boston, MA: Harvard Business School Press.

Use the editor's name (last name and first and middle initials) and *Ed.* (for "editor").
Use *Eds.* ("editors") if the book has more than one editor.

TRANSLATED BOOK

Freire, P. (1995). *Pedagogy of the oppressed* (M. B. Ramos, Trans.). New York, NY: Continuum. (Original work published 1970).

Add the translator's name (first and middle initials and last name) and *Trans.* (all in parentheses) after the title of the book.

Printed Articles

Articles appear in newspapers and periodicals (journals or magazines). While newspapers are usually published daily, magazines are usually published weekly or monthly, and journals are published quarterly or even biannually.

ARTICLE IN A MAGAZINE

Appenzeller, T. (2007, June). The big thaw. *National Geographic, 211,* 56–71.

Include the date (year, month, day) directly after the author name. Do not abbreviate months. Give the volume number in italics after the magazine title, followed by issue number (if available) in parenthesis. End with the page numbers of the article.

ARTICLE IN A NEWSPAPER

Swartz, J. (2014, May 5). Market won't friend social media. *USA Today,* B1.

If no author appears, give the title of the article first, followed by the date. After the title of the newspaper, include any section letters before the page numbers.

ARTICLE IN A JOURNAL PAGINATED CONTINUOUSLY

Most academic journals number the pages of each issue continuously through an annual volume. The second issue does not begin with page 1, but with the number after the last page of the previous issue.

Fiske, S. T. (2010). Envy up, scorn down: How comparison divides us. *American Psychologist, 65,* 698–706.

Place the volume number in italics directly after the journal title, before the page numbers.

Batt, H. W. (2001). Value capture as a policy tool in transportation economics. In L. S. Moss (Ed.), *City and country* (pp. 195–228). Malden, MA: Blackwell.

After the author and date, give the title of the article/chapter. Then write *In* and the first and middle initials and last name of the editor(s). The abbreviation *Ed.* or *Eds.* (in parentheses) should follow the editor(s). End with the title of the book, the page numbers on which the article or chapter appears, and the publication information.

ENCYCLOPEDIA ARTICLE

Aesthetics. (2005). In *Encyclopaedia Britannica* (15th ed., Vol. 13, pp. 9–23). Chicago, IL: Encyclopaedia Britannica.

Begin with the author (if given) and date. Then give the title of the article. The name of the encyclopedia (after *In*) should be in italics. The volume number and page number(s) should be in parentheses.

Other Sources

BROCHURE

Masonic Information Center. (n.d.). *A response to critics of freemasonry* [Brochure]. Silver Spring, MD: Masonic Services Association.

Use *n.d.* to indicate "no date," which is often necessary for brochures. After the title, add the descriptor *Brochure* in square brackets before the publication information.

PERSONAL INTERVIEW OR LETTER

APA style recommends citing personal communications only with in-text citations—not in the References. In the in-text citation, give the name of the interviewee, the title *personal communication*, and the date.

(L. Jackson, personal communication, March 4, 2010).

TELEVISION PROGRAM

Martin, J. (Writer), & Moore, R. (Director). (1992). A streetcar named Marge [Television series episode]. In A. Jean & M. Reiss (Producers), *The Simpsons.* Los Angeles, CA: Twentieth Century Fox.

Begin with the name and title of the script writer, then the name and title of the director and the date. Give the title of the episode or segment, followed by *Television series episode* in square brackets. Next, list the producer and the title of the program (italicized). End with the city and state (of the broadcasting company) and the company name.

GOVERNMENT PUBLICATION

U.S. Census Bureau. (2010). *Statistical abstract of the United States.* Washington, DC: U.S. Government Printing Office.

If no author is given, use the government agency as the author, followed by the date, the title (in italics), and the publication information that appears on the title page. If a report number is given, include that information in parenthesis just after the title.

Electronic Sources

As with print sources, citations for electronic sources require author(s), publication date, title, and publication information. Authors and titles are formatted in the same manner as print sources. The difference occurs with publication information: Publishers of electronic work sometimes assign a digital object identifier, which is a kind of persistent virtual address. The DOI is sometimes, not always, located at the top of the article. If a source has a DOI, you need not include a retrieval date or URL. If no DOI was assigned, however, provide a URL. When adding the URL to your citation, break it only before punctuation and do not add hyphens. The APA Style Guide says, "No retrieval date is necessary for content that is not likely to be changed or updated, such as a journal article or book." In other words, if the content is likely to stay the same, no retrieval date is needed. Especially with electronic sources, remember the basic principle behind citing sources: *to provide a guide for finding the sources you used.*

Activity

In small groups, discuss the following:

1. The APA Style Guide urges researchers not to put the name of a database in a reference—even if the source was retrieved from a database. Imagine APA's reasoning.

2. APA invites researchers to use DOIs when possible. But much of the information on the Internet has not been assigned a DOI. How would you, then, deal with that discrepancy?

3. Given that style guides like those of MLA and APA cannot account for every emerging type of source, what should researchers do? How should writers and researches develop a uniform strategy for documenting their work?

ARTICLE IN AN ONLINE JOURNAL OR RETRIEVED FROM A DATABASE

Nolan, K. P., & Harold, C. M. (2010, September). Fit with what? The influence of multiple self-concept images on organizational attraction. *Journal of Occupational & Organizational Psychology, 83,* 645–662. doi:10.1348/096317909X465452

Wright, Jr., K. P., McHill, A. W., Birks, B. R., Griffin, B. R., Rusterholz, T., & Chinoy, E. D. (2013, August 19). Entrainment of the human circadian clock to the natural light-dark cycle. *Current Biology, 23*(16), 1554–1558. doi:10.1016/j.cub.2013.06.039

If the article has been assigned a *digital object identifier* (DOI), place that after the period that follows the page number, even if you accessed the article in print.

Pavur, Claude. (2009, November). Classical Humanism has everything to do with justice. *Electronic Antiquity, 13*(1). Retrieved from http://scholar.lib.vt.edu/ejournals/ElAnt

If the article does not have a DOI assigned, include the URL for the journal's home page after the words *Retrieved from*. If the journal is published only electronically, it may not have page numbers, in which case none appear in the References entry.

OFFICIAL WEBSITE

American Society for Aesthetics. (n.d.). *Aesthetics on-line.* Retrieved August 10, 2010, from http://www.aesthetics-online.org

As with all sources in APA format, begin with the author's or editor's name(s) (inverted), if available, and the date of electronic publication. Give the title of the site (italicized). Write *Retrieved* and then the date of access (if the information is likely to be edited or revised), followed by *from* and the URL (no final period).

DOCUMENT FROM WEBSITE (AUTHOR OR DATE STATED)

Seligson, H. (2014, 4 May). High manxiety: Thirtysomething men are the new neurotic singles." Retrieved May 6, 2014 from http://www.thedailybeast.com/

Begin with the author name (normal APA format), followed by the date (in parentheses), the title of the specific document, the word *Retrieved*, the access date if necessary, *from* and the URL.

DOCUMENT FROM WEBSITE (NO AUTHOR OR DATE STATED)

Equestrian handbook. (n.d.) Retrieved April 28, 2014 from http://www.sca.org/

Begin with the title. In place of the date, write *n.d.* in parentheses for "no date." Then, give the title of the specific document (if applicable), *Retrieved* and the access date if necessary, and finally *from* and the URL.

McNair, P. (2014, May 4) *Patricia Ann McNair: On all things writerly and read-erly*. Retrieved May 6, 2014, from patriciaannmcnair.com/

Begin with the creator's name, followed by the date of the most recent update, the title, *Retrieved*, the date of access if needed, and *from* and the URL.

ONLINE PRESENTATION OR VIDEO

Groshelle, Z. (2014, April 23). *Visualizing your pitch* [Prezi slides]. Retrieved from prezi.com/oerqtrj5ie3y/visualizing-your-pitch/

Denton, C. (2012, August 21). *WeVideo sample* [Video file]. Retrieved from vimeo.com/47979624

HBO. (2014, May 3). *Julia Louis-Dreyfus and Joe Biden: White House corre-spondents' dinner 2014* [Video file]. Retrieved from https://www.youtube.com/watch?v=da5tjfpKyac

Give the author or corporate name, date of publication, and the title of presentation in italics. Then give the digital file format in brackets, *Retrieved from,* and the URL.

SAMPLE RESEARCH ESSAYS

Sample MLA-Style Research Essay

Samantha Tengelitsch
Professor Jones
English 111
17 December 2013

Sage Femme: An Argument in Support of Home Birth

Last Sunday, I gave birth at home. It was my third baby, second homebirth. Nobody delivered my baby; I did it—on my bed, holding on to my husband with the support of a certified midwife and her apprentice. My children were in the other room sleeping soundly. My mother was downstairs on the couch, waiting to hear the baby's first cries. Another friend, who had helped watch my children as I labored throughout the day, slept on the floor beside the bed where my children slept. The dog took little notice. Laboring and birthing at home seemed as normal as the spaghetti we had had for dinner that night.

My husband and I chose homebirth for our second and third babies and a local midwife to serve as guardian over these births. The practice of midwifery is ancient. Midwives have attended women at home for hundreds of thousands of years, with knowledge passed from one generation to the next. The majority of traditional midwives are educated through apprenticeships. They understand that birth is a normal event in a woman's life and allow this process to unfold naturally with little to no intervention.

In other countries around the world women labor and birth in the safety and comfort of their own homes. Consequently, women in these countries experience less obstetrical intervention and lower infant/maternal mortality rates. One study conducted in the Netherlands reported that "women who had given birth previously had significantly better outcomes in planned home births" (Brodsky 92). Sound scientific evidence has proven in recent years that midwives are as safe as or safer than doctors for primary care and using midwives greatly reduces the rates of unnecessary obstetrical interventions (Wagner 1226). Despite this, the United States has seen a dramatic decrease in home-based maternity care in the last century: In 1900 less than five percent of women gave birth in a hospital; by 1940 half of all women, and seventy-five percent of all urban women, had their children in a hospital (Edmonson and Kassen). While the United States Centers for Disease Control reports a slight increase in home births for the period 2005–06, they accounted for only 0.59% of all births (MacDorman et al. 12).

Begins with personal narrative

Provides relevant background information about midwifery.

Uses research to argue about advantages of homebirth..

Tengelitsch 2

The decline of midwifery in the United States from the early 1900s to the present is due in part to misconceptions about midwifery and in part to the introduction of man-midwives (later called "obstetricians") into the birth space. Significant advancements at the turn of the century in human understanding of the anatomy and physiology of birth helped spur the *medicalization* of childbirth. In her article "The Home-birth Choice," Jill Cohen writes:

> Since women were barred from attending medical schools, men became the birth practitioners. Having never had a baby themselves, they were unable to approach women and childbirth with the inner knowledge and experience of a woman. Childbirth became viewed as pathological rather than natural. Medical techniques and interventions that were unnecessary and often dangerous became commonplace.

Provides background on the mainstream perspective of childbirth.

Midwifery changed rapidly as midwives were unable to obtain licensures and in some cases even forbidden to legally practice.

When my husband and I first informed our family of the decision to have our second child at home, the question most often posed was, "Why would you want to do that?" There was confusion over why I wanted to experience birth, including the pain of labor. And despite the evidence for the safety of homebirth, misconceptions lingered that homebirth was dangerous and that we were somehow putting our baby at risk. The opposition came for the most part from the older generation; a generation mostly numb to birth, women who were unconscious or semi-conscious for their deliveries, having been given analgesics like Twilight Sleep.

Description of hospital protocol for childbirth

When their generation was giving birth to ours, hospital protocols called for women to deliver on their backs, their feet in stirrups, their genital hair was shaved, they were given enemas, their perineum was surgically cut, and their babies were often pulled from their bodies with steel forceps as the drugs severely depressed the body's natural urge to "bear down." It is no wonder women of this generation elected to forget the experience of childbirth. Although they were home-born babies themselves, by the time these women were of childbearing age, a medical model had taken the place of midwifery and the hospital swiftly overshadowed home as the most appropriate place to give birth.

When men entered the attendant space, the beauty and empowerment of birth was stripped away in favor of procedure and positions that were better suited for the attendant, rather than the laboring woman. Hospitals enacted protocols to ensure delivery of the baby within twenty-four hours of admittance into the maternity ward. Some of these protocols included inducement or augmentation of labor with synthetic hormones, routine episiotomy, and delivery by Cesarean. The percentage of women in the United States who give birth by major abdominal surgery soared from 5.5% in 1970 to an astounding 32.8% in 2012, according to the United States Centers for Disease Control (Goer 21; Osterman and Martin 2). That is, nearly a third of babies born in the United States today are born surgically. Women are left in the dark about the looming risks of hemorrhage or infection and the ongoing pain associated with major abdominal surgery.

Provides a government statistic as support.

Birth is almost taboo in American culture. The movie and television portrayal of labor and birth is so far askew from normal that it is no wonder women are choosing an intrusive approach to delivering their babies. But I hoped for something less invasive and institutional. When my husband and I found out we were expecting our first baby, we researched our options. We knew we wanted a natural birth and read everything we could find on the topic. It was then that I first noticed a peculiar trend: The books written from the obstetrical point of view emphasized what would be done to me, while the books about homebirth were typically written by women or midwives and told the stories of their births.

Makes an evaluative distinction between the secondary sources on the topic.

These books were inspirational and renewed within me a trust in the process. We interviewed a homebirth midwife, but pressure from our families and the misrepresentation of birth as dangerous in the media deterred us from having the baby at home. We choose to labor in the hospital with a CNM, a certified nurse-midwife. The experience wasn't unpleasant, though we were offered drugs (despite the fact that we had insisted on none) and I was kept on the electronic fetal monitor for short durations throughout the labor, which meant I had to be on my back. Prior to my labor, I had gone so far as to call the hospital to request a list of all procedures and standard protocols. We went in knowing what to expect, armed with knowledge and a newly inspired trust in my body.

As that first labor progressed to the pushing stage, the nurse-midwife had me push while on my back or on my side, but I just wasn't moving the baby down. Pushing felt awkward and uncomfortable. Finally, instinctively, I flipped around onto my hands and knees. I felt suddenly empowered and was able to move with the contractions, pushing as I needed. I ignored the screams of the nurses to *PUSH*! and let my body work the baby out. Within ten minutes, my first daughter was born. No tears, no complications, no cord wrap, no intervention. Just birth, as it has existed for hundreds of thousands of years: unflawed, powerful, and beautiful.

Develops argument through personal narrative (next several paragraphs)

Tengelitsch 4

I knew I wanted to be at home the second time around. I needed a space and a woman attendant who would respect my body and allow me to do what I needed to bring the baby into the world. I chose a midwife who lived in town and was certified with a state organization. She had already attended over 250 births and her soft voice and gentle demeanor left me feeling very comfortable. During my labor, she seemed to disappear into the shadows of the room, leaving my husband and me to do our dance.

The second birth was fast and easy. I labored in a tub of warm water and then got up and found myself once again in the familiar hands and knees position, pushing with ease. This time the midwife held onto my husband's hands as our baby came into the world. He, too, felt a sense of empowerment in catching our second daughter as she was born.

Last Sunday, we did it all over again. Same position, same bed, same midwife. All was so familiar. Candles lit the room, my children slept soundly, the dog took little notice. Why wouldn't anyone want this? The pain is fading fast in my memory, replaced with the sights and sounds of labor. The flickering of candles, the midwife's soft touch, my hand in my husband's hands and the reassurance of his presence.

Women actually experience less pain at home. During labor, oxytocin—the hormone which causes contractions and helps the baby to be born—works in harmony with endorphins—the body's own pain-relieving hormone. During a homebirth, the woman's body will release these hormones according to her needs and she will usually cope well with the sensation of labor (Wickham). The pain of labor is what guides our bodies into the position best suited for birth. Squatting and kneeling (the position I naturally assume in labor) have remained some of the most common postures in traditional cultures throughout the world (Kitzinger). As the baby's head descends into the birth canal, these positions take pressure off of the perineum, decreasing the chance of tearing. They also open the pelvis and allow more room for the baby to maneuver.

Back at the hospital, my fellow new mothers are delivering on their backs. Many are suffering from unnecessary procedures such as episiotomy due in part to the supine position and in part because this is simply the way it has been done in hospitals for the last half-century despite warnings to the contrary from the World Health Organization (WHO). In its report "Classification of Practices in Normal Birth," the WHO suggests both the "freedom in position and movement throughout labor" and "encouragement of non-supine position in labor" (35).

Refers to authority—the World Health Organization. The authority supports the point stated at the beginning of the paragraph.

In the supine, or on-the-back position, women are more likely to feel vulnerable; it's a death position, a sleep position. In their book *Women Giving Birth*, Astrid Limburg and Beatrijs Smulders describe the vital importance of a non-supine position:

> The upright position is an optimistic position, making [a woman] feel strong. She can trust her body, which has been made to give birth and deliver with her own strength. She has equal status with those around her. This is not the case when a woman is in the supine position. She lies in a bed as if ill, and people tower above her, making her feel small and dependent. When the delivery does not go smoothly, she tends to surrender to the specialist and gives up responsibility. (2)

The supine position is simply not conducive to birthing. *Would you poop lying down? Of course not!* Gravity is beneficial! Upright positions encourage the baby to move down into the birth canal and are often far more comfortable for laboring women. Movement is essential in speeding up or maintaining good momentum in labor and yet, in the hospital, women are limited not only by their sterile surroundings, but also by tradition and technology. While I'm not suggesting that all medical advancements are without merit, some are simply used too often and in many cases incite, rather than prevent, further intervention.

In addition to external interventions, drugs are still a major part of the birth equation in hospitals. The majority of women are opting to say no to the pain of labor. According to Judy Slome Cohain, "In Western countries, roughly 50-70% of birthing women have epidurals for pain relief." The main reason, Cohain explains, is simple word of mouth. Women hear about positive experiences from friends and family members and then opt for the drugs when the question inevitably comes from the attending physician.

Sheila Kitzinger, world-renowned midwife and birth advocate, writes, "It is ironic that the phrase 'Just say no,' invented for the anti-drug campaign, is now being used to promote drugs for pain relief" (284). Women are more likely to request pain relief and less likely to experience normal birth when they are in a space that elicits feelings of vulnerability or fear. (A hospital in itself is a place for sick people, so the association is immediately negative for many.) Drugs, especially epidural medication, leave women without the ability to move about freely and they have side effects that doctors must address. According to Judith Rooks, a certified nurse midwife:

> Women who have epidurals often need additional procedures, treatments and other elements of care to deal with the unintended effects

Side notes:

Blends information from source into text. See pages 338–349.

The quotation supports and extends the idea stated at the top of the paragraph.

Qualifier: Not all medical advancements are without merit.

Quotes an authority—Kitzinger. In an appositive phrase describes her credentials.

of epidurals, including oxytocin to strengthen labor, an intravenous infusion (to prevent hypovolemia and hypotension), urinary catheters, continuous electronic fetal monitoring, and forceps or vacuum to deliver the baby. Depending on which drugs are used, the women may need medications and personal care and support to deal with itching, nausea, vomiting, and shivering.

Soon the body is no longer laboring; the entire process has been augmented by the so-called "miracle" of modern medicine.

Concession: Homebirth isn't for everybody.

However, when women are left alone to labor as they wish, they reach into a place that is older than our hospitals and our medical invention and birth from within.

Concludes with appeal to value: Home is familiar and intimate.

Homebirth isn't for everyone. In some cases, women need to be in the hospital setting. We are, however, the only country that relies on routine obstetrical care for all women, despite their risk factors. Perhaps if we began treating women like thinking individuals, if we returned the trust in them, women would not feel obligated to choose a hospital delivery. They would recognize the safety and comfort of their own homes and likely opt to stay there during their births, where they can labor standing, sitting, squatting, in a tub of warm water or on their hands and knees. In a place where they are surrounded by family and friends, where their children sleep soundly in the other room, and where the dog takes little notice.

Works Cited

Brodsky, Archie. "Midwifery's Rebirth." *National Review*, 11 Aug. 1997, p. 46+.

"Classification of Practices in Normal Birth." *Care in Normal Birth: A Practical Guide*, World Health Organization, Department of Reproductive Health and Research, 1996, apps.who.int/iris/bitstream/10665/63167/1/WHO_FRH_MSM_96.24.pdf.

Cohen, Jill. "The Homebirth Choice." *Midwifery Today*, Sept. 2008, www.midwiferytoday.com/articles/homebirthchoice.asp.

Cohain, Judy Slome. "The Epidural Trip: Why Are So Many Women Taking Dangerous Drugs During Labor?" *Midwifery Today*, no. 95, 2010, www.midwiferytoday.com/articles/epiduraltrip.asp.

Edmonson, James M., and Julian Kassen. "Obstetrical Literature and the Changing Character of Childbirth." Case Western Reserve U, 2002, Dittrick Medical History Center.

Goer, Henci. *Obstetric Myths versus Research Realities: A Guide to the Medical Literature*. Bergin & Garvey, 1995.

Kitzinger, Sheila. "Who Would Choose to Have a Caesarean?" *British Journal of Midwifery*, vol. 9, no. 5, May 2001, pp. 284–85.

Limburg, Astrid, and Beatrijs Smulders. *Women Giving Birth*. Celestial Arts, 1993.

MacDorman, Marian F., et al. "Trends and Characteristics of Home and Other Out-of-Hospital Births in the United States, 1990–2006." *National Vital Statistics Reports*, vol. 58, no. 11, United States, Department of Health and Human Services, Centers for Disease Control and Prevention, National Center for Health Statistics, National Vital Statistics System, 3 March 2010, www.cdc.gov/nchs/data/nvsr/nvsr58/nvsr58_11.pdf.

Osterman, Michelle J.K., and Joyce A. Martin. "Primary Cesarean Delivery Rates, by State: Results From the Revised Birth Certificate, 2006–2012." *National Vital Statistics Reports*, vol. 63, no. 1, United States, Department of Health and Human Services, Centers for Disease Control and Prevention, National Center for Health Statistics, National Vital Statistics System, 23 Jan. 2014, www.cdc.gov/nchs/data/nvsr/nvsr63/nvsr63_01.pdf.

Rooks, Judith P. "Epidural Analgesia as Used During Childbirth in the United States." *Japanese Journal for Midwives*, vol. 54, no. 10, 2000, pp. 9–14. *MidwifeInfo*, edited by Nancy Sullivan, midwifeinfo.com/topic-epidurals.php. Accessed 22 Nov. 2013.

Wagner, Marsden. "Midwifery in the Industrialized World." *Journal of the Society of Obstetricians and Gynaecologists of Canada*, vol. 20, no. 13, Nov. 1998, pp. 1225–34.

Wickham, Sarah. "Homebirth: What Are the Issues?" *Midwifery Today*, no. 50, Summer 1999, www.midwiferytoday.com/articles/homebirthissues.asp.

Works Consulted

Feldhusen, Adrian E. "The History of Midwifery and Childbirth in America: A Time Line." *Midwifery Today*, 2000, www.midwiferytoday.com/articles/timeline.asp.

Running head: FILLING IN THE BUBBLES   1

Filling in the Bubbles:
An Investigation of Standardized Tests

Kate Pottoff
Northwestern Michigan College

Filling in the Bubbles:
An Investigation of Standardized Tests

It is inevitable. It is no use trying to escape or avoid it; at some point during everyone's academic career, he or she will be required to take a standardized test. Everyone knows the routine: The alarm clock going off at a ridiculous hour of the morning prompting a search for that early-morning coffee on the way to the testing facility. People are then directed to the proper seat, and for the duration of the day they are expected to take the infamous test. The desks are too small for comfort, the pencil tips eventually dull filling in the bubbles, and soon hands start to shake and sweat as students realize they are taking the first step towards their future.

But what if this test does not measure aptitude and, by extension, intelligence, like it is assumed to? Suddenly, the weight society places on test scores seems a little skewed. The SAT and ACT have been used to evaluate future college students since the mid-twentieth century, and for decades the integrity of these tests has been questioned. Each year, it is becoming more and more apparent that perhaps standardized testing, specifically the SAT and ACT, does not provide an accurate portrayal of an individual's intelligence and should be weighted accordingly by college admissions personnel.

Standardized testing has been under serious scrutiny for good reason. There are many known and even more unknown flaws behind the logic of standardized testing. Over the years, standardized tests have been blamed for favoring certain races and genders and hindering others. As Christina Perez (2002) argues, the SAT does little more than reinforce the gaps in wealth. Ultimately, Perez says, the SAT "tilts the playing field even further against low-income and minority applicants." Cultural biases have shaped test questions as well as format, and the project to erase all biases from the tests is an ongoing process. It is imperative that every student tested is tested fairly, especially in a country where all "men are created equal" and guaranteed equal rights. Equality is a concept that our society has struggled with throughout history. Racism and prejudice towards all groups of people have been condemned and people now expect the same rights as their neighbors, no matter what their race, sex, religion or ethnicity. Those rights should extend to the right to be tested and evaluated fairly. According to the National Center for Fair and Open Testing, many university leaders now realize that "the preoccupation with test scores hinders educational equity and has come at the expense of students' other high school experiences" (n.d.).

General scenario.

Proposes a *line of reasoning*. If A, then B, then C

Explains that standardized tests are culturally biased

Quotation from the source supports the main idea of the paragraph.

Standardized admissions tests (such as the SAT, ACT, GRE, and MCAT) fail to predict achievement, and they block access to higher education for otherwise qualified students. For example, when test scores are used to determine eligibility for scholarships, "students of color receive disproportionately fewer scholarships due to their lower test scores" (National Center for Fair and Open Testing, n.d.). And those who doubt the connection between test scores and family income might consider the following: Studies show that good coaching programs can raise a student's score by 100 points or more (National Center for Fair and Open Testing, n.d.). Many of these courses—which teach little more than test-taking strategies—are expensive, costing $800 or more. While the standardized test-makers claim that their tests measure "skills and knowledge learned over a long period of time" (National Center for Fair and Open Testing, n.d.), the coaching programs undermine such claims and expose one type of income-related bias.

Test scores vary by gender, family income, and ethnic group. For the SAT in 2012, males scored 498 and females scored 493 in critical reading. Those with a family income over $140,000 scored in the 4th percentile, while average scores drop consistently in accordance with a drop in family income: $120,000–$140,000: 5th percentile; $100,000–$120,000: 10th percentile; $80,000–$100,000: 11th percentile; $60,000–$80,000: 13th percentile; $40,000–$60,000: 14th percentile; $20,000–$40,000: 17th percentile. Scores vary based on ethnicity as well. Asians, Asian American/Pacific Islanders scored 518 in critical reading; Whites, 527; Other Hispanic or Latino, 447; Mexican or Mexican American, 448; African American or Black, 428. Results for the ACT follow the same trends (College Board, 2012). However, there is plenty of evidence to show that these scores do not correlate to intelligence or even success in college. "Colleges that have made the SAT optional report that their applicant pools are more diverse and that there has been no drop off in academic quality" (National Center for Fair and Open Testing, n.d.).

Although these biases are probably far from intentional, they are an injustice all the same. Obviously, the tests are far from perfect, favoring some cultures and even genders over others. Since these tests are not perfect by a long shot, this means the tests themselves are flawed, and we should not be expected to accept the results as a true representation of a person's intelligence. Especially in a culture where test results can determine a student's acceptance into college or make or break an applicant's future career, biased test results cannot be tolerated. If our society is going to weight tests heavily, those tests should at least be fair and unbiased.

Not only can the practice of standardized testing harm certain groups of individuals by inaccurately measuring their intelligence, it can also harm the way education is viewed in schools. Teachers have been accused of trying to "teach to the test" in order to boost students' scores. This new style of teaching can lead teachers to ignore crucial core elements of the curriculum and classify information as important or irrelevant to the test. But education is not regurgitating answers on a test; it is asking questions, problem solving, and learning to think in new ways. As David Owens (1985), author of *None of the Above: Behind the Myth of Scholastic Aptitude,* puts it, "The cult of mental measurement beguiles us into forgetting that the numbers are less important than the learning they are supposed to represent" (p. xix). To limit education down to a crash course in how to ace the SAT not only hurts students but eventually the society they live in as well by devaluing education and intelligence.

Transition to another problem with standardized testing.

Apparently, the SAT and ACT both have their downfalls. However, perhaps the problem does not begin with inaccurate, biased tests, but with how society views testing in general. Besides these obvious flaws of standardized testing, many more lurk beneath the surface. Standardized testing presumes to measure a person's aptitude for college, and by extension, his or her intelligence, all stemming from only a couple hours of test taking in a classroom. The idea that tests measure intelligence is not a new one; it permeates our culture in every aspect. Whether a person is applying for a driver's license or taking the bar exam, tests are everywhere. They are used as a rite of passage and a measuring tool of accomplishment.

Smeared throughout life is the notion that tests accurately measure intelligence and competence. However, to assume it is possible to measure a person's intelligence in a single isolated behavior known as "filling in the bubbles" is a stretch. Intelligence is not a black-and-white, tangible aspect of a person; it is a vast gray area, which can only be explored through avenues a little more extensive and involved than filling in dots on a Scantron. Simon Benlow (2004) shares the same view of intelligence. Benlow explores how consumerism has infiltrated academia and promoted passivity in students. He argues that students must take an active role in their learning instead and challenge themselves: "In college, students cannot simply consume knowledge. Even in its most packaged form, the textbook, knowledge must be regenerated, revised, reinterpreted and remembered to be anything beyond an answer on a multiple choice test" (p. 131).

Counterargument: Challenges the position that tests measure intelligence.

Refers to authority, Benlow, for support.

Benlow realizes that intelligence is more involved than memorization and regurgitation and values a more intensive view of intelligence, one that standardized testing fails to acknowledge. The majority of most standardized tests are multiple-choice questionnaires, and do not require the critical thinking and creativeness that should be considered an important part of intelligence.

The term "intelligence" refers not only to a person's "textbook knowledge" but also to a person's talents and intellectual skills. "Textbook knowledge" is material essentially copied out of students' books and pasted onto a test page. It is important information, but it is hardly brain surgery. On the other hand, intellectual skills such as creativity, cleverness, inventiveness, and problem-solving abilities all comprise a person's intelligence as well. These skills and abilities are as crucial to intelligence as textbook knowledge. However, measuring these skills poses quite a challenge. Impersonal tests cannot presume to measure these skills. Therefore, test results offer an incomplete portrayal of a person's intelligence. According to Perez (2002), "No matter how promoted, no three-hour test can measure habits of mind such as creativity, perseverance or judgment, so important in college and life." Standardized tests can measure a person's basic knowledge, but fail to factor in the other elements of intelligence.

> The source blends in and directly supports the point already stated in the paragraph.

Not only does standardized testing lack the ability to measure a person's entire range of knowledge, but it also assumes people who are knowledgeable will test well. However, due to testing anxiety and improper preparation in high schools, many students have poor test-taking skills. It is easy to imagine how students with inadequate test-taking skills could be at a disadvantage when it comes to the practice of standardized testing. For example, imagine a student, Stacey. Stacey has worked hard throughout high school, performing to her full potential and working hard in all of her classes. When other students were out socializing at football games, shopping with friends, or simply sitting at home on the couch watching television, she was studying. When students were sitting in the hallway before class furiously scribbling answers to material due two weeks ago, she was already planning her approach to the end-of-the-year research project.

> Uses a scenario as a support strategy.

However, when it came to the ACT, Stacey's preparations did not pan out. Time after time, she took the test, attending classes and doing test booklets in her spare time, and her score never improved. At the end of her senior year, Stacey ended up as class valedictorian with an almost perfect GPA. Although her work ethic and dedication far exceeded those of her fellow students, Stacey was rejected from many of her choice colleges, colleges that many of her peers were accepted to. Students with lower GPAs, easier classes, and a less impressive work ethic were considered to be more promising college students than she. Undoubtedly, there is something wrong with that picture. Certainly, a student's GPA and study habits should be a better indicator of future success in college than a score on a standardized test. A GPA reflects students' attitudes toward their education and how much they value getting a quality education. A GPA also reflects students' work ethics over an extended period of time, so it should be considered more representative of a student's success or failure than a simple score on a college entrance exam.

Since the practice of standardized testing is flawed, the weight placed upon test scores seems somewhat absurd. As Lemann (1999) recognized, "The [SAT] is widely believed to be the key to admission into a selective college, which in turn is widely believed to be the key to a life of prestige and prosperity. People can't help thinking of the score as a permanent measure of their innate worth." Although some colleges deny that standardized testing contributes heavily to the admissions process, many would disagree. According to Marklein, colleges promote high standardized testing scores. She states, "College admissions deans often downplay the significance of the exam in the application process—but then tout their schools' rising average scores in glossy recruitment brochures" (2002).

> Uses sources to detail recent attitudes and developments regarding colleges and standardized tests.

Despite the hype over standardized testing scores, some colleges are wising up and eliminating such scores from their admissions process. For example, Chatham College in Pittsburgh dropped all standardized test score requirements for admissions, and now encourages applicants to submit graded test papers, high school GPA, and portfolios. According to Michael Poll, vice president for admissions, "Standardized tests only reveal verbal and mathematical aptitude within a very controlled environment . . . but Chatham also considers qualities like creativity, ingenuity, leadership or reasoning that better indicate a successful college student" (as cited in Chatham College, 2005). And in recent years, plenty of other institutions have begun to break away from the big two (SAT and ACT) tests. According to John Fraire (2014), "there is a growing trend to reduce the role of standardized testing in college admissions and scholarships. More than 800 colleges and universities, mainly on the East Coast, now use some form of testing-optional practice in their admissions office."

Contrary to the concerns of testing advocates, standards at such schools have not spiraled downward. The National Center for Fair and Open Testing (n.d.) reports: "Schools that have dropped or sharply restricted their use of standardized admissions tests are widely pleased with the results. Regardless of size or selectivity, these institutions have seen substantial benefits, including increased student diversity, more and better-prepared applicants, and positive reactions from alumni/ae, students, guidance counselors, and the public." And in the fall of 2008, the National Association for College Admission Counseling urged colleges throughout the country to omit both the ACT and SAT as required components of admission. Citing a variety of institution-specific studies, the NACAC argued that ACT and SAT scores may not be the most reliable indicators of college success and may, in fact, skew the entire process of admission (Jaschik, 2008).

Concession: Standardized testing has some merit.

Standardized testing fails to take into account flawed testing or the idea that perhaps intelligence cannot be measured by one lone test, but yet, it is still weighted heavily by most colleges. Although the practice of standardized testing has some merit, it may not be the answer to evaluating future college students. Testing has been accepted in our culture because it often *can* measure what an individual does or does not know, but testing is far from a perfect science, and so it should be weighted accordingly.

Counterargument: Many people would argue X. However, Y.

Many people would argue that standardized testing is the most economical and efficient way of measuring intelligence and predicting performance. However, in the long run, the investment to reduce dependence on standardized testing would pay off. Certainly, portfolios and interviews, combined with previous GPAs, give colleges a more realistic and tangible representation of a person's intelligence than a stack of impersonal and perhaps flawed test scores.

In the end, standardized testing is simply inadequate as a tool to determine potential collegiate success because it fails to measure intelligence accurately. Intelligence is too complex to be measured by a test booklet and accompanying Scantron sheet. Also, biased tests fail to evaluate all people fairly. Testing has its pros as well as its cons, but higher education needs to consider the flaws. Other avenues should be pursued to replace testing, or at the very least, the weight of tests should be reduced significantly.

References

Benlow, S. (2013). "Have it your way": Consumerism invades education. In J. Mauk & J. Metz (Eds.), *The composition of everyday life* (4th ed., pp. 130–132). Boston, MA: Wadsworth.

Chatham College implements "SAT-optional" applications policy. (2005, November 17). *College Campus News*. Retrieved from http://www.collegenews.org

College Board. (2012). College bound seniors 2012. Retrieved from http://professionals.collegeboard.com/data-reports-research/

Fraire, J. (2014, April 28). Why your college should dump the SAT. *Chronicle of higher ed*. Retrieved from http://chronicle.com/article/Why-Your-College-Should-Dump/146209/

Jaschik, S. (2008, September 22). Dramatic challenge to SAT and ACT. *Inside higher ed*. Retrieved from http://www.insidehighered.com/news

Lemann, N. (1999, September 6). Behind the SAT. *Newsweek*. Retrieved from
    http://www.newsweek.com

Marklein, M. B. (2002, August 27). Love it or hate it, the SAT still rules. *USA
    Today*. Retrieved from http://www.usatoday.com

National Center for Fair and Open Testing. (n.d.). University testing. Retrieved
    April 28, 2014, from http://www.fairtest.org

Owens, D. (1985). *None of the above: Behind the myth of scholastic aptitude*. Boston,
    MA: Houghton Mifflin.

Perez, C. (2002, March 28). Get rid of SAT, similar tests. *USA Today*. Retrieved
    from http://www.usatoday.com

PART FOUR

Argument Anthology

Every argument is a response.

John Mauk

15

Politics

Politics comes from the Greek *polis*, or "city"—the public place where many people gather and live. Whenever different people come together, they are bound to disagree on some very basic ideas: how to share resources, how to maintain order, how to organize social space, and so on. And from those disagreements comes the art of politics. Some people say that they are not interested in government or politics. But the truth is they probably don't enjoy typical conversations about politics, which can degenerate into tirades. Unless they live under a rock, most people are deeply political. They hold a collection of assumptions about the role of education, religion, the military, business, or the medical field in their own lives.

We have all accumulated some basic assumptions about government. (Even the notion that we should allow the government to continue in its present form—that we shouldn't tear it down and start all over again—is a political assumption, one that is lived out every day by most Americans.) And government itself is not some dry or detached subject. It constantly touches our daily lives. From the moment we wake up and face the day, most of us are enabled or impacted by governmental regulations: electricity, airwaves, fuel, roads, sewers, water, education, and nearly all financial exchanges.

Many (perhaps most) of the arguments in this book indirectly involve the government. But the readings in this section put forth explicit arguments about the nature of government—what it should do, how it should do it, what impact it might have on people's lives.

Readings about Politics in Chapters 1–14

"Speech on the Land," Chief Seattle

"Warfare: An Invention—Not a Biological Necessity," Margaret Mead

"Red (White and Blue) Scare," Stephen Pell

"A Nation Made of Poetry," Joannie Fischer

Above: This sign was posted on the back of a semi-trailer. The picture was taken in the spring of 2007.

The Audacity of Hope

BARACK OBAMA

Sen. John Kerry was nominated as the Democratic presidential candidate at the 2004 Democratic National Convention. Barack Obama, then a state legislator in Illinois running for the U.S. Senate, gave the following keynote address. It was his first major political speech—and it launched him into "stardom" within the party, as he won his seat in the Senate by a landslide.

Thank you so much. Thank you. Thank you. Thank you so much. Thank you so much. Thank you. Thank you. Thank you, Dick Durbin. You make us all proud.

On behalf of the great state of Illinois, crossroads of a nation, Land of Lincoln, let me express my deepest gratitude for the privilege of addressing this convention.

Tonight is a particular honor for me because, let's face it, my presence on this stage is pretty unlikely. My father was a foreign student, born and raised in a small village in Kenya. He grew up herding goats, went to school in a tin-roof shack. His father—my grandfather—was a cook, a domestic servant to the British.

But my grandfather had larger dreams for his son. Through hard work and perseverance my father got a scholarship to study in a magical place, America, that shone as a beacon of freedom and opportunity to so many who had come before.

5   While studying here, my father met my mother. She was born in a town on the other side of the world, in Kansas. Her father worked on oil rigs and farms through most of the Depression. The day after Pearl Harbor my grandfather signed up for duty; joined Patton's army, marched across Europe. Back home, my grandmother raised a baby and went to work on a bomber assembly line. After the war, they studied on the G.I. Bill, bought a house through F.H.A., and later moved west all the way to Hawaii in search of opportunity.

And they, too, had big dreams for their daughter. A common dream, born of two continents.

My parents shared not only an improbable love, they shared an abiding faith in the possibilities of this nation. They would give me an African name, Barack, or "blessed," believing that in a tolerant America your name is no barrier to success. They imagined—they imagined me going to the best schools in the land, even though they weren't rich, because in a generous America you don't have to be rich to achieve your potential.

They're both passed away now. And yet, I know that on this night they look down on me with great pride.

They stand here—and I stand here today, grateful for the diversity of my heritage, aware that my parents' dreams live on in my two precious daughters. I stand here knowing that my story is part of the larger American story, that I owe a debt to all of those who came before me, and that, in no other country on Earth, is my story even possible.

Tonight, we gather to affirm the greatness of   10 our Nation—not because of the height of our skyscrapers, or the power of our military, or the size of our economy. Our pride is based on a very simple premise, summed up in a declaration made over two hundred years ago:

> We hold these truths to be self-evident, that all men are created equal, that they are endowed by their Creator with certain inalienable rights, that among these are Life, Liberty and the pursuit of Happiness.

That is the true genius of America, a faith—a faith in simple dreams, an insistence on small miracles; that we can tuck in our children at night and know that they are fed and clothed and safe from harm; that we can say what we think, write what we think, without hearing a sudden knock on the door; that we can have an idea and start our own business without paying a bribe; that we can participate in the political process without fear of retribution, and that our votes will be counted—at least most of the time.

Source: Senator Barak Obama's speech at 2004 Democratic National Convention.

This year, in this election we are called to reaffirm our values and our commitments, to hold them against a hard reality and see how we're measuring up to the legacy of our forbearers and the promise of future generations.

And fellow Americans, Democrats, Republicans, Independents, I say to you tonight: We have more work to do—more work to do for the workers I met in Galesburg, Illinois, who are losing their union jobs at the Maytag plant that's moving to Mexico, and now are having to compete with their own children for jobs that pay seven bucks an hour; more to do for the father that I met who was losing his job and choking back the tears, wondering how he would pay 4,500 dollars a month for the drugs his son needs without the health benefits that he counted on; more to do for the young woman in East St. Louis, and thousands more like her, who has the grades, has the drive, has the will, but doesn't have the money to go to college.

Now, don't get me wrong. The people I meet—in small towns and big cities, in diners and office parks—they don't expect government to solve all their problems. They know they have to work hard to get ahead, and they want to. Go into the collar counties around Chicago, and people will tell you they don't want their tax money wasted, by a welfare agency or by the Pentagon. Go in—go into any inner-city neighborhood, and folks will tell you that government alone can't teach our kids to learn; they know that parents have to teach, that children can't achieve unless we raise their expectations and turn off the television sets and eradicate the slander that says a black youth with a book is acting white. They know those things.

15   People don't expect—people don't expect government to solve all their problems. But they sense, deep in their bones, that with just a slight change in priorities, we can make sure that every child in America has a decent shot at life, and that the doors of opportunity remain open to all.

They know we can do better. And they want that choice.

In this election, we offer that choice. Our Party has chosen a man to lead us who embodies the best this country has to offer. And that man is John Kerry.

John Kerry understands the ideals of community, faith, and service because they've defined his life. From his heroic service to Vietnam, to his years as a prosecutor and lieutenant governor, through two decades in the United States Senate, he's devoted himself to this country. Again and again, we've seen him make tough choices when easier ones were available.

His values and his record affirm what is best in us. John Kerry believes in an America where hard work is rewarded; so instead of offering tax breaks to companies shipping jobs overseas, he offers them to companies creating jobs here at home.

John Kerry believes in an America where all   20 Americans can afford the same health coverage our politicians in Washington have for themselves.

John Kerry believes in energy independence, so we aren't held hostage to the profits of oil companies, or the sabotage of foreign oil fields.

John Kerry believes in the Constitutional freedoms that have made our country the envy of the world, and he will never sacrifice our basic liberties, nor use faith as a wedge to divide us.

And John Kerry believes that in a dangerous world war must be an option sometimes, but it should never be the first option.

You know, a while back—a while back I met a young man named Shamus in a V.F.W. Hall in East Moline, Illinois. He was a good-looking kid—six-two, six-three, clear-eyed, with an easy smile. He told me he'd joined the Marines and was heading to Iraq the following week. And as I listened to him explain why he'd enlisted, the absolute faith he had in our country and its leaders, his devotion to duty and service, I thought this young man was all that any of us might ever hope for in a child.

But then I asked myself, "Are we serving   25 Shamus as well as he is serving us?"

I thought of the 900 men and women—sons and daughters, husbands and wives, friends and neighbors, who won't be returning to their own hometowns. I thought of the families I've met who were struggling to get by without a loved one's full income, or whose loved ones had returned with a limb missing or nerves shattered, but still lacked long-term health benefits because they were Reservists.

When we send our young men and women into harm's way, we have a solemn obligation not to fudge the numbers or shade the truth about why they're going, to care for their families while they're gone, to tend to the soldiers upon their return, and to never ever go to war without enough troops to win the war, secure the peace, and earn the respect of the world.

Now—now let me be clear. Let me be clear. We have real enemies in the world. These enemies must be found. They must be pursued. And they must be defeated. John Kerry knows this. And just as Lieutenant Kerry did not hesitate to risk his life to protect the men who served with him in Vietnam, President Kerry will not hesitate one moment to use our military might to keep America safe and secure.

John Kerry believes in America. And he knows that it's not enough for just some of us to prosper— for alongside our famous individualism, there's another ingredient in the American saga, a belief that we're all connected as one people. If there is a child on the south side of Chicago who can't read, that matters to me, even if it's not my child. If there is a senior citizen somewhere who can't pay for their prescription drugs, and having to choose between medicine and the rent, that makes my life poorer, even if it's not my grandparent. If there's an Arab American family being rounded up without benefit of an attorney or due process, that threatens my civil liberties.

30 It is that fundamental belief—it is that fundamental belief: I am my brother's keeper. I am my sister's keeper that makes this country work. It's what allows us to pursue our individual dreams and yet still come together as one American family.

Epluribus unum: "Out of many, one."

Now even as we speak, there are those who are preparing to divide us—the spin masters, the negative ad peddlers who embrace the politics of "anything goes." Well, I say to them tonight, there is not a liberal America and a conservative America— there is the United States of America. There is not a Black America and a White America and Latino America and Asian America—there's the United States of America.

The pundits, the pundits like to slice-and-dice our country into Red States and Blue States; Red States for Republicans, Blue States for Democrats. But I've got news for them, too. We worship an "awesome God" in the Blue States, and we don't like federal agents poking around in our libraries in the Red States. We coach Little League in the Blue States and yes, we've got some gay friends in the Red States. There are patriots who opposed the war in Iraq and there are patriots who supported the war in Iraq. We are one people, all of us pledging allegiance to the stars and stripes, all of us defending the United States of America.

In the end—in the end—in the end, that's what this election is about. Do we participate in a politics of cynicism or do we participate in a politics of hope?

John Kerry calls on us to hope. John Edwards 35 calls on us to hope.

I'm not talking about blind optimism here—the almost willful ignorance that thinks unemployment will go away if we just don't think about it, or the health care crisis will solve itself if we just ignore it. That's not what I'm talking about. I'm talking about something more substantial. It's the hope of slaves sitting around a fire singing freedom songs; the hope of immigrants setting out for distant shores; the hope of a young naval lieutenant bravely patrolling the Mekong Delta; the hope of a millworker's son who dares to defy the odds; the hope of a skinny kid with a funny name who believes that America has a place for him, too.

Hope—hope in the face of difficulty. Hope in the face of uncertainty. The audacity of hope!

In the end, that is God's greatest gift to us, the bedrock of this nation. A belief in things not seen. A belief that there are better days ahead.

I believe that we can give our middle class relief and provide working families with a road to opportunity.

40 I believe we can provide jobs to the jobless, homes to the homeless, and reclaim young people in cities across America from violence and despair.

I believe that we have a righteous wind at our backs and that as we stand on the crossroads of history, we can make the right choices, and meet the challenges that face us.

America! Tonight, if you feel the same energy that I do, if you feel the same urgency that I do, if you feel the same passion that I do, if you feel the same hopefulness that I do—if we do what we must do, then I have no doubt that all across the country, from Florida to Oregon, from Washington to Maine, the people will rise up in November, and John Kerry will be sworn in as President, and John Edwards will be sworn in as Vice President, and this country will reclaim its promise, and out of this long political darkness a brighter day will come.

Thank you very much, everybody. God bless you. Thank you.

Analyzing Argument

1. What is the dominant form of appeal in Obama's address?

2. Besides promoting John Kerry's candidacy for president, what else is Obama arguing for?

3. Describe Obama's voice and provide several excerpts from the speech to support your description.

4. What basic assumptions, values, or beliefs are important to Obama's speech?

Laugh Baby Laugh, Cry Baby Cry

PAT SMITH

Pat Smith, a college writing instructor, wrote the following essay to explore deeper into the cause of the 2010 BP oil spill in the Gulf of Mexico. Smith attempts to dig past the reasons mentioned in the essay's opening paragraph and get at the reason for those reasons.

The cause of the 2010 oil spill in the Gulf of Mexico will be investigated and debated for decades. Was it a bad cement job by Halliburton? Or did environmentalists force oil companies into deeper and deeper water? Is Obama to blame? This oil well was approved on his watch. Shouldn't the buck stop there?

One of the giddy triumphs of the 2008 National Republican Convention and presidential campaign was the chanting prompted by national leaders like Rudy Giuliani and Sarah Palin: *Drill Baby Drill! Drill Baby Drill! Drill Baby Drill! Drill Baby Drill! Drill Baby Drill! Drill Baby Drill!* Chanting a slogan is the opposite of serious, analytical thought. And anytime—without exception—you find a group of people repeatedly shouting a slogan, emotion and irrationality have replaced reason and rationality in the minds of the chanters. Political and corporate leaders know this, so they like to hear the masses chanting, and they're the ones that get them chanting. The people are not left to come up with their own slogans to repeat, but instead are led to them by their national and international cheerleaders.

While the chanting of a slogan may seem spontaneous, there's more to it. In the case of *Drill Baby Drill,* the chant emerges from an ongoing national debate. One group hopes to protect the environment from things like global warming and oil spills. The other group denies that global warming exists and insists that big oil companies like BP know what they're doing. Just stay out of their way. They've got a handle on things, and regulation is not necessary.

It's actually harmful because in a capitalistic system the best, most efficient, and most responsible corporations and individuals rise to the top. The circular reasoning goes: we know they're the best because they have risen to the top, and the reason they have risen to the top is because they're the best. They run things for us, and they run things well. And if they don't, capitalism will take care of it.

For example, if there is an oil spill or a banking crisis, the people (the chanters) withdraw their financial support from these corporations and their CEOs, then new and better ones take their place. The problem is, nobody's boycotting BP or Morgan Stanley because it turns out they are *too big to fail.* The idea of capitalism as sold to the masses turns out to have a catch, a fly in the ointment: You can't boycott the local BP stations because, you are told, they're not actually owned by BP. Plus, if you boycott them you're just hurting the girl who works the cash register, and she's got bills to pay and mouths to feed. You're hurting the truck drivers who deliver the gas and cupcakes and the workers at Hostess and the corn farmers in Iowa we depend on for the high fructose corn syrup. And so on. You can't refuse to use gas or oil, unless you're willing to walk to work and freeze in the winter. Your world has been set up that way, and so have you. While the ideal of capitalism, like democracy, might work at the more local level, on the global scale, the ideal crumbles under too much weight.

Before the industrial revolution, if you needed a new hat, you went to a local hat maker, a hatter, and you ordered a hat which he then made for you. After the industrial revolution, because of technology and assembly lines, it was possible to make a thousand hats a day, and to make them more cheaply. The problem was, people didn't need that many hats. Tribal war chants have been around since there have been tribes (though a Google search of war chants brings up mostly information about the Florida State Seminoles War Chant or the Atlanta Braves Tomahawk Chop). But corporate, consumerist (war) chants emerged from the public relations (or propaganda) ideas of the early PR men such as Edward Bernays and Ivy Lee. When technology allowed the very few to quickly and cheaply produce more than the many actually needed, a new need was created—a need for consumers, and for the PR men who would create, maintain, and control them.

Based on the new ideas of Sigmund Freud (Bernays's uncle) and longtime knowledge about human psychology (Julius Caesar writes in *Commentaries on the Gallic War* about how to conquer the masses by dividing them against each other), the people who ran corporations (a new concept that also emerged from the industrial revolution) learned to advertise differently. Advertisements no longer said, *We make hats. Our hats are of good quality. They cost 25 cents. Next time you need a new hat, buy one from us.* Now advertisements said, *You need a new hat. You deserve a new hat. Your neighbor has lots of new hats and so should you. That opera singer that is all the rage, she has lots of new hats, and so can you. Just go buy a hat!* And they showed celebrities wearing the hat they wanted you to buy, just as they now say you need oil because you need a Hummer because Arnold drives one and you're like him or you could be if you had a Hummer too. All this leads to chanting.

This is not to say that all chanting is bad. Chants and mantras are commonly used in spiritual practice. And this fall college football fans across the country will have fun chanting, *Let's go Big Green,* *let's go! Let's go Big Green, let's go!* It will be good for the college spirit, good for the Big Green Nation. The hardship caused by the 2010 oil spill was caused by enthusiastic, psychologically manipulated, emotional, irrational, wise-guy chanting, which was caused by a complex and fascinating combination of history, psychology, sociology, economics, and rhetoric, which are (coincidentally?) some of the subjects least valued and most pooh-poohed by the chanters, and on some level by their leaders. This is why the chanting takes place, why it's possible, why it has real and serious consequences, and why those chanting don't think so.

Analyzing Argument

1. What is Smith's main claim?

2. How is the main claim supported? Explain how at least two strategies (listed on page 26) support Smith's main claim.

3. How does Smith's argument help complicate the reader's thinking about capitalism? (What is the fly in the ointment?)

4. Why does Smith connect tribal war chants, consumerist chants, and sports chants? How might this connection help the reader understand and accept the main claim?

5. How does Smith use a particular situation (the oil spill) to reveal a new way of thinking?

America's Real Death Panels

DIANA NOVAK

In "America's Real Death Panels," Diana Novak uses the case of Cameron Willingham, executed for setting a fire that he did not set, to point out a problem with jury selection in capital (death penalty) cases. This essay was published October 28, 2009 in a news magazine, *In These Times.*

Next spring, Texas will decide whether or not to become the first state to admit it executed an innocent man. Cameron Willingham was put to death in February 2004, 12 years after being convicted of killing his three infant children in a fire at their Corsicana, Texas, home. In August, the International Association for Fire Safety Science (IAFSS) released a report that concluded none of the evidence from the fire indicated it was set intentionally and that the state fire marshal who testified the fire was arson lacked "any realistic understanding of fires."

The IAFSS was asked to investigate the case by the Texas Forensic Science Commission, which was created in 2005 to re-examine questionable forensic evidence. The TFSC plans to continue its examination of the fire, but admits the report is a "major step" toward exonerating all that is left of Willingham: his name. As in any jury trial in the United States, Willingham, who maintained his innocence to the end, was convicted by a group of his peers—12 men and women who supposedly represented the community in which he lived. However, the prosecution in his case sought the death penalty, and that automatically changed the pool of people allowed to serve on his jury. For capital cases in which the jury will debate whether or not to sentence a convicted defendant to death, the Supreme Court mandates that jurors be "death-qualified"—that is, they must pledge during the jury selection process that they morally support capital punishment and that they would have no problem signing a sentence that will result in the death of another human being.

Social science research indicates that this selection process seriously limits juries in capital cases to people who share similar moral viewpoints. During the last four decades, U.S. researchers have found that in capital cases the people most likely to be chosen during the jury selection process are those with "authoritarian" personality types—people who believe that strict enforcement of laws is needed to maintain social stability. Authoritarians follow convention. They think the function of disciplinary action is to control criminals. They predictably tend to convict anyone (both the guilty and the innocent) who is unfortunate enough to be indicted and brought to trial before a jury. In other words, they believe one is guilty until proven innocent, and are thus more likely to accept the prosecution's case rather than the defendant's.

Psychologist and litigation consultant Brooke Butler's research has shown that those on death-qualified juries tend to believe in a fundamentally just world—people get what they deserve and that everything that happens in a person's life is a direct result of things they control. She found that such jurors are more likely to make decisions based on aggravating circumstances (the morbid facts surrounding a victim's death, etc.) rather than mitigating ones. They are more racist, sexist and homophobic than their unselected counterparts, and less likely to accept mental illness or age as a defense. Death-qualified jurors are typically "male, Caucasian, moderately well-educated, politically conservative, Catholic or Protestant, and middle-class," she says.

Victoria Springer, social science researcher 5 and sentencing expert, argues that the people with authoritarian personality types who are typically selected to serve on death-qualified juries will face a serious mental conflict. These pro-crime-control jurors are required to "adopt the attitude that the individual to be tried before them is innocent until proven guilty—which stands in direct opposition to their attitudes, orientation, and personality that has been specifically selected for."

From there, it is easy to understand how for such people the fundamental presumption of innocence conflicts with what the prosecution presents to them as "the facts"—the evidence, regardless of strength. Springer says that if the assumption of innocence clashes with the death-qualified juror's desire to remove a criminal from the streets, then the decision to render a guilty verdict reinforces what these jurors feel is their purpose on the jury in the first place.

Cameron Willingham, wrongfully convicted and executed by a Texas jury selected through the filter of "death qualification," was robbed of the right to have a jury of his peers decide his fate. Instead, he was put to death by those of his neighbors who innately believe that the American judicial system is a bastion of truth.

Analyzing Argument

1. How does Novak's essay complicate the reader's thinking about *a jury of one's peers?*

2. According to Novak, why might "death qualified" jurors be more likely to find an innocent person guilty?

3. What is Novak's main claim?

4. How does Novak support the main claim? Name specific support strategies from pp. 26–47.

5. Describe Novak's voice as a writer. Why is it inviting, alienating, persuasive, etc? Provide examples to support your claim.

The Irrefutable Jefferson

ROBERT "FRANK" JAKUBOWICZ

In the following essay, Robert "Frank" Jakubowicz uses two events, the Fourth of July and a recent Texas Board of Education textbook decision, to argue the history and meaning of the Declaration of Independence and the American Revolution. The essay was published in the July 4, 2010, *Berkshire Eagle* newspaper.

Thomas Jefferson, until this year, was revered in American history textbooks as the Founding Father who wrote the Declaration of Independence. His document is the reason we celebrate the fourth of July as this country's independence day. This is a holiday to remind Americans about the history and significance of that document.

But earlier this year, religious conservative members of the Texas Board of Education decided to push for a revision of this history by downplaying Jefferson's influence in the founding of our nation because the notion of the "separation of church and state" has been traced to him. These religious rightists believe this country was founded as a Christian nation and decided to make their point by revising American history in their public school textbooks. The effect of this kind of revision of American history would be to celebrate the founding of this country as a religious event rather than the secular event it is.

One does not have to be an American history scholar to understand that the American Revolution was not fought as a religious war against anti-Christian forces or an Antichrist. It occurred as a reluctant solution to a struggle by colonists against an imperial British government. The leaders of the Revolution considered this rebellion a secular matter. Their goal was to establish the colonies as free and independent states concerned with matters of this world and the new land in which they existed, rather than establish a Christian nation. As a matter of historical fact, America entered into the Treaty of Tripoli in 1797 which included in part the following statement: "the Government of the United States of America is not, in any sense, founded on the Christian religion." I wonder if the Texas Board would consider inserting this item in their textbooks?

The drafting of this treaty began during George Washington's presidency. The final draft was read in full in the Senate where it was approved unanimously and then signed by Washington's successor, President John Adams. The full text of the treaty was also published in three American newspapers in Philadelphia and New York. The American diplomat who authored this treaty was a close friend of Jefferson.

Jefferson made history with the help of John 5 Adams and Ben Franklin in writing the Declaration of Independence to abolish British colonial rule. His document, as noted by Karen Armstrong in her book "The Battle For God," was an "Enlightenment" document, not a religious one. It was based on a 17th and 18th century political theory of philosophers like John Locke and others which was considered self-evident to Jefferson's generation. This political theory is at the heart of the document we celebrate today, namely, that individuals "are created equal" with rights to "Life, Liberty, and the pursuit of Happiness" to be secured by a government empowered by the consent of the governed.

Jefferson, according to American historian Gordon S. Wood, later explained that his purpose with this document was to firmly and plainly state self-evident, common sense principles with which sensible people would agree and which would justify the colonist's independence.

Jefferson's Declaration of Independence, approved by Congress on July 4, 1776, was read in public just a few days later in Philadelphia to the ringing of bells and band music. The following year

"The Irrefutable Jefferson" by Robert "Frank" Jakubowicz. From *The Berkshire Eagle*, July 4, 2010. Reprinted with permission from *The Berkshire Eagle*.

it was observed in the same city with an adjournment of the Continental Congress and celebrated with bonfires, the ringing of bells, fireworks and a parade. The celebration then spread nationally.

The Massachusetts legislature passed a resolution to celebrate the event in 1781 and Boston was reportedly the first municipality to do so in 1783. The celebration of this day in cities like Pittsfield with its big parade and fireworks display and similar celebrations in other parts of Berkshire County and throughout the nation differ little from the earlier celebrations that have been ongoing for 234 years. The Pittsfield Parade Committee and its volunteers not only put on a great entertainment spectacle; they continue a great tradition to honor one of the key historic events of the birth of this nation. This is a day to memorialize the country's independence in breaking with the old order of governance and going forward with one based on new ideas.

It is fitting that such celebrations continue because the idea of human rights expressed in the Declaration of Independence is indeed timeless and self-evident. These rights expressed by Jefferson became an important part of the Constitution through the first 10 amendments (the Bill of Rights) and the 14th Amendment. They also served as a basis for reform movements elsewhere. His

memorable words have become immortal, and shame on the Texas Board of Education for trying to downplay him and his document as important parts of American history.

Analyzing Argument

1. Explain how the tension or conflict that propels Jakubowicz's essay emerges from two events, the Fourth of July and the Texas Board of Education decision.

2. What evidence supports Jakubowicz's claim that the American Revolution was a secular, and not religious, matter?

3. Jakubowicz's essay is journalistic, not academic. That is, it appeared in a local newspaper and was not written for a college class. If the essay were intended for an academic audience, for what sources would Jakubowicz provide formal documentation?

4. Summarize Jakubowicz's argument by writing out his main and supporting claims in paragraph form.

5. Research the Texas Board of Education's decision, and then explain how the board members might respond to Jakubowicz's argument.

16

Men and Women

The Declaration of Sentiments, prepared for the 1848 Seneca Falls Convention on women's rights and issues, states:

> The history of mankind is a history of repeated injuries and usurpations on the part of man toward woman, having in direct object the establishment of an absolute tyranny over her. To prove this, let facts be submitted to a candid world.

The Declaration goes on to submit the facts, in part:

- He has never permitted her to exercise her inalienable right to the elective franchise.
- He has compelled her to submit to law in the formation of which she had no voice.
- He has withheld from her rights which are given to the most ignorant and degraded men, both natives and foreigners.

Conversations about gender, from Seneca Falls (and before) to the more contemporary examples found in this chapter, are complex and get more complicated as one explores further. Although the readings here focus primarily on women, they are not about just women. As journalist Susan Faludi explains:

> I don't see how you can be a feminist and not think about men. One of the gross misconceptions about feminism is that it's only about women. But in order for women to live freely, men have to live freely, too. Feminism has shown us that what we think of as feminine is actually defined by cultural messages and political agendas. The same holds true for men and for what constitutes masculinity. Being a feminist opens your eyes to the ways men, like women, are imprisoned in cultural stereotypes.

Readings about Men and Women in Chapters 1–14

"No Sex Please, We're Middle Class," Camille Paglia

"Sage Femme: An Argument in Support of Home Birth," Samantha Tengelitsch

Fantastic Ideals

JENNIFER WORLEY

Jennifer Worley, a graphic design major, wrote this argument for her college composition course. The assignment called on her to argue for an unconventional way of seeing a topic.

I know what beauty looks like. She is on the cover of magazines, in all the hit movies, she is a computer-generated character in a video game, she is the centerfold men admire, and a doll we play with and dress up. She has long, skinny legs, her hair shines like water, her skin is smooth like silk and free of scars and pimples, her hands are soft, with long painted fingernails, her breasts are just right (not too big, not too small, not too saggy or too perky, not too round or too flat), her butt is tight and perfectly rounded, her lips are full and pink, her teeth pearly white, her eyes wide and intriguing, her waist is narrow and her stomach flat, her legs, armpits, and bikini line are free of unwanted hair, and even her eyebrows are strategically tweezed to just the right shape. Her bra matches her panties every day of the week, her clothes cling snugly to every curve of her body, just enough to make everyone who sees her wonder what's underneath. She struts along, sporting shoes that add three inches to her height, but rub her heels raw. On the outside, she appears sweet, innocent, independent, and strong. She is the idealized image of beauty and perfection consistently shown to men and women. She tells us what to eat, drink, wear, buy—and what women are supposed to be.

At twenty years old, I'm 5' 2" and 115 pounds, and every time I look in the mirror, I think, "Ten pounds would do it. If I could just lose that much, everything in my life would be better." I have thought this way since I was thirteen years old. Dieting and exercise have been unsuccessful, yet I still believe that someday I can look like her. I can be beautiful and perfect. These thoughts often consume my days. I feel guilty about everything I put in my mouth. I never feel pretty enough or sexy enough. My question is: If beauty is so painful, why do I even want to be beautiful, and who made these damned rules?

Over my first two semesters of college, I took the first and second part of Western Art History. Again and again, I was amazed at the difference between the shape of women centuries ago and the images we see today. In much of the past, art has depicted women as voluptuous, and even heavyset. By today's standards many of the women in these images would be considered overweight, while in their time, they were very attractive. They were the standard of beauty. It was even common for painters to remove wrinkles, scars, emotions, etc., yet the models would not meet today's standards of feminine beauty.

One of the most recognized beauties in American history is Marilyn Monroe. She was certainly considered a beauty in her own time, and still is, but she was no size one—probably not even a three or a five. Yet she was adored by men and women alike, and her image graced advertisements, paintings, and much more. It seems today, however, that women are shrinking. If beauty is measured in dress size, it seems to be getting smaller and smaller each year, making it more impossible to live up to (or down to!). According to Jean Kilbourne, "it has been estimated that twenty years ago the average model weighed 8 percent less than the average woman; today she weighs 23 percent less" (125).

Idealization of women is nothing new. Nathaniel 5 Hawthorne's 1846 short story "The Birthmark" illustrated the tragedy of seeking ideal beauty. In the story, a scientist attempts to remove a birthmark from his wife's face in order to perfect her appearance. Although he is successful at ridding her of the mark, the process kills her. In a recent essay, Chester McCovey discusses "The Birthmark" and its relevance to our own culture:

> As for physical imperfection in the twenty-first century, it seems odd that on one level we promote

Jennifer Worley, "Fantastic Ideals." Reprinted with the permission of the author.

respect for all sorts of human "imperfections," yet on another level, we strive as we do to eliminate them whenever we can. It seems odd because so many times they are not imperfections at all. (613)

In other words, what we consider imperfections are also what make us unique, a quality we are told is important. Still, we make great effort to get rid of imperfections so we can get closer to the ideal.

The ideal is getting thinner and thinner. Flawlessness is required. In a culture where obesity is on the rise and imperfection is everywhere, images of super-thin beauty are causing women to doubt their worth. Next to every image of the super-thin ideal model, there should be a sign that reads: "Caution. Do not try to achieve this body at home. It could be harmful to your health and may cause psychological damage." An ad from The Body Shop comes close to such a statement. It reads: "There are 3 billion women who don't look like supermodels and only 8 who do" (qtd. in Kilbourne 124–25). This is the painful truth. Unfortunately, it is much more common to see images that make us believe something different: that every woman should look like a supermodel, or die trying.

Feelings of worthlessness can drive women to diet excessively and have plastic surgery, Botox injections, liposuction, and facelifts. And all of these have side effects. "Research has . . . found that dieters often experience a temporary drop in mental abilities and thus have less energy to focus on tasks other than controlling their food" (Kilbourne 125). Women, in general, are expected to eat less than men, and to eat and drink things that are low in fat and calories. That's not to say that men don't diet, but it is true that women are more likely to. Unfortunately, many of the popular diets are unhealthy. They cause women to become malnourished and develop vitamin deficiencies, the effects of which can be difficult to reverse. And, even though diets may help drop unwanted pounds, the weight often returns once the diet is stopped. A 2002 issue of *Adbusters* gives some shocking statistics about women and dieting: "71% of girls diet, 11% use diet pills, 8% induce vomiting, 45% skip meals" ("Appetite").

Beyond the physical costs, these methods of "perfecting" ourselves cost money, which is why women are the targets of advertising. The advertising companies are well aware of women's self-consciousness and use it against us to sell their products. They make us feel ugly and inadequate so that we will spend our money on products that claim to make us perfect. It is within the rights of the companies to portray whatever image will best sell their product, but their repeated attempts steer away from selling a product and toward projecting an image.

Early in life, most girls are exposed to one of the 10 purest forms of idealization: the Barbie doll. According to the *New York Times,* "if the 11 1/2-inch doll were 5-foot-6, her measurements would be 39-21-33. . . . One academic expert calculated that a woman's chances of having Barbie's figure were less than one in 100,000" (qtd. in Solomon 8). Even with the knowledge that common ideals are nearly impossible to live up to, women are taught from childhood that these ideals are the essence of beauty. On the flip side, with every Barbie comes a Ken. It could be argued that Ken is also idealized, and this is true. The difference, however, is that the Ken ideal is one of physical strength. Barbie, along with most idealized images of women, appears weak, hungry, and fake.

The ideal woman is imprinted in the minds of both men and women so early that it strongly affects the way we look at and interact with each other. Women are constantly doubting themselves, and men are often defining the women in their lives according to the ideal. As Kilbourne puts it:

> Male college students who viewed just one episode of *Charlie's Angels* . . . were harsher in their evaluations of the attractiveness of potential dates than were males who had not seen the episode. In another study, male college students shown centerfolds from *Playboy* and *Penthouse* were more likely to find their own girlfriends less sexually attractive. (133)

This certainly is not the case for everyone, but with so many images being thrown at us, it becomes difficult to draw our own conclusions about beauty. I remember being told by boys in junior high what kind of butt I had, as well as all the other things that were wrong with the way I looked, acted, and dressed. It's pretty safe to say that without idealized images telling us how to look, think, and act, people would act differently toward each other.

Behind the ideal beauty, behind the advertisements and fashion show runways, there is a reality that most people do not see. Behind the perfection, models go to extremes to be ideal, literally starving themselves, over-exercising, and constantly being told they aren't good enough, just to work a few years in the business before they are too old or too fat. Somewhere in our minds, most average women understand models have unrealistic and unhealthy bodies. Yet, even with this understanding, we desire to achieve the ideal once it has been shown to us. We come to accept it. We want to be taller and thinner, have bigger boobs, smaller butts. The danger is that average women get so wrapped up in wanting to meet these expectations that we, too, go to extremes. We develop depression, low self-esteem, and eating disorders. We endure self-doubt, self-criticism, and even self-destruction. As Susan Griffin explains:

> We are full of defect. Our brows, for instance, are lined. . . . Our flesh is aging. Our chins sag. . . . We call the furrows over the bridge of our noses "worry lines." We try not to worry; we try not to move the muscles of our faces. . . . We are wizened. Our lips are pursed. . . . Our cheeks and our temples sag. . . . Our jaws droop; our necks have folds. . . . We find wrinkles cover our faces. . . . (88)

Like the models, average women go through hell before realizing that the ideal is unnecessary and unattainable.

15   But I know what beauty looks like. She is short, she is fat, she is tall, she is thin, she is black, brown, yellow, white. Her hair is frizzy, curly, dull, dry, colored, short. She runs, she jumps, she climbs, she works, she plays, and she drives people crazy. She's your mother, your sister, your aunt, cousin, niece, wife, daughter, friend. She has scars, pimples, and wrinkles, and she's flabby, saggy, and pear shaped. Her skin is dry, her lips are cracked, she's tired, grumpy, and bloated. She likes pizza, chocolate, burgers, fries, ice cream, and candy. She is you, she is me. She is real, she is beauty.

Works Cited

"Appetite." *Adbusters*, Nov.–Dec. 2002.

Griffin, Susan. *Woman and Nature: The Roaring inside Her*. Sierra Club Books, 1978. Counterpoint, 2000.

Kilbourne, Jean. *Deadly Persuasion: Why Women and Girls Must Fight the Addictive Power of Advertising*. Free Press, 1999.

McCovey, Chester. "The Parting Breath of the Now-Perfect Woman." *The Composition of Everyday Life: A Guide to Writing*, by John Mauk and John Metz, 3rd ed., Wadsworth, 2010, pp. 612–13.

Solomon, Norman. "Still Not Good Enough: From Barbie to Botox." *Humanist*, vol. 62, no. 4, July 2002, pp. 7–8. *Academic Search Elite*, 6858013.

Analyzing Argument

1. What argument in disguise does Worley uncover? (See Arguments in Disguise, pages 79–83).

2. How is the argument disguised? What helps hide it?

3. In a group, examine the following, which form Worley's line of reasoning in paragraph 11. Where, and for what reason, might people disagree?

   • Behind the ideal beauty, there is a reality most people do not see.

   • The reality is: models go to extremes.

   • Most average women understand that models have unrealistic and unhealthy bodies.

   • YET, these women desire to achieve the ideal once they come to accept it.

   • The danger is: average women going to extremes to meet unrealistic expectations.

   • Going to extremes causes depression, low self-esteem, and eating disorders.

Declaration of Sentiments

ELIZABETH CADY STANTON

In the early nineteenth century, a spirit of reform spread throughout the United States. Many of the reformers were women, who worked for the rights of others but lacked rights of their own. In 1848 Lucretia Mott and Elizabeth Cady Stanton, two activists in the movement to abolish slavery, organized the Seneca Falls Convention, the first conference to address women's rights and issues. Stanton drafted the Declaration of Sentiments for the convention, where it was signed by sixty-eight women and thirty-two men. The Declaration, deliberately modeled on the Declaration of Independence, demanded that women have equality with men before the law, in education, and in employment. This revolutionary document also demanded that women be allowed to vote, a right they received seventy-two years later with the Nineteenth Amendment in 1920.

Sentiments

When, in the course of human events, it becomes necessary for one portion of the family of man to assume among the people of the earth a position different from that which they have hitherto occupied, but one to which the laws of nature and of nature's God entitle them, a decent respect to the opinions of mankind requires that they should declare the causes that impel them to such a course.

We hold these truths to be self-evident: that all men and women are created equal; that they are endowed by their Creator with certain inalienable rights; that among these are life, liberty, and the pursuit of happiness; that to secure these rights governments are instituted, deriving their just powers from the consent of the governed. Whenever any form of government becomes destructive of these ends, it is the right of those who suffer from it to refuse allegiance to it, and to insist upon the institution of a new government, laying its foundation on such principles, and organizing its powers in such form, as to them shall seem most likely to effect their safety and happiness.

Prudence, indeed, will dictate that governments long established should not be changed for light and transient causes; and, accordingly, all experience has shown that mankind are more disposed to suffer, while evils are sufferable, than to right themselves by abolishing the forms to which they were accustomed. But when a long train of abuses and usurpations, pursuing invariably the same object, evinces a design to reduce them under absolute despotism, it is their duty to throw off such government and to provide new guards for their future security. Such has been the patient sufferance of the women under this government, and such is now the necessity which constrains them to demand the equal station to which they are entitled.

The history of mankind is a history of repeated injuries and usurpations on the part of man toward woman, having in direct object the establishment of an absolute tyranny over her. To prove this, let facts be submitted to a candid world.

He has never permitted her to exercise her 5 inalienable right to the elective franchise.

He has compelled her to submit to law in the formation of which she had no voice.

He has withheld from her rights which are given to the most ignorant and degraded men, both natives and foreigners.

Having deprived her of this first right as a citizen, the elective franchise, thereby leaving her without representation in the halls of legislation, he has oppressed her on all sides.

He has made her, if married, in the eye of the law, civilly dead. He has taken from her all right in property, even to the wages she earns.

He has made her morally, an irresponsible being, 10 as she can commit many crimes with impunity, provided they be done in the presence of her husband. In the covenant of marriage, she is compelled to promise obedience to her husband, he becoming, to all intents and purposes, her master—the law giving him power to deprive her of her liberty and to administer chastisement.

He has so framed the laws of divorce, as to what shall be the proper causes and, in case of separation, to whom the guardianship of the children shall be given, as to be wholly regardless of the happiness of the women—the law, in all cases, going upon a false supposition of the supremacy of man and giving all power into his hands.

After depriving her of all rights as a married woman, if single and the owner of property, he has taxed her to support a government which recognizes her only when her property can be made profitable to it.

He has monopolized nearly all the profitable employments, and from those she is permitted to follow, she receives but a scanty remuneration. He closes against her all the avenues to wealth and distinction which he considers most honorable to himself. As a teacher of theology, medicine, or law, she is not known.

He has denied her the facilities for obtaining a thorough education, all colleges being closed against her.

15 He allows her in church, as well as state, but a subordinate position, claiming apostolic authority for her exclusion from the ministry, and, with some exceptions, from any public participation in the affairs of the church.

He has created a false public sentiment by giving to the world a different code of morals for men and women, by which moral delinquencies which exclude women from society are not only tolerated but deemed of little account in man.

He has usurped the prerogative of Jehovah himself, claiming it as his right to assign for her a sphere of action, when that belongs to her conscience and to her God.

He has endeavored, in every way that he could, to destroy her confidence in her own powers, to lessen her self-respect, and to make her willing to lead a dependent and abject life.

Now, in view of this entire disfranchisement of one-half the people of this country, their social and religious degradation, in view of the unjust laws above mentioned, and because women do feel themselves aggrieved, oppressed, and fraudulently deprived of their most sacred rights, we insist that they have immediate admission to all the rights and privileges which belong to them as citizens of the United States.

In entering upon the great work before us, 20 we anticipate no small amount of misconception, misrepresentation, and ridicule; but we shall use every instrumentality within our power to effect our object. We shall employ agents, circulate tracts, petition the state and national legislatures, and endeavor to enlist the pulpit and the press in our behalf. We hope this Convention will be followed by a series of conventions embracing every part of the country.

Resolutions

Whereas, the great precept of nature is conceded to be that "man shall pursue his own true and substantial happiness." Blackstone in his Commentaries remarks that this law of nature, being coeval with mankind and dictated by God himself, is, of course, superior in obligation to any other. It is binding over all the globe, in all countries and at all times; no human laws are of any validity if contrary to this, and such of them as are valid derive all their force, and all their validity, and all their authority, mediately and immediately, from this original; therefore,

Resolved, that such laws as conflict, in any way, with the true and substantial happiness of woman, are contrary to the great precept of nature and of no validity, for this is superior in obligation to any other.

Resolved, that all laws which prevent woman from occupying such a station in society as her conscience shall dictate, or which place her in a position inferior to that of man, are contrary to the great precept of nature and therefore of no force or authority.

Resolved, that woman is man's equal, was intended to be so by the Creator, and the highest good of the race demands that she should be recognized as such.

25 *Resolved,* that the women of this country ought to be enlightened in regard to the laws under which they live, that they may no longer publish their degradation by declaring themselves satisfied with their present position, nor their ignorance, by asserting that they have all the rights they want.

Resolved, that inasmuch as man, while claiming for himself intellectual superiority, does accord to woman moral superiority, it is preeminently his duty to encourage her to speak and teach, as she has an opportunity, in all religious assemblies.

Resolved, that the same amount of virtue, delicacy, and refinement of behavior that is required of woman in the social state also be required of man, and the same transgressions should be visited with equal severity on both man and woman.

Resolved, that the objection of indelicacy and impropriety, which is so often brought against woman when she addresses a public audience, comes with a very ill grace from those who encourage, by their attendance, her appearance on the stage, in the concert, or in feats of the circus.

Resolved, that woman has too long rested satisfied in the circumscribed limits which corrupt customs and a perverted application of the Scriptures have marked out for her, and that it is time she should move in the enlarged sphere which her great Creator has assigned her.

30 *Resolved,* that it is the duty of the women of this country to secure to themselves their sacred right to the elective franchise.

Resolved, that the equality of human rights results necessarily from the fact of the identity of the race in capabilities and responsibilities.

Resolved, that the speedy success of our cause depends upon the zealous and untiring efforts of both men and women for the overthrow of the monopoly of the pulpit, and for the securing to woman an equal participation with men in the various trades, professions, and commerce.

Resolved, therefore, that, being invested by the Creator with the same capabilities and same consciousness of responsibility for their exercise, it is demonstrably the right and duty of woman, equally with man, to promote every righteous cause by every righteous means; and especially in regard to the great subjects of morals and religion, it is self-evidently her right to participate with her brother in teaching them, both in private and in public, by writing and by speaking, by any instrumentalities proper to be used, and in any assemblies proper to be held; and this being a self-evident truth growing out of the divinely implanted principles of human nature, any custom or authority adverse to it, whether modern or wearing the hoary sanction of antiquity, is to be regarded as a self-evident falsehood, and at war with mankind.

Analyzing Argument

1. What argument is made by modeling this argument on the Declaration of Independence?

2. How does modeling the Declaration of Independence make the Declaration of Sentiments more compelling?

3. In groups, discuss what relationship the document suggests between the Declaration of Independence and the Declaration of Sentiments.

4. What common assumptions and values underlie the Declaration?

5. Write a Declaration of Sentiments for a movement or cause of your own. Then compare it to the Declaration of Sentiments for the Seneca Falls Convention.

What Happened to the Women's Movement?

BARBARA L. EPSTEIN

Barbara L. Epstein, a professor in the History of Consciousness program at the University of California at Santa Cruz, is author of *The Politics of Domesticity: Women, Evangelism, and Temperance in Nineteenth Century America* (1981) and *Political Protest and Cultural Revolution: Nonviolent Direct Action in the 1970s and 1980s* (1991). This article appeared in *Monthly Review* in 2001. Following this essay is a response, "Different Strategies Are Necessary Now," by Joan Acker.

From the late 1960s into the 1980s there was a vibrant women's movement in the United States. Culturally influential and politically powerful, on its liberal side this movement included national organizations and campaigns for reproductive rights, the Equal Rights Amendment (ERA), and other reforms. On its radical side it included women's liberation and consciousness raising groups, as well as cultural and grassroots projects. The women's movement was also made up of innumerable caucuses and organizing projects in the professions, unions, government bureaucracies, and other institutions. The movement brought about major changes in the lives of many women, and also in everyday life in the United States. It opened to women professions and blue-collar jobs that previously had been reserved for men. It transformed the portrayal of women by the media. It introduced the demand for women's equality into politics, organized religion, sports, and innumerable other arenas and institutions, and as a result the gender balance of participation and leadership began to change. By framing inequality and oppression in family and personal relations as a political question, the women's movement opened up public discussion of issues previously seen as private, and therefore beyond public scrutiny. The women's movement changed the way we talk, and the way we think. As a result,

arguably most young women now believe that their options are or at least should be as open as men's.

Despite the dramatic accomplishments of the women's movement, and the acceptance of women's equality as a goal in most sectors of U.S. society, gender equality has not yet been achieved. Many more women work outside the home but most continue to be concentrated in low-paying jobs; women earn, on the average, considerably less than men; women are much more likely than men to be poor. Violence against women is still widespread. Responsibility for childcare remains largely the responsibility of women; despite the fact that most women work outside the home, nowhere is it seen as a societal rather than a familial responsibility. In the 1960s and 1970s feminists protested the imbalance in power between men and women in family and personal relations. But these continue to exist.

Worst of all, there is no longer a mass women's movement. There are many organizations working for women's equality in the public arena and in private institutions; these include specifically women's organizations such as the National Organization for Women, and in environmental, health care, social justice, and other areas that address women's issues. But, where there were once women's organizations with large participatory memberships there are now bureaucratic structures run by paid staff. Feminist theory, once provocative and freewheeling, has lost concern with the conditions of women's lives and has become pretentious and tired. This raises two questions. Why is there so little discussion of the near-disappearance of a movement that not so long ago was strong enough to bring about major changes in the social and cultural landscape? What are the causes of the movement's decline?

Why the Silence?

The decline of the women's movement has coincided with a right-wing attack on feminism, and with the decline of other activist movements. The civil rights and Black Power movements are considerably weaker and more fragmented now than they were a few decades ago. The environmental activist and gay and lesbian rights movements have lost coherence and direction. Many feminists and other progressives have resisted public discussion of the weaknesses of these movements, arguing that any acknowledgement of them provides the right with ammunition. But this is not a valid reason to avoid examining a movement's problems. There is no place other than the public arena for holding such a discussion. The causes of the decline of these movements are more complicated than can be dealt with by circling the wagons. Right-wing attacks have played a role in damaging some feminist projects, such as abortion rights, but the overall decline of the women's movement has much more to do with a loss of a sense of urgency within than with attacks from without.

5   It is my impression that the real reason for avoiding or suppressing criticisms within the movement is fear that discussing the movement's problems will hasten a process of unraveling that is already well underway. Movements are fragile; the glue that holds them together consists not only in belief in the causes that they represent, but also confidence in their own growing strength. Especially when a movement is in decline it is tempting to silence criticism and turn to whistling in the dark, in the hope that no one will notice that something has gone wrong. But problems that are not acknowledged or discussed are not likely to go away; it is more likely that they will worsen. Understanding why a movement has declined may not lead to the revival of that movement as it was in the past, but it may help in finding new directions.

     Reluctance to look at the weaknesses of the current women's movement may also have to do with the fear that second wave, or contemporary, feminism could disappear, sharing the fate of first wave feminism. The first women's movement in the United States, which took place in the latter part of the nineteenth and the early twentieth century, was almost wiped from historical memory during the four-decade interlude between the two waves of feminist activism. It was the weaknesses of first wave feminism, most of which have not been shared by feminism's second wave, that made this possible. First wave feminism was largely confined to white, middle, and upper-middle class women. First wave feminism also moved, over the course of its history, towards a narrowness of vision that isolated it from other progressive movements. The first feminist movement in the United States originated in the abolitionist movement. In its early years feminism's alliance with the anti-slavery movement, and its association with other protest movements of the pre–Civil War decades, gave it a radical cast. But when the Civil War ended and suffrage was extended to former slaves but not to women, much of the women's movement abandoned its alliance with blacks. In the decades between the Civil War and the turn of the twentieth century, racist and anti-immigrant sentiment spread within the middle class. In the last decades of the nineteenth century and the first two decades of the twentieth the women's movement narrowed its focus to winning woman's suffrage, and leading feminists turned to racist and anti-immigrant arguments on behalf of that goal. Other currents in the women's movement, such as the women's trade union movement, avoided racism and continued to link feminism with a radical perspective. But by the late nineteenth century the mainstream woman suffrage organizations dominated the women's movement. By the time woman's suffrage was won, first wave feminism had abandoned any broader agenda and had distanced itself from other progressive movements. Feminism was easily pushed aside by the conservative forces that became dominant in the twenties.

     The impact of second wave feminism has been broader and deeper than that of the first wave. Whatever direction U.S. politics may take it is hard to imagine feminism being wiped off the slate as it was in the thirties, forties, and fifties. In the last three decades feminism has changed women's lives and thinking in ways that are not likely to be reversed. Where first wave feminism collapsed into a single-issue focus, second wave feminism has in many respects broadened. Second wave feminism had its limitations in its early years. Though participants included women of color and of working-class backgrounds, their route into the movement was through the same student and professional circles through which white middle-class women found feminism. The presence of women of color and working-class women did not mean that feminism was being adopted within these communities. Second wave feminists, especially in the intoxicating early years of the movement, tended to believe that they could speak for all women. Such claims contained a small grain of truth, but ignored the composition of the movement, which was overwhelmingly young, white, college educated, heterosexual, and drawn from the post–Second World War middle class.

Unlike first wave feminism, the second wave broadened over time, in its composition and, in important respects, in its perspective. In the 1970s and 1980s, lesbian feminism emerged as a current within the movement. Women of color began to articulate their own versions of feminism, and working-class women, who had not been part of the movement's early constituency of students and professionals, began to organize around demands for equal treatment at the workplace and in unions, for childcare, and for reproductive rights. Where first wave feminism pulled back, over time, from its early alliances with the black movement and other radical currents, second wave feminism increasingly allied itself with progressive movements, especially with movements of people of color and with the gay and lesbian movement. Second wave feminists also developed increasing sensitivity to racial differences, and differences of sexual orientation, within the women's movement.

From a Movement to an Idea

The heyday of the women's movement was in the late 1960s and early 1970s. During the 1980s and 1990s a feminist perspective, or identity, spread widely and a diffuse feminist consciousness is now found nearly everywhere. There are now countless activist groups and social and cultural projects whose goals and approaches are informed by feminism. There are women's organizations with diverse, grassroots constituencies focusing on issues of concern to working-class women and women of color. There is the National Congress of Neighborhood Women, dealing with the problems of working-class women and women of color. There are many local groups with similar concerns; an example from California is the Mothers of East Los Angeles, which has played an important role in environmental justice struggles. There is Women's Action for New Directions (previously Women's Action for Nuclear Disarmament), bringing women of color and white women together around issues of health and the environment. There are many others. Nevertheless, grassroots activism is not the dominant, or most visible, sector of the women's movement. Public perception of feminism is shaped by the staff-run organizations whose concerns are those of their upper-middle class constituencies and by the publications of feminists in the academy. The mass diffusion of feminist consciousness, the bureaucratization of leading women's organizations, and the high visibility of academic feminism are all consequences of the acceptance of feminism by major sectors of society. But these changes have not necessarily been good for the movement. Feminism has simultaneously become institutionalized and marginalized. It has been rhetorically accepted, but the wind has gone out of its sails.

Feminist activism has not ceased, nor have the numbers of women engaged in feminist activity or discussion declined. Millions of U.S. women talk to each other about women's concerns, using the vocabulary of feminism. There are countless

10

organized feminist projects, focusing on domestic violence, reproductive rights, and women's health. There are international networks of women continuing efforts begun at the international meeting of women at Beijing in 1995. Young feminist writers are publishing books addressed to, or speaking for, their generation.

The proliferation of feminist activism is part of a broader pattern. The numbers of people involved in community, social justice, and progressive activism generally appears to have increased since the 1970s (though there is no way of counting the numbers of people involved). Feminist activism is not an exception to this trend, especially if one includes in this category women's involvement in the environmental and public health movements, addressing women's issues among others. The fact that feminist perspectives have been adopted by movements outside the women's movement, by organizations that also include men, is itself an achievement. Women play a role in leadership of the environmental and anti-corporate movements that is at least equal to men's; feminism is understood by most of these groups to be a major element in their outlook. But these activist projects do not shape the public image of feminism. The organizations and academic networks that shape public perceptions of feminism have become distant from the constituencies that once invigorated them, and have lost focus and dynamism.

Feminism has become more an idea than a movement, and one that often lacks the visionary quality that it once had. The same could be said about progressive movements, or the left, generally: we now have a fairly large and respectable arena in which feminist and progressive ideas are taken for granted. And yet we seem to have little influence on the direction of politics in the United States as a whole, and a kind of "low-grade depression" seems to have settled over the feminist/progressive arena. This is both result and cause of the weakness of the left in recent decades, a response to the widespread acceptance of the view that there is no alternative to capitalism. The women's movement has been weakened along with other progressive movements by this loss in confidence in the possibility that collective action can bring about social change.

Why the Decline of the Women's Movement?

In the 1960s and early 1970s the dominant tendency in the women's movement was radical feminism. At that time the women's movement included two more or less distinct tendencies. One of these called itself Socialist Feminism (or, at times, Marxist Feminism) and understood the oppression of women as intertwined with other forms of oppression, especially race and class, and tried to develop a politics that would challenge all of these simultaneously. The other tendency called itself Radical Feminism. Large-R Radical Feminists argued that the oppression of women was primary, that all other forms of oppression flowed from gender inequality.

Feminist radicals of both stripes insisted that the inequality of the sexes in the public sphere was inseparable from that in private life; radical feminism demanded equality for women in both spheres. And despite disagreements among themselves about the relationship between the oppression of women and other forms of oppression, radical feminists agreed that equality between women and men could not exist by itself, in a society otherwise divided by inequalities of wealth and power. The goal of radical feminism was an egalitarian society, and new kinds of community, based on equality.

During the 1960s and 1970s the radical current 15 within the women's movement propelled the whole movement forward, but it was the demand for women's entry into the workplace, on equal terms with men, that gained most ground. The more radical feminist demands for an egalitarian society and new kinds of community could not be won so easily. Though the liberal and radical wings of the women's movement differed in their priorities, their demands were not sharply divided. Radical feminists wanted gender equality in the workplace, and most liberal feminists wanted a more egalitarian society. Affirmative action was not only a tool of privileged women. In an article in the Spring 1999 issue of *Feminist Studies,* Nancy McLean points out that working women used this policy to struggle for equality at the workplace, both opening up traditionally male jobs for women and creating a working-class component of the women's movement. As long as the women's movement was growing and was gaining influence, demands for equal access to the workplace and for broad social equality complemented one another.

But a movement's demands, once won, can have different consequences than intended. Affirmative action campaigns were on the whole more effective in the professions than elsewhere, and it was educated, overwhelmingly white, women who were poised to take advantage of these opportunities. This was in large part due to the failure of the labor movement to organize women and people of color. The class and racial tilt of affirmative action was also a result of the accelerating stratification of U.S. society in the 1970s, 1980s, and 1990s, the growing gap between the lower and higher rungs of the economy. The gains made by working women for access to higher-paid jobs could not offset the effects of widening class divisions. From the early 1970s on, the standard of living of workers generally declined. Women, who were poorer to begin with, suffered the worst consequences.

The radical feminist vision became stalled, torn apart by factionalism and by intense sectarian ideological conflicts. By the latter part of the 1970s, a cultural feminism, aimed more at creating a feminist subculture than at changing social relations generally, had taken the place formerly occupied by radical feminism. Alice Echols' book *Daring to Be Bad: Radical Feminism in America 1967–1975* describes these developments accurately and empathetically. Ruth Rosen's recent survey of the women's

movement, *The World Split Open: How the Modern Women's Movement Changed America,* includes a clear-eyed account of the impact of these developments on the women's movement generally. Ordinarily, such sectarianism occurs in movements that are failing, but the women's movement, at the time, was strong and growing. The problem was the very large gap between the social transformation that radical feminists wanted and the possibility of bringing it about, at least in the short run. The movement itself became the terrain for the construction of, if not a new society, at least a new woman. The degree of purity that feminists demanded of one another was bound to lead to disappointment and recriminations.

I think that radical feminism became somewhat crazed for the same reasons that much of the radical movement did during the same period. In the late 1960s and early 1970s many radicals not only adopted revolution as their aim but also thought that revolution was within reach in the United States. Different groups had different visions of revolution. There were feminist, black, anarchist, Marxist-Leninist, and other versions of revolutionary politics, but the belief that revolution of one sort or another was around the corner cut across these divisions. The turn toward revolution was not in itself a bad thing; it showed an understanding of the depth of the problems that the movement confronted. But the idea that revolution was within reach in the United States in these years was unrealistic. The war in Vietnam had produced a major crisis in U.S. society. Protest against the war, combined with protest against racism and sexism, led some to think that it had become possible to create a new society. In fact, the constituency for revolution, however conceived, was limited mostly to students and other young people, and this was not enough for a revolution. When the war ended the broad constituency of the protest movement evaporated, isolating its radical core. Radical feminism lasted longer than other insurgencies due to the continuing strength of the women's movement as a whole, and the ongoing receptivity of many feminists to radical ideas. But by the 1980s radical feminism, at least as an activist movement with a coherent agenda, also became marginal to politics in the United States.

Affirmative action for women constituted an effort toward gender equality in the workplace, a goal not yet achieved. But the success of the women's movement in opening up the professions to women, ironically, has had the effect of narrowing the movement's perspective and goals. When it was mostly made up of young people, and infused with radical ideas, feminism was able to develop a perspective that was in many ways independent of, and critical of, the class from which most feminists were drawn. Now, although there are important new, younger feminist voices, the largest part of the organized women's movement consists of women of my generation, the generation that initiated second wave feminism. I am not suggesting that people necessarily become less radical as they get older. I think that what happens to people's politics depends as much on the times, and the political activity that they engage in, as it does on their age. In a period when radicalism has been made to seem irrelevant even for the young, it is easy for a movement whose leadership is mostly made up of middle-aged, middle-class professionals to drift into something like complacency.

20   This of course does not describe the whole women's movement. What we now have is a women's movement composed on the one hand of relatively cautious organizations such as the National Organization for Women, the National Women's Political Caucus, and others, as well as more daring but also less visible organizations concerned with specific-issue grassroots organizing. What we do not have is a sector of the women's movement that does what radical feminism once did, that addresses the issue of women's subordination generally, and places it within a critique of society as a whole. Liberal feminism lost the ERA, but it did accomplish

many things. Largely due to liberal feminist organizing efforts, young women and girls now have opportunities that did not exist a few decades ago, and expectations that would have seemed wildly unrealistic to earlier generations.

Radical versions of feminism still exist, but more in the academy and among intellectuals than among organizers. Some feminists have continued to work at bridging this gap, both in their intellectual work and in engagement with grassroots movements. The growing numbers of women, including feminists, in the academy, has meant that many students have been introduced to feminist and progressive ideas, and feminist and progressive writings have influenced the thinking of a wide audience. But on the whole, feminists in the academy, along with the progressive wing of academics generally, lack a clear political agenda, and have often become caught up in the logic and values of the university. In the arena of high theory, and to some extent cultural studies, both of which are closely associated with feminism, the pursuit of status, prestige, and stardom has turned feminist and progressive values on their head. Instead of the 1960s' radical feminist critique of hierarchy, we have a kind of reveling in hierarchy and in the benefits that come with rising to the top of it.

Though the contemporary women's movement has avoided the racial and ethnic biases, and the single-issue focus, that plagued the early feminist movement, it resembles first wave feminism in having gradually lost its critical distance from its own middle- and upper-middle class position. First wave feminism narrowed, over the course of its history, not only in relation to the issue of race but also in relation to the issues of capital and class. In the pre–Civil War years, first wave feminism was part of a loose coalition of movements within which radical ideas circulated, including critical views of industrial capitalism. In the late nineteenth century, as the structures of industrial capitalism hardened and class conflict intensified, feminists played important roles in the reform movements that championed poor and working-class people, and some sections of the women's movement criticized capitalism and reached out to labor. The Women's Christian Temperance Union, for instance, criticized the exploitation of labor by capital and entertained support for "gospel socialism" as "Christianity in action." In the early years of the twentieth century the alliance between feminism and socialism continued within the Socialist Party. But after the turn of the century mainstream feminists moved away from any critique of capitalism, instead identifying women's interests and values with those of the upper middle class. By the time first wave feminism disappeared it had lost any critical perspective on capitalism or on its own class origins.

Feminism Has Absorbed the Perspective of the Middle Class

Like first wave feminism, contemporary feminism has over time tended to absorb the perspective of the middle class from which it is largely drawn. Meanwhile the perspective of that class has changed. Over the last several decades, under the impact of increasing economic insecurity and widening inequalities, the pursuit of individual advancement has become an increasingly important focus within the middle class. Community engagement has weakened for many, perhaps most, middle-class people. For many people, especially professionals, work has become something of a religion; work is the only remaining source of identity that seems valid. Meanwhile the workplace has become, for many, more competitive and more stressful. This is not just a problem of the workplace, but of the culture as a whole. This country has become increasingly individualistic, cold, and selfish. And feminism has not noticeably challenged this. The feminist demand for equal workplace access was and remains important; for most women this demand has not been achieved. But the most visible sector of the women's movement appears to have substituted aspirations toward material success for the demand for social equality and community. This evolution, from the radical and transforming values of its early years, has been so gradual that it has been easy for those involved not to notice it. But it is a reflection of the shifting perspectives of women who were once part of a radical movement and now find themselves in settings governed by a different set of values.

In the 1970s and 1980s, many feminists thought that if only we could get more women into the universities, the universities would be transformed and would become less elitist, less competitive, more humane, and more concerned with addressing social problems. We now have a lot of women in the universities, and it is not clear that the universities have changed for the better. Indeed, in many respects the universities are worse, especially in regard to the growing pursuit of corporate funds and the resultant spread of the market ethos. But so far neither women in general nor feminists in particular have been especially prominent in challenging these trends and demanding a more humane, less competitive, or less hierarchical university. Feminist academics have not in recent years been particularly notable for their adherence to such values. There are some areas of academic feminism where there is open discussion, where people treat each other with respect, and where everyone involved is treated as an equal participant towards a common purpose. But in too much of feminist academia this is not the case. In the arena of high theory, the most prestigious sector of academic feminism, competition and the pursuit of status are all too often uppermost.

The shift in values that has taken place in the women's movement has been part of a broader trend. In a period of sharpening economic and social divisions, characterized by corporate demand for greater and greater profits and the canonizing of greed, a whole generation has been seized by the desire to rise to the top. Feminists are no exception to this. The image of the feminist as careerist is not merely a fantasy promulgated by hostile media. Put

25

differently, feminists, at least those in academia and in the professions, have been no more overtaken by these values than other members of the middle class. But to say this is to admit that feminists have lost their grip on a vision of a better world.

Contemporary feminism emerged out of the rebellion of young middle-class women against domesticity, and their demand for careers outside the home, which was one side of the gender politics of the 1960s and early 1970s. The other side was rebellion against work in a corporate-driven society on the part of the young men of the New Left, and their never fully defined demand for something more meaningful. Christopher Lasch's posthumously published collection of essays, *Women and the Common Life* (Norton, 1997), argues, in an essay entitled "The Sexual Division of Labor, The Decline of Civil Culture, and the Rise of the Suburbs," that these critiques were both correct and were in principle complementary. He argued that each view suffered from failing to take the other into account, and that the division between these critiques reflected the excessive distance between the spheres of work and family. He called for equal participation of the sexes in the home and a workplace made more human by incorporation of a feminist critique.

I think that we need an updated version of 1960s radicalism, which would include both socialist and feminist perspectives and address itself to the increased power of the corporations and influence of marketplace values. Most feminists would disavow the individualism and the pursuit of success that has become such a prominent part of culture in the United States. But I think that most of us live according to these values anyway: we measure our value by our success at work, and we let little stand in the way of it. It is taken for granted that success in life can be measured, in large part, by the achievement of wealth and status, through work. These values may have taken hold most strongly within the professional middle class, but they have extended far beyond it as well; they are reinforced by economic insecurity, the fear of falling behind, losing one's job, falling to the bottom.

It is difficult, even for radicals, to maintain a different set of values when institutions and social relations outside of work have become so weakened, when nothing but achievement at work seems to hold much social value. Our communities have dwindled. We regret this but most of us respond by further throwing ourselves into our work. I think we need a critique of, and an alternative to, an increasingly unfettered capitalism, which intensifies social divisions, puts a price on everything, and draws all arenas of life into its vortex. One can think of the radical feminist demand for equality and community as quaint, or one can see it as a precondition for a contemporary radical program.

Analyzing Argument

1. In a sentence, what is Epstein's main claim?

2. In a paragraph, summarize Epstein's argument.

3. What does Epstein value?

4. Epstein concludes: "I think we need a critique of, and an alternative to, an increasingly unfettered capitalism, which intensifies social divisions, puts a price on everything, and draws all arenas of life into its vortex." How might a critique of capitalism be helpful or harmful?

Different Strategies Are Necessary Now

JOAN ACKER

Joan Acker teaches sociology at the University of Oregon and has been involved in feminist activities since the late 1960s. She is the author of *Doing Comparable Worth: Gender, Class and Pay Equity* (1989). The following essay was published in *Monthly Review* in response to Barbara Epstein's "What Happened to the Women's Movement?" (pp. 413–420).

Barbara Epstein's answer to "What Happened to the Women's Movement?" (*Monthly Review*, May 2001) explains much of the decline of the intense, exciting, radical and socialist feminist organizing of the 1960s and 1970s, with its visions of societal transformation and women's emancipation. However, I think that she underemphasizes, or even ignores, some important parts of a comprehensive answer. These have to do with the daunting reality facing revolutionary visions, the strength of opposition to women's equality with men, and changes in economic and political relations that now seem to require new visions and ways of organizing.

Before I discuss these issues, I want to add to her comments on first wave feminism. Abandonment of a broad agenda and of links to radical organizations were not the only reasons for the decline of first wave feminism. Decline was also a consequence of deep-seated but hidden antipathy to feminist claims within radical organizations, as well as a consequence of the successes of first wave feminism. My own experiences in the 1940s lead me to those conclusions. I grew up in the late '30s and early '40s with the firm belief that the women's movement had been a success, that women were equal to men, and that I could do and be anything I wanted, an individualistic perspective, I admit. The radical organizations I joined had campaigns against racism, but generally denied that any problems with democracy or equality existed for women within their own organizations. What problems there were in the larger society would be solved automatically as the working class triumphed. I began to see the fallacy, and the male privilege, in these claims only as I had children and my low wage-earning capacity forced the decision that I be the homebound caregiver. I think that young women today have similar difficulties in seeing the continuing inequalities and subordinations. The second wave movement accomplished a great deal, as Epstein says. Young women do face a different world of possibilities than second wave feminists faced. It is easy to believe that all the problems are solved. But, they too may have rude awakenings.

The daunting reality facing radical and socialist feminist visions was, and is, not only that we have no gender- and race-egalitarian alternative to capitalism, but that the interweaving of gender and race with the economic, political, and social relations of capitalism is much more complicated and pervasive than we had imagined. To fundamentally change the situation of women, almost everything else must change. But, as Epstein recognizes, the constituency for revolution was never large, and the vision of revolution was unrealistic. In any case, a revolution led by New Left male radicals would probably have been disastrous for women and for the ideals of the New Left itself. Instead, radical, socialist, and liberal feminists turned to specific and immediate projects for change. Much of the grassroots organizing, and the radical spirit of the movement, was focused on struggles for Affirmative Action, comparable worth, women's health care, and legal abortion, among many other issues. This division of labor within the feminist movement has achieved many, if somewhat separate, victories. And these victories should not be attributed only to liberal feminists. This is the strength of the women's movement and one reason it has survived. The general understanding of women's subordination within a critique of capitalist societies still exists, but, as many now recognize, this critique is too general to fuel specific organizing. I think that Epstein makes too broad a generalization when she says "feminists have lost their grip on a vision of a better world." I don't fundamentally disagree with her, but I would temper her nostalgia a bit.

Opposition to feminist demands has something to do with the decline of the women's movement as grassroots, radical organizing. This opposition has appeared in many forms, from silent resistance to the well-known backlash in legal attacks on Affirmative Action, and media caricatures of unattractive feminists. The struggle for pay equity, or comparable worth, provides examples of the multifaceted opposition to changes that could fundamentally improve the economic situation of many women. First, opposition from politicians, employers, and bureaucrats, in both the public and private sectors, forced equity advocates to settle for restrictive definitions of which jobs should be equalized. These definitions limited efforts to the public sector, and to jobs in one employing organization, rather than attacking inequities in the labor market generally. Job evaluation specialists enlisted to assist with determining inequities wanted to protect their evaluation systems from changes sought by feminists because such changes might radically increase pay to women and upset private sector employers, the usual clients of job evaluation specialists. Only the grossest inequities could be identified using these systems. Employers opposed pay equity because they feared high costs. Working-class men were afraid that their own wages would be cut to increase women's wages, and some employers argued for this. Sometimes working-class men's sense of masculine superiority was threatened by the idea that women's work might be of equal worth to theirs. Opposition increased as free market ideology began to dominate public discussions. Comparable worth worked where it was really tried, but this happened in only a few states and in a larger number of municipalities.

Economic and employment changes driven by 5 capitalist efforts to achieve "flexibility," maximize profits, and weaken the labor movement also undermined pay equity efforts. These efforts occurred in the early 1980s, at the time that employers began downsizing, refusing wage increases, and demanding wage givebacks, all part of the war on labor. Working-class men were seriously threatened, as they have continued to be. Male support for pay equity was difficult to mobilize under these conditions. Similarly, access to the higher-paying, skilled, male-dominated jobs was, and continues to be, difficult under these conditions. This is one reason that Affirmative Action was more effective in the upper-level professional and managerial jobs than in working-class jobs. Excluded groups can be let in with less fear when job opportunities are expanding than when they are contracting.

Changes such as these suggest that different strategies are necessary now, and some are appearing. Many of these are labor movement strategies, not necessarily linked to feminism, such as organizing home care workers in Los Angeles, or hotel workers in Hawaii. Feminist strategies that might mobilize a movement today must have a race focus, a cross-class focus, and possibly a global focus. One issue that might meet these criteria, and at the same, build a radical critique of current social arrangements and values is the issue of who is going to care for our children and our sick. As more and more women are in paid labor, as work hours get longer, as work and economic survival become more stressful, caring is at the bottom of the list in rewards. Women remain responsible for care giving, with little or no pay, and no thanks. These problems affect women across all areas of our society, although resources to deal with them vary widely. Women on welfare and women professionals face similar challenges, in this regard. The societal cost is tremendous, but hidden. This is a radical issue, because its roots are in the fundamental organization of U.S. capitalism, in the structures of our cities, in our lack of public transportation, in the devaluing of women and their work.

Like Barbara Epstein, I yearn for a rebirth of radicalism and the heady feeling of participating in a broad movement for economic justice and humane values. This time it will have to be a radicalism that integrates critiques of gender and racial subordination in ways that have not been achieved by men working in radical and socialist traditions. A go-it-alone feminist movement will not be broad enough. But, can the men adapt?

Analyzing Argument

1. What is Acker's disagreement with Epstein's argument? How might Epstein respond to Acker?

2. What assumptions do Epstein and Acker share?

3. How does Acker support her argument? What support is most or least engaging?

4. Describe Acker's voice. Is it curious, engaging, alienating, rigorous, or something else? Use specific sentences or passages from Acker to help support your point.

5. In groups, discuss Acker's final sentence. What argument does it suggest? How does that argument relate to Acker's main line of reasoning?

Ad Urges Students to Think Twice about Colleges with a Rape Problem

ROBIN WILSON

According to Robin Wilson's author statement, she writes articles "that often examine [a] matter in a new light and sometimes run contrary to conventional wisdom." This article was published in *The Chronicle of Higher Education* on May 15, 2014, after a gender-equality group UltraViolet intensified its public campaign against rape on college campuses.

At a gathering last month for students admitted to Dartmouth College's Class of 2018, a father asked Lorelei Yang, a junior there, whether the campus was a dangerous place for women. He'd heard about sexual assaults at Dartmouth, says Ms. Yang, and wondered if the campus's problems were unique.

Dartmouth is the primary target in a hard-hitting new advertising campaign by the national gender-equality group UltraViolet. "Accepted to Dartmouth?" reads one of the ads that appeared last month on Facebook and other websites, drawing more than 200,000 views. "You should know about its rape problem."

The campaign comes as colleges are under increasing pressure from students and the federal government to improve their response to reports of sexual assault. In personal accounts and in complaints filed with the U.S. Department of Education, students and alumni have alleged that their institutions brushed off or mishandled their reports. And dozens of investigations have ensued, along with much media attention and strong assurances from college presidents that they are committed to this important issue.

This month UltraViolet dialed up the intensity, expanding its ad campaign to Occidental College; American, Brandeis, Harvard, and Florida State Universities; and the Universities of California at Berkeley and of Michigan at Ann Arbor. With the exception of American and Brandeis, the targeted institutions are among 55 colleges and universities now under federal investigation for possible violations of the gender-equity law known as Title IX, which requires campus officials to investigate and resolve reports of sexual harassment and assault whether or not the police are involved.

UltraViolet's online ad campaign is an in-your-face attempt to get prospective students and campus officials to recognize the severity of sexual assault, says Karin Roland, the group's organizing director. "The goal is to make sure that students considering these schools know what they're getting into," she says. "And it's to make sure administrators know they can't hide from this problem. Universities can either take student safety seriously, or we'll bring the grass-roots pressure to push them over the edge to do it."

Ms. Yang, a government major and member of a campus group at Dartmouth that educates students about sexual misconduct, believes the ad campaign is more about fear-mongering than about fixing the problem. In response to the concerned father at the Class of 2018 gathering, she recalls saying that while Dartmouth does have a sexual-assault problem, it isn't alone. "I said, 'It's a problem at every university campus.'"

Dartmouth, meanwhile, created its own ad campaign last month. Its ads refer people to a "sexual-assault awareness resource page," which says the university is poised to institute tough new sanctions for students found responsible for rape, to open a resource center for victims, and to host a national conference in July.

"We think we're on the leading edge of where higher ed is right now in terms of ways to prevent sexual assault and punish students," says Justin Anderson, a Dartmouth spokesman. "UltraViolet is ignoring the actions Dartmouth is taking."

'If Bad PR Is What It Takes …'

UltraViolet prefers to be pointed. Like other staff members there, Ms. Roland used to work for MoveOn.org, a nonprofit group that backs Democratic politicians and is known for its early use of email and online communication to spread information and raise money.

10 UltraViolet, which also speaks out on abortion, pay equity, birth control, and gender discrimination, took aim at Dartmouth and the seven other campuses, Ms. Roland says, either because they were the site of high-profile sexual-assault cases or because students there were pushing administrators to step up their response to sexual assault.

At Dartmouth this year, a first-year student came forward and said that her name had appeared in an online "rape guide," in which a male classmate gave tips on how to persuade her to perform oral sex. The student said she was later assaulted at a fraternity party. In April of last year, the college canceled classes for a day of dialogue after students protested at an event for prospective students, decrying incidents of sexual assault, racism, and homophobia on the campus. Last May, Dartmouth students announced they had filed a federal complaint over the college's alleged misreporting of sexual-assault cases.

"Dartmouth has one of the most rampant sexual-assault problems in the country," says Ms. Roland. And UltraViolet wants to get that message out. "If bad PR is what it takes to get these schools to act," she says, "we'll bring them bad PR."

Florida State is part of the ad campaign, says Ms. Roland, because in 2012 an undergraduate woman accused the university's high-profile quarterback, Jameis Winston, of rape. Critics have said university officials did nothing to deal with the allegation. A local prosecutor, meanwhile, said he lacked evidence to charge Mr. Winston.

Florida State can't comment on the case, a university spokeswoman says. But "the university agrees with UltraViolet," she adds, "on the importance of shining a light on the issue of sexual assault."

'What's the End Goal?'

It's unclear what effect the UltraViolet campaign 15 may have. Spring is when admitted students decide where to enroll, but many factors influence their college choices.

During a program for prospective students this year at Dartmouth, students and parents asked questions about sexual assault, Mr. Anderson says. The university's applications dropped 14 percent this year over last year, to 19,235, a decline officials there are studying. But at the same time, its yield, or the proportion of admitted students who enroll, hit an all-time high of 54.5 percent. "For the first time in seven years," says Mr. Anderson, "we won't have to go to our wait list."

Susan Struble, a 1993 Dartmouth graduate, applauds the UltraViolet campaign and any additional attention and resources the college may commit to the issue. Two years ago she started a group of faculty members, students, and alumni called DartmouthChange.org to persuade the university to pay more attention to sexual violence. "It was bad when I was on campus," she says, "and it's bad now." Ms. Struble was sexually assaulted by a male undergraduate when she was a prospective student visiting Dartmouth, she says, and then again after she enrolled. She never filed a report.

To put more pressure on campuses and further raise awareness, UltraViolet has also asked Princeton Review Inc. to survey students about sexual assault on their campuses and include that information in its college rankings. But while the company added a page on its website last month devoted to student safety, it does not plan to ask students to rank campuses specifically on sexual assault, says Robert Franek, senior vice president there.

"The creation of a student-opinion ranking based on sexual assault," he says, "is not the ranking list we can create at the Princeton Review." Any information it provides about sexual assault, he believes, should be based on quantitative data, not students' opinions.

20   Alison Kiss, executive director of the Clery Center for Security on Campus, thinks UltraViolet's "scare tactics" may be counterproductive. The Clery Center, a nonprofit group created to lobby for consumer information on campus crime, continues to monitor and advocate for student safety.

"What's the end goal?" Ms. Kiss asks about the ad campaign. "It sounds like it is to shame the institution," she says. "How is that improving the community or the culture for students there now? I don't think it takes an evidence-based approach to eradicate sexual violence on campus."

Analyzing Argument

1. How is this article a kind of argument analysis? Explain any specific passages that analyze the ongoing argument or UltraViolet's campaign.

2. Beyond analysis, what is Wilson doing? What claims (of fact, value, or policy) can you detect or point out in the article?

3. What values or assumptions are competing in the public debate about campus rape? (Wilson may not state these directly, so try to infer the subtle or unstated opposition.)

4. Explain how the quotation from Alison Kiss is a counteragument. What particular position is Kiss refuting?

5. How do the quotations by college administrators function in the article? What claims, values, or assumptions do they reinforce or express?

The Problem No Longer Nameless

HANNAH REMMERT

Hannah Remmert, a professional writing major at Miami University of Ohio, developed this project for a first-year English course. The assignment asked students to examine a text that pushed against mainstream or conventional thinking. Remmert selected Betty Friedan's influential work, *The Feminine Mystique* (1963).

After WWII, women were encouraged not to work out of the home but to focus on perfecting their families—what Betty Friedan's *The Feminine Mystique* calls "the problem that has no name." The problem, put briefly, was that women were unhappy simply being housewives. Their lives provided little to no intellectual challenge, making each day as boring, monotonous, and unsatisfying as the day before. Additionally, each woman thought she faced this problem alone, making it all the more serious as each thought herself delusional for questioning a life in which she had the perfect appliances, the perfect home, and the perfect family. Through its wide circulation, *The Feminine Mystique* introduced to the mainstream an idea that would have otherwise remained silent.

While *The Feminine Mystique* connected to a wide population, its success was often discredited. Many people did not take Friedan seriously, claiming her work to be "unscientific" or "too obvious and feminine." Similarly, people often discredit her text as an outlet of her own personal frustrations with a failing marriage and being locked into housewifery (Schuessler).

Friedan exhibited passion for learning throughout the entirety of her life, graduating at the top of her class from Smith University with a major in psychology. She then won a prestigious scholarship to pursue a Ph.D. from the University of California, Berkeley (Dreier). During her time there, Friedan questioned her decision to accept this scholarship, which would funnel into a career as a professional psychologist. As Friedan admits, "Nothing was important to me that year but love. We walked in the Berkeley hills and a boy said: 'Nothing can come of this, between us. I'll never win a fellowship like yours'" (70). Friedan gave up the scholarship, happy at the time to let go of the fear associated with becoming a career woman. She married and began her family. So perhaps critics who proclaim her work simply an outlet for her own personal frustrations about housewifery are true. But the very nature of this problem lay in personal frustration. It could not be thought of as a simple political problem, with a simple solution. Rather, it was transpersonal: many women felt this frustration and dissatisfaction.

Despite the criticism it received, Friedan's text was able to serve as a catalyst for fundamental change. Women began to think differently and realize that they shouldn't have to simply be housewives. Friedan enabled women to come to grips with their feelings that they wanted a purpose in life greater than a "server of food, a putter-on of pant and a bedmaker, somebody who can be called on when you want something" (Friedan 21). Friedan gave women both the "ok" to be dissatisfied with their mundane lives and the blessing to embark on changing it. Women had had enough. They were ready for a change.

This change came in the form of second-wave feminism. As Peter Dreier explains in his *Huffington Post* article, women began to organize and fight for rights beyond the vote, a battle many of their grandmothers before them fought as first-wave feminists. This time, women wanted equality in all aspects, from careers to reproductive rights, equal salaries to sports. Betty Friedan herself became very involved politically. In 1966, she helped form the National Organization for Women, or NOW, to lobby and organize for the civil rights of women. NOW elected Friedan as their first president, a position she held until 1970. Friedan also helped in the formation of the National Abortion Rights Action League and the Women's Strike for Equality in honor of the 50th anniversary of the 19th Amendment (Dreier). Through the efforts of those in these groups, many important steps for women were reached. As more and more got accomplished, more and more women became aware of the action taken for their rights, and subsequently the movement grew until society could no longer ignore these women pleading for true equality, making so many sacrifices to give them a chance at a life any white man of the time was simply born with. The power of this movement lay in the fact that it affected multitudes of women. All had felt society's pressures at some point, encouraging them to stay at home, to marry early, to avoid getting mixed up with a career, to find themselves fulfilled by motherhood. Women could apply this problem to their own understanding and personal experiences, creating a deeper emotional connection across America, creating a deeper connection in the need for change.

While *The Feminine Mystique* was not the only feminist text circulating at this time, Friedan wrote it with a particular, influential group in mind. The struggles she addresses apply primarily to white, middle-class women of the time. Friedan left out women of color entirely, and did not begin to fight for the rights of lesbians until much later. While leaving out certain groups of women gives her argument a definite bias, had Friedan included the minority groups in her argument, it may have been weakened by the social frictions of the era—specifically, the Civil Rights battles.

Despite the fact that Friedan didn't explicitly include all women in her initial work, her intended audience clung to the ideas she introduced and became the empowered women that began significant change. These were the women who worked closely with Friedan and others as they created numerous events and organizations to better vocalize their argument. *The Feminine Mystique* ignited something critical. It equipped middle-class white women with the knowledge that they were not alone, and that together they could do something.

Works Cited

Dreier, Peter. "The Feminine Mystique and Women's Equality—50 Years Later." *The Huffington Post*, 18 Feb. 2013, www.huffingtonpost.com/peter-dreier/the-feminine-mystique-betty-friedan_b_2712355.html.

Friedan, Betty. *The Feminine Mystique*. W.W. Norton, 1963.

Schuessler, Jennifer. "Criticisms of a Classic Abound." *The New York Times*, 18 Feb. 2013, www.nytimes.com/2013/02/19/books/50-years-of-reassessing-the-feminine-mystique.html?_r=0.

Analyzing Argument

1. What is Remmert's main claim about Friedan's book? Is it, in your estimation, a claim of fact or value?

2. How does Remmert deal with opposition? Where and how does she counter or concede?

3. What are Remmert's two main support strategies? Explain how each reinforces her main claim.

4. Remmert alludes to first- and second-wave feminism. How do these concepts fit into her overall argument about Friedan's book?

There are **3 billion** women who **don't** look like **supermodels** and **only 8** who **do.**

Image courtesy of The Advertising Archives

This ad is from an internal poster campaign of The Body Shop, an international toiletries and cosmetics retailer.

Analyzing Argument

1. What argument does this ad make?

2. What details of the poster convey the argument, and how?

3. What is the ad a response to?

4. What values does the ad appeal to?

5. Whom does the ad target, and how?

A suffrage parade in New York City, 1912.

Analyzing Argument

1. How is marching in a parade an argument? What other groups participate in parades, and what arguments do they make by doing so?

2. What other public actions make arguments? List examples, and specify what arguments you think each action makes.

3. How might people have responded to this image in 1912? How might they respond today? What assumptions, values, and beliefs have changed? What ones haven't changed, but should?

4. How do particular details of the image contribute to the argument?

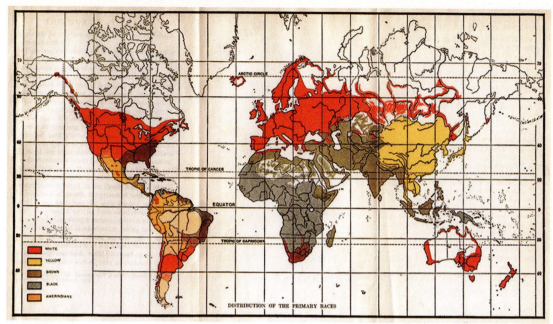

17 Race

In America, race has figured into national boundaries, education, religious doctrine, law enforcement, reproductive rights, economic principle, war, and even the act of writing history. In short, race has been fused to every conceivable public policy and debate. Meanwhile, the concept itself has been called into question. Today, some scholars are asking: Is race a biological fact or social construction?

Race continues to be a complex and controversial issue that affects average people's lives and every nation. Whether we consider race biologically or socially, it continues to be a major topic in the ongoing discussion about issues that matter deeply in American society. These readings explore race and invite the reader to participate in the national dialogue about race in the United States.

Readings about Race in Chapters 1–14

"Speech on the Land," Chief Seattle

"Seattle's Rhetoric," Andrew Buchner

"Progressive Profiteering: The Appeal and Argumentation of *Avatar*," Ben Wetherbee

"The Hearts of Argument: Benetton's Advertising Appeal," Megan Ward

"Disparities Demystified," Pedro A. Noguera and Antwi Akom

Above: Lothrop Stoddard's personal rendering of racial distribution, from *The Rising Tide of Color Against White World-Supremacy*, published in 1920. In this book, Stoddard argues that "yellow" and "brown" races would challenge white supremacy in the coming decades—that Chinese and Japanese expansion, along with Islamic "fanaticism," would push against white global dominance.

What Is Race?

VICTOR M. FERNANDEZ

Discussion, dialogue, and debate frequently fall short of insight or revelation because people begin arguing the issue before they have explored what the key term(s) might mean. The following essay invites the reader to stop for a moment and consider his or her understanding of the commonly used term "race." Fernandez, a nurse, asks the reader to step back from the debate about particular racial issues and ask a more radical question: What is race? This essay is from the Cultural Diversity in Nursing website, www.culturediversity.org.

In the Emergency Department the radio squawks with the familiar greetings: "MGH this is rescue 3 inbound with a 56-year-old black male with complaint of chest pain. . . ." The patient arrives and is received by the nurse who assesses the patient while the admissions clerk begins with a stream of questions, including one about race. The patient is treated and admitted to the ICU (Intensive Care Unit), where the nurse begins the admission assessment; again, the question of race comes up on the assessment form. In reviewing the chart the physician's notes read as follows: "This is a 56-year-old black male who presents to the ER with . . ." Flip to the nurse's notes: ". . . 56 yo black male, diaphoretic . . ." But what exactly is race?

Many Americans, and it would appear many in our health care system, put an emphasis on classifying everyone by race, not region, or culture. There exist laws that protect people from racial bias, there are racial relation issues, and proportional representation of racial groups. Words like "racial groups," "race," and "racial conflict" are quite common terms in the English language, and they keep cropping up in the press, in TV news, and in casual conversations, but the meaning of the term *race* frequently seems ambiguous and vague.

The AAPA (American Association of Physical Anthropology) Statement on Biological Aspects of Race (1996) describes the popular concept of race as "being derived from 19th and early 20th century scientific formulations." The popular American folklore of the three great racial groups has its roots in a system developed in Europe and North America in the 18th century. It was for some time common to divide people into three main races. Caucasian or the so-called white race, for example, are native residents of Britain, France, and Germany. Natives of Uganda, Somalia, and Nigeria in Africa are considered Negroid or part of the black race. Koreans, Chinese, and American Indians are all Mongoloid or members of the yellow race. The distinguishing characteristics of these races are based on their visibly observable traits such as skin color, hair form, bone structure, and body shape. We must keep in mind that the American system of categorizing groups of people on the basis of race was developed by what was then a dominant white, European-descended population, and serves as a means to distinguish and control other "non-white" populations in various ways.

Though many definitions exist, there appears to be no established agreement on any scientific definition of race. What we do find though, is the general belief among the scientific community that race has no biological or natural basis and that the "race"-related physical variations found in humans have no real significance except for the social/cultural importance put on them by people. Race is a cultural term that Americans use to describe what a person's ancestry is, and that unfortunately brings with it many misconceptions and erroneous biological connotations. The popular tendency to attribute a general inferiority or superiority to a particular race, based on these biological differences, fails to notice that these differences in humans are not only genetic but also influenced by environmental factors.

5   Furthermore, those features considered significant for the survival of the species, such as the genetic capacity for intellectual development, have not been found, nor known to occur, more frequently in one population than in any other. In spite of our apparent differences, which are only skin deep, all humans around the world are biologically quite similar.

"The concept of race is a social and cultural construction. . . . Race simply cannot be tested or proven scientifically," according to the policy statement issued by the American Anthropological Association. "It is clear that human populations are not unambiguous, clearly demarcated, biologically distinct groups. The concept of 'race' has no validity . . . in the human species." Race is a socially defined concept that is used to categorize people according to their physical characteristics, and as such, a biologically meaningless category. It would be obvious by now that most people misuse the term "race," since the "pure races" or genetically homogeneous human populations alluded to do not exist, nor is there any valid evidence that they have ever existed. Unfortunately, these antiquated racial concepts persist as social conventions that serve to foster institutional discrimination. Race has a social and political significance because of racism: Such ideas as biological superiority or deficits among races, the assumption that intelligence, learning ability, physical endurance and such are somehow linked with genetic characteristics that differ systematically between "races" have often been used to support this racism.

In an apparent attempt to change some of the national attitudes towards the concept of race, the AAPA recommended the U.S. government drop the term "race" from its census categories in favor of a more useful term such as ethnicity. While *race* refers to the categorization of people, *ethnicity* has to do with group identification and reflects the person's culture. Even though nearly all college textbooks have long since dropped the idea that humanity can be neatly divided into races, racial categories were not completely abandoned; instead U.S. censuses now permit people to list themselves in several races if they so choose. As an example from another perspective, the Canadian Census does not collect data by racial categories, only by country of birth. Blacks and whites from Jamaica could classify themselves as British. There remains much debate regarding the concept of race, ethnicity, and appropriate categorization.

Keep in mind the concepts of race and ethnicity are strictly cultural constructs, and there is simply no physical evidence that ethnic groups are much different from one another. However, there does exist cultural differences and material culture evidence of people's self-defined ethnicity. "Race et culture" (Lévi-Strauss 1979 [1971]) begins with a critique of the idea of race: Lévi-Strauss shows how pervasive notions of racial difference are in human societies, and how they contribute to the integrity of the group. He further states that far from it being the case that culture is the product of race, "race— or that which one generally means by this term—is one of several functions of culture" (Lévi-Strauss 1979, 446).

I will continue to use the term "race" but with occasional reminders that social and behavioral differences among human beings are not genetic or biological and therefore not racial. It would be foolish not to recognize that regardless of whether biological differences exist or not, race plays a role and we need to include it, but with extreme caution.

Educating people in the United States is not   10 likely to correct their terminology; however, there is a tendency to disregard the wishes of the people affected, and they will likely continue labeling people as they (selfishly) see fit. We may have to continue correcting misconceptions and erroneous biological and genetic connotations to race as we encounter them. It is not your job to sensitize the U.S. population, but it seems we will wallow in stupidity until somebody teaches us otherwise.

References

American Association of Physical Anthropology: Statement on Biological Aspects of Race. Published in the *American Journal of Physical Anthropology,* vol. 101, pp. 569–570, 1996. For further information on Statement on Biological Aspects of Race, see American Association of Physical Anthropologist, www.physanth.org /about/position-statements/biological-aspects-race.

Lévi-Strauss, Claude. (1979 [1971]). "Race et histoire," in Raymond Bellour and Catherine Clément, eds., *Claude Lévi-Strauss,* pp. 427–462. Paris: Gallimard, originally published in *Revue internationale des sciences sociales,* 23(4).

Analyzing Argument

1. Fernandez argues for a particular definition of *race*. What is it?

2. What form of support is most critical to Fernandez's argument? Explain how that support strategy helps to make his case about the nature of race.

3. Why might the reader disagree with Fernandez about race? Make a list of potential points of contention. How might Fernandez respond to each point?

4. To whom does Fernandez seem to be speaking in his conclusion? How does the concluding strategy relate to the rest of his argument?

Another Inconvenient Truth: Race and Ethnicity Matter

WILLIS D. HAWLEY AND SONIA NIETO

For years, scholars, teachers, and lawmakers have been examining a trend known as "the achievement gap" among different races and ethnicities in American education. Consistently, African-American, Hispanic, and Native American students have lagged behind their Caucasian counterparts in nationwide tests and graduation rates. This article, published in the academic journal *Educational Leadership,* proposes a range of strategies for confronting that gap.

Given the shameful differences in the academic outcomes and graduation rates of students of color compared to many Asian and white students, one would expect policies and practices related to students' race and ethnicity to be high on the reform agenda. Of course, there is widespread discussion of the "minority achievement gap," but solutions on the public agenda are invariably colorblind. It is widely assumed that what works for white and Asian American students will work for students of color—if only we did it more often.

We need, however, to recognize an inconvenient truth—that when it comes to maximizing learning opportunities and outcomes for students from racially and ethnically diverse backgrounds, race and ethnicity matter. Race and ethnicity influence teaching and learning in two important ways: They affect how students respond to instruction and curriculum, and they influence teachers' assumptions about how students learn and how much students are capable of learning.

Being more conscious of race and ethnicity is not discriminatory; it's realistic. Research on race and ethnicity related dispositions suggests that almost all of us, regardless of our skin color, are biased against, or at least relatively uncomfortable with, people whose race and ethnicity are different from our own (Greenwald, Pohlman, Uhlman, & Banaji, 2007). Moreover, people of different races and ethnicities see the incidence of discrimination and the availability of educational and economic opportunity differently (McIntosh, 1988; Nieto & Bode, 2008; Sleeter, 1994).

Clarifying Terms

We use the expression race and ethnicity responsive rather than more comfortable terms like diversity or cultural responsiveness to draw attention to the importance of addressing issues related to skin color in improving students' learning opportunities. Also, when we focus on race alone, we sometimes see only black and white, neglecting the wide range of ethnicities in our schools and society.

Effective implementation of race and ethnicity-responsive approaches to school improvement that benefit all students requires that educators take three steps.

Step 1: Understand How Race Affects Teaching and Learning

Commitment to race and ethnicity conscious strategies for school improvement begins by understanding the influence of race and ethnicity on behavior and on attitudes about racial and ethnic differences.

There are three important lessons in this regard. First, differences among people to whom we assign racial and ethnic identities have no biological bases and are, instead, the product of socially constructed beliefs. When these beliefs disadvantage one group more than another, we can change them through social action. For example, one study found that teachers who became active in antiracist projects broadened their understanding and were able to use

Source: "Another Inconvenient Truth: Race and Ethnicity Matter," by Willis D. Hawley & Sonia Nieto, 2010, *Educational Leadership* 68(3), pp. 66–71. © 2010 by ASCD. Reprinted and adapted with permission. Learn more about ASCD at www.ascd.org.

their new skills in creating affirming learning environments for all their students (Donaldson, 2001).

Second, most of us are not fully aware of our dispositions toward people of races and ethnicities different from our own (Ayres, 2001). Thus, we do not understand how others see our behavior or the extent to which latent beliefs shape our actions. Learning how to question our beliefs is essential.

Finally, despite progress in race relations, many people of color see their opportunities as limited and fear they will experience discrimination. Given years of neglect and discrimination in public education, these perceptions are neither surprising nor unwarranted. Nevertheless, communities of color have, in general, great faith that education is their best hope for improving their children's life chances.

Examining Some Common Nonproductive Beliefs

10 This first step involves looking at some common beliefs about teaching and learning that often undermine students' opportunities to learn but which we sustain because they seem sensible and are, in many cases, well-meaning.

- To be fair to all students, one should be colorblind and ignore racial differences. To acknowledge that focusing on students' race or ethnicity affects how one should teach is to acknowledge that racial and ethnic discrimination has been, and continues to be, a significant influence on what and how students learn. This is not a comforting thought in a nation whose public stance is one of equity and fairness for all. Indeed, it is quite common to hear educators say that they are color-blind, as though this were a positive value. Although color-blindness is a good thing when it means that people do not discriminate on the basis of race, it can have negative consequences when educators refuse

to see their students' racial, ethnic, cultural, and linguistic differences. Instead, teachers need to respect and build on differences to foster student learning.

- One can build student self-esteem by reducing academic rigor. This particularly harmful belief leads to lowered expectations and, inevitably, to lower academic outcomes. Compelling evidence shows that when teachers hold high expectations for students who have been marginalized by their schooling experiences, student learning is enhanced, as long as high expectations are linked to greater resources and support (Ferguson, 2004). Without appropriate support in place, the often-stated "all students can learn" is an empty slogan.

- Teaching should be adapted to students' learning styles. A simplistic understanding of learning styles often leads to stereotypes about students from particular backgrounds, as though all students from a shared background learn in exactly the same way. Not only do students learn in different ways, but also students of color are often more dependent on school for learning how to learn than are more economically advantaged students who may have had more varied learning opportunities. Although differentiating instruction is important, ultimately teachers' misuse of the term *learning styles* may limit the cognitive development of students from disadvantaged groups.

- Students must have good basic skills before teachers can engage them in more complex learning activities. This belief belies the reality that even the youngest students can learn complex material while at the same time developing basic skills. For example, in her thought-provoking book about her work with 1st and 2nd graders from culturally diverse backgrounds, Mary Cowhey (2006) shows that while the students were learning to read, write, add, and subtract, they were also having conversations about philosophy, learning about the civil rights movement, and even engaging in a successful voter registration drive—activities that not only are cognitively demanding but that also make the curriculum more pluralistic and engaging.

Step 2: Use Race and Ethnicity Responsive Teaching Practices

Despite the research-based and common sense proposition that the key to effective schools is effective teaching—particularly in racially and ethnically diverse schools—public policy focuses more on teacher qualifications than on teaching quality. Efforts to improve teaching are often generic ("good teaching is good teaching") and typically are based on the idea that what works for one student works for another. A concomitant belief is that struggling students just need more of the same. Unfortunately, most measures of good teaching do not deal explicitly with culturally relevant pedagogy, in spite of the fact that research has documented that this approach to teaching can be effective with all students (Gay, 2010; Ladson-Billings, 2009; Murphy & Alexander, 2006).

Numerous researchers have investigated the kind of teaching that makes a difference, particularly for students whose culture, race, and language differ from the majority (Garcia, 1999; Gay, 2010; Haberman, 1988; Ladson Billings, 2009; Michie, 2009; Nieto, 2003). The following practices illustrate the interdependence of good instructional practice and of caring and trustful relationships among students and teachers:

- Respecting and being interested in students' experiences and cultural backgrounds.

- Supporting higher-order learning (for example, engaging students in complex problem solving while developing basic skills).

- Building on students' prior knowledge, values, and experiences.

- Avoiding stereotyping of students.

- Using ability grouping flexibly and sparingly.

- Adapting instruction to students' semantics, accents, dialects, and language ability.

- Applying rules relating to behavior fairly and sensitively.

- Facilitating learning of challenging material by knowing how to deal with stereotype threat, that is, some students' beliefs that cultural myths about racial differences in abilities may be valid.

- Engaging families directly in their children's learning.

Step 3: Promote Supportive School Conditions. Looking at School Culture

School structures, processes, and cultures affect student dispositions and their opportunities to learn. Under the best of situations, these racially and ethnically responsive conditions are aligned and reinforcing. The source of this coherence is a belief shared by teachers, administrators, and school staff that they have both the ability and the responsibility to significantly influence student learning, regardless of students' backgrounds.

We call such coherent sets of understandings and commitments race- and ethnicity-responsive school cultures. School practices in such cultures include targeted and flexible grouping for instruction; access to and support for learning high-level content (such as advanced placement courses); inclusive and affirming curriculums; and fair disciplinary rules and processes.

In schools with race- and ethnicity-responsive school cultures, teachers and administrators demonstrate respect and affirmation for their students' identities and experiences and make it clear that drive, or what Jaime Escalante called ganas—the desire and motivation to succeed—can overcome even brutal structural inequalities. Numerous studies have found this to be the case. For example, in a three-year investigation of

15

academic achievement among Mexican American students in a Texas high school, Valenzuela (1999) located the problem of student under-achievement not in students' identities or in family culture or poverty, but rather in uncaring school-based relationships and ineffective organizational structures.

Seeing Assets, Not Deficits

All students bring cultural values and experiences to their education, yet schools frequently disregard them, particularly teachers who are unfamiliar with their students' cultures. Gonzalez, Moll, and Amanti (2005) show teachers how to investigate, document, and use students' funds of knowledge—their experiences, skills, and competencies—through home visits and interviews with families. Teachers have found that families' competencies range from medicinal know-how to skills in arts and crafts to literary expertise to entrepreneurial knowledge, yet these funds of knowledge are frequently overlooked simply because of families' social class, ethnicity, or race.

A belief in students' identities also includes knowing something about their cultural and historic experiences. Working with a group of Latino and African American incarcerated young men, artist-educators Patty Bode and Derek Fenner developed a study of public murals and street art in the United States. They initiated the unit with Aaron Douglas's Harlem Renaissance era murals. Making authentic cultural connections to the artists and their work supported the young men's academic achievement; they expressed their learning in vibrant paintings, collages, and documentaries (Bode & Fenner, 2010).

But there is a danger in over-generalizing about cultural effects. What is needed instead is knowledge and awareness of the history and valued practices of students and their communities (Gutierrez & Rogoff, 2003). Therefore, it makes sense for teachers to learn about the students in their classrooms as well as about their families, prior experiences, cultural practices, and values.

Honoring Youth Culture

Many young people, regardless of their ethnicity or race, relate to today's youth culture; affirming this part of their identity is also a way of demonstrating a belief in students' identities.

For instance, in their research with high school students, Morrell and Duncan-Andrade (2002) used students' involvement with hip-hop culture to transform their curriculum and pedagogy and successfully engage students in literacy learning. At the same time, these researcher/practitioners have taught urban high school students such texts as *Beowulf, The Canterbury Tales, Othello, Macbeth, Hamlet,* and *The Odyssey* because they believe that all students should engage with demanding material whether it is based on urban and popular culture or on canonical texts that can—and indeed must—be made relevant and exciting for students.

Engaging Students in Race- and Ethnicity-Related Inquiry

Teachers and schools can also show respect for students by involving them in classroom-based research. Using participatory action research as a pedagogical approach, researcher Jason Irizarry and a group of high school students with whom he was working conducted a two-year ethnographic study examining the policies and practices that affected their education experiences. Irizarry and his students created a curriculum that focused on learning about Latinos' historic struggle for equal education and on developing the skills needed to conduct research relating to Latinos' education experiences and academic outcomes.

Demonstrating skills that schools purport to be important—such as the ability to analyze information and use data to construct written and oral persuasive arguments—students presented the findings of their research as well as recommendations to inform school reform efforts at various conferences and professional meetings. Recommendations to teachers included holding students to high standards and providing supports for students to meet them, honoring students' cultural and linguistic diversity, and building mutually edifying relationships with students and families. Most notable, Irizarry and his students share this experience in *The Latinization of U.S. Schools,* a book they wrote to inform the work of educators and policymakers.

Developing a Responsive School Culture

Changing a culture requires changing more than just attitudes and beliefs—it requires changing behaviors. Schools can accomplish this by focusing on the following practices.

Targeted Professional Development

People seldom believe in practices they don't know how to implement. It follows that urging teachers to have high expectations for themselves and students, without enhancing their expertise, is not only inadequate but may be counter-productive (Ferguson, 2004).

25   School-based professional learning communities can improve teaching and learning and lead to a fundamental change in teachers' work. To enhance their learning, teachers can, for example, shadow students during the day and do collaborative inquiry (Zemelman & Ross, 2009). By shadowing students, teachers can learn which content and activities most motivate students as well as how and with whom students prefer to learn. As a result, teachers could investigate what it would mean to create culturally responsive learning environments for particular students. Administrators could support teacher collaborative inquiry by providing needed resources, such as books and other materials, time before or after school, or simply moral support for teachers' work.

Surfacing Issues Related to Race and Ethnicity

When schools examine data on student achievement, they invariably look at differences among racial groups—although they may not look beyond superficial categories of racial difference, such as Asian American or Latino. But, ironically, proposals for improvement seldom suggest that student difficulties could be related to race or ethnicity. Nevertheless, instruction that is unresponsive to such differences and to ethnicity-related tensions in schools and classrooms may partially explain low achievement.

    Most schools are not characterized by open discussions of issues related to race and ethnicity. Educators may believe that focusing on race and ethnicity could be divisive and that strategies to enhance the achievement of students of color will undermine other students' learning opportunities. Yet such discussions are essential to a race- and ethnicity-responsive school culture.

    Professional learning communities can provide the structure, shared respect, and trust needed for collaboratively addressing these issues. Although many teachers and administrators may be reluctant to focus on the thorny issues of racism and privilege, most students are eager to begin the conversation. One helpful resource for surfacing these issues in the classroom is Mica Pollock's *Everyday Antiracism* (New Press, 2008), which includes insightful essays by more than 60 researchers who each propose a single action that educators can take to counteract racism in schools and society. These include such actions as challenging cultural messages about who can and cannot do science and using photography to wrestle with questions of racial identity.

Witnessing Effective Practice

Seeing is believing. Teachers need opportunities to witness diversity-responsive practices. By closely and openly examining evidence on student performance, schools can identify teachers who are more effective than others with students of diverse backgrounds. In some cases, teachers will be more effective with students of one race than with students of another. School districts can identify people from whom and places in which others can learn, and they should provide time and resources to do so.

Engaging with Families

30 The families of students of diverse racial and ethnic backgrounds often feel unwelcome and uncomfortable in schools and can be reluctant to engage in the kinds of activities that schools sanction. As a result, teachers and other educators may conclude that these families do not value education. In fact, in general, African American, Latino, American Indian, and Pacific Island families have a great deal of respect for education and view it as the best way out of poverty and hopelessness (see Bouffard, Bridglall, Gordon, & Weiss, 2009).

Family involvement strategies that are responsive to racial and ethnic diversity reject the idea that language or cultural differences are insurmountable barriers. They encourage educators to:

- Learn about their students' families by communicating with them consistently and respectfully.

- Learn about the communities in which they teach by becoming familiar with the community resources.

- Learn to speak at least one of the native languages of the students they teach.

- Learn how to engage families in their children's education in ways that enrich the curriculum, family support for learning, and teachers' knowledge of students.

- Listen to what the families need and want for their children (Hidalgo, Sui, & Epstein, 2004).

Good for All

Often, schools marginalize special efforts to meet the needs of students of racially and ethnically diverse backgrounds, treating them as actions that take time away from the central tasks of improving academic achievement.

But there is no zero-sum game here. Indeed, it is ironic that policies and practices that are particularly responsive to the needs of students of color are likely to be the best things we could do to enhance the learning of all students.

School structures, processes, and cultures affect student dispositions and their opportunities to learn.

Authors' note: The concerns addressed in this article are the focus of the Southern Poverty Law Center's Teaching Diverse Students Initiative. Extensive resources for improving the learning opportunities of students of color can be found on the initiative's website at *www.tolerance.org/tdsi*. Resources include articles, learning activities, interactive cases, interviews, and examples of promising practices.

References

Ayres, I. (2001). *Pervasive prejudice? Unconventional evidence of race and gender discrimination.* Chicago: University of Chicago Press.

Bode, P., & Fenner, D. (2010, April). Incarcerated youth and integrated arts education. Paper presented at the annual convention of the National Art Education Association, Baltimore.

Bouffard, S., Bridglall, B., Gordon, E., & Weiss, H. (2009). Reframing family involvement in education. Cambridge, MA: Harvard Family Research Project.

Cowhey, M. (2006). *Black ants and Buddhists: Thinking differently and teaching creatively in the early grades.* Maine: Stenhouse.

Donaldson, K. M. (2001). *Shattering the denial.* Westport, CT: Bergin and Garvey.

Ferguson, R. (2004). Professional community and closing the student achievement gap. Retrieved

from Teaching Tolerance at www.tolerance.org/tdsi
/asset/professional-community-and-closing-stude

García, E. E. (1999). *Student cultural diversity*. Boston: Houghton Mifflin.

Gay, G. (2010). *Culturally responsive teaching*. New York: Teachers College Press.

Gonzalez, N., Moll, L. C., & Amanti, C. (2005). *Funds of knowledge*. Mahwah, NJ: Erlbaum.

Greenwald, A., Pohlman, T., Uhlman, M. S., & Banaji, M. (2007). Predictive validity of the IAT: Understanding and using the Implicit Association Test. Retrieved from www.tolerance.org/tdsi/asset /predictive-validity-iat.

Gutierrez, K. D., & Rogoff, B. (2003). Cultural ways of learning. *Educational Researcher*, 32(5), 19–25.

Haberman, M. (1988). *Preparing teachers for urban schools*. Bloomington, IN: Phi Delta Kappa Educational Foundation.

Hidalgo, N. M., Sui, S-F., & Epstein, J. L. (2004). Research on families, schools and communities. In J. A. Banks & C. A. M. Banks (Eds.), *Handbook of research on multicultural education* (2nd ed., pp. 631–655). San Francisco: Jossey-Bass.

Irizarry, J. (Ed.). (2011). *The Latinization of U.S. schools*. Boulder, CO: Paradigm.

Ladson-Billings, G. (2009). *The dreamkeepers: Successful teachers of African American children* (2nd ed.). San Francisco: Jossey-Bass.

McIntosh, P. (1988). White privilege and male privilege (Work Paper No. 189). Wellesley, MA: Wellesley College Center for Research on Women.

Michie, G. (2009). *Holler if you hear me* (2nd ed.). New York: Teachers College Press.

Morrell, E., & Duncan-Andrade, J. (2002). Promoting academic literacy with urban youth through engaging hip-hop culture. *English Journal* 9(6), 88–92.

Murphy, P. K., & Alexander, P. A. (2006). *Understanding how students learn: A guide for instructional leaders*. Thousand Oakes, CA: Corwin Press.

Nieto, S. (2003). *What keeps teachers going?* New York: Teachers College Press.

Nieto, S., & Bode, P. (2008). *Affirming diversity* (5th ed.). Boston: Allyn and Bacon.

Sleeter, C. E. (1994). *White racism*. Multicultural Education, 1(4), 5–8, 39.

Valenzuela, A. (1999). *Subtractive schooling*. Albany: State University of New York Press.

Zemelman, S., & Ross, H. (2009). *13 steps to teacher empowerment*. Portsmouth, NH: Heinemann.

Analyzing Argument

1. How do Hawley and Nieto work to convince readers of a crisis?

2. Explain how Hawley and Nieto take on the hidden layers of the issue. How do they address the quiet assumptions or the underlying values of their readers?

3. Consider Hawley and Nieto's counterargument strategy: how do they analyze and reveal the logic of a particular opposing position?

4. Explain how concessions and qualifiers work in the argument. Describe particular passages in which Hawley and Nieto use a concession or qualifier to enrich their own ideas.

5. The achievement gap has been discussed widely in education journals. How do the authors acknowledge their rhetorical situation? In other words, how do they engage what has been said prior to their article?

It's Racism, Stupid: Bias, Not Affirmative Action, Stigmatizes People of Color

TIM WISE

Tim Wise, an anti-racist writer and educator, has written about 175 essays on race over the past 15 years. He has spoken on over 400 college campuses in 48 states and published several books, including *Affirmative Action: Racial Preference in Black and White* (2005).

Sometimes an argument gets made with such regularity that no matter how silly, it nonetheless requires an answer. Indeed the more often it gets made, the more often it calls for rebuttal, since its repetition indicates someone just isn't getting it.

Such is the case with the oft-repeated claim, usually by whites, that affirmative action stigmatizes blacks and other persons of color who benefit from its presumed generosity. As such, they note—and owing to their deep concern for the psychological well-being of their dark-skinned brothers and sisters—the elimination of such programs would be in the best interest of those persons they were meant to help.

By casting their opposition to affirmative action in such seemingly altruistic terms, critics seek to avoid the impression that they are motivated by racial resentment at the opening up of opportunities to long-marginalized groups. See, they seem to be saying, we don't mind black folks. Heck, we *love* black folks, and just want what's best for them. And what's best for them, presumably, is no more "preferential treatment" in college admissions, jobs, or contracting.

Putting aside the simple reality that all of this so-called preferential treatment has hardly put a dent in the edifice of white domination—white men still get 93% of all government contract dollars, hold over 90% of top jobs and 85% of tenured professorships—the notion that affirmative action stigmatizes beneficiaries and therefore should be scrapped for the sake of black and brown mental health is disingenuous and even racist on several levels.

First, since affirmative action has opened up opportunities that would otherwise have remained off-limits to people of color (and few deny this, despite the above data indicating that white men are still very much running the show), such arguments seem to imply that people of color would have been better off not to have gotten the jobs, college slots, or contracts they received. We are asked to believe that they would have been better off with, say, one percent instead of three percent of federal contract dollars; or perhaps half a percent instead of four percent of tenured faculty positions.

In other words, we are to believe that *less* opportunity to demonstrate their abilities would have been better for black and brown self-esteem, while more opportunity thanks to affirmative action was harmful. That few people of color would trade the added opportunities they have received for the sake of their self-image attests to how utterly asinine such an argument really is.

Secondly, this feigned white concern (occasionally parroted by black conservatives whose paychecks are almost always signed by whites) seems especially hypocritical when one considers that the same folks making this argument said nothing when *The Bell Curve* was published and greeted merrily by the conservative right. After all, here was a book that said blacks were genetically less intelligent than whites, predisposed to crime, out-of-wedlock childbirth, and all forms of social pathology. If the right

5

Tim Wise, "It's Racism, Stupid: Bias, Not Affirmative Action, Stigmatizes People of Color" from ZNet Daily Commentary (www.zmag.org), December 7, 2003. Reprinted with the permission of the author.

believes that affirmative action creates self-doubt, or implies that people of color are less capable and need special help to succeed, then how much more harmful must a book like *The Bell Curve* be, which doesn't imply that such persons are less capable, but rather screams it quite openly?

Yet, not only did whites not condemn this volume upon its publication—and no prominent conservative said a critical word, while several like William Bennett praised it openly—but indeed white consumers made it a best-seller within weeks and its primary author, Charles Murray, became a media star. Such is white concern for black people's self-esteem.

Thirdly, that blacks themselves overwhelmingly support affirmative action leaves proponents of the stigma argument with only one of two possible beliefs from which to choose: either that blacks are too stupid to intuit their own interests and too dim-witted to see how badly they are being damaged by affirmative action, or alternately, that blacks are so gullible (and thus also stupid) as to be deceived into supporting affirmative action by scheming civil rights activists. Either way, this argument requires a belief in the ignorance of black people, and their utter inability to think rationally. Such a position is of course flatly racist not to mention utterly vapid.

10   Additionally, whatever stigma could even theoretically attach to benefiting from affirmative action surely dissipates once one has to prove themselves on the job or in school. Indeed, persons of color know well that they will likely have to work twice as hard to get half as far or be considered half as good as whites; and they have known that since long before affirmative action came around. But at least with affirmative action they get the chance to work twice as hard and demonstrate their capabilities.

What's more, once given that chance, persons of color rise to the occasion. A comprehensive analysis of over 200 studies on the work performance of affirmative action beneficiaries, published a few years ago in the *Journal of Economic Literature,*

found that said beneficiaries performed just as well and often better than their white male counterparts. So much for stigma. If these workers were given to doubting their own abilities due to having received a bump from affirmative action, surely this self-doubt would have translated to weakened job performance.

Furthermore, to the extent such beneficiaries perform equal to or better than white men on the job, any lingering biases on the part of whites, such as beliefs that blacks are less capable and qualified, can hardly be blamed on affirmative action, but are rather the fault of white ignorance and racism itself.

As for college performance the same is true. Yes, students of color fail to graduate from colleges at the same rate as their white counterparts, but this hardly indicates that they were less qualified and thus came to doubt their abilities once admitted to schools that were "above their level," thanks to affirmative action. After all, at several top colleges, including all of the Ivy League schools, black and white graduation rates hardly differ. Furthermore, even when the rates of matriculation differ widely there is no reason to suspect stigma or that these students of color were over their heads academically.

For example, even black students with SAT scores of 1400 or better (out of 1600)—academically "qualified" to attend any school—fail to graduate from their chosen colleges at rates that are up to nine times higher than their white counterparts. Since they were clearly capable students, other factors must be to blame, among them, hostile racial climates or feelings of isolation on mostly white campuses (both of which have been documented by years of studies), and financial concerns that are more common for people of color. Indeed, as Dalton Conley documents in his groundbreaking book, *Being Black, Living in the Red,* once family economic status, including wealth and asset background, is controlled for (and thus, only truly similar black and white students compared), there is no racial difference between blacks and whites in terms of college graduation rates. So whatever graduation gaps do exist can be explained by economics, not stigma associated with affirmative action.

15 And finally, one has to wonder why no similar concern arises over white self-esteem? After all, the history of white America has been a history of affirmative action; one in which we received nonstop preferential treatment and continue to do so. Yet do those who shed crocodile tears over the stigmatizing effects of affirmative action for people of color likewise argue that whites who benefit from preferences, or have done so in the past, have been stigmatized?

Is George W. Bush stigmatized because his daddy got him into Yale?

Are the white baby-boomers who are currently inheriting nearly $10 trillion of property and wealth from their parents—wealth that was accumulated under conditions of formal apartheid with its attendant preference for whites—stigmatized by receipt of said wealth? If so, when are they going to relinquish the wealth in the name of their mental health, and if not, why not, if "preference" is inherently stigmatizing? Will conservatives now seek to raise the inheritance tax, perhaps to 100%, so as to save trust fund kids years of expensive therapy for their damaged self-concepts?

Bottom line: if black and brown folks are being stigmatized by affirmative action, we whites must be the most self-hating bunch around. Years of racial privilege must surely have brought us to the point of near paralysis, such that it quite literally boggles the mind to contemplate how we manage to persist in our daily routines at all.

But luckily there is a solution; a way for whites to safeguard our self-images, made evident by a recent study, which found that job applicants with white-sounding names are fifty percent more likely to be called in for an interview than those with black-sounding names, even when the applicants are of identical qualifications. Given the unfair preference for those who appear to be white, and the stigma that must therefore assault every Biff, Skyler or Chloe, forced to wonder if they got their jobs due to their lily-white names, perhaps the critics of racial preferences should start a campaign for whites to change our names to Tamika, Shamika, Andre, and Tyrone, just to even things out a bit and avoid the damage that would otherwise come from an unfair head start.

Lamont Bush. Yeah, that ought to do it. 20

Analyzing Argument

1. Summarize the argument to which Wise is responding.

2. Summarize Wise's argument; what is his main claim and support?

3. Highlight three appeals to logic and explain how each connects to Wise's main claim.

4. How does Wise use his analysis of the opposing argument as support for his own argument?

John Metz

18 Environment

C oncerns about the environment have been steadily growing over past decades, and today the environment is one of the most commonly debated issues in the United States and throughout the world. (Perhaps you have calculated your "carbon footprint" and taken steps to become carbon neutral.) As the national and international debate about the environment develops, new questions, issues, and arguments emerge.

We hear so much about "the environment" that we may come to think of it as an abstract issue. But we are all connected in very personal and immediate ways to the environment: air, water, soil, and other living creatures. The environment is what surrounds us. It's what we swim in, walk on, eat, and breathe. It's what lifts our spirits and makes us feel alive. And it can kill us.

As we explore particular environmental issues, we also explore ways of thinking about the environment: What is it? What is the cause of current environmental concerns, such as global warming, toxic rivers, and so on? What changes are we willing to make in our lifestyle? What crises face us now, and what crises loom ahead?

Readings about the Environment in Chapters 1–14

"A Community of Cars," Ryan Brown

"In Defense of Darkness," Holly Wren Spaulding

"Speech on the Land," Chief Seattle

"More Than Cherries," Samantha Tengelitsch

"Big House in the Wilderness: Moratoriums on Building and Individual Irresponsibility," Tracy Webster

"The Idols of Environmentalism," Curtis White

> There are no passengers on Spaceship Earth. We are all crew.
>
> —*Marshall McLuhan*

Lunar Eclipse: November 8, 2003

ED BELL

On November 8, 2003, there was a lunar eclipse. Ed Bell, an English professor, wrote this essay later that night.

The moon is gently orange with a thin, star-white bottom; its dark top disappears into the blackness surrounding it. Thirty-seven miles north, in town, it lacked the magically dull glow it has here eleven miles south of the store and gas station and twenty miles north of the next nearest bright lights. Driving east while it was still light out, I noticed a crescent moon, but knew it was a full-moon night. An eclipse! I watched as the crescent got smaller and smaller; I was hoping to find a dark spot where I could pull off to the side of the road and take in the full beauty of a lunar eclipse. I was approaching town, though.

I grew up in the country, then moved to the city in my early twenties. I must have seen many star-filled skies as a child. I don't remember any. After a young adulthood of city lights, I remember the first night I saw the stars again. I was in my mid-thirties, traveling west, and we stopped to camp for the night. The rest of that summer we traveled the west, camping in Utah, Oregon, Arizona, pitch-black nights and a billion stars, uncountable, so many that shooting stars were not rare to see and the constellations were so full of other stars I had trouble making them out.

Before that, we drove out to the country, away from the city lights, to see Midwestern stars. We had star books and maps of the sky. Here, it was different. I couldn't help thinking of Anasazi men and women, from birth to death looking up each night at the miraculous sky. Who needs TV? No wonder the Bible says:

> The heavens tell of the glory of God.
> The skies display his marvelous craftsmanship.
> Day after day they continue to speak;
> night after night they make him known.
> They speak without a sound or word;
> their voice is silent in the skies;
> Yet their message has gone out to all the earth,
> and their words to all the world.

(*Holy Bible*, Ps. 19.1–4)[1]

Because of light pollution, some people have never seen a dark sky. "In most cities, there's little point in gazing at the sky—unless you're fascinated by the sight of a few stars and some airplanes against a glowing background," says David Tenenbaum, a science, health, and environment writer (for ABC-NEWS.com, *Technology Review, BioScience, Environmental Health Perspectives, American Health,* and other publications). "If you have not seen a truly dark sky, you may not know that the urban glow conceals a network of uncountable stars in intriguing constellations."

And what about the animals? According to Johannes Andersen, general secretary of the International Astronomical Union, animals that are "programmed to prefer the dark may avoid brightened habitat. Sea turtles can get lost searching for a beach to lay eggs, and their hatchlings may confuse over-lit beachfront resorts for the ocean horizon, wasting precious energy needed to find the sea and escape predators" (qtd. in Tenenbaum). Plants, too, which require a certain degree of not just light but also darkness, are bound to suffer. In "Where Has the Night Sky Gone, and Why Should We Care?" Cliff Haas reminds us that every green plant "needs a measure of darkness to properly complete its

5

Ed Bell, "Lunar Eclipse: November 8, 2003." Reprinted with the permission of the author.
[1] The King James Version reads, The heavens declare the glory of God; and the firmament sheweth his handywork. Day unto day uttereth speech, and night unto night sheweth knowledge. There is no speech nor language, where their voice is not heard. Their line is gone out through all the earth, and their words to the end of the world. (Ps. 19.1–4)

circadian rhythm." Until recently, this process continued on schedule.

Light pollution may also affect how we understand the universe. Some deep-space observatories, which astronomers use to examine the early days of our universe, are becoming unusable (Tenenbaum). But not just astronomers care about light pollution. And not just plants and animals are affected by it. Haas says that "two generations now live on our world never having seen our address in the Universe." He means the Milky Way, which gets erased each night by the washed-out skyglow that is caused by too much wasted lighting.

"Light pollution affects everyone, whether they appreciate the night sky or not," Haas claims. It "costs us more in taxes, operating expenses for businesses, and in the price of goods that we purchase." But isn't all that light necessary? Where I live, a rarely used rest stop burns bright lights every night. And I wonder what the Morgans (the name on the mailbox across from the rest stop) must think of all that light. How it must have changed their lives: dark one night, all lit up the next. I suppose they have "gotten used to it." I admit that while traveling I have sought out such well-lit places to sleep: a rest stop, a Wal-Mart parking lot, a 24-hour truck stop. But lighting does not, contrary to popular belief, make a place safer. And even if it does, the issue becomes the quality—instead of the quantity—of lighting.

One solution, according to Tenenbaum, is pretty simple: "Avoid making excess light, and use reflectors and shields to direct light toward the ground." Haas reminds us that "we use lampshades in our homes to shield the bulbs' glare from our eyes so we can see everything better. For some strange reason, when bringing artificial lighting outdoors into the night this wisdom is quickly forgotten." We send vast amounts of light up into the sky where it is of no value to anyone, and where it is harmful to us all. Wasted light, according to Andersen, produces glare that "prevents you from seeing rather than helps you [to see]" (qtd. in Tenenbaum).

Don't really care? Since wasted light wastes money, the hope is that "economics may someday overpower the urge to turn night into day" (Tenenbaum).

The National Parks and Conservation Association, a private watchdog group found that "[g]lare emitted by towns up to 150 miles away obscures the stars above two-thirds of the 189 American parks surveyed—a long-distance phenomenon called 'skyfog'" (Reynolds). Haas argues, "The amount of electricity wasted by ill designed outdoor illumination has been estimated at 30%, resulting in well over $4 billion annually in unnecessary energy costs." The impact of all this smears across the economy and the environment. Wasted lighting, for example, is likely to come from coal-fired plants that are not environment friendly. And better ideas about how to create quality lighting will not hurt the economy overall. "To correct the problem would hurt business and we certainly could never do that," Haas begins. Then he continues: "[But] correcting the problem would help business more than most people presently realize." It would help the environment too, and more people could experience one of life's great blessings—the stars in the sky.

The problem isn't confined to the United States. Paul Brown and Ian Sample, writers for the British newspaper the *Guardian,* report that "only the most thinly populated parts of [Great Britain] remain dark—11%"; that "more than half the present generation of children has never seen the Milky Way, the luminescent band of interstellar gases and stars that is 'our galaxy'"; that "at least five of the 12 signs of the zodiac are now impossible to see in most of Britain"; that "billions of watts are poured into the heavens from signs and . . . street lamps"; that "light pollution got 24% worse between 1993 and 2000"; that "of 800 members of the Society for Popular Astronomy, nearly 80% could not see the Milky Way, 58% had to travel between five and 50 miles to see it, and one in eight had to travel over 50 miles"; and that "in Liverpool 30 years ago it was possible to see 7,000 stars in the Milky Way, now it is possible to see only between 50 and 200 on a clear night."

During blackouts, authorities report a phenomenon in which city dwellers call to ask about, or report, the stars in the sky. There are so many. They have never seen them before. Is something going on, they ask? They are surprised, just as I was that one night camping, to see what is really up there!

Works Cited

The Bible. Authorized King James Version, Oxford UP, 1998.

Brown, Paul, and Ian Sample. "The Sky You Won't See at Night." *The Guardian*, 7 Oct. 2003, www.theguardian.com/life/news/story/0,12976,1057703,00.html.

Haas, Cliff. "Where Has the Night Sky Gone, and Why Should We Care?" *Light Pollution Awareness*, AOL, Apr. 2000, members.aol.com/ctstarwchr/nightsky.htm.

Holy Bible. New Living Translation, Tyndale, 1996.

Reynolds, Gretchen. "Blinded by the Light." *Outside*, Nov. 1999, www.outsideonline.com/1889656/blinded-light.

Tenenbaum, David. "Blinded by the Light." *The Why Files*, U of Wisconsin, 2000, whyfiles.org/shorties/055darksky/.

Analyzing Argument

1. What is Bell's argument? In a paragraph, summarize his main claim and support.

2. What type of support does Bell use to develop his argument?

3. Most people probably do not see light pollution as a crisis, so Bell has to pull readers into a new way of thinking. In what particular passages can you see him working to do this? How effectively does he help the reader to see the crisis?

4. How do Bell's first three paragraphs strengthen or weaken his overall argument?

Squeaky Clean

MONICA POTTS

"Squeaky Clean" was published July 8, 2010, on The American Prospect website. At the time, the *Deepwater Horizon* offshore oil drilling rig had been gushing oil into the Gulf of Mexico since April 20. Monica Potts is associate editor for the *Prospect*.

As oil continues to spew into the Gulf of Mexico and disheartening images of oil-covered birds permeate our national consciousness, at least one commercial lifts our spirits. In a television ad for Dawn soap, a duck waddles by, a fluffy otter splashes, and other happy water creatures are gently cleansed of oil by a pair of rubber-gloved hands. A voice tells us that thousands of animals in oil spills have been saved using the dishwashing liquid made by Dawn, and now our purchase can help. A trip to the local grocery store to buy a cheap bottle of soap can save the life of a furry friend. Dawn, owned by Procter & Gamble, is donating $1 to wildlife-rescue organizations for every special bottle of Dawn soap purchased. The campaign started a year ago but has gotten more attention and a renewed push in the wake of the Deepwater Horizon disaster.

There's a catch: Each donation has to be "activated." Consumers who buy the bottle have to fill out an online form before the bottle turns into a donation. It's not automatic. Total donations for the two groups receiving the money, the International Bird Rescue Research Center and the Marine Mammal Center, were capped at $500,000, and Procter & Gamble says it's reached $460,000. Spokesperson Susan Baba says the company now plans to extend its campaign with a new goal of $1 million over two years total.

Consumers may think they are supporting a company that saves animals, but it's not so simple. While the soap is used by some wildlife-rescue organizations to clean animals affected by oil spills, Procter & Gamble is far from a green company: It tests cosmetics on animals, sells consumer products laden with chemicals, and spends millions lobbying against consumer and environmental protections. (There also is some debate over the survival rate of birds covered in oil. A German scientist recently advocated against cleaning the birds at all because less than 1 percent survive, but other scientists say that it's impossible to give a survival rate and that cleaning birds is worth the effort.) This is, as ever, an example of how good Procter & Gamble is at marketing its products: Dawn is just dish soap, but its special characteristics have earned it the loyalty of wildlife-rescue organizations, and so should win yours, too. This is an organization with $79 billion in sales in 2009, 29 percent of which came from generic household products like Dawn whose sales advantage depends entirely on creating the public impression that they are somehow different. The company spends $7 billion a year on advertising and, according to Advertising Age, is the No. 1 advertiser in the U.S.

Procter & Gamble also dominates the wildlife soap donation field. Mark Russell is part of the Gulf team for the International Bird Rescue Research Center and says the center has been using Dawn since the 1970s. After testing different substances, the center found that Dawn met all its criteria for removing oil from animals. The center, while testing other soaps periodically, has been using Dawn since, partly because Procter & Gamble began donating the dish soap after the center approached the company in the 1980s.

Ironically, the salvation for these birds creates demand for the very thing harming them. Some environmental groups say Dawn is part of the broader problem. It's a petroleum-based product packaged in plastic. Russell says the center often hears calls to test new, greener products, but those calls come at a time of a disaster when testing a new

5

product is impractical. "If another product with the same characteristics but with greener qualities presented itself, we may use it, but it would have to be readily available countrywide," he says.

While individuals may be able to donate a dollar to these worthwhile organizations by buying Dawn, the reality is that Procter & Gamble's profit goes to lobbying against environmental regulations. The company spent more than $4 million in lobbying last year and $1 million in lobbying in the first quarter of this year, fighting efforts to restrict or regulate the household chemicals in its products and to ban animal testing. Though the company does not have to disclose its position on proposed legislation, Procter & Gamble lobbied against a 2009 effort to disclose ingredients in household cleaning products, instead supporting an industry-led voluntary-disclosure effort. It also lobbied against bans in various states on dishwashing detergent containing high levels of phosphorus and fought to delay the bans' implementation.

One of the main issues for the company's public action committee, its lobbying arm, is chemical regulation. The group opposes state and local laws banning chemicals and supports instead "uniform regulations at the federal level, when needed." The company opposed stricter household chemical regulations in the European Union in 2003 and is rated poorly by Greenpeace for the chemical content of its household products. Those chemicals, including ones banned in the EU because they can be harmful to fish and humans, end up in the environment. Animal-rights groups have long called for advocates to boycott Procter & Gamble because it tests cosmetics on animals. In addition, a complaint filed by People for the Ethical Treatment of Animals against a facility that researched Iams pet food (the brand is owned by Procter & Gamble, but the company did not run the facility) for animal cruelty sparked a Department of Agriculture investigation. It resulted in $33,000 in civil penalties in 2006.

Promoting charity alongside consumerism isn't new territory for Procter & Gamble. In 2009, the company launched a charity-themed Tide bottle, "Loads of Hope," as part of a disaster-relief campaign for victims of Hurricane Katrina. Commercials for the detergent featured survivors talking about what a relief it was to do their laundry. By that time, the company had handled 30,000 loads of laundry for the people of New Orleans.

For Procter & Gamble's part, Baba says getting consumers to register their bottle of Dawn online allows them to learn more about the wildlife organizations and choose whether to donate a larger amount. But donating still requires visiting the website, which means many consumers could be buying the bottles without understanding the extra steps needed to make a donation. Consumers could believe they are helping simply by buying Dawn. One of the goals of this campaign, which started a year ago, is raising consumer awareness for the wildlife-rescue organizations involved. However, it also clearly benefits Procter & Gamble. Baba would not share the number of bottles shipped to stores or the percentage activated for donations, because she says it is proprietary information. "We will make sure that people who buy bottles are able to activate those bottles," she says.

Other companies (sic), including BP, the oil 10
company responsible for the spill in the Gulf, also promotes a similarly green image and worked hard to present itself as a reformed petroleum company. No longer British Petroleum, it started its "Beyond Petroleum" campaign a decade ago and advertised its renewable-energy efforts. It regularly touts its investments in wind energy (BP owns eight wind farms in the U.S.) and growing solar-energy sales. BP's commercials talk about reducing carbon emissions and moving beyond the use of fossil fuels. This is all despite anti-environmental actions before and leading up to the spill. The company spent $16 million lobbying for more deepwater offshore drilling, making it one of the highest spenders on lobbying in the U.S.

Surely, the organizations partnering with Dawn welcome the donations and attention. But the bigger questions are how much do environmentally questionable companies like Procter & Gamble profit from disaster, in money or in image, and why do we buy into their "goodwill" campaigns without making them reform their practices.

Analyzing Argument

1. Potts writes, "Consumers may think they are supporting a company that saves animals, but it's not so simple." How does Potts help readers complicate their thinking about the issue? How does Potts encourage readers to think differently?

2. Write down Potts's main claim and several supporting claims that create a line of reasoning for her argument.

3. List the strategies used to support the main claim.

4. Potts writes, "Promoting charity alongside consumerism isn't new territory for Procter & Gamble." How does Procter & Gamble promote charity alongside consumerism? With peers, think of examples of other companies that do this. What argument are the companies making by doing so?

Rice Bowl, Dust Bowl: Agribusiness and the Future

LISE MARING

Lise Maring worked for several years at NASA's Langley Research Center and briefly at the Goddard Space Flight Center in various capacities as a contractor employee. She is currently working as a technical editor and writer in the private sector. In this essay, first published in the *Alternative Press Review* in 2003, Maring takes the reader beyond the more commonly argued environmental issues (declining fisheries, for example) and reveals a less apparent and extremely important concern: the commercial mining of our soils and groundwater.

We've all read the articles concerning our declining fisheries. It was in the *Washington Post,* the *New York Times,* and even our local newspapers. For the first time, we began to hear about how the oceans are being "mined" by large commercial interests with their miles and miles of nets.

But the world's fisheries aren't the only renewable resources that are suddenly becoming nonrenewable. Two other very vital resources are also in danger of being depleted. What you haven't read much about yet is that corporate interests—similar to those that are mining the oceans—are also in control, either by direct ownership or indirectly through ownership of food processing facilities, of much of the world's agricultural lands, and they are in the process of mining our soils and groundwater.

These interests comprise a handful of transnational food companies that distribute an amazing abundance of food products to the thousands of supermarkets across the country each and every day. Some days it seems as if there is an infinite supply of food, and the stores are veritable cornucopias with shelves that are always stocked full. These companies include such giants as Kraft Foods, ConAgra, and ADM. They depend on "economies of scale," which means large-scale processing and worldwide supply and distribution; this in turn requires consolidated farming and huge numbers of acres dedicated to monocultures of crops like wheat, corn, and soybeans.

Essentially, the small farms cannot compete with the huge industrialized factory farms with their large pieces of specialized equipment. Many of these family farms end up being sold for housing developments or to the neighboring industrialized farms. Thus the number of small farms decreases each year, while the acreage per farm increases.

The six founding countries of Europe's Common Agricultural Policy had 22 million farmers in 1957; today that number has fallen to 7 million. Just 20 percent of the European Union's wealthiest and largest farmers get 80 percent of EU subsidies. Canada lost three-quarters of its farmers between 1941 and 1996, and the decline continues. In 1935 there were 6.8 million working farmers in the U.S.; today the number is under 1.9 million.[1] Agribusiness has had a great impact on our society, one we pretty much take for granted. Many colleges have now changed the title of their programs from Agriculture to Agribusiness. Here, students learn as much about economics, import and export law, international relations, and the stock exchange as they do about the various varieties of corn, the diseases of beef cattle, and the latest irrigation techniques.

So, that's progress, right? Technology and the market at their best. If this approach lowers our food prices, makes more food available to everyone, and gives us such a great variety to pick from, what's the problem?

Well, let's back up a minute and look at some other numbers—let's see what our cultural and economic prejudices have cropped out of the big picture. According to the latest figures from the U.S. Census Bureau, there are over 291,000,000 people in the

Lise Maring, "Rice Bowl, Dust Bowl: Agribusiness and the Future" from *Alternative Press Review* (2003). Reprinted with the permission of the author.

[1] www.newfarm.org/depts/gleanings/0503/peasantrevolt.shtml.

United States with one new hungry mouth being added every 10 seconds. The world population, on the other hand, is currently at 6,300,872,412 people and rising. The estimated population for the year 2050 is now at 9,078,850,714.

Landscape ecologist Eric Sanderson and his team found that 83 percent of the surface of our planet is already in use by us humans for such things as farming, mining, fishing, and as a place to live. They also found that most of the land that can be farmed for rice, wheat, or corn is already being used for that purpose.[2]

Between 1950 and 1981, the area in grain expanded from 587 million hectares (ha) to 732 million ha. By 2000 it had fallen to 656 million ha, and between 1950 and 2000, the cropland area per person shrank from 0.23 to 0.11 ha—an area half the size of a housing lot in suburban America.[3] To bring it down to a more personal level, David Pimentel, a professor of ecology and agricultural science at Cornell University, has estimated that each person in the United States requires 1.9 ha of cropland and pasture per year for their food needs, while a person in China requires only 0.4 ha because of the primarily vegetarian diet.[4]

10 And where is your 1.9 hectares of land located? It most likely isn't in your backyard. In essence, there are little pieces of it scattered all over the world. Most of our food travels an average of 1,200 to 1,500 miles before getting to our plates.

But, with all the technology and latest scientific knowledge that agribusiness has available, aren't they making the most efficient use of the land and increasing the yield each year? The answer is no. It turns out that the small farm, with its smaller acreage, but greater variety of crops, *actually yields more per acre than the industrial farm*. The reason for this is partly due to the very economies of scale that characterize agribusiness.[5]

In the United States, current agricultural practices are destroying the topsoil about 18 times faster than it can be replenished, and we depend more and more heavily on artificial fertilizers to fill the gap.[6] Moreover, as Europe and Asia adopt the American agribusiness ways of agriculture, they can expect to see similar results.

"In fact, corn cultivation in this country is, for the most part, an energy-consuming environmental disaster," according to David Pimentel. "Corn is the number one cause of erosion or total soil loss in the United States. It uses more fertilizer than any other crop. It's the largest user of insecticides. And it's the largest user of herbicides."[7]

Furthermore, just as bacteria are evolving faster than our antibiotics, and insects faster than our insecticides, so are weed plants evolving faster than the herbicides can keep up, thus more and more herbicide is needed to kill them each year on larger and larger pieces of land.[8]

15 It's not just Western countries' agricultural lands that are suffering topsoil loss. According to Janet Larsen of the Earth Policy Institute (EPI), the growing demands of the world's current human population are turning productive land into desert on every continent. The cultivation of marginal lands has caused extensive soil erosion everywhere, while billions of cattle, sheep, and goats have pushed pastures beyond their sustainable limits. In the western United States, cattle have left about 10 percent of already arid lands barren, and about two-thirds substantially degraded. Larsen believes desertification plagues up to one-third of the Earth's land area, affecting more than 1 billion people in 110 countries.[9]

In March 2002, the FAO admitted that the number of chronically hungry people in the world is not decreasing as fast as they predicted in 1996.

---

[2] news.nationalgeographic.com/news /2002/10/1025_021025_HumanFootprint.html.
[3] www.earth-policy.org/Updates/Update21.htm.
[4] dieoff.org/page136.htm.
[5] www.foodfirst.org/pubs/backgrdrs/1999/w99v6n4.html.
[6] dieoff.org/page136.htm.
[7] Rick Weiss, "Corn-Burning Benefits Hinge on How It's Grown," *Washington Post*, 27 Jan. 2003: A8.
[8] Michael McCarthy, "Superweeds Signal Setback for GM Crops," *Independent.co.uk*, 23 June 2003.
[9] Robert Glennon, *Water Follies: Groundwater Pumping and the Fate of America's Fresh Waters* (Island, 2002).

FAO concluded that the world's grain production would have to rise every year by 1.2 percent to meet the needs. This is 17 percent higher than what was being produced in the 1990s. But since we are already using all available croplands, this means the increase would have to come from the existing lands. Unfortunately, according to Lester Brown of the EPI, it may be a losing battle since grain yields have actually decreased rather than increased.[10]

In other words: Bottom line, what we are doing to the fisheries, we are doing to the land. We are currently in the process of "mining" our soils. Because whatever value is in food comes from the soil, the air, and the fertilizer we put on it—and the fertilizer comes from soil (if it is manure) or from oil (if it is synthetic)—and oil is running out.

Now, let's take a look at the water situation. Only about 3 percent of the water on our planet is freshwater. Groundwater accounts for about 14 percent of that 3 percent, while ice sheets and glaciers account for about 85 percent. The rest is in lakes, streams, reservoirs, the air and soil, and rivers. In the United States, groundwater supplies about 50 percent of our drinking water, 40 percent of the water used for irrigation, and about 25 percent of the water used by various industries.

Just to give some idea of how much water it takes to keep things going in today's society, according to the EPA and John Ryan it takes about:

- 700 gallons of water to make a cheeseburger

- 25 gallons of groundwater to irrigate each 2 square foot area of wheat field

- 1,851 gallons of water to refine one barrel of crude oil

- 25 gallons of water to make one pound of plastic.[11]

World water demand has tripled over the last half-century. According to Lester Brown of the EPI, governments are satisfying the growing demand for food by overpumping groundwater, a measure that virtually assures a drop in food production when the aquifer is depleted. Knowingly or not, governments are creating what Brown calls a "food bubble" economy.[12]

According to Brown: "Aquifers are being depleted in scores of countries, including China, India, and the United States, which collectively account for half of the world grain harvest. Under the North China Plain, which produces more than half of China's wheat and a third of its corn, the annual drop in the water table has increased from an average of 1.5 meters a decade ago to up to 3 meters today."[13]

"In the United States, the water table has dropped by more than 30 meters (100 ft.) in parts of Texas, Oklahoma, and Kansas—three key grain-producing states. As a result, wells have gone dry on thousands of farms in the southern Great Plains."[14] In California's San Joaquin Valley, where large quantities of vegetables such as tomatoes and lettuce are grown, the land subsided around 9 meters (27 ft.) between 1925 and 1977 due to the extraction of groundwater.[15]

In other words, we are in the process of "mining" our very finite freshwater supplies, and it is a process that is invisible to most of us until our wells start to run dry.

We are pushing the sustainable limits of our world and are threatening to overwhelm it. It is not only the world's fisheries and fossil fuels that are becoming depleted. It is also our precious, life-sustaining resources of water and soil. To add to the uncertainty, we are changing our climate in ways that will transform the areas we now consider our prime

[10] www.newscientist.com/news/news.jsp?id-ns99993457.
[11] John C. Ryan and Alan T. Durning, "Stuff: The Secret Lives of Everyday Things," Northwest Environmental Watch, Seattle, January 1997.
[12] www.earth-policy.org/Updates/Update22.htm.
[13] Ibid.
[14] Ibid.
[15] Glennon.

agricultural lands into desert. But, according to Eric A. Davidson in his book *You Can't Eat GNP*, "One economist argued that we need not worry much about the effects of global warming on the economy, because the only sector of the economy that he considered strongly influenced by the climate is agriculture, which contributes only 3 percent of the United States' GNP." One can only hope that this economist will not someday have to eat his own words.

25 We in the industrialized nations enjoy a fantastic range of foods, literally from soup to nuts, including a vast variety of seafood, grain products, meats, fruits, and vegetables. But many of us don't realize the heavy price we are paying for the luxury of importing food items from all over the world and at every season of the year. Unlike the prodigal son, we have no other home to return to if we choose to squander our inheritance and that of the future generations.

Analyzing Argument

1. What is the essay's main claim?

2. What specific passages help the reader accept Maring's main claim?

3. The academic audience is informed, skeptical, and curious. How does Maring's argument appeal to an informed audience? A skeptical audience? A curious audience?

4. Which of the following does Maring appeal to: logic, emotion, character, value, need? Provide examples to support your response.

5. Why might the reader have trouble accepting Maring's view of the future? What changes might help the reader accept her view?

Common Climate Change Myths

NATIONAL PARK SERVICE

The following article was published on the National Park Service (NPS) Climate Change Response Program (CCRP) website. The site explains that NPS created CCRP "to take a proactive role on the issue [of climate change]" and to "foster communication and provide guidance, scientific information, and recommendations that support stewardship actions to preserve our natural and cultural heritage from the detrimental impacts of global climate change."

Despite scientific evidence about the realities of climate change, we are still faced with persistent and confusing myths in the media. To allow the National Park Service to manage for climate change, we have dissected and examined these myths and found the realities of potential climate forecasts sobering. Not only will climate change impact the natural, cultural and historic resources we protect, but also how we serve the National Park Service mission and maintain a high-quality visitor experience.

The climate change story is more than dire predictions of the future. There are compelling reasons for federal agencies, as well as individuals, to act quickly to reduce greenhouse gas emissions. The future is not written yet. The actions we take today will determine the future Earth we leave our children and grandchildren. Will they be proud that we embraced the challenges of climate change? Or will they be dismayed at our excuses to avoid controversy and challenge? We find hope in the fact that we still have time to create a better, more livable planet.

As the National Park Service moves forward in a world where climate change is a reality, we find common ground where all Americans can stand. First, we are charged with preserving some of the most amazing resources in this country, resources that American livelihoods are based on, and these special places provide a connection with nature and offer personal inspiration. Second, the actions we can take to reduce our greenhouse gas emissions ultimately create a better world through energy efficiency, healthy ecosystems, energy independence and improved human health. These are all desirable outcomes that benefit everyone, regardless of climate change.

Myth 1: *The current warming trend is a natural process, the Earth has done this before and nature is capable of coping.*

The Earth's temperature fluctuates naturally over what humans view as very long periods of time; tens of thousands to millions of years. The temperature increase attributed to a sharp rise in atmospheric carbon dioxide occurred over a few decades. So while life on this planet copes with gradual change in a dynamic environment, the current warm up, and the speed at which it happens, is unprecedented over the last 1,300 years.

Myth 2: *Scientists are in disagreement.*

A recent survey of climatologists reveals that 97% of those scientists think that global climate change is occurring presently and that human activity is the primary cause. The myth that scientists disagree about the existence of climate change persists because the scientific method is pitted against an apparent societal need for absolute certainty portrayed in the media. 5

When faced with a question, scientists first develop a "hypothesis" and then subject their hypothesis to rigorous experimentation and observation. Multiple proven hypotheses may be collected into a "theory," which summarizes several experiments and observations. Theories are lines of thinking that scientists accept as true, but scientists always make room for an exception, or for science to come along with new discoveries that can disprove previously accepted hypotheses and theories. A theory need not have 100% agreement to be valid, and theories seldom achieve unanimous approval.

Source: www.nature.nps.gov/climatechange/myths.cfm.

Scientists may disagree about certain aspects of climate change, but this is part of the scientific process, not a sign that a theory is inaccurate. As new facts come to light, science adjusts its theory. A "law" is a predicted set of observations with no significant exceptions. Theories do not "grow up" to be laws once they are proven. In fact, scientists are still refining Newton's laws of gravity.

Let's be clear. Climate change is happening all around us, and human activities are accelerating it. The evidence is overwhelming, and the theory of global warming is sound. The Intergovernmental Panel on Climate Change (IPCC), which conducted the [aforementioned] survey, consists of thousands of scientists from all over the world who specialize in difference aspects of climate science. A separate study by the National Academy of the Sciences drew the same conclusions.

As a scientific agency, the National Park Service has learned to adapt our management practices to new evidence as it becomes available. For example, we used to manage forest fires by putting them out as quickly as possible. We now realize that fire is a natural process, and this process must remain active in fire-dependent ecosystems to promote healthy forests, and healthy forests release less carbon into the atmosphere in the long run.

We acknowledge that uncertainty remains over how fast and how much the temperature will increase. Nor are we certain about rainfall levels and the number or severity of storms. Some scientists think that the outcomes will slowly increase like turning a dial; while other scientists think it will be more like flipping a switch. Despite the uncertainty, we believe it far riskier to do nothing. We will move forward with the best science we have today. Our mission demands that we do so.

10 **Myth 3:** *Global climate change is not human caused we can't possibly affect something as big as the planet.*
Our history is alive with examples of human impacts on global systems, from something as large-scale as damming mighty rivers to a myriad of small actions like shooting the last passenger pigeon. We all have the ability to add and take away in small amounts to a global system. We find evidence of how humans have affected natural and cultural resources in our national parks. Petrified Forest National Park was once covered with pieces of petrified wood—not today. The park is facing the possibility that it may lose the singular thing that defines it—because some visitors have taken just one piece of petrified wood. When it comes to climate change, it is not just individual impacts but the collective impact that changes the global system.

Myth 4: *If climate change were true we would be seeing the impacts already.*
We ARE seeing the impacts in many places around the world. The most obvious impacts are currently visible in more northern latitudes, along the coasts, and in high-elevation habitats. The glaciers in Glacier National Park, for example, are shrinking—the park once had 150 glaciers larger than 25 acres in size, and now only 25 are left, and they are predicted to be completely gone by 2020. Plants like Joshua trees in Joshua Tree National Park or sugar maples in many eastern parks need a particular temperature zone to survive. They have already begun a shift across the landscape to reach the right growing conditions. Fire seasons in the West appear to start earlier and last longer into the fall. Park facilities and homes in Alaska are sinking due to thawing permafrost. Once gone, these fragile ecosystems and cultural resources are gone forever.

Myth 5: *Cold weather disproves global warming.*
While we may say "climate" when we mean "weather," and vice versa, they are two very different things. As Mark Twain put it, "Climate is what we expect, weather is what we get." Weather is what we get on a day-to-day basis, whereas climate is the average weather conditions over long periods of time. With the 2010 heavy snowstorms in the Washington DC area, some declared that climate change was

over. But climate scientists tell us that with climate change we can expect more flooding, more drought, extended heat waves, and more severe storms. Furthermore, one cold winter does not by itself change the long-term average (the climate) much. Both the overall climate and the extremes of weather are a concern for national parks. In 2006, huge floods damaged many of the main roads in Mount Rainier National Park in Washington state. The park was closed to visitors for many months to repair damaged roads and make it safe for visitors to reenter the park. Those storms may not be directly attributable to climate change, but the increased frequency of such storms will certainly impact parks.

Myth 6: *Climate change is being caused by the sun?* Recent records of the sun's activity show that solar radiation reaching the Earth varies by about 0.1%. That change is too small to explain documented warming over the past 50 years, and scientists haven't found any long-term trend in solar output that would explain it. Two factors control how much energy the Earth receives from the sun. First, subtle wobbles in our planet's orbit around the sun vary the amount of solar radiation received and changes the seasonal cycles. These "Milankovitch Cycles" affect the Earth on timescales of thousands of years and their impact on climate change is well understood. Second, the sun's energy output changes following the 11-year sunspot cycle, but also may vary gradually over longer periods of time.

Myth 7: *Alternative energy is too expensive and cannot solve our energy needs.*
We need to compare short-term and long-term costs to settle this myth. In the short-term, today's alternative energy producers are often more expensive than traditional' energy sources. However, when long-term costs such as pollution, global warming, and quality of life are factored into the economics of energy, alternative energy shines. When faced with the need to change, America produces innovative solutions that lead the world. Many of these changes were very expensive and limited at the beginning. America's national parks were another innovative idea, sometimes called "America's best idea." They were expensive and controversial 100 years ago. Now they are priceless gems that reconnect us with nature, our heritage, and the larger world around us.

Myth 8: *There is plenty of time to react to climate change.*
Changes in the Earth's climate, because of the increased level of greenhouse gases like carbon dioxide, already affect our national parks and visitors' experiences in the parks. Let's say we could stop pumping greenhouse gases into the atmosphere today. The amount we have already released would linger for decades and continue to raise the temperature at the surface of the Earth where we already see the effects of climate change. In the Rocky Mountains, for example, pine trees have already been infested by the mountain pine bark beetle, a blight brought on by the stresses of climate. Acres of dead trees have increased the threat of more severe fire activity, changed the visitor experience and created a hazard for campers in some national parks. By the time we realize such climatic effects, it is often too late to do something about it; a planned response to climate change is much better than a hasty reaction.

Myth 9: *There's nothing I can do to change this, so why should I care?*
One individual CAN make a difference, a difference that is compounded when others join in. We need your help to make changes so we can fulfill the mission of the National Park Service: to conserve our natural, cultural and historic resources for the enjoyment of this and future generations. We need your help to ensure generations to come experience the tallgrass prairie, see spectacular waterfalls, mountains and hear the call of the pika among wildflowers in the alpine tundra. Please join us.

Analyzing Argument

1. In your own words, write down a main claim for "Common Climate Change Myths."

2. What support strategy or strategies does the article use to counter the myth that scientists are in disagreement about climate change?

3. According to the article, how is the difference between "climate" and "weather" important to the debate?

4. "Common Climate Change Myths" is one part of a larger website, "Climate Change Response Program." What points from the article might the website treat in more depth?

ROMEO RANOCO/Reuters/Corbis

19

Education

W hat is education? At first, the response may seem obvious. But one quickly discovers that education is a complex topic that is challenging to define. Arguments about education can be more than arguments about school: we learn not just in the classroom but throughout life. And while we probably equate being educated with going to school and earning a degree, we also can think of education as something broader, as something that happens every day outside of classrooms.

Education impacts everyone's life, whether a lack of education or an abundance of it, whether formal (Harvard) or informal (School of Hard Knocks). People debate such things as the purpose of education, teaching styles, learning styles, the student-teacher relationship, the role of technology, and the No Child Left Behind Act. As long we live in a democracy, education will be a central topic of debate. It is not something to be solved and then forgotten, but something to be monitored, retooled, and debated continually so that it responds to and maintains the complexities of our civilization.

Readings about Education in Chapters 1–14

"Communication: Its Blocking and Its Facilitation," Carl R. Rogers

"Standardized Testing vs. Education," Justin James

"Disparities Demystified," Pedro A. Noguera and Antwi Akom

"Somewhere in the Past: Clarksville's School and Community Life," Cameron Johnson

"Evaluation of 'The Education of Ms. Groves,'" John Adams

"Investing in Futures: The Cost of College," Charles Nelson

"Filling in the Bubbles: An Investigation of Standardized Tests," Kate Pottoff

Going Down the Drain

DAN COOK

Many writers have discussed "brain drain," a situation in which educated adults leave a city or region that lacks opportunity. But Daniel Cook takes the issue in a different direction. He finds that education itself—the belief in its inherent value—is being driven away from his state. He does not blame the government or business or other states. Instead, he points the finger at everyday citizens. Specifically, he blames a prevailing attitude about learning, and he explains how that attitude undermines the people who cling to it.

I got home from work one day and turned on the news. The Governor of Michigan, Jennifer Granholm, was talking to CNN's Wolf Blitzer about the "Brain Drain" in her state. Apparently, this phenomenon involves educated, creative, and/or entrepreneurial individuals leaving Michigan for opportunities in other states. The focus of the show then switched to something about a celebrity smoking crack. I turned the channel and found a commercial for "Are You Smarter than a Fifth-Grader". I made it back to CNN in time to learn that it is dangerous to type text messages while driving a car (they do official studies to make sure).

While watching all of this on television, I looked back on the workday that I had just come home from. Many of my co-workers ascribe very little value to education. In fact, some of them are downright hostile to it. Knowledge pertaining to anything outside of everyday practical usage is disregarded. Foreigners, minorities, books, science, art, music (except country) and technology are all perceived in a negative light. These attitudes are ubiquitous in Northern Michigan, and they exist all over the country.

The "Brain Drain" that Governor Granholm was talking about is a real thing. People are leaving Michigan every day. The problem manifests itself at the local level (it seems that we all know someone who moved away to find work elsewhere), at the state level (what Granholm mentions), and at the national level as well (more on this later). It can't help to have a populace that neither values nor welcomes educated people.

A connection between this everyday resistance to "progress" and the vapid content of my television is hard to ignore. There is an aspect of our cultural identity that values rugged individualism more highly than education. This has become an encumbrance. In previous decades, a lack of education was not a great barrier to the American Dream. This is no longer the case. The market forces of the global economy demand that America's workforce be more educated if it wishes to maintain its standard of living. The expansion of the labor market has reduced the value of "grunt labor" dramatically. If Michigan cannot provide opportunities for the "best and brightest", then some other place will. Likewise, if Michigan can't provide the "best and brightest", then some other place will (i.e. labor outsourcing). Anyone that wants to discourage intellectual advancement is an obstacle that we can no longer afford to tolerate.

This is not about class-snobbery. As a working-class guy, I am talking about people whom *I work with*. I interact with them every day and many are friends. It is not a mean-spirited swipe at those who have below average intelligence either. These are people who (having average smarts and being the products of public education) should know better than to believe the nonsense that they do. They *can* help it. It's frustrating to be having a good conversation with one of your peers and then hit a wall built from bricks of ignorance. For instance, pointing out that racism is bad for society raises hackles. The homogenized ethnic majority actually feels threatened. The same people that easily accept things like racism and blind nationalism tend to reject serious political theory. Science and technology are things to be feared (we can probably blame Hollywood for some of this). Anything that requires organized thought is rejected in favor of knee-jerk reaction. Superstitions and prejudices taint a good person's judgment. The problem is an attitude, and an attitude is a choice. I'm talking about individuals who choose (though, perhaps not consciously) to perpetuate a negative situation. The rejection of a more developed worldview is as symptomatic of the "brain drain", as it is a contribution to it.

I understand that a lot of intellectual activities can be considered impractical and a "waste of time", but if one has time to drive around on a snowmobile while drunk on Natural Light, he might have time to think about his role in human society. Maybe take a break from "deer-shining" and encourage his kids to learn something about the world they've been burdened with. The future, after all, *will* happen.

The whole country has some issues in the smarts department. The local attitudes discussed here are not really unique. They're more of a microcosm for something happening with America. We love to say that this is *the greatest country in the world*, but, according to a 2007 article on the Washington Post's website, we're not even average. The piece, written by Maria Glod titled: "U.S. Teens trail Peers Around World on Math-Science Test" discusses something called the PISA test. The PISA (Program for International Student Assessment) test compares high-school students from thirty different countries in several different academic categories. Glod writes that "The average score of U.S. students lagged behind those in 16 of 30 countries. . ." and that they were "11 points below the average of the 30 countries."

That many Americans care little for academic achievement is all too apparent. Who hasn't seen a *my kid beat up your honor student* bumper sticker? We have pejorative terms for kids that do well in school. We call them nerds and geeks and marginalize them socially. We use these terms for adults that are well-versed in any subject. This is *the greatest country in the world?* A country that actively discourages intelligence is *the greatest country in the world?*

Most Americans are concerned about the education of young children, but we don't seem to agree on what to do about it. Some agree with newly elected congressman Rand Paul, who wants to eliminate the Department of Education. Paul and his Tea Party supporters represent a strain of American thought that is very suspicious of public education. I know, personally, some Tea Partiers. They're the same co-workers that I mentioned earlier in this essay. These guys will go off about how the government is "stealing their money" and "throwing it away" to fund public education, libraries, or community colleges. A little learning wouldn't hurt any of them one bit. In fact it might help them avoid being manipulated by those who exploit superstition and paranoia. Writing on WorldNetDaily.com, Devvy Kidd reiterates the argument against the Department of Education. The article, subtly titled, "Department of Education Must Be Abolished" forwards the idea that the federal government's plan is to forward a communist agenda. Kidd points out that "The tenth plank of the 'Communist Manifesto' reads: 'Free education for all children in public schools,' and this is one of the highest goals of communitarians" (Kidd). She does not, however, indicate why this is bad (other than to tie it to past national enemies' economic systems). Certainly, this is an extreme viewpoint, but the fact that someone with a parallel policy can be elected to Congress says something about the electorate. America, being the representative democracy that it is, can only change if its constituents change. No top-down approach to re-emphasize education is going to work for long if voters are afraid of it. Therefore, government policies will prove ineffective at solving the problems caused by the "brain drain". The phenomenon itself fights against a solution.

One thing that we can do is to stop encouraging 10
media companies that generate mindless content. We need to think about what messages are being sent to society and decide whether these are things that we want to see more of. Not censorship, but grass-roots selectivity. The power of the consumer

should never be underestimated. Everything we buy and everything we watch sends a message to corporate America that we want more of it. Do we need more brainless country music suggesting that the South should have won the Civil War? Do we want more movies that glorify criminals? John Wayne and Elvis were great for their time, but now we have to support a new kind of role model. The future that we should want needs a general population that is well-versed in mathematics and economics. Tomorrow's cultural icons could be yesterday's nerds. If we can get there, then maybe we can get by with a little less attitude.

What is America going to be like thirty years from now? The wealth generated over the past sixty-years has made us complacent. This complacency doesn't manifest in our being soft and effeté, as one might suspect, but it manifests in our being dull and crass. Because the "Brain Drain" phenomenon is worsened by public ignorance and provincial attitudes, we must make education a higher cultural priority. America will be slow to change. The resistance will be strong. It took us a long time to get this way, and it will take perseverance to improve.

Policy changes are easy to suggest. Entrenched attitudes, however, are hard to work around. The real change that we need to make is a cultural one. This is something that any of us can do by rejecting the aspects of society that hold us back and accepting those that help us move forward.

Works Cited

Glod, Maria. "U.S. Teens Trail Peers Around World on Math-Science Test." *The Washington Post*, 5 Dec. 2007, www.washingtonpost.com/wp-dyn/content/article/2007/12/04/AR2007120400730.html.

Kidd, Devvy. "Department of Education Must Be Abolished." *WorldNetDaily.com*, 7 Dec. 2004, www.wnd.com/2004/12/27895/.

Analyzing Argument

1. Is your response to this essay a knee-jerk reaction? Explain how it is or isn't and why.

2. What is the essay's main claim?

3. What support strategies from Chapter 3 does Cook use to help the reader understand and accept the main claim?

4. Is the following sentence the main idea of paragraph four? "Anyone that wants to discourage intellectual advancement is an obstacle that we can no longer afford to tolerate." Explain why it is or isn't.

5. In a paragraph, define "education" as Cook sees it: What is the purpose of education? What is the value of education? What does education look like? What definitions of education would Cook reject and why?

The High Cost of Food

DARRA GOLDSTEIN

"The High Cost of Food" by Darra Goldstein appeared in *Gastronimica: The Journal of Food and Culture* (Winter 2008). Goldstein, who is Editor in Chief of the journal, explains: "*Gastronomica* uses food as an important source of knowledge about different cultures and societies, provoking discussion and encouraging thoughtful reflection on the history, literature, representation, and cultural impact of food. The fact is, the more we know about food, the greater our pleasure in it." As you read Goldstein's essay, consider how her argument necessarily involves issues far beyond the simple act of eating.

Lately I've been hearing dire economic forecasts about a slide into recession, with the sharp rise in U.S. food and oil prices of special concern. I understand economic misery and am not going to suggest that we would all be better off paying more for our oil and for our food—or am I? The more we pay for oil, the less we'll use. Or is that logic too simplistic, given our ingrained driving habits and desires? I'll leave that determination to the energy pundits, but I do want to raise my voice in favor of higher food prices.

Like many others, I worry about the accessibility of food to all who are struggling. But I worry just as much about a nation that feeds itself so poorly that the population ends up malnourished. The low cost of non-nutritious food in the United States is ultimately hurting people, particularly the disadvantaged, more than it is helping them.

Whenever I go to Europe, I'm struck by the radical differences in our attitudes towards food. There, people pay for food that is good. Quality is important to them. They recognize and value the labor that goes into farming and gathering and producing; they understand that they get what they pay for in terms of both taste and nutritional value. The problem is not that we can't find excellent food here in the U.S., but that as a nation we have been schooled to believe that food should not cost very much. Cheap is good. Fast and cheap is even better. Thus the wholesome, more nutritious stuff ends up in fancy stores beyond the pocketbooks of most consumers, who are left to buy ever more highly processed foods—now often labeled as "organic" or containing added nutrients as "functional foods" to make up for their lack of natural goodness.

Perhaps the real problem is that we have not taken the time to educate ourselves sufficiently about *taste*. Instead, we've been suckered by synthetic sweeteners and flavors. Ours is a culture of denial, in which we spend billions of dollars on artificial diet foods instead of recognizing the pleasure that flavorsome, high-quality foods bring. Real foods may sometimes be high in cholesterol, or fat, or whatever the latest demon is. Therefore we need to practice moderation—but not denial. In this regard we remain far behind Europe in our government's understanding of what is needed to keep our national body—not to mention our psyche—fit.

I've written earlier in these pages about the 5 Council of Europe, which stands at the fore in promoting awareness of the importance of food not only to individual health but also to the health of the collective, whether a nation or a culture. Following the publication of *Culinary Cultures of Europe: Identity, Diversity and Dialogue,* the Council has broadened its thinking to include issues of health and their impact on culture. Thus, as part of the 2007–2008 Europalia festival in Brussels, I recently participated in a roundtable that celebrated the riches and benefits of Mediterranean food—the heart-healthy fats, the reliance on plant sources instead of on animals, the glass of wine with dinner.

Like the Europeans, we must begin to value food and its producers. And what better time to do so than in this election year? The *New York Times* reports that our presidential candidates are talking a lot about diet—but only in terms of their own efforts not to gain pounds on the fried-food-strewn campaign trail. Why aren't they seizing this opportunity to focus on the sources of wholesome food, to promise support for the American family farm, to find ways to make fresh foods available to all, even in blighted neighborhoods where local stores carry only highly processed items?

Our politicians try to get cheap votes by promising cheap food and generous farm subsidies. But do we need more corn syrup? When our leaders bemoan the high cost of health care, they rarely mention that cheap foods are an underlying problem. Nor do they like to explain the long-term truth: that although good food may initially cost more at the farmstand or grocery, bad food exacts a far greater cost. Food is an intimate issue, a family issue, one that touches our deepest nerves. But it is also a crucial *societal* issue. Our candidates should seek to inspire us, to change the national mindset, so that Americans will begin to see food not merely as fuel but as a meaningful product in its own right. Is that really asking too much?

It's only human nature: if we pay a high price for something, we tend to value it more. That's precisely what we need to do with food: move it from the realm of the cheap and undervalued to a respected place at the table, where it will be recognized for the life-nourishing gift that it is.

Analyzing Argument

1. Goldstein compares American and European attitudes about food. How does this comparison help to support her main claim?

2. According to Goldstein, why should food be more expensive?

3. With a group of peers, discuss how Americans become educated about food. What most determines Americans' knowledge and attitudes about food?

4. How does Goldstein's essay use food as an important source of knowledge about different cultures and societies? How does it provoke discussion and encourage thoughtful reflection on the history, literature, representation, and cultural impact of food?

5. Describe Goldstein's voice as a writer. What makes it inviting or alienating?

What Is a Freethinker and Why Does It Matter?

FRED EDWORDS

"What Is a Freethinker and Why Does It Matter?" was first published in the *Humanist* magazine, Mar/Apr 2006. Fred Edwords (1948–) is a leading voice for humanism. From 1994–2006, he was editor of the *Humanist,* and from 1984–1999, he was executive director of the American Humanist Association. He is currently AHA director of communications and board chair of Camp Quest, a summer camp for free-thinking youth.

In his 1957 essay, "The Value of Free Thought," Bertrand Russell writes:

> What makes a freethinker is not his beliefs but the way in which he holds them. If he holds them because his elders told him they were true when he was young, or if he holds them because if he did not he would be unhappy, his thought is not free; but if he holds them because, after careful thought he finds a balance of evidence in their favor, then his thought is free, however odd his conclusions may seem.

By this definition, a wide range of people have been freethinkers: not only agnostics and atheists but also deists, liberal religionists, religious innovators, and those who have challenged the predominant orthodoxies in every field of endeavor, from science to politics to the arts. That adds up to a lot of people. And what it tells us is that almost every great individual in history had to, in some way or another, think free—else they likely wouldn't have stood out enough to become famous in the first place.

A more useful definition is that provided by most dictionaries, which tell us that a freethinker is one who has rejected authority and dogma, particularly in religious thinking, in favor of rational inquiry. The term first came into use in England toward the end of the seventeenth century as a designation for those who inquired into traditional religious beliefs, tested them against experience, and drew their own conclusions. According to the *Oxford English Dictionary* the label was "claimed especially by the deistic and other rejecters of Christianity at the beginning of the eighteenth century." But as Gerald A. Larue demonstrates in *Freethought Across the Centuries* (Humanist Press, 1996), there have been freethinkers in nearly every historical period and on every continent.

For example, in ancient Egypt, at the time of Cheops, builder of the Great Pyramid of Giza (circa 2550 BCE), we find wisdom schools for the sons of wealthy men where secular ideas were taught. Out of this tradition grew the secular songs of harpists, who sometimes brought critical thinking to bear on religious belief. Similar wisdom schools of ancient Israel produced ideas reflected in a number of biblical proverbs as well as the Book of Ecclesiastes, written during the fourth century BCE.

In the Indian subcontinent, some divisions that developed within Hinduism during and after the sixth century BCE were decidedly godless. Moreover, breaking off from Hinduism at that time were Jainism and Buddhism, both nontheistic systems. Meanwhile, Lao Tsu developed Taoism in China, a quietist form of agnostic mysticism, and Confucius emerged to offer humanistic wisdom teachings aimed at creating ethical integrity. These latter became widely accepted three centuries later merged with a system of social regimentation to become China's state ideology.

In ancient Greece, the pre-Socratic Ionian 5 philosophers tried out a variety of new ways of accounting for the universe and explaining nature without reference to gods—Xenophanes going so far as to say the gods had been created by humans in their own image. Then, during the Golden Age of Athens, a humanistic circle of thinkers led by Aspasia

Fred Edwords, "What Is a Freethinker and Why Does It Matter?" from *The Humanist*, vol. 66, no. 2, Mar./Apr. 2006, pp. 44–45. Reprinted with the permission of the author.

included Protagoras and Socrates. And the tragedian Euripides wrote plays that criticized religious fanaticism, superstition, patriarchy, and war. From that point on, freethinking ideas became a regular part of European history.

Because the social experiment known as the United States of America was a product of the European Enlightenment, it's no surprise that freethinkers figured prominently in the nation's early history and that freethought went on to become a vital part of American culture. Nobody has made this point more clearly today than Susan Jacoby in *Freethinkers: A History of American Secularism* (Metropolitan Books, 2004). She illuminates the central, often germinal, role played by prominent freethinkers and freethought organizations in the nation's defining struggles. One simply cannot correctly understand the American abolition movement or the movements for suffrage, labor, public health, birth control, civil liberties, civil rights, sexual freedom, peace, or ecology (among others) without understanding the freethought movement. Trying to grasp American culture and history while remaining ignorant of freethinking would give as distorted an image as trying to do so while ignorant of Protestant evangelicalism. Indeed, in many of the leading cultural conflicts both were intertwined, often in direct confrontation, and from the beginning of the nation's history.

For example, immediately after the end of the American Revolution Patrick Henry sought to displace the position of the Episcopal Church as the official state religion of Virginia by introducing in the Virginia General Assembly a liberalizing bill that would tax all Virginians to support "teachers of the Christian religion." The aim was to replace one established church with a multiplicity of established churches. But James Madison objected, holding that no state government should be in the business of supporting any religion, and issued his now famous "Memorial and Remonstrance against Religious Assessments."

Its impact was profound. Jacoby writes that "although Madison was speaking from the perspective of an Enlightenment rationalist, his presentation of the pernicious possibilities for state interference with religion appealed powerfully to nonconformist Protestants, including small Quaker and Lutheran sects as well as the more numerous Baptists and Presbyterians, who had long resented the domination of the Episcopalians." Thus, at that moment in history, "the interests of the evangelicals and the Enlightenment rationalists coincided and coalesced in a common support for separation of church and state." As a result, not only did Patrick Henry's assessment bill disappear but it was replaced by one from Thomas Jefferson, the Virginia Statute for Religious Freedom, advancing complete church–state separation. It became law on January 16, 1786.

In the matter of the nation's subsequent conflict over the issue of slavery, memories have become distorted with time. Today many evangelicals and others seek to have passages added to U.S. history textbooks proclaiming the positive contributions of Christianity to American life. And they cite religious objections to slavery as a primary example. But Jacoby sets the record straight:

> The religiously correct version of American history has never given proper credit to the central importance of the Enlightenment concept of natural rights—or to the anticlerical abolitionists who advanced that concept before the public—in building the case against slavery. Throughout the three decades preceding the Civil War, the anticlerical ethos of the radical abolitionists was used against them by religious opponents of emancipation, who frequently trotted out the specter of the French Revolution and even described abolitionism itself as an atheist plot.

It was the same with the struggle for women's rights.

> From the 1848 Seneca Falls [women's rights] convention to the current battle over abortion, no cause has better demonstrated the conflict between America's religious and secular values than the drive for women's rights. As soon as

news of the Seneca Falls convention began to circulate, feminism began to be portrayed by its opponents as a threat to religion.

Regarding other freethought social action, Jacoby acknowledges the role of Ethical Culture but neglects to mention that, in 1877, Ethical Culturists established the Visiting Nurse Service, the first of its type that did not do missionary work for organized religion but focused exclusively on physical care. In the 1880s Ethical Culturists founded the City Club to fight political corruption in New York City, established the first U.S. settlement house to address the social needs of urban slum communities, launched the Legal Aid Society, campaigned against child labor, and worked for improved public health. In the twentieth century they helped found the National Association for the Advancement of Colored People, engaged in union arbitration, and helped launch the American Civil Liberties Union.

10   Jacoby also mentions Humanism but not enough on individual Humanists, like Corliss Lamont, who successfully stood up to the House Un-American Activities Committee and Senator Joseph McCarthy and went on to win major litigation against government surveillance. Nor does she mention facts about the American Humanist Association, such as its founding of the National Commission for Beneficent Euthanasia in 1974 that issued the groundbreaking "A Plea for Beneficent Euthanasia" signed by medical, legal, and religious leaders. It called for "a more enlightened public opinion to transcend traditional taboos and move in the direction of a compassionate view toward needless suffering in dying" long before the activism of the Hemlock Society and Jack Kevorkian and before the current growth in interest in right-to-die legislation—all efforts of which have been top-heavy with freethinkers and Humanists.

But the message is clear nonetheless; freethought isn't just a set of abstract philosophical ideas or critiques of religion. It is and always has been a commitment to social change and social action, having a profound and positive impact on the advancement of civilization.

Analyzing Argument

1. What does Edwords value, and what outside values does Edwords bump heads with?

2. What is Edwords's main claim, and how does he support it?

3. In paragraphs 6–9, what point does Edwords make by discussing slavery and feminism?

4. What assumptions, values, or beliefs allowed both evangelicals and rationalists to support separation of church and state?

5. Provide examples of your own thoughts and actions to explain to what degree you are, or are not, a freethinker.

Learning, Styles, Freedom, and Oppression

SIMON BENLOW

In the following essay, Simon Benlow takes on a popular educational trend: learning styles. The trend asserts that every student can be categorized into a particular group according to his or her supposed style of learning. Benlow takes on the trend and the thinking that drives teachers to accept it. Notice how he counters, concedes, and qualifies his claims.

During the Cold War, when people conjured nightmarish visions of life in Soviet Russia, they imagined long lines of comrades waiting to be told their lot in life. If the communist rulers told Alexi to be a plumber, then plumber he was. If Nikoli was good at jumping, then he would be deemed long jumper for the Soviet Olympic team; if Marta was good with her fingers, she'd be a filing clerk at the Kremlin. Americans, on the other side of the world, shuddered at the idea of limiting the range of possibility for individual human growth. Based on enlightenment philosophy, the American belief in human potential stood opposed to the nightmarish cookie-cutter identity politics of the Soviets. But since the Cold War, American education has done a fine job of making Soviet identity protocols a reality.

In the United States, we have not had absurd degrees of control foisted upon us from our rulers; instead, we have run willingly toward oppression, control, and reductionism. In an increasingly disorienting and saturated society, we have become enamored with the ring of truth that *seems* to accompany simplicity. We have given increasingly younger children (as young as twelve) battery tests that recommend careers—hence education tracks. And in college, we are moving away from intellectual potential and toward direct career paths that correspond to particular *learning styles*.

Today, as the post–Cold War generation comes to college, students are not told exactly *what* they should be. It's far creepier than that: After taking long multiple-choice surveys, students are told *how* they think—and presumably how they have always thought and how they will always think. After one survey, they are categorized as one of only three types: visual, auditory, or kinesthetic. These categories, or "modalities," say the researchers, define the three basic ways that people learn. Increasingly, on campuses, instructors and students alike are proclaiming, "I'm an auditory learner, so . . .," "I'm kinesthetic," etc.—people proudly announcing their intellectual labels as though they were characters in Aldous Huxley's horrific futuristic tale *Brave New World*. (But even Huxley's genius for imagining reductionist horrors could not compare to the learning styles perspective. Huxley, after all, could whittle down humanity to *five* human categories. Learning styles fans trumped him with *three*.) And amazingly, the learning styles movement has not been drummed off campuses; it's been embraced by an alarming number of administrators, counselors, and academic departments around the country.

Beyond its wild reductionism, there are many deep logical flaws with the research that grounds the learning styles movement. It dismisses years of research that shows a significant (if not dramatic and direct) cause/effect relationship between socioeconomic factors and education. It rests on a set of non sequiturs and indirect measures. (For instance, if a student says, through a battery of test questions, that she likes to study at home in a chair, this, say the researchers, helps them to determine how she learns. But there is no direct correlation between *liking* something and *learning from* it. In fact, the opposite could be entirely true, but the surveys do not acknowledge the correlation either way.) The surveys ignore the huge impact of situational contingencies on learning,[1] and, like most battery tests of their kind, assume that when someone chooses option A (out of possible options A or B), that A is inherently true. Of course, much

---

[1] The test asks many questions about situational contingencies, but only as a means to discover something internal and presumably permanent in the individual, so that environmental factors in an educational situation are not seen as influential but as elements in the bigger profile of a coherent, self-enclosed, and consistently systematic individual consciousness.

research has been done to show that even if people could choose among A, B, C, D, E, F, G, H, I, J, K, L, M, N, O, P, Q, R, S, T, U, V, W, X, Y, Z, their choice is not necessarily related to the truth of their behavior or personality or thought processes or anything outside of the specific language of survey question itself.

5   But this argument is not necessarily about invalidity. If the logical holes of the theory do not prompt educators to shun the fad outright, then the implications for students should. Imagine a student, Jennifer. She didn't do well in her K–12 education. She hated the town she lived in; she suffered constantly from a chaotic home life, and spent much of her time with friends—outside of the home and away from school. When she goes to a local community college, someone gives her a learning styles survey, which asks where she is comfortable learning, what kinds of environments most help her to feel energized, etc. After the test, she is told that she is a kinesthetic learner. The test, which ignores the relationship between academic learning and Jennifer's lived experiences, prompts her to internalize a reductive label. So rather than evaluate her education (analyze the system itself or the pedagogy which introduced her to literature or calculus or chemistry), Jennifer learns that she is a particular *type*. She has been given a tool for limiting herself, a terminology for pigeon-holing her entire intellectual constitution. If she takes the new category seriously, she will learn to permanently close off certain intellectual pathways that were, perhaps because of her prior experiences (and not her innate learning style), hardly ever opened. If she's a dutiful student and listens to the results of the impressive-looking survey, she will come to believe that she does not have the intellectual wherewithal to do physics or read *Moby-Dick*.

People steeped in learning styles discourse ask questions, such as "How do we teach philosophy to concrete thinkers?" We should reveal the absurdity of such a question, which is based on a false binary. Thinking is not simply concrete or abstract. How could thinking be only concrete? It's thought. Thought is abstract. An idea is abstract.

Certainly, there are layers to thought—ranging from basic comprehension to meta-theory, but to say that thinking is *either* concrete *or* abstract not only reduces the complexity of thinking; it totally misrepresents what thinking *is*. To ask people if they are concrete or abstract thinkers is tantamount to asking them if they use their skin or bodies more. Imagine someone asking, "Do you use your skin or body more when you run? How about when you write? How about when you take a shower?" The questions are absurd because the skin is an organ of the body. It is not a separate entity. Similarly, theoretical thought processes are not separate from comprehension. Students who aren't good at "abstraction" are simply not good at juggling various abstractions at once. But, despite the discourse of the learning styles movement, they can learn. Given close attention, guidance, and thoughtful pedagogy, students who have become their own worst learning enemies can, in fact, be more than one of three types.

Absurd categorizations (e.g., concrete/abstract, visual/auditory/kinesthetic) defeat students. Such monstrosities rarely, if ever (and I would argue strongly for *if ever),* benefit students. Most often, students get pinned beneath such contraptions. When given labels for their personalities or intellectual habits, they think of the hardships they have had in their education, pin themselves beneath one of those labels, and dismiss any future association with the others. And rather than diffuse this intellectual self-abuse, the learning styles movement enables it. Rather than free students from self-defeating categories or helping them to crawl out from under bad experiences, the movement trains students to limit themselves, to defeat themselves, to adopt a harmful language about their own potential.

Some have argued that the movement has had one good outcome: It's prompted teachers to rethink the habit of lecture. Of course, this is a positive effect. But we did not need the learning styles movement to teach us that students learn better when they participate actively in building ideas. John Dewey argued this point, without the fallacies, distortions and pseudo-science, early in the 20th century. Many scholars before and since have developed theories of participant knowledge-making without reducing human identity into silly categories.

Certainly, learning styles advocates are not evil-minded people. They want to help students. But the grounding assumptions of the movement emerge from some dubious intellectual traditions—from the tendencies of 19th and 20th century pop psychologists, phrenologists, Nazi regimes, and Cold War propagandists to codify human identity—to see behavior as the consequence of human types rather than a complex web of forces (biological, sociological, political, and spiritual). In some ways, it is an echo of a scientifically aggressive but naïve time—a time when people believed they could, quickly and easily, determine *who you are*.

10   Contrary to the learning styles movement and its ghastly scientific cousins of the past, neurologists are recently uncovering the wild complexity of learning. In the past few years, neurologists have been substantiating what philosophers have thought for millennia: that humans are *not* hardwired for a particular type of learning; rather, the processes of learning change the person—the wiring of the brain. In a variety of studies, neurologists have shown that the adult brain (not only the brains of children and infants) actually reorganizes with new experiences ("A New Window"). Synapses, the connections between neurons, actually form and reform according to experience. That is, experiences prompt the brain to reorganize how it processes information—and in the world of the brain, that amounts to reconstitution. Such a revelation has huge implications for education. James Zull, a biology professor at Case Western Reserve University, describes teaching as "The Art of Changing the Brain," also the title of his latest book. "What the title says is that learning is a physical change in the brain. This is one thing neuroscience has shown us, and if it is true, then it must be that successful teachers produce change in the learner's brain" (Zull). And the more neurologists learn, the more

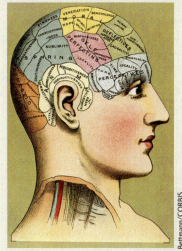

A phrenological chart of presumed character traits and their locations in the brain. Phrenology was popular in the early 19th century but is now considered a pseudoscience.

they shun fads like learning styles as oversimplified "folk psychology" that poisons the educational climate for students (Geake 130–32).

As science on learning gets more sophisticated and as we reconnect with the powerful insights of past philosophers, we should continue to evaluate the habits of education. And we should be careful enough to teach students out of their habits as well. We should help them to be free of oppressive categories. If we are truly interested in teaching "lifelong learning," a commonly celebrated phrase in higher education, we should give students tools for intellectual transformation—not stagnation and pigeon-holing. Rather than helping students to remain entrenched in their intellectual habits, we ought to give them tools for digging out of the past, out of the present, and out from under any bizarre categories that get dropped on them in the future.

Works Cited

Geake, John. "Neuromythologies in Education." *Educational Research*, vol. 50, no. 2, June 2008, pp. 123–133, amyalexander.wiki.westga.edu/file/view/neuromythologies-p.pdf.

"A New Window to View How Experiences Rewire the Brain." *Howard Hughes Medical Institution*, 19 Dec. 2002, www.hhmi.org/news/new-window-view-how-experiences-rewire-brain.

Zull, James E. "The Art of the Changing Brain." *New Horizons for Learning*, May 2003, education.jhu.edu/PD/newhorizons/Neurosciences/articles/The%20Art%20of%20the%20Changing%20Brain/.

Analyzing Argument

1. What is Benlow's main claim? Is it a claim of fact, value, or policy?

2. How do concessions and qualifiers function in this argument? What points do they soften—or appear to soften? What do they accomplish?

Point to specific passages to help with your explanation.

3. Explain the role of allusion in Benlow's argument. For instance, how does the Cold War allusion function? How does it relate to the rest of his argument?

4. Where does Benlow use analogical reasoning? Point to a particular passage and explain how the reasoning works—how a comparison leads to or supports a claim.

5. Point to the most heated or contentious passage in Benlow's argument. Why do you think Benlow goes so hard? Why the intensity?

20

Consumption

D o you ever feel like you live in a culture of Consumption Gone Mad? As citizens of a thriving capitalistic nation, Americans are confronted each day with decisions about what and how to consume. Should one buy an SUV, shop at Walmart, keep up with new technology? How should one shop for food? What is the effect of consuming natural resources such as trees, wetlands, fish, and petroleum? Should one buy waxed or unwaxed dental floss, and what flavor?

Ten days after September 11, 2001, President George W. Bush spoke to the nation, saying, "I ask your continued participation and confidence in the American economy. Terrorists attacked a symbol of American prosperity; they did not touch its source." Consumption is, it seems, integral to individual and national identity. Perhaps even more than the other topics in the Argument Anthology, this chapter touches other issues: consumption and environment, consumption and education, consumption and popular culture, and so on.

In economics, consumption is the use of goods and services to achieve utility. (Utility is the happiness or gratification gained by consumption.) Consumerism, a related concept, is defined in part as equating personal happiness with the consumption of goods and services. Many of the readings throughout this book make either implicit or explicit arguments about consumption and consumerism.

Readings about Consumption in Chapters 1–14

"A Community of Cars," Ryan Brown

"Disconnected," Lynda Smith

"The Fashion Punk Paradox," Andrew Hyde

"No Sex Please, We're Middle Class," Camille Paglia

"Citizens and Consumers," Amber Edmondson

"Big House in the Wilderness: Moratoriums on Building and Individual Irresponsibility," Tracy Webster

Letter to Kohl's

K. T. GLENCY

K. T. Glency wrote this letter to the chairman and CEO of Kohl's in 1999 after the situation he describes in his letter.

K. T. Glency
23 Maple
Toledo, OH 43609

Bill Kellogg
Kohl's Chairman & CEO
N56 W17000 Ridgewood Dr.
Menomonee Falls, WI 53051-5660

Dear Mr. Kellogg:
I am writing you what I consider to be an important letter. While it is a longer letter than I would normally send to a busy executive, I hope that you'll take time to read it and consider what I am about to say.

A week ago, I had an experience at your Kohl's store on Monroe Street in Toledo, Ohio. I had never been to a Kohl's store before, but I was looking for a golf shirt, couldn't find what I wanted, so I tried Kohl's. I purchased a few shirts in your store (one golf shirt and two tee-shirts), the total coming to about forty dollars. At the checkout, the clerk (associate, or whatever Kohl's calls people who work the checkout) said that if I "applied for" a Kohl's charge, I would save 15 percent on my purchase. I am sure you are familiar with the routine.

I didn't want a Kohl's charge. I have just one charge card which I use frequently, and having only one charge card suits me fine. I don't see a reason for collecting a lot of different ones. Still, I agreed to "apply for" a Kohl's charge, imagining that I would use it rarely, if ever. I filled out the forms as the line behind me grew longer.

The clerk then went to a computer and checked my credit. She returned and said that my credit had been approved and that I would save 15 percent on my forty-dollar purchase. Then she said, "I'll put this [purchase] on your Kohl's charge for you."

When I told her I didn't want to use my Kohl's 5 charge today, she said I had to (or else I could not receive the 15 percent discount). But she hadn't said that before. Your clerk deceived me. To put it simply and honestly, the Kohl's clerk as a normal part of her job *lied* to me. She had said that if I "applied" for the card I would save 15 percent, but she had not said that I had to use the charge card today, or ever.

While I did not push for the 15 percent discount (even though she had said it would be given if I just applied for the card), I did try explaining what I thought was the problem with what had just happened. But your clerk didn't seem to care much that she had *said* one thing yet all along and knowingly *meant* another. She became annoyed at me even though I was careful to be very polite the whole time.

My complaint has nothing to do with not having saved $3.50. I am not the type of person who will apply for a credit card to save a little money. Instead, it bothered me that your store says one thing but then slides that one thing into another. Your clerks are obviously trained to say very nicely, "I'll just go ahead and put that on your Kohl's credit card." I think they even say "for you" to make it sound like they're doing you a favor, even though they are really just making it harder for people to say "no." Your marketing specialists know that if your clerks say it that way, the customer will generally go along with it. They know not to say, "Do you want it on your Kohl's credit card, some other credit card, or would you like to pay cash?" They know not to give the customer a choice. And they know not to say up front that you have to use the card today; they know to say that you only have to "apply." It is fine if Kohl's requires the customer to use the credit card on that purchase, but you should say exactly *that* right up front instead of saying that you get a discount just for "applying."

Shortly after my Kohl's experience, I got a call from a telemarketer. It could have been the clerk at

Kohl's, her sister, or her best friend. She used the same technique. She wanted me to purchase premium cable channels and said that the first month would be free and the cost of hook-up would be waived. She talked and talked, then she said, "Which day is better for you, Mr. Glency? Thursday or Friday?" Of course I said that I didn't want the service. But I think a lot of people who don't want a premium cable channel say, "Well, I guess Thursday is a better day for me than Friday is." You know this, Mr. Kellogg. The cable company knows this. And that's why you do it.

Executives such as yourself perpetuate this culture of dishonesty. I know it sounds overdramatic, but it is not. Your clerk is, as a normal part of her job, taught to deceive each customer that comes by—each customer including the woman her grandmother plays bridge with (or the woman *your* grandmother plays bridge with). And then when your clerk goes home, someone just like her calls her on the telephone and does the same thing to her that she has been doing all day to everyone else.

10   I know that you are in business to make money. You want lots of people to have Kohl's credit cards, and this is a way of getting one into their wallets. I know you are competing with K-Mart, Wal-Mart, J.C. Penney, and Sears, who are probably doing the same thing. But, you all are contributing to a culture of dishonesty. And you are trying to get credit cards into the hands of people who can't handle them. While we are concerned about guns and drugs in this country, we should be just as concerned with credit. I am certain, Mr. Kellogg, that as a department store executive you are aware of the careless spending habits of many Americans. According to a recent article in the *Boston Review,*

> About two-thirds of American households do not save in a typical year. Credit card debt has skyrocketed, with unpaid balances now averaging about $7,000 and the typical household paying $1,000 each year in interest and penalties. These are not just low-income households. Bankruptcy rates continue to set new

records, rising from 200,000 a year in 1980 to 1.4 million in 1998.

I wonder how serious you consider this problem to be. Stores like Kohl's and executives such as yourself are nothing less than "the candy man." You might as well be selling drugs or guns to customers who you know will use them irresponsibly. Enabling someone to spend $7,000 they don't have and then $1,000 in interest and penalties is harmful. It is only a slight variation on the old Company Town in which an employee lived more like a slave than an employee: he and his family were put in debt and were likely to stay in debt. The employee of the Company Town didn't know what he was getting into. The first-time heroin user didn't imagine she would become hopelessly addicted. And who begins collecting credit cards imagining that in a few years he will be so in debt that he must file for bankruptcy (and be bailed out by taxpayers like you and me)? It is strong language, and deservedly so.

After the girl told me the truth—that I had to put my purchase on my Kohl's card—and ended up charging me the undiscounted price, I walked back to your Customer Service counter to make the same point there that I am making to you now. Of course I waited in line, investing my time just to make the point that Kohl's conducts business dishonestly. I knew that back there I would just be talking to another employee whose job it is to support Kohl's policy, whatever it be. The woman there said two interesting things:

1) She said that no one else has ever complained about this situation. I believe her. For one, I knew going into it that it'd be somewhat unpleasant, would take at least a half hour, and that nothing would change. So why bother, right? Most people don't complain, Mr. Kellogg, but that doesn't mean they like what's going on. Did she assume that because most people don't take thirty minutes (or an hour) to express their dissatisfaction that they are pleased? The selling technique plays on the fact that people go along with things, that they will not

take time out of their busy day to say that they don't appreciate the deception.

I accept the responsibility of speaking up for all the people who for various reasons put a purchase on a credit card even when they don't want to. Some people just think they have to (because the store said they have to). Others are nice and don't want to cause trouble. Others I'm sure say that it's just too late—it has already happened. Others feel like they got a real deal (15 percent off!) and depending upon circumstances, maybe they did. But some people don't speak up because they are timid, shy, polite, afraid, not-very-smart, and so on (whatever the case, we cannot assume that it's because they like what just happened). You know this, and your customer service representative's second comment indicated that she knew it too.

15   2) When I complained that you should not be required to put your purchase on your credit card (my complaint, of course, being that you shouldn't be required to because you are told you need only "apply"), she said that it (the sales technique) "wouldn't work" if the customer weren't required to put the purchase on the credit card. (She said something like, "It wouldn't work then.")

As you know, at one time stores would give you something if you just applied for credit. Then they would check your credit and send you a card if you were accepted. Now stores check the credit right there and require that the purchase be put on the store's card. This makes sense. I understand it. I am one who might never use the card again. Your store is now unwilling to take the risk of someone never using the card. Fine. I have no objection. But, you shouldn't lie and tell the customer that "applying" is all that they need to do. You should be honest and say that the customer must use the new card to pay for today's purchase. If you require the customer to put the purchase on the Kohl's credit card, you should say that.

The woman in Customer Service said, "Well, most people figure that out." Her statement suggests the point that you may want to argue: *use* of the credit card is implied. And it is, especially to those customers who shop a lot at a variety of stores. They know now, after an initial experience, that *use* of the credit card is most likely required. Others do not know this. And whether or not people figure it out depends upon their degree of "consumer literacy." Those who are the least literate are deceived and taken advantage of, while those who are the most literate accept a deceptive technique as being normal. Either case (as well as the ones that fall somewhere in between) is unfortunate. That some are "onto" or "into" the game and willing to play it does not make it right. For the record, I suspected that I might be required to use the card today, especially after the clerk went over to the computer terminal to check my credit. (I am not really "out of" the game.)

The point is that you tell people one thing and then sneakily slide that statement into something else. It is dishonest, and you are making anyone who works for you do it hundreds of times a day. Mr. Kellogg, what impact does that have on the employee, as well as on the customer who gets it not just from you but elsewhere? It is tricky, especially to certain vulnerable groups who are likely to shop at your store (the elderly, for example). You are requiring as a normal part of an entry-level, fairly low-paying job that one hard-working person mislead another, then another, over and over again.

Do you think this chips away at something? Do you feel any responsibility? How do you feel when someone applies this treatment (which pervades our culture) to you or to your mother or father or to your wife or child? Do you see how big a part of it YOU are? Do you see how YOU contribute to it? Does it bother you at all?

What does bother you? Violent lyrics in rap 20 songs? Violence on TV? Maybe you wonder why movies today must be so violent. Perhaps you, like many others, think that they are negatively affecting young people and society overall. But movies get more and more violent because violence sells. It works. And if you want to make money making movies, you have to make the next movie more violent than the last one. It's the same with deceptive marketing at department stores. You are doing something that is bad for society because you feel that you have to in order to keep up with Wal-Mart and K-Mart. So, all the big department store executives such as yourself must turn to deceptive means in order to compete with each other.

I suspect that you are all pretty nice men and women with nice families. I suspect that the clerk at Kohl's and the Customer Service representative are pretty nice too. Yet, all are lying. It's their job to lie. And to me it is very sad in all of your cases. Perhaps you sit around with friends and wonder about public situations in which people are rude to each other or dishonest while never thinking that thousands of people a day are lied to as a matter of normal business at *your* store.

Perhaps you don't think there is any impact on your employees when the entity from which they get paid requires them to regularly enact these little deceptions on normal people just like themselves. What does the clerk at Kohl's think when she has a confused, elderly customer applying for a credit card in order to save 15 percent? What does the clerk think when the elderly customer (just as planned) goes along with everything she says: "I'll go ahead and put this on your Kohl's card FOR YOU?" Is she happy that she has signed up another customer *for the store?* Does she think that she has tricked a stupid, old lady? Does she think it's right? Does she feel good? Does she feel bad? Does she feel anything at all?

I noticed in talking with the two Kohl's employees that they were very pleasant—more precisely, that they made a point of speaking in a very pleasant tone of voice. I think one reason why they were so pleasant was that I was pleasant. I did not push them very far in thinking about what they were saying, and I purposely pulled back when I saw them getting irritated. I dropped the matter because I could see that they weren't getting what I was saying. Yet, they *were* pleasant to start out with and remained pleasant, although both (especially the sales clerk) were getting tired of me and quickly developing different attitudes, which caused me to drop the matter and go away.

I suspect that they felt like they were doing an honest job because they were speaking in a pleasant tone of voice and thus being nice to a complaining customer. But they were confusing "pleasant tone of voice" with "being nice." This is very disturbing, Mr. Kellogg. Speaking politely is not the same as being nice or honest. And I fear that while you require your employees to be nice or friendly or pleasant to customers, that really just means in tone of voice, not in actions (or in actuality). You could also require that they treat the customers honestly. Conmen, Mr. Kellogg, are nice; otherwise, their con (to use the language of your Customer Service representative) "wouldn't work." Show me an unfriendly conman.

I am glad that your employees seem to be friendly, but saying one thing while knowing that you mean something else is not right, nice, or honest just because it was said in a pleasant tone of voice. I fear that your employees think that it is. Here is where *you* have a responsibility to show people through store policy what honesty really is. Here is where you, an important executive who can affect the actions of many people (not just your employees but your customers through your employees and even people who have never entered your store—we are all connected), can help to teach people that being nice to one another is not merely speaking in a nice tone of voice, but also requires being honest. This is a serious responsibility that carries with it the potential to have a real positive impact on all of our daily lives.

You can help to teach people what honesty is. You can teach people that if they leave out important information or define words in ways others would not define them, they are *not* being honest. Honesty involves seeing where the other person might get the wrong idea and clarifying things up front—not trying to confuse things a little and then say, "Well, you should have figured it out."

I agree with you that people should be able to figure *some* things out. Undoubtedly, certain things are implied. Some people will be able to figure out more than others. And some people will be able to figure out very little. Of course Kohl's employees cannot spell out every detail of a situation, but they should not take any action to purposely deceive. Society has a responsibility to educate people enough so that they can figure things out on their own. And influential executives such as you have a responsibility to *not* deceive the public.

"What is the harm?" Dishonesty is everywhere. It's common. It's accepted. It's not much thought about. And, it must have some negative impact on society and its individual members. The Kohl's employee misleads a customer who is a telemarketer, and that telemarketer misleads a computer salesperson, and that salesperson misleads someone who sells cars, and that person misleads an employee at Kohl's, and they all find themselves on a treadmill of dishonesty. Your sales clerk makes her commission on sales of new credit card accounts, but then spends it on what? And what is her attitude when she works hard, though dishonestly, then gets taken by the telemarketer or someone else? What is the impact of all this on one's quality of life?

I am asking you three things:

30   1) Are you personally contributing to a chipping away of honesty and integrity, and does this have a negative impact on our society? This is not an easily answered question. As you consider your answer, think of your employees, who are taught to deceive the customer (and of all those customers who are routinely misled).

2) Will you change the way your store does business by taking an honest approach in all matters with your customers and employees? Will you require this honesty of all your employees?

3) Will you publicly encourage other important business executives to do the same?

I hope you have safely reached the end of this letter, will take time to consider my ideas, and even let me know what you think. I hope you are well.

Sincerely,
K. T. Glency

Analyzing Argument

1. How is the Kohl's sales clerk participating in a "culture of dishonesty" (paragraph 10)?

2. How does Glency appeal to logic?

3. Identify Glency's most explicit or direct appeal to value. Then identify his most subtle or indirect appeal to value.

4. Glency compares an unsuspecting credit card user to a heroin addict. How is this analogy an appeal to value? (What might Glency hope to accomplish with the analogy?)

5. Examine the following passage from Glency's letter:

   What does bother you? Violent lyrics in rap songs? Violence on TV? Maybe you wonder why movies today must be so violent. Perhaps you, like many others, think that they are negatively affecting young people and society overall. But movies get more and more violent because violence sells. It works. And if you want to make money making movies, you have to make the next movie more violent than the last one. It's the same with deceptive marketing at department stores. You are doing something that is bad for society because you feel that you have to in order to keep up with Wal-Mart and K-Mart. So, all the big department store executives such as yourself must turn to deceptive means in order to compete with each other.

   Explain how Glency's comparison of movies and department stores supports his main claim.

6. In groups, discuss the length of Glency's letter. Why might he have chosen to write such a long letter? Make a list of advantages and disadvantages of a letter that is this developed. Assuming that Glency was aware of potential drawbacks to his letter's length, why might he have decided to stick with the longer, more developed approach?

Credit Cards on Campus

ROBERT D. MANNING

The following essay was published in 2006 on the Center for a New American Dream website, which provides the following mission statement: "The Center for a New American Dream helps Americans consume responsibly to protect the environment, enhance quality of life, and promote social justice." Robert D. Manning is a research professor and director for the Center for Consumer Financial Services at the Rochester Institute of Technology. He is author of *Credit Card Nation* (2000) and *Give Yourself Credit* (2007).

It's not only possible—but crucial—to teach teens good money habits *before* they go to college.

For a generation where "cash is so five minutes ago" and 18-year-old basketball stars flout $90 million sneaker deals, old school values like saving and long-term planning can seem pretty fuddy-duddy. But with debt and personal bankruptcies for young adults rising at alarming rates, teaching financial literacy to our kids *before* they go off on their own could save them from a future of stress and frustration.

"Plastic Money" Doesn't Come Cheap

Giving young people unfettered access to easy consumer credit—before they have demonstrated the ability to manage a personal budget or obtain a full-time job—can create a host of emotional and psychological problems. The unrestrained use of "plastic money" can fundamentally undermine teens' cognitive ability to understand the relationship between income and standard of living. Poor payment habits can also lead to abysmal personal credit reports with shocking results for naive twenty-somethings: rejections for apartment rentals, home mortgages, auto loans, car insurance, graduate school loans, professional school admission, and even jobs.

Twenty years ago, who could have foreseen that college graduates would have their consumer credit scores scrutinized as carefully as their GPAs? So much for American Express saving the day. (Do teenagers wonder if Jerry Seinfeld has a problem paying *his* credit card bills?)

With credit lines and material expectations 5 progressively increasing on American campuses, many teens now view consumer credit as a social entitlement rather than an earned privilege. A recent Citibank/Sony Visa campaign promotes credit cards as the "Currency of Fun," offering electronic gadgets as rewards for high levels of purchasing—implying that the more you spend, the more "fun" you will enjoy and the more "toys" you will receive. Conversely, limiting access to material goods is portrayed as depriving students of their right to pursue happiness through shopping.

Credit card companies encourage fantasies of easy money because students are so profitable: teens have financial naivete, high material expectations, responsiveness to relatively low-cost marketing campaigns, high potential earnings, and future demand for financial services. Not surprisingly, companies are approving credit lines for students at progressively earlier ages, including high school seniors. Most college freshmen now receive their first credit card before taking their first mid-term exam. Cross-marketing with retail affiliates (such as Visa-issued Gap cards) make impulse shopping even easier.

The Campus Gold (and Platinum) Rush

Since the onset of banking deregulation in 1980, the increasingly concentrated U.S. financial services industry has become more dependent on high-interest revolving credit card loans, which are about three times more profitable than the average banking product. The top 10 banks now control over four-fifths of the credit card market (compared to less than one-fourth in the late 1970s), and these trillion-dollar conglomerates are less cautious with their lending policies than the community banking systems they supplanted.

As profits from revolving debt escalated in the late '80s, the institutional pressure to expand credit card portfolios intensified. Banks began strategizing over how to penetrate the desirous but risky college market. Financial institutions learned that excluding parents from the credit approval process was a lucrative policy that increased students' discretionary purchases, leading to mounting finance charges and fees. By the beginning of the 1989–91 recession, about one-half of college students at four-year institutions had their own credit cards, but few had accumulated over $5,000 in revolving debt. This quickly changed as banks marketed credit cards to juniors and sophomores. By the late 1990s, over 70 percent of college students at four-year institutions had credit cards and banks commonly marketed them to freshmen. With more time to accumulate debt and much higher lines of credit, students began amassing much larger debt burdens, with $15,000 to $20,000 in cumulative "plastic" balances a not uncommon experience.

College administrators have not been passive bystanders. Marketing agreements have proliferated on college campuses which grant credit card companies exclusive promotional access to students in exchange for *millions* of dollars. This is especially common at public institutions, since the largest 250 public universities account for nearly two-thirds of the students at four-year institutions. It is noteworthy that none of the "royalties" from these lucrative contracts have been used to fund financial literacy or debt consolidation programs.

10   Today, three-fourths of college students have bank-issued credit cards. And, at public institutions, students commonly use their college loans (whose repayment schedule is deferred until after graduation) to pay down their monthly credit card balances—a perverse form of a savings account. This trend is encouraged by the largest credit card issuer and student loan provider, Citibank, which essentially reduces its risk by encouraging students to shift their high interest credit card debt into low-interest,

federally guaranteed college loans. It should not be surprising, then, that combined student loan and credit card debt levels are ascending to new heights. In a 2001 survey of its student loan borrowers, Nellie Mae found that the average combined student debt was $20,402—including $17,140 of student loans and $3,262 of credit card debt.

Of course, access to consumer credit cards need not entail student debt problems. If students understand the cost-efficient use of bank credit cards, having them at an earlier age may actually result in fewer debt problems later on.

Less Plastic and More Freedom

It is imperative for parents to discuss the potential social and economic consequences of debt-based consumption with their children as soon as they are able to recognize the advertising messages that define the pop culture of their youth. Persistence and determination are needed to counteract these pervasive messages of instant gratification—but it is possible to break the cognitive chains that associate "fun" with purchasing more "toys."

You can emphasize the positive power of savings to kids at a very early age. Encourage or enforce a savings plan with young children, such as putting 20 percent of his or her allowance into a special bank account, to demonstrate that spending is linked to the money he or she has available. Calculate the cost of a desired activity or toy in terms of the number of weeks your child must wait to earn it with savings. The child may become frustrated by this process—especially if he or she is accustomed to mom or dad buying the toys—but it will be more significant to the child through the process of using his or her own money, and waiting to earn it teaches the power of delayed gratification.

As children enter the early teen years, many will want credit cards—especially since credit is commonly used to facilitate online transactions. Before jumping into the world of credit with your child, establish a joint checking account as a reward for attaining earlier savings goals. Teach him or her how to balance a checkbook, emphasizing that this convenience requires a great deal of personal responsibility. Just like saving up allowance, the money can only be spent if it is available—do not permit the bank to offer overdraft protection. Monitor how your child handles this responsibility. If you are satisfied with your child's spending habits, you may consider a check-cashing or debit card in the early teenage years to access the checking account.

15   As your teen assumes greater responsibility with money—and perhaps with other duties, such as household chores—a credit card can be a good option, if chosen and monitored carefully. There are many forms of pre-paid bank cards which function like debit cards and teach kids that deferring payment is not the same as having "free money." It is important to demonstrate that the power of credit can quickly exceed its convenience through high cost finance charges and fees. Use a calculator . . . to show the real cost of purchases on a card with a revolving balance, and how increasing monthly payments and lowering annual percentage rates will lower overall costs. The key is to emphasize that impulse buying on credit entails paying more later—sometimes much more—which can mean painful future sacrifices.

In addition to chaperoning your child through different financial lessons, it is important throughout this time to discuss the temptation of money, the lure of advertising, and the blurring of "needs" with "desires." Balance savings objectives with rewards for meeting specific goals, discuss money matters clearly and often, and of course, model responsible habits in your own financial life, or many of these lessons will be lost.

Today, the mantra of "buy now, pay later," is portrayed in the mass media and popular culture as the new values of the "Just Do It!" generation. Too often, financial irresponsibility is portrayed as a benign rite of passage as our youth make the transition to the personal responsibilities of adulthood. In reality, many youth find their personal relationships and professional careers ruined without an informed view of the power of plastic. By equipping our teens with appropriate financial skills, we can replace the seduction of "stuff" with the rewards of personal empowerment and self-fulfillment.

Analyzing Argument

1. According to Manning, how do credit card companies appeal to students? Why are such appeals effective?

2. According to Manning, how can the cognitive chains that associate "fun" with purchasing more "toys" be broken? How does this idea relate to Manning's line of reasoning?

3. Manning concludes with a strong assertion: "In reality, many youth find their personal relationships and professional careers ruined without an informed view of the power of plastic." How does the rest of the article support this claim?

4. Why might the reader accept or reject Manning's main claim? What assumptions or values might keep someone from understanding or accepting the argument?

Intoxitwitching: The Energy Drink Buzz

SIMON BENLOW

We argue the value of almost everything in our lives: food, clothing, education, entertainment, jobs, pay, perks, and so on. Benlow, a writer and college instructor, wrote this argument about the value of energy drinks as a sample for students.

In mainstream America, beverages are fantastic—glitzy, intense, extreme, luxurious, radical, decadent. They come at us via loud vending machines and frenetic commercials. We drink super-yellow, neon-fizzy liquids from a vast array of bended plastics: with handgrips, large mouth holes, long necks, and extra reservoirs for big gulpers. When we drink in America, we zoom past the subtle, the nuanced, the basic, the fundamental, the organic. We often pass up a *fresh* drink and reach for the zippy, artificially colored, coagulated, syrupy goo that's labeled "fresh!"

In this continuum of products comes the energy drink: Monster, Full Throttle, AMP, and Red Bull. Such drinks are the zenith of extreme beverages. They have maximized caffeine and sugar; in fact, the drinks themselves are merely vessels for the buzz-inducing agents (in the same way that cigarettes are vessels for nicotine). Red Bull's slim, sensible-looking can promises a range of benefits: "Improves performance, especially during times of increased stress or strain. Increases concentration and improves reaction speed. Stimulates the metabolism." If all this were true, Red Bull would be more than an energy drink; it'd be superhero serum. But it's not true—or possible. Anything that quickens reaction time and increases the metabolism is bound to *decrease* concentration. In fact, when we see the first three ingredients (water, sucrose, glucose), it is easy to imagine the opposite of concentration: distractibility and twitchiness. Alertness and zingy reflexes are simply not the same as concentration.

My evaluation may sound harshly negative—as though I'm anti-stimulant. But I'm a caffeine fiend.

I drink anywhere from 3 to 6 cups every day. Two years ago, after a few cups of morning coffee, I found my way to a Red Bull just before a hike in the woods. It was new to me, but I figured that an "energy drink" would prompt a more rigorous pace and a heartier workout. I didn't anticipate scaling trees (some without branches), running escaped-lunatic style through the woods, brandishing sticks, leaping down ravines, yelling "Kill the Halflings!" à la the Uruk-hai in the recently released *Lord of the Rings* movies. I also didn't anticipate staring at the ceiling that night (many hours after the Red Bull) feeling the call of the wild in each heartbeat. As a mild-mannered, 30-something college professor, I hadn't anticipated such drama—from a drink that my preteen niece could buy if she could tolerate the taste.

This Red Bull experience parallels Sam Eifling's more formal exploration of energy drinks. In his article "Booster Shot," the reporter narrates his sampling of Red Bull, Monster, AMP, Full Throttle, SoBe No Fear, and other similar concoctions. He experiences a range of feelings, none of which measure up to the advertised effects: "wooziness," "distractibility," "disappointment," a sour stomach, and a few headaches. In Eifling's personal study, most of the drinks generate a fleeting lack of focus, and those that prompt alertness (what might translate as *energy*) also prompt distractibility.

Some might argue that Red Bull and its cousins are merely thirst quenchers—that the super-charged ingredients are inconsequential. Certainly, it is fair to say that caffeine affects some people more dramatically than others. But if people are *not* catapulted into a twitchy buzz, given the level of fructose and glucose, what's occurring biologically? What does it suggest that some consumers *don't* feel jolted after pounding a Monster or a Red Bull? Perhaps a good number of energy drinkers have become immune—so saturated with our culture's hyped-up sweeteners that they're unable to detect a sudden super-sugar intrusion. Have we reached maximum sugar capacity?

At best, the zingy energy drink beverage line is another indication of our broader cultural habit for overindulging. At worst, it is another implement of intellectual distraction. It is no secret that K–12 and college students are increasingly less able to focus, less apt to read a novel than they have been in the past. The upswing in short attention spans has been blamed on everything from MTV to video games, from childhood inoculations to super-charged digital media advertising. But for anyone who's ever been in a public school classroom, and who has witnessed the post-lunch collective neurosis that comes after students pound down a few soda pops, one culprit is obvious: fructose—or its simple-headed cousins, glucose and sucrose. And in the hierarchy of super-sugared beverages, the energy drinks far exceed standard Coca-Cola or Mountain Dew. In short, energy drinks are exactly what most students don't need. The culture they live in begs them not to pay attention—to anything for more than few seconds. The constant barrage of speedy images yanks their attention away from one thing and onto the next. By the time a student is ready to begin reading, she has intellectual whiplash; by the time she enters college, she has internalized the culture's zing. (Good luck with chemistry, calculus, or literature.)

As with all products, the truth of the energy drink lies beneath its name—beneath the language and the allure concocted by the language. The drinks don't actually yield *energy.* Energy can be controlled, sensed, nuanced. Energy transfers itself into more energy. But a Red Bull or an AMP gives a twitchy buzz, a subtle, maybe even unconscious, jitter. Granted, sugar in all forms (or artificial forms) equals energy to the human body. But we should be suspicious of energy that manifests itself as nothing but a twitchy buzz or as distractibility. And according to Alicia Shively, a writer for the *White Pine Press,* we have good reason to be more than suspicious. Officials in Canada and Ireland have publicly denounced Red Bull, and French officials made it illegal to sell, "categorizing the drink as a medicine because of the level of taurine . . . an amino acid that assists in Red Bull's energy inducing buzz" (10).

If energy drinks were labeled according to their effects, they might have been called *distraction* drinks, *dare-you-to-focus* drinks, *try-sitting-down-and-follow-one-idea* drinks, *ruin-your-taste-buds* drinks. Instead, the corporations have waxed over the real intellectual effects of the hyper-caffeinated goo-in-a-can. They used the most positive spin for twitchiness and distractibility: *energy.* But despite the lovely name, the last thing in the world that the American population needs are the effects brought on by a Red Bull. We're a distracted and distractible people. We don't need over-the-counter assistance.

The Romans went down, some say, because of lead in the drinking water. They all went nuts—followed their leaders right over the cliffs of reason. Maybe beverages are, indeed, the pivotal element in the rise and fall of civilizations. If I wanted to take over a country, I'd start by giving everyone a Red Bull . . . and then another. Then, I'd give everyone a cell phone. I'd say to my generals and admirals waiting just outside the borders, "Now, watch how everyone stays distracted. First, you'll notice a steep decline in literacy."

Works Cited

Eifling, Sam. "Booster Shot." *Slate*, 20 Sept. 2005, www.slate.com/articles/life/shopping/2005/09/booster_shot.html.

Shively, Alicia. "Warning: This Product Contains Hype." *White Pine Press* [Traverse City], 10 Oct. 2005, pp. 1+.

Analyzing Argument

1. Summarize Benlow's argument: What is his main claim and support?

2. How does the argument appeal to logic? How does it appeal to emotions, character, values, or need? Point to specific passages.

3. Point to the essay's use of counterargument, concession, and qualifier. How does each strategy figure into the overall argument? What effect does each have on the argument?

4. How does Benlow's voice impact the argument? How might it help or hurt the success of the argument for readers?

The Origin of Rhubarb

BARCLEY OWENS

Like most people, Barcley Owens, a writer and English professor, was entirely uninterested in the origins of rhubarb. Then he stumbled upon the topic and researched it for several weeks. According to Owens, "This essay suggests that fostering an intellectual life requires curiosity—a willingness to digress, to exchange the mundane humdrum of routine chores for the thrill of discovery."

"Rhubarb pie."

"What about it?"

"You like it?"

"Nope, never have. Apple's my favorite, then cherry—and pumpkin at Thanksgiving."

5   "So you don't like rhubarb?"

"Nope, too bitter."

"Sugar sprinkled on top helps."

"Maybe, I don't know. My aunt served it on the Fourth of July. She never used water."

"No water?"

10   "Nope, she told us it does well enough on its own."

"Didn't it scorch?"

"Guess not. Aunt Aileen's pies were a big deal. She always said, 'Rhubarb's good for what ails you.'"

"Didn't your aunt have corns?"

"No, warts—warts on her knees. Not very pretty."

15   "Well, I guess rhubarb didn't help so much with the warts."

"Nope, I don't suppose it ever did."

What about rhubarb?

It's mostly used in pies, homegrown in gardens, emblematic of rural Americana, a summer delight.

Certainly rhubarb was not something I was thinking of as I flipped through a dictionary, blithely speeding along toward the word *rhododendron*, a word I misspell even as I write this sentence. I've long since forgotten why I ever needed to know how to spell *rhododendron*, but on the way, I overshot and ran smack into *rhubarb* and a curious note regarding its etymology.

The ancient Greeks knew all about *rha bar-* 20 *barum*. To them it was a valuable pharmaceutical imported from the barbarous lands to the north, from beyond the Volga River, in those times known as the Rha, hence their word for the plant, *rha barbarum* ("rhubarb"). Properly dried and in good condition, it was worth its weight in salt. To find out why, we must tell a story about how knowledge is acquired.

Our story begins with Empedocles of Acragus (circa 450 BC), the Father of Rhetoric, who may or may not have thrown himself into the volcanic maw of Mt. Etna. All they could find was one sandal. At any rate, Empedocles proposed a cosmology which associated common elements with four of the Greek gods: air with Zeus, earth with Hera, fire with Hades, and water with Persephone (Burnet). Fifty years later, another local expert known as Hippocrates of Cos (circa 400 BC), the Father of Medicine, formulated the theory of humors. To Hippocrates' credit, the oath bearing his name required physicians, by all means available, to help patients recover instead of causing them more harm. Hippocrates subscribed to Empedocles' notion of four fundamental elements and furthermore speculated there were four specific properties: *cold, dry, wet,* and *hot.* He found that earth (composed of dirt, sand, rocks) was mostly cold and dry, whereas air was often hot and wet, and so forth.

This is the way the ancients reasoned, and we have to admire their serious pursuit of logic. One popular story about Hippocrates was that he peered into a vial of blood, stirred it with a swizzle stick, and mostly saw red. Yes, quite likely, but wait, under that mask of red, he could make out a faint, silky froth of snowberry white, a light hint of cadmium yellow, and a deep undertow of onyx black. Behold a vision, a clarifying moment of true epiphany. He had discovered bile (Riley 10).

So far, so good.

Now, the next beautiful leap of logic, known as the theory of humors, added an elegant symmetry.

Barcley Owens, "The Origin of Rhubarb." Reprinted with the permission of the author.

Although it was based on nothing more real than pure speculation, it led to a resilient and wildly complicated medical theory that survives to this day under the various guises of herbal folklore, the sort of backwoods homilies based on pseudo-science touted by alternative-medicine practitioners. Yet, for all its arcane mysticism, the theory of humors was really based on one simple precept: Each person's body is a microcosm of the vast empyrean. Storms, earthquakes, volcanoes, plagues, droughts, floods, falling stars, all the assorted ills of nature were conjectured to have their miniature counterparts within the human body. Ergo sum, the all-too-common improper mixing of blood and bile led to topsy-turvy humors, creating all manner of constitutional ailments in the frail wrack of human existence.

25   Like any respectable, evolving organism, a long-lived theory tends toward increasing complexity, passing along its DNA through the ages, promulgated by scribes copying manuscripts from papyrus to vellum to paper, with all manner of sundry local experts ad-libbing footnotes, ad infinitum, exegeses upon exegeses, until, voilà, a theory arrives at the end of line bearing an ancient and honorable pedigree, corroborated by a vast, venerable database and accepted as simple truth.

Ah, truth. That sublime, singular, ephemeral moment of consensual agreement.

Onward.

Skip to Galen of Pergamum (circa 150 BC), physician to gladiators, a local expert on the fighting habits of weasels, much celebrated for a very logical assertion that experiments lead to empirical knowledge. Unfortunately Galen's logical assertion did not stop him from inventing whole-cloth the notion that the humors were exceedingly intermingled in a state of dangerous flux, and that, namely, all too often, misbegotten bile was ascending when it should have been descending, putrefying when it should have been coagulating, or vaporizing when it should have been liquefying in the small gut. Such an awful state of affairs required the constant vigilance of the best local experts, day and night. The difficult task for physicians, then, was to combat bad humors. They had to be expunged, expelled, expatiated, re-circulated, and finally, if all went as planned, restored to a natural balance. This resounding culmination of Greek logic resulted in some very aggressive treatments, including bleeding, vomiting, and the vigorous evacuation of bowels. And through the sheer force of established truth, these malpractices were continued through the ages, killing untold numbers of patients (Foust 15).

So how does rhubarb figure into our story? Because it's a mild purgative, less astringent than coffee beans, less unsavory than castor oil, less bulky than flax seed or marshmallow root. So, if one was playing the heroic medicine game, dried rhubarb became a necessary pharmaceutical. By all accounts, it was really quite pleasant, more cordial than bitter pill, less intrusive than an enema. But wait, not just any rhubarb will do! Certainly not the inferior, garden variety rhubarb, the kind of rhubarb we eat in pies today. No, if you were living in Europe during the Middle Ages, and were of some means, your learned physician would prescribe only the best, the one Very True and Authentic Rhubarb, said to originate somewhere in the wilds of China, south of the Great Wall, or maybe farther to the west, in the highlands. Some claimed Mongolia, while others swore by Tibet. Alas, there was cheaper rhubarb by the bagful coming out of Turkey along the Siberian trade routes, but this poor substitute was not as effective in the vital, all-important evacuation of bowels. It had limited potency and did not even look much like the much renowned True Rhubarb. No, True Rhubarb was a giant, tall as a dragon, Hydra-headed with rhizomes. It arrived to the markets of Europe sliced in a particular manner, sun-dried, striated, pierced with holes, strung on branches. And it was unlike any other rhubarb on earth (Foust 24). This was accepted by local experts everywhere as a fact, the simple truth.

The resulting European frenzy for True Rhubarb, known today as the Great Rhubarb Mania, reached a feverish pitch during the eighteenth and nineteenth centuries. Like our own era's UFO encounters, there was a rash of True Rhubarb sightings. Extravagant claims were made and then investigated—with mixed results. Gold medals and cash prizes were offered by scientific societies in a sort of "rhubarb sweepstakes." In 1769, James Inglish produced an astounding twelve-pound plant standing twelve feet high, dwarfing the spindly garden varieties (Foust 119–21). Apothecaries and physicians through-out Europe tried in vain to isolate and reproduce the essential traits of various claimants. Explorers set out on great expeditions across the formidable Middle Kingdom, collecting impressive specimens of white rhubarb, bloody rhubarb, Canton rhubarb, Russian rhubarb, Himalayan rhubarb, and so forth. Despite the best efforts of these intrepid souls—scaling the high shale peaks above Lake Zaisan, scouring the icy gorges of Kalmyk, shivering in the plains of Sikkim, braving the drenching monsoons of the Indus Valley—nothing definitive was ever confirmed. All the tantalizing importations, care-fully and lovingly tended for decades in gardens throughout Europe, still could not produce the roots and stalks of the fabled True Rhubarb. Much specu-lation and many theories followed. Perhaps it was the soil. Perhaps the weather. On and on it went, seedlings hauled thither and yon, nourished, trans-planted, studied—all with mixed results. Nobody could get any closer to the supposed Shangri-la of the One True Rhubarb.

Manchu chieftains, fully cognizant of their lucrative monopoly, were noticeably tight-lipped when questioned. "What? Rhubarb? No, not around here. Very sad, so sorry. Maybe try to the north, across the next river, over that big mountain."

And so it went.

By the 1870s, our epic draws to a rather exhil-arating close. With the inertia of rhubarb mania drained and spent, several matters gradually became accepted as commonsensical. A revealing editorial comment, almost an aside, in an 1878 issue of the *Journal of Botany,* noted that, perhaps, just perhaps, there was not a single species of True Rhubarb—a betrayal of faith many enthusiasts nevertheless must have long suspected (Foust 158–79). Although it took several centuries of intense effort, local experts everywhere proved quite capable of changing their minds. Imagine that! Savor the sheer wonder of it. Based solely on the slow accrual of plain facts, people were compelled via the inductive power of science, from both field studies and laboratory experiments, to give up their much-cherished, centuries-old mythology of rhubarb in exchange for nothing more than facts—namely, that commercial rhubarb was in reality several species which varied tremendously depending on environmental factors such as soil, climate, maturity, time of harvest, the drying process, shelf life, and most critically, the elevation at which it was cultivated. In short, there was no mystery, no golden fleece, no single species of the one Very True and Authentic Rhubarb.

Never had been.

Ironically this non-discovery came just as the 35 medicinal market for rhubarb crashed. Twenty-five hundred years of quackery finally gave way to the evidence of Louis Pasteur's germ theory, so that by the turn of the twentieth century, doctors no longer needed the unfashionable theory of bodily humors. Within one generation, modern medicine had sup-planted Greek logic and the market demand for dried rhubarb vanished (*From Quackery;* Osler).

So what about rhubarb?

Maybe you shouldn't care. It doesn't matter if you feel fine about being duped by the residuals of wrong-headed folk beliefs foisted on us by advertise-ments, pop-psychology surveys of personality types, aptitudes and learning styles. After all, only histori-ans need to know that George Washington died on December 14, 1799, after three local experts drained five pints of his blood—just to relieve a sore throat! (Wallenborn; Witt). And odds are you won't be given a porcelain bleeding bowl or a fine set of French scarifying cups on your next birthday. You really only need to know about such things if you're curious. Or if you find yourself one day scoring "melancholy" on a personality test. Or rated as a "kinesthetic learner who prefers shady environments." Or your career aptitude reads "beekeeper." Or your mood ring turns orange so you climb into your Geo Metro and head to Wal-Mart for aspirin but instead find yourself reaching for St. John's wort. And, really, who needs rhubarb when you already know how to spell *roadadendren . . . rhodadendrin . . . rhododendron?*

Works Cited

Burnet, John. "Empedocles of Acragas." *Exploring Plato's Dialogues*, edited by Anthony F. Beavers, U of Evansville, 1998.

Foust, Clifford M. *Rhubarb: The Wondrous Drug.* Princeton UP, 1992.

From Quackery to Bacteriology: The Emergence of Modern Medicine in 19th Century America: An Exhibit October 12–December 30, 1994. Ward M. Canaday Center, Toledo,1994.

Osler, William. "The Rise and Development of Modern Medicine." *The Evolution of Modern Medicine: A Series of Lectures Delivered at Yale University on the Silliman Foundation in April, 1913,* Project Gutenberg, 2006, www.gutenberg.org/files/1566/1566-h/1566-h.htm.

"Rhubarb." *The American Heritage Dictionary*, 3rd ed., 1992.

Riley, Mark T. "Hippocrates." *Great Thinkers of the Western World*, Harper, 1999.

Wallenborn, White McKenzie. "George Washington's Terminal Illness: A Modern Medical Analysis of the Last Illness and Death of George Washington." *The Papers of George Washington*, U of Virginia, 2000, gwpapers.virginia.edu/history/articles/illness/.

Witt, Charles B., Jr. "The Health and Controversial Death of George Washington." *Ear, Nose & Throat Journal*, vol. 80, no. 2, Feb. 2001, pp. 102–05, www.thefreelibrary.com/The+health+and+controversial+death+of+George+Washington.-a076636540.

Analyzing Argument

1. In one sentence, write down the essay's main claim. Then list the ways the author develops his argument.

2. How does the concluding paragraph shed light on the essay's main idea? What specific references are especially helpful?

3. Describe Owens's voice as a writer, and explain how it is or is not appropriate for this argument.

4. What does Owens value? What does he want the reader to value?

5. How does the wide range of sources function in Owens's "story" about rhubarb? How do the sources help to make it a story about human understanding?

Consumed by the Other: What Spam Means

JUDY CHU

In the following essay, Judy Chu, a professor at Northwestern Michigan College, explores the role Spam has played in her life—and what Spam means. Chu's essay was sparked by the discovery of a can of Spam in a friend's kitchen cupboard. Like Simon Benlow (energy drinks), Barcley Owens (rhubarb), K. T. Glency (sales techniques), and other arguers, Chu takes a closer look at an ordinary subject. Looking closely results in discovery—and not just a discovery of answers but a discovery of complexities and further questions. When we begin to look, we do not know what we will find or where our search will take us.

"Something happens when you fry it. Its sugars caramelize during the browning process, imparting additional flavor and succulence."

Karen and I smiled at her brother's observation, more intently focused on shaping mounds of steamed sticky rice into inch-thick rectangles than waxing philosophical over the finer gastronomic points of a cultural icon. We were, after all, hungry. And in the midst of helping my best friend pack up her apartment in New England three summers ago, as she prepared to relocate to the Bay Area, the three of us were attempting to draw down the contents of her refrigerator and cupboards before she moved.

I have pointed out that we were hungry and do so again, to provide context for those who might cringe at our main ingredient. For on that mid-July evening just outside of Hartford, Connecticut, we three—who had grown up together in the San Gabriel Valley east of Los Angeles, conditioned by our Chinese immigrant parents to recoil at the prospect of food gone to waste—were not about to pitch out a can with an expiration date still several years away. Instead, we were frying up slices of Spam to prepare the Hawaiian favorite *Spam musubi,* otherwise known as Spam sushi.

I never tasted Spam sushi until my mid-twenties when I dated a guy from Hawaii and managed to spend two consecutive summers loafing around in Oahu, eating the stuff on a regular basis. But I did grow up eating Spam during the 1970s and '80s, often chopped up into my family's version of fried rice, a dish we made with leftover rice, preferably cold from the fridge, which we scrambled together with green onions, eggs, and diced bits of whatever luncheon meat we had on hand. Hot dogs were best, but cold cuts would do. And so, of course, would Spam.

Spam sliced straight from the can into a white 5 bread sandwich was another favorite childhood meal, one I associate in particular with memories of my family's summer vacations when we'd load up a box of provisions, pack our bags, and pile into our dusky green Ford Falcon station wagon to explore the national parks of the wild, wild West. My dad figured out the itinerary of these trips by identifying the ultimate destination (Yosemite, the Grand Canyon, or Yellowstone) and plotting a strategic course toward it via the Motel 6 chain. Each morning, we'd start out before sunrise, and each afternoon, we'd pull into some highway rest stop to eat our Spam sandwiches and potato chips (typically a generic version of Ruffles or Lay's, though I recall being especially enamored as a child with the whole concept of Pringles—uniformity pressed into a can—an unsurprising fascination, perhaps, given the nature of Spam itself).

I remember being mesmerized, as an eight- or nine-year-old, by the gleaming blue and neon yellow can. I remember pulling the key off the top and slipping it into the notched side tab. I remember my mom warning me to be careful of the jagged edges that emerged as I twisted my way around the tin, and my dad taking over when I neared the end, so to finish the job cleanly. After disposing of the lid, he would pierce the side of the exposed meat with a pair of chopsticks to pry it out and then slide it

Judy Y. Chu, "Consumed by the Other: What Spam Means." Reprinted with the permission of the author.

onto a plastic plate. I remember the mottled pink protein block glistening with its infamous gelatin, as my brother and I salivated in anticipation. We were, after all, hungry.

These images steeped in personal nostalgia—of childhood meals, vacation picnics, and more grown-up culinary adventures—invariably swim to the surface of my consciousness whenever Spam comes up in a conversation (which is more often than you might think). Depending on my audience, I will be met with similar enthusiasm, curious disbelief, or outright disdain. Spam, it seems, is not the greatest food to admit to eating, let alone liking.

"Spam, spam, spam, spam, spam, lovely spam, wonderful spam."

Mention the word "Spam" these days, and most will think of unwanted e-mails, a fact of our wired contemporary life that must surely discourage the public relations division of the Hormel Corporation, creators and makers of the spiced ham and pork shoulder concoction.[1] More irreverent followers of pop culture can explain how Spam, unveiled to the consuming public in 1937, evolved, at least nominally, into the bane of the Internet age. In a recent debate in the English House of Lords on food safety regulations (specifically dangerous, or annoying, product packaging like certain cans) and unsolicited e-mails (that too may be dangerous or annoying), the Lord Faulkner of Worcester enlightened his unknowing peers: "My Lords, I can help . . . with the origin of the word. It comes from aficionados of Monty Python, and the famous song, 'Spam, spam, spam, spam.' It has been picked up by the Internet community and is used as a description of rubbish on the Internet" ("This Potted Meat" 22–23).

10   While Spam's cybersignificance is a worthy subject in itself, I am drawn to a more fundamental and slippery question about the original meat product: Just what does it mean to eat Spam? Evoking visceral responses among consumers and citizens worldwide, Spam rivals the iconic status of Coca-Cola and McDonald's, which is not so surprising given its place in America's history of twentieth-century modernization and globalization. Having come of age during World War II, it is inextricably linked with our nation's ideals of democracy as well as its military presence abroad. While some, like a chef friend of mine, decry it as a nightmare of food technology, countless others, including most residents of our 50th state, relish its savory sweetness and rely upon its shelf life. Late-night comedians can count on it for laughs and, in doing so, reveal much about our nation's complicated attitudes toward class; yet many, including my parents, eat it without a smirk or trace of ironic self-awareness. So how is it that all these different implications and concerns converge? What does Spam mean?

Most of us will readily concede, either literally or metaphorically, the following cliché: We are what we eat. Yet in his book *American Foodways*, folklorist Charles Camp helpfully complicates this truism when he observes that "we may be what we do *not* eat" (21). Drawing on this tension, then, between those who assert that our food choices signify who we are and those who object to such gastronomic profiling, I offer my own theory about why Spam invokes such a multiplicity of responses. For if Camp and other folklorists are right and our cultural identity is defined by what we want to eat as well as what we refuse to eat, then Spam's significance may reside in its capacity to tell us who we are. Or who we are not.

I've been thinking a lot these days about how one's identity is shaped by what one embraces or denies—values, certainly, but not abstract concepts so much as those embodied in the physical world: in the company we keep, the places we frequent, the things we consume or don't. Perhaps Spam matters because it invites us to know ourselves in terms of our response to it. It asks us to look in that mirror through which we see ourselves, in darkness or light. It offers us the opportunity to reject our reflection as mere distortion or acknowledge it as somehow

---

[1] Incidentally, its name is derived from its key ingredient: *spiced ham* = Spam.

authentic. For Americans especially (though others around the world are involved), Spam allows us to idealize who we are and displace our anxieties about who we might be. Reassuringly familiar yet paradoxically exotic, Spam is the Other; and as the Other, it reinforces, in all its baffling complexity, our sense of self.

In order to see Spam as the Other, however, and hence some version of ourselves, we first consider Spam on its own terms. And while many will object, I nonetheless maintain it as fact: Spam tastes good. The Hormel Corporation understands that Americans love fat and salt. Spam has plenty of both. (Even Lite Spam and Low Sodium Spam contain shocking amounts for anyone apt to read nutrition labels.) Given its resonance with the American palate, Spam reveals something significant about our country itself. Food writer Jonathan Gold got it right back in 1999 in his column "Counter Intelligence" for the independent *LA Weekly*. In a review of Mago's, a burger joint in West Los Angeles with a largely Japanese-Hawaiian-American clientele, his particular praise of the Spamburger yielded a deeper insight about who we are as a nation: "A Spamburger is all about the Spam, its cloying, porky essence, the overgenerous nature of salty, fatty food manufactured for and revered by folks for whom salty, fatty food is, or used to be, the ultimate in unobtainable luxury. Spam is what this country is all about, a pig in every can and two cars in every garage. Spam tastes like America." While Gold's rhetorical style is admittedly (and deliciously) hyperbolic, his insights into the American palate in context of our lifestyle are on the mark. Back when it first hit the market, Spam may have offered some assurance against the poverty of the Great Depression and the looming specter of wartime privation. Nowadays in our fast-food nation, however, where the Atkins diet thrives (despite its creator's recent autopsy that revealed a host of health maladies)

and a mad cow in Washington state sends tremors through Wall Street, Spam appeals not only to our biological necessity and cravings, but also to our socialized desires for convenience and ubiquity.

Precisely because Spam can so readily satisfy the appetite, however, it invites critique. The very fact that it falls short of any kind of culinary or nutritional standard most of us would aspire to, yet insinuates itself so easily into the way we live, speaks volumes about how we become accustomed to, and often ultimately celebrate, that which seems initially suspicious, reprehensible, or unnatural. How does this happen, one might ask? How does the Other—a foreign custom, a baffling behavior, a pig in a can—become that which is natural, wholesome, and welcome as our very own self?

The answer to this question might lie in our 15 contemporary culture of instant gratification and mindless consumption. Though Spam doesn't contain, according to its labeled ingredients, any mysterious "natural flavorings" or "artificial colorings," its unstated purpose is the same as that of most processed, convenience, fast, junk food: eat, enjoy, and don't think about it. In Spam's case, this seamless assimilation between consumer and product relies in part on a perfectly calibrated balance of salt, fat, and sugar. In addition, Spam's texture is telling; there's no bone to contend with. In fact, other than the can and the meat, there's only the gelatin that, if anything, facilitates its ease of access (imagine getting Spam out of the can without it) and quick passage down the throat.[2] Indeed, all the physical properties of Spam suggest a product that caters to the lowest common gastronomic denominators.

This is ironic, of course. Because while we, as Americans, want it our way, we don't like to think that we take the easy way out. Due to our Puritan legacy perhaps, we deem absolute pleasure in consumption somehow uncivilized. Relishing what we eat (especially with indiscriminate gusto) might

---

[2] The gelatin itself is disturbing for some, a fact which the Hormel Corporation recognizes. In fact, according to *Spam: A Biography*, Hormel has figured out how to solidify, and hence dispense with, the gelatin for their Korean market, in deference to their cultural palates (Wyman 83). That Spam continues to be sold to Americans with gel intact must suggest something about how Hormel perceives our taste.

strike some of us as morally questionable, coarse and vulgar perhaps, immodest at the very least. While psychologists Richard I. Stein and Carol J. Nemeroff agree that "'Morality' may seem too strong a word to describe beliefs or feelings about food in modern American culture," they nonetheless assert that "people make moral judgments of others based on the types of foods they eat" (480–81). In this sense, then, Spam may ask unsettling questions about our moral fiber, or lack thereof.

Such moral uncertainty may not be so surprising, given the actual constitution of a can of Spam. In other words, the fact that Spam exists in the uncomfortably ambiguous, nether world of meat products, as opposed to just meat, makes it inherently troubling. Of course, this wasn't always the case. In 1937, when America was just hitting its stride with processed and manufactured food, Spam debuted on the market as "The Miracle Meat," along with Pepperidge Farm Bread, Kraft Macaroni and Cheese, and Ragu Spaghetti Sauce (Trager 492–93). As America endured the Great Depression, shifted into World War II, and reconsidered its attitude toward food (think rationing, victory gardens, and sacrifice for "our boys"), tinned meat might have seemed like a miracle indeed, possessing its own sort of moral clarity. Yet now, almost 70 years later, warier about what we ingest, many Americans would rank Spam somewhere below those other suspiciously processed meat products, hot dogs and bologna, and barely above the lowest standard for queasily uncertain protein: the public school cafeteria's infamous mystery meat. First advertised as a wholesome, all-American meat product, that qualifier itself, *product,* is perhaps simply too disconcerting nowadays for the average American consumer.

Not only are Spam's contents uncertain and potentially scary, so too is the social status it potentially signifies. In his analysis of the habits of consumption that characterize different socio-economic classes, including attitudes toward food and eating, French sociologist Pierre Bourdieu has theorized that those in the middle class (or aspiring to be middle class, which some have suggested might describe practically all Americans), are particularly identified in terms of their "cultural capital" (176), the social status acquired through one's discriminating taste and ability to make distinctions among cultural practices and things consumed.[3] This sheds light on what Spam signals, to others and even ourselves, about our social sophistication or lack thereof. Those who admit to eating Spam (let alone liking it) might very well open themselves up to the contempt of others with more cultural capital.

Late-night humorists offer a different take on Spam's cultural and class implications. Witness David Letterman's apt insight into the multitasking middle-class American self (and the eerie resemblance between two products we'd never think to link): "Spam-on-a-rope for those who like to snack and shower." Or Jeff Foxworthy's litmus test: "You might be a redneck if you've ever barbecued Spam on the grill." Both jokes get laughs of discomfiting recognition. We can make fun of those others who eat Spam, because we'd never stoop so low. Or would we?

Jane and Michael Stern, correspondents for 20 *Gourmet* magazine and National Public Radio's show *The Splendid Table,* include Spam in their *Encyclopedia of Bad Taste* and offer their own hypothesis for its place in American history. They assert that Spam's popularity after World War II was due to the Stockholm Syndrome, "that paradoxical condition in which captive people come to feel affection for their captors. Forced to live with Spam during the war, many soldiers and civilians didn't want to give it up" (Stern and Stern 278).[4] Theirs is a whimsical theory that resonates some truth. American and Russian soldiers, English civilians, Hawaiian residents, and

---

[3] Though Bourdieu focuses on the French, his work is applicable throughout the industrialized West. Indeed, his assertion that for the working class, "food is claimed as a material reality . . . hence the emphasis on heavy, fatty, strong foods, of which the paradigm is pork—fatty and salty" (197), resonates with Jonathan Gold's reflections on Spam.

[4] The Sterns actually base their theory on the "Helsinki syndrome." Yet unless there is another Nordic group that explains this syndrome, I believe they meant to attribute it to the Swedes in Stockholm.

my parents, too (who left China in the late 1940s fleeing the communists and came to this country in the mid-1960s seeking the American dream)—all can ascribe their taste for Spam to a gastronomical relationship forged in a wartime context of fear, distress, loss, dislocation, and hunger.

But what fascinates me even more in the Sterns' entry on Spam is their observation that "aspiring gourmet housewives, eager for any kind of convenience food and for a bit of exotic culinary adventure, too, embraced Spam as the basic ingredient for vast numbers of Polynesian and Cantonese-flavored casseroles, in which the luncheon meat gets chunked, then combined with maraschino cherries, grape jelly, soy sauce, cans of bamboo shoots, and corn starch" (278). For if the Sterns are right, then what many American housewives of that greatest generation did in their own kitchens, their own homes, was nothing short of an attempt to meet the Other.

Though I'm not sure how maraschino cherries and grape jelly fit in with an Asian (or Oriental, as those housewives probably called it) gastronomic vocabulary, I recognize and appreciate their search for exoticism on a plate. Who among us in our astonishingly diverse country hasn't at some point eaten something that wasn't, by cultural heritage, his own? Who hasn't, if she has cable access, dallied for just a few seconds on the Food Network to watch Nobu Matsuhisa make *sashimi*, Mario Batali prepare *gnocchi*, or Emeril Lagasse offer up *etouffée*? The more adventurous among us, those driven by gastronomic curiosity, even recreate these other cultures in our own kitchens.

So the question lingers disconcertingly, for discriminating gourmands loaded with cultural capital and, yes, me: Just how were those aspiring gourmet housewives with their cans of Spam any different?

Not much, I suppose. For I remember how exotically wonderful mashed potatoes and gravy sounded when I was growing up, compared to my family's daily servings of steamed rice. And while Peter Brady's "Pork chops and applesauce" sketch made no sense to me as a ten-year-old in terms of sitcom humor, I resolved back then (while watching

a bafflingly perfect, blended TV family of three blonde girls, three brunette boys, two preternaturally cheerful parents, and one housekeeper named Alice) that, if given the chance, I would try a dish comprised of meat and fruit, as strange as it seemed, and no doubt enjoy it. Indeed, once I ventured out of the family room and into the kitchen for my initial culinary experiments as a kid, these yearnings for the Other persisted. After reading *Little House on the Prairie* for the seventh time, for example, I decided to make cornmeal mush, which proved disappointing once I discovered it was really just that: mushy cornmeal. (Of course, my disappointment as a child was transformed when I grew up and rediscovered the charms of cornmeal mush in its more exotic, and hence palatable, guise as *polenta*.)

Given my stints these days in my Northern Michigan kitchen that find me fine-tuning my method for pistachio biscotti, pad thai noodles, and curried chickpea stew, who am I now to scoff at those women of a different time and era, bravely venturing into foreign culinary territory, earnestly melding chunks of Spam with soy sauce, bamboo shoots, and cornstarch? Who am I to dismiss those housewives, enthralled by some notion of the exotic, conjuring the Other in their strange recipes with a can of Spam? Who am I to draw a line between their Polynesian Chinese-flavored casseroles and my own family's Chinese American fried rice? Who am I to say that they differ so much from me?

There is, I suppose, one difference: What was exotic for those housewives back then is for me now simply that which is familiar. Soy sauce, bamboo shoots, and cornstarch are all staples of my own kitchen cupboard, not to prepare a foreign cuisine but to help me reflect on my experiences as a Chinese American miles away from her Southern California childhood home. Whereas their meals might have represented an exploration of the alluringly unfamiliar, a fleetingly safe expedition to the Orient, a quick and tasty consumption of the Other, mine serve now to reconnect me with something inherently paradoxical about myself.

I am an American who grew up negotiating her immigrant parents' essential Otherness. While my mother and father traveled around the world to a new life in a foreign county, I traded my West coast address for one in the Midwest. Mine was a mere shift across a couple of time zones within the country of my birth, which is not so grand in the larger scheme of things. Still, my own modest migration has helped me to appreciate more fully what my parents dared some forty years ago. For I, too, have moved far away (though not so far, really) from a familiar landscape. And sometimes, the place where I came from, the Chinese diaspora community of the San Gabriel Valley in Los Angeles, feels continents away from the place where I now live on the shores of Lake Michigan in a Midwestern resort town that bills itself the Cherry Capital of the World.

Funnily enough, though, it's not the Chinese ingredients that bring me back home. Instead, it's the can of Spam in my Michigan basement. I bought it over two years ago in a fit of nostalgia, despite my husband's doubts, but I haven't touched it since, as I'm older now and thinking more carefully about my food choices.[5]

Maybe one day, when my husband's not looking, I'll stir up a pan of Spam fried rice. Or better yet, I'll save it for when my friend, Karen, comes for a visit, so we can whip up a batch of Spam sushi. Because one of these days, after all, someone will be hungry. Hungry enough to reach for that can. Until then, however, it'll keep. It'll definitely keep.

Works Cited

Bourdieu, Pierre. *Distinction: A Social Critique of the Judgement of Taste*. Translated by Richard Nice, Harvard UP, 1984.

Camp, Charles. *American Foodways: What, When, Why and How We Eat in America*. August House, 1989.

Gold, Jonathan. "Spamming the Globe." *LA Weekly*, 29 Oct.–4 Nov. 1999, www.laweekly.com/restaurants/spamming-the-globe-2131284.

Stein, Richard I., and Carol J. Nemeroff. "Moral Overtones of Food: Judgments of Others Based on What They Eat." *Personality and Social Psychology Bulletin*, vol. 21, no. 5, May 1995, pp. 480–90.

Stern, Jane, and Michael Stern. *The Encyclopedia of Bad Taste*. HarperCollins, 1990.

"This Potted Meat, This England." *Harper's*, Aug. 2003, pp. 20–23.

Trager, James. *The Food Chronology*. Henry Holt, 1995.

Wyman, Carolyn. *Spam: A Biography*. Harcourt Brace, 1999.

Analyzing Argument

1. According to Chu, what does it mean to eat Spam?

2. How, according to Chu, is Spam "Other"?

3. What connection does the essay make between Spam and social status?

4. What type of support (allusions, definitions, personal testimony, and so on) does Chu use? Provide an example of three types of support, and explain why each example is important to her argument.

5. How does Chu use outside sources to support its claims?

---

[5] The last time I checked their cupboards, my parents had a can of Spam, several years old. "Too much salt," said my dad, shaking his head. Though such gastronomic caution would have been inconceivable to him (and me) twenty-five years ago, he too is becoming more health conscious as he approaches his seventies.

Antibacterial Soap

AMY ZACHARY

Amy Zachary, a visual communications major, developed the following argument over several weeks during her second-semester college English course. Once she started inventing ideas for the topic, she found several ways that antibacterial soaps had come up in her own life. These realizations gave way to helpful lines of reasoning.

My cousins were visiting from Indiana. We had been to Leelanau Sands, playing slot machines and nervously fingering betting chips as we waited for the next card from the blackjack dealer. The next stop was a tavern, where we ordered drinks and a variety of appetizers to share. Only one of us had carried away more money from the casino than we went in with, but all of us had left the casino with more germs than usual on our hands. Mentioning I was glad that I had washed my hands in the restroom upon arrival brought a childhood look of contrition to the rest of the gang, and the table cleared with an earnest rush in the direction I had come from.

Throughout the states, Americans are increasingly conscious of the dangers lurking on public surfaces. Nobody wants to pick up some dreaded ailment because they touched a coin or doorknob that a stranger recently handled. New diseases such as the avian flu appear in the news every week. There is still no cure for the common cold, although quicker relief from symptoms currently rules advertising proclamations. We don't have time to be sick; we are in fear for our lives; our sons, daughters, and spouses may bring home invasive germs from school or work!

Fear of germs is embedded in our psyches from childhood. Admonishments of "Don't put that in your mouth—you'll get sick," the aforementioned "Wash your hands before supper," and "Oooohhhh—YUCKY!" are constant reminders that it's a dirty world out there and Mommy and Daddy want to protect their children from it. Grade-school classes give young pupils their first microscopic view of writhing bacteria, which are surely out to get them. Junior high–age children attending sociology and culture classes learn of diseases caused by the terrible filth endured in third-world countries. As we grow up, we realize Mommy, Daddy, and teachers can't do everything, and that it's really up to oneself to protect oneself. As we become mommies and daddies, we swear we'll do our best to protect our children better than the last generation. Human nature thrives on progress. A cleaner world with fewer germs would seem the ideal claim. It's a wonder that we are not all obsessive-compulsive about hand-washing.

We easily fell into a consumerist trap the soap and detergent manufacturers made, perhaps without malice in mind, when they came out with new "antibacterial" products for home use. Formerly reserved for hospitals, the products would apparently give your home and skin sterile properties beyond the ordinary. Dial Corporation led the way in 2002, opening the sales of their new line with the theme "you're not as clean as you think" (qtd. in Macarthur and Neff). With our mindset of "cleaner is better," we bought all we could get our hands on. And the new products literally got on our hands, in the form of antibacterial soap, filling matching bathroom accessories, public restroom dispensers and dishwashing detergent bottles.

USA Today quotes the Soap and Detergent 5 Association and the Cosmetic, Toiletry, and Fragrance Association as stating, "More than thirty years of research has proven that antimicrobial washes reduce or eliminate bacteria that can lead to skin infections, intestinal illnesses or other commonly transmitted diseases" (Rubin). The key word in that statement is "reduce." Antibacterial soaps are a danger because of the way they *attack* bacteria, disabling weaker strains while stronger ones

Reprinted by permission of Amy Zachary.

survive, particularly if the hand-washing process is too short. The weaker bacteria that are killed are most likely harmless to begin with. The remaining bacteria, stronger and retaining a greater chance of virulence, are then left with space to evolve into a strain of infection we have no cure for (Thomas). Consequently, a new threat to our immune systems emerged.

It took forty years for medical science to concede the consequences to our immune systems of doctors prescribing antibiotics for every little illness, including illnesses caused by viruses, which are not even affected by antibiotics—or antibacterial soap (Thomas). People who frequently swallow down antibiotics to combat illness find that the effectiveness of one type diminishes over time, and a different antibiotic must be tried. The germs that cause illness build resistance, while our bodies lose the capacity to fight them without aid. Will everyday use of antibacterial soaps (which are known to kill bacteria selectively) follow the same trail? Remember, antibiotics are drugs, available only with a physician-written prescription, while antibacterial soaps line supermarket shelves.

The most sinister ingredient of antibacterial soap is *triclosan*. Triclosan destroys bacteria in a way parallel to how penicillin-derivative antibiotics work at preventing an organism from replicating, by producing a genetic change (Thomas). Triclosan resistant strains of bacteria are developing due to overexposure to this cleaning solution ingredient, including three types of *E. coli* (Thomas). The parallels are significant enough, pointing out we shouldn't wait four decades (three have already passed) to concur that everyday use of antibacterial soap is "too much of a good thing."

Why aren't other commonly home-stocked cleaners creating super-strong bacteria? While triclosan's manufacturer, Ciba, claims, "Triclosan works continuously for many hours, staying on the skin after washing" ("Triclosan"), common cleaners don't leave a residue to facilitate the selective process. With ordinary soap and water, the soap *loosens*

dirt and germs, weak and strong alike, and they are all washed down the drain together.

For the most part, regular soap is diluted by water to a level safe for the environment. Bleach, a cleaning mainstay, is labeled with warnings and cautions, not recommended for hand-washing. It kills *all* of the immediate bacteria, fungus, and viruses, yet dilutes enough in water that it is used to disinfect drinking-water wells. A list of more modern products includes alcohol-based hand sanitizers, whose formulas kill bacteria by drying them out, and evaporation removes any environmental danger.

Unlike antibacterial soap, triclosan-less cleaners aren't converted by sunlight into hormone-disrupting dioxins or altered by chlorine to create harmful chloroform gas. (I always link chloroform to murder mysteries, when the killer sneaks up behind the victim with a chloroform-soaked handkerchief to knock her unconscious.) Triclosan has also been found to be "toxic to aquatic life," especially to a major player in the oxygen production cycle of photosynthesis—algae (Thomas). Environmentally, the destruction of algae by global warming is finally being acknowledged by the United States; it seems to have taken the hurricanes of 2005 to wake President Bush up to the fact that global warming is going to affect us in this lifetime. (While we haven't actually started choking to death due to the lack of oxygen, the predictions of global warming's effect are coming true.) What will it take to initiate governmental action on triclosan? Some people won't believe there's a problem until they *personally* know someone directly affected by antibacterial soap use. Will they also believe that a tree falling in the woods does not make noise if no one is there to hear it? That AIDS doesn't exist until their brother dies of it? Must a stealthy, silent killer become a mass murderer before getting attention?

Further proof that antibacterial soaps are toxic lies in a discussion I had with Steve Westphal, purchasing director of Northwestern Michigan College. While he assured me that NMC does not use antibacterial soaps for reasons already stated, he added that in order to use antibacterial hand soap in restrooms the college would have to buy all new dispensers, because antibacterial soap would *atomize* the gaskets in ordinary dispensers. That doesn't sound like anything I want to rub around on *my* hands.

According to the United States Food and Drug Administration's Office of Cosmetics and Colors, personal products are defined as cosmetics or drugs depending upon their intended use. Intended use is established by promotional claims, consumer perception, and, as the FDA states, "ingredients that may cause a product to be considered a drug because they have a well known (to the public and industry) therapeutic use." Originally, "soap" was made from animal fat and wood ashes. Today, the FDA considers a product "soap" if it "primarily consists of alkali salts of fatty acids" and is only labeled as "soap." Plain soap is not regulated. Once claims of beautification or health are made, soaps' intended purposes change and regulations fall into place. Cosmetic soap must include all ingredients on the label, while soap that is, according to the FDA, "intended to . . . cure, treat, or prevent disease" (which includes any using the word "antibacterial") is regulated as a drug and must be labeled with active ingredients first, separated from the rest of the ingredients. Triclosan is most often the active ingredient listed. So, while not all antibacterial/drug-category soap contains triclosan, all soap containing triclosan (a known antibacterial agent) must be regulated as a drug. We can toss out the idea that "antibacterial" was just a new marketing strategy. Yet, they are not stocked in the pharmaceutical aisles of our grocery stores, and only the informed consumers may realize they are buying something more potent than simply "cleaner is better."

Although antibacterial soap was not officially brought out for home use until the 21st century, I think back to 1995, when I was working at a manufacturing plant. I remember Kay, who brought in her own bar of soap because using the new antibacterial liquid brought out a rash on her hands. Brian, one of the bosses, figured the eczema on his hands was acting up due to added stress. No one questioned why the new soap dispensers appeared in the restrooms; they routinely changed when our company switched to a different vendor. Following governmental regulations, we had Material Safety Data Sheets available in a book in every department. They contained all the information of composition, properties, handling, and hazard recommendations, supposedly, for every type of grease and chemical used in the plant. Hand soap didn't seem important; some people are allergic to the *weirdest* things.

However, there is now an MSDS available on Safeguard Liquid Antibacterial Hand Soap issued by Procter & Gamble on November 2, 2005. It may be the beginning of a trend, as the document supersedes no other, and "may be required by law, but is not an assertion that the substance is hazardous." Health hazards are rated as "1 = Slight," the active ingredient listed is "triclosan," and "Section III–Hazards Identification" states: "Skin Contact: May cause mild, transient superficial effects similar to [those] produced by other mild hand soaps. Use on irritated or extremely dry skin may aggravate the existing condition." Additional information on the form states that "Safeguard is not regulated by TSCA [Toxic Substance Control Act]" and "Do not use this product on infants 6 months of age" (Procter & Gamble). While the information given may not be extraordinarily alarming, it should be kept in mind that these sheets are based on safety for workers, and are not issued frivolously. It would be interesting to know if the information about not using the product on babies is only due to thoughts of sensitive skin, or if it also relates to the fact that babies' immune systems are reacting to the world around them and building resistance. While we take care to keep our babies clean, vying for a sterile environment inhibits the natural process; people who get chicken pox early in life rarely suffer from another case.

15   We all need to "get a little dirty" now and then to maintain healthy immune systems. Unless a person's immune system is already disabled, it is not recommended he or she live in a plastic bubble. We should not attempt to sterilize our world because "our world" will always be part of a larger world that is not sterile; if a body has never met the contender, it will not be prepared to defend itself. We inoculate ourselves against several diseases by injecting a tiny portion of the selected ailment. To turn the scenario around, when we do gain an infection, it's better that the bacteria causing it face antibiotics for the first time. Using antibacterial soaps every day could be like giving bacteria an inoculation, so that when we really need to destroy them, they are able to brush off our efforts.

Some people may say they use antibacterial soaps because they have a severe illness and the soaps may reduce the chances of infection. But such concerns arise from a misconception about bacteria: It's the duration of hand washing, not the chemical in the soap, that removes the germs. The average hand washing only lasts three to five *seconds*, not nearly enough time to remove infection-causing bacteria (Underwood).

But most important is the marketing and product placement. If a product is on the same grocery store shelf as similar, familiar products that don't need warnings, chances are that people will completely bypass reading the label. Grocery stores and supermarkets could stock antibacterial products in the pharmaceutical aisles; however, since that doesn't announce directly *why* the store rearranged, the reason could easily be ignored. Requiring a prescription (the same as for their antibiotic counterparts) would remove them from easily accessible shelves, if we can talk pharmacies into making room for the vast array. Could the manufacturers simply admit they made a mistake and stop marketing antibacterial soap to the general public?

It's unlikely that manufacturers will want to do that. According to Alan Eshleman, MD, on the Kaiser Permanente website in August 2004, "75% of the liquid soaps and 30% of the bar soaps currently marketed in the USA contain antibacterial chemicals. The most common of these chemicals is a substance known as triclosan" (Eshleman). Imagine the scope of the money involved *now,* when Dial Corp. spent twenty to twenty-five million just on the opening "You're not as clean as you think" advertising campaign back in 2002 (qtd. in Macarthur and Neff). American consumers let their "cleaner is better" ideology push the popularity of the products to that ratio; interest waned for soap that had not been "improved."

The question remains: why did the manufacturers let it get out of hand? Greed and reliance on research similar to that (previously mentioned) by the Soap and Detergent Association were probably the main contributors to painting the market into a corner. Ciba, not a soap manufacturer, but the actual manufacturer of triclosan, touts in bold on their website, "A long and beneficial history," "Triclosan is safe and effective," and "Triclosan— the added layer of hygiene." The site explains how triclosan is "a secret protection" and that it stays on the skin, providing "long-lasting action against germs." However, the most revealing portion of the website states that "it shouldn't be used mindless [sic] and without a justified reason. The use should go along with a personal assessment of the need of the use of an antimicrobial substance. Ciba supports the use of triclosan only if there is a benefit to human beings" ("Triclosan"). Why were antibacterial soaps containing triclosan then allowed to take over our grocery store shelves—especially after year-long studies conducted by Columbia University's School of Nursing Associate Dean for Research, Elaine Larson, and controlled the same as pharmaceutical studies, showed antibacterial soap not to be any more effective in decreasing the number of germs on subjects' hands than ordinary soap (Underwood)? "People *think* they're cleaner" does not stand as justified reason.

20   Since 2000, the list of countries discouraging the use of antibacterial products has grown, including Finland, Denmark, and Germany (Thomas). And in October 2002, the Center for Disease Control recommended that even hospitals use alcohol-based, waterless germicides verses [sic] antibacterial cleaners (Underwood). Given such recommendations, and given a basic understanding of bacteria biology, the American public should re-examine the hyped status of antibacterial soaps. As we weigh the possibilities of increasingly devastating bacteria, and other looming risks yet to be evaluated, the everyday public may find antibacterial soap a hazard we should live without.

Works Cited

Eshleman, Alan. "Antibacterial Soaps: Will They Keep You Healthy?" *Kaiser Permanente*, Aug. 2004. Accessed 2 Nov. 2005.

Macarthur, Kate, and Jack Neff. "Dialing for Dollars Is a Dirty Business." *Advertising Age*, vol. 73, no. 2, 14 Jan. 2002, p. 3. *Academic Search Elite*, 5870748.

Procter & Gamble. "MSDS: FH/C/2004/BCWT-67PKX7." 2 Nov. 2005, www.woodfruitticher.com/documents/044255Safeguard_Antibacterial_Hand_Soap.pdf.

Rubin, Rita. "Antiseptic Soaps Bubble Up Again." *USA Today*, 20 Oct. 2005, usatoday30.usatoday.com/news/health/2005-10-19-antiseptic-soaps_x.htm.

Thomas, Pat. "The Dawn of the Domestic Superbug." *Ecologist*, vol. 35, no. 6, July–Aug. 2005, pp. 42–48, www.theecologist.org/investigations/health/268802/the_dawn_of_the_domestic_superbug.html.

"Triclosan Information." *Ciba Specialty Chemicals*, 20 Oct. 2005, www.triclosan-info.com. Accessed 19 Nov. 2005.

Underwood, Anne. "The Real Dirt on Antibacterial Soaps." *Newsweek*, 4 Nov. 2002, p. 53, www.newsweek.com/real-dirt-antibacterial-soaps-142205.

United States, Food and Drug Administration. *Is It a Cosmetic, a Drug, or Both? (or Is It Soap?)*. 8 July 2002, www.fda.gov/Cosmetics/GuidanceRegulation/LawsRegulations/ucm074201.htm.

Analyzing Argument

1. What is Zachary's main claim against antibacterial soap?

2. What is the best supporting passage in the argument?

3. In paragraph 10, Zachary alludes to the global warming debate. How does that allusion function in the argument? In what way does it support her point about antibacterial soap?

4. Chart the line of reasoning in paragraph 6. What are the stated and unstated premises?

AP Images/Jason DeCrow

21

Popular Culture and the Media

P opular (pop) culture is the culture of the masses. It includes all forms of media (such as TV, Internet, books, film, newspaper, magazines); music, sports, fashion, and other everyday interests; issues such as race, religion, gender, and entertainment; and so on. Because of its extensive nature, pop culture overlaps with other topics in the Argument Anthology. In fact, most readings in *Inventing Arguments* relate in some way to popular American culture.

In the ongoing national discussion of important issues, we ask the following types of questions: Is the news media a watchdog of government? How does popular music influence behavior? Are Americans more concerned with sports and entertainment than with poverty and discrimination? Should restaurants prepare their food differently? Should they serve smaller portions? What is the relationship between overweight children and fast food? To what extent should popular forms of media be used in the classroom? Why are both licit and illicit drugs so popular? Should I drive to work alone, carpool, ride a bike, or walk? Why is it important to study pop culture?

Everyone stands back and analyzes pop culture to some degree. Yet while we analyze certain aspects of it, because we are so intertwined with our own culture, we uncritically accept other aspects. The readings here invite you to consider a few of the many issues related to the media and popular American culture.

Readings about Popular Culture and the Media in Chapters 1–14

Still Missing: Women in the Media

MEGAN TADY

In the following essay, Megan Tady argues that "mostly men are deciding how to represent and portray a majority of our population in the media. Their choices often end up degrading, stereotyping or ignoring women." Tady's essay examines the causes and consequences of women's presence or lack of it in today's media. "Still Missing: Women in the Media" was published April 13, 2010, at InTheseTimes.com. Tady is a blogger and video producer for Free Press, the national nonprofit media reform organization, and she writes a monthly InTheseTimes.com column on media issues.

A week before I graduated from college in 2002, my adviser called me into his office for a "welcome to the real world" chat.

"I know you want to be a writer, but I want to give you a dose of reality first," he said. He pulled open a drawer jammed with rejection letters. "I don't want to discourage you, but this industry is tough. Don't take rejection personally—just keep writing."

And so I have. But what happens when the media industry isn't rejecting my work, it's rejecting my gender? The fact of the matter is that women still don't start on an equal playing field in the media.

Sure, we've made great strides—we've got Rachel Maddow and Katie Couric and Oprah. But our work for gender equality in the media is far from over. It's as important as ever to tie the media reform movement to the advancement of women.

Where Are the Women?

5   In early April, National Public Radio's ombudswoman, Alicia Shepard, released the results of her own gender survey in a blog post titled, "Where are the women?" She found that although the radio network is an industry leader when it comes to female hosts and correspondents, it doesn't have the same record for female commentators and news sources. On NPR's 104 shows between April 13, 2009, and Jan. 9, 2010, just 26 percent of the sources were women.

To be clear, NPR isn't the only news organization with shameful stats. A recent report from the Global Media Monitoring Project found that worldwide, women make up only 24 percent of the people "interviewed, heard, seen or read about in mainstream broadcast and print news." And an article in *Newsweek* in March headlined "Are We There Yet?" outlines the longstanding and troubling gender bias in the industry, where "female bylines at major magazines are still outnumbered by seven to one."

In her blog post, Shepard said NPR has plans to improve, but also rationalized the network's behavior:

> Admittedly, the relative lack of female voices reflects the broader world. The fact remains that even in the fifth decade after the feminist revolution; men are still largely in charge in government at all levels, in corporations and nearly all other aspects of society. That means, by default, there are going to be more male than female news sources.

This oft-repeated justification begs the chicken-and-the-egg question: Are female voices less prominent in the media because they hold fewer positions of power and authority, or are women holding less positions of power and leadership because they're not given an equal platform in the media? Today, just like decades ago, women have to overcome negative and sexualized images in the media to obtain high-ranking political positions.

It's Still a Man's World

It is also rare to see women at the helm of media institutions. A 2007 study by Free Press, the organization I work for, found that while women comprised

51 percent of the U.S. population, they owned less than 6 percent of television stations and 8 percent of all full-power commercial broadcast radio stations. Again, we're back to the chicken or the egg.

10   These alarming statistics mean that mostly men are deciding how to represent and portray a majority of our population in the media. Their choices often end up degrading, stereotyping or ignoring women. Even throwaway headlines like CNN's "Women Blamed in Moscow Suicide Blasts" are damaging to women, and point to both a strange fascination with and objectification of the gender in the media. As a writer on the blog Femonomics wrote, "To see how backwards this headline is, imagine the consummately uninformative "Men blamed for 9/11.""

I'm not saying that CNN's newsroom editors maniacally set out to hurt women with that headline, or that it was particularly egregious. In fact, the editors probably didn't give it a second thought— and that's where the problem lies. Gender bias is so rooted in our culture, and so subtle, that we can barely recognize it. And if we can't recognize it, we can't condemn it.

High Stakes for Gender Equality

Even as women struggle now to break into the media industry as journalists and commentators, or to find media they can relate to as female consumers, the situation could get worse.

This year, we're watching one of the biggest media mergers in history, as Comcast prepares to take over NBC. Comcast has already sheepishly confessed to having only one woman on its board of directors—that's just one woman helping to direct one of the most massive media empires in the country.

And because of a recent federal court ruling in favor of, again, Comcast, the future of the Internet as we've known it—a force that has leveled the playing field for women and allowed us to be our own voice and establish healthy images—is also in jeopardy.

So the stakes are now even higher: Women must   15 get involved and fight for a better media system. Taking the media into our hands means claiming our power as women, and taking ownership over our viewpoints. And for you men reading this: Joining this movement means you won't stand aside while the women in your lives are routinely maligned by the media.

After all, a more consolidated media system and a corporate-controlled Internet will only serve to deepen the entrenched sexism and gender bias that is so damaging to women and our collective consciousness.

Analyzing Argument

1. What is the essay's main claim?

2. What appeals does Tady use to develop her argument? Point to particular passages in your response.

3. Explain how Tady uses an example to help the reader better recognize gender bias.

4. Explain how Tady uses counterargument, concessions, and/or qualifiers to manage opposition.

The *Daily Show* Generation

MARY ZEISS STANGE

From ancient civilizations to today's popular culture, comedians have been political. *The Daily Show with Jon Stewart* fits into a long tradition. As the television show has gained a huge audience for its insightful parody, it has also gained a political power of its own. In fact, politicians now see it as the main stage for reaching American youth. Mary Zeiss Stange, a professor of women's studies and religion at Skidmore College, addresses the program's undeniable political and cultural draw in an article in *USA Today* on September 12, 2006.

Is Jon Stewart a corruptor of youth or a political mentor?

The question is wacky enough to be a *Daily Show* headline. But it has been seriously posed by a number of academics, most recently in a study published in May by two political science professors in the journal *American Politics Research*.

A Better Understanding

They reached this conclusion by contrasting the responses of students who had viewed 2004 presidential election coverage on the *Daily Show* to those of students who had viewed similar reportage on CBS's *Evening News*. The study had an ironic edge to it, however: The cynical and potentially more apathetic *Daily Show* viewers also seemed to be "more confident about their own ability to understand politics" than those who had "consumed" the network news.

The "*Daily Show* effect" study made media waves when *The Village Voice* ran a story about it in its education issue for this fall. Suddenly, pundits showed more interest in the political thinking of college students than they had since the 2004 elections. In August, MSNBC's Chris Matthews featured the issue on his Sunday morning talk show, putting former CBS news anchor Dan Rather on the spot to explain why young viewers might have opted for Stewart over him. In reply, Rather said something about how that age group wasn't really his demographic.

As a college professor who, among other things, serves as faculty adviser to our progressive student organization, I was immediately struck both by the rightness of Rather's response, and by the wrong-headedness of the assumption that educated young adults cannot discern a relationship between Stewart's satire (which Baumgartner/Morris persistently call "sarcasm") and pointed political commentary.

Because the courses I teach—in women's and environmental studies, and in American religion—have contemporary "real world" implications, I customarily build a current-events component into them. These assignments serve two functions: One is for students to relate news items from various sources—newspapers, magazines, broadcast media, and the Internet—to course content. The other, more important, one is for students to pay close attention to the way the news is being "packaged." Are there politically or otherwise skewed stories, editorial content masquerading as straight news, and so on?

Based on my experience with them, I can attest that the current college-age generation is generally, and increasingly, media savvy when it comes to critically "consuming" the news. I would further argue that this is more so because of shows such as Stewart's (and more recently its spinoff, *The Colbert Report*) as well as websites such as that of *The Onion* newspaper. After all, in order to "get" their humor, one has to already know something substantial about the stories they parody.

As it turns out, two other academic studies, both from the Annenberg Public Policy Center of the University of Pennsylvania, bear out my classroom experience.

Mary Zeiss Stange, "The Daily Show Generation" from *USA Today* (September 12, 2006). Reprinted with the permission of the author, Professor of Women's Studies & Religion, and Director of the Women's Studies Program, at Skidmore College.

At Home on the Internet

These viewers were also younger, better educated, and more likely to identify themselves as moderates or liberals.

10   Where did these hip, young *Daily Show* viewers get their knowledge of politics?

I'd say that over the years, the current-event reports in my classes have mirrored this pattern, bearing in mind that many people read newspapers online now.

A second set of facts emerged from this study: Reading newspapers (presumably, on- or off-line) increases political awareness, but searching the Internet increases both political awareness and civic engagement. The *Daily Show* generation, in other words, is not only apt to be more concerned about politics but also more likely to be spurred to do something with that concern.

The apparent sharp upsurge in the past several years of political activism—both liberal and conservative—on college campuses nationwide would seem to bear this out. Whether that activism will translate into significant voter turnout this November remains to be seen. But apathy it is not.

Are these same young people cynical about politicians and newscasters? If the "serious" national news media are irked at being called to account by a show whose lead-in is "puppets making crank phone calls," they have no one to thank but themselves.

Analyzing Argument

1. Stange suggests "a relationship between Stewart's satire . . . and pointed political commentary." In your own words, explain this relationship.

2. Consider the following: "Based on my experience with them, I can attest that the current college-age generation is generally, and increasingly, media savvy when it comes to critically 'consuming' the news. I would further argue that this is more so because of shows such as Stewart's (and more recently its spinoff, *The Colbert Report*) as well as websites such as that of *The Onion* newspaper." Why does Stange use quotations around *consuming*? What is she suggesting about mainstream news, and about mainstream news viewers?

3. A Pew research study published in 2007 found that viewers of *The Daily Show* and *The Colbert Report* scored the highest on a survey of political knowledge. Viewers of Fox News scored the lowest. How does this finding correspond to Stange's claim about *The Daily Show*?

4. Jon Stewart often condemns mainstream or "serious" news outlets for being anything but serious or news. Consider the arguments by John Adams (pages 182–184). How does Adams's argument overlap with Stewart's condemnation of mainstream news or with Stange's understanding of her students?

Text Me All about Yourself: The Rise of Mobile Networking

CLAYTON DACH

New technological gadgets constantly enter the marketplace and get plugged into people's daily lives. These devices become fused with common expectations and basic assumptions about identity—how one should behave, how one should interact with and treat other people. In a sense, technologies help make popular culture what it is. This article from *Adbusters Magazine*, June–July 2007, shows how people often uncritically accept the latest gadget into their lives, into their thinking, and into the common culture.

If you've ever felt the need to know what every single one of your chums is doing at every hour of every day, then count yourself lucky. They may now volunteer to surveil themselves for your amusement and edification, all thanks to an emerging breed of mobile messaging services with names like Jaiku, Twitter, and Dodgeball.

The idea is simple: you sign up, your buddies sign up, you send texts via your mobile phone to the messaging service, and then it routes those texts to everyone on your contact list. At the coffee shop with nothing to entertain you? Let them all know. Walking your dog in the park? Let them know. With your mom shopping for socks? Dammit, let them know.

Only, you have to do it in 140 characters or less, which is a wee bit longer than the sentence that you've just finished reading.

Biz Stone is the co-founder of Twitter, the most pared-down and quite likely the fastest-growing of the pack. He's quick to clarify that Twitter is technically a "device agnostic message routing system," which to most of us means that you can send and receive messages—"tweets" in the brand lingo—in a number of ways, including the Twitter website, mobile phones, instant messaging clients, and downloadable desktop applications.

"The day-to-day advantage," notes Stone, "is 5 the ability to stay connected with friends and family members any time using a variety of devices."

Sound nifty? It can be. Consider the ease of checking in to see if anybody wants to join you in an hour for yakisoba, or to catch the *Porky's* retrospective at that eastside rep cinema.

Take a look at the public message history on the Twitter homepage, though, and it becomes apparent that this isn't the only way, or even that primary way, that people are using the service. The first thing you'll notice, at least as an outsider, is the relative banality of the tweets—there's a preponderance along the lines of "Watching Jimmy Kimmel embarrass a couple of high school kids in Scrabble," or the shorter and sweeter "Wasted. Loving it."

Charles Klein is an Arcata, California–based web designer who has been using Twitter for the last five months or so. "I find I use Twitter as a mini-blog," he explains, "tending to post random thoughts and feelings in addition to things that I am doing. I also like to post links to random things I find throughout the day."

Klein even has praise for the pithy nature of the medium, saying, "I tend to favor the use of Twitter over a blog because it is so quick and to the point, and can accomplish basically the same thing."

Fellow Californian and Twitterer "Adora" might 10 agree. The self-described "web 2.0 voyeur" got onboard a couple of months ago and says, "I try to update with items of interest to everyone following me. Neat geeky things I do through my job and website, the wacky things that I catch myself doing . . . I recently cut my thumb in half with a butter knife (don't ask) and after I pulled the knife out my first thought was, 'Oh man, I know I'm bleeding everywhere, but I just have to Twitter this.'"

Adora and Klein have one more thing in common, an expected consequence of granting people the ability to spontaneously contact just about everyone they know, wherever they are: They've both had to nix people who Twittered too often, too inanely.

"It was a person that I did not know except through Twitter," Klein reveals. "Once he posted one too many play-by-play accounts for that evening's *Dancing with the Stars,* I promptly removed him from the list. As ridiculous as this service is, that somehow seemed to push the limit."

While Stone acknowledges that some users require "an adjustment period coupled with feedback from friends to find just the right level of participation," he also points out that Twitter lets people manage how, when, and from whom they receive messages. As to why certain users don't easily glom onto the fact that they might be pestering their pals, Stone suggests that Twitter differs from other means of communication because "users do not expect replies to their updates nor do they feel obligated to review friends' updates with any significant comprehension. This shift in expectations means friends and family members can stay connected in real time as it suits them in an ambient, non-disruptive manner."

Connecting without disrupting? If that sounds like an unlikely combination, perhaps you've been wasting too much time rubbing elbows with other messy flesh bags, and not enough time amassing armies of "friends" on MySpace and Facebook. Much like those other social networking revelations, Twitter is—for better or for worse—a love letter to the open-door policy, and for every user who is merely there to keep in touch, there has to be at least one crashing bore of a showboat, careerist self-aggrandizer, or compulsive self-archivist.

Happily, since Twitter's one-text-for-all spirit 15 allows you to treat the individual entries in your contact list as essentially interchangeable, you can afford to be a bit mercenary in dealing with such riffraff.

"The majority of the people I've added are people I've never met," explains Adora, "but if their updates aren't consistently humorous or inspirational, I'm not getting much value and I'll stop following that person. It sounds a bit harsh, but we are talking about immediate 24/7 interruption here."

"The people I really know," she adds, "I put up with whatever they broadcast."

Analyzing Argument

1. *Adbusters Magazine* describes itself as "an ecological magazine, dedicated to examining the relationship between human beings and their physical and mental environment." According to Dach's article, how might mobile messaging services (Jaiku, Twitter, Dodgeball) impact the relationship between humans and their physical or mental environment?

2. In a sentence, what is the main claim of the article?

3. What does the opening sentence communicate about Dach's stance on the topic? What other sentences communicate a similar stance? What sentences provide an opposing position?

4. What does Adora value about instant messaging? Do you share Adora's assumption that inspiration can come from a stranger's daily broadcast? Why or why not?

The Origin of Grunge

JAY HARRINGTON

An extended e-mail conversation about the origins of music styles prompted Jay Harrington, a writer and alumnus of the University of Toledo, to write the following essay.

> **"He most honors my style who learns under it to destroy the teacher."**
> **—Walt Whitman, "Song of Myself"**

In order to discern the origin and meaning of the term *grunge,* it will be useful to look at another American cultural phenomenon which similarly seems to cross musical boundaries into fashion, politics, and social identity: namely, *punk.* Both grunge and punk represented watershed moments along the continuum of what has come to be known as "alternative culture." In other words, they developed out of an artistic, political, and social movement not within, but against, popular culture. As Pat Blashill notes in *Noise from the Underground:*

> Alternative culture wasn't invented by Nirvana in 1992. They just brought an anthem of disaffection and anger to the top of the charts, to the malls, to the army bases, and into the living rooms of a nation that had spent most of the eighties trying to convince itself that it was a kind and gentle place . . . America was all about shiny surfaces, and mainstream culture was about as deep as Bobby McFerrin's 1988 hit song, "Don't Worry, Be Happy." . . . Hollywood was again becoming a factory for empty escapism. The best-seller lists were rocked by *Slaves of New York, Less Than Zero,* and *Bright Lights, Big City,* three very hip novels about people with nice clothes, cocaine, and hardly anything to say. (16)

It's no accident that punk occurred during a similarly vacuous period in American popular music. Bloated, vapid, sexy, dope-addled rock bands like Aerosmith, Zeppelin, Styx, and Boston were the norm in the average teen record collection and disco was king with the young adults (along with coke and cheap sex). This hedonistic, consumerist culture was ripe for an attack from the disaffected, disenfranchised, and not-so-pretty people who lived on the underbelly of the American dream, and punk rock was the rallying cry.

But, like any movement of the people against an oppressive, greedy system, there is a tendency for that system to co-opt, corrupt, and assimilate the movement before it can do any real damage to the machinery already in place. This is one of the more tragic and pathetic aspects of both the grunge and punk movements: before any real momentum, many of their best and brightest were turned into shills for the same corporate giants they had earlier stood up to, neutralized like Kesey's protagonist in *One Flew Over the Cuckoo's Nest.* Before they could create a real stir, original artists were snatched up by major labels, which persuaded them to put profits and sales before art. As it usually happens in the music business, bands sought out a way to achieve greater exposure and actually make a decent living doing what they love, but they quickly became imprisoned in the business, where their music suffered, they wound up alienating their core followers, their sales plummeted, and they ended up owing their record companies more money than they could ever hope to repay via royalties. As the song goes, "Another One Bites the Dust."

It isn't just the record companies that contribute to this gradual corruption of artists, though. The major radio and television programming, publishing, fashion, and merchandising industries are equally to blame. Like a pack of sharks in a feeding frenzy they rip, shred, and squeeze every cent possible out of a band or trend, forcing it down the throats of the public until, gorged and stupefied, they move on to the next kill. For example, to modern consumers, punk means Sum 41, Good

Charlotte, The Get Up Kids, and the Vines. These are the bands we see in *Details, Spin, Rolling Stone,* and on MTV. However, all of these bands borrow only minimally from the musical ideas of their forebears while borrowing HEAVILY (and expensively) from the fashion closets of bands like the Clash, the Exploited, and the Sex Pistols. Early "punks" had their clothes safety-pinned together because (a) that was all they could afford, and (b) it was a reaction against the polyester, wide-collared, bell-bottomed society they were surrounded by. Today the same look can be achieved at Hot Topic in any mall in America for hundreds of dollars.

5   The documentary film *Hype!* features a montage of malls and catalogs across the country circa 1992 trying to market the "grunge look" to wealthy teen consumers eager to adopt the styles made popular by the media's portrayal of their heroes, Nirvana and Pearl Jam. "Grunge" kids in Seattle in the eighties, on the other hand, wore flannel and long johns because it's wet and cold there most of the time. And before those kids could say "sellout," they saw a slew of L.A. imports like Alice in Chains start tromping around their city in their Doc Martens looking for the money (and finding it) while great Northwest rock bands like the Fastbacks, the Posies, and the Supersuckers got passed over by the major label A&R people because they didn't conform closely enough to their hometown "look" and "sound" to be marketable. Caveat emptor, baby.

As we have seen, by the time a name like *grunge* gets affixed and is widespread enough to penetrate the national consciousness, the music and attitudes that originally inspired it have been all but destroyed. According to some "experts," grunge began in Seattle. But if Neil Young is truly the "Godfather of Grunge" (as some say), then it must be a Canadian import. Some say it was just a resurgence of punk rock, but punk's origins are also hotly contested. The Brits say it started with the Sex Pistols and the Damned (circa 1976), but they clearly took their cues from the burgeoning New York scene and bands like the Ramones, Richard Hell and the

Voidoids, and Johnny Thunders and the Heartbreakers, who were already in place by 1974–75. This, of course overlooks the contributions of other important American bands like Akron, Ohio's Devo and west-coasters like the Wipers, the Dead Kennedys, Black Flag, Big Boys, and the Avengers. It also ignores the very convincing argument that this new, dangerous, rebellious musical and cultural movement had its roots in the Midwest with bands like the MC5 and the Stooges, who were playing rock music with as yet unheard-of abandon in the late sixties, not to mention mixing in a liberal dose of revolutionary politics. Still others point us back to the Northwest and the early sixties for the genesis of both punk and grunge with the classic, non-commercial garage rock of the Seeds and the Sonics. At this point we are forced to conclude that it all began with rock and roll in the fifties, which of course evolved out of jazz and the blues. And so we see that both punk and grunge, like most of the significant trends in American music, are a product of both the black man's blues and the white man's marketing savvy. God Bless America.

In *The Decline of Western Civilization,* a great film by Penelope Spheeris, a young kid named Eugene sums up what punk means to him: "Punk rock . . . that's stupid, y'know . . . I just call it rock and roll . . . because that's what it is . . . and it's fast, and it's rockin', and it's for real, y'know . . . there's no rock stars." Punk rock icon Mike Watt says that punk is more a state of mind than a style. It's what you get when the rules imposed by commerce, society, talent, or taste are ignored in the name of art or expression: "Art is used by us to prove to each other that we are alive."

Whatever the case, music industry people and purists will tell you that both punk and grunge are merely fashionable anomalies in the development of modern rock music, little more than brief fads or marketing ploys at best. Or, at worst, they represent periods when talentless, crazed hacks tried to seize the reins of the American rock machine and use it for their own nefarious purposes and ruin rock and roll. This may be partly true, but we should welcome the attempt. The pioneers of both grunge and punk ruined rock and roll in the same way that Walt Whitman ruined poetry and Einstein and Heisenberg ruined reality. In other words, we owe them a great debt for it.

Works Cited

Blashill, Pat. *Noise from the Underground: A Secret History of Alternative Rock*. Simon and Schuster, 1996.

Spheeris, Penelope, director. *The Decline of Western Civilization*. Viacom, 1981.

Watt, Mike. Interview by Daniel Robert Epstein. *SuicideGirls.com*, 2 May 2004, www.suicidegirls. com/girls/anderswolleck/blog/2678966/mike-watt/.

Whitman, Walt. "Song of Myself." *The Walt Whitman Reader: Selections from* Leaves of Grass. Courage Books / Running Press, 1993.

Analyzing Argument

1. Why is it helpful to talk about punk when exploring the origins of grunge?

2. How is this an argument of definition? What particular term or concept is in question?

3. Harrington paraphrases Mike Watt when he writes, ". . . punk is more a state of mind than a style. It's what you get when the rules imposed by commerce, society, talent, or taste are ignored in the name of art or expression." How does Harrington describe that state of mind?

4. Based on Harrington's argument, why should we be grateful to pioneers of grunge and punk?

5. What about Harrington's voice as a writer makes his argument more convincing?

Working Stiffs by George Dila: A Review

JOHN MAUK

Book reviews are a common and popular genre. They show up in many, if not most, national magazines and newspapers. Because they span so many media outlets, book reviews vary significantly—from brief to extensive, from quirky to formal, from harsh to sober. They all, however, tend to include a few key elements: they give brief and strategic summaries; they explain the type of book in question (such as memoir, mystery, fantasy, or literary fiction); they make some claim of value about the book; finally, they offer some criteria or standard for that judgment. The following review, originally published on *The Compulsive Reader* website, is one approach to the genre.

Anyone who's ever been promoted knows the ugly truth about work: advancing through the ranks means saying *yes* to some rotten stuff—stuff that will get other people demoted, bamboozled, fired, hurt, or killed. Of course, colleges won't teach this—and maybe they shouldn't—but professional success often requires treachery, not flagrantly deceitful behavior but participation in widely accepted nastiness. As George Dila's new collection shows, good workers get beyond the moral quandaries. They survive. They say *yes*—eventually or right away—to whatever orders roll down from the top.

The characters in *Working Stiffs*[1] don't openly embrace the company's mean-spirited, oppressive, or murderous policies. They get talked or lulled into them. Out of exhaustion, fear, or basic survivalism, they accept their superiors' language and logic—however it comes. In the first story, "Eyes to Wonder, Tongues to Praise," the narrator, Baker, learns that he's bound for a promotion but only because his buddy is getting fired. Baker has to keep it secret, and it eats him up. He's riddled with anxiety, but he manages the discomfort and accepts his own complicity. He's even surprised at how well he staves off his buddy's suspicion: "I'm lying fluidly now, seamlessly," he tells us. And as the story climaxes, we learn just how complicit he becomes.

In "90 Million," the narrator, Howard, has a loyalty problem. His almost-former boss, Martin Harpoonian, has sold the company to new investors but can't quite let it go. Things get complicated when Harpoonian locks himself in his office and refuses to hand over power. The old guy knows that the new investors will eventually sell off his beloved company and let hundreds of loyal employees go. It's a standoff between value systems. And Howard becomes the go-between. The new investors call him persistently in hopes that he might lure Harpoonian out of the office. They make promises:

> "We're going to need good people, Howard. Folks who know the business. People we can rely on." "Help us out, Howard." We'd be grateful. You understand."

And so Howard has a problem. Will he help to usher in the future? Will he help his boss to defend the past? The answer comes after days (pages) of rich tension. And it's not so much the decision but the way Howard manages to halfway participate—to remain only somewhat involved—that feels so creepy and poignant.

Lest we think that workplace dilemmas are the province of modern offices, Dila hurls us back to an Old Testament tale in "Shaft Men." The workers are grunts in Joshua's army. They complain a little but eventually get with the program: kicking away the bodies of their fellow soldiers and gutting the Canaanites when it's time. The narrator, Stephen, isn't bothered by the ethics of war. The problem for him isn't existential or ethical; it's simply how to get beyond tedium:

> The next morning we form up and march around Jericho again. Our feet thud, we sing, the horns blare. We return to camp. Do not question authority, Jeb tells us. There is a plan.

5

[1]One Wet Shoe Publishing, 2014.

The next day we march around the city again,
and the next day, and the next, and the next.
The spring is gone from our step, the gusto from
our voices. Shem asks, How many officers does
it take to lead an ass? I cannot repeat his answer.

These stories are not simply about work and its
quotidian nastiness. They're about the needling questions beneath it all. They're about our own participation in awful contests and forms of domination. And
what's most interesting, and most terrifying, is that
the narrators are self-aware. Whether killing a hud-
dled family of Canaanites or accepting a promotion
to middle management, these guys all understand
what they're supporting. As first-person narrators,
they are both acting out and articulating (observing
and reporting) what we conclude about working life.

Working Stiffs is not Dila's literary debut. His
first full-length collection, *Nothing More to Tell*
(Mayfield Press), was plenty celebrated. Dila has a
steady hand, a superior eye for narrative tension,
and an undeniable rhythm. His scenes cruise along
like old-time films: with controlled grace and perfect crescendos. The plots are leak-proof. The occupational entanglements are rotten and real, and the
narrators lie only to themselves. In short, it's great
fiction. Granted, it's a chapbook—with only three
brief stories—but it's a thoroughly dark (and darkly
funny) study of workplace carnage.

And beyond its artistic prowess, Dila's little gem
will make you want to quit your job and be better
off for it.

Analyzing Argument

1. Book reviews usually forward claims of
   value. In other words, the reviewer offers an
   evaluation of the work in question. What is
   Mauk's claim of value?

2. A good book review offers a strategic summary:
   it includes just enough information to allow the
   audience a sense of the book without getting
   too caught up in details. Where does Mauk
   attempt strategic summary?

3. Evaluations also rely on *criteria* or standards of
   judgment. (See page 200 in Chapter 9.) What
   criteria are functioning in this review?

4. Why does Mauk spend so much time discussing the narrator of each story? Why do the narrators matter to this review?

5. How does the reference to Dila's earlier work,
   Nothing More to Tell, function in the review? What
   claim does it help to support?

6. Where do you sense concessions or qualifiers?
   Explain what any specific concession or qualifier
   does for the review.

Martin Luckner/stockchng.com

22

Technology

I n the twenty-first century, technological advances can be dizzying. New technology designed to make life better threatens to be overwhelming, time consuming, expensive, and downright harmful. Technology serves us, but how? What are the intended and unintended consequences of particular technologies and of our cumulative use of various technologies?

Technology is ubiquitous, and it impacts other topics, such as consumption, the environment, popular culture, and media. Consider how technology impacts education:

- One reason for the steady increase in college tuition is new technology: computer technology has replaced inexpensive chalkboards.

- Educators and taxpayers explore the value of computers and particular software in the college, high school, and elementary school classrooms.

- We try to figure out how technology outside of school (video games, iPods, cell phones) affects students when they are in school. Does it make people think or learn differently? Does technology make today's students different from previous generations?

Because technology is fused to everyday life and is increasingly linked to basic human affairs, it gets pulled into various argumentative topics, and it is a central focus of much analysis and debate.

Readings about Technology in Chapters 1–14

Finding the Robot Chauffeur

DANIEL ALBERT

Daniel Albert, a freelance writer, was the curator of transport at Science Museum, London. Albert has written extensively about cultural adaption of technology, automobiles specifically. This article was published in *N+1*, a magazine of "literature, culture, and politics," in 2013.

The footnotes to car ads have grown more interesting of late. They started decades ago with the innocuous boilerplate, "Professional driver, closed course." But then someone let the copywriters have their snarky fun. The Ford Fusion Hybrid's features an enduring classic that appears as the sedan leaps off a cliff: "Fictionalization. Professional driver on closed course. Do not attempt. Cars cannot fly."[1]

Silly as these warnings sound, the latest fine print inadvertently reveals our automotive future. Since 2010, when it debuted an automatic braking technology that keeps you from mowing down pedestrians, Volvo has been running vague disclaimers like, "City Safety is not a substitute for safe driving." Mercedes Benz shows its cars racing across the frozen north thanks to its intelligent traction system with the countervailing footnote, "Drive cautiously based on weather conditions." Jeep, of all brands, has to remind buyers, "Electronic driver assistance features are not substitutes for active driver involvement." Chevrolet warns you, "Never rely on its Crash Imminent Braking feature to brake the vehicle." Yes, the feature stops the Impala from going Titanic and hitting an iceberg while the driver's eyes wander. But that's just in the ad.[2]

The prize for covering the bottom of the screen with advice goes to Toyota's "May You" commercial, which helpfully explains that "Vehicle Stability Control is not a substitute for safe driving," "Lane Keeping Assist is not a substitute for attentive driving," "Pre-Collision system is not a substitute for attentive driving." To that effect, "Do not rely exclusively on the Blind Spot Monitor to determine if lane changing is safe."[3]

These warnings are all baldfaced lies. City Safety is a substitute for safe driving. You can drive as madly as you like thanks to the electronic stability of your Mercedes. Your Jeep is too polite to tailgate. Your Toyota knows better than you do when it can safely change lanes. Lane Keeping Assist and Pre-Collision braking are not just substitutes for attentive driving—*inattentive* driving is their raison-d'être. Add to these safety features gimmicks such as self-parking and remote starting by mobile phone ("Siri, start the car") and you have machines that look an awful lot like robot cars.

The American "love affair" with the automobile is often mistaken for a love affair with driving. We think driver distraction arose with the smartphone, but truth be told most Americans never liked driving much. When Oldsmobile debuted Motoring's Magic Carpet on the eve of World War II, it lamented the struggles of the little lady with a standard transmission: "After nineteen distinct manual operations, she's finally ready to drive." Relief came from the Hydra-Matic drive, the original automatic transmission. Times have changed but the dream has not. Today, Mercedes promises a "flying carpet" ride from its laser-guided Magic Body Control active suspension system. Let them wrestle with their overtaxed motors among the dark satanic mills of Europe. Americans invented power steering. Come to think of it, flying carpets don't even need steering wheels, do they?[4]

Those who read robot news may think I'm on about the Google Car, the result of Pentagon funding, Stanford computer genius Sebastian Thrun,

---

"Finding the Robot Chauffeur," by Daniel Albert. nplusonemag.com/online-only/online-only/finding-the-robot-chauffeur/. Reprinted with permission of the publisher.

[1] 2013 Ford Fusion "Cliff" Commercial.
[2] The Volvo XC60 & City Safety: From Sweden with Löv; 4Matic Four Wheel Drive "Badges"; 2013 Jeep Grand Cherokee "Desolation"; 2014 Chevrolet Crash Imminent Braking through Radar.
[3] Toyota Let's Go Places Safely — "May You."
[4] Oldsmobile Presents Motoring's Magic Carpet Hydra-Matic B-44 (1942 Oldsmobile Playlets), 1941; Mercedes Benz Magic Body Control.

and of course money from all those little internet adverts. The origin of Google's small self-driving fleet—each with sixty-four spinning laser beams mounted to its roof and hacker wires running down to the wheels—dates to the 2005 DARPA Grand Challenge, where Stanley, Stanford's VW SUV (now on display at the Smithsonian), beat twenty-three other teams in a race through the desert. In 2007, Stanford placed second in DARPA's urban version of the race, in which cars had to cope with stop signs and other annoyances. They were bested by Carnegie Mellon, but ran ahead of MIT, Virginia Tech, and the rest. Who says college is a waste?

No doubt the people who brought us the remote-controlled drone, the stealth bomber, and persistent, ubiquitous surveillance have great plans for these self-driving systems. An automated fuel truck won't be wearing a Pakistani suicide vest or be mourned by folks back home like a brave young military contractor. Self-driving vehicles built by Lockheed Martin have already had their first tour of duty in Afghanistan. They didn't help win the war, of course, but they did help win Lockheed Martin a contract.

But it's not just Elon Musk, Sergey Brin, and the Pentagon who are bringing us robot cars. There are cars on the road today that could, with just a little tweaking, drive themselves in most situations. They could at the least ply the interstates. That they do not is a failure of marketing imagination and law, not technology.

Society is already groping toward the few changes needed to make robot cars a reality. Automakers will need a new marketing plan to replace their current sales messages. The appeals to economy and quality will still hold water, but what about those that promise the thrill and competition of driving? Snaking along wet mountain roads, ramming through walls, and outpacing other traffic—such kicks are lost on robots. Violence—both the threat and exhilaration of it—has been a persistent and of late seemingly more prevalent theme in advertising. The 2014 Cadillac XTS Vsport literally "blows the doors off" the competition in its latest ad. Perhaps the worst was a BMW film that featured Clive Owen as a professional driver beating the vanity out of Madonna with his BMW M5. At the other end of the spectrum, Mitsubishi's 2014 Outlander commercial shows a woman badly injured on the road before the arrival of the SUV, with Frontal Collision Mitigation ("It is not a substitute for safe and careful driving").[5] Surely the ad agencies will come up with new pitches when robot cars end what has been more than a century of highway violence.

And of course many of us invest our egos in our vehicles—whether driving ovate maxivans, equine pickups, or phallic coupes. Whether cars can continue to do that cultural work—can continue to serve as the ultimate symbol of consumption and success—remains to be seen.

Government will have to rethink much of the regulatory regime that surrounds cars and driving. This is a bigger problem than you might imagine because so much of our system for regulating traffic is not really about making traffic smoother or safer. It's about social control. A century ago, as cars suddenly made it possible for Americans to slip local bonds, government responded with rules and regulations to keep track of who was driving what. Whether intentionally or not, traffic regulations became a national dragnet serving all manner of police purposes, suppressing everything from sex trafficking to adolescent rebellion. More recently, traffic laws have nabbed terrorists and funded police operations through civil forfeiture rules. We'll have to figure out how to weave a new dragnet in the age of robot cars. As luck would have it, the NSA is already on the case.

It is little exaggeration to say that the automobile served as the cornerstone of American economic growth for much of the 20th century. Production created middle-class jobs while consumption and

10

---

5 "Doors," The All-New 2014 Cadillac XTS Sport; "The Hire," BMW Films, 2002; 2014 Mitsubishi Outlander, "New Safety."

infrastructure generated economic activity. A transition to robot cars could reignite this economic engine. No other society is as deeply committed to a future of individualized mass transportation, so we are the obvious nation to begin the transition to driverless cars. The savings in lives, aggravation, and energy would be enormous. The robot car could jump-start the economic engine even as it displaces taxi drivers and long-haul truckers. This is not to promise a techno-utopia—only to point out that a lot of money has been made selling American cars to the world and we might as well try for an encore.

Truth be told, many people gave up driving long ago, yet there they sit, behind the wheel. The robot cars are here. If only we'd let them drive.

Analyzing Argument

1. What is Albert's main claim? What kind of claim is it (fact, value, or policy)?

2. How do the warnings, what Albert calls "bald-faced lies," relate to his main claim? In other words, how do the allusions to car ad footnotes function in his argument? What idea do they help him to establish?

3. In his fifth paragraph, Albert says, "Times have changed, but the dream has not." What does he mean? And how does this line work in his argument about robotic cars?

4. Explain how Albert concedes or qualifies his claims? Refer to specific passages or statements in your response.

5. How does Albert's characterization of the past help him to paint a picture of the future? Refer to specific passages or statements in your response.

The Technology Slaves

ROSS WHEATLEY

In the following essay, Ross Wheatley responds to "Isolated by the Internet," an excerpt from Clifford Stoll's book *High Tech Heretic* (1999). Stoll argues that using the Internet causes "serious negative long-term social effects, ranging from depression to loneliness."

In "Isolated by the Internet," an excerpt from his book *High Tech Heretic,* Clifford Stoll argues that using the Internet causes "serious negative long-term social effects, ranging from depression to loneliness" (269). He refers to the research of Carnegie Mellon University psychologists Robert Kraut and Vicki Lundmark who found "an average increase in depression by about 1 percent for every hour spent online per week." They also found that "online activity resulted in increased loneliness." Stoll asks: "Depression. Loneliness. Loss of close friendships. This is the medium that we're promoting to expand our global community?" (270)

Stoll claims that time spent online "steal[s] our lives and undermine[s] our communities" (277), and that greater use of the Internet contributes to "small but statistically significant declines in social involvement" (271). According to Stoll, "Psychologists point out that the best predictor of psychological troubles is a lack of close social contacts" (272), and while he acknowledges throughout his argument that people do make connections with others through the Internet ("a support group for an obscure medical condition"; a "soon-to-be married couple [who] met through postings to a Usenet news group" [269]; and so on), he makes clear that these connections "simply aren't deep." He says, "Online friends can't be depended on for help with tangible favors . . ." and he refers to one participant in a study who "noted that when her daughter was homesick or depressed, she reverted to telephone calls to provide support" (271). He concludes:

The price of computing at home—as in school and at work—is far more than the cost of the hardware. The opportunity cost is our time, and it is taken out of our individual lives and our very real neighborhoods. The time you spend behind the monitor could be spent facing another person across a table or across a tennis court. Disguised as efficiency machines, digital time bandits steal our lives and undermine our communities. (276)

While Stoll argues that we should be out playing tennis, others would no doubt respond with various arguments about how Internet use doesn't hurt, but actually helps to develop, social skills and community. (They might claim that Stoll is just an old fuddy-duddy who doesn't understand *virtual* communities.) But while Stoll dismisses financial cost ("The price of computing . . . is far more than the cost of the hardware"), financial cost is, in fact, an extremely important issue (and one that somehow slips under the radar as other issues take center stage). It could be argued that the *dollars and cents* cost of using the Internet—along with all the other technologies we are committed to—is largely responsible for a lot of the negative social effects about which Stoll is concerned.

Stoll makes a variety of points that he could, but doesn't, connect to the *financial* cost of using technology. For example, he says, "One report suggested that parents, busy from work which they've brought home, spend only six to eight minutes a day talking with their children" (272). His insight is that because parents are using the Internet at home, as well as at work, they're not spending much time with their children. One might look at it another way: Because Americans are spending so much money on technology these days, they are working more; therefore, they have less time to talk to their children. (Incidentally, the children are happy not to talk, as they are busy consuming the technology.)

Certainly Stoll is right when he says that "technology also blurs the line between work and play. 5

Thanks to telephones, pagers, and cell phones, work seeps into our private time, forcing shallow, impersonal communication into quiet hours and intimate moments" (274). All this time spent online, on the phone, listening to iPods, trying to figure out what's wrong with your iPod, trying to figure out how to work your new iPod, and so on may intrude on our private space and be detrimental to our social lives. And, one could argue the opposite as well—that all this time spent using technology enhances one's social life. But isn't this looking for subtlety or debate when something much more obviously detrimental is staring you right in the face, whacking you over the head, reaching into your pocket?

Stoll argues that "with houses increasingly wired for communication, electronic messages invade our home life" (275). Right again. But we should also keep in mind that we're working more so that *we can pay* to wire our houses. Every year families spend money "wiring" themselves with computers, TVs, cell phones, iPods—money that they could have spent to go on a family vacation, or two.

- We're working more to pay for all the technology.

- Parents are so busy working that they only spend 6 to 8 minutes a day talking with their children.

- It is as if the parent is a slave to technology.

Stoll quotes an Intel psychologist who is defending the Internet against the claim that it is "building shallow relationships, leading to an overall decline in feeling of connection to other people" (271). The psychologist says, "This is not about the technology, per se; it's about how it is used. It points to the need for considering social factors in terms of how you design applications and services for technology" (271). While this response takes us to another interesting place, full of issues that we could and should debate, it ignores an issue just as worthy of debate, if not more so: How much *money* does all this technology cost us, and is it worth it?

Stoll tells us that in the Kraut and Lundmark study, "[The researchers] provided computers, software, modems, accounts, and training . . ." (270). Like the Intel psychologist, the researchers gloss over the financial toll technology takes on our lives. Require the study subjects to purchase computers *and* software *and* accounts; let them go without training or pay for the training on their own; make them purchase a new version of Microsoft Office, spending hours researching how to get the best price; be realistic and leave it to up to them to upgrade other unrelated products, getting everything compatible, including the software required to protect the whole system from attack; *then* study how depressed they are. And they might be lonely too. And all the hours of working to pay for the pleasure may have distanced them from an old friend or two.

According to Daniel Gross in "Buy Cell: How Many Mobile Phones Does the World Need?" (2004), an analyst at Bank of America projects that "650 million wireless handsets would be sold this year and 730 million next year." Trikon Technologies Inc. said that "the worldwide handset market is 'forecasted to reach 1 billion units by 2006.'" Adding up the numbers, Long points out that "one in every 10 humans will buy—not possess, but *buy*—a new cell phone this year" (Gross). People are not purchasing their cell phones for the long term: they realize a cell phone will last a couple years at most and then they'll have to get a new one. It's the same for their iPod, Blackberry, Bluetooth, and so on—all products that may be obsolete if you are reading this a year or two after it is written. Yesterday (January 10, 2007), Steve Jobs announced Apple's entry into the cell phone market with iPhone, a smart phone costing $499. Every year, similar innovations require Americans to either get on board (spend the money and learn the technology) or be left behind. Some people consider the technology they use to be a necessity, while others see it as a worthwhile luxury. Is a cell phone necessary, and will the new, smart iPhone become a necessity? If a person works a particular type of job, it may be a necessity to what is required for doing that job. The same is true of desktop or laptop computers, Internet service, and software; of digital cameras for some; of iPods for others; and so on.

10   One could argue that this technology boom will not continue. At some point, we will have what we need and will be able to keep it a while, and the cost will be minimal. But there's no evidence of that happening. It might; it might not. So far, the evidence suggests that from now on, if it's not one technology cost, it will be another.

The story of two determined detractors illustrates the hidden costs of today's technology. Replacing batteries is something we haven't considered yet. When Casey and Van Neistat, two brothers from New York City, found out how much it cost to replace the battery in an iPod, they, "recorded a phone call to the Apple help line, where they were told the smartest thing was to buy a new iPod." Then they videotaped themselves "stenciling 'iPod's unreplaceable battery lasts only 18 months' on iPod posters; and posted it all online as a three-minute video." In his *New York Times* article describing what happened, Nat Ives makes sure he reminds us how inexpensive the protest was: "The clip cost them $40 to produce."

Not really, Mr. Ives. The brothers have no doubt spent thousands on computers, software, cell phones, iPods, and other technology, just to be savvy enough to (cheaply) protest the high cost of it all. Ives tells us that "Apple computer . . . soon began offering a cheaper battery-replacement program" (Ives). But what does Apple care? It seems that most Americans—unlike the Neistats—simply accept that all the charges are worth paying for. Ives's attitude is typical of Americans in general: He underestimates the real cost of their protest, simplistically suggesting that it was done for just forty dollars.

Stoll argues that sitting at a computer instead of strolling through the park is bad for one's social skills, social life, and community. He may be right. And if we can't say for certain that he's right, we can say that he raises an important issue that Americans should explore and debate. But in the last twenty years Americans have been handed an additional bill—their monthly technology bill. There's no need to provide examples of how much all this costs. Each person can add up his or her own monthly technology bill, the new "tax" nearly all Americans pay these days in order to participate fully in the American dream. That bill has been steadily rising, and it has become more and more a necessity (and less optional). The days of free TV and a Smith-Corona are gone forever.

IDE Corp., Innovative Designs for Education, is an educational consulting firm specializing in helping educators rethink instruction to better prepare students for the 21st century. Their website states:

> Today, computers are assisting in the development of new innovations, significantly speeding up the development process. New advances in technology are rendering computers of a year ago obsolete. No sooner is a computer model manufactured than the next one has rolled off the design presses, and no end is in sight. Computer designers are now moving beyond silicon chips to using DNA chips . . . a move from geologic roots to biologic roots, making the computer an even closer representation of man.

New advances in technology are being introduced   15 at greater and greater speeds. Today's workers learn to use new technology every few months. How can students learn to embrace change and acclimate to new technologies as they emerge? What can schools do to help?

How much MONEY is all this going to cost? How much time and energy will it take to earn the money? And what all will be sacrificed along the way? If Americans are more depressed and lonely, it might have a lot to do with how hard they have to work now to pay for all the stuff that makes them more lonely and depressed. It sounds like most Americans are slaves to technology. Many would tell you they aren't slaves, and that they enjoy their gadgets. (They might have Stockholm syndrome.) We could debate whether or not it is even possible to break free from our bondage to technology. Is escape possible, or does technology have a death grip on us? Are we dependent on it? Is it worth the cost?

Works Cited

Gross, Daniel. "Buy Cell: How Many Mobile Phones Does the World Need?" *Slate*, 2 June 2004, www.slate.com/articles/business/moneybox/2004/06/buy_cell.html.

Ives, Nat. "Marketing's Flip Side: The 'Determined Detractor.'" *The New York Times*, 27 Dec. 2004, www.nytimes.com/2004/12/27/business/media/marketings-flip-side-the-determined-detractor.html.

"Rapid Advances for Teaching." *IDE Corp.*, 19 Dec. 2006. Accessed 8 Jan. 2007.

Stoll, Clifford. "Isolated by the Internet." *Writing in the Disciplines*, by Mary L. Kennedy, et al., 5th ed., Pearson, 2004, pp. 269–277.

Analyzing Argument

1. What is Wheatley's main disagreement with Stoll? On what points do Wheatley and Stoll agree?

2. Explain how Wheatley makes a concession to Stoll and then builds on the concession to further develop his argument.

3. What is the essay's main claim?

4. List the essay's major types of support. How might one type of the support be developed further?

5. How is Wheatley's argument about value? What particular value or principle is at stake?

Advances in Medical Technology: The Flip Side

JAN POTTS

We often write, argue, or invent because two (or more) things come together and grab our attention. Jan Potts's argument below was triggered by two things: (1) noticing a trend in recent news reports on health and (2) reading Amy Zachary's "Antibacterial Soap" (pages 494–498). Prompted by Zachary's argument, Potts takes a "yes and" approach, agreeing with Zachary and adding support to her argument. While the essays agree in general, the arguments are different. Potts makes different claims, provides different examples, and speaks with a different voice.

As reported on the *CBS Evening News,* December 14, 2006, "A new analysis documents a staggering 7 percent drop in U.S. breast cancer rates in 2003." This is such a large decrease that Donald Berry, head of the Division of Quantitative Sciences at the University of Texas MD Cancer Center, said, "When I saw it, I couldn't believe it" ("U.S. Breast Cancer Rates Plunge"). As of right now, the experts think the drop is because many women stopped taking hormone pills—pills that their doctors had prescribed.

According to CBS, "The 7.2 percent decline came a year after a big federal study linked menopause hormones to a higher risk of breast cancer, heart disease, and other problems. Within months, millions of women stopped taking the pills" (Serrano). If the doctors are right today, the pills they had been prescribing for the last 10 years were causing breast cancer. Of course the doctors aren't sure.

Today's story about the drop in breast cancer rate is good news, indeed. But it raises the question, how often does the prescription drug or modern medical solution create a new health problem?

Just last week another common medical practice was called into question. In 1994, doctors started inserting stents, tiny metal devices, into blood vessels to prop them open, the way tent posts hold up a tent. But over time, some patients' arteries have narrowed where the stents are, and it looks like blood clots are forming around the stents. These stents, inserted into the patient's blood vessels in order to prevent heart attacks, can "choke off the blood supply in the artery, leading to a sudden heart attack, and potentially, to death" (Dakss).

The FDA (Federal Drug Administration) concluded that "in about 40 percent of the situations in which the stents are used, the blockage involves just one artery, and the patient's heart is not significantly damaged" (Dakss). That's the good news. The bad news is: 60 percent of the time *more than one* artery gets blocked and "the patient suffers a serious heart attack, or other complications are involved."

Nearly every night there is a story on the evening news about a new scientific or medical study that calls into question some common medical practice. We progress medically as if rolling and tumbling down a hill all arms and legs. Every night during the news, people watch advertisements for drugs. In a single news broadcast, one sees ads for: Prilosec OTC. Aricept. Spiriva. There's something for restless leg syndrome. Bristol-Meyers-Squibb has an ad, not for a particular drug, but for the company overall. There are also ads for Tylenol, Benefiber, Cepacol, Gold Bond Lotion, Bayer, V8, and Crest. These ads pay for the evening news, which regularly reports on the benefits and side effects of prescription and over-the-counter drugs.

The combination of drug ads and news stories raises serious questions: Are we really that sick? If we are, why? Do we need all these drugs? To what extent do the drugs help us or make us worse? To what extent does the advertising encourage us to have faith in uncertain remedies? To what extent does the news broadcast itself encourage us?

According to the United States government:

• Prescription drug use is rising among people of all ages, and use increases with age.

- Five out of six persons 65 and older are taking at least one medication and almost half the elderly take three or more.

- Adult use of antidepressants almost tripled between 1988–1994 and 1999–2000. Ten percent of women 18 and older and 4 percent of men now take antidepressants.

- The National Health and Nutrition Examination Survey found a 13 percent increase between 1988–1994 and 1999–2000 in the proportion of Americans taking at least one drug and a 40 percent jump in the proportion taking three or more medicines. Forty-four percent reported taking at least one drug in the past month and 17 percent were taking three or more in the 2000 survey (Longley).

What is the effect on Americans of all this drug taking? One might argue that Americans are better off: "The latest report shows continued improvements in Americans' health, with life expectancy at birth up to 77.3 years in 2002, a record, and deaths from heart disease, cancer and stroke—the nation's three leading killers—all down 1 percent to 3 percent" (Longley). But what about the side effects?

In drug ads, the side effects are no longer squeezed in at the end, too fast to hear. For some reason, pharmaceutical companies now feel comfortable announcing the side effects slowly, deliberately. While couples ride bikes or sail boats, a seductive velvety voice proclaims:

> Get immediate medical help if you have any of these signs of allergic reaction: hives, difficulty breathing, swelling of your face, lips, tongue, or throat. Other less serious side effects are more likely to occur, such as: stomach pain, gas, nausea, vomiting, diarrhea, or headache. Stop using and talk to your doctor if you experience: drowsiness or dizziness, nausea, vomiting, or decreased appetite, abnormal abdominal pain, diarrhea, muscle cramps, insomnia or vivid dreams, sleepwalking or dry mouth. Although

not all of these side effects may occur, if they do occur they may need medical attention: Arm, back or jaw pain, chest pain or discomfort, chest tightness or heaviness, fast or irregular heartbeat, nausea, shortness of breath, sweating, cough, difficulty swallowing, dizziness, hives, painful blisters on trunk of body, puffiness or swelling of the eyelids or around the eyes, face, lips or tongue, skin rash, tightness in chest, unusual tiredness or weakness, wheezing.

While these side effects strike us as undesirable, 10 they seem tolerable and worth the risk. But what about the more serious side effects that are revealed as important medical discoveries years later? When the brain gives way to Alzheimer's, who is to say that it's not the result of a lifelong concoction of prescription drugs? Yet a Google search turns up only information about how prescription drugs are used to *treat* Alzheimer's. There is no hint of a suggestion that prescription drugs might *contribute to* Alzheimer's.

Americans have been down this road before. In her essay "Antibacterial Soap," Amy L. Zachary explains how a seemingly innocent and beneficial product turns out to be not what it seems. She says, "We easily fell into a consumerist trap the soap and detergent manufacturers made, perhaps without malice in mind, when they came out with new 'antibacterial' products for home use" (494). As she explains, while the antibacterial soap industry claimed that "you're not as clean as you think" and "[m]ore than thirty years of research has proven that antimicrobial washes reduce or eliminate bacteria that can lead to skin infections, intestinal illnesses, or other commonly transmitted diseases" (qtd. in Zachary 494), this turns out to be a dangerous oversimplification.

Antibacterial soap, originally marketed as a solution, turns out to be hazardous. Zachary compares its compromising and ultimately harmful effects to a similar mistake doctors and patients made with antibiotic drugs: "It took forty years for medical science to concede the consequences to our immune systems of doctors prescribing antibiotics for every little illness" (495). She explains: "The germs that cause illness build resistance, while our bodies lose the capacity to fight them without aid" (495). The unintended side effects can be worse than the solution.

Many examples (such as the antibiotics, antibacterial soap, breast cancer/hormone treatments, or stents following angioplasty) suggest that our remedies can be what kill us. This phenomenon has occurred throughout the history of medicine and is unavoidable. But through advertising, pharmaceutical companies have persuaded both patients and doctors that we need what they are selling. They have created a mindset. As soon as drug companies were allowed to come into our living rooms and snuggle up with us and appeal to our innermost values and fears, they persuaded us that we want what they were selling. They told us that it's a good thing they have these drugs, because these drugs are just what we need. They became godlike in our minds.

In many cases prescription drugs are a godsend, of course. But we should look carefully at the influence big pharmaceutical companies have on our thinking. Certainly, drugs are appealing. If something hurts and X makes us feel better, it makes sense to consider taking X. But if the drugs we're taking today hurt us more in the long run, we may need to lay off some of our drugs. If an individual drug has serious side effects (and side effects we don't discover until later), how much more difficult is it to discover the long-term consequences of combinations of drugs? At what cost do we take our medicine?

Works Cited

Dakss, Brian. "Mixed Verdict on Drug-Coated Heart Stents." *CBS News*, 11 Dec. 2006, www.cbsnews.com/news/mixed-verdict-on-drug-coated-heart-stents/.

Longley, Robert. "Almost Half of Americans Take at Least One Prescription Drug." *About.com: US Government Info*, 4 Dec. 2005, usgovinfo.about.com/od/federalbenefitprograms/p/meddrugpro.htm.

Serrano, Alfonso. "U.S. Breast Cancer Rates Plunge." *CBS News*, 14 Dec. 2006, www.cbsnews.com/news/us-breast-cancer-rates-plunge/.

Zachary, Amy L. "Antibacterial Soap." *Inventing Arguments*, by John Mauk and John Metz, 4th ed., Cengage Learning, 2016, pp. 494–498.

Analyzing Argument

1. Briefly summarize the argument by writing down its main claim and support.

2. How does the essay rely on appeals to value? How do the appeals to value help the reader understand and accept the claim?

3. How does the argument appeal to logic? What main line of reasoning develops throughout the essay?

4. Compare this essay with Amy Zachary's essay "Antibacterial Soap":

   - Write down the main idea of each essay. Then discuss with classmates how the ideas differ or are the same.

   - What aspects of the issue does Potts draw attention to?

   - Compare Potts's and Zachary's voices. Does one sound more urgent? Is one more austere? How would you describe each writer's voice? How are the voices different? What is engaging or alienating about each voice?

5. In groups, discuss different ways one might enter the argument. Describe each point of entry. For example, is it a disputed assumption, value, belief, fact, or line of reasoning? Try pinpointing the point of contention.

Isolated Community: Hidden Dangers of MMORPGs

RACHEL SCHOFIELD

As J. Noel Trapp argues (pages 161–164), massive multiplayer online role-playing games have become a huge entertainment phenomenon. Trapp argues that MMORPGs have succeeded largely because people crave belonging, and the "real world" social conditions of mainstream capitalist culture do not cultivate community, belonging, or intimacy for millions of people. But Rachel Schofield is suspicious of MMORPGs and the communities they create. In this argument, written for her first-year college writing course, Schofield tries to uncover the hidden layers of these virtual communities.

Across the world, millions of aching fingers feverishly dart over keyboards. Carpal tunnel sets in, and innumerable eyes water from staring at computer screens for countless hours. A young man pops caffeine pills to stay awake long into the night. As morning creeps up, his alarm clock goes unheard, his phone goes unanswered as an angry boss calls about his absence from work, and unpaid bills pile up in his mailbox. A Korean couple leave their child unattended for hours as they play World of Warcraft in an Internet café down the street—fanatically devoted to a game, while left at home their four-year-old dies of neglect (Levin). Friends, family, and entire countries worldwide are concerned about loved ones as massive multiplayer online role-playing games (MMORPGs) slowly erode true community. There is a growing concern about what happens when we ignore those around us and concentrate on an only partially real world that lies not in true space, but in cyberspace—when we forsake our immediate community and become entangled in an isolated community. While MMORPGs seem to exemplify true community, they actually undermine its core principles.

In a recent controversial survey, clinical psychologist Dr. Maressa Hecht Orzack concluded that forty percent of World of Warcraft's players are addicted to the game (Levin). According to its website, World of Warcraft (WoW) is the world's largest and most popular MMORPG, with more than eight million gamers worldwide. Part of the lure of massive multiplayer games like WoW is the sense of community gamers feel when working with others. But is this truly community, or just the elusive shadow of a fast-fading foundation of our society?

When we think about our culture's traditional definition of community, most would agree that a healthy community encourages mutually beneficial relationships and communication between its members, yet supports freedom and individuality. We like to keep a balance between group cohesion and personal expression. On the surface, MMORPGs' virtual community seems to fit both parts of this definition. According to Richard Ryan, a professor in the department of clinical and social psychology at the University of Rochester in New York, two of the main reasons that gamers play MMORPGs are that they "give [gamers] a sense of freedom maybe that they are not experiencing elsewhere or opportunities to connect with players" (Smith). Groups of players work together in tight-knit "parties" or "guilds" to achieve common goals, earning items and status in the process. By helping each other, gamers are able to achieve higher levels more quickly than players who go it alone. At the same time, players are able to express themselves through their avatars (in-game personas) in novel ways that are more accepted in the virtual world than in everyday life. For instance, male gamers often create attractive female avatars, yet in the real world expressing themselves in this way would generally be considered abnormal behavior.

Gamers themselves may see MMORPGs as just any other community, but when we look closer, we find that there are underlying differences. Granted, MMORPG members share a common interest in gaming, and help each other to accomplish group goals. However, teams of gamers have less of an interest in individuals' well being than in successfully raiding a dungeon. Perhaps this is because of the anonymous environment inherent in a form of communication that takes out the human element.

5   True communities foster human interaction as a means of preserving our relationships to other members. MMORPGs lack physical human-to-human interaction, a key component of communication and relationships. I'm not saying that gamers do not talk to other players. Rather, players do not have "real" face-to-face communication. For them, communication is mediated by a cold, unfeeling computer screen, unable to convey the true complexity of human emotion and subtle nuances of body language that we would otherwise pick up on in our real lives. Players who submerse themselves in this virtual world limit themselves to mere machine and fail to realize their own bodies' potential as a vastly complex organism of multifaceted communication.

Another downfall of MMORPGs' lack of physical interaction is that people can deceive others more readily. In many cases gamers don't even know their teammates' real names, ages, or gender. Danger can develop when the gamer isolates themselves from their immediate community, becoming involved in contrived, unnatural, distanciated relationships with people they hardly know. (The abundance of online predators is ample proof of this.) To counteract the long-distance relationships' tendency to become dangerous to true community, some guilds, such as my brother's, choose to meet each other in real life, recognizing the value of real human interaction—leaving behind the virtual world for a face-to-face meeting.

In addition to the so-called "social" aspect of MMORPGs, many gamers see them as arenas for self-expression and experimentation with personal identity as they create their individual in-game personas. However, Darian Leader, writer for the UK's *Sunday Times,* points out a darker aspect of this activity: "Creating new identities often goes with social isolation and exclusion. Joining a virtual community . . . just gives us another way of putting barriers between ourselves and others" (Leader). Moreover, players' identities are ultimately disposable. Players can change their own identities easily and leave behind so-called friends and associates. Players can ditch whomever they want, whenever they want. They don't have a pressing personal responsibility to help others. The fellow gamers are "out of sight, and out of mind." And of course, this thinking becomes dangerous when it is subtly, subconsciously applied to real-life relationships.

Players utilize gaming as an escape from the pressures of their physical world. People seek gaming as relief from real-life pressures stemming from society and social life, but in fact this causes more problems than it relieves—actually making it harder for them to interact in real life. They begin to ignore real-world problems that only get worse as time passes. When gamers neglect their real-world relationships for virtual ones, they are in fact undercutting true community. Family, friends, coworkers, and neighbors lose a member of their lives. There are even websites devoted to supporting "WoW widows." Shelly Quintana set up one of these sites because "WoW has taken a serious toll on my relationship. My husband still goes to work and supports his children and still has family time, but there is just not room for relationship time and World of Warcraft" (Levin). Gamers even neglect themselves: their hygiene, health, and future. It is not uncommon for a WoW addict to go days without showering or brushing his teeth, cooping himself up in his room, not interacting with friends, family, or the opposite sex. When the real world becomes less of a priority than the false world, there is a problem. MMORPGs crumble family values and ruin friendships. They create a distance between the gamer and those people whom he has a responsibility to help, and those who would help him.

Realizing gamers' desire for community, WoW's developers created tools in the game to help create their version of "community." The Guild Relations Program invites guilds into a rewards program "based on the level of activity demonstrated in regard to constructive community interaction" (worldofwarcraft .com). This interaction includes creating movies, writing fan fiction, and making game guides for the use of other players. This is not really developing community, but rather helping generate propaganda. These materials do not foster relationships or promote individuality. In the end, the intent of the game is to make money for the developers. It is not designed to encourage individuality or community, but rather the illusion of it, in order to lure more gamers into paying next month's fee.

10   We have seen that MMORPGs create isolated community. This is different from a true community because isolated communities are distanciated, lack human-to-human interaction, and, therefore, do not foster the kind of communication and concern for others that should be valued in a healthy community. Is this a sign that our culture as a whole is becoming more geared toward isolated communities? It is widely accepted among sociologists that America is now the "salad bowl" instead of the "melting pot." We, as a culture, are becoming more isolated. We need to reevaluate the role of technology in our lives. Is it facilitating communication, or rather creating a false sense of community? Are we utilizing technology to keep in touch with family members or help those around us, or are we caught up in the frenzy of a contrived fantasy world?

Works Cited

Leader, Darian. "Comment: Identity Crisis." *The Sunday Times*, 10 Dec. 2006, Culture section p. 10, www.thesundaytimes.co.uk/sto/culture/ article175786.ece.

Levin, Derren. "A Virtual Escape from Reality." *The Sydney Morning Herald*, 1 Mar. 2007. Accessed 7 Mar. 2007.

Smith, Tammie. "Gripped by Games: Playing Satisfies Basic Needs, Study Says." *Richmond Times-Dispatch*, 3 Jan. 2007. *Academic Search Elite*.

World of Warcraft Community Site. Blizzard Entertainment. Accessed 7 Mar. 2007.

Analyzing Argument

1. What is Schofield's line of reasoning?

2. How does this argument depend on the definition of *community*? Does Schofield have to convince us of a particular understanding of community?

3. Read J. Noel Trapp's essay about MMORPGs (in Chapter 8, Arguing Causes). Despite the obvious differences between Trapp's and Schofield's arguments, what values or assumptions do both writers share?

4. Read either Jan Potts or Ross Wheatley—both in this chapter. What are the shared values and assumptions between Schofield and Potts or Schofield and Wheatley?

Letters from the Past

LAURIE SCHUTZA

Often, arguments about technology are actually arguments about human affairs—social, psychological, political, even spiritual issues. This is the case with Laurie Schutza's argument about letter writing, a traditional and nearly forgotten technology replaced by other, faster technologies. Schutza developed this essay for her first-year college writing course.

I recently came across a box of old photographs while visiting my parents. I was thrilled to see photos of my dad as a kid hanging from trees, playing football, on vacations, and interacting with his family. At the bottom of the box, I was surprised to find a bundle of forty or so letters from the early to mid 1950s, still in their postmarked envelopes. I didn't know what to expect and I hoped I wasn't prying, but my curiosity got the best of me.

The letters, I discovered, were written by my dad to his parents in New York from the day he started college as an engineering major, through graduation, and after he acquired his first job in Houston, Texas, where he met my mother. I never even knew these letters existed. Once I started reading, I was hooked. Each one told a story, a firsthand account of what was going on in his life at that given time. His letters went into great detail, sometimes five or six pages long, in his own beautiful cursive handwriting. I voraciously read each letter and as I did, they revealed a side of my dad I never knew. A vulnerable, sweet, and somewhat naïve kid who loved his parents and was reaching out to them. I could grasp his feelings, his hopes and dreams, as well as his fears as if he were speaking directly to me. As I continued to read each one in sequence, I saw that kid grow up to be the father I know today.

What a treasure I had found in these letters. I could touch and feel the actual paper and ink that my father had lovingly written to his parents. I had a record, a history in detail of the events of his life at that time. (I'm sure he left out a few details; he

was a college student, and they were his parents.) Although the photos were wonderful to see, they couldn't tell the whole story. The letters conveyed the emotions, feelings, and history behind the pictures.

Through my dad's letters, I was taken back to a time before e-mail, computers, and cell phones, when the postal system was one of the only ways to communicate with loved ones. Phone calls and telegrams, considered expensive luxuries, were kept as brief as possible. My dad's only choice was to write letters; he made that commitment to his parents and in return they wrote back to him. The words flowed as if he were there conversing in person. His handwriting made the words seem more authentic and from the heart. Obviously, his words were treasured, or the letters would not have been saved all these years. I could see, as never before, how the letters kept their deep, personal relationship alive.

These days, people are just too busy to sit down and take the time to handwrite a letter. It takes time and effort, something our fast-paced society doesn't seem to have the patience for. We have so many choices and the temptation to reach for any given time-saving device is great. From e-mail to cell phones, we have opted for convenience, but something is lost. Sadly, it appears that the close, personal connections created by handwritten letters may become a thing of the past and are being further diminished by our busy society's need for faster, more efficient forms of communication.

We seem to be living in an age of time-warp speed that encompasses every portion of our lives. From fast food to fast cars, our obsession is unyielding and there is no time for slowing down. Affectionately known as "snail mail," old-fashioned letters are becoming obsolete and are slowly being eliminated from society by faster, more immediate technologies. Gone are the days when we opened the mailbox with great anticipation in hopes of receiving a long, leisurely letter from someone we care about. Now we approach our mail with either indifference

5

or dread because most of our boxes are full of junk mail or bills. Occasionally greeting cards will arrive and although thoughtful, they are written by corporate writers and poets, composed of generic clichés and humorous anecdotes. A signature is all that is required of us.

Today, picking up a phone is so easy and cheap; we almost take it for granted. A telephone conversation can be a wonderful experience, hearing a loved one's voice over the line, but sometimes we hold back our emotions and often don't convey what we want to say. Expressions such as love, affection, apologies, and condolences are best said through writing, rather than over the phone or even face to face. The act of letter writing forces one to think through thoughts and feelings, plus it gives a permanent record of that time and place. Phone conversations are lost forever.

Some say correspondence is alive and well through the Internet. Admittedly, e-mail has its advantages. It is instantaneous and convenient. With the push of the send button our messages can be read in seconds anywhere in the world. E-mail is truly an amazing and useful tool. It is encouraging friends and family to write to each other more than ever, but are we really "in touch" with our loved ones? Is this form of instant communication bringing us closer, or are we distancing ourselves further from one another?

We chat but the conversation never runs too deep. There seems to be less feeling behind the message. Something is missing. E-mail somehow seems artificial and so casual that the message can become meaningless and so easy that we sometimes forget about the importance of the recipient. A glowing screen can almost act like a mask, concealing our true identities, and disconnecting the bonds between us. The screen does not encourage intimacy or reflection, as we hammer away at our keyboards.

10   The cold, impersonal nature of a computer-generated letter cannot replace the handwritten letter. Many e-mails are quick, choppy, and abbreviated, full of acronyms and errors. Their brevity almost seems hostile and rude. We are reduced to using "emoticons," combinations of keyboard characters that are used to convey moods and emotions. Although clever, a cute sideways smiley face doesn't give us the nuances or freedom we have when we write by hand. We can't reveal our individuality through the typed word like we can with the pen. The ink practically flows through the fingertips to the paper with every slant and every loop. There is a certain warmth and honesty in beautiful penmanship, even in the imperfections. The style can convey emotions, and the personality of the writer comes through. One can hear their voice, feel their presence, even smell their scent. The crispness and folds of the paper and even the postage stamp adds to the allure. Letters are tangible, something one can hold and keep, to read over and over again. Handwritten letters form human connections between us and tell others that we care enough to take the time to write. We are thinking only of that person and no other at that particular time as we carefully construct our letter. This can form very meaningful and special bonds. And once again, unless printed out, e-mails tend to be deleted and lost forever in cyberspace.

Letters live on and give us glimpses of the past the way it truly was. They are extremely valuable to historians. Letters have described most of the world's major events, and have reflected social and cultural trends. They have revealed a more personal side of our famous historical figures. The letters of presidents such as Adams, Truman, and Reagan revealed worried parents, affectionate husbands and wives, and doubting leaders. They became more human in our eyes. The letters of ordinary people are perhaps the most interesting, because they bring us into their world and daily lives as it's really happening. The letters of immigrants leaving home, pioneers heading west, and soldiers off to war communicated across the distances separating them from their families and friends.

Many letters have been lost over the years, but many have been so treasured that they have survived for centuries. In her book *Breath Escaping Envelopes,* Betty Beeby has compiled letters from her ancestors who first settled in Northern Michigan in 1875. She writes:

> Because much of the wealth comes in letter form, it offers a uniquely personal perspective on the past, putting readers inside history—not as it is refracted through memory, but as it is actually happening. The voices on these pages speak in the here-and-now, sharing the unfolding of their lives as events occurred. . . . I see things because my grandmother wrote about them; I have vivid mental pictures, painted in her own words. These are the insights no history book can give and that I wish to share. . . . For readers, the effect is to stumble into an intimate relationship, of which we are an immediate part. (xi–xiii)

Beeby's grandmother had kept hundreds of these letters in the old family barn. They spoke to her. Even the title of her book evokes a human quality to the letters. As if the letters have awoken from a deep sleep, once read again, they have become living and breathing beings. They seem to be alive with a soul and a spirit.

My dad's letters spoke to me, too. I found myself entranced by his letters, full of admiration for this other part of my dad I didn't know. I was transcended to another time and place with his stories of hitchhiking cross-country, how to live reasonably well on a dollar or two a week, and his fear and anxiety writing the dreaded college essay. He shared all this and much more with his parents. Although Dad could probably recall some bits and pieces of these memories, they would be fuzzy at best. The letters filled in the gaps between the photographs and his memory giving me a "vivid mental picture" (Beeby xii). Reading his life as it happened made it come alive.

Letters reveal the rich tapestry of everyday life and provide a legacy we can pass down to future generations. But what kind of letters will we be leaving to our children fifty years from now? A collection of a few hurried, mindless e-mail messages to one another. They are a marvelous convenience and tool but unfortunately, e-mails are usually deleted as soon as they are received. They are read on impersonal, soulless screens that are difficult to curl up with. Handwritten letters can be held and touched, revealing the writer's character and personality with every stroke of the pen, but sadly, letters are few and far between these days. They may become a relic of the past just like the art of penmanship.

My college-aged kids were never taught cursive writing and are much more comfortable in front of a keyboard than behind a pen. They are also more comfortable picking up the phone, but conversations can not be preserved. With all these time-saving devices, one would think we would have more time on our hands than ever. It seems life is too hectic to even notice the disappearance of the handwritten letter. We will be losing a valuable treasure if we allow this to happen. If we could just slow down and take the time, we could reconnect with our loved ones the way I did with my Dad and revive the art of letter writing. Finding those letters has inspired me to write to my loved ones more often. I just hope I can leave that same legacy to my children.

Work Cited

Beeby, Betty. *Breath Escaping Envelopes*. Edited by Mary Frey, Pearl Press, 2000.

Analyzing Argument

1. Often, people make arguments that celebrate "the good ol' days" and fall into a trap of oversimplifying the past as a time of pleasure and positive values. How does Schutza avoid that trap? How is her argument more than a celebration of the "good ol' days"?

2. What connection does the essay make between handwritten letters and a particular value?

3. How does Schutza support her claim that hand-written letters have important advantages over e-mail (paragraphs 8–10)? How important is this claim to her argument? How else might she have supported it?

4. What are the shared values and assumptions between Schutza and Rachel Schofield's essay in this chapter?

5. This essay depends largely on personal testimony. How does Schutza's testimony reveal something important? Could a list of statistics reveal the same thing?

Richard Styles/stockchng.com

23

Philosophy and Humanity

Philosophy and humanity may seem like esoteric topics, meant for and understood by only a small group. But they are as common and important as other topics such as race, environment, or education. Philosophy can be defined as follows:

- the love or pursuit of wisdom;
- the critical analysis of fundamental assumptions or beliefs;
- a set of ideas or beliefs relating to a particular field or activity, or an underlying theory;
- a system of values by which one lives.

These dictionary definitions only scratch the surface of what philosophy can mean. Humanity is an equally rich concept; it can mean

- the human race;
- the condition or quality of being human;
- the quality of being humane.

The writers in this section take on big questions. They make claims related to broad categories and concepts, but the arguments also focus on particular situations or discoveries. While the writers argue points about an entire species (humans), they also stay grounded in specific debates.

Readings about Philosophy and Humanity in Chapters 1–14

"Communication: Its Blocking and Its Facilitation," Carl R. Rogers

"In Defense of Darkness," Holly Wren Spaulding

"Seattle's Rhetoric," Andrew Buchner

"The Pack Rat among Us," Laurie Schutza

"Live Forever," Raymond Kurzweil

The Great Extinction

JUSTIN E. H. SMITH

Justin E. H. Smith is professor of history and philosophy of science at the prestigious University of Paris Diderot. On May 5, 2014, this article was published in the *Chronicle of Higher Education*, a widely read journal for scholars, professors, and academic administrators.

There is a great die-off under way, one that may justly be compared to the disappearance of dinosaurs at the end of the Cretaceous, or the sudden downfall of so many great mammals at the beginning of the Holocene. But how far can such a comparison really take us in assessing the present moment?

The hard data tell us that what is happening to animals right now is part of the same broad historical process that has swept up humans: We are all being homogenized, subjected to uniform standards, domesticated. A curiosity that might help to drive this home: At present, the total biomass of mammals raised for food vastly exceeds the biomass of all mammalian wildlife on the planet (it also exceeds that of the human species itself). This was certainly not the case 10,000 or so years ago, at the dawn of the age of pastoralism.

It is hard to know where exactly, or even inexactly, to place the boundary between prehistory and history. Indeed, some authors argue that the very idea of prehistory is a sort of artificial buffer zone set up to protect properly human society from the vast expanse of mere nature that preceded us. But if we must set up a boundary, I suggest the moment when human beings began to dominate and control other large mammals for their own, human ends.

We tend to think about history as human history. Yet a suitably wide-focused perspective reveals that nothing in the course of human affairs makes complete sense without some account of animal actors. History has, in fact, been a question of human–animal interaction all along. Cherchez la vache is how the anthropologist E. E. Evans-Pritchard argued that the social life of the cattle-herding Nuer of southern Sudan might best be summed up—"look for the cow"—but one could probably, without much stretching, extend that principle to human society in general. The cattle that now outweigh us are a mirror of our political and economic crisis, just as cattle were once a mirror of the sociocosmic harmony that characterized Nuer life.

Most of history, to the extent that it is understood narrowly as a human affair, has consisted in a patchwork of interconnected but still largely autonomous human societies; or at least they were autonomous in their self-conception, even if they were always intricately interconnected by trade, war, and migration. In the 18th century, Immanuel Kant came to understand history precisely as the process whereby European civilization radiates out and progressively engulfs the Arctic, the Americas, and the South Sea Islands—bringing them, that is, into the fold of history.

And however we define history, it is certain at least that these areas were enfolded into something new and unprecedented. When Kant was writing, the Inuit, for example, lived more or less independently, as hunters and foragers, in a mode of life that was directly adapted to and integrated with their environment. Today the Canadian Inuit live under the administration of a Euro-American colonial state, and many depend for their food on transport of mass-produced, processed commodities from the urban, industrial south.

What is often overlooked in the familiar summaries of this process—overlooked, perhaps, for fear of appearing disrespectful by running indigenous peoples and wild animals together—is that it has not been limited to a single species. Animals are swept up in the same frenzy: Either join up with what is increasingly the only game in town, and you will grow fat and homogeneous, and your body will be instrumentalized for economic ends; or die out. Mammalian biodiversity is dropping, while the biomass of cattle is skyrocketing. Cattle are even driving indigenous humans out of their habitats, most notably in the Amazon, either to assimilate into the urbanized proletariat or, likewise, to die off.

We do not need to exaggerate the analogy between human cultures and biological species in order to appreciate the unitary nature of the process that is under way. History has always been the history of humans within their environments, and it is crucial to understand history in this trans-species way in order to place the recent idea of the Anthropocene in proper perspective.

It may seem presumptuous to propose that the principal characteristic of the present period of the Cenozoic era is the presence of human beings. After all, these are divisions in a geological time scale, and the rocks go deep. But all of the epochs and eons, going back to the boundary of the Archean, 2.5 billion years ago, have been named according to their representative life forms, and no life form represents the present better than Homo sapiens.

10 But we couldn't have done it without the animals. We brought the world to its present state, but we did so by putting nonhuman nature to work for us. A crucial part of this has been the exploitation of, and occasional cooperation with, animals, and it is not surprising that, as we appear to be approaching some sort of climactic finish, the animals that remain are principally the ones that have been incorporated into the process in some way or another—the ones that are regulated, conserved, bred, consumed.

There are, however, many losers in this history, many animals that cannot, by reason of their niche or behavior, be incorporated into the Anthropocene. These are the victims of the "sixth extinction" described by Elizabeth Kolbert in her recent book of the same name. The subtitle declares it an "unnatural history," but it makes little sense to view this massive die-off as unnatural: Human history is natural history.

Strictly speaking, the earth does not itself mind being brought into the Anthropocene. There is nothing about the earth that justifies any talk about the temperature it "ought" to maintain, or the size of the polar ice caps it "should" have. The fact that recent climate change is, beyond any reasonable scientific doubt, anthropogenic in nature makes no difference to the earth.

The environmental philosopher and anthropologist Thom Van Dooren writes of "incredible loss" in his penetrating new book, *Flight Ways: Life and Loss at the Edge of Extinction* (Columbia University Press). But a loss to whom? Or to what? Van Dooren gives us intimate, detailed biographies of a handful of imperiled species of birds. We learn, for example, of the American whooping crane (*Grus Americana*), now being taught to discover new migratory routes by conservationists guiding them in ultralight aircraft. And we learn of the Indian vulture (Gyps indicus), whose bloody sanitation work makes it both a fearsome sight for humans (its head is featherless, better to insert it into the innards of carcasses) and a link in the chain of life and death. The crane's prospects are looking better than those of the vulture at present, thanks largely to the differing attitudes and policies of the humans around them. Humans can occasionally help the animals, though even here, as Van Dooren clearly sees, there is a troubling mixture of care and violence. When we guide cranes along new routes, we are making choices about life and death, just as when we slaughter or let an animal die by neglect.

In all of this, again, nature itself is indifferent. The earth does not resent its humans, nor does it have any interest in preserving its polar bears or its rain forests. In fact, many species would do very well in a significantly hotter environment. Snakes like the giant Titanoboa thrived during the late Paleocene, as the tropics approached one of several thermal maxima. Attempts have been made to account for the current state of the earth as the one that is fitting and "healthy." But unless one accepts the Gaia hypothesis, there are no plausible grounds for supposing that the earth is an organism, and thus that it might really be healthy or sick, or that it might have a suitable body temperature or ideal set of charismatic megafauna. We talk about "saving the earth," but what we really want is to save ourselves.

Not that there's anything wrong with that. But 15 we must be clear about the motive for our conservation efforts, if for no other reason than that it will help us to better understand the true character of the misfortune of animal extinction. This improved understanding could, in turn, have significant policy implications. For one thing, more honesty about the fact that we wish to save polar bears because we love them, and not because the earth loves them, could help to reorient conservationist arguments in a direction that skeptics would find more compelling.

Ironically, much conservationist thinking involves an implicitly mythological conception of species diversity that agrees in its essentials with the creation account offered in Genesis. In the scriptural tradition, God looked upon his work and deemed it good, and what ensued was a stable order of fixed, discrete, and well-bounded kinds, with no relations of descent among them. The best metaphor for conceptualizing biodiversity in this view is Noah's ark, where each kind can be neatly separated from the others in its own compartment. The conservationist view generally leaves the creator out of the picture, yet the creatures are still deemed good, intrinsically good, and if they do not remain fixed and unchanging, then we may conclude that something is out of order—or "unnatural," to use Kolbert's term.

Darwinism, properly understood, is the opposite of this mythological outlook. It tells us that no particular arrangement of biodiversity is good in itself, and that no species has any absolute reason to exist. For a given species to be "better" than another is simply for it to have an adaptation that enhances its likelihood of surviving to reproductive age. Are humans better than fish? It is impossible to answer, without specifying whether the contest is to take place on land or under water. Should there be air-breathing animals at all? That depends on whether the planet has a breathable atmosphere. If not, it would be better to live in the ocean and to breathe through one's gills. And so on.

The point here is not to relativize the current ecological crisis, or to call for an approach to mass extinction that simply says, *que cera, cera*. Rather, it is to suggest that conservationism might do well to acknowledge the endurance and the strength of the mythopoetical conception of nature, the one that sees our fellow creatures not only as more or less well adapted, but also as good, truly good. This would not require any overt theology, as it is already implicit in conservationist thinking, and many if not most conservationists have no patience for cosmological arguments for the existence of God. But it would require an abandonment of our piecemeal wisdom about animals and our relations with them, a wisdom thrown together out of sloppy scientism, utilitarian half-measures, and basic ontological mistakes.

We try to convince ourselves that our commitments to animals flow from their neurophysiology alone, from a recognition of their capacities to experience pain, to have episodic memories, or to plan for the future. We blame ourselves for inconsistency when the well-being of an animal with lesser capacities concerns us more than that of one with higher capacities—a pet cat, for example, as opposed to a pig bred for food. In thinking this way, we fail to note that the boundaries of moral community have never in human history been drawn along species lines alone, nor have they been drawn in view of a theory of the complexity of other beings. Rather, moral commitments emerge out of the way creatures, human and nonhuman, enter into meaningful exchange with one another.

At the same time, somehow, a strange, vestigial 20 Platonism coexists with this crude utilitarianism, and attributes a moral status to kinds themselves. There is, to be precise, a peculiar, implicit equivalence in the way we tend to think about killing animals, and about driving animal species to extinction: One animal species is morally equivalent to one human individual. Thus we say that the Steller's sea cow was hunted to extinction, in much the same way we might say that the vicar has succumbed to gout. This switch, as we move from humans to animals, is significant for a number of reasons. It helps to explain why the argument that slaughter, at the end of a happy, free-ranging, species-appropriate life, is acceptable for a lamb but not for a child. It explains why culling zebra herds is "for their own good," while Jonathan Swift's plan for Irish population control is self-evidently satirical.

Errol Fuller's *Lost Animals: Extinction and the Photographic Record* (Princeton University Press) calls to mind the sort of commemorative volume that might follow a singular human disaster, such as September 11, which aims to testify to the unique, irreducible existence of each of the victims. But each of the victims in Fuller's book is not an individual at all but a species. Many of his short biographies of the recently vanished are touching, even revelatory. There is the Yangtze River dolphin (Lipotes vexillifer), whose existence remained unconfirmed until 1917, when the 17-year-old Charles Hoy shot one with his rifle, ate some meat, and took a photo. He contracted a parasitic flatworm in that same river and died, back in the United States, in 1922. Mao's so-called Great Leap Forward placed dams throughout the Yangtze and cut interbreeding populations of dolphins off from one another. The last of them, Qi Qi, died in captivity in 2002. Qi Qi's funeral was broadcast on Chinese national television.

There is the Tasmanian thylacine (Thylacinus cynocephalus), which looks like a dog or wolf but belongs to an ancient marsupial lineage and is far closer to a kangaroo than a canine. The last known thylacine died in captivity in 1936, though it lives on in cryptozoological circles of varying degrees of reputability. The thylacine, previously known as the Tasmanian wolf, had been a great success in the zoos of Europe, and numerous photographs survive showing the creature, behind bars, gaping.

One cannot help reflecting, in reading this profound volume, on the way photography, as a medium of representation of the natural world, both bears witness to the process of destruction and, in a way, emblematizes and perhaps even facilitates this process. As with war photography, the technology that testifies coevolves with, and is set up alongside, the technology that kills. The period of history that has witnessed some of the worst violence, both ecological and military, is also the best documented. We have unprecedented electronic surveillance not just of human settlements but also of all of nature, and yet this surveillance seems to be doing nothing at all to turn back the process of homogenization and reduction of biodiversity. On the contrary, the two developments seem to be of a piece.

And yet one can't help wishing that the photographic record extended much further back still, that there were a way of recovering images of species lost well before the late 19th century. We have cave paintings of woolly rhinoceroses and mammoths, and these are precious, but they allow us to go on imagining these vanished animals as fantastical, as the products of human phantasm, rather than as our fellow beings in every sense but the temporal one. Iconic war photographs, of flaming monks or naked children fleeing napalm, are said to humanize their subjects, and therefore to help turn public opinion against violence. What do photographs of extinct species do? There is no word for it. We cannot say "animalize," since that means something very different, and indeed the fact that it does could very well be a sign of the depth of the problem.

It is for the same reason that our true fellowship, in spite of centuries of spurious theological and scientific arguments to the contrary, cannot be contained within the boundaries of our own species, but extends out to all the creatures with which, or with whom, we enter into meaningful interaction.

Intensive livestock production and other abhorrences suppress the meaning of human-animal relations, deny that there could be such relations at all, and attempt to convince us that we are dealing with a mere commodity. Those practices deprive the animals of their creaturehood and take away the possibility of recognizing fellowship with them. But what we see when we are forced to look— by, say, the activists who bring hidden cameras into the slaughterhouses—are fellow creatures greatly reduced: ghoulish shadows, living ghosts.

These animals are the ones that have been caught up in the system. In some respects, it is psychologically less demanding to recognize the fellow-creature status of the ones that remain outside the system, and that therefore are now threatened with extinction. They are the noble natives, adorned with feathers and shells, while the cattle are the rude and lowly workers that polite society does not wish to see. Still, this very psychology can help us confirm the point that our judgments about where community lies are not determined by species boundaries, despite our modern efforts to have them so. What is lost when the thylacine goes extinct is a history of community and any possibility of future community. And that is a loss to be mourned.

Aristotle wrote more than 2,300 years ago that hunting is "a form of war." He wrote this, appropriately, in a treatise called Politics. This was the Iron Age, and it was already clear to Aristotle that humanity had definitively won this war, at least against our fellow top predators. For the most part, ancient Athenians did not have to live in fear of other carnivores.

Yet now, at the beginning of the Anthropocene, we find that the war continues, in new and vastly more destructive forms. For one thing, we no longer discriminate between friend and foe; we don't hunt only those who hunt us. History proceeds apace, on both sides of the boundary we pretend

to maintain at the limits of our species. Literally and slightly less literally, in both forms of war we've entered the napalm era. We're smoking out the jungle now, and we need as much testimony as possible, from photographs and from lucid witnesses and critics and from every other imaginable source, to not let us forget that our fellow creatures are being massacred.

Analyzing Argument

1. What is Smith's main claim? And what type of claim is it? (Fact, value, or policy?)

2. According to Smith's argument, how are conservationists and creationists similar? What assumption do they share?

3. What is the "mythopoetical conception of nature" and why does Smith argue against it?

4. Where do you sense concessions and/or qualifiers? Explain what positions or claims Smith concedes to or what ideas he qualifies.

5. How does the allusion to Aristotle function in Smith's concluding paragraphs?

Natural Passions

LAURA TANGLEY

Tangley's article was first published in *International Wildlife* (Sept./Oct. 2001), a magazine of the National Wildlife Federation, which was founded in 1936. The federation's mission is to help educate citizens and politicians about people's relationship to the natural world.

As a biologist working for the Amboseli Elephant Research Project in Kenya, Joyce Poole has seen plenty of fascinating behaviors since she began studying these behemoths more than a quarter century ago. Among her favorites are what elephants do at the "greeting ceremonies" she observes when members of the same family or group meet after a separation. According to Poole, up to 50 of the animals rush together loudly, flap their ears wildly and spin in circles, all the while emitting a chorus of rumbles, roars, screams, and trumpets. She's convinced "that greeting elephants feel a deep sense of joy at being reunited with friends and that their rumbles and roars express something like: 'Wow! It's simply fantastic to be with you again.'"

Primatologist Jane Goodall also has seen her share of joyful behavior among chimpanzees living in Tanzania's Gombe National Park. But she was perhaps most touched by the sorrow she witnessed once after a 50-year-old matriarch of the troop she was studying died. Throughout the day following the old female's death, her eight-year-old son sat vigil by his mother's lifeless body, occasionally taking her hand and whimpering. Over the next few weeks, he grew increasingly listless, refused food and finally withdrew from the troop. Three and a half weeks after his mother's death, the formerly healthy young chimp also was dead. "He died of grief," concludes Goodall.

Field biologists such as Poole and Goodall, who've each spent decades studying the behavior of animals in their natural habitats, do not doubt that elephants, chimpanzees, and other creatures feel intense, humanlike emotions—from happiness, sadness, and anger to perhaps even love and embarrassment. But among many other scientists, the idea that animals feel emotion has long been, and remains, controversial. Their skepticism is driven in part by professional aversion to anthropomorphism, the very nonscientific tendency to attribute human qualities to nonhuman animals. Some researchers also point out that it is impossible to prove animals have emotions through standard scientific methods—repeatable observations that can be manipulated in experiments—leading them to conclude that such feelings therefore cannot exist.

These days, however, amid mounting evidence to the contrary, "the tide is turning radically and rapidly," says Marc Bekoff, a biologist at the University of Colorado-Boulder. Research by Bekoff and others—in fields ranging from ethology to neurobiology—is beginning to provide scientific support for the notion that animals feel a wide range of emotions. These findings, they believe, have profound implications for how humans and other species will interact in the future.

Even scientists who are most opposed to the idea of animal passion acknowledge that many creatures experience "primary emotions"—feelings such as aggression and fear that are instinctive and require no conscious thought. Essential to escaping predators and other dangers, fear, in particular—along with predictable freeze, flight or fight responses—seems to be hardwired. A laboratory rat that has never encountered a cat, for example, will still freeze if it is exposed to the smell of this predator.

But beyond such instinctive behavior, "secondary emotions" such as happiness and sadness have been flatly denied by most scientists for the past several hundred years, with one notable exception: In *The Expression of the Emotions in Man and Animals*, published in 1872, Charles Darwin argued that there is continuity between the emotional lives of humans and other animals, attributing differences to degree rather than kind. "The lower animals, like man, manifestly feel pleasure and pain, happiness and misery," he wrote. But in contrast to his theory of evolution by natural selection, Darwin's ideas about animal emotions did not catch on among mainstream biologists.

There's no question that emotions are difficult to study. "I can't prove that another human being is feeling happy or sad," says Bekoff, "but I can deduce how they're feeling through body language and facial expression." As a biologist who has conducted field studies of coyotes, foxes, and other canids for the past 30 years, Bekoff also believes he can tell what these animals are feeling by looking for clues such as changes in posture, facial expression, pupil size, and vocalization. Subsequent behavior—a fight following the appearance of aggression, for instance—can confirm these hunches.

Growing acceptability of such field observations, or anecdotes, has been key to making today's case for animal emotions. Long maligned among most researchers, the anecdote "must be revalued and reinstated into science under its old and honored descriptor: the case study," writes Harvard University's Stephen Jay Gould in the forward to a recent book, *The Smile of a Dolphin*. Edited by Bekoff, the book features essays from more than 50 scientists who have spent their careers watching animals. As Bekoff points out to critics of this case-study approach, "the plural of anecdote is data."

Take pleasure. Anyone who's ever held a purring cat, or been knocked down by a leaping, barking, tail-wagging dog, knows that animals often appear to be happy. Beastly joy seems particularly apparent when animals play with one another. According to Bekoff, virtually all young mammals as well as some birds play, as do the adults of many species, including, of course, humans.

10   Dolphins, for example, are often seen chasing each other through the water like frolicsome puppies or riding the wakes of boats like surfers.

According to Goodall, young chimpanzees "chase, somersault, and pirouette around one another with the abandon of children." In Colorado, Bekoff once saw an elk race back and forth across a patch of snow (even though plenty of bare ground was available), leaping and twisting its body on each pass. Recent research suggests that play helps young animals develop skills they need in adulthood. But they're also having fun, says Bekoff. "Animals at play are symbols of the unfettered joy of life."

So, too, can be creatures that seem to be in love. The most widespread displays of affection are between parents and offspring. But some researchers also have reported what looks like romantic love. Bernd Wursig, a Texas A&M University biologist, was studying right whales off the coast of Argentina when he saw a female choose just one of many suitors pursuing her (in contrast to "normal" behavior marked by promiscuity). After mating, the two whales lingered side-by-side, stroking each other with their flippers, then rolled together in what looked like an embrace. Finally the cetaceans departed, yet remained touching as they swam away slowly, diving and surfacing in unison.

As a scientist, Wursig believes his observation should be considered no more than "an alternative mating strategy." But he still entertains the notion that the animals acted as they did "because they were the 'right' right whales for each other."

Love's flipside, heartbreak, also is reported by researchers, particularly when animals lose a mate, parent, offspring, or close companion. A female sea lion, for instance, wails forlornly if she sees a killer whale eating her pup. Geese, which mate for life, hang down their heads and droop their bodies dejectedly following the death of a partner. And like the chimp Goodall observed in Gombe, creatures ranging from great apes and monkeys to bears, moose, and antelope stand vigil beside the bodies of deceased family members, sometimes succumbing to withdrawal, sickness, and death themselves.

Elephants, well-known to biologists like Poole for their rambunctious displays of pleasure, take grief to an extreme as well. She and other field researchers have recorded many instances of the animals standing quietly beside the body of a dead elephant, occasionally reaching out and touching it with their trunks. Elephants also carry the tusks and bones of their departed kin great distances and may even try to cover them with dirt or leaves. After nearly three decades studying the animals, Poole says that elephants' behavior toward the dead "leaves me with little doubt that they experience deep emotions and have some understanding of death."

15   There is "hard" scientific evidence for animal emotions as well. Neuroscientists who study the biology of emotions, a discipline still in its infancy, have discovered key similarities between the brains of humans and other animals. In all species studied so far, including our own, emotions seem to arise from long-evolved parts of the brain—particularly the amygdala, an almond-shaped structure in the brain's center. Working with rats, they have found that stimulating one part of the amygdala invariably induces a state of intense fear. Rats with damaged amygdalae exhibit neither normal behavioral responses to danger (such as freezing or running) nor the physiological changes associated with fear (such as higher heart rate and blood pressure).

Brain imaging studies show that when humans experience fear, their amygdalae, too, become activated. And like the rats, people who have suffered damage to this part of the brain are unable to be afraid, even when circumstances warrant it. New York University neuroscientist Joseph LeDoux, whose lab conducted many of the rat experiments, concludes that the amygdalae of humans and rats are "basically wired the same way."

Research on brain chemistry also bolsters the case for animal feelings. Stephen Siviy, a behavioral neuroscientist at Gettysburg College in Pennsylvania, has found that when rats play with each other, their brains secrete large amounts of dopamine, a chemical that is associated with pleasure and excitement in humans. In one experiment, he placed pairs of rats in distinctive Plexiglas chambers and allowed them to play. A week later, Siviy realized that he could place one rat by itself in a chamber and, anticipating play, the animal "becomes very active, vocalizing, and pacing back and forth with excitement." But if he gave the same animal a drug that blocks dopamine, all such activity ceased. Jaak Panksepp, a neuroscientist at Bowling Green State University in Ohio, discovered that rats also produce opiates when they play, chemicals that, like dopamine, are involved in the experience of pleasure in people.

Another chemical, the hormone oxytocin, is associated with both sexual activity and maternal bonding in humans. Now it seems that the same hormone governs attachment among some animals. To investigate oxytocin's role in bonding between mates, University of Maryland neuroscientist C. Sue Carter studied a mouselike rodent called the prairie vole, one of the few mammal species known to be monogamous. Carter discovered that female voles, which ordinarily spend a day selecting a mate, will choose one within an hour (often the first male she sees) if she's just received an injection of oxytocin. But females given a drug that blocks the hormone never pick a mate no matter how much time they have. According to Carter, oxytocin triggers behavior in voles that looks much like people who are "falling in love."

Looks can be deceiving, though. Even the most ardent believers in animal passion warn that humans can easily misinterpret what they're seeing. The shape of a dolphin's mouth, for example, leads to the conclusion that the animal is smiling or laughing, even when it is afraid or in distress. Chimpanzees have a facial expression signaling fear that also is misunderstood as smiling. "It's both presumptuous and dangerous to blindly assume that animal emotions are the same as ours," says Bekoff.

20   Such caveats help fuel the arguments of skeptics. "A whale may behave as if it's in love, but you cannot prove what, if anything, it is feeling," says LeDoux, author of *The Emotional Brain*. LeDoux believes the

question of feelings ultimately boils down to whether or not animals are self-conscious. And though they "may have snapshots of self-awareness," he says, "the movie we call consciousness is not there." University of Wisconsin neuroscientist Richard Davidson agrees that very few species (higher primates and, most recently, dolphins) have demonstrated self-consciousness so far. Yet he suspects that at least some other animals "may have the antecedents of feelings."

Or maybe more. Biologists such as Bekoff say their most convincing argument comes from the theory of evolution itself. Citing remarkable similarities between the brain anatomy and chemistry of humans and other animals, Siviy asks: "How can you believe that feelings suddenly appeared, out of the blue, in human beings?" Goodall adds that neuroscientists who study animals to learn about the human brain, then deny that those animals have emotions, are "illogical."

But if in fact there is continuity between the emotional lives of humans and other animals, where does one draw the line? Even Bekoff says, "We're not going to talk about jealous sponges and embarrassed mosquitoes."

Yet happy iguanas are another matter. In experiments with these tropical reptiles, Michel Cabanac, a physiologist at Laval University in Quebec, found that when they're in a comfy, warm spot—which the animals prefer over areas that have food but are cooler—they show physiological changes that are associated with pleasure in mammals. Frogs and fish, on the other hand, do not. Cabanac proposes that emotions evolved somewhere between amphibians and the first reptiles.

In the end, though, what difference does it make if an iguana is happy but a frog is not? Many scientists maintain that resolving the debate over animal emotions is much more than an intellectual exercise. If animals do experience a wide range of humanlike feelings, they say, it has implications for how they are treated by our own species. Bekoff, for one, would like to see a world where people ate no meat or animal products, and circuses, zoos, and marine parks were shut down. But he's also realistic, hopeful that the new case for animal emotions will at least spur changes in regulations governing the use of animals everywhere from zoos and biomedical labs to farms, pet stores, and animal shelters.

Bekoff and his colleagues also hope that the debate over animal emotions and consciousness will soon shift—from whether nonhuman species have them to how they experience them. Sitting outside his Boulder home one sunny afternoon, Bekoff turned to his big, friendly dog, Jethro. "I know that Jethro's consciousness is not the same as mine," he acknowledged. "But there's no question that he has dog consciousness." 25

Analyzing Argument

1. What situation does Tangley's essay explore? What does she define?

2. Why does Tangley think it is important to define this topic correctly?

3. Write out Tangley's line of reasoning. In other words, describe how she develops a series of premises that supports her main claim.

4. How does Tangley deal with viewpoints different from her own? What points does she refute (counterargue) or acknowledge (concede)?

5. Identify three support strategies (examples, allusions, and so on) in the essay and describe how each supports Tangley's main claim.

The Cell That Makes Us Human

HELEN PHILLIPS

For decades, science has discovered more and more genetic connections between humans and other animals. But a few researchers recently have discovered a particular neuron unique to the human species and certain primates. In this report, first published in *New Scientist* in 2004, Helen Phillips describes researchers' assumptions about this neuron—and points to the bigger arguments that it might create.

John Allman spends a lot of time counting brain cells. He often sets out from his home turf at the California Institute of Technology in Pasadena to visit pathology labs, museums, and anthropology departments around the world on the lookout for interesting brain tissue, so he can count some more. Sometimes he'll be after samples from gorillas or chimps, at other times a collection from a psychiatric hospital or from a stillborn infant. Allman practices the old-fashioned discipline of histology, and has a rare kind of patience to stare down his microscope for hours on end, often documenting tens of thousands of cells in any one brain. "Let's say it's absorbing," he admits.

In this age of brain scanners, genetic profiling, and bioinformatics, Allman's absorption sounds pretty low-tech, and frankly, quite dull. What possible scientific interest could there be in counting brain cells?

His answer is surprising. He thinks he has found an important key to our humanity—an explanation for our ability to love, empathize, feel guilt or embarrassment, to understand deception and cooperation. While the definition of what makes us human may include language, our large brains and intelligence, or the ability to use tools and fire, these complex social emotions set us apart from other animals too. They are judgments made not by reasoning or logic but by a type of rapid intuition which allows us to function in the most complex social environment faced by any animal. And this social intuition is special, Allman says, because, of all the traits that make us human, only these quick-fire signals seem to be carried by a recently evolved type of brain cell, unique to higher primates.

The cells that interest Allman are known as spindle cells. They were first noted by anatomists more than 100 years ago, but until recently no one had paid them much attention. Then in the late 1990s, graduate student Esther Nimchinsky, working with Patrick Hof, an expert on neurodegeneration at Mount Sinai Medical Center in New York, took an interest. She was mapping a region of the brain called the cingulate cortex—an evolutionarily ancient structure common to all mammals, which lies beneath the midline of the cerebral hemispheres. There she spotted a group of brain cells that were strikingly large, with unusually long spindle-shaped bodies. She and Hof found that the cells appeared only in the front, or anterior, part of the cingulate cortex, the ACC. While normal brains held very few of them, patients who had died of Alzheimer's disease had even fewer—only around a quarter of the usual number. With their unusual size and shape, and appearing as they often did in small clusters, these cells looked as though they might be doing something special, Nimchinsky recalls.

She subsequently found spindle cells in the same area of the brains of chimpanzees and gorillas, though not in macaque monkeys. She and Hof decided to contact Allman, an expert in primate brain evolution and anatomy. He helped them gather more brain tissue and make a huge survey of the cells in more than 50 different species—enough to be sure that the cells appeared in orangutans but not gibbons, as well as in all the African apes: humans, gorillas, chimpanzees, and bonobos. But monkeys and other primates lacked the cells, as did non-primate mammals.

5

In other words, only humans and our very closest relatives seem to share spindle cells. The numbers were interesting, too. Orangs had just a few, humans tens of thousands. Gorillas, chimps and bonobos fell in between—the numbers seeming to reflect the animals' distance from us on the evolutionary tree.

Nimchinsky moved on, but Allman was too intrigued to let the work drop. He noticed that a handful of old anatomy studies mentioned another brain area, the orbitofrontal cortex, behind the orbits of the eyes, and along with colleagues Atiya Hakeem and Nicole Tetreault he started looking there. Within the area he found that a region named the frontoinsular, or FI, cortex was bursting with spindle cells, this time only in humans and other African apes. And that was it—the cells don't occur anywhere else. So what are these unique cells doing in just two distinct parts of the brains of only the most developed primates?

According to Christof Koch, a neuroscientist from Caltech with a particular interest in the neural basis of consciousness, there are just a few big differences that set the minds of humans apart from those of mice or monkeys: Humans can talk and introspect, and they have high levels of self-awareness. "But we are hard-pressed to tell the difference in the brain tissue," he says. This is what makes the spindle cells interesting. "As far as we know they are the only cell that is unique to humanoids."

Allman agrees that spindle cells might be doing something special, but what? When he began to explore what was known about these two anatomical regions and what was showing up in brain imaging studies, he realized that there might be a common theme. The anterior cingulate region has many functions: guiding attention, sensing pain and errors, and tapping into the control systems for breathing, heart rate, and other internal organs. But in all these, it acts as a hub between thought, emotion, and the body's response to what the brain is feeling.

Area FI also seems to have a role in emotional responses—specifically, our reactions to others. It is active when a mother hears an infant cry or when we sense the pain felt by a loved one. Sean Spence from the University of Sheffield in the U.K. found the same region lit up in brain scans when people were being deceived. And Andreas Bartels and Semir Zeki from University College London showed that FI as well as ACC were active when people looked at a picture of a person they loved. Tania Singer from University College London has published a study showing that when someone was judged to be a fair player, the brain response to that person's face included activity within FI. "All these responses have something in common—they all represent value judgments within a social context," Allman says. They reflect how people see you and how you respond to that. "I think [spindle] cells are the home of the complex social emotions."

But there are other brain regions, in the prefrontal cortex, which become active in some social situations yet contain no spindle cells. Can he really say that these cells have the monopoly on social emotions? For example, psychologist Josh Greene from Princeton University showed that the frontal polar region, near FI, but completely devoid of these cells, was active when people made ethically charged decisions, such as judging whether to save someone's life but endangering others, or when punishing those who did not comply with rules. This might be seen as a strong argument against a vital role for spindle cells in complex social emotions.

But Allman points out that the sorts of social situations that trigger neural activation outside FI and ACC tend to be more deliberate: They take the past and future into account, or involve complex calculations. He suggests that our brains have two separate systems. One is more deliberating, thinking about issues of fairness, punishment, moral judgments, and the like. The second, faster, system mediated by spindle cells controls more intuitive behavior during social interactions. If you love

10

someone, you know instantly how to react to them. You don't have to think. This is where spindle cells are important, Allman believes. "The main thing [spindle cells] do is to adjust your behavior in a rapid real-time interaction in a complex social environment," he says.

It certainly looks as though spindle cells are built for speed. Their most striking feature is that they are huge. The body is up to 0.1 millimetres [sic] long, and four times the volume of the surrounding cells. And they have a very wide and long axon and dendrites—the branching extensions that act as the wiring in the brain. "Velocity increases as axon size increases," Koch says, "so we can probably say that the output zips along at high speed."

Such thinking rings true to primatologist Louise Barrett from the University of Liverpool in the U.K. "What is unique about humans is the speed at which we run," she says. Speed is vital for juggling more complex social information of the type that we deal with, she says. Antonio Damasio of the University of Iowa, the author of three books about emotions, agrees that relating spindle cells to emotions is "entirely reasonable." Clearly the cells don't work in isolation, he points out. But there is no doubt that the areas where spindle cells are found are important for social emotions and most other emotions. "However, the interpretation must be regarded as speculative, for the time being," he adds.

15   One reason this sounds an incredible claim is that it seems a big job for a relatively small number of cells. At most there are just over 100,000 spindle cells in our brains, a tiny fraction of the billions of brain cells. "That doesn't sound like a lot of neurons to carry this freight, to be such an important player in social cognition," says Roger Bingham, who works on the evolution of the mind at the University of California at San Diego. But it's not unheard of, he points out. Signals such as moods, reward, and pleasure are also carried by a small number of cells that have a widespread influence all over the brain.

The anatomy backs the idea that a few cells can be very influential. The cortex of the brain is built up of neat layers of cells running parallel to the brain's undulating surface. Each layer has a specific role: One takes in information fed from our senses; another sends feedback; another relays information to the next brain region in the circuit. Spindle cells are always in layer 5, the layer that sends the final signal, the result of all the calculations and activity in a particular region, onto other brain regions. This means that they carry the weight of all the important activity of the region. Allman suggests the signal they convey to other parts of the brain may be very simple: something like "I feel good about this" or "I don't feel good about this." This is an important component of social intuition, he says, and it may also extend to non-social situations as a feeling of luck or a hunch. "It is so simple that I think it is entirely reasonable that it could be performed by about 100,000 neurons," he says.

Although Allman has not been able to measure any of the electrical properties of spindle cells, he has been able to study some of their chemical properties. He and his colleague Karli Watson found receptors on the cells for the neurotransmitters serotonin, dopamine, and vasopressin. These transmitters have known links with behaviors such as reward value, bonding, love, and mood, which reinforces the brain imaging findings.

A decade ago, for example, Thomas Insel, director of the U.S. National Institute of Mental Health in Bethesda, Maryland, discovered that vasopressin and a related hormone, oxytocin, were vital for the formation of pair bonding in voles. Both hormones are released during mating. Blocking their activity prevents bonding in animals that have mated, and giving these hormones encourages unmated animals to bond. "The relevant circuits have either oxytocin or vasopressin receptors," he says. "It appears that dopamine pathways in the brain are specifically involved."

Insel admits that he has wondered whether looking for vasopressin receptors in the human brain might tell us which circuits are important for human social bonding too. We often attribute love and bonding to our heart, but maybe our feelings for loved ones are actually carried by the spindle cells. "I think this is a fascinating hypothesis, but one that will be difficult to prove or disprove," he says.

20   One way to test the idea that spindle cells are vital for quick-fire social emotions would be to look at brains that you would not expect to have such social skills, and see what sort of cell populations they have. For example, people with autism are often extremely capable in predictable environments where rules, logic, and calculations work, but in a complex, ever-changing social setting they often fail to behave in appropriate ways. So are spindle cells found in autistic people's brains?

It is rather early to say, according to Allman. But he thinks that during the development of autistic brains the spindle neurons may fail to migrate to their normal positions. Hof also has some intriguing results suggesting that the spindle cells in schizophrenic brains appear abnormal too—though here other cell types may also be affected. And then there is the early discovery that spindle cells are particularly vulnerable to neurodegeneration in Alzheimer's disease. Humans are the only primates that suffer such age-related neurodegenerative illnesses, he points out. Exactly why spindle cells are vulnerable will be an important question in understanding and treating these devastating diseases.

Allman explains it at an evolutionary level: "Because this class of neurons has recently evolved, natural selection has had just a short time to work on the circuits that they are involved in and therefore they may be more vulnerable to dysfunction," he says. But Hof is also trying to understand the protein chemistry and unique structures that make the cells vulnerable. Meanwhile, Allman is busy seeking tissue from brains with all kinds of neuro-psychiatric disorders. He is considering a number of disorders, he says, including obsessive-compulsive disorder and anorexia, which he thinks have all the hallmarks of an overactive spindle system.

As well as helping us understand brain dysfunction, research into spindle cells also offers an intriguing insight into the evolution of the human mind. Allman suspects that spindle cells have been around for some 10 million years, most likely appearing in the common ancestor of African apes and orangutans. If he is correct, and they are the home of complex social emotions, then some of the mental traits we consider to be most distinctly human actually have deep origins.

This makes perfect sense to Barrett and her colleague Robin Dunbar, who have identified big differences between the social structures of great apes and monkeys. They believe that the superior abilities of apes in general cognitive tasks and in social settings have their origins in their so-called fission-fusion societies, where animals live as part of a social group, but one that is not together all of the time.

"Great apes have a much more dispersed social 25 system," Barrett says. They may spend time on their own, but they also know all the other individuals around. "When in a dispersed system, you have to keep in mind the animals that are not there, and keep track of them through time," she says. The increased complexity in what they call the "social environment" may have driven the evolution of bigger brains and some of the complex skills we think of as uniquely human.

Bingham agrees. Evolutionary psychologists have concentrated their efforts to understand human nature on considerations of the social pressures on the minds of our ancestors, he says. But the origins of human characteristics such as guilt, remorse, love, and empathy began much earlier than we might think. Brains evolved to deal with an uncertain environment, he says, and for apes, problems of the environment are largely social cognition problems: trying to work out what the other player is thinking, believing, and how they will act.

"You can see how resentment, a sense of fair play, righteous anger, and other complex social emotions come into our everyday lives," Bingham says. "We come by all these sentiments and responses over evolutionary time. Finally we are actually getting to look inside the black box to see where it happens."

Analyzing Argument

1. Consider the following claim: "Brains evolved to deal with an uncertain environment." Why might people reject this claim? What assumptions (about human behavior, the human brain, one's environment) oppose the claim?

2. Phillips says that if spindle cells are the "home of complex social emotions, then some of the mental traits we consider to be most distinctly human actually have deep origins." What does she mean by "deep origins"?

3. What basic assumptions do the researchers in this article share with those in Tangley's article (pp. 535–538)?

The Mystery of the Missing Links

MARY WAKEFIELD

"The Mystery of the Missing Links" was published October 25, 2003, in the *Spectator,* a British magazine.

A few weeks ago I was talking to a friend, a man who has more postgraduate degrees than I have GCSEs. The subject of Darwinism came up. "Actually," he said, raising his eyebrows, "I don't believe in evolution."

I reacted with incredulity: "Don't be so bloody daft."

"I'm not," he said. "Many scientists admit that the theory of evolution is in trouble these days. There are too many things it can't explain."

"Like what?"

5 "The gap in the fossil record."

"Oh, that old chestnut!" My desire to scorn was impeded only by a gap in my knowledge more glaring than that in the fossil record itself.

Last Saturday at breakfast with my flatmates, there was a pause in conversation. "Hands up anyone who has doubts about Darwinism," I said. To my surprise all three—a teacher, a music agent, and a playwright—slowly raised their arms. One had read a book about the inadequacies of Darwin— Michael Denton's *Evolution: A Theory in Crisis;* another, a Christian, thought that Genesis was still the best explanation for the universe. The playwright blamed the doctrine of survival of the fittest for "capitalist misery and the oppression of the people." Nearly 150 years after the publication of Charles Darwin's *Origin of Species,* a taboo seems to be lifting.

Until recently, to question Darwinism was to admit to being either a religious nut or just plain thick. "Darwin's theory is no longer a theory but a fact," said Julian Huxley in 1959. For most of the late 20th century Darwinism has seemed indubitable, even to those who have as little real understanding of the theory as they do of setting the video-timer. I remember a recent conversation with my mother: "Do you believe in evolution, Mum?" "Of course I do, darling. If you use your thumbs a lot, you will have children with big thumbs. If they use their thumbs a lot, and so do their children, then eventually there will be a new sort of person with big thumbs."

The whole point of natural selection is that it denies that acquired characteristics can be inherited. According to modern Darwinism, new species are created by a purposeless, random process of genetic mutation. If keen Darwinians such as my mother can get it wrong, it is perhaps not surprising that the theory is under attack.

10 The current confusion is the result of a decade of campaigning by a group of Christian academics who work for a think-tank called the Discovery Institute in Seattle. Their guiding principle—which they call Intelligent Design theory or ID—is a sophisticated version of St Thomas Aquinas's *Argument from Design.*

Over the last few years they have had a staggering impact. Just a few weeks ago, they persuaded an American publisher of biology textbooks to add a paragraph encouraging students to analyse theories other than Darwinism. Over the past two years they have convinced the boards of education in Ohio, Michigan, West Virginia, and Georgia to teach children about Intelligent Design. Indiana and Texas are keen to follow suit. They sponsor debates, set up research fellowships, publish books, distribute flyers and badges, and conduct polls, the latest of which shows that 71 percent of adult Americans think that the evidence against Darwin should be taught in schools.

Unlike the swivel-eyed creationists, ID supporters are very keen on scientific evidence. They accept

Mary Wakefield, "The Mystery of the Missing Links" from *The Spectator* (October 24, 2004). Reprinted with the permission of *The Spectator*, www.spectator.co.uk.

that the earth was not created in six days, and is billions of years old. They also concede Darwin's theory of microevolution: that species may, over time, adapt to suit their environments. What Intelligent Design advocates deny is macroevolution: the idea that all life emerged from some common ancestor slowly wriggling around in primordial soup. If you study the biological world with an open mind, they say, you will see more evidence that each separate species was created by an Intelligent Designer. The most prominent members of the ID movement are Michael Behe, the biochemist, and Phillip E. Johnson, professor of law at the University of California. They share a belief that it is impossible for small, incremental changes to have created the amazing diversity of life. There is no way that every organism could have been created by blind chance, they say. The "fine-tuning" of the universe indicates a creator.

Behe attacks Darwinism in his 1996 book, *Darwin's Black Box: The Biochemical Challenge to Evolution.* If you look inside cells, Behe says, you see that they are like wonderfully intricate little machines. Each part is so precisely engineered that if you were to remove or alter a single part, the whole thing would grind to a halt. The cell has irreducible complexity; we cannot conceive of it functioning in a less developed state. How then, asks Behe, could a cell have developed through a series of random adaptations?

Then there is the arsenal of arguments about the fossil record, of which the most forceful is that evolutionists have not found the fossils of any transitional species—half reptile and half bird, for instance. Similarly, there are no rich fossil deposits before the Cambrian era about 550 million years ago. If Darwin was right, what happened to the fossils of all their evolutionary predecessors?

15 Phillip E. Johnson, author of *Darwin on Trial,* hopes that these arguments will serve as a "wedge," opening up science teaching to discussions about God. Evolution is unscientific, he says, because it is not testable or falsifiable; it makes claims about events (such as the very beginning of life on earth) that can never be recreated. "In good time new theories will emerge and science will change," he writes. "Maybe there will be a new theory of evolution, but it is also possible that the basic concept will collapse and science will acknowledge that those elusive common ancestors of the major biological groups never existed."

If Johnson is right, then God, or a designer, deposited each new species on the planet, fully formed and marked "made in heaven." This is not a very modern-sounding idea, but one whose supporters write articles in respectable magazines and use phrases such as "Cambrian explosion" and "irreducible complexity." Few of us then (including, I suspect, the boards that approve American biology textbooks) would be confident enough to question it. Especially intimidating for scientific ignoramuses is the Discovery Institute's list of 100 scientists, including Nobel prize nominees, who doubt that random mutation and natural selection can account for the complexity of life.

Professor Richard Dawkins sent me his rather different opinion of the ID movement: "Imagine," he wrote, "that there is a well-organised and well-financed group of nutters, implacably convinced that the Roman Empire never existed. Hadrian's Wall, Verulamium, Pompeii—Rome itself—are all planted fakes. The Latin language, for all its rich literature and its Romance language grandchildren, is a Victorian fabrication. The Rome deniers are, no doubt, harmless wingnuts, more harmless than the Holocaust deniers whom they resemble. Smile and be tolerant, just as we smile at the Flat Earth Society. But your tolerance might wear thin if you happen to be a lifelong scholar and teacher of Roman history, language, or literature. You suddenly find yourself obliged to interrupt your magnum opus on the *Odes* of Horace in order to devote time and effort to rebutting a well-financed propaganda campaign claiming that the entire classical world that you love never existed."

So are all Intelligent Design supporters fantasists and idiots, just wasting the time of proper scientists and deluding the general public? If Dawkins is to be believed, the neo-Darwinists have come up with satisfactory answers to all the conundrums posed by ID proponents.

In response to Michael Behe, the Darwinists point out that although an organism may look essential and irreducible, many of its component parts can serve multiple functions. For instance, the blood-clotting mechanism that Behe cites as an example of an irreducibly complex system seems, on close inspection, to involve the modification of proteins that were originally used in digestion.

20 Matt Ridley, the science writer, kindly explained the lack of fossils before the Cambrian explosion: "Easy. There were no hard body parts before then. Why? Probably because there were few mobile predators, and so few jaws and few eyes. There are in fact lots of Precambrian fossils, but they are mostly microbial fossils, which are microscopic and boring."

Likewise, palaeontologists say that they do know of some examples of fossils intermediate in form between the various taxonomic groups. The half-dinosaur, half-bird archaeopteryx, for instance, which combines feathers and skeletal structures peculiar to birds with features of dinosaurs.

"Huh," say the Intelligent Designers, who do not accept poor old archaeopteryx as a transitory species at all. For them, he is just an extinct sort of bird that happened to look a bit like a reptile.

It would be fair to say that the ID lobby has done us a favour in drawing attention to some serious problems, and perhaps breaking the stranglehold of atheistic neo-Darwinism; but their credibility is damaged by the fact that scientists are finding new evidence every day to support the theory of macro-evolution. There is also something a little unnerving about the way in which the ID movement is funded. Most of the Discovery Institute's $4 million annual budget comes from evangelical Christian organisations. One important donor is the Ahmanson family, who have a long-standing affiliation to Christian Reconstructionism, an extreme faction of the religious Right that wants to replace American democracy with a fundamentalist theocracy.

There is a more metaphysical problem for Intelligent Design. If we accept a lack of scientific evidence as proof of a creator's existence, then surely we must regard every subsequent relevant scientific discovery, each new Precambrian fossil, as an argument against the existence of God.

25 The debate has anyway been confused by the vitriol each side pours on the other. Phillip Johnson calls Dawkins a "blusterer" who has been "highly honoured by scientific establishments for promoting materialism in the name of science." Dawkins retorts that religion "is a kind of organised misconception. It is millions of people being systematically educated in error, told falsehoods by people who command respect."

Perhaps the answer is that the whole battle could have been avoided if Darwinism had not been put forward as proof of the non-existence of God. As Kenneth Miller, a Darwinian scientist and a Christian, says in his book *Finding Darwin's God,* "Evolution may explain the existence of our most basic biological drives and desires but that does not tell us that it is always proper to act on them. . . . Those who ask from science a final argument, an ultimate proof, an unassailable position from which the issue of God may be decided will always be disappointed. As a scientist I claim no new proofs, no revolutionary data, no stunning insight into nature that can tip the balance in one direction or another. But I do claim that to a believer, even in the most traditional sense, evolutionary biology is not at all the obstacle we often believe it to be. In many respects evolution is the key to understanding our relationship with God."

St. Basil, the 4th-century Archbishop of Caesarea in Cappadocia, said much the same thing: "Why do the waters give birth also to birds?" he asked, writing about Genesis. "Because there is, so to say, a family link between the creatures that fly and those that swim. In the same way that fish cut the waters, using their fins to carry them forward, so we see the birds float in the air by the help of their wings." If an Archbishop living 1,400 years before Darwin can reconcile God with evolution, then perhaps Dawkins and the ID lobby should be persuaded to do so as well.

Analyzing Argument

1. What is the argument's main claim and support?

2. What support strategies (forms of evidence, examples, or appeals) are most important to the development of Wakefield's argument? Point out specific passages in your response.

3. How do authorities help develop the argument?

4. Why does Wakefield want to redefine the debate? Why might someone object to her way of presenting the debate?

The Comfort of Silence

WILLIAM GRAHAM

William Graham, a medical science major at Miami University, developed this essay for a first-semester English course. The assignment asked students to develop a public argument. While students could choose their own topics, they were asked to "show us a part of the topic that we do not usually consider so that we not only accept your position but also re-think the very nature of the topic itself."

> **"You talk when you cease to be at peace with your thoughts; And when you can no longer dwell in the solitude of your heart you live in your lips, and sound is a diversion and a pastime. And in much of your talking, thinking is half murdered."**
> **— Kahlil Gibran, *The Prophet***

Silence. That's all we heard as we sat on the stone wall. The three of us overlooked the bay, enveloped in darkness. The moving date seemed so far away at one time, but it came quickly upon us. So there we sat, one day away from our friend's move across the country. I wanted to bring up the good times we had, perhaps throw in an inside joke for all of us to enjoy. However, when I opened my mouth to speak, I was quickly quieted. It irritated and puzzled me. The silence felt unnatural as if after a year, we couldn't muster what to say. But there we sat listening to the rhythm of the waves crashing on the shore. And it became comforting. It seemed odd to sit there in silence having so much to say but I'm glad I did. Whatever wasn't said was already known and it allowed all of us a chance to review our friendship without having to explicitly state it.[1]

Silence is something our culture undervalues. It's not necessarily our fault. As humans, we are attracted to sound to identify possible danger. It's evolutionary. It's in our genes. Sound is something that is, by our nature, hard to ignore.

Imagine the sounds of a typical day walking around. For myself, a college student, cars, buses, and chatter fill the streets of the campus. The bells of the tower chime the melody of a song I can never seem to grasp. People all around are talking to their friends face-to-face or via phone. Add this to the sound of nature as the animals scurry around and the wind bustles the trees. The amount of sound we have added to our environment is unsettling to think about.

Now before I come off as completely against sound, I am not arguing for a life of solace and separation. Sound creates a feeling of inclusion. I sing in a choir, and so it is my job to tell the story or message conveyed in the piece. For this reason, when my choir starts to sing, we take upon the ethos of the song. We become part of the piece. I'm also a big fan of listening to music. In a way, it feels as if I become part of the performance or the music video. There are times when I just sit and listen to a melancholic song, as it seems to depict exactly what I am going through. Or I'll blast my favorite song and dance (if I may call it that), sing along, or picture myself at a concert. Regardless, it improves my mood.

Biologically, we are social creatures with one of the most complex forms of communication. It would be a shame to live a life in complete silence. However, moderation is key. There is a balance between sound and silence, and we as a society are gravitating more towards sound. When silence arrives, we are quick to dismiss it with headphones or phones, but we should start to embrace it.

For starters, there's the simple stress relief in silence. As reported by Wolfgang Babisch, "Noise activates the pituitary-adrenal-cortical axis and the sympathetic-adrenal-medullary axis. Changes in stress hormones including epinephrine, norepinephrine and cortisol are frequently found in acute and chronic noise experiments" (1). In simpler terms, sound activates our nervous systems, it activates the flight or fight response, it excites our

---

Reprinted with permission by William Graham
[1]The epigraph and introduction of this piece were inspired by Holly Wren Spaulding's "In Defense of Darkness."

body. Therefore, silence, defined in my case as in the absence of man-made sound, spares our body the external stimulation. It allows our bodies to relax and our minds to settle.

Silence allows us to disconnect from society, if only for a moment. By not having sound call our attention and focus, we are able to retreat into our own thoughts and imaginations. It's a chance to reflect back on good memories or to think about our future. It won't always be some moment insight or epiphany (it could be though). However, it draws us away from the hectic day-by-day routines we too often find ourselves in.

Remember back to when you actually started *thinking*. I'm not talking about thinking about deadlines or projects, what to eat or where you should go. I'm talking about conceptualizing, questioning, imagining. Was it perhaps in your bed at night where all your day's assignments had been completed? Or perhaps was it on a weekend afternoon when you decided to take a walk around the beach? It seems our most relaxing and thought-provoking moments have been those in silence. An environment of silence doesn't beckon us to act, but rather to think. In the words of philosopher Francis Bacon, "Silence is the sleep that nourishes wisdom." So before you hit play on your I-pod or click that call button, turn it off and listen to the world. Maybe even shut your eyes. Just embrace the silence.

Works Cited

Babisch, Wolfgang. "The Noise/Stress Concept, Risk Assessment and Research Needs." *Noise Health*, vol. 4, no. 16, 2002, pp. 1–11.

Bacon, Francis. *BrainyQuote.com*, www.brainyquote.com/quotes/quotes/f/francisbac165288.html.

Works Consulted

Prochnik, George. *In Pursuit of Silence: Listening for Meaning in a World of Noise.* Doubleday, 2010.

Spaulding, Holly Wren. "In Defense of Darkness." *Inventing Arguments*, by John Mauk and John Metz, 4th ed., Cengage Learning, 2016, pp. 74–78.

Analyzing Argument

1. What is Graham's main claim about silence?

2. How is Graham's argument a counterargument?

3. Where does Graham concede or qualify his claims? What opposing idea or assumption seems to drive the concession or qualifiers?

4. Describe Graham's voice. Point to specific passages or statements to support your characterization.

5. What assumption or value underlines Graham's argument? In other words, what unstated belief warrants his claims?

1993 Patrick Hardin

What's it all about?

Analyzing Argument

1. What does this cartoon argue?

2. What elements, words and visuals, make the argument?

3. What assumptions underlie the argument?

4. Answer the question "What is it all about?"

GLOSSARY

Academic Argument A type of argument that focuses on written text in an academic setting. Academic arguments are different from the fleeting hit-'em-when-they-least-expect-it rhetoric of consumer society. Academic arguers explore complexities to develop new ways of thinking on a topic. In academic argument, both claim and support are the result of focused exploration, a sincere attempt to understand other points of view, and a willingness to question one's own current way of thinking. (See Argument; Academic Audience.)

Academic Audience The audience for academic writing (including academic arguments). *Audience* usually refers to a collection of readers rather than one particular person. For example, although instructors ultimately read and assess student writing in college, academic writing most often addresses a broader community of potential readers—not merely the instructor and students in a class but also the community they create as participants in college life. Academic audiences are aware of themselves as an audience and are constantly thinking about the messages being sent and the way the ideas can be received. Academic audiences expect and value qualities that are not expected in popular culture: revelatory rather than familiar points; appeals to logic rather than to emotion; analysis rather than packaging; inclusion rather than exclusion. (See Audience; Academic Argument.)

Ad Hominem (Latin for *to the person*) A logical fallacy that attacks an arguer rather than examining the logic of the argument: *We shouldn't listen to their claims about social justice because those people are crazy.*

Allusion A reference to some bit of public knowledge (from history, current events, popular culture, religion, or literature). Allusions are commonly used to support ideas in formal essays, informal articles, and literary works. Allusions are also common in everyday argument, especially as presented in movies, songs, and TV shows. *You're a real Einstein* is an allusion to Albert Einstein, for example, and most audiences will understand what this allusion means. In a sense, allusions are like outside sources because they add depth and meaning to an argument. By making connections to culturally shared bits of knowledge, allusions link an argument to the world beyond it. (See Support.)

Analogy An extended comparison in which two things share several characteristics or qualities, or in which two situations or scenarios are presented as the same. Usually, an unfamiliar or lesser known thing is compared to something more familiar, thereby making the unfamiliar more familiar. Analogies also can be used to bring out a particular quality: *The U.S. military faced the same kind of consistent attacks in Iraq as the Russian military did in Afghanistan. Eventually, the attacks prompted the Russians to pull out their forces.* (See Support.)

Anecdote A short account of a particular event or incident. Anecdotes are often given in the form of a brief story that supports an arguer's point. While testimony, another form of support, comes from an eyewitness ("I saw the train coming around the mountain"), an anecdote is told by the arguer as though he or she were an objective reporter of events ("The incident on the train tracks started with the train coming around the mountain"). The details in an anecdote can provide powerful support because they help to draw an audience into a specific scene. (See Support.)

Antonomasia A figure of speech in which a description of someone is used in place of an actual name, such as *The King of Pop* to refer to Michael Jackson, *The King* to refer to Elvis, or *Ol' Blue Eyes* to refer to Frank Sinatra. (See Figurative Language.)

Appeal A major form of support in argumentation that requires the arguer to *create* a connection between the audience and the topic. Appeals call on the reader's sense of logic, emotion, character, value, or need. They differ from forms of evidence (statistics, facts, illustrations, etc.) in an important way. An arguer can simply point to something as a fact or statistic. But an appeal must be constructed out of logical steps, shared values, beliefs, or needs; the arguer must *create* the bridge between the topic and the audience. For this reason, Aristotle called appeals *artistic proofs* and forms of evidence *inartistic proofs*.

Appeal to Character (*Ethos*) Drawing attention to the arguer's personal nature, integrity, experience, wisdom, or personality. Appeals to character are an explicit strategy for building trust or confidence in the arguer, which helps the audience to accept the arguer's claims.

Appeal to Emotion (*Pathos*) Connecting the audience's emotions (sympathy, anger, happiness, etc.) to the topic. Appeals to emotion are not usually used in academic arguments.

Appeal to Logic (*Logos*) Engaging the intellectual/reasoning capacity of the audience. Appeals to logic are key in academic argument and constitute the primary rhetorical moves in all academic disciplines. (See Deductive Reasoning; Inductive Reasoning; Syllogism; Enthymeme; Logical Fallacies.)

Appeal to Need Making a connection between the topic and a basic human need (food, shelter, belonging, intimacy, self-realization, etc.). Like appeals to value, appeals to need tap into a broad layer of human affairs. They work by reaching inside of an audience, into their essential requirements.

Appeal to Value Making a connection between the topic and a general value (such as fairness, equality, honor, kindness, selflessness, duty, responsibility, economics, pragmatics). While an argument emerges from a particular situation, the claims made in an argument emerge from value systems of its participants. Appeals to value may be the most intense and abundant appeals in popular arguments about political, social, and cultural issues. In everyday life, we often use values to persuade others to accept points: Any argument based on equality, justice, duty, responsibility, security, or honesty is an appeal to value. When arguers can make the connection between a particular point and a broader value, they have tapped into something beyond their particular argument; they have called on the belief system of both the audience and the broader public. (See Ideology.)

Arguable Claim Any assertion that could be challenged on various grounds that invites or directly addresses opposition. (See Claim.)

Argument The act of asserting, supporting, and defending a claim. Argument is an intellectual and a social process. People are surrounded by argument almost constantly. It can be said that public life is argumentative—that people are vying to be heard, trying to assert their vision of the world to anyone who will hear it. But argument can work in much more subtle ways in the form of advertisements, songs, billboards, posters, slogans, and even stories. While our daily language may not be full of explicit debate, it is full of suggestions about our beliefs. When people make a subtle point about a favorite song or an interesting class, they are suggesting an entire argument, which entails a set of values and assumptions about social worth. (See Academic Argument.)

Arguments in Disguise See Objectivity Disguise; Personal Taste Disguise; Propaganda; Spin.

Arrangement The organization of ideas in an argument. Arrangement involves putting ideas in a particular order and creating connections between those ideas. But it also involves structuring the logic and creating lines of reasoning. When arguers structure ideas, they create the reader's journey through their argument. (See Unity; Coherence; The [Five] Canons of Rhetoric.)

Artistic Proofs Support that must be created by the arguer. Aristotle called appeals *artistic proofs* because the writer must create the bridge between the topic and the audience. Writers also use inartistic proofs (facts, statistics, testimony), which they do not create. Inartistic proofs already exist. (See Appeal; Inartistic Proofs; Support.)

Asides Comments, usually placed in parentheses, that allow writers to add more. Although the parenthetical comment is used for a broad range of purposes, three uses are dominant: (1) to give more detailed information; (2) to add an informal and often more opinionated assertion; (3) to emphasize or extend a point.

Association Fallacy Claiming that two people or things share a quality just because they are somehow associated, connected, or related.

Assumption An assumption is a logical connection between a claim and support. Every argument (every claim and support) contains an assumption that is crucial to its validity. Assumptions are sometimes stated and sometimes unstated. They can be obvious and easily accepted, or hidden and highly debatable. Claim: You should dress nicely for your interview. Support: You want to make a good impression on the employer. Assumption: Dressing nicely makes a good impression on potential employers. (See Warrants.)

Audience The people receiving, or potentially receiving, a message (a written, spoken, crafted, or performed argument). Especially in everyday argumentation, a specific audience may be known—a friend, colleague, family member, employer, etc. But in academic writing, *audience* usually refers to a collection of readers rather than one particular person. (See Academic Audience.)

Authorities Experts in a given field who offer specialized knowledge. A type of support, authorities are used in arguments to give credibility to a writer's claims, to illustrate outside or opposing perspectives, to help explain a topic, or to give a sense of popular opinion or historical context. Authorities, or references to outside sources, can be used in a variety of ways, but they usually are used to give an idea credence or believability. (See Support.)

Backing In Toulmin analysis, support for the warrant.

Begging the Question A type of logical fallacy that attempts to prove a claim by using an alternative wording of the claim itself: *We should vote for the school levy because it is the best thing to do.* Also called *circular reasoning.*

The (Five) Canons of Rhetoric Invention, arrangement, style, memory, and delivery. Since classical times, rhetoric has been divided into five categories or canons. (Rhetoric has been thought about and categorized in various other ways as well.) These canons are used as intellectual tools for developing, extending, and shaping ideas.

Claim An assertion made about a given topic. In argument, claims are supported or argued for. An argument consists of a main claim (or thesis) and support. Claims can be categorized as claim of fact, claim of value, or claim of policy.

Claim of Fact A type of claim that argues that a condition exists, has existed, or will exist. We often associate fact with truth (hence, with being beyond dispute), but facts themselves are always in dispute. For instance, a historian must prove that Rome influenced all the societies of Europe; another historian might suggest a region that was beyond the influence of Rome. Claims of fact include *The Roman Empire influenced all of Europe. The Earth is not flat. The Packers will win the Super Bowl this year.*

Claim of Policy A type of claim that argues that some action should be taken or some change made. Claims of policy call for a particular change in behavior, policy, approach, or even attitude: *The Confederate flag should not be flown above a state capital building. Voluntary prayer should be allowed in public schools. We should get out of class early today.*

Claim of Value A type of claim that argues that something has or reflects a particular quality (that it is good, bad, just, unreasonable, practical, unfair, etc.). It may assert approval or disapproval. Any claim that argues the worth of an issue is a claim of value; usually an adjective, or a *predicate of value,* can be found in the claim. For instance, in the following, *good, underhanded,* and *wrong* are all predicates of value: *The Packers are not a very good team this year. The governor's strategies for getting elected are underhanded. Abortion is wrong.*

Coherence The flow and connection of ideas within the text. (See Arrangement.)

Concession Granting value or credit to an opposing claim. Concessions are closely related to *qualifiers,* which acknowledge the limits of one's own claims. Conceding certain points and qualifying others are important strategies for strengthening an argument. When we write arguments, it is easy to become fixated on our own opinions and to draw firm boundaries between our own perspective (which we assume is correct) and others' (which we assume are less correct or flat-out wrong). Concessions allow us as arguers to cling less tightly to our own perspectives, which allows us to invent more nuanced points. This does not mean that *conciliatory* arguments (those that concede points) are wishy-washy. It means that they are more engaged with the opinions swirling around in the rhetorical situation. (See Counterargument; Qualifiers; Rogerian Argument.)

Counterargument Refuting the claims or positions that are opposed to those being forwarded by the arguer. In academic argument, simply projecting one's opinion is not enough. Good arguers must engage what others believe and must take on opposing viewpoints; they must *counterargue.* Perhaps other positions are unethical, unreasonable, logically flawed, or impractical. Whatever their shortcomings, opposing viewpoints must be addressed head on. Dismissing opposing positions too easily can shortchange one's argument. Good arguers carefully examine others' positions, and even try to imagine contrary points, and this helps them draw clear boundaries between their positions and others'. (See Concessions; Qualifiers.)

Deductive Reasoning This type of reasoning builds a conclusion from accepted premises or general principles. Often, this means relying on classes (all dogs, all men, all raincoats, and so on). For example: *All birds* have beaks. Polly the parrot is *a bird.* Therefore, Polly has a beak. Here, a conclusion has been built from a general premise about birds. Deduction may also rely on, or build from, a definitional statement—a statement that says what something is: *Bipeds are* animals with two legs. *Ostriches are* two-legged animals. Therefore, Ostriches are bipeds. Also, notice

the definitional statement in the previous example: Polly the parrot *is a bird.* (See Inductive Reasoning.)

Delivery The presentation of ideas in an argument. Delivery is one of the five canons of rhetoric. In ancient Greece, and through much of the history of argument, *delivery* referred to the physical oral performance of an argument. But since the move to written text, it now refers to all the processes involved in presenting ideas to an audience. Although we can make a distinction between invention (discovering and developing ideas) and delivery (shaping the final presentation of ideas for readers), the two are intertwined, deeply rooted together. As people invent ideas, they often simultaneously think about their readers and even consider certain phrases that might resonate with others. And, as people shape ideas for others, they may also reinvent them. Perhaps the most helpful distinction between invention and delivery is that invention emphasizes the discovery of what the arguer knows, and delivery emphasizes what the audience knows and how it will react. (See The [Five] Canons of Rhetoric.)

Dialectical Reasoning (*Hegelian Logic*) A process of critical thinking put forth by philosopher Georg Wilhelm Friedrich Hegel (1770–1831), who believed that all human thought developed through various stages from personal to social to spiritual. Progression through those stages depends upon a type of reasoning: First, we believe or put forward an idea (thesis); then we inevitably doubt it (antithesis); then we come to new understanding (synthesis). In other words, in order to grow intellectually, we must move beyond our initial ideas (our theses) by doubting. But doubting everything is not complete growth. We must reconcile our doubt with the original thought. In argument, Hegelian logic helps us get beyond our initial opinions (thesis statements) and into increasingly sophisticated ideas. For example:

- Thesis: School uniforms deny students freedom of expression.
- Antithesis: School uniforms do not deny freedom of expression because expression is not exclusively about clothing.
- Synthesis: School uniforms make clothing irrelevant as the sole form of personal expression.

Either/Or Reasoning A type of logical fallacy that offers only two choices when more exist: *You either agree with the policy, or you are anti-American.* (See Logical Fallacies.)

Enthymeme Statements or passages that contain unstated premises or assumptions. *Because the dog is scratching at the back door, someone should let her out* is an enthymeme because it contains a claim, support, and an unstated premise. The claim is *someone should let the dog out.* The support is *because she is scratching at the back door.* And the unstated premise or warranting assumption is *when the dog scratches at the back door, that means she wants to go outside.* Enthymemes are the most basic form of reasoning in everyday arguments, and they also function in formal arguments. Sometimes unstated premises, or assumptions, are not entirely acceptable, and so an entire argument can be called into question. (See Warrants; Syllogism.)

Ethos See Appeal to Character.

Evidence A type of support that includes reference to authority, facts, statistics, and testimonies. Evidence does not require an arguer to create it but only to employ what already exists. Merely mentioning evidence, for example, simply giving a fact, is not usually enough. Arguers must also explain the relevance of the evidence. (See Authorities; Facts; Statistics; Testimony; Support; Appeal.)

Examples Particular occurrences of a phenomenon. Whenever arguers support a claim with particular versions of a point, they are using examples. An example of a horse is Secretariat; an example of a bad idea is diving off a bridge into shallow water. (See Support.)

Exigence The critical moment in a rhetorical situation; the moment that requires someone to speak or write. The exigence is created when something happens (or fails to happen) that calls for someone to speak out and persuade others to think or act in a particular way. An exigence may be something as direct and intense as a power outage, which might prompt an official to persuade everyone to "stay calm" or to "assist those in need." An exigence may be more subtle or complex, like the discovery of a new virus, which might prompt medical officials to persuade the public how to change its behavior. Exigence is part of a situation. It is the critical component that makes people ask the hard questions: What is it? What caused it? What good is it? What are we going to do? What happened? What is going to happen? (See Rhetorical Situation; Stasis Theory; Kairos.)

Facts Agreed-on bits of knowledge that do not require further support in an argument. Facts are verified or verifiable claims. This is not to say that facts cannot be disputed; they often are. But when arguers use a fact, they assume that it carries its own support. (See Support.)

False Analogy A type of logical fallacy that makes a comparison between two things that are ultimately more unlike than alike. The differences between the things compared make the comparison ineffective or unfair, or the comparison misrepresents one or both of the things involved: *Running a college is a lot like running a corporation: if you provide a better service, then you get more customers.* (See Logical Fallacies.)

Faulty Cause/Effect A type of logical fallacy that confuses a sequential relationship with a causal one. Faulty cause/effect wrongly assumes that Event A caused Event B because Event A occurred first: *the sun rose because the rooster crowed.* (See Logical Fallacies.)

Figurative Language Language that is not literal; language that redirects meaning away from the literal definitions of words. Figurative language is used to help arguers portray ideas, and, if used appropriately, it can add layers of richness to an argument. Some types of figurative language include antonomasia, analogy, hyperbole, irony, metaphor, metonymy, personification, simile, and understatement.

Formality/Informality Formality is the adherence of a text to conventions of style and format. Writing that stays within conventions and does not draw attention to itself by digressing or breaking with convention is considered formal. While many other features dictate the degree of formality, the following are major factors:

Formal Writing:
- Adheres to conventions of grammar and sentence structure.
- Does not draw attention to itself with novel phrasing or dramatic shifts in tone.
- Does not use much figurative language (metaphors or similes).
- Attempts to remain transparent; draws attention to ideas rather than the sentences, words, and phrases themselves.

Informal Writing:
- Veers away from standard conventions.
- Intentionally breaks conventional grammar or sentence structure rules.
- Draws attention to itself with unique or quirky phrasing.
- Freely uses slang or street phrasing.
- Draws attention to the writer (*I, me*), the audience (*you*), or both (*we*).

Golden Age Fallacy Characterizing the past as broadly and inherently better.

Hasty Generalization Drawing a conclusion about a group of people/events/things based on insufficient examples. This is often the logical flaw behind racist, sexist, or bigoted statements: *German Shepherds are vicious.* (See Logical Fallacies.)

Hegelian Logic See Dialectical Reasoning.

Hyperbole A figure of speech involving a deliberate exaggeration: *Look out! That puddle's the size of Lake Erie.* (See Figurative Language.)

Ideology The collection of unstated values and beliefs that inform people's understanding of the world. This collection of values and beliefs is not readily apparent to us; it is camouflaged by the sayings and behaviors of everyday life. You might think of ideology as the most invisible, most indirect or unstated, layer of an argument. Ideology is not usually directly addressed in arguments, but it does give birth to people's opinions about particular issues, and more sophisticated writers will dig deep enough to expose this layer. That is, they will try to explain the system of unstated beliefs and assumptions beneath their own argument or the arguments of others. Political ideologies include communism, conservativism, fascism, feminism, liberalism, and so on.

Illustrations Graphic descriptions or representations of an idea. Sometimes writers illustrate a point with words only. They carefully describe the details of an idea so that an image is created in the mind of readers. In essence, writers draw a picture with words so that readers imagine it visually. But illustrations, in the strict sense of the word, use actual graphics. (See Support.)

Inartistic Proofs Support that already exists, such as facts, statistics, and testimony. Aristotle called appeals artistic proofs and evidence inartistic proofs because with appeals, arguers must create a bridge between the topic and audience; with evidence, the arguer utilizes evidence that already exists. (See Artistic Proofs; Appeal; Evidence; Support.)

Inductive Reasoning This type of reasoning builds from specific premises and leads to a general claim. For example: Two cars collided at the intersection last week. A pedestrian was nearly hit at the intersection yesterday. Today a motorcycle rear-ended a car at the intersection. Therefore, this is a dangerous intersection. When we come to a conclusion based on several specifics, we are reasoning inductively. Inductive reasoning is the primary engine of scientific research because researchers conduct specific tests or experiments to arrive at general conclusions. (See Deductive Reasoning.)

Informality/Formality See Formality/Informality.

Invention The discovery and development of ideas. Because the goal of argument is to *reveal* a new way of seeing a topic (and thus to persuade people to rethink their positions and beliefs), good invention strategies are key to success. Invention is the first of the five canons of rhetoric. (See Rhetoric.)

Inventive Research A type of research that is exploratory. It may involve seeking out opposing points of view, reexamining a familiar topic from a different angle, finding new layers in a topic, and so on. In short, inventive research is adventurous research. (See Seeking Research.)

Irony The act (or art) of saying one thing and meaning the opposite. In other words, an ironic statement means the opposite of what it says. When people proclaim, "Nice job, Grace!" after someone has tripped, they are being ironic. They really mean, "That wasn't very graceful." As an argumentative strategy, irony is a way to connect with the audience—to share a secret understanding, like a wink. Because the arguer assumes that the audience knows the real meaning behind the words, a bond develops.

Kairos Greek for *opportune moment.* It refers to the moment in a rhetorical situation that is ripest with opportunity—the moment when the right statement can have the most impact and influence on an audience. (See Rhetorical Situation.)

Logical Fallacies Flaws in the structure of an argument that make the claims invalid. A fallacy is a falsehood, so a logical fallacy is a logical falsehood that makes no sense within a given situation. (See Ad Hominem; Begging the Question; Either/Or Reasoning; Faulty Cause/Effect; False Analogy; Hasty Generalization; Non Sequitur; Oversimplification; Red Herring; Slippery Slope; Strawperson.)

Logos See Appeal to Logic.

Main Claim The primary assertions made about a given topic. (See Claim.)

Memory The fifth of the five canons of rhetoric; the recollection of prepared points. In ancient Greece, when the five canons were vital to the teaching of rhetoric, rhetors memorized lengthy arguments and delivered them as speeches. However, the rhetorical situation has changed dramatically since then. Now that we depend so heavily on written text, and less on a dramatic performance (or delivery), memory is hardly a vital part of argument. But memory has been replaced by revision (or reseeing): we no longer need to see our argument in our mind for purposes of remembering, but since others will read it, we resee it to imagine how readers will understand it. Then we make adjustments.

Metaphor A comparison in which one thing takes on the characteristics of another: *Our economy is on the edge, and one wrong move could send it plunging downward.*

Metonymy A figure of speech that names something using only part of that thing. For example, people use *Washington* to refer to the U.S. government or *the pen and the sword* to refer to writing and military action.

Non Sequitur (Latin for *it does not follow*) A statement that does not follow logically from what has preceded it. This is the result of skipping several logical steps in drawing a conclusion: *Alphie is good-looking; therefore, he will be happy.*

Objectivity Disquise Fools the audience into thinking that the presented information is entirely unbiased.

Oversimplification A type of logical fallacy that does not acknowledge the true complexity of a situation: *If Bill and Lisa would just get married, they would solve their problems.*

Paraphrase A rewording of the original source using your own words and expressions. Unlike summary, paraphrase covers the detail and complexity of the original text.

Pathos See Appeal to Emotion.

Personal Taste Disguise Camouflages an argument as or within an appeal to the audience's personal tastes and desires.

Personification Treating a nonhuman thing as though it were human: *So the house just sat there through the years, minding its own business while the world built up around it.*

Plagiarism The act of using other writers' words or ideas without attribution or proper quotation. It is stealing others' ideas in large chunks (entire essays or passages) or in small bits (a sentence or phrase). Most writing instructors recognize two different types of plagiarism: (1) sloppy paraphrase, which occurs when writers do not sufficiently reword the ideas from a source, and (2) intentional theft, which involves buying or stealing others' words, passages, or entire projects.

Post Hoc, Ergo Propter Hoc See Faulty Cause/Effect.

Premise Any claim that provides reasoning for another claim. Premises work like support in that they substantiate claims. But premises are single statements that set up or make an intellectual path for other claims. Premises are most often discussed as statements that lead to a conclusion or to a claim that has been proven. For instance, *if A and B, then C. A and B* are premises that lead to C: *If the rain has been coming down for two days, and if your shoes have been outside the whole time, your shoes are probably ruined.*

Proof A broad term that refers to support strategies. *Proof* is sometimes used synonymously with *support*. Aristotle split proofs into two categories: inartistic (forms of evidence) and artistic (appeals). (See Support.)

Propaganda A complex set of strategies used to drive audiences into a uniform way of thinking and feeling. It may involve the objectivity disguise, the personal taste disguise, vague or ill-defined words, slogans, strong appeals to emotion, need, and character, intellectual or moral certainty, demarcation of groups, and logical fallacies.

Qualifier A word or phrase that limits the meaning of another word or phrase. A qualifier acknowledges the limits of one's own claims. Qualifiers are closely related to concessions, which grant value to someone else's claims. The difference is that concessions focus on others' ideas and qualifiers focus on the arguer's own claims. If you qualify your point, you draw attention to its limitations. We often qualify our claims in everyday conversations: *I'm not saying that all politicians are bad, but many of them seem to distort the truth. Granted, some country music is good, but a lot of it just rubs me the wrong way.* Qualifiers also show up as words and phrases that make statements seem less extreme. Words such as *perhaps, seems, maybe, could,* and *might* qualify argumentative claims.

Rebuttal In Toulmin analysis, circumstances that could invalidate the claim.

Red Herring A type of logical fallacy that tries to shift attention away from the original focus of the argument: *I might have*

wrecked your car joy riding, but you shouldn't have left the keys in it in the first place.

Revelatory Claim An argumentative assertion that challenges a common perspective, reveals a hidden dimension, or encourages a fresh way of thinking. (See Claim.)

Rhetoric A process of recognizing and using the most effective strategies for influencing thought. Aristotle defined rhetoric as "the ability in each particular case to see the available means of persuasion." In other words, rhetoric is more than a tool for changing people's minds; it is also the *study* of how people get persuaded into their beliefs. People who study rhetoric and writing are interested in how people's opinions form and change; they study the relationship between language and belief; and they examine the cultural conditions around people and their everyday use of language. In its classical origins (which most scholars note as the fifth century BCE), rhetoric was a primary field of study. In many ways, it was the glue between various academic pursuits because it focused on how ideas (regardless of content) get used, shared, communicated, implemented, and manipulated in the world. The study of rhetoric was the study of social and intellectual activity.

The study of rhetoric is still at the heart of contemporary writing classes. That is, students learn not simply about correct grammar but about the relationship between language and thought. Rhetoric is key in the study of argument (the deliberate and calculated use of rhetoric to influence or change thought). Aristotle's lessons on rhetoric are still in place. In writing, debate, communication, and speech courses, students still study the five categories or *canons* of rhetoric passed down from the ancient Greeks:

- **Invention:** The discovery and development of ideas.
- **Delivery:** The presentation of ideas.
- **Arrangement:** The organization of ideas in a coherent and engaging fashion.
- **Style or Voice:** The personal or individualized use of language conventions, with attention to appropriateness, situation, and audience.
- **Memory:** The recollection of prepared points.

Rhetorical Situation An opportunity to address a particular audience about a disputed or disputable issue (in other words, a chance to use rhetoric—to study the available means of persuasion—in a particular set of circumstances). A rhetorical situation involves an *exigence*, or an occasion when something happens or does not happen that results in some uncertainty. The rhetorical situation also involves the speaker/writer, the audience, the method of communication, and the rules of communication (whether directly stated or implied). No aspect of the situation exists independently of the others: what can and should be said (the message or text) depends upon the other elements. All elements of the rhetorical situation exist in time and place. All of the thinking and living that goes on in that place—and that has gone on before—impacts what can and should be said. Good rhetoricians (good arguers) understand how to use particulars within a setting. The ancient Greeks called this *kairos,* or the opportune moment. The particulars of a situation actually bring an argument into being and help writers and speakers to develop ideas. And attention to the details of the rhetorical situation creates an effective argument. Making powerful arguments, then, involves not merely attention to language but also an awareness of surroundings (the intellectual, physical, and social layers of a situation). (See Rhetoric; Exigence; Kairos; Audience.)

Rhetorician An expert in or teacher of rhetoric. Rhetoricians do more than find the best language to change someone's mind; they study the whole situation (the real-life conditions and details, the rules and institutions involved, the values of potential audiences). They are interested in the relationships between what has happened in the situation, what is said or written, and what might happen. In a way, rhetoricians are part sociologist, part language theorist, part psychologist, and part philosopher.

Rogerian Argument An approach to argument based on the work of Carl Rogers (1902–1987), in which the arguer attempts to build common ground between value systems. According to Rogerian theory, arguers should first seek to understand opponents' views. Once we know the terrain of our opponents, we can build a bridge to it. The goal, then, is not to uncover weaknesses in opponents' thinking, but to uncover the key similarities between our own perspectives and those of others. Only then can we genuinely determine the nature of our own positions and effectively change how we think, which is a key element in Rogerian theory. This strategy is related to dialectical reasoning, or Hegelian logic, which attempts to find synthesis between two opposing claims. (See Hegelian Logic; Dialectical Reasoning.)

Sarcasm A type of irony characterized by a slant toward mean-spiritedness. Sarcasm is often used in a playful manner between people who are familiar enough not to offend one another with playful poking. But in academic argument, and more formal situations generally, sarcasm should be used very discriminately—or not at all. Because academic audiences are not necessarily familiar with a writer, they do not expect to participate in much sarcasm. In the wrong situation, sarcasm can make a writer (or speaker) seem dismissive of audience's expectations or of the situation itself.

Scenarios Fictional or hypothetical accounts. As a persuasive tool, scenarios can support nearly any argumentative claim. When arguers use scenarios, they signal the audience that they are in hypothetical territory. This can involve a simple cue such as *Imagine that* or something even more subtle: *If one student were to score a 93%, another 95%, and another 100%, they would all receive a 4.0. However, the final grade would be. . . .* (See Support.)

Seeking Research Research done to find particular pieces of information, such as data, a specific historical account, or examples. (See Inventive Research.)

Simile A comparison using like or as in which one thing takes on the characteristics of another: "You are like a hurricane. There's calm in your eye" (Neil Young).

Slippery Slope A type of logical fallacy that assumes that a certain way of thinking or acting will necessarily continue or extend in that direction (like a domino effect). Such an argument suggests that once we begin down a slope, we will inevitably slip all the way down, and so the effects of a particular action/idea are exaggerated: *If the Supreme Court allows the police to set up informational roadblocks, it will soon grant law enforcement full license to inspect anyone at any time.*

Spin A heavily biased portrayal of information. Spinning an event or statement involves turning its obvious or apparent meaning into something else—usually a meaning that is favorable to the spinner's cause or position.

Stasis Theory A system or approach involving four questions that help one to understand the nature of a disagreement and the precise nature of opposing claims. The term "stasis" comes from the Greek root *sta,* "to stand." Arguers ask a series of questions that help them determine the issue to be argued, the point of contention, or the place at which an arguer "takes a stand." In any rhetorical situation, there are many possible positions and opinions—and without some process of narrowing the scope, arguers might be left to simply bounce from point to point, never settling on real differences between positions. Stasis theory provides a framework that helps arguers to narrow in on a given point and to say, in effect, "*This* is the point of contention." The process involves four general questions:

1. **Conjecture:** Does it exist? Did something happen? (All questions related to origin and cause.)
2. **Definition:** What is its nature? What do we call it? (All questions related to meaning.)
3. **Quality:** Is it right or wrong? What or whom does it involve or affect? (All questions related to value.)
4. **Procedure:** What should be done? (All questions related to policy or procedure.)

An argument (even several different arguments) could emerge from each question. Arguers use the four questions (or stases) as investigation tools to ask, *Is this the disagreement?*

Statistics Numerical data drawn from surveys, experimentation, and data analysis. (See Support.)

Strawperson A type of logical fallacy that misrepresents an argument by oversimplifying it so that it can easily be proven wrong: *People against the war think that the U.S. shouldn't defend itself from dangerous forces.*

Style The personal or individualized use of language conventions, with attention to appropriateness, situation, and audience. An arguer's style is the particular way he or she uses language to engage an audience. Style is closely related to (and sometimes used synonymously with) voice. While both terms have long histories and have come to mean many different things, there is an important distinction for academic writing: Style is most often associated with a personalized set of mannerisms that a writer carries from situation to situation (or assignment to assignment). Ernest Hemingway had a style. Emily Dickinson had a style. Voice, on the other hand, is seen as something that changes from situation to situation, sometimes dramatically. Writers can change the nature of their voices depending on the audience, topic, time, place, and shared expectations. This ability to change is key to rhetoric, and key to good argumentative writing. (See Voice.)

Summary Expressing ideas from a source in your own words. Unlike a paraphrase, summary removes much of the detail from the original passage.

Support Sometimes called *grounds* or *proofs,* support gives substance and legitimacy to a claim or thesis. Support comes in various forms: authorities, facts, statistics, evidence, allusions, anecdotes, examples, illustrations, scenarios, appeals to logic, appeals to emotion, appeals to character, appeals to value, appeals to need. Through the ages, scholars have categorized and recategorized these support strategies. One long-standing perspective casts them into three main groups:

    Types of Appeal: to logic, emotion, character, value, need
    Types of Evidence: authorities/testimony, facts, statistics
    Types of Example: allusion, anecdote, illustration, scenario

While the groupings are interesting (and helpful in the broader study of rhetoric), they are not essential. Most arguments depend on various forms of support; however, there are common tendencies. For instance, arguments about value tend to use appeals, while claims of fact tend to rely heavily on evidence. Appeals to logic are key to all types of formal, academic arguments. Support gives substance and legitimacy to a claim or thesis. (See Appeal; Evidence; Authorities; Facts; Statistics; Allusion; Anecdote; Examples; Illustrations; Scenarios.)

Syllogism A line of deductive reasoning that requires three steps: *If reason A is true and reason B is true, C must be true.* Or put another way: *A is true and B is true; therefore C is true.* Often, A and B are referred to as *premises.* The premises create an intellectual pathway to the final claim. Notice the following popular example about Socrates, the ancient Greek philosopher:

    All humans are mortal.
    Socrates is human.
    Therefore, Socrates is mortal.

Testimony An eyewitness account: *I watched as the crescent got smaller and smaller; I was hoping to find a dark spot where I could pull off to the side of the road and take in the full beauty of a lunar eclipse.* (See Support.)

Toulmin Argument An important system for analyzing arguments, based on the work of Stephen Toulmin (1922–2009).

Originating from the formal study of logic, Toulmin's framework suggests that an argument has six primary components: main claim, support, warranting assumption, backing, modal qualifier, and rebuttal. The first three are most widely discussed in the field of rhetoric; the warranting assumption is the most notable element because of its wide range of use. (See Warrants.)

Understatement A figure of speech in which a deliberately less forceful or dramatic expression than expected is used: *Antarctica is a little chilly.*

Unity The cohesive quality of ideas. If a text has unity, it develops a primary line of reasoning without significant digression. Although many different points (and sometimes seemingly unrelated points) may be addressed in a single argument, they are all directly related to the main claim or thesis. Writers use transitions between major points to achieve unity and logical connections among ideas.

Voice The writerly identity created within a text. Voice is closely related to style (the personal or individualized use of language conventions) but changes from situation to situation. When we read a text and comment about the author, we are commenting only on the identity in the particular text: *Clark is very formal here. Tamera seems curious.* This identity is referred to as the *voice* of the writer, or the presence and character of the writer as it appears in the text. All texts have a voice; it may be formal, barely noticeable, formulaic, or monotone. Some writers create a strong voice, one that comes out of the text boldly, while others keep their voices understated. (See Style.)

Warrants (Warranting Assumptions) The reasons that connect claims with their support. As philosopher Stephen Toulmin explains, inside every argument lies a warranting assumption, but it is often unstated. The assumption may seem so obvious to the arguer that he or she feels no need to announce it, or perhaps the assumption rests so deeply and quietly in the arguer's mind that he or she does not even recognize it. Warranting assumptions rest deeply in our thoughts. In a sense, they are part of our ideologies: the collection of unstated values and beliefs that inform people's understanding of the world. When we discover a warranting assumption, we reveal the hidden support structure of an argument and can more accurately determine the argument's strengths and weaknesses.

For example, the statement *We should not withdraw our troops from Iraq just because the war isn't going well after four years* rests on an unstated assumption: that people want to withdraw troops because the war isn't going well. People may want to withdraw troops for other reasons; people may be against the war whether it is going well or not, or they may want to withdraw troops because they feel the war has been managed incompetently. Because of an unstated warranting assumption, the audience may be led in a particular direction without realizing it, and ultimately led to a particular conclusion that is not based on sound logic or evidence.

INDEX

Analysis
  of arguments, 85–106
  of film, 102
  pitfalls of, 89–91
  summary and, 88–89
  visual arguments, 97–99
Analytical posture, 85–87
Anecdotes, as support, 31
Animal Farm (Orwell), 44–45, 82
"Another Inconvenient Truth: Race and Ethnicity
    Matter" (Halwey and Nieto), 435–441
Answers, arguing the future and, 304–305
Anthologies, MLA citation format, 361–362, 363
"Antibacterial soap" (Zachary), 494–498
Appeals
  to character, 43–44
  classical argument, 5
  to emotion, 44–45
  to logic, 36–43, 273
  to need, 45
  support and, 35–47
  to value, 46, 139–140, 201–203, 273
  visual arguments and, 98–99
Appositives, 27
Arguable claims, 18–19
Argument(s)
  about the future, 278–306
  about the past, 244–277
  academic, 4–6
  analysis of, 85–106
  on bumper stickers, 132
  causal arguments, 147–178
  cause/effect arguments, 268
  classical, 5
  crisis arguments, 207–243
  defined, 3
  disguised arguments, 78–83
  evaluation arguments, 268–269
  invention and, 11–12
  in politics, 395–405
  proposal arguments, 209
  Rogerian argument, 5–6
  on signs, 133

Toulmin argument, 6
  value arguments, 179–206
  visual arguments, 97–99
Aristotle, 7, 35
"Around the Table in Traverse City" (Papcun),
    291–293, 300–301
Arrangement
  arguing the future and, 302–303
  arguing the past and, 274–275
  in causal arguments, 173–175
  in crisis arguments, 239–240, 243
  definitions and, 142–143
  of ideas, 9
  value arguments and, 203
Artistic proof, 35
Artworks, MLA citation format for, 365
Asides, in value arguments, 204–205
Association fallacies, 43
Assumptions
  activities, 71, 78
  basic principles, 67–71
"The Audacity of Hope" (Obama),
    396–399
Audience
  arguing the future and, 303–305
  arguing the past and, 274–276
  in causal arguments, 175–177
  in crisis arguments, 241–243
  definitions and, 143–145
  value arguments, 204–205
Authorities
  arguing the future with, 300–301
  arguing the past and, 271, 276
  causal arguments and, 172
  in crisis arguments, 238
  evidence from, 27
Author's intent
  analysis and description of, 90
  credibility of research sources and,
    330–331
Authors' names
  APA citation format for, 370–371
  MLA citation format, 353–354

causal arguments and, 172
in research, 310
in research sources, 332–333
"Higher Education through Discombobulation"
    (Chitwood), 29, 190–192, 201
"The High Cost of Food" (Goldstein),
    464–465
Hilliard, Michael C., 185–189, 201–203,
    499, 511
Historical research, 310
    secondary research and, 322
Huxley, Aldous, 271
Hyde, Andrew, 123–127, 141–143, 473, 499

I

Ideas, invention and, 11–12
Ideology
    disguised arguments and, 80–83
    spin as tool of, 81–82
"The Idols of Environmentalism" (White),
    210–214, 237–240, 445
Illustrations, as support, 31–32
Images
    arguing the future and, 294
    arguments concerning, 134
    causal arguments in, 165
    crisis arguments and, 232
    of history, 261–263
    of philosophy, 550
    research using, 327–328
    as value arguments, 193
    of women, 429–430
Inartistic proof, 35
Inclusion, in rhetoric, 10
"In Defense of Darkness" (Spaulding), 46, 74–78,
    88, 445, 511, 529
Inductive reasoning, 39
Informality
    audience and voice and, 144–145
    in crisis arguments, 241, 243
Ingersoll, Robert G., 295
Inquiry, Toulmiin argument, 6
Internet research sources, 326–328

Interviews
    APA citation format for, 372
    MLA citation format for, 363
    in primary research, 312–314
In-text citations
    APA style, 367–368
    MLA style, 352–353
"Intoxitwitching: The Energy Drink Buzz"
    (Benlow), 482–483
Invention
    activities, 138
    arguing the future and, 299
    arguing the past and, 264–267, 273
    of claims, 17–18, 136–138, 168–171, 197–199
    classical argument, 5
    crisis arguments, 234–236
    defined, 11–12
    of support, 138–142, 171–173, 200–203
    workshop on, 135–136, 168, 196, 234,
        265–266, 273–275, 299
Inventive research, 309–310
"Investing in Futures: The Cost of College"
    (Nelson), 29, 288–290, 300–305, 460
"I" pronoun, voice in writing and, 177
"The Irrefutable Jefferson" (Jakubowicz), 404–405
"Isolated Community: The Hidden Dangers of
    MORPGs" (Schofield), 522–524
"It's Racism, Stupid: Bias, Not Affirmative Action,
    Stigmatizes People of Color" (Wise), 442–444

J

Jakubowicz, Robert "Frank," 404–405
James, Justin, 46, 72, 128–131, 145, 348, 460
Johnson, Cameron, 26–27, 37
    on appeals, 85–86, 91
    on arguing the past, 257–260, 266–267,
        272–276
    on education, 460
Journals, 324–325
    APA citation format, 371–372
    online journals, APA citation format for, 373–374
    online journals, MLA citation format for, 362
    printed articles citation format, MLA style, 362